GREAT WRITERS STUDENT LIBRARY

20th-CENTURY
DRAMA

GREAT WRITERS STUDENT LIBRARY

Editor: James Vinson
Associate Editor: D. L. Kirkpatrick

20th-CENTURY DRAMA

INTRODUCTION BY
SIMON TRUSSLER

First published 1983 by
THE MACMILLAN PRESS LTD
London and Basingstoke
Associated Companies throughout the world

ISBN 0 333 28355 4   hard cover edition

ISBN 0 333 28354 6   paperback edition

Printed in Hong Kong

CONTENTS

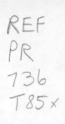

EDITOR'S NOTE

The entry for each writer consists of a biography, a complete list of his published books, a selected list of published bibliographies and critical studies on the writer, and a signed critical essay on his work.

In the biographies, details of education, military service, and marriage(s) are generally given before the usual chronological summary of the life of the writer; awards and honours are given last.

The Publications section is meant to include all book publications, though as a rule broadsheets, single sermons and lectures, minor pamphlets, exhibition catalogues, etc. are omitted. Under the heading Collections, we have listed the most recent collections of the complete works and those of individual genres (verse, plays, novels, stories, and letters); only those collections which have some editorial authority and were issued after the writer's death are listed; on-going editions are indicated by a dash after the date of publication; often a general selection from the writer's works or a selection from the works in the individual genres listed above is included.

Titles are given in modern spelling, though the essayists were allowed to use original spelling for titles and quotations; often the titles are "short." The date given is that of the first book publication, which often followed the first periodical or anthology publication by some time; we have listed the actual year of publication, often different from that given on the title-page. No attempt has been made to indicate which works were published anonymously or pseudonymously, or which works of fiction were published in more than one volume. We have listed plays which were produced but not published; librettos and musical plays are listed along with the other plays; no attempt has been made to list lost or unverified plays. Reprints of books (including facsimile editions) and revivals of plays are not listed unless a revision or change of title is involved. The most recent edited version of individual works is included if it supersedes the collected edition cited.

In the essays, short references to critical remarks refer to items cited in the Publications section or in the Reading List. Introductions, memoirs, editorial matter, etc. in works cited in the Publications section are not repeated in the Reading List.

INTRODUCTION

If the United Kingdom and the United States are two nations divided by a common language, seldom can the division have been more manifest than in the development of their dramatic literatures during the present century. With the more recently emergent theatres of the "old" and "new" commonwealth also staking their claims to consideration in any survey such as this, generalizations about English-speaking drama of the 20th century must be very tentative indeed. Perhaps the only safe statement is that the notorious linguistic chauvinism of the English-speaking nations has tended to leave them even further distant from the artistic and theatrical innovations of continental Europe than from each other's.

Such isolationism was one of the themes of William Archer's influential *English Dramatists of Today* (1882) – though "sardoodledom," as Bernard Shaw dubbed it, was still busy adapting the worst of French drama into lifelessly "well-made" fare. Henry Arthur Jones and Arthur Wing Pinero were, in truth, providing mildly more thoughtful and domesticated versions of this kind of play as much as they were weaning English audiences into an acceptance of Ibsen. Thus, for all the fulminations of Clement Scott and his like against Pinero's *The Second Mrs. Tanqueray* (1893) – its central character "a woman with a past" – the play's morality was staidly Victorian, however discreetly it picked at the hem-stitching of a subject more usually left veiled.

Pinero's own earlier work in farce – which he had largely forsaken for the "social drama" – remains eminently more worth reviving, just as it is, for that matter, often more striking in its implicit comments on middle-class morality. Similarly, the much-derided burlesques and melodramas which flourished on the Victorian stage often called social and artistic assumptions more effectively (if elliptically) into question than the floundering "legitimate" drama. But the social divide in theatre audiences, reflected also in the rise of the music hall, perpetuated a false distinction between "art" and "entertainment" which would have been entirely foreign to Shakespeare and the Elizabethans. Indeed, in looking at the attempts to drag the British drama unwillingly into the 20th century, one must not forget the flourishing state of the variety stage, and the important role it played in the birth of the animated picture, before the happy partnership of "cine-variety" gave way to the cut-throat competition of the 1920's.

It was a Dutchman, J. T. Grein, whose formation of the Independent Theatre in 1891 was the first serious attempt to create a British equivalent to the "free theatre" advocated and practised by Antoine. Its first production was, almost inevitably, Ibsen's *Ghosts*, and although its six-year life was mainly devoted to introducing foreign works to limited audiences, its influence in sustaining the efforts of Archer and Shaw to create a new British drama was considerable. Thus, it launched Shaw's own belated dramatic career with *Widowers' Houses* in 1892, the year after he had avowed his idiosyncratic dramatic discipleship in *The Quintessence of Ibsenism*.

Shaw was to remain more influential as a critic than as a dramatist throughout the decade: and although the Stage Society, which took up the work of the Independent Theatre in 1899, opened with the first production of what is now one of his most assuredly commercial plays, *You Never Can Tell*, it was not until the momentous partnership of Granville-Barker with J. E. Vedrenne, in their management of the Court Theatre from 1904 to 1907, that Shaw's plays began to win the acceptance of the general theatrical public.

In addition to the works of Shaw, and Barker's own over-discussive plays, the Court helped to establish the theatrical reputations of Galsworthy and of St. John Hankin; and, after Vedrenne had departed for the Savoy, it was here that Somerset Maugham made his name with *Lady Frederick* (within the next year, no less than three more of his plays shared its success, to run simultaneously in the West End). Barker's *Waste* had, however, been refused a licence by the Lord Chamberlain, and was staged in "club" conditions; but, as the first edition of *The Stage Year Book* commented, "had *Waste* been free to go to the public it is unlikely that they would have wanted the play." What they evidently did want was such dramatic candy-floss as writers like Alfred Sutro were churning out — "extremely clever in idea and treatment," *The Stage* article considered them, and "often very fresh in their outlook," though it conceded "a certain want of nature" in the characters.

If the new century did see a number of promising new British dramatists emerge, the newness of their plays was thus of a rather old-fashioned kind — typically, the dramatization of a pin-downable social "issue" explored through its effects on a family circle, with set-piece discussions between ostensibly naturalistic characters who in fact embodied tidy sets of ideas and assumptions. Shaw certainly employed the formula, however phlegmatically he kept his tongue in his cheek, and only in *Heartbreak House* can one begin to sense the pain behind the protocol. For in spite of the socialist apologetics, Shaw's characters were no less securely of the middle or upper classes than Sutro's: even honest John Galsworthy — notably in *Strife* and *Justice* — could produce working-class characters a mite more believable than Henry Straker or Alfred Doolittle.

Shaw was a selfless supporter of the limited-run system employed at the Court, which Archer and Barker were already advocating should be developed into a true repertoire of regularly programmed plays in their elaborate proposals for a National Theatre — not to be fully realized for another 60 years. Some attempts were made in the regions to establish theatres based on the repertoire principle, but in most cases this degenerated into the oft-derided system of "weekly" or "fortnightly rep." However, when Annie Horniman took over the old Gaiety in Manchester in 1908 she was not only laying the foundations of the modern repertory movement, but helping to create what became known as the "Manchester school" of dramatists, of which Stanley Houghton, Harold Brighouse, and Allan Monkhouse are the best-remembered writers. Such plays as Houghton's *Hindle Wakes* and Brighouse's *Hobson's Choice* did capture more than a caricatured regional flavour: but it was symptomatic of metropolitan prejudices that only *Hobson*, with its safe moral of a strong woman successfully standing up for "her man," found favour in London, while the more genuinely emancipated *Hindle* was unliked in the capital. Indeed, its understanding of the role of the sexes was more truly revolutionary than Shaw's in the all-too-aptly-titled *Man and Superman*.

Thus, even the "play of ideas" could often only succeed by getting so unobtrusively under the guard of bourgeois audiences that they never really noticed that their conventions were meant to be under attack. And, of course, there were plenty of dramatists only too ready to reassure them that all was for the best in the best of possible worlds. It is not at all surprising that two of the most theatrically enduring of the plays of the period before the First World War were both by that most perversely nostalgic of writers, Sir James Barrie — *Peter Pan*, about little boys who did not wish to grow up, and *The Admirable Crichton*, about a paragon of a servant capable of rising to the occasion, but content to acknowledge his "place" with the return to normalcy. The "message" of those plays was paradoxically both prophetic and deeply reactionary.

The British theatre was little affected by innovations on the Continent. All it could offer by way of a native version of the symbolism of Maeterlinck's *Pelléas and Mélisande* was Stephen Phillips's *Paolo and Francesca* — one of his half-dozen or so short-lived but highly acclaimed poetic dramas, which actually caused William Archer to greet Phillips as a new Milton. No British writer achieved the harsh, politicized realism of a Hauptmann or a Gorky. And even the *fin de siècle* fancy for aestheticism found Oscar Wilde far less shocking as a dramatist than he appeared to his age as a poet, or, for that matter, as a person. In Gordon Craig, the aesthetic movement did find a theoretician of lasting (if tangential) influence on the modern theatre, but as a director he was even less concerned with contemporary dramatists than he was with actors (who proved steadfastly reluctant to become marionettes). It's notable, too, that Granville-Barker, who went on from the Court to rescue Shakespeare from the spectacular "realism" of Irving and Tree, lacked the stylistic perception to free his own characters from naturalistic clutter – just as William Poel, in helping to rediscover Shakespeare's contemporaries for the living stage, had applied none of the lessons he learned to contemporary work.

So there were no British playwrights to follow the lead of the new novelists in exploring the artistic paths opened up by Freudian psychology – even James Joyce's single work for the theatre was a verbose, sub-Ibsenesque affair, and Lawrence's plays, little performed and certainly undervalued, mined a solidly naturalistic vein, almost documentary in its local colour. The London theatre offered no such early intimations of the absurdist or expressionist response to the human condition as did Jarry, Wedekind, or Strindberg – a response which was to seem so starkly appropriate after the futilities of the First World War. As for the war itself, it marked, for the British theatre, little more than a four-year interlude of musicals and other entertainments deemed to be the stuff for the troops on leave. Plays with such titles as *The Man Who Stayed at Home*, *The War Baby*, *Shell Out*, and *Brave Women Who Wait* filled uncritical houses. Even the eclipsed Stephen Phillips produced a ramblingly patriotic work called *Armageddon*, replete with the Shade of Attila, the Spirit of Joan of Arc, and Moloch, presumably in the flesh.

If the renewal of the British drama at the turn of the century was less than revolutionary, the renaissance in the Irish theatre that occurred in the same period coincided with and helped to swell a rising tide of nationalistic fervour. It was in 1899 that Lady Gregory, Yeats, George Moore, and Edward Martyn set up the Irish Literary Theatre; and Lady Gregory and Yeats, together with J. M. Synge, were to be the leading writers for the Abbey Theatre in Dublin when Miss Horniman took a lease on the building in 1905. While Yeats was able to tap the mythic roots of Irish consciousness, Lady Gregory was more at home with the anecdotal elements of her nation's folk-lore – and Synge somehow combined the soaring spirit of the one with the microcosmic domesticity of the other.

Although Synge died in 1909, and neither Yeats nor Lady Gregory wrote specifically for the Abbey after 1912, the craftsmanlike Lennox Robinson tended the theatre through the difficult years of civil war and independence, to await the new creative turbulence caused by the plays of Sean O'Casey. The stormy receptions accorded alike to Synge's *The Playboy of the Western World* in 1907 and to O'Casey's *The Plough and the Stars* nearly 20 years later may be instructively contrasted with the regard in which English audiences came to hold their own acerbic Irishman Shaw, the laughing, licensed jester of the British theatre.

American drama before the First World War was plentiful but largely pedestrian. If the subject-matter of writers such as William Gillette and Edward Sheldon was distinctively American, their work was of little stylistic originality – and, as in the case of Sheldon and the prolific Clyde Fitch, was often flawed by a persistent descent into sentimentality. James Herne's *Margaret Fleming* (1890) almost uncannily paralleled *The Second Mrs. Tanqueray* both in its date and in its "shocking" theme, but achieved nothing like Pinero's success, even *de scandale*. It was left to William Vaughn Moody to strike a more serious note, and in *The Great Divide* (1906) he attempted that combination of surface realism with the archetypal concerns of the American consciousness which has generally been realized only in the more expansive novel form.

The unadventurous state of the American theatre at the turn of the century was perpetuated if not caused by the vice-like hold exerted by "the Syndicate," a monopolistic group of agents and managements whom only the lightweight fare of such a writer as George M. Cohan could please. Their power was seriously challenged only by the independent spirit (and equally lightweight fare) of David Belasco, whose own managerial skills were happily combined with those of a spectacular melodramatist. His plays, though of little lasting interest, did at least whittle away at the power base of the Syndicate, which was finally destroyed by the rise of the no less monopolistic Shubert family, and the death of the leading Syndicate manager, Charles Frohman, in 1915.

Among the honourable band of actors who braved the wrath of the Syndicate had been James O'Neill, a matinee idol before his time, whose son Eugene was by 1915 already studying under George Pierce Baker at Harvard, where Baker's influential course in dramatic literature had been established ten years earlier. This was arguably the single most important development in the history of the American drama in the first decade of the century: but its pioneering influence was not to be felt in the theatre until after the First World War.

If that war proved to be a watershed for American and continental drama, for the British theatre it was little more than a backwater from which, with peace, the sturdy old oarsmen returned; and only with the economic depression and growing threat from fascism at the end of the 1920's could new currents be detected. But it must be said that, measured purely in terms of the quantity of work produced, the decade saw an enormous blossoming of interest in the theatre, not only in the West End but in the enormous number of clubs, play producing societies, drama guilds, and amateur groups for which the newly formed British Drama League provided a focal point – and this interest was not only in the traditional petty-cultural strongholds of the suburbs and the shire towns, but in working-class districts as well. A flourishing market in one-act plays sprang up in response to this phenomenon, and although almost all are now deservedly forgotten the importance of the movement in beginning to recreate a more broadly based audience for the theatre, particularly in the regions, should not be underestimated.

But the most notable theatrical regimes of the decade were of Lilian Baylis at the Old Vic, and Nigel Playfair at the Lyric Theatre, Hammersmith, which were concerned, respectively, with solid, educational Shakespeare, and with stylish productions of the minor classics. By and large, contemporary dramatists still had to succeed – or fail – in the West End, where the old actor-managers had finally bowed out to the commercial entrepreneurs, though theatregoing itself remained largely a social obligation for upper-middle-class audiences. Shaw, Galsworthy, and Barrie continued to write for these audiences, but it was the work of Somerset Maugham that was most closely tailored to their requirements. His plays have suffered since for this restricted *milieu,* but in one of his last dramatic works, *For Services Rendered* (1932), Maugham did show himself capable of cutting through conventional morality to write with bitterness and truth about the aftermath of war. R. C. Sherriff's *Journey's End* (1928) – a curious combination of contempt for militarism and regret for lost comradeship – was the only other British war play of much note, and it, too, was the product of a period when the war could be recollected with rationality if not tranquillity: it was left to an Irish writer, Sean O'Casey, to employ in *The Silver Tassie* the harsher vocabulary of expressionism to encompass the horrors of the trenches.

For the most part, writers in the 1920's were content rather to reflect the prevailing mood of desperate gaiety, most clearly captured in the palatably outrageous work of Noël Coward. Many of his comedies of superficial modern manners have proved too formulaic to survive: but when, in his farces, moral conventions are apparently preserved with a straighter face – so that they may *almost* be outraged, as the form demands – he struck a more enduring vein, and works like *Hay Fever* and *Blithe Spirit* stand alongside the vintage farces of Ben Travers as the major achievements of the period in that underestimated genre.

Miles Malleson's *The Fanatics* (1924) and Frederick Lonsdale's *Spring Cleaning* (1923), along with Coward's *The Vortex* (1924), questioned moral values in the brittle, mildly titillating manner of the "bright young things," while for their parents the later Lonsdale and A. A. Milne were perhaps most prominent among the many writers whose plays would typically be set in the sitting rooms of small country houses, well stocked with explicatory domestics and comforting bound volumes of *Punch*. Clifford Bax and Laurence Housman were the most craftsmanlike of those who sought the different kind of solace offered by the costume drama, while John Drinkwater attempted a more serious investigation of the lessons of history, though he never repeated the success of *Abraham Lincoln* (1918). Clemence Dane tackled a curious mixture of literary, historical, and contemporary themes, and St. John Ervine tried his hand at most forms from problem play to light comedy, while Sutton Vane's *Outward Bound* (1923) and Basil Dean and Margaret Kennedy's *The Constant Nymph* (1926) were very different examples of "one-off" successes, never to be repeated. At the other extreme, the year 1928 saw three thrillers by the perennial Edgar Wallace running simultaneously in the West End. But few of the plays of any of these writers now do more than gather dust on the shelves of second-hand bookshops.

The decade before the Second World War reflected in the British theatre the division in the country, between those who anticipated the conflict, and those who took refuge from its inevitability, whether in the glories and problems of the past, as in Gordon Daviot's *Richard of Bordeaux* (1933), in the downright myopic patriotism exemplified by Coward's *Cavalcade* (1931), or in the simpler reassurances of the family circle. The period was notable for the number of plays which were, in Robert Graves's phrase, "simple and clean," like Dodie Smith's encomium for domesticity, *Dear Octopus* (1938). Polished comedies were turned out by John van Druten, polished melodramas by Emlyn Williams, polished studies of character by James Bridie, and polished paradoxes about the nature of time by J. B. Priestley – who, like Shaw, proclaimed himself a socialist, but included few working-class characters in his plays, except below stairs. Other West End plays of the period showed no greater awareness of the lower orders, or of the social consequences of the depression – though Walter Greenwood's *Love on the Dole* (1935), adapted with Ronald Gow from his own novel, and Emlyn Williams's *The Corn Is Green* (1938) were honourable exceptions.

In the main, it was left, ironically, to the poetic dramatists from the public schools to inject politics into playwriting. The Group Theatre, formed in 1933, staged plays by W. H. Auden, Christopher Isherwood, Louis MacNeice, and Stephen Spender, in which moral archetype was duly set against moral archetype in the cause of the proletarian revolution. In the event, however, this body of work was more important to the development of post-war poetic drama – of which T. S. Eliot's *Murder in the Cathedral* (1935) was the most important forerunner – than to the creation of a theatre for working people. But the workers' theatre movement, which had had its beginnings in the 1920's, did now begin to bear fruit, in the early work of Joan Littlewood in Manchester, and the formation of Unity Theatre in London, followed by its various regional namesakes. None of these looked, at least initially, to native talent for their product, but rather to the techniques of political theatre developed in pre-fascist Germany, in the Soviet Union before the dead hand of "socialist realism" descended, and, most accessibly, in the United States. Glasgow Unity did begin to foster its own small school of Scottish writers during the war, but most of the political theatres took their inspiration from the play with which London Unity opened its doors in 1936, Clifford Odets's *Waiting for Lefty*.

Odets was a writer with the Group Theatre, New York, which first staged *Lefty* in the United States, and such close links between a playwright and a particular company had been a new and fruitful characteristic of the American theatre ever since the formation of the Provincetown Players in 1915. The most important of the Provincetown writers was, of course, Eugene O'Neill, who had been able to use the company as an outlet for his more experimental plays even after he had won wider acceptance from Broadway audiences. Much of O'Neill's work remains deeply flawed, but is the more astonishing for its formal range in the light of the previous conservatism of the American theatre. His brooding power is as alert in *The Iceman Cometh* – written in 1946 after a twelve years' silence – as in *Bound East for Cardiff* three decades earlier. O'Neill handled stylistic experiment with a sometimes disconcerting lack of self-awareness, was prone to linguistic bathos, and often used theatrical sledgehammers where nutcrackers were called for; but his figure continues to dominate the American theatre, to which for the first time he gave entirely distinctive shape.

The Washington Square Players and the Neighbourhood Playhouse were formed in the same year as the Provincetown Players, and in 1926 came Eva Le Gallienne's Civic Repertory Theatre. Not all were long lived, but it was from the remnants of the Washington Square Players that the more enduring Theatre Guild was created, to introduce professionalism into the struggle against the commercially-motivated managements. These groups were especially notable for bringing the work of the major European playwrights to the United States, and they prepared the soil in which the new writers encouraged by the Group Theatre, itself formed in 1929, could flourish.

Meanwhile, the protean 1920's in the American theatre saw the early verse dramas of

Maxwell Anderson alongside the satirical farces of George S. Kaufman, the abrasive naturalism of Sidney Howard alongside the amiable moralities of George Kelly, and the high comedies of Philip Barry alongside the distinctly lower comedies of S. N. Behrman. Elmer Rice introduced expressionism to America, while the diffuse talent of Paul Green began its exploration of the national folkways. It was a time of relaxed, expansive writing, befitting a period of prosperity which had also seen a boom in theatre building on Broadway – and which was to be brought so abruptly to a close by the great slump of 1929.

Although dedicated primarily to exploring the relevance of Stanislavskian techniques to the American stage, the Group Theatre inevitably found its work reflecting the radical climate of the post-depression years, in plays by such writers as John Howard Lawson (an early exponent of vaudevillian techniques in drama, and of the strip-cartoon-like style of living newspaper), the idealistic Irwin Shaw, the soft-centered Sidney Kingsley – and, most notably, the young Clifford Odets, who wrote more characteristically in the social-realist mould than in the agitprop form of *Waiting for Lefty*, his first produced play.

Such freer techniques were taken up less by the Stanislavskian Group Theatre than by the Federal Theatre Project, launched in 1935 as part of the Works Progress Administration programme. Of vital importance in its main task of giving work to unemployed actors, often in areas which had previously been theatrical deserts, the Federal Theatre also produced a number of its own "living newspapers," and was prominent in promoting the cause of black theatre, as well as helping to create the Mercury Theatre under Orson Welles and John Houseman. When the project was closed in 1939 it had contributed significantly to bringing the American theatre to maturity – healthily self-aware, and able to assimilate useful foreign influences without being overwhelmed by them. Not insignificantly, the FTP's director, Hallie Flanagan, was, like Eugene O'Neill, a student of George Pierce Baker.

Both Maxwell Anderson and Thornton Wilder had been in turn hailed as inheritors of the mantle of O'Neill, though in the event he was to outwrite both the humanistic but formally conventional Anderson and the innovative, resoundingly theatrical Wilder. Two lesser (though certainly individual) writers of the period, William Saroyan and Lillian Hellman, took, respectively, facile optimism and facile pessimism to equally irritating extremes, while Robert Sherwood reflected the more balanced if woolly liberalism of his age. All helped to assert that individuality of the American character which the company loyalties and the shared social concerns of the 1930's had to some extent softened, but which the ensuing quarter-century was to see once again in the ascendant.

It is significant that the major American contribution to the theatre during and immediately after the Second World War was in the musical: as well as providing a necessary morale-booster for an age of austerity, its typically large scale was ideally suited to combat the growing threat from television, and to accommodate the need for instant success (or failure) which the shrinking number of theatres and productions on Broadway created. The outwardly flamboyant temperament of Tennessee Williams was also well-suited to an all-or-nothing climate, and he succeeded in rousing his audiences with claustrophobic plays bursting at their own seams with sexuality, expressed, repressed, or sublimated. William Inge for a while appeared to be following in Williams's footsteps, in plays which tackled similar themes in a more sentimentalized manner, and Robert Anderson and Paddy Chayevsky also produced a few post-war plays of more than passing interest.

But these paled beside the work of Arthur Miller. More thoughtful though no less introspective than Williams, he had to battle for audiences against greater odds: but his *Death of a Salesman* (1949) succeeded, largely because of the shock of recognition it induced, in establishing itself as perhaps the first world classic of the American theatre. Miller continued to encourage the American public to question its own more insidious life-lies – notably in *The Crucible* (1953) – and might almost be said to have written himself out of a job when national self-questioning became endemic in the 1960's. But by that time such guerilla groups as the Living Theatre had prepared the ground for a generation of more militant dramatists and theatre workers – and had also begun to break the long stranglehold of Broadway over the American theatre.

The analogous influence of the West End over the British theatre began to wane rather sooner than this, in part under continuing pressure from the "little" and club theatres, and in part due to the happy wartime accident which created the Council for the Encouragement of Music and the Arts, in the belief that culture would help alleviate the rigours of the blitz and the blackout. As the Arts Council, this body was to play an increasingly important part after the war not only in funding but in shaping the direction of the arts – the theatre the most profoundly, as the most public of them all. Local government support for the arts was also encouraged, and these twin sources of subsidy were respectively to help decommercialize and decentralize the "serious" British theatre in the following decades.

In the immediate aftermath of war, the drama of social protest found itself largely burnt out by its own political success, while the middlebrow drama was agonizedly adjusting to the radically changed conditions of austerity. It is scarcely surprising, in retrospect, that the importance of the new poetic drama should have been overestimated. E. Martin Browne, who had first encouraged T. S. Eliot to turn to the stage, now made the little Mercury Theatre, where *Murder in the Cathedral* had first been seen in London, a permanent home for poetic drama, and here were produced Ronald Duncan's *This Way to the Tomb* and Christopher Fry's *A Phoenix Too Frequent*. Fry went on to achieve considerable commercial success with his mixture of poetic whimsy and profundity, and Eliot's continuing work in the medium – in most cases first seen at the newly-founded Edinburgh Festival – contributed to the impression that a new poetic renaissance in the drama was indeed under way.

But the renaissance proved short-lived, and Eliot's plays, for all their loose classical trappings, came increasingly to resemble drawing-room comedies of eccentric upper-class manners, which just happened to be set in verse and to be pregnant with metaphysical overtones. There were, in truth, enough writers now emerging to produce such plays without any such pretensions – notably Terence Rattigan, with his over-crafted models of English understatement; N. C. Hunter, with his well-made laments for the declining status and values of the bourgeoisie; William Douglas Home, who observed with wry detachment political and domestic manoeuvres slightly higher up the social ladder; and the more original Peter Ustinov, whose eternal promise never quite developed beyond the level of witty anecdotage. The novelist Graham Greene also passed through a theatrical phase, while the poet Dylan Thomas contributed in *Under Milk Wood* a brilliant dramatic sport, without antecedent or successor. That the play was, however, originally written for radio is a pertinent reminder that the BBC was helping to keep dramatic invention alive amidst the prevailing doldrums, with the quirky Giles Cooper and the erudite parodist Henry Reed the brightest innovators in a challenging but too-often neglected medium.

The Arts Theatre Club in London had provided a home for interesting and experimental work during and after the war, and it was here that the first play by John Whiting to reach the stage, *Saint's Day*, was greeted with howls of protest and counter-protest in 1951. That Whiting was virtually driven out of the theatre after a few more attempts to breach the defences of the West End suggests the low water-mark to which the British theatre had sunk by the mid-1950's. But though it was to be at the Royal Court in 1956 that those defences were at last to give way, it is only fair to stress that the tide had, almost unnoticed, begun to turn with the arrival of Joan Littlewood's Theatre Workshop at its permanent home in Stratford, East London, in 1953. Meanwhile, another production at the Arts Theatre was raising more perceptible storm signals along the tranquil waterfront of the British theatre in 1955, when a new young director, Peter Hall, directed the British premiere of a play by Samuel Beckett – *Waiting for Godot*.

Beckett, like so many Irish playwrights, wrote from exile. But, like his fellow-exile and early master Joyce, he remained profoundly influenced by the *mores* and the idiom of his native land. (The Abbey Theatre in Dublin had duly driven its only major inter-war discovery, Sean O'Casey, into exile in England, and although its pioneering role was in part taken over by the Gate Theatre under Micheál MacLiammóir and Hilton Edwards, Denis Johnston was the only writer of much importance to emerge from the Irish theatre before that broth of a dramatist, Brendan Behan, erupted into the early seasons of Theatre

Workshop, and drank himself to an early death.) Beckett had made his reputation as a novelist, writing in French, before creating in *Godot* one of the seminal plays of the post-war years. The later *Endgame* carried its own influential, apocalyptic message, and Beckett has continued to refine his art – as it sometimes seems, almost out of existence. But those two tramps, eternally expecting the arrival of Godot, and in their waiting running through a sort of inverted paradigm of the conventions of comedy, have remained the most enduring of Beckett's metaphors for the ways in which men try to reconcile themselves to their own absurdity and probable extinction.

When George Devine created his "playwrights' theatre" at the Royal Court in 1956, and cannily spotted the promise of a young actor-playwright called John Osborne, aspiring writers suddenly recognized with the success of *Look Back in Anger* that the theatre was, once more, a medium in which challenging things could be said – if necessary, as *Godot* had shown, in unconventional ways. No matter that *Look Back in Anger* now seems a fairly orthodox psychological drama about a mixed-up marriage: the fact that it drew for its characters upon the disillusioned young, in a scruffy setting far from the sitting rooms of Hampstead or the Surrey suburbs, struck a chord of recognition in many writers for whom the political watershed of 1956 – with its dying twitch of British imperialism in the Suez adventure, and flexing of Soviet muscles in Budapest – had provided other causes for rethinking received positions. For the theatre, the first visit in the same year to Britain of the Berliner Ensemble provided a jolt of a different kind – to accepted attitudes concerning the relationship between performers and audience.

An explosion of energy followed, at first with the Royal Court and Theatre Workshop as its twin epicentres, then increasingly fed by shock waves from the regions, where the relative affluence of the late 1950's and early 1960's led to a boom in the building and reconstruction of theatres subsidized by local authorities. In 1960 Peter Hall took over the direction of the Shakespeare Memorial Theatre at Stratford-upon-Avon, rechristened his ensemble the Royal Shakespeare Company, and opened a London home for them at the Aldwych Theatre. Three years later the long-awaited National Theatre took up residence at the Old Vic, while its own grandiose concrete home began its lengthy struggle from the drawing board. And in 1964 the newly elected Labour government created, for the first time in Britain, a Ministry for the Arts, under which Arts Council resources increased dramatically. In all these developments – only the most notable in that period of hectic activity – it is difficult to separate cause from effect. What is certain is that the dozen years between 1956 and 1968 saw more important work in British theatre than had been accomplished in as many decades previously.

John Osborne continued to write for the Court with more or less success during the period, his talent increasingly recognized as highly individual rather than representative of his generation – though it was, sadly, apparently extinguished with the onset of irritable middle age. A more typical figure of the time was probably Arnold Wesker, whose early work was presented at one of the first of the new civic theatres, the Belgrade in Coventry, but soon transferred to the Royal Court, with which theatre he quickly became identified. Like Osborne, Wesker at first used fairly conventional, naturalistic, three-act formats: again, it was his subject-matter – in the *Trilogy*, effectively the history of two generations of an East End family of Jewish socialists – that was so startlingly original.

Both Osborne and Wesker explored new formal possibilities as they developed, but the third major writer to emerge from the Royal Court in its early years, John Arden, was remarkable for striking out from the first in his own stylistic directions. He has ranged from the episodic, mythic quality of his first play to reach the main stage, *Serjeant Musgrave's Dance*, through modern *commedia dell'arte* and council-estate naturalism, to Aristophanic farce and historical chronicle. He has also been unusual among writers of his generation in evolving from an early dispassionate political attitude towards the polemical, avowedly socialist viewpoint of his later work – whereas Osborne has long since discarded his own rather romantic socialism for a sort of pastoral angst, and Wesker, while remaining true to his ideals, has shifted the emphasis in his writing from public affairs to private pain.

Down in the East End, Theatre Workshop developed its own tradition in parallel rather than collaboration with the Royal Court. Apart from the burnt-out Behan, the most promising product of its early years was Shelagh Delaney – whose *A Taste of Honey*, according to legend written in disgusted reaction to a play of Terence Rattigan's, displayed with raw authenticity and some poetry the facts of life and love in a northern industrial slum. Deeply influential, the play remained Shelagh Delaney's only important work, and raises the question of how far it was indebted to the creative process of reshaping to which Joan Littlewood subjected most material in rehearsal. By such methods Theatre Workshop fostered a school of minor East End dramatists, and both the title and the tempo of the cockney musical *Fings Ain't Wot They Used T'Be* typify the breezy if slightly self-conscious style which Joan Littlewood rough-hewed into the unpolished perfection of *Oh, What a Lovely War!* before effectively leaving the company in 1963.

Many writers both for the Court and Theatre Workshop produced only one or two interesting plays before sinking into relative obscurity – one thinks of Ann Jellicoe with *The Sport of My Mad Mother* and *The Knack*, Bernard Kops with *The Hamlet of Stepney Green*, and Alun Owen with *Progress to the Park*, all of which caught in different ways the spirit of their place and times, yet whose authors have never quite been able to repeat their success. Others who were perhaps first persuaded of the potentiality of theatre by the work of the Royal Court – John Mortimer, for example – received their first productions there, but have since become accepted as West End playwrights. Yet others found their way into the theatre by the more conventional routes – in the cases of Robert Bolt and Peter Shaffer, straight into the West End, where, indeed, their spiritual homes have proved to be, though Shaffer's upmarket expansions of psychological dramas into quasi-epic moulds have latterly required the resources of the National Theatre (which finally moved into its purpose-built permanent home, with three auditoriums, in 1976).

David Mercer also earned his spurs in the commercial theatre – strangely, for a writer who has continued to combine his socialism with an interest in Laingian psychology. He has now, more appropriately, become a sort of "house" dramatist for the Royal Shakespeare Company, which came relatively late to the encouragement of new writing. But its short experimental season at the Arts Theatre in the early 1960's introduced no less than three dramatists to full exposure in live theatre – Giles Cooper, who turned briefly from his radio work to create a couple of chilling black comedies before his premature death; Henry Livings, whose anarchic farces have never found a permanent spiritual home; and David Rudkin, who only recently shook off the image of the "one-play" author of *Afore Night Come* to produce major new work, again for the RSC. Michael Hastings was another writer who, after the early success of *Yes, and After*, seemed to lie fallow, until returning creatively to the scene – and it is perhaps significant that he, like Rudkin, was difficult to "place" in the early years after 1956, when the critical tendency was to categorize most dramatists as either socially-conscious or absurdists.

It was, therefore, inevitable that Harold Pinter should have been first regarded as a follower of the so-called "theatre of the absurd," once the disastrous reception of *The Birthday Party* had given way to the success of *The Caretaker*, which transferred for a long West End run after opening at the still-influential Arts. Enough has already been written on Pinter to fill a dozen volumes of the present size, but just as he is certainly the most widely explicated of contemporary dramatists, so also is he among the most resolutely silent, outside the chosen confines of his terse, increasingly mannered plays. His success, however enduring it may prove, has certainly been a strongly personal one, and soon paid off whatever debts it owed to Beckett. Apart from the sadly short-winded verbal energies of N. F. Simpson, who more truly belonged to the tradition of English comic eccentrics than to the French absurd school, there were thus relatively few new British writers who could be credited as its alumni.

Among the talents of the "second wave" of new writers, even fewer conformed to convenient critical stereotypes. The first of these individualists to emerge was Tom Stoppard, whose *Rosencrantz and Guildenstern Are Dead* stepped straight from a student production on the "fringe" of the Edinburgh Festival into the National Theatre. Stoppard has continued to produce plays combining sprightly metaphysical high jinks with cunningly crafted plots and cardboard characters: the veneer of profundity overlaying his undoubted wit has naturally endeared him to West End audiences, who, though of much the same social composition as ever, will cheerfully assimilate in time the cultural influences they at first despise. Even Joe Orton enjoyed posthumous commercial success, when some of the taboos he had helped to trample over lost a little of their sanctity in the process. (The new style of stringent satire first employed in 1961 in the revue *Beyond the Fringe* also did its share of taboo-trampling, but its initiatives were sustained on television and in the press rather than in the theatre, though one of the *Fringe* writers, Alan Bennett, did go on to write some gentler satiric comedies for the West End.) Orton's sexually freebooting farces owed something of their impish energy to the tradition of Ben Travers, while their distinctive language often resembled an unlikely combination of Congreve and the civil service.

The most important writer to emerge during the 1960's was Edward Bond, whose vision was uniquely his own, but whose concerns prophetically foreshadowed those of the coming decade. His plays, from the close social realism of *Saved* to the eloquent myth-making of *Lear*, managed to blend a high seriousness of purpose with extreme precision of theatrical execution – and a gift for interdependent verbal and physical imagery unequalled since Brecht. Both Orton and Bond found themselves in frequent trouble with the Lord Chamberlain in his role as censor, which was becoming increasingly anachronistic and was finally abolished in 1968 – just one of the kaleidoscopic events of a year which was to prove a further turning point in the history of the British theatre, as indeed in the climate of international affairs.

The renewal of energies in the American theatre sprang from different causes. Though one of its impulses – the beginnings of the movement for small "off-off-Broadway" theatres, which dates from Café Cino's opening in 1958 – was more or less contemporaneous with the breaking of the English "new wave," here it was slower to develop and flourish. Thus, whereas the creation of permanent repertory companies by the National Theatre and the RSC had undoubtedly been a major factor contributing to the strength of the British theatre, the opening in New York in 1965 of the Lincoln Center for the Performing Arts proved a source of continuing disappointment. Joe Papp's humbler Public Theatre, which had its origins in the parks during the 1950's, was, however, the direct ancestor of the new Public Theatre which opened in 1967 with *Hair,* the musical which "defined" the decade as *Oklahoma!* had the 1940's, and *West Side Story* the 1950's. The growth of non-profit regional theatre in some ways mirrored the increase in decentralized activity in Britain, but the needs of the geographically immense United States made each new centre more truly its own focal point, rather than part of a national cultural network.

But alongside the new playhouses and companies that flourished (and as often fell by the wayside) off-off-Broadway – most notably, Café La Mama, opened in 1961 by Ellen Stewart – arose a number of small, sometimes itinerant companies, often regionally based. The oldest of them all, the Living Theatre, continued also to be the most avant-garde under the direction of Julian Beck and Judith Malina, and here Jack Gelber's influential, spontaneous-seeming drugs play, *The Connection,* had been premiered in 1959. But by the later 1960's the Living Theatre had largely abandoned the use of existing scripts and, often in exile, preferred constantly to renew its own penchant for highly physical, ostensibly improvised theatre. Other important companies included Joe Chaikin's Open Theater, the San Francisco Mime Troupe founded by Ronnie Davis, and the Bread and Puppet Theatre, under Peter Schumann. Later, Richard Schechner's Performance Group and the Chicano company El Teatro Campesino reflected the new concern respectively with environmental and ethnic theatre: but all the groups shared an interest in non-naturalistic modes of performance, and in exploring new kinds of relationship between actors and their audiences.

Amidst this hive of communal activity, it is not surprising that the names of companies stand out rather than those of playwrights. Of the writers who emerged in the 1950's, Lorraine Hansberry died tragically young, and Arthur Kopit worked out his own erratic, satirical variations on the American Dream, while Edward Albee was the only figure to achieve international status. From his absurdist early work Albee passed through the starkly realistic mood of *Who's Afraid of Virginia Woolf?* into a phase of aesthetic exploration which took him from the lucidly downbeat *A Delicate Balance* to the labyrinthine *Tiny Alice*. Among writers to emerge more recently, the most original and the most prolific has been Sam Shepard, whose wild, image-rich genius sets American media-myths in startling new lights, using language of strength, subtlety, and often stunning rightness.

The upsurge of ethnic consciousness in the 1960's saw the creation for the first time of an extensive body of black plays for black audiences – whereas Hansberry and even James Baldwin had found themselves using forms (and sometimes looking for audiences) inherited from the "white" theatre. The Free Southern Theatre was founded in New Orleans in 1964, and the short-lived but influential Black Arts Repertoire Theatre in the following year. From its ashes sprang a nationwide complex of black groups, of which the most important were the militant Spirit House, Newark, formed in 1966, the New Lafayette Company in 1967, and the integrationist Negro Ensemble Company a year later. Spirit House was the inspiration of LeRoi Jones, who now writes under his Muslim name of Amiri Baraka, and whose work ranges in mood from the despairing to the poignant, and in style from the abrupt naturalism of *Dutchman* to the neo-expressionism of *Slave Ship*. Ed Bullins, who works largely with the New Lafayette Theatre, is a more expansive, indeed expansionist writer, mainly concerned with large-scale explorations of the realities of negro life in the United States.

No British black writers of equivalent stature have yet appeared, though Barry Reckord, Michael Abbensetts, and Mustapha Matura are probably the most notable of the Caribbean dramatists now working in London. The major West Indian playwright is undoubtedly Derek Walcott, born in St. Lucia but now settled in Trinidad, the only writer of the area to have achieved an international reputation for his bittersweet evocations of Caribbean life. Among African writers in English, the Nigerian Wole Soyinka writes with gentle irony of the contrasts between the new, developing Africa and the certainties of the old tribal homelands, while in South Africa the white dramatist Athol Fugard has shown a continuing concern for the oppressed black majority of that country – though his plays have been the more forceful for their recognition of human complexity and cussedness, and their idiomatic portrayal of the "poor whites" whose needs counterpoint those of their black compatriots.

Fugard has acknowledged his indebtedness to the work and writings of the Polish theatrical innovator Jerzy Grotowski, and throughout the English-speaking world the late 1960's saw a new concern with the non-verbal elements of theatre which Grotowski stressed. Sometimes the results were highly disciplined but extremely stylized (as in the productions of the late Naftali Yavin and The Other Company), sometimes brutally physical or stridently sexual, as in the more blatant misinterpretations of the ideas of Antonin Artaud. So, in Britain, just as the visit of the Berliner Ensemble had had a shaping influence on the direction taken by the theatre after 1956, among the factors which helped to make the year 1968 a new turning point were the visits of various of the pioneering American companies, and the work of three expatriate American directors – Charles Marowitz, Jim Haynes, and Ed Berman.

The "events" in Paris in the May of 1968, the bitter brevity of Dubcek's "Prague spring," and the mounting protests in the United States against American involvement in the Vietnam War had little lasting effect on politics in Britain, but did contribute to the radical change in the cultural mood. Though many of the dramatists of the "generation of 1956" continued to write and develop, the turn of the decade saw quite different kinds of relationships between emergent writers and the small, often itinerant theatre groups that began to spring up – at first in such venues as Jim Haynes's short-lived but seminal Arts Lab as part of a self-consciously "underground" spirit of protest, but gradually beginning to make their contribution to the mainstream of theatre activity.

In the West End, the steady decline in the commercial theatre continued, with only a few writers of even middling seriousness making much appeal – typically, with the mixtures of sexual and mild intellectual titillation offered by the academic love-games of Simon Gray, or the infinite changes upon middle-class, menopausal philanderings rung by Alan Ayckbourn. Peter Nichols offered a wider-ranging but modishly cynical kind of serio-comedy, and

Christopher Hampton produced stylish work which owed some of its success to the very schematic quality by which it was flawed. But just as the West End was increasingly filled with transfers from the regional theatres, or from the subsidized national companies, so the work even of such commercially successful dramatists had been "discovered" first in these more adventurous outlets. Ayckbourn, in particular, is an intriguing exception to every rule: the nearest to a purely "boulevard" dramatist writing in Britain, he is nevertheless loyal to the little theatre-in-the-round in provincial Scarborough for which virtually all of his work is first produced.

David Hare is another writer whose well-rounded attacks on liberalism have come to appeal to the more masochistic instincts of West End audiences, yet who first worked with one of the most influential of the small groups, the aptly-named Portable Theatre. And it was here that the bleak political visions of Howard Brenton and the imagistic, dream-like plays of Snoo Wilson also reached their first audiences. Though, like Hare and Brenton, many other writers of their generation now write for whichever national, regional, or commercial management will take their plays (and a few, like Trevor Griffiths, have turned to the huge audiences offered by television), the number whose earliest work is closely associated with one or another of the smaller companies remains substantial. David Edgar, for instance, whose anti-fascist chronicle *Destiny* was eventually produced by the Royal Shakespeare Company to become one of the seminal works of the period, began his prolific career with the General Will. But such continuing loyalties as those of John McGrath for the 7:84 Companies of England and Scotland, and of Steven Berkoff for his own London Theatre Group, are now exceptional, while Pip Simmons and the People Show are the sole survivors of any importance among the numerous groups once dedicated to collectively-created performance.

Not that the number of small companies has diminished, but they have tended to concentrate in particular areas, either speaking to specific sections of the community – children, women, or the various ethnic and sexual minorities – or working closely within the defined area of a particular local community. Meanwhile, many of the national and regional companies have created their own "studio" theatres (the Royal Court's Theatre Upstairs was among the first), where the experimental work once associated with the freewheeling "underground" companies now enjoys the benefits – and the associated dangers – of being institutionalized. Even the Royal Shakespeare Company has opened its own studio theatre spaces both in Stratford and London. Its productions of the work of such writers as Howard Barker, Barrie Keeffe, and Stephen Poliakoff at the Warehouse in London have, in particular, demonstrated not only the huge advantages of providing younger writers with better technical facilities and a larger company than they might otherwise enjoy, but also underlined the dangers of allowing an almost predictable set of "company" attitudes, both political and stylistic, to develop – in this case, a sort of broadly left-wing despondency in the face of an exploitative, urbanized, violent society – from which both the theatre and the writers may find it difficult to escape.

Inevitably, any such survey as this must hedge its critical bets in assessing the recent past. To the new writers already mentioned could be added (in order not of importance but, very roughly, of their emergence as writers for live theatre) the names of James Saunders, Charles Wood, David Halliwell, Peter Terson, C. P. Taylor, Brian Friel, Peter Gill, Stanley Eveling, Peter Barnes, Heathcote Williams, Caryl Churchill, E. A. Whitehead, Pam Gems, and Steve Gooch – all of whom have a body of promising work behind them, and plenty of creative years ahead. Lists equally long could, of course, have been drawn up for almost any decade of the century, had not history already sorted out most of the winners from the also-rans. Yet the prospects for the present generation do look more hopeful in two respects. Firstly, the very conception of dramatists as "winners" or "losers" in some desperate race along the corridors of a hall of fame is becoming, thankfully, less appropriate, in an age when the decline of the commercial sector is changing the idea of theatre as just another packaged cultural commodity. Secondly, and consequently, the writers of the present day are less restricted by the "received" styles or conventions, social or theatrical, needed for commercial success, and so are writing for (if not always reaching) a more broadly based audience than any generation of dramatists in history – not excluding the Elizabethan.

State subsidy for the theatre is often maligned – from the political right for its featherbedding effects, from the left for its inherent dangers of political censorship. But it has in practice contributed enormously to the wide social spread of new theatre writing – not only in Britain, but, for example, in Australia, where the 1960's and 1970's saw a burgeoning new theatre, for the first time drawn from and contributing to a distinctively national style and idiom. Meanwhile, in the United States the National Endowment for the Arts, though created as recently as 1966, has already caught up with the Arts Council of Great Britain in its funding for the theatre, relative to the much larger population it serves. The stronger existing American tradition of subsidy for the arts from private foundations (and the "hidden" subsidy of the widespread network of university theatres) has, however, given the explosion in regional theatre a much more varied and pragmatic form than in Britain – at its worst simply substituting one set of commercial pressures for another, but at its best proving healthily regenerative.

In America too, the dramatists who achieve – or need to achieve – old-style Broadway success are getting fewer, though their numbers do include the phenomenally successful Neil Simon, to name but half-a-dozen. More and more writers are thus emerging from the off-off-Broadway theatres or from the regions – where a sometimes competitive effort to include the "best of new writing" is an increasingly regular feature of "prestigious" programming (ironically, the quality of the classical repertoire is now more often to be deplored than that of the newly premiered productions). It's notable that the worst of the false glitter and stylistic affectations of the late 1960's is also disappearing, to give way to a harder slog to win regular and (most important) wider audiences. And the range of attitudes and styles employed by such writers as Lanford Wilson, Terrence McNally, Paul Foster, Israel Horovitz, Tom Eyen, Kenneth H. Brown, Jean-Claude van Itallie, John Guare, Michael Weller, David Rabe, Thomas Babe, and David Mamet covers a spectrum no less wide than that of their British counterparts.

For most of the 20th century, it should be remembered, the theatre has felt itself to be fighting for its very survival, against the successive counter-attractions of film, radio, and television. Further electronic miracles notwithstanding, the fact that the theatre *has* not only survived such threats, but is actually flourishing throughout the English-speaking world as at no other period in the present century, suggests that the unpredictable "event" that occurs whenever live actors perform before live audiences does meet (and can exploit, whether for better or worse) a continuing human need. And it is partly the very success of the newer media in providing the more instant and easily assimilable kinds of satisfaction that has led to the decline of the commercial theatre – except, significantly, in such spectacular areas as the musical. The theatre that survives is not an art form forced to admit that it enjoys only a minority appeal, needing to be constantly underwritten by subsidy of one sort or another, but one which is looking with increasing flexibility at the *kind* of appeal it exerts, and the kind of experience that can only be offered by its unique blending of talents. The playwright is just one of the contributors to this combination, but, after the brief and no doubt necessary flirtations with forms of "collective creation" of the late 1960's, is now once more recognized as the most important. I would cheerfully and with real confidence predict that, in ten years time, an edition of the present work would need to be twice as thick.

READING LIST

1. Bibliographies, handbooks, etc.

Parker, John, editor, *Who's Who in the Theatre,* 1912; 16th edition, edited by Ian Herbert, 1977.

Logasa, H., and W. Ver Nooy, *An Index to One-Act Plays,* 2 vols, 1924; 5 supplements, 1932–66.

Ottemiller, J. H., *Index to Plays in Collections,* 1943; 4th edition, 1964.

Ryan, P. M., *History of the Modern Theatre: A Selective Bibliography,* 1960.

Stratman, Carl J., *A Bibliography of British Dramatic Periodicals 1720–1960,* 1962.

Burton, E. J., *The Student's Guide to British Theatre and Drama,* 1963.

Thomson, R. G., and N. O. Ireland, editors, *Index to Full Length Plays, 1895–1964,* 3 vols., 1964–65.

Faxon, F. W., and others, editors, *Dramatic Index 1909–49,* 2 vols., 1965.

Rigdon, Walter, *The Biographical Encyclopedia and Who's Who of the American Theatre,* 1966; revised edition, as *Notable Names of the American Theatre,* 1976.

Adelman, I., and R. Dworkin, *Modern Drama: A Checklist of Critical Literature on 20th-Century Plays,* 1967.

Long, E. Hudson, *American Drama from Its Beginnings to the Present,* 1970.

Mikhail, E. H., *A Bibliography of Modern Irish Drama 1899–1970,* 1972.

The Brock Bibliography of Canadian Stage Plays in English 1900–1972, 1972; supplement, 1973.

Nicoll, Allardyce, *English Drama 1900–1930: The Beginnings of the Modern Period,* 1973.

Vinson, James, editor, *Contemporary Dramatists,* 1973; revised edition, 1977.

Breed, Paul F., and Florence M. Sniderman, *Dramatic Criticism Index,* 1973.

Mikhail, E. H., *Contemporary British Drama 1950–76: An Annotated Critical Bibliography,* 1976.

Mikhail, E. H., *English Drama 1900–50: A Guide to Information Sources,* 1976.

2. General histories

Reynolds, E., *Modern English Drama: A Survey of the Theatre since 1900,* 1949; revised edition, 1950.

Trewin, J. C., *Theatre since 1900,* 1951.

Meserve, Walter, *An Outline History of American Drama,* 1965.

Nicoll, Allardyce, *English Drama 1900–1930: The Beginnings of the Modern Period,* 1973.

Rees, Leslie, *The Making of Australian Drama: An Historical and Critical Survey from the 1830's to the 1970's,* 2 vols., 1973.

3. Themes, topics, and short periods, etc.

Clurman, Harold, *The Fervent Years: The Story of the Group Theatre,* 1945.

Bentley, Eric, *The Modern Theatre: A Study of Dramatists and the Drama,* 1948.

Speaight, Robert, *Drama since 1939,* 1948.

Gassner, John, *Form and Idea in Modern Theatre,* 1956.

Trewin, J. C., *The Gay Twenties: A Decade of the Theatre,* 1958; *The Turbulent Thirties: A Further Decade of the Theatre,* 1960.

Donoghue, Denis, *The Third Voice: Modern British and American Verse Drama,* 1959.

Kitchin, Laurence, *Mid-Century Drama,* 1960; revised edition, 1962.

Taylor, John Russell, *Anger and After: A Guide to the New British Theatre*, 1962; as *The Angry Theatre*, 1962; revised edition, 1969.

Weales, Gerald, *American Drama since World War II*, 1962; *The Jumping-Off Place: American Drama in the 1960's*, 1969.

Himelstein, Morgan Y., *Drama Was a Weapon: The Left-Wing Theatre in New York 1929–1941*, 1963.

Corrigan, Robert W., editor, *Theatre in the Twentieth Century*, 1963.

Freedman, M., editor, *Essays in the Modern Drama*, 1964.

Rabkin, Gerald, *Drama and Commitment: Politics in the American Theatre of the 1930's*, 1964.

Bogard, Travis, and W. I. Oliver, editors, *Modern Drama: Essays in Criticism*, 1965.

Brustein, Robert, *The Theatre in Revolt: An Approach to Modern Drama*, 1965.

Merchant, W. M., *Creed and Drama: An Essay in Religious Experience*, 1965.

Kitchin, Laurence, *Drama in the Sixties*, 1966.

Bigsby, C. W. E., *Confrontation and Commitment: A Study of Contemporary American Drama*, 1967.

Hogan, Robert, *After the Irish Renaissance*, 1967.

Taylor, John Russell, *The Rise and Fall of the Well-Made Play*, 1967.

Spanos, W. V., *The Christian Tradition in Modern British Verse Drama: The Poetics of Sacramental Time*, 1967.

Marowitz, Charles, and Simon Trussler, editors, *Theatre at Work*, 1967.

Kostelanetz, Richard, *The Theatre of Mixed Means*, 1968.

Laurence, Margaret, *Long Drums and Cannons: Nigerian Dramatists and Novelists*, 1968.

Cohn, Ruby, *Currents in Contemporary Drama*, 1969.

Gilman, Richard, *The Confusion of Realms*, 1970.

Taylor, John Russell, *The Second Wave: British Drama for the Seventies*, 1971.

Turner, Darwin T., *Black Drama in America*, 1971.

Lewis, Allan, *The Contemporary Theatre*, 1971.

Lewis, Allan, *American Plays and Playwrights*, 1971.

Cohn, Ruby, *Dialogue in American Drama*, 1971.

Elsom, John, *The Theatre Outside London*, 1971.

Brown, John Russell, *Theatre Language*, 1972.

New, W. H., editor, *Dramatists in Canada*, 1972.

Mason, Bruce, *New Zealand Drama: A Parade of Forms and a History*, 1972.

Kurdys, Douglas Bellamy, *Form in Modern Verse Drama*, 1972.

Valgemae, Mardi, *Accelerated Grimace: Expressionism in the American Drama of the 1920's*, 1972.

McLeod, Stuart R., *Modern Verse Drama*, 1972.

Bell, Sam Hanna, *The Theatre in Ulster*, 1972.

Schechner, Richard, *Environmental Theatre*, 1973.

Worth, Katharine, *Revolutions in Modern English Drama*, 1973.

ÓhAodha, Mícheál, *Theatre in Ireland*, 1974.

Hinchcliffe, Arnold P., *British Theatre, 1950–70*, 1974.

Gilman, Richard, *The Making of Modern Drama*, 1975.

Hogan, Robert, and James Kilroy, editors, *The Modern Irish Drama: A Documentary History*, 1975—

Anderson, Michael, *Anger and Detachment*, 1976.

Trewin, J. C., *The Edwardian Theatre*, 1976.

Elsom, John, *Post-War British Theatre*, 1976.

Graham-White, Anthony, *The Drama of Black Africa*, 1976.

Bogard, Travis, and others, *American Drama*, 1977.

Hunt, Hugh, John Russell Taylor, and Kenneth Richards, *The Revels History of Drama in English*, vol. 8: *1880 to the Present*, 1978.

Hayman, Ronald, *British Theatre since 1955*, 1979.

4. Anthologies of primary material

Mantle, Burns, and others, editors, *The Best Plays of 1920,* 1920, and later volumes.

Famous Plays of Today, 1929, and later volumes to 1954.

Trewin, J. C., editor, *Plays of the Year 1948–49,* 1949, and later volumes.

Bentley, Eric., editor, *The Modern Theatre*, 6 vols., 1955–60.

New English Dramatists 1, 1959, and later volumes.

Miller, Jordan Y., editor, *American Dramatic Literature,* 1961.

Weales, Gerald, editor, *Edwardian Plays,* 1962.

Hogan, Robert, editor, *Seven Irish Plays 1946–64,* 1967.

Rowell, George, editor, *Late Victorian Plays 1890–1914,* 1968.

Okpaku, J., editor, *Contemporary African Drama: A Critical Anthology,* 1971.

Kalman, R., editor, *A Collection of Canadian Plays,* 3 vols., 1973.

ALBEE, Edward (Franklin, III).   American.   Born in Washington, D.C., 12 March 1928. Educated at Lawrenceville School; Valley Forge Military Academy, Pennsylvania; Choate School, Connecticut, graduated 1946; Trinity College, Hartford, Connecticut, 1946–47. Served in the United States Army. Worked as a radio writer, WNYC, office boy, Warwick and Legler, record salesman, Bloomingdale's, book salesman, G. Schirmer, counterman, Manhattan Towers Hotel, messenger, Western Union, 1955–58, all in New York. Producer, with Richard Barr and Clinton Wilder, New Playwrights Unit Workshop, later Albarwild Theatre Arts, and Albar Productions, New York; also a stage director. Founder, William Flanagan Center for Creative Persons, Montauk, Long Island, New York, 1971. United States Cultural Exchange Visitor to Russia. Recipient: Berlin Festival Award, 1959, 1961; Vernon Rice Award, 1960; Obie Award, 1960; Argentine Critics Award, 1961; Lola D'Annunzio Award, 1961; New York Drama Critics Circle Award, 1964; Outer Circle Award, 1964; Antoinette Perry Award, 1964; Margo Jones Award, 1965; Pulitzer Prize, 1967, 1975. Litt.D.: Trinity College, 1974. Member, National Institute of Arts and Letters, 1966. Lives in Montauk, New York.

PUBLICATIONS

Plays

The Zoo Story (produced 1959).   In The Zoo Story, The Death of Bessie Smith, The
    Sandbox, 1960.
The Sandbox (produced 1960).   In The Zoo Story, The Death of Bessie Smith, The
    Sandbox, 1960.
The Death of Bessie Smith (produced 1960).   In The Zoo Story, The Death of Bessie
    Smith, The Sandbox, 1960.
The Zoo Story, The Death of Bessie Smith, The Sandbox: Three Plays.   1960; as The
    Zoo Story and Other Plays, 1962.
Fam and Yam (produced 1960).   1961.
The American Dream (produced 1961).   1961.
Bartleby, with James Hinton, Jr., music by William Flanagan, from the story by
    Melville (produced 1961).
Who's Afraid of Virginia Woolf? (produced 1962).   1962.
The Ballad of the Sad Café, from the story by Carson McCullers (produced
    1963).   1963.
Tiny Alice (produced 1964).   1965.
Malcolm, from the novel by James Purdy (produced 1966).   1966.
A Delicate Balance (produced 1966).   1966.
Breakfast at Tiffany's, music by Bob Merrill, from the story by Truman Capote
    (produced 1966).
Everything in the Garden, from the play by Giles Cooper (produced 1967).   1968.
Box and Quotations from Chairman Mao Tse-Tung: Two Inter-Related Plays (as Box-
    Mao-Box, produced 1968; as Box and Quotations from Chairman Mao Tse-Tung,
    produced 1968).   1969.
All Over (produced 1971).   1971.
Seascape (produced 1975).   1975.
Listening (broadcast 1976; produced 1977).   In Two Plays, 1977.
Counting the Ways (produced 1976).   In Two Plays, 1977.
Two Plays.   1977.
The Lady from Dubuque.   1978.

Radio Play: Listening, 1976.

Bibliography: *Albee at Home and Abroad: A Bibliography, 1958–June 1968* by Richard E. Amacher and Margaret Rule, 1970.

Reading List: *Albee* by Ruby Cohn, 1969; *Albee* by Richard E. Amacher, 1969; *Albee* by C. W. E. Bigsby, 1969, and *Albee: A Collection of Critical Essays* edited by Bigsby, 1975; *Albee* by Ronald Hayman, 1971; *From Tension to Tonic: The Plays of Albee* by Anne Paolucci, 1972; *Albee: The Poet of Loss* by Anita M. Stenz, 1978.

*   *   *

At age fifty, after two decades of playwriting, Edward Albee remains the most controversial playwright of the United States. Critics are divided as to whether he is a realist or absurdist. Critics and public are divided as to the quality of his writing after *Who's Afraid of Virginia Woolf?* Actors and directors are divided as to whether he is wise to direct his own plays. Never one to soar above the battle, Albee wittily attacks his attackers. More importantly, he continues to write plays in his own restless search for new dramatic forms.

The Zoo Story, completed in 1958 when he was thirty years old, played in New York City on the same bill as Beckett's *Krapp's Last Tape*, and Albee was immediately pigeonholed as absurdist. Rather than dramatize a metaphysical impasse, however, Albee creates a protagonist who is a martyr to brotherly love and cultural vigor. In arousing smug Peter to enact a zoo story, Jerry strikes hard at complacent conformity, and Albee strikes hard at conventional theater.

Albee's next few plays in the next few years are more traditionally satiric. *The Death of Bessie Smith* lacerates white racism; *The American Dream* and *The Sandbox* ridicule American materialism and mindlessness. *Fam and Yam*, a slight piece which Albee continues to direct, confronts an old established playwright with a bright young novice.

For all the energetic idiom of *The Zoo Story* and the satiric verve of his other short plays, Albee remained a fringe playwright until his very full evening of theater, *Who's Afraid of Virginia Woolf?* The play has been misunderstood as a marital problem play, a campus satire, or veiled homosexuality, but, even misunderstood, its verbal pyrotechnics attracted audiences. Slowly, its symbolic import has seeped through an apparently realistic surface. George and Martha, ostensibly an American academic couple but related by name to the father (and mother) of the United States, have based their union on the illusion of a child. On the eve of the child's twenty-first birthday, the fantasy parents return home from a campus party. Drinking heavily, the older couple uses a younger couple for "flagellation." As in O'Neill's *Long Day's Journey into Night* alcohol proves confessional and penitential for all four characters. In the play's third act "Exorcism" George kills their imaginary son. The middle-aged couple, alone at daybreak, has to learn to live with naked reality.

A direct challenge to O'Neill's *The Iceman Cometh*, *Who's Afraid of Virginia Woolf?* is a noteworthy contribution to American dramatic preoccupation with illusion, in the lineage of Williams's *Streetcar Named Desire* and Miller's *Death of a Salesman*. In this big four O'Neill and Williams are the romantics, Miller and Albee the realists, and yet *Virginia Woolf* reveals hints of nostalgia for illusion. Moreover, with time, the play's verbal vitriol seems diluted, clarifying the theatricalization of a crisis in Western culture.

All Albee's subsequent plays hinge on this theme, for which he finds new forms. He continues the corruscating dialogue of *Virginia Woolf* into the first scene of *Tiny Alice* but then shifts to slower rhythms of mystery — both murder and metaphysics. As in *Zoo Story* and *Virginia Woolf*, the protagonist of *Tiny Alice* seeks the reality beneath the surface, and the surface glitters theatrically with such devices as a model castle, a Cardinal who keeps caged cardinal-birds, a beautiful woman disguised as an old crone, an operatic staircase, and visual reminders of the Pietà and Crucifixion. Brother Julian claims to be "dedicated to the reality of things, rather than the appearance." Abandoned on his wedding day by his bride Alice and her entourage, literally shot into reality, Julian finally lies in cruciform posture, clinging to illusion as he really dies.

A Delicate Balance returns to a more realistic surface; as in *Virginia Woolf* a love relationship in one couple is explored through the impact of another couple. In Friday's Act I terrorized friends seek refuge with Tobias and Agnes; in Saturday's Act II Tobias welcomes them, but his daughter Julia reacts hysterically. In Sunday's Act III the friends know they are not welcome, know that they would not have welcomed, and they leave. The passion leads not to resurrection but restitution of a delicate family balance.

After two related and exploratory plays, *Box-Mao-Box*, Albee returns in *All Over* to the upper middle-class American milieu that he stylizes deftly. He brings to the center of this play a theme at the periphery of his other plays – the existential impact of death. In spite of the title, "all" is not quite "over," for a once powerful man is dying behind a stage screen. Waiting for his death are his wife, mistress, best friend, son, and daughter, whose mannered conversation traces the man's presence everywhere or "all over." Death precariously joins these people, only to sunder them again, as each is suffused in his/her own unhappiness.

Between *A Delicate Balance* and *All Over*, upper middle-class plays in credible settings, Albee wrote "two inter-related" and experimental plays, *Box* and *Quotations from Chairman Mao Tse-Tung*. In *Box*, "a parenthesis around *Mao*," a brightly lit cube usurps the whole stage while the audience hears nearby an associational monologue of a middle-aged woman. Apparently rambling, the speech is carefully structured: "When art hurts. That is what to remember." *Quotations* theatricalizes art hurting. Within the cube appears a steamship deck with four characters on it – a silent minister, Chairman Mao speaking only in the titular quotations, a shabby old woman speaking only doggerel verse of Will Carleton, and a middle-class, middle-aged, long-winded lady whose discourse further develops the themes of art and suffering. Skillfully and movingly counterpointed, the three voices dramatize the frailty of art – how it is nourished by suffering and how it suffers.

After the jejune lapse of *Seascape* Albee created another two short experimental plays, *Listening* and *Counting the Ways*. *Listening*, "a chamber play" translated from radio, resembles a chamber quartet in its blend of four voices – a recorded voice announcing the twenty scenes, a fifty-year old man, a fifty-year old woman, and a twenty-five year old "girl." Grouped about a fountain pool, the three visible characters engage in non-linear dialogue through which certain themes recur, particularly the girl's charge: "You don't listen.... Pay attention, rather, is what you don't do." Though the characters seem to speak in a limbo beyond life, the play is climaxed by a shocking suicide and a last reiteration of the girl's charge countered by the fifty-year old woman: "*I* listen." Less resonant but nevertheless witty and inventive is the two-character *Counting the Ways*, "A Vaudeville" in twenty-one scenes varying the moods of a love affair as Bergman does that of a marriage.

The corpus of Albee's work shows more stylistic variety and closer attention to the nuances of language than the work of any American playwright, living or dead, Rarely facile, never clumsy, recently mannered, Albee continues to dramatize deep themes in distinctive theatrical forms.

—Ruby Cohn

ANDERSON, Maxwell. American. Born in Atlantic, Pennsylvania, 15 December 1888; grew up in North Dakota. Educated at Jamestown High School, North Dakota, graduated 1908; University of North Dakota, Grand Forks, 1908–11, B.A. 1911; Stanford University, California, 1913–14, M.A. 1914. Married 1) Margaret C. Haskett in 1911 (died, 1931), three sons; 2) Gertrude Maynard in 1933 (died, 1953), one daughter; 3) Gilda Oakleaf in 1954. Teacher, Minnewaukan High School, North Dakota, 1911–13, and Polytechnic High School,

San Francisco, 1914–17; Professor and Head of the English Department, Whittier College, California, 1917–18; Staff Member, *New Republic* magazine, New York, 1918–19, New York *Evening Globe*, 1919–21, and New York *World*, 1921–24; Founder-Editor, with Frank Ernest Hill, *Measure* magazine, New York, 1921; Founder, with Robert E. Sherwood, Elmer Rice, S. N. Behrman, Sidney Howard, and John F. Wharton, Playwrights Company, 1938. Recipient: Pulitzer Prize, 1933; New York Drama Critics Circle Award, 1936, 1937; American Academy of Arts and Letters Gold Medal, 1954. *Died 28 February 1959.*

PUBLICATIONS

Collections

Dramatist in America: Letters 1912–1958, edited by Laurence G. Avery.   1977.

Plays

White Desert (produced 1923).
What Price Glory?, with Laurence Stallings (produced 1924).   In *Three American Plays,* 1926.
First Flight, with Laurence Stallings (produced 1925).   In *Three American Plays,* 1926.
The Buccaneer, with Laurence Stallings (produced 1925).   In *Three American Plays,* 1926.
The Feud.   1925.
Outside Looking In, from the novel *Beggars of Life* by Jim Tully (produced 1925).   With *Gods of the Lightning,* 1929.
Forfeits (produced 1926).
Saturday's Children (produced 1927).   1926.
Gypsy (produced 1929).   Shortened version in *The Best Plays of 1928–29,* edited by Burns Mantle, 1929.
Gods of the Lightning, with Harold Hickerson (produced 1928).   1929.
Elizabeth the Queen (produced 1930).   1930.
Night over Taos (produced 1932).   1932.
Sea-Wife (produced 1932).
Both Your Houses (produced 1933).   1933.
Mary of Scotland (produced 1933).   1934.
Valley Forge (produced 1934).   1934.
Winterset (produced 1935).   1935.
The Masque of Kings (produced 1937).   1936.
The Wingless Victory (produced 1936).   1936.
High Tor (produced 1937).   1937.
The Feast of Ortolans (broadcast 1937; produced 1938).   1938.
The Star-Wagon (produced 1937).   1937.
Knickerbocker Holiday, music by Kurt Weill (produced 1938).   1938.
Second Overture (produced 1940).   1938.
Key Largo (produced 1939).   1939.
Journey to Jerusalem (produced 1940).   1940.
The Miracle of the Danube (broadcast 1941).   In *The Free Company Presents,* edited by James Boyd, 1941.
Candle in the Wind (produced 1941).   1941.
The Eve of St. Mark (produced 1942).   1942.

Your Navy, in *This Is War!* 1942.
Letter to Jackie, in *The Best One-Act Plays of 1943,* edited by Margaret Mayorga. 1944.
Storm Operation (produced 1944). 1944.
Joan of Lorraine (produced 1946). 1947.
Truckline Cafe (produced 1946).
Anne of the Thousand Days (produced 1948). 1948.
Joan of Arc (screenplay, with Andrew Solt). 1948.
Lost in the Stars, music by Kurt Weill, from the novel *Cry the Beloved Country* by Alan Paton (produced 1949). 1950.
Barefoot in Athens (produced 1951). 1951.
The Bad Seed, from the novel by William March (produced 1954). 1955.
A Christmas Carol, music by Bernard Heermann, from the story by Dickens (televised 1954). 1955.
The Masque of Pedagogues, in *North Dakota Quarterly,* Spring 1957.
The Day the Money Stopped, from the novel by Brendan Gill (produced 1958).
The Golden Six (produced 1958).

Radio Plays: *The Feast of Ortolans,* 1937; *The Bastion Saint-Gervais,* 1938; *The Miracle of the Danube,* 1941; *The Greeks Remember Marathon,* 1944.

Television Play: *A Christmas Carol,* 1955.

Screenplays: *All Quiet on the Western Front,* with others, 1930; *We Live Again,* with others, 1934; *So Red the Rose,* 1935; *Joan of Arc,* with Andrew Solt, 1948; *The Wrong Man,* with Angus MacPhail, 1957.

Verse

You Who Have Dreams. 1925.
Notes on a Dream, edited by Laurence G. Avery. 1971.

Other

The Essence of Tragedy and Other Footnotes and Papers. 1939.
The Bases of Artistic Creation: Essays, with Rhys Carpenter and Roy Harris, 1942.
Off Broadway: Essays about the Theatre. 1947.

Bibliography: *A Catalogue of the Anderson Collection* by Laurence G. Avery, 1968; *Anderson and S. N. Behrman: A Reference Guide* by William Klink, 1977.

Reading List: *Anderson: The Man and His Plays* by Barrett H. Clark, 1933; *Anderson: The Playwright as Prophet* by Mabel Driscoll Bailey, 1957; *Life among the Playwright's Producing Company* by John F. Wharton, 1974; *Anderson* by Alfred S. Shivers, 1976.

*   *   *

Maxwell Anderson became a playwright by accident, but once committed to a career in the theater, he set out to base his work on carefully wrought principles of composition. His dramatic theories were based on the practices of ancient Greece and the Elizabethan period, and he was fiercely dedicated to the ideal of the theater as the democratic cultural institution.

He reintroduced the idea of poetic tragedy and attracted large audiences to his historical verse plays though there are few striking passages of poetry in his work.

For Anderson the theater was both a spiritual experience and a commercial medium. While he agreed with Aristotle that the audience should be led by the playwright to experience strong emotions, he was sure that the proper mark of success was ticket sales. He accepted the maxim that no playwright deserves or will get posthumous adulation who has not attracted an enthusiastic audience during his lifetime. He attacked the New York critics for short-circuiting the gleaning process with their first-night reviews, but was personally willing to accept the audience's spontaneous judgment. He rejected the notion of government subsidization because he thought it would interfere with the natural selection process and resisted the lure of off-Broadway production on the grounds that only the more rigorous Broadway circuit was an ample test. Anderson successfully countered the commercial forces of Broadway for more than a quarter of a century and dominated American theater in the 1930's.

Anderson believed in theater of ideas. In an essay called "Keeping the Faith" he enunciated as rule number one the necessity of having a central idea or conviction which cannot be excised without killing the play. His *Joan of Lorraine* dramatizes the process of making concessions to the realities of play production while trying to protect the central core of the play's integrity. Though his convictions changed markedly during his career, his use of the stage to express them did not. He attacked big government, defended democracy, preached pacifism, and urged commitment to war. As his ideas about war, for instance, changed from the cynicism of *What Price Glory?* (written with Laurence Stallings) to the patriotic fervor of *The Eve of St. Mark* and *Storm Operation*, he presented each new certainty with as much strength as the one before.

Anderson's overriding theme is the spiritual victory of humanity. In his essay "Off Broadway" he defined theater as "a religious institution devoted entirely to the exaltation of the spirit of man." He tried through the disillusionment of the 1920's, the depression of the 1930's, and the global war of the 1940's to present the triumphant human spirit. He has been accused of being a pessimist, but his view is essentially that of an optimistic humanist. He emphasized the importance of individual choice and the necessity of commitment. King McCloud of *Key Largo*, for instance, having failed to make a stand in the last days of the Spanish Civil War, finds it hard to stop running. His spirit triumphs only when he finds something for which he is willing to die. Mio of *Winterset*, emotionally crippled by lust for revenge, becomes a complete person only when he accepts love.

In many plays Anderson used the lives of historical characters to illumine broad questions of power and choice. He wrote plays about Christ, Socrates, Elizabeth I, Mary Stuart, George Washington, and Peter Stuyvesant. A comparison of *Elizabeth the Queen* with *Masque of Kings* illustrates the major problem in Anderson's method of historical tragedy. He is able to delineate Elizabeth's choice to have her lover Essex beheaded as a triumph of wise government over personal weakness, but Rudolph's suicide will not fit into such a neat pattern. As a result the third act of *Masque of Kings* takes a different direction from the one we might reasonably expect after the recognition scene of Act II, and the ending is weak and inappropriate.

The high seriousness of his subject matter is often a mistake. It is unfortunate that he did not leaven his work with comedy more often. In *High Tor* and *Knickerbocker Holiday* (music by Kurt Weill) he demonstrated a rich gift for humor. *Both Your Houses*, a play about Congressional corruption, makes excellent use of satire and was highly praised by critics.

Anderson's deficiences as a playwright seem to be related to conflicts between his intellectual approach to form and his spontaneous ideas for content. He wanted to emphasize the primacy of individual choice, for instance, but Aristotelian tragedy, which he chose to emulate, best communicates the powerful forces that neutralize free will. He wanted to write plays constructed around a second act recognition scene followed by spiritual triumph in physical defeat, but some of the historical characters he chose do not fit this pattern. He wanted to show the triumph of the human spirit, but one of his most successful plays, *The*

Bad Seed, demonstrates the victory of congenital evil. He wanted to treat universal themes, but in plays such as *Gods of the Lightning* and *Wingless Victory* he got bogged down in heavy social commentary.

Anderson has been criticized for lack of innovation, and that is a fair criticism. His approach and subject matter are quite traditional. Echoes of *Medea* are clear in the plot of *Wingless Victory*, and the parallels between *Winterset* and *Romeo and Juliet* are obvious. His concern is less with striking out into new territories than with re-vitalizing the old. The actors in *Elizabeth the Queen* actually use Shakespeare's lines, for instance, but the effect is to illuminate the Queen's character and judgment.

Anderson was a prolific writer whose work attracted audiences and made money; by his own criteria he was a success. In comparison with his fellow writers in the American theater he must also be rated a success; only O'Neill outshone him in his time. Anderson did not always overcome the problems posed by his own methods, but he did illuminate the mazes of power, freedom, and faith he set out to explore. For over a quarter of a century, especially with works such as *Elizabeth the Queen*, *High Tor*, and *Winterset*, he dramatized the human condition in some striking scenes and created some high moments in American theater.

—Barbara M. Perkins

ARDEN, John. English. Born in Barnsley, Yorkshire, 26 October 1930. Educated at Sedbergh School, Yorkshire; King's College, Cambridge, B.A. 1953; Edinburgh College of Art, diploma in architecture, 1955. Served as a Lance-Corporal in the British Army Intelligence Corps, 1949–50. Married the actress Margaretta Ruth D'Arcy in 1957; has four sons. Architectural Assistant, London, 1955–57; Fellow in Playwriting, University of Bristol, 1959–60; Visiting Lecturer in Politics and Drama, New York University, 1967; Regents Lecturer, University of California at Davis, 1973; Writer-in-Residence, University of New England, Armidale, New South Wales, 1975. Co-Founder, Corrandulla Arts Centre, County Galway, Ireland, 1973. Recipient: BBC Northern Region Prize, 1957; *Evening Standard* award, 1959; Trieste Festival Award, 1961; Vernon Rice Award, 1966; Arts Council award, 1973. Lives in County Galway, Ireland.

PUBLICATIONS

Plays

    All Fall Down (produced 1955).
    The Waters of Babylon (produced 1957). In *Three Plays*, 1964.
    When Is a Door Not a Door? (produced 1958). In *Soldier, Soldier and Other Plays*, 1967.
    Live Like Pigs (produced 1958). In *Three Plays*, 1964.
    Serjeant Musgrave's Dance: An Unhistorical Parable (produced 1959). 1960; revised version (produced 1972).
    The Happy Haven, with Margaretta D'Arcy (produced 1960). In *Three Plays*, 1964.
    Soldier, Soldier (televised 1960). In *Soldier, Soldier and Other Plays*, 1967.
    The Business of Good Government: A Christmas Play, with Margaretta D'Arcy (produced, as *A Christmas Play*, 1960). 1963.

Wet Fish (televised 1961).   In *Soldier, Soldier and Other Plays,* 1967.

Ironhand, from a play by Goethe (produced 1963).   1965.

The Workhouse Donkey: A Vulgar Melodrama (produced 1963).   1964.

Three Plays.   1964.

Armstrong's Last Goodnight: An Exercise in Diplomacy (produced 1964).   1965.

Ars Longa, Vita Brevis, with Margaretta D'Arcy (produced 1964).   1965.

Fidelio, from a libretto by Joseph Sonnleithner and Friedrich Treitschke, music by Beethoven (produced 1965).

Left-Handed Liberty: A Play about Magna Carta (produced 1965).   1965.

Friday's Hiding, with Margaretta D'Arcy (produced 1966).   In *Soldier, Soldier and Other Plays,* 1967.

The Royal Pardon: or, The Soldier Who Became an Actor, with Margaretta D'Arcy (produced 1966).   1966.

Soldier, Soldier and Other Plays.   1967.

The True History of Squire Jonathan and His Unfortunate Treasure (produced 1968).   In *Two Autobiographical Plays,* 1971.

The Hero Rises Up: A Romantic Melodrama, with Margaretta D'Arcy (produced 1968).   1969.

The Soldier's Tale, from a libretto by Ramuz, music by Stravinsky (produced 1968).

Harold Muggins Is a Martyr, with Margaretta D'Arcy and the Cartoon Archetypical Slogan Theatre (produced 1968).

The Bagman; or, The Impromptu of Muswell Hill (broadcast 1970).   In *Two Autobiographical Plays,* 1971.

Two Autobiographical Plays.   1971.

The Ballygombeen Bequest, with Margaretta D'Arcy (produced 1972).   In *Scripts 9,* September 1972.

The Island of the Mighty: A Play on a Traditional British Theme, with Margaretta D'Arcy (produced 1972).   1974; section, as *A Handful of Watercress* (produced 1976).

The Non-Stop Connolly Show: A Dramatic Cycle of Continuous Struggle in Six Parts, with Margaretta D'Arcy (produced 1975).   3 vols., 1978 (first four parts).

Radio Plays: *The Life of Man,* 1956; *The Bagman,* 1970; *Pearl,* 1978.

Television Plays: *Soldier, Soldier,* 1960; *Sean O'Casey* (documentary), with Margaretta D'Arcy, 1973.

Other

To Present the Pretence: Essays on the Theatre and Its Public.   1978.

Reading List: *Arden* by Ronald Hayman, 1968; *Theatre Language: A Study of Arden, Osborne, Pinter, and Wesker* by John Russell Brown, 1972; *Arden* by Simon Trussler, 1973; *Arden: A Study of His Plays* by Albert Hunt, 1974; *Arden* by Gloria Leeming, 1974; *Anger and Detachment: A Study of Arden, Osborne, and Pinter* by Michael Anderson, 1976.

*   *   *

A consciousness of society and politics as well as the individual informs John Arden's work as a playwright, critic, and actor. In almost any context one attempts to place him he appears, to his credit, abrasive and anomalous. Loosely implicated in the "angry young men" group of the 1950's, he countered the commitment of their work with a resolute disengagement; as the universities have expanded to include modern drama in the syllabus of the academy, he observes the tyranny of the "literary" text of the play and the mistaken valuation of the "objective"; and as state subsidies have created a secure and, some might say, "entrenched" British theatre, Arden criticises a system where selection and production of plays are determined by a director-administrator whose policies are administrative rather than artistic. In an age where writers of all kind accept their isolation even when they do not prize it, Arden stresses collaboration – with other playwrights, and of playwrights with directors, actors, and production workers.

In an article reprinted in *To Present the Pretence*, Arden acknowledges a debt to Jonson rather than Shakespeare, distinguishing between Jonson's concrete and Shakespeare's impressionist language. But in its energy, catholicity, and virtuosity the achievement of Arden's plays is Shakespearian, while the richness of the worlds of his plays reveals a more general influence of Renaissance drama as a whole. Arden's own descriptions of this richness of content and form indicate other of its contexts: in the Preface to *The Workhouse Donkey* he calls for "the old essential attributes of Dionysus" which include noise, disorder, generosity, corruption, fertility, and ease; and in *The Hero Rises Up* (about Nelson) he and Margaretta D'Arcy unfavourably contrast the rectilinear Romans with the curvilinear natives of ancient Britain who endearingly "muddle through"; both the Dionysiac and the curvilinear point to his marked preoccupation with natural man, and the modes of popular, and Brechtian, theatre.

Although the plays before 1970 share a similar kind of disengagement, and the plays after evident commitment, and though they all include prose and verse, there is no other single common language or style, as one finds in Pinter for example. A prodigious range of class, education, region, and historical period is manifest in the language of the plays. In the comedies set in the present, such as *The Waters of Babylon*, *Live Like Pigs*, and *The Workhouse Donkey*, the verse is balladic, the prose colloquial, and the mode at times melodrama, but in some of the British history plays, such as *Left-Handed Liberty* (on Magna Carta) and *Armstrong's Last Goodnight*, both the verse and prose are more poetic and in a high, literary style which is in part due to the strangeness to Arden's audience of medieval English and sixteenth-century Scots respectively. The fables, too, such as *Serjeant Musgrave's Dance* and *The Bagman*, share this poetic quality of language, which is conceived so as to be taken in on first hearing rather than only when read.

In several of his prefaces to the plays Arden links them to contemporary political situations (*Armstrong* with the Congo and *Musgrave* with Cyprus), in the way that Arthur Miller treats McCarthyism in *The Crucible*, but Arden's distance from all his characters in the earlier plays forces the audience to tolerate the more culpable characters along with the more innocent so that complete identification of the audience with the "good" is prevented; at the same time Arden provides a certain sympathy and room for imperfect men who verge on the repugnant such as Musgrave; and through this technique two recurring, rather sordid characters, Charlie Butterthwaite and Krank, take on Falstaffian proportions and complexity. But overall Arden curtails our interest in individual character and forces us to see the archetype, and the social and political implications of his characters' decisions.

The preface to *The Bagman* and the play itself chart the immediate circumstances of Arden's move from detachment to commitment in his life and work. Not surprisingly, however, even plays after this shift, *The Island of the Mighty* (on the Arthurian legends) and *The Ballygombeen Bequest* (on absentee landlordism and exploitation in Ireland) attest to Arden's virtuosity, the first being an epic of three very complex and poetic plays, and the latter a melodramatic but documented treatise.

In addition to these works, Arden has written several plays for children, opera libretti, drama for television and radio, and fascinating criticism – in the often ample prefaces to the plays and in *To Present the Pretence*. He is prolific, and his work is original, independent, ambitious, and memorable, if somewhat uneven. With Samuel Beckett, he appears as one of the principal innovators on the contemporary British scene.

—Laurel Brake

AUDEN, W(ystan) H(ugh).   American.   Born in York, England, 21 February 1907;
emigrated to the United States in 1938; naturalized, 1946. Educated at St. Edmund's School,
Grayshott, Surrey; Gresham's School, Holt, Norfolk; Christ Church, Oxford (exhibitioner),
1925–28. Served with the Loyalists in the Spanish Civil War; with the Strategic Bombing
Survey of the United States Army in Germany during World War II. Married Erika Mann in
1935. Schoolmaster, Larchfield Academy, Helensburgh, Scotland, and Downs School,
Colwall, near Malvern, Worcestershire, 1930–35. Co-Founder of the Group Theatre, 1932;
worked with the G.P.O. Film Unit, 1935. Travelled extensively in the 1930's, in Europe,
Iceland, and China. Taught at St. Mar's School, Southborough, Massachusetts, 1939–40;
American Writers League School, 1939; New School for Social Research, New York,
1940–41, 1946–47; University of Michigan, Ann Arbor, 1941–42; Swarthmore College,
Pennsylvania, 1942–45; Bryn Mawr College, Pennsylvania, 1943–45; Bennington College,
Vermont, 1946; Barnard College, New York, 1947; Neilson Research Professor, Smith
College, Northampton, Massachusetts, 1953; Professor of Poetry, Oxford University,
1956–61. Editor, Yale Series of Younger Poets, 1947–62. Member of the Editorial Board,
Decision magazine, 1940–41, and *Delos* magazine, 1968; The Readers' Subscription book
club, 1951–59, and The Mid-Century Book Club, 1959–62. Recipient: King's Gold Medal for
Poetry, 1936; Guggenheim Fellowship, 1942; American Academy of Arts and Letters
Award of Merit Medal, 1945, Gold Medal, 1968; Pulitzer Prize, 1948; Bollingen Prize, 1954;
National Book Award, 1956; Feltrinelli Prize, 1957; Guinness Award, 1959; Poetry Society
of America's Droutskoy Gold Medal, 1959; National Endowment for the Arts grant, 1966;
National Book Committee's National Medal for Literature, 1967. D.Litt.: Swarthmore
College, 1964. Member, American Academy of Arts and Letters, 1954; Honorary Student,
Christ Church, 1962, and in residence, 1972–73. *Died 28 September 1973.*

PUBLICATIONS

Collections

   The Collected Poems, edited by Edward Mendelson.   1976.

Plays

   The Dance of Death (produced 1934; as *Come Out into the Sun,* produced 1935).   1933.
   The Dog Beneath the Skin; or, Where Is Francis?, with Christopher Isherwood
      (produced 1936; revised version, produced 1947).   1935.
   No More Peace! A Thoughtful Comedy, with Edward Crankshaw, from the play by
      Ernst Toller (produced 1936).   1937.
   The Ascent of F6, with Christopher Isherwood (produced 1937).   1936; revised edition,
      1937.
   On the Frontier, with Christopher Isherwood (produced 1938).   1938.
   The Dark Valley (broadcast, 1940).   In *Best Broadcasts of 1939–40,* edited by Max
      Wylie, 1940.
   Paul Bunyan, music by Benjamin Britten (produced 1941).   1976.
   The Duchess of Malfi, music by Benjamin Britten, from the play by John Webster
      (produced 1946).
   The Knights of the Round Table, from the work by Jean Cocteau (broadcast, 1951;
      produced 1954).   In *The Infernal Machine and Other Plays,* by Jean Cocteau, 1964.
   The Rake's Progress, with Chester Kallman, music by Igor Stravinsky (produced
      1951).   1951.

Delia; or, A Masque of Night, with Chester Kallman (libretto), in *Botteghe Oscure XII.* 1953.

The Punch Revue (lyrics only) (produced 1955).

The Magic Flute, with Chester Kallman, from the libretto by Schikaneder and Giesecke, music by Mozart (televised, 1956).   1956.

The Play of Daniel (narration only) (produced 1958).   Editor, with Noah Greenberg, 1959.

The Seven Deadly Sins of the Lower Middle Class, with Chester Kallman, from the work by Brecht, music by Kurt Weill (produced 1959).   In *Tulane Drama Review,* September 1961.

Don Giovanni, with Chester Kallman, from the libretto by Lorenzo da Ponte, music by Mozart (televised, 1960).   1961.

The Caucasian Chalk Circle (lyrics only), with James and Tania Stern, from the play by Brecht (produced 1962).   In *Plays,* by Brecht, 1960.

Elegy for Young Lovers, with Chester Kallman, music by Hans Werner Henze (produced 1961).   1961.

Arcifanfarlo, King of Fools; or, It's Always Too Late to Learn, with Chester Kallman, from the libretto by Goldoni, music by Dittersdorf (produced 1965).

Die Bassariden (The Bassarids), with Chester Kallman, music by Hans Werner Henze (produced 1966).   1966.

Moralities: Three Scenic Plays from Fables by Aesop, music by Hans Werner Henze.   1969.

The Ballad of Barnaby, music by Wykeham Rise School Students realized by Charles Turner (produced 1970).

Love's Labour's Lost, with Chester Kallman, music by Nicholas Nabokov, from the play by Shakespeare (produced 1973).

The Entertainment of the Senses, with Chester Kallman, music by John Gardner, (produced 1974).   In *Thank You, Fog,* 1974.

The Rise and Fall of the City of Mahagonny, with Chester Kallman, from the opera by Brecht.   1976.

Screenplays (documentaries, in verse): *Night Mail,* 1936; *Coal Face,* 1936; *The Londoners,* 1938.

Radio Writing: *Hadrian's Wall,* 1937 (UK); *the Dark Valley,* 1940 (USA); *The Rocking-Horse Winner,* with James Stern, from the story by D. H. Lawrence, 1941 (USA); *The Knights of the Round Table,* from a work by Jean Cocteau, 1951 (UK).

Television Writing (with Chester Kallman): *The Magic Flute,* 1956 (USA); *Don Giovanni,* 1960 (USA).

Verse

Poems.   1928.

Poems.   1930; revised edition, 1933.

The Orators: An English Study.   1932; revised edition, 1934, 1966.

Poems (includes *The Orators* and *The Dance of Death*).   1934.

Look, Stranger!   1936; as *On This Island,* 1937.

Spain.   1937.

Letters from Iceland, with Louis MacNeice.   1937.

Selected Poems.   1938.

Journey to a War, with Christopher Isherwood.   1939; revised edition, 1973.

Ephithalamion Commemorating the Marriage of Giuseppe Antonio Borghese and Elisabeth Mann.   1939.

Another Time: Poems (includes *Spain*).   1940.
Some Poems.   1940.
The Double Man.   1941; as *New Year Letter,* 1941.
Three Songs for St. Cecilia's Day.   1941.
For the Time Being.   1944.
The Collected Poetry.   1945.
Litany and Anthem for St. Matthew's Day.   1946.
The Age of Anxiety: A Baroque Eclogue (produced 1954).   1947.
Collected Shorter Poems 1930–1944.   1950.
Nones.   1951.
The Shield of Achilles.   1955.
The Old Man's Road.   1956.
Reflections on a Forest.   1957.
Goodbye to the Mezzogiorno (bilingual edition).   1958.
Auden: A Selection by the Author.   1958; as *Selected Poetry,* 1959.
Homage to Clio.   1960.
Auden: A Selection, edited by Richard Hoggart.   1961.
Elegy for J.F.K., music by Igor Stravinsky.   1964.
The Common Life (in German, translated by Dieter Leisegang).   1964.
The Cave of Making (in German, translated by Dieter Leisegang).   1965.
Half-Way.   1965.
About the House.   1965.
The Twelve, music by William Walton.   1966.
Marginalia.   1966.
Collected Shorter Poems, 1927–1957.   1966.
River Profile.   1967.
Selected Poems.   1968.
Collected Longer Poems.   1968.
Two Songs.   1968.
A New Year Greeting, with *The Dance of the Solids,* by John Updike.   1969.
City Without Walls and Other Poems.   1969.
Academic Graffiti.   1971.
Epistle to a Godson and Other Poems.   1972.
Auden/Moore: Poems and Lithographs, edited by John Russell.   1974.
Poems, lithographs by Henry Moore, edited by Vera Lindsay.   1974.
Thank You, Fog: Last Poems.   1974.

Other

Education Today – and Tomorrow, with T. C. Worsley.   1939.
The Intent of the Critic, with others, edited by Donald A. Stauffer.   1941.
Poets at Work: Essays Based on the Modern Poetry Collection at the Lockwood Memorial Library, University of Buffalo, with others, edited by Charles D. Abbott.   1948.
The Enchafèd Flood; or, The Romantic Iconography of the Sea.   1950.
The Dyer's Hand and Other Essays.   1962.
Selected Essays.   1964.
Secondary Worlds.   1968.
A Certain World: A Commonplace Book.   1970.
Forewords and Afterwords (essays), edited by Edward Mendelson.   1973.
The English Auden: Poems, Essays, and Dramatic Writings, 1927–1939, edited by Edward Mendelson.   1977.

Editor, with Charles Plumb, *Oxford Poetry 1926.*   1926.

Editor, with C. Day Lewis, *Oxford Poetry 1927.*   1927.
Editor, with John Garrett, *The Poet's Tongue: An Anthology.*   2 vols., 1935.
Editor, *The Oxford Book of Light Verse.*   1938.
Editor, *A Selection from the Poems of Alfred, Lord Tennyson.*   1944; as *Tennyson: An Introduction and a Selection,* 1946.
Editor, *The American Scene, Together with Three Essays from "Portraits of Places,"* by Henry James.   1946.
Editor, *Slick But Not Streamlined: Poems and Short Pieces,* by John Betjeman.   1947.
Editor, *The Portable Greek Reader.*   1948.
Editor, with Norman Holmes Pearson, *Poets of the English Language.*   5 vols., 1950.
Editor, *Selected Prose and Poetry,* by Edgar Allan Poe.   1950; revised edition, 1955.
Editor, *The Living Thoughts of Kierkegaard.*   1952; as *Kierkegaard,* 1955.
Editor, with Marianne Moore and Karl Shapiro, *Riverside Poetry 1953: Poems by Students in Colleges and Universities in New York City.*   1953.
Editor, with Chester Kallman and Noah Greenberg, *An Elizabethan Song Book: Lute Songs, Madrigals, and Rounds.*   1955.
Editor, *The Faber Book of Modern American Verse.*   1956; as *The Criterion Book of Modern American Verse,* 1956.
Editor, *Selected Writings of Sydney Smith.*   1956.
Editor, *Van Gogh: A Self-Portrait: Letters Revealing His Life as a Painter.*   1961.
Editor, with Louis Kronenberger, *The Viking Book of Aphorisms: A Personal Selection.*   1962; as *The Faber Book of Aphorisms,* 1964.
Editor, *A Choice of de la Mare's Verse.*   1963.
Editor, *The Pied Piper and Other Fairy Tales,* by Joseph Jacobs.   1963.
Editor, *Selected Poems,* by Louis MacNeice.   1964.
Editor, with John Lawlor, *To Nevill Coghill from Friends.*   1966.
Editor, *Selected Poetry and Prose,* by Byron.   1966.
Editor, *Nineteenth Century British Minor Poets.*   1966; as *Nineteenth Century Minor Poets,* 1967.
Editor, *G. K. Chesterton: A Selection from His Non-Fiction Prose.*   1970.
Editor, *A Choice of Dryden's Verse.*   1973.
Editor, *George Herbert.*   1973.
Editor, *Selected Songs of Thomas Campion.*   1974.

Translator, with Elizabeth Mayer, *Italian Journey 1786-1788,* by Goethe.   1962.
Translator, with Leif Sjöberg, *Markings,* by Dag Hammarskjöld.   1964.
Translator, with Paul B. Taylor, *Völupsá: The Song of the Sybil,* with an Icelandic Text edited by Peter H. Salus and Paul B. Taylor.   1968.
Translator, *The Elder Edda: A Selection.*   1969.
Translator, with Elizabeth Mayer and Louise Bogan, *The Sorrows of Young Werther, and Novella,* by Goethe.   1971.
Translator, with Leif Sjöberg, *Evening Land/Aftonland,* by Pär Lagerkvist.   1975.

Bibliography: *Auden: A Bibliography 1924-1969* by Barry C. Bloomfield and Edward Mendelson, 1972.

Reading List: *The Poetry of Auden: The Disenchanted Island* by Monroe K. Spears, 1963, and *Auden: A Collection of Critical Essays* edited by Spears, 1964; *Auden's Poetry* by Justin Replogle, 1969; *Changes of Heart: A Study of the Poetry of Auden* by Gerald Nelson, 1969; *A Reader's Guide to Auden* by John Fuller, 1970; *Auden* by Dennis Davison, 1970; *The Later Auden* by George W. Bahlke, 1970; *Auden as a Social Poet* by Frederick H. Buell, 1973; *Man's Place: An Essay on Auden* by Richard Johnson, 1973; *Auden: A Tribute* edited by Stephen Spender, 1975.

*   *   *

One of the most recurrent features of W. H. Auden's poetry is the *paysage moralisé* (an early poem is actually called this) in which the landscape becomes the emblematic topography of a spiritual condition. Auden, whose earliest reading was in geology and mining and who first thought of becoming an engineer, has always believed that the way we locate ourselves in space, in a specific landscape we alter and adapt to, both determines and reveals our moral being, our sense of personal destiny and collective responsibility. Thus, in those fine "Horatian" *Bucolics* from the 1950's he can playfully link our neuroses with our choice of locale, as in "Mountains" –

> And it is curious how often in steep places
>   You meet someone short who frowns,
> A type you catch beheading daisies with a stick

– or prescribe the curative powers of "Lakes" (which always recall the "amniotic mere" of the womb): "Moraine, pot, oxbow, glint, sink, crater, piedmont, dimple ...?/Just reeling off their names is ever so comfy." While in "Plains" he can express his aversion to those flats "where all elsewheres are equal," "nothing points," and the tax-collector's writ is unchallengable ("where roads run level,/How swift to the point of protest strides the crown./ It hangs, it flogs, it fines, it goes"). "In Praise of Limestone" (1948) sets the tone for much of this later work, making a limestone landscape symbol of both our yearning for stability and our actual transience, beginning

> If it form the one landscape that we, the inconstant ones,
>   Are consistently homesick for, this is chiefly
> Because it dissolves in water

and ending with a wistful confession:

> Dear, I know nothing of
> Either, but when I try to imagine a faultless love
>   Or the life to come, what I hear is the murmur
> Of underground streams, what I see is a limestone landscape.

The tone is more relaxed in these post-war poems, but the technique is the same as that employed in those poems of quest, pursuit, and flight which dominate his earlier writings, poems whose terrain is best described by Caliban in *The Sea and the Mirror*, that extended commentary in verse and prose on Shakespeare's *Tempest* which enables Auden to dramatize his views on the relation between life and art. Caliban, spokesman of the carnal and material, of "history," speaks with sympathy of the spirit Ariel's obligation to deliver us from "the terrible mess that this particularized life, which we have so futilely attempted to tidy, sullenly insists on leaving behind," translating "all the phenomena of an empirically ordinary world" into "elements in an allegorical landscape":

> a nightmare which has all the wealth of exciting action and all the emotional poverty of an adventure story for boys, a state of perpetual emergency and everlasting improvisation where all is need and change.

Certainly, John Buchan seems as much an influence as Marx or Nietzsche on those early poems in which the young, proud inheritor finds himself unexpectedly turned into an outsider, as in "The Watershed," "frustrate and vexed" in face of an abandoned, derelict landscape racked by depression and unemployment, "already comatose,/Yet sparsely living"; one who "must migrate" ("Missing") to become a leader, turn into a "trained spy"

("The Secret Agent"), and ("Our Hunting Fathers") "hunger, work illegally,/And be anonymous" in a world of suspicion, insecurity and betrayal, as "all the while/Conjectures on our maps grow stranger/And threaten danger" ("No Change of Place"). The Auden of these early poems, walking a dangerous tightrope between "Always" and "Never" ("Between Adventure") saw his personal anxieties bodied forth in the world at large, and found a refuge for his public-school hauteur and élitism in a communism which rationalized his contempt for an age of mediocrity, impotence and defeat. In "Family Ghosts," for example, he sees "the assaulted city" surrounded by "the watchfires of a stronger army," and it isn't possible to decide whether this is a personal allegory of love or a political poem which looks towards class-struggle as release from the "Massive and taciturn years, the Age of Ice." Christopher Isherwood, Auden's collaborator in the verse-plays *The Dog Beneath the Skin*, *The Ascent of F6*, and *On the Frontier*, wrote of him in these terms in 1937, speaking of Auden's love for the Norse sagas: "The saga world is a schoolboy world, with its feuds, its practical jokes, its dark threats conveyed in puns and riddles and understatements"; in *Paid on Both Sides*, Auden's early, expressionist charade, he adds, "the two worlds are so inextricably confused that it is impossible to say whether the characters are really epic heroes or only members of a school O.T.C." Stephen Spender, also one of Auden's "Gang" during this period, has written of the "schoolboy ruthlessness" and latent fascism of *The Orators*, and the once-popular plays in which Auden and Isherwood tried to explore the contemporary crisis in the terms of Ruritanian allegory, knockabout, and morality-play which rob it of all urgency, are dismissed by Spender as virtuoso exercises, "a hash of the revolutionary and pacifist thought of the 1930s, reduced to their least convincing terms," which "provide considerable evidence that one aspect of the 1930s was a rackety exploitation of literary fashions."

Letter to Lord Byron perhaps best sums up the ambivalence of Auden's mood in the 1930's. Written in a skilful pastiche of Byron's own insouciant rhythms and rhymes, it expresses an aristocratic, Byronic disdain for the cant and hypocrisy of the "well-to-do" Home Counties, with their bland, self-deceiving smugness, against which Auden sets the urgencies of a more desolate world:

> To those who live in Warrington or Wigan,
> It's not a white lie, it's a whacking big 'un.
> There on the old historic battlefield,
>   The cold ferocity of human wills,
> The scars of struggle are as yet unhealed;
>   Slattern the tenements on sombre hills,
>   And gaunt in valleys the square-windowed mills
> That since the Georgian house, in my conjecture
> Remain our finest native architecture.

Yet that shift in the last couplet from moral outrage to sober aesthetic appreciation, together with the easy abstraction and the typecast imagery, reveals Auden's basic remoteness from his subject; indeed, a stanza later he can confess openly to his twentieth-century delight in that landscape: "Tramlines and slagheaps, pieces of machinery,/That was, and still is, my ideal scenery."

"Journey to Iceland" (1936) explains the rationale of Auden's travelogues: "North means to all *Reject*"; but such rejection also brought with it a new perspective that extended his control of his material and made possible a larger, clearer vision, revealed in that mythic conspectus of human evolution "Sonnets from China," originally included in the travel book *Journey to a War*. After the claustrophobic, cryptic, furtive atmosphere of the earlier poems, Auden here perfected the new straightforwardness already evinced in "Spain 1937," where "the menacing shapes of our fever/Are precise and alive." Significantly, the latter's explicit commitment to communism led a censorious later Auden to excise it from the canon (those patriarchal, castrating imagos, the Censor and the Scissor Man, have made themselves felt again and again in his poetic career). His reasons are interesting. Of the last stanza of "Spain" –

> The stars are dead. The animals will not look.
> We are left alone with our day, and the time is short, and
> History to the defeated
> May say alas but cannot help or pardon

– he has said: "To say this is to equate goodness with success. It would have been bad enough if I had ever held this wicked doctrine, but that I should have stated it simply because it sounded to me rhetorically effective is quite inexcusable." But what the poem in fact stresses is the openness of human choice and the tragic discrepancy between history and morality (success may involve "The conscious acceptance of guilt in the necessary murder"), between – in Pascal's terms – Nature and Justice. There is nothing here which belies Auden's later conversion to Kierkegaard's Christian existentialism: the belief that man is responsible for his acts, and must make his leap of faith in fear and trembling, knowing that it may be a wrong and corrosive choice.

That faith is best expressed in *For the Time Being*, a "Christmas Oratorio" which recreates the Christian myth in contemporary terms (casting Herod, for example, as a well-intentioned liberal statesman whose massacre of the innocents is for the public good). History is now for Auden seen in the perspective of eternity:

> To those who have seen
> The Child, however dimly, however incredulously
> The Time Being is, in a sense, the most trying time of all.
> For the innocent children who whispered so excitedly
> Outside the locked door where they knew the presents to be
> Grew up when it opened. Now, recollecting that moment
> We can repress the joy, but the guilt remains conscious.

For Auden, who had originally identified with "Voltaire at Ferney" (1939), perennial oedipal rebel –

> Cajoling, scolding, scheming, cleverest of them all,
> He'd led the other children in a holy war
> Against the infamous grownups

– this "growing up" expressed, in terms of traditional theology, his final transfer of allegiance from the Son to the Father, effected, ironically enough, through the advent of that Child to a world at war. The transfer can be seen occurring in his fine poem "In Memory of Sigmund Freud" (1939), where that liberating discoverer of the unconscious is seen both as wide-eyed child and benevolent father who

> showed us what evil is, not, as we thought,
> deeds that must be punished, but our lack of faith,
> our dishonest mood of denial,
> the concupiscence of the oppressor.

The same affirmation animates "In Memory of Ernst Toller," acknowledging the great gift of both Freud and Marx to human self-understanding: the disclosure of those unconscious determinations of our identity – whether biological or socio-economic, each shaping the other – which constrain our existential freedom only when unrecognized:

> We are lived by powers we pretend to understand:
> They arrange our loves; it is they who direct at the end

The enemy bullet, the sickness, or even our hand.
It is their tomorrow hangs over the earth of the living
And all that we wish for our friends: but existence is believing
We know for whom we mourn and who is grieving.

For the later, Anglican, Auden, finally expatriate in an alien and yet familiar America, acknowledgment of our guilt is the ground of freedom. Rosetta, one of the four "displaced persons" lining a wartime bar in New York in *The Age of Anxiety*, at a time when "Many have perished, more will," daydreams of

> one of those landscapes familiar to all readers of English detective stories, those lovely innocent countrysides inhabited by charming eccentrics with independent means and amusing hobbies to whom, until the sudden intrusion of a horrid corpse onto the tennis court or into the greenhouse, work and law and guilt are just literary words.

As the 1936 poem "Detective Story" and the essay "The Guilty Vicarage" make clear, this landscape is Auden's own peculiar version of the myth of the Fall: to live in history is to accept complicity, and to accept complicity is the beginning of grace: "But time is always guilty. Someone must pay for/Our loss of happiness, our happiness itself." Each of the "travellers through time" of *The Age of Anxiety* sets out "in quest of his own/Absconded self yet scared to find it" (for it will turn out to be the culprit). In *New Year Letter* Auden resolves, in his own person, to accept responsibility for his fallen condition. History is the middle way, that Purgatory where, "Consenting parties to our lives," we may "win/Truth out of Time. In Time we sin./But Time is sin and can forgive"; in Time too we learn "To what conditions we must bow/In building the Just City now." But the world remains one in which "Aloneness is man's real condition."

What underlies all Auden's poetry, in fact, early and late, is this tension between aristocratic disdain and a humble and, at times, humiliating love for the things of this world. It is there in his love poetry, whether in the early and beautiful "Lullaby" ("Lay your sleeping head, my love,/Human on my faithless arm") or the innocuous narcissism of the last poem in his *Collected Poems* (1976), also called "A Lullaby" – "now you fondle/your almost feminine flesh/with mettled satisfaction" – but with its last line, "Sleep, Big Baby, sleep your fill," almost an epitaph. The explicit homosexual lust of "Three Posthumous Poems" suggests that translation of *Eros* into *Agape*, of sensual into spiritual love, was no more difficult for Auden than it was for the Sufi poets. His perennial movement between renouncing and embracing, *askesis* and indulgence, is embodied in his very language, which at once delights in the rich multiplicity of an abundant world and yet keeps it at bay with a deliberate, distancing artificiality that defamiliarizes the accustomed, or calls attention to the medium itself through nonce-words and neologisms, arcane or archaic usages, portentous polysyllables cut short by sudden racy slang, magpie gauds and macaronics. By turns demotic and hieratic, shifting peremptorily in rhythm, tone, and register, skittish, hoydenish, and haughty, polyglot and jargonish, ruminative and aphoristic, shocking and coy, Auden's language corresponds in its variety to a frame of mind, to that master of disguises (Sherlock Holmes was always a hero) his poems expose from first to last. If his later poetry is more domestic and muted, full of thanksgivings and valedictions, elegies and reminiscences, it can still rise to pyrotechnic heroisms of language. But perhaps the best of these later volumes is *Homage to Clio*, a series of poems dedicated to Auden's first and last love, the matronly Muse of History:

> Madonna of silences, to whom we turn

> When we have lost control, your eyes, Clio, into which
>   We look for recognition after
> We have been found out....

I have seen
Your photo, I think, in the papers, nursing
A baby or mourning a corpse: each time

You had nothing to say and did not, one could see,
Observe where you were, Muse of the unique
Historical fact, defending with silence
Some world of your beholding....

With this one poem alone Auden could establish his claim to be a serious and a major poet, fulfilling that specifically human vocation, the ability "with a rhythm or a rhyme" to "Assume ... responsibility for time."

—Stan Smith

BAGNOLD, Enid. English. Born in Rochester, Kent, 27 October 1899. Educated at Prior's Field, Godalming, Surrey, and in Marburg, Germany, and at the Villa Leona, Paris; studied painting with Walter Sickert. Married Sir Roderick Jones in 1920 (died, 1962); three sons and one daughter. Served as a driver with the French Army during World War I. Recipient: Arts Theatre Prize, 1951; American Academy of Arts and Letters Award of Merit, 1956. C.B.E. (Commander, Order of the British Empire), 1976. Lives in Rottingdean, Sussex.

PUBLICATIONS

Plays

Lottie Dundass (produced 1942). 1943.
National Velvet, from her own novel (produced 1945). 1961.
Poor Judas (produced 1946). In Two Plays, 1951.
Two Plays (includes Lottie Dundass and Poor Judas). 1951.
Gertie (produced 1952; as Little Idiot, produced 1953).
The Chalk Garden (produced 1955). 1956.
The Last Joke (produced 1960). In Four Plays, 1970.
The Chinese Prime Minister (produced 1964). 1964.
Call Me Jacky (produced 1967). In Four Plays, 1970; (revised version, as A Matter of Gravity, produced 1975).
Four Plays (includes The Chalk Garden, The Last Joke, The Chinese Prime Minister, Call Me Jacky). 1970.

Fiction

The Happy Foreigner. 1920.

Serena Blandish; or, The Difficulty of Getting Married.   1924.
National Velvet.   1935.
The Squire.   1938; as *The Door of Life,* 1938.
The Loved and Envied.   1951.
The Girl's Journey: Containing The Happy Foreigner and The Squire.   1954.

Verse

The Sailing Ships and Other Poems.   1918.

Other

A Diary Without Dates.   1918.
Alice and Thomas and Jane (juvenile).   1930.
Autobiography: From 1889.   1969.

Translator, *Alexander of Asia,* by Princess Marthe Bibesco.   1935.

*   *   *

The title of Enid Bagnold's first novel proclaims a preoccupation with a character type that has dominated most of her work: *The Happy Foreigner* concerns, in Katherine Mansfield's words, "an unknown young woman, secret, folded within herself." Gradually, the young woman has become older, and the non-fictional substructure indicated in the autobiographical *Diary Without Dates* has become less obvious. *The Squire,* for example, offers the vision of a lady literally "folded within herself" by pregnancy, and isolated from her family and household by her social status; this may be seen as the prototype of Bagnold's dramatic protagonists, almost all of whom find human relationships impossible or illusory.

Though her novel *Serena Blandish* was dramatised by S. N. Behrman in 1929, it was only after *The Squire* that Miss Bagnold turned seriously to drama, and initially she appears to have been unable to reconcile the objectivity of stage presentation with the characteristically introverted nature of her human material. The stage version of *National Velvet* lacks both the semi-documentary impact of her novel and, more importantly, the subjectivity which has given the novel an identification appeal for two generations of youngsters. Plays like *Lottie Dundass* and *Poor Judas* retain a degree of power through their convincing presentation of unpleasant characters, but all of these early plays reveal an uncertain handling of a somewhat fanciful story-line which would be more easily acceptable in prose form.

The Chalk Garden is Miss Bagnold's most famous play, celebrated for its spectacular stage successes, for the response of critics like Tynan, and for its Chekhovian parallel between human and vegetable life. But it also marks the playwright's most complex essay in the relationships among variously abrasive and isolated characters, with the action developing easily from the depth of female characterisation in a way that is lacking in the somewhat self-indulgent perspective of the three later plays. *The Last Joke* is based on an episode in Miss Bagnold's *Autobiography,* and appears to have been limited dramaturgically by fidelity to this extraordinary source material. The play includes a character who may be seen as somewhat authorial but who remains towards the periphery of the action. In *The Chinese Prime Minister* and *Call Me Jacky,* however, such a character is at the core of the play, so that the action emanates largely from the whims of a leisurely and eccentric lady without the effective counterweight of other characters such as those in *The Chalk Garden.*

Enid Bagnold's reputation as a playwright may be gauged by the number of celebrated actors and actresses who have appeared in her works, but none of her plays is in any sense merely a vehicle for a performer. Indeed, though most of them pose formidable casting problems, their literary sophistication has ensured a popularity in the library to plays which have failed on the stage, so that *Call Me Jacky* is as satisfying reading as mature novels like *The Loved and Envied.*

—Howard McNaughton

BARAKA, Amiri.   See **JONES, LeRoi.**

BARKER, Harley Granville -.   English.   Born in London, 25 November 1877. Served in the Red Cross and the British Army Intelligence during World War I. Married 1) the actress Lillah McCarthy in 1906 (divorced, 1917); 2) Helen Huntington Gates in 1918. Worked as child entertainer with his mother, then as a stage actor: London debut in 1892; acted and directed for the Stage Society, London 1900–04; campaigned for a National Theatre, and successfully ran a pilot scheme for such a theatre at the Court Theatre, London, 1904–07; established Shaw's reputation as a dramatist; in management, with Lillah McCarthy, at the Little, Kingsway, St. James's, and Savoy theatres before 1914; toured America, 1915; ceased to work in the theatre, except intermittently, after his second marriage, and began to hyphenate his name; lived in Paris after 1930. Clark Lecturer, Cambridge, 1930; Romanes Lecturer, Oxford, 1937; Director of the British Institute of the University of Paris, 1937–39; Visiting Professor, Yale University, New Haven, Connecticut, 1940, and Harvard University, Cambridge, Massachusetts, 1941–42, 1944–45. Member of the Executive Committee of the Fabian Society, 1907–12; Chairman of the British Drama League, 1919–32. LL.D.: University of Edinburgh, 1930; Litt.D.: University of Reading, 1937; D. Litt.: Oxford University, 1937. Fellow, and Member of the Academic Committee, Royal Society of Literature. *Died 31 August 1946.*

PUBLICATIONS

Collections

Collected Plays.   1967 (one volume only published).
Three Plays (includes *The Marrying of Ann Leete, The Voysey Inheritance, Waste*), edited by Margery Morgan.   1977.

Plays

The Weather-Hen, with Berte Thomas (produced 1899).
The Marrying of Ann Leete (produced 1902).   1909; in *Three Plays,* 1977.

Prunella; or, Love in a Dutch Garden, with Laurence Housman (produced 1904).   1906; revised version, 1930.

The Voysey Inheritance (produced 1905).   1909; revised version, 1913, 1934; in *Three Plays,* 1977.

Waste (produced 1907).   1909; revised version (produced 1936), 1926; in *Three Plays,* 1977.

A Miracle (produced 1907).

The Madras House (produced 1910).   1910; revised version, 1925.

Rococo (produced 1911).   In *Rococo ...,* 1917.

Anatol (includes *Ask No Questions and You'll Hear No Stories, The Wedding Morning, A Christmas Present, An Episode, Keepsakes*), from plays by Schnitzler (produced 1911).   1911 (includes also the play *A Farewell Supper,* translated by Edith A. Browne and Alix Grein); edited by Eric Bentley, in *From the Modern Repertory 3,* 1956.

Das Märchen, with C. E. Wheeler, from the play by Schnitzler (produced 1912).

The Morris Dance, from the novel *The Wrong Box* by Robert Louis Stevenson and Lloyd Osbourne (produced 1913).

The Harlequinade: An Excursion, with D. C. Calthrop (produced 1913).   1918.

The Dynasts, from the play by Hardy (produced 1914).

Vote by Ballot (produced 1917).   In *Rococo ...,* 1917.

Rococo, Vote by Ballot, Farewell to the Theatre.   1917; as *Three Short Plays,* 1917.

Deburau, from a play by Sacha Guitry (produced 1920).   1921.

The Romantic Young Lady, with Helen Granville Barker, from a play by G. Martinez Sierra (produced 1920).   In *The Plays of Martinez Sierra,* 1923.

The Two Shepherds, with Helen Granville Barker, from a play by G. Martinez Sierra (produced 1921).   In *The Plays of Martinez Sierra,* 1923.

The Kingdom of God, with Helen Granville Barker, from a play by G. Martinez Sierra (produced 1923).   In *The Plays of Martinez Sierra,* 1923.

Wife to a Famous Man, with Helen Granville Barker, from a play by G. Martinez Sierra (produced 1924).   In *The Plays of Martinez Sierra,* 1923.

The Secret Life.   1923.

Doctor Knock, from a play by Jules Romains (produced 1926).   1925; edited by Eric Bentley, in *From the Modern Repertory 3,* 1956.

Six Gentlemen in a Row, from a play by Jules Romain (produced 1927).   1927.

Four Plays, with Helen Granville Barker, from plays by S. and J. Alvarez Quintero (includes *A Hundred Years Old, Fortunato, The Lady from Alfaqueque, The Women Have Their Way,* produced 1928).   1927.

His Majesty.   1928.

Take Two from One, with Helen Granville Barker, from a play by G. Martinez Sierra.   1931.

Four Comedies (includes *Love Passes By, Don Abel Wrote a Tragedy, Peace and Quiet, Doña Clarines*), with Helen Granville Barker, from plays by S. and J. Alvarez Quintero.   1932.

Fiction

Souls on Fifth (stories).   1916.

Other

Scheme and Estimates for a National Theatre, with William Archer.   1904; revised edition, 1907.

The Red Cross in France.   1916.
The Exemplary Theatre.   1922.
Prefaces to Shakespeare.   5 vols., 1927–47; revised edition, 2 vols., 1946–47; *More Prefaces to Shakespeare,* edited by Edward M. Moore, 1974.
A National Theatre.   1930.
On Dramatic Method (lectures).   1931.
The Use of the Drama.   1945; revised edition, 1946.

Editor, *The Players Shakespeare.*   7 vols., 1923–27 (prefaces also published separately).
Editor, *The Eighteen-Seventies.*   1929.
Editor, with G. B. Harrison, *A Companion to Shakespeare Studies.*   1934.
Editor, *Eight Letters from T. E. Lawrence.*   1939.

Reading List: *The Court Theatre 1904–07* by Desmond MacCarthy, 1907, edited by Stanley Weintraub, 1966; "Granville Barker: Some Particulars" by G. B. Shaw in *Drama,* Winter 1946; *The Lost Leader* by W. Bridges Adams, 1954; *Granville Barker, Man of the Theatre, Dramatist, and Scholar* by C. B. Purdom, 1955 (includes bibliography by Frederick May and Margery Morgan), and *Bernard Shaw's Letters to Granville Barker* edited by Purdom, 1956; *A Drama of Political Man: A Study in the Plays of Granville Barker* by Margery Morgan, 1961.

*   *   *

Harley Granville-Barker wrote his first plays as a young actor, and his mature drama was one aspect of his total effort to carve out the model of an English national theatre. His various books and articles advocating such a theatre and discussing the art of acting (e.g., *A National Theatre, The Exemplary Theatre,* "The Heritage of the Actor") are matched by the public themes and challenging techniques of his plays. These demand large casts of experienced actors and prolonged, intensive rehearsal. The unusual degree of intelligence and imagination needed for their presentation has to call out like qualities from an attentive audience. Barker's early retirement from active stage work meant that he did not break theatrical ground for the two plays he wrote in the 1920's (*The Secret Life* and *His Majesty*), and in the lengthy interval before the growth of civic theatre after the World War II most of his other work was neglected and forgotten. The simplest piece, *The Voysey Inheritance,* has had regular revivals, but otherwise Barker has had to wait for the 1970's, and conditions in the major subsidised theatres approximate to what he sought for the theatre as a whole, for any measure of re-discovery.

His close professional and personal association with G. B. Shaw has delayed recognition of the individuality of Barker's drama. Comparison of *The Marrying of Ann Leete* with his later plays can establish precisely what additions to his dramatic resources he drew from Shaw. First among these is a greater explicitness, accessory to the occasional use of broader styles of comic characterisation (e.g., Booth Voysey and Major Thomas and Eustace Perrin State in *The Madras House*), the rhetorically constructed monologue (as given to Constantine in Act III of *The Madras House* or to Lord Clumbermere in *The Secret Life*), and the orchestrated debate, or discussion, among a stageful of characters focussing on the themes of the play (e.g., *Waste,* Act III; *The Madras House,* Act III; *The Secret Life,* Act III, scene ii); the introduction of elements of fantasy into a predominently naturalistic context (e.g., the Moorish Room and the mannequins in *The Madras House*) was partly anticipated in the grotesque wedding scene of *Ann Leete,* an animated Hogarth caricature. Certainly Shaw and Barker stimulated each other's thinking, and whole groups of their plays are interlinked by common themes and images, but the two minds had opposite tendencies, Barker's being introspective, questing, exact, and sensitively alert. The structure of thought in his plays is close and continuous, and in place of Shaw's galvanic energy he offers dramatic concentration and a more finely turned, subtle style of dialogue.

Most of his early unpublished plays which survive were written, to varying degree, in collaboration with an older actor, Berte Thomas. They are concerned with aspects of the emancipation of women and the moral transformation it entails. After this phase, the lessons of Ibsen are most evident in the extensions of naturalism Barker practises. His use of the idiom of evangelical Christianity ("salvation" and "soul" are key terms) dates the plays, though it is not dogmatic religion he is interested in, but the difficult search for values, vision, and a far-reaching purpose beyond self-interest facing those who (like Trebell in *Waste*) "grew up in the late nineteenth-century, neo-Polytechnic belief that you couldn't take God seriously and be an F.R.S." For the far regions of experience he wanted to explore, he relied largely on the trained ability of actors to bring out meanings implicit in the text and between its lines, as indicated in his essay "The Coming of Ibsen." To this end he writes a loaded but deliberately fractured dialogue, and incidentally anticipates Harold Pinter's technique of scoring the text. The loading is achieved by devices learnt mainly from Shakespeare: verbal repetition, running imagery, puns, multi-faceted lines open to delivery with varying patterns of stress and inflection, when the actor's awareness of the discarded possibilities may inform the reading he chooses. Fully developed, in his later plays and the revised version of *Waste*, these techniques emerge as a symphonic structure reinforcing, or virtually replacing, the more obvious line of dramatic action.

Although these features are embryonic in *The Marrying of Ann Leete*, the spareness and astringency of the writing help establish this play as a fable of late nineteenth-century consciousness in late eighteenth-century guise. In *The Voysey Inheritance* and *The Madras House*, the move towards surrogate musical composition allows Barker to subdue narrative interest, as happens in the modernist novel, while combining a novelistic richness of detail with plot-forms better suited to documenting and discussing the condition of contemporary England. Barker's socialism is most directly active in his satiric treatment of middle-class capitalist society in *The Voysey Inheritance* and the more impressive survey of economic imperialism and the relations of the sexes, interlocked into a single system and its supporting mental structures, in *The Madras House*. But he is not primarily a polemical, let alone propagandist, writer, and it is the trapped anti-hero, conscious of his own impotence, who brings each of these plays home. Faced by the trivialisation of politics in Edwardian England, the central character in *Waste* is more heroic, and his ultimate suicide shows his potent refusal to be assimilated. Undoubtedly Barker's personal dilemmas and reflections on leaving the theatre have informed the meditative, lyrical elements in his two last plays, perhaps to a morbid extent in *The Secret Life*, but there is no narrowing of relevance. War-devastated Europe is the implied background to both these plays: *The Secret Life*, concerned with the unstrung will, integrity, and commitment in political life; and *His Majesty*, in which realism is intermeshed with Ruritanian fable, and the mystique of leadership and authority is examined in the context of rising fascism.

The wit and elegance of Barker's naturalistic dialogue distinguish his English versions of foreign plays, including the translations from the Spanish in collaboration with his second wife. His interest in theatrical tradition, his practical theatre-craft, and a dry-eyed, slightly bitter quality seem to have been his contributions to the plays written in collaboration with Laurence Housman and D. C. Calthrop. The *Prefaces to Shakespeare* remain the outstanding example of academic criticism combined with full awareness of the practical theatre.

—Margery Morgan

BARRIE, Sir J(ames) M(atthew).   Scottish.   Born in Kirriemuir, Forfarshire, now Angus, Scotland, 9 May 1860. Educated at Glasgow Academy, 1868–70; Forfar Academy, 1870–71;

Dumfries Academy, 1873–78; University of Edinburgh, 1878–82, M.A. 1882. Married the actress Mary Ansell in 1894 (divorced, 1909). Drama and Book Critic, *Edinburgh Courant*, 1879–82; Leader Writer, *Nottingham Journal*, 1883–84. Lived in London after 1885: worked as a journalist, contributing to the *St. James's Gazette* and *British Weekly*, 1885–90; wrote for the theatre from 1890. President, Society of Authors, 1928–37, and Dramatists' Club, 1934–37. LL.D.: University of St. Andrews, 1898; University of Edinburgh, 1909; D.Litt.: Oxford University; Cambridge University. Rector, University of St. Andrews, 1919–22; Chancellor, University of Edinburgh, 1930–37. Created Baronet, 1913; Order of Merit, 1922. *Died 19 June 1937.*

PUBLICATIONS

Collections

Letters, edited by Viola Meynell. 1942.
Plays and Stories, edited by Roger Lancelyn Green. 1962.

Plays

Caught Napping. 1883.
Ibsen's Ghost; or, Toole Up-to-Date (produced 1891).
Richard Savage, with H. B. Marriott Watson (produced 1891). 1891.
Walker, London (as *The Houseboat*, produced 1892). 1907.
The Professor's Love Story (produced 1892). In *Plays*, 1942.
Becky Sharp (produced 1893).
Jane Annie; or, The Good Conduct Prize, with Arthur Conan Doyle, music by Ernest Ford (produced 1893). 1893.
The Little Minister, from his own novel (produced 1897; as *Little Mary*, produced 1903). In *Plays*, 1942.
A Platonic Friendship (produced 1898).
The Wedding Guest (produced 1900). 1900.
The Admirable Crichton (produced 1902). 1914.
Quality Street (produced 1902). 1913.
Peter Pan; or, The Boy Who Wouldn't Grow Up (produced 1904; revised version, produced 1905). In *Plays*, 1928.
Pantaloon (produced 1905). In *Half Hours*, 1914.
Alice Sit-by-the-Fire (produced 1905). 1919.
Josephine (produced 1906).
Punch (produced 1906).
When Wendy Grew Up: An Afterthought (produced 1908). 1957.
What Every Woman Knows (produced 1908). 1918.
Old Friends (produced 1910). In *Plays*, 1928.
A Slice of Life (produced 1910).
The Twelve-Pound Look (produced 1910). In *Half Hours*, 1914.
Rosalind (produced 1912). In *Half Hours*, 1914.
The Dramatists Get What They Want (produced 1912; as *The Censor and the Dramatists*, produced 1913).
The Will (produced 1913). In *Half Hours*, 1914.
The Adored One: A Legend of the Old Bailey (produced 1913; as *The Legend of Leonora*, produced 1914; shortened version, as *Seven Women*, produced 1917). *Seven Women* included in *Plays*, 1928.

Half an Hour (produced 1913).   In *Plays*, 1928.

Half Hours   1914.

Der Tag (produced 1914; as *Der Tag; or, The Tragic Man*, produced 1914).   1914.

Rosy Rapture; or , The Pride of the Beauty Chorus, music by H. Darewski and Jerome Kern (produced 1915).

The Fatal Typist (produced 1915).

The New Word (produced 1915).   In *Echoes of the War*, 1918.

The Real Thing at Last (produced 1916).

Irene Vanbrugh's Pantomime (produced 1916).

Shakespeare's Legacy (produced 1916).   1916.

A Kiss for Cinderella (produced 1916).   1920.

The Old Lady Shows Her Medals (produced 1917).   In *Echoes of the War*, 1918.

Reconstructing the Crime (produced 1917).

Dear Brutus (produced 1917).   1922.

La Politesse (produced 1918).

A Well-Remembered Voice (produced 1918).   In *Echoes of the War*, 1918.

Echoes of the War.   1918.

Barbara's Wedding (produced 1927).   In *Echoes of the War*, 1918.

The Truth about the Russian Dancers (ballet), music by Arnold Bax (produced 1920).   1962.

Mary Rose (produced 1920).   1924.

Shall We Join the Ladies? (produced 1921).   In *Plays*, 1928.

Neil and Tinntinabulum.   1925.

Representative Plays (includes *Quality Street, The Admirable Crichton, What Every Woman Knows, Dear Brutus, The Twelve-Pound Look, The Old Lady Shows Her Medals*).   1926.

The Plays of Barrie (includes *Peter Pan, The Admirable Crichton, Alice Sit-by-the-Fire, What Every Woman Knows, A Kiss for Cinderella, Dear Brutus, Mary Rose, Pantaloon, Half an Hour, Seven Women, Old Friends, Rosalind, The Twelve-Pound Look, The New Word, A Well-Remembered Voice, Barbara's Wedding, The Old Lady Shows Her Medals, Shall We Join the Ladies?*).   1928; augmented edition, edited by A. E. Wilson (includes *Walker, London; The Professor's Love Story; The Little Minister; The Wedding Guest; The Boy David*), 1942.

The Boy David (produced 1936).   1938.

Screenplay: *As You Like It*, with Robert Cullen, 1936.

Fiction

Better Dead.   1887.

When a Man's Single: A Tale of Literary Life.   1888.

The Little Minister.   1891.

Sentimental Tommy: The Story of His Boyhood.   1896.

Tommy and Grizel.   1900.

The Boy Castaways of Black Lake Island.   1901.

The Little White Bird.   1902; as *The Little White Bird; or, Adventures in Kensington Gardens*, 1902; revised material for children, as *Peter Pan in Kensington Gardens*, 1906.

Peter and Wendy.   1911; as *Peter Pan and Wendy*, 1921.

Farewell Miss Julie Logan: A Wintry Tale.   1931.

Verse

Scotland's Lament: A Poem on the Death of Robert Louis Stevenson.   1895.

Other

The New Amphion. 1886.
Auld Licht Idylls. 1888.
A Window in Thrums. 1889.
An Edinburgh Eleven: Pencil Portraits from College Life. 1889.
My Lady Nicotine. 1890.
Allahakbarries C. C. (on cricket). 1893.
Margaret Ogilvy, by Her Son. 1896.
The Allahakbarrie Book of Broadway Cricket for 1899. 1899.
George Meredith 1909. 1909; as *Neither Dorking nor the Abbey,* 1910.
The Works (Kirriemuir Edition). 10 vols., 1913.
Charles Frohman: A Tribute. 1915.
Who Was Sarah Findley? by Mark Twain, with a Suggested Solution of the Mystery. 1917.
The Works. 10 vols., 1918.
The Works (Peter Pan edition). 14 vols., 1929–31.
The Greenwood Hat, Being a Memoir of James Anon, 1885–1887. 1930; revised edition, 1937.
M'Connachie and J. M. B.: Speeches. 1938.

Bibliography: *Barrie: A Bibliography* by B. D. Cutler, 1931.

Reading List: *Barrie* by F. J. Harvey Darton, 1929; *Barrie* by Denis Mackail, 1941; *Barrie* by Roger Lancelyn Green, 1960; *Barrie: The Man Behind the Image* by Janet Dunbar, 1970; *Barrie* by Harry M. Geduld, 1971; *Barrie* by Allen Wright, 1976; *Barrie and the Lost Boys* by Andrew Birkin, 1978.

*   *   *

J. M. Barrie, wrote a critic at the time of his death, was "a romantic who could suddenly turn round and write the realists off the stage. It is customary nowadays to make fun of his excursions into fairyland. That he made greater excursions elsewhere is too easily forgotten."

The irony of Barrie's career is that his most famous and most frequently performed play, *Peter Pan*, probably the greatest children's play ever written, has prevented him from being taken seriously as a major dramatist. Yet even *Peter Pan* has its undertones of tragedy, certainly for the adult play-goer or reader – and for them the true ending is Peter's last despairing glance through the closed window of the Darling nursery: "He had ecstasies innumerable that other children can never know; but he was looking through the window at the one joy from which he must be for ever barred."

Although Barrie had already written in his novels *Sentimental Tommy* and *Tommy and Grizel* of "the boy who could not grow up," it is unsafe to treat Tommy Sandys as a complete self-portrait, though the grim pessimism of the second follows his own part-predicament mercilessly to its probable conclusion if that predicament had been complete. At the date of writing this predicament could not be followed in absolute detail – only hinted at by Grizel: "He did not love her. 'Not as I love him,' she said to herself, 'Not as married people ought to love, but in the other way he loves me dearly.' By the other way she meant that he loved her as he loved Elspeth [his sister], and loved them both just as he had loved them when all three played in the den. He was a boy who could not grow up." Barrie's personal predicament, that he was nearly though not quite impotent, brought about the break up of his marriage ten years later, but by then he had finished with novel writing as his triumph in the theatre became complete.

His novels and short stories are most unduly neglected: Conan Doyle lamented that the theatre had "diverted from literature the man with the purest style of his age," and Stevenson had greeted his most popular novel, *The Little Minister*, as holding the promise of real genius. But the theatre was already claiming Barrie in 1891–2 when the one-act parody, *Ibsen's Ghost*, and the full-length farce, *Walker, London,* both achieved long runs and high acclaim.

Barrie was still, however, known for his "Thrums" novels and stories, and his next play, *The Professor's Love Story*, was an amusing and charming triviality set in his native Kirriemuir. Real success came with the dramatised version of *The Little Minister*. His attempt at the problem play in the new Ibsen tradition which Shaw and Pinero were bringing into fashion (*The Wedding Guest*) was less successful, and he wisely turned to his own individual kind of play with *Quality Street* and *The Admirable Crichton*.

With these he entered truly into his kingdom. They are plays of charm, fancy, even at times whimsy, which hide a real problem, social and personal, that might easily have been the subject of tragedy. Yet the treatment sends the audience away with the conscious joy of escape and the, perhaps unconscious, feeling also of having been posed with a problem as potentially "real" as anything in Ibsen or Galsworthy or Granville-Barker, and as thought-provoking as Shaw at his best. When Captain Brown comes back from the wars and finds his first love, Phoebe Throssell, old and tired in her working clothes teaching her school in Quality Street, he turns from her to her niece who seems all that Phoebe had been before he went away. That the niece turns out to be Phoebe herself making her one desperate bid to win back his love – and succeeds – does not take away from the "problem," and the possibility of a tragic ending.

The basic idea for *The Admirable Crichton* was a remark by Conan Doyle that "if a King and an able seaman were wrecked together on a desert island for the rest of their lives, the sailor would end as King and the monarch as his servant." From this grew Barrie's parable of the Earl of Loam and his party, cast away on their island and helpless in this new setting until Crichton, the butler, who in the first act has been the perfect servant in an aristocratic household, takes control and shows himself to be the natural master in the given circumstances. By the end of the third act the situation is approaching its remorselessly logical conclusion, with Crichton, as undisputed king, about to choose the Earl's eldest daughter as his bride, when the rescue party reaches the island – summoned by Crichton who fires the beacon at the supreme moment, though he knows what the result will be. In the last act Crichton is once more the butler in Lord Loam's Mayfair house, while all the party have slipped back almost into their original characters, and their reactions to their island experience point the moral and underline the quiet satire on the values of civilisation.

Peter Pan followed, between two lesser plays, and then came *What Every Woman Knows*, which remains the best-known and most frequently revived after *Peter Pan* itself. Here again we have Barrie's unique mixture of romance and realism as Maggie saves her husband's career and their marriage without him realising that both depend on her superior courage, wit, and understanding.

His next outstanding play, *Dear Brutus*, employed fantasy as well as realism, and is held by many to be Barrie's greatest play; it has been revived many times.

Its theme is contained in the quotation from *Julius Caesar*: "The fault, dear Brutus, is not in our stars, but in ourselves": guests at a house party, after revealing their characters and blaming various chance mistakes for their failures, go out in Lob's magic wood at the end of act one. In the wood we see most of them throwing away their second chances in the same way as their first; and in act three they return and wake to a far deeper understanding of their own characters, though only one couple, the Dearths, are given real hope of a lasting change. "Barrie with a plot," wrote Denis Mackail, "and Barrie expressing a philosophy on which he had mused for years and in its own mood and convention, as near as almost nothing to a flawless play." *Mary Rose*, with a greater use of fantasy, was even more popular in its early years, but has not worn so well.

Barrie was also a master of the one-act play. The best known are *The Twelve-Pound Look*, *The Will*, *The Old Lady Shows Her Medals*, and *Shall We Join the Ladies?*, which is the first act of a thriller which for various reasons Barrie did not finish – though not, as if often said, because he was unable to complete the plot.

Towards the close of his life he turned back to the Scottish scenes of his youth with the short-story *Farewell Miss Julie Logan*, and to his early journalistic days in *The Greenwood Hat*, both more enjoyable for the modern reader than his early Auld Licht sketches and journalism.

Barrie has been out of favour with critics for a longer time than usually follows an author's death. But recent revivals have delighted audiences and shown Barrie's supreme skill in the basic mechanics of the dramatist's art. Some at least of his plays, besides *Peter Pan*, may confidently be claimed for immortality.

—Roger Lancelyn Green

BARRY, Philip. American. Born in Rochester, New York, 18 June 1896. Educated in public schools in Rochester; Yale University, New Haven, Connecticut (Editor, *Yale Review*), A.B. 1919; studied with George Pierce Baker at Harvard University, Cambridge, Massachusetts, 1919–22. Worked in the Code Department of the U.S. Embassy, London, 1918–19. Married Ellen Semple in 1922; two sons. Professional playwright from 1922; wrote for M.G.M., Hollywood, from 1934; lived in France, 1938–39. Member, National Institute of Arts and Letters. *Died 3 December 1949.*

PUBLICATIONS

Collections

States of Grace: Eight Plays, edited by Brendan Gill.   1975.

Plays

A Punch for Judy (produced 1921).   1922.
You and I (produced 1922).   1923.
God Bless Our Home.   1924.
The Youngest (produced 1924).   1925.
In a Garden (produced 1925).   1926.
White Wings (produced 1926).   1927; revised version, music by Douglas Moore
    (produced 1935).
John (produced 1927).   1929.
Paris Bound (produced 1927).   1929.
Cock Robin, with Elmer Rice (produced 1928).   1929.
Holiday (produced 1928).   1929.
Hotel Universe (produced 1930).   1930.
Tomorrow and Tomorrow (produced 1931).   1931.
The Animal Kingdom (produced 1932).   1932.
The Joyous Season (produced 1934).   1934.

Bright Star (produced 1935).

Spring Dance, from a play by Eleanor Golden and Eloise Barrangon (produced 1936). 1936.

Here Come the Clowns (produced 1938).   1939.

The Philadelphia Story (produced 1939).   1939.

Liberty Jones (produced 1941).   1941.

Without Love (produced 1943).   1943.

Foolish Notion (produced 1945).   Abridged version in *The Best Plays of 1944–45,* edited by Burns Mantle, 1945.

Second Threshold, completed by Robert E. Sherwood (produced 1951).   1951.

Fiction

War in Heaven.   1938.

Reading List: *The Drama of Barry* by Gerald Hamm, 1948; *Barry* by Joseph Roppolo, 1965.

*   *   *

American theater has never been particularly congenial to that honorable but somewhat amorphous genre *high comedy.* Philip Barry is one of the very few American playwrights who is a celebrated practitioner of the form. In plays like *Paris Bound, The Animal Kingdom, Without Love,* and – most famously – *Holiday* and *The Philadelphia Story,* he places articulate and well-to-do people in well-appointed homes and forces them to face domestic crises – usually a marriage in danger – with an equanimity that might be called courage and a wit which demands – but does not always get – audiences willing to listen for the precise meaning of lines which will direct them to the seriousness which lies at the heart of all the plays. That Barry is not simply an elegant entertainer can be seen in the variety of work in his canon – in which the successful comedies share space with a satirical extravaganza (*White Wings*), a Biblical play more concerned with theology than anecdote (*John*), a mood play in which characters find spiritual regeneration through psychodrama (*Hotel Universe*), a parable of good and evil among vaudevillians (*Here Come the Clowns,* based on Barry's own novel *War in Heaven*), a symbolic political drama (*Liberty Jones*), and a mixture of the real and the imaginary (*Foolish Notion*).

The comedies tend to be more effective than the overtly earnest plays, in which art sometimes loses out to exposition. But the important thing about Barry as a serious playwright is that, light or heavy, his work is informed by a major theme. Most of his plays, from *You and I* to *Second Threshold,* deal with man's need to be faithful to himself and his possibilities, personal and professional. The Barry protagonists have to escape the rigidities dictated by family (*The Youngest*), convention (*The Animal Kingdom*), society (*Holiday*). Sometimes, as with John and Herodias in *John,* the characters are trapped by their own preconceptions, and the luckier among them learn to live by discovering that, however benign their intentions, they too are manipulators (Nancy in *The Youngest,* Linda in *Holiday*) or by accepting their own imperfect, human condition (Tracy Lord in *The Philadelphia Story*). Barry's central concern is supported by recurrent minor themes – marriage as a bond of love, not a legal or religious ritual; work as a self-fulfilling activity, not a social imposition – and by the implicit religious assumptions that mark him even at his most secular. That *Holiday* and *The Philadelphia Story* are likely to remain Barry's most popular plays should not hide the fact that a number of the others – particularly the neglected *In a Garden* – deserve a place in the working American repertory.

—Gerald Weales

BAX, Clifford. English. Born in London, 13 July 1886; brother of the composer Sir Arnold Bax. Educated privately; studied art at the Slade School, London. Married 1) Gwendolen Bishop Smith in 1910 (died, 1926), one daughter; 2) Vera May Young in 1927. Lived in Germany, Belgium, and Italy; returned to England and gave up painting to concentrate on literary and dramatic work: Editor, *Orpheus* magazine, 1909–14, and the Orpheus series of books, 1909–17. Chairman, Incorporated Stage Society, 1929. Fellow, Royal Society of Literature, and Society of Antiquaries. *Died 18 November 1962.*

PUBLICATIONS

Plays

The Poetasters of Ispahan (produced 1912). In *Antique Pageantry,* 1921.
The Masque of the Planets, in *Orpheus 17,* 1912.
The Game of Death, in *Orpheus 23,* 1913.
The Marriage of the Soul (produced 1913).
The Sneezing Charm (produced 1918).
Square Pegs (produced 1919). 1920.
Antique Pageantry: A Book of Verse Plays (includes *The Poetasters of Ispahan, The Apricot Tree, The Summit, Aucassin and Nicolette*). 1921.
The Apricot Tree (produced 1922). In *Antique Pageantry,* 1921.
Old King Cole. 1921.
Shakespeare, with Harold F. Rubenstein. 1921.
The Impresario from Smyrna, in *Four Comedies by Goldoni.* 1922.
Mine Hostess, from a play by Goldoni (produced 1924). In *Four Comedies by Goldoni,* 1922.
Polite Satires (includes *The Unknown Hand, The Volcanic Island, Square Pegs*). 1922.
The Unknown Hand (produced 1926). In *Polite Satires,* 1922.
Polly, music by Frederic Austin, from the play *The Beggar's Opera* by John Gay (produced 1922). 1923.
And So Ad Infinitum (The Life of the Insects), with Nigel Playfair, from a translation by Percy Selver of a play by Karel Capek (as *The World We Live In,* produced 1922; as *The Insect Play,* produced 1923). 1923.
Up Stream (produced 1925). 1922.
The Cloak (produced 1923). 1924.
Midsummer Madness, music by Armstrong Gibbs (produced 1924). 1923.
Nocturne in Palermo. 1924.
Prelude and Fugue (produced 1927). 1924.
Studio Plays (includes *Prelude and Fugue, The Rose and the Cross, The Cloak*). 1924.
Mr. Pepys: A Ballad-Opera, music by Martin Shaw (produced 1926). 1926.
Rasputin, from a work by A. N. Tolstoy and P. E. Shchegolev (produced 1929).
Socrates (produced 1930). 1930.
The Chronicles of Cupid, Being a Masque of Love Throughout the Ages, with Geoffrey Dearmer. 1931.
The Venetian (produced 1931). In *Valiant Ladies,* 1931.
The Immortal Lady (produced 1931). In *Valiant Ladies,* 1931.
The Rose Without a Thorn (produced 1932). In *Valiant Ladies,* 1931.
Valiant Ladies. 1931.
Twelve Short Plays, Serious and Comic. 1932.
April in August (produced 1934). 1934.
The Quaker's Cello. 1934.

Tragic Nesta. 1934.
The House of Borgia (produced 1935). 1937.
Battles Long Ago, in *Eight One-Act Plays of 1936,* edited by William Armstrong. 1937.
Hemlock for Eight, with Leon M. Lion (broadcast 1943). 1946.
Golden Eagle (produced 1946). 1946.
The Buddha: A Radio Version of His Life and Ideas (broadcast 1947). 1947.
The Play of St. Lawrence: A Pageant Play. 1947.
Circe (as *A Day, A Night, and a Morrow,* produced 1948). 1949.

Radio Plays: *Mr. Williams of Hamburg,* 1943; *Hemlock for Eight,* with Leon M. Lion, 1943; *Out of His Senses,* 1943; *The Buddha,* 1947; *The Shrouded Candle,* 1948; *The Life That I Gave Him,* from a play by Pirandello, 1951.

Fiction

Many a Green Isle. 1927.
Time with a Gift of Tears: A Modern Romance. 1943.

Verse

Twenty Chinese Poems Paraphrased. 1910; augmented edition, as *Twenty-Five Chinese Poems,* 1916.
Poems Dramatic and Lyrical. 1911.
Japanese Impromptus, with Daphne Bax. 1914.
A House of Words. 1920.
The Traveller's Tale. 1921.
Farewell, My Muse. 1932.

Other

Friendship. 1913.
Inland Far: A Book of Thoughts and Impressions. 1925.
Bianca Capello (biography). 1927.
Leonardo da Vinci. 1932.
Pretty Witty Nell: An Account of Nell Gwynn and Her Environment. 1932.
That Immortal Sea: A Meditation upon the Future of Religion and Sexual Morality. 1933.
Ideas and People. 1936.
Highways and Byways in Essex. 1939.
The Life of the White Devil (on Vittoria Orsini). 1940.
Evenings in Albany. 1942.
Whither the Theatre −? A Letter to a Young Playwright. 1945.
The Beauty of Women. 1946.
Rosemary for Remembrance (autobiography). 1948.
Some I Knew Well. 1951.
W. G. Grace (biography). 1952.
Who's Who in Heaven: A Sketch. 1954.

Editor, *Four Comedies by Goldoni,* translated by Bax, Marguerite Tracy, and Eleanor and Herbert Farjeon. 1922.
Editor, *Letters,* by Florence Farr, Bernard Shaw, and W. B. Yeats. 1941.

Editor, *Never Again!* 1942.

Editor, *Vintage Verse.* 1945.

Editor, *The Silver Casket, Being Love Letters and Love Poems Attributed to Mary Stuart.* 1946.

Editor, *All the World's a Stage: Theatrical Portraits.* 1946.

Editor, *The Poetry of the Brownings.* 1947.

Editor, with Meum Stewart, *The Distaff Muse.* 1948.

Translator, *Initiation and Its Results,* by Rudolf Steiner. 1909.

Translator, *The Age of Gold: A Chorus Translated Out of Tasso's L'Aminta.* 1944.

*　　*　　*

Clifford Bax's background was affluent and cultured (the composer Arnold Bax was his eldest brother), and he began his career as a student of art at the Slade School, combining this training with an interest in the occult which led him to the Theosophical Society. In the 1920's and 1930's he was associated with such noncommercial theatrical organizations as the Incorporated Stage Society, the Phoenix Society, and the Three Hundred Club, and collaborated with Nigel Playfair in several ventures at the Lyric, Hammersmith. His view of the stage was set forth in a pamphlet, *Whither the Theatre —?*

Although Bax produced a range of works encompassing poetry, translations from Capek and Goldoni, a biography of the cricketer W. G. Grace, several volumes of reminiscences, and a romantic novel chronicling the inter-war years, his reputation chiefly rests on his stage adaptations and original plays. His unexacting light entertainments were an attractive contribution to the London theatre of their day, but when he essayed the handling of strong situations or significant themes, certain deficiencies were apparent beneath the professional gloss. Thus in the novelettish *Up Stream*, a drama of conflict and emotion set in the Amazonian jungle, clumsy exposition, stilted dialogue, and implausible behaviour vitiate the plot's latent possibilities.

After 1925 Bax wisely chose to write primarily "costume plays" on historical and literary subjects, although *Socrates*, arguably the best of these, is unlike any other "period" drama of its time. Its episodes are largely skilful adaptations of Plato's dialogues, which when staged can prove unduly static, but a sympathetic yet unsentimentalized portrait of Socrates emerges. Bax avoids a total dissipation of theatrical interest by sensibly focusing on the successful campaign to destroy the philosopher. His more romantic treatments of historical materials, if livelier, were less satisfactory, depending on incident rather than insight for their success: hence, because of the lightweight psychological motivation of its protagonists, *The Venetian*, a spirited attempt at an Italianate drama of love-intrigue on Jacobean lines, fails to build to the required climax. *The Immortal Lady*, a tribute to the Countess of Nithsdale who rescued her Jacobite husband from the Tower in 1716, is accomplished and entertaining, yet contrives to present the escape with only the seriousness and suspense appropriate to a schoolgirls' escapade, while the highly popular *The Rose Without a Thorn*, in seeking to demythologize and humanize Henry VIII, comes dangerously close to trivializing him. Again, there is a basic lack of conviction in the reasons for the characters' conduct (most notably Katheryn Howard), and the contemporary idiom in which the Queen and her lovers converse is fatally defective in Tudor resonance. Although this was part of the author's deliberate intention, Bax was not the only twentieth-century playwright to discover that the themes of historical high romance blended unhappily with characters, situations, and diction drawn from modern Mayfair. While Bax enjoyed some well-deserved celebrity during his working life, it must be admitted that there is a certain facile quality about all but his best plays, and that even these do not satisfy now at a very deep or permanent level.

—William M. Tydeman

BAXTER, James K(eir). New Zealander. Born in Dunedin, 29 June 1926; son of the writer Archibald Baxter. Educated at Quaker schools in New Zealand and England; Otago University, Dunedin; Victoria University, Wellington, B.A. 1952. Married Jacqueline Sturm in 1948; two children. Worked as a labourer, journalist, and school-teacher. Editor, *Numbers* magazine, Wellington, 1954–60. Spent 5 months in India studying school publications, 1958; started commune in Jerusalem (a Maori community on the Wanganui River), 1969. Recipient: Unesco grant, 1958; Robert Burns Fellowship, Otago University, 1966, 1967. *Died 22 October 1972.*

PUBLICATIONS

Plays

    Jack Winter's Dream (broadcast, 1958).   In *The Wide Open Cage and Jack Winter's Dream*, 1959.
    The Wide Open Cage (produced 1959).   In *The Wide Open Cage and Jack Winter's Dream*, 1959.
    The Wide Open Cage and Jack Winter's Dream: Two Plays.   1959.
    The Spots of the Leopard (produced 1963).
    The Band Rotunda (produced 1967).   In *The Devil and Mr. Mulcahy and The Band Rotunda*, 1971.
    The Sore-Footed Man, based on *Philoctetes* by Euripides (produced 1967).   In *The Sore-Footed Man and The Temptations of Oedipus*, 1971.
    The Bureaucrat (produced 1967).
    The Devil and Mr. Mulcahy (produced 1967).   In *The Devil and Mr. Mulcahy and The Band Rotunda*, 1971.
    Mr. O'Dwyer's Dancing Party (produced 1968).
    The Day Flanagan Died (produced 1969).
    The Temptations of Oedipus (produced 1970).   In *The Sore-Footed Man and The Temptations of Oedipus*, 1971.
    The Devil and Mr. Mulcahy and The Band Rotunda.   1971.
    The Sore-Footed Man and The Temptations of Oedipus.   1971.

    Radio Play: *Jack Winter's Dream*, 1958.

Verse

    Beyond the Palisade: Poems.   1944.
    Blow, Wind of Fruitfulness.   1948.
    Hart Crane.   1948.
    Rapunzel: A Fantasia for Six Voices.   1948.
    Charm for Hilary.   1949.
    Poems Unpleasant, with Louis Johnson and Anton Vogt.   1952.
    The Fallen House: Poems.   1953.
    Lament for Barney Flanagan.   1954.
    Traveller's Litany.   1955.
    The Night Shift: Poems of Aspects of Love, with others.   1957.
    The Iron Breadboard: Studies in New Zealand Writing (verse parodies).   1957.
    In Fires of No Return: Poems.   1958.
    Chosen Poems, 1958.   1958.

Ballad of Calvary Street. 1960.
Howrah Bridge and Other Poems. 1961.
Poems. 1964.
Pig Island Letters. 1966.
A Death Song for M. Mouldybroke. 1967.
A Small Ode on Mixed Flatting: Elicited by the Decision of the Otago University Authorities to Forbid This Practice among Students. 1967.
The Lion Skin: Poems. 1967.
A Bucket of Blood for a Dollar: A Conversation Between Uncle Sam and the Rt. Hon. Keith Holyoake, Prime Minister of New Zealand. 1968.
The Rock Woman: Selected Poems. 1969.
Ballad of the Stonegut Sugar Works. 1969.
Jerusalem Sonnets: Poems for Colin Durning. 1970.
The Junkies and the Fuzz. 1970.
Jerusalem Daybook (poetry and prose journal). 1971.
Jerusalem Blues (2). 1971.
Autumn Testament (poetry and prose journal). 1972.
Four God Songs. 1972.
Letter to Peter Olds. 1972.
Runes. 1973.
The Labyrinth: Some Uncollected Poems, 1944–1972. 1974.
The Bone Chanter: Unpublished Poems 1945–1972. 1977.
The Holy Life and Death of Concrete Grady: Various Uncollected and Unpublished Poems, edited by J. E. Weir. 1977.

Other

Recent Trends in New Zealand Poetry. 1951.
The Fire and the Anvil: Notes on Modern Poetry. 1955; revised edition, 1960.
Oil (primary school bulletin). 1957.
The Coaster (primary school bulletin). 1959.
The Trawler (primary school bulletin). 1961.
New Zealand in Colour, photographs by Kenneth and Jean Bigwood. 1961.
The Old Earth Closet: A Tribute to Regional Poetry. 1965.
Aspects of Poetry in New Zealand. 1967.
The Man on the Horse (lectures). 1967.
The Flowering Cross: Pastoral Articles. 1969.
The Six Faces of Love: Lenten Lectures. 1972.
A Walking Stick for an Old Man. 1972.

Reading List: *The Poetry of Baxter* by J. E. Weir, 1970; *Baxter* by Charles Doyle, 1976; *Baxter* by Vincent O'Sullivan, 1976.

*   *   *

At his best one of the finest English-language poets of the past thirty years, James K. Baxter is the one New Zealand poet of undeniable international reputation. Although he died in his mid-forties, his literary career lasted for over thirty years. Its fruits were many volumes of poems, a number of plays, works of literary commentary or criticism, essays on religious topics, and a small amount of fiction (he was a fine exponent of the parable).

With publication of his first book, *Beyond the Palisade,* when he was eighteen, Baxter at once became a figure of note in New Zealand letters. Within a few years, he already occupied a central position in the literary scene, so that his booklet, *Recent Trends in New Zealand Poetry*, a beautifully condensed commentary, was from the first accepted as authoritative. Alongside his literary reputation, Baxter quickly began to build one as a maverick and a bohemian. When, late in the 1940's, he moved to Wellington and began his long friendship and collaboration with Louis Johnson, they became the focus of the "romantic" element in New Zealand writing, which found its centre in Wellington for the next dozen years or so.

Throughout the 1950's Baxter produced a prolific variety of poems, plays, stories, and criticism, work which ranged from makeshift to brilliant. With Johnson and Charles Doyle (and, latterly, others) he edited the characteristically erratic periodical *Numbers*, then the only alternative to the few "establishment" periodicals such as *Landfall*.

1958 was a crucial moment in Baxter's career. Until then, his adult life had been a strange compound of Christian concern and rip-roaring bohemianism. That year he stayed for a long spell in the Trappist monastery at Kopua, Hawke's Bay, and was converted to Roman Catholicism. At the same time, his superb collection *In Fires of No Return* drew upon the work of his whole career to that point. *Howrah Bridge and Other Poems* followed in 1961 and was composed of new poems plus fine pieces ranging back to the 1940's; but Baxter's talent as a poet for a time seemed to lose focus. It was typical of Baxter that he made little or no effort to become known outside his own country; untypical as he was, he was very deeply a New Zealander, though anguished at his country's unspiritual puritanism.

After a low-energy period, Baxter's career gathered momentum again when he was awarded a Burns Fellowship at the University of Otago. Writing in the *Dominion* on 23 October 1965, Louis Johnson suggested that "the Burns scholarship may well mark a turning-point in his career" and this proved to be the case in remarkable ways. First, it produced what many consider to be Baxter's best verse collection, *Pig Island Letters*, a book in which he learned from, and transcended, the unlikely twin influences of Lawrence Durrell and Robert Lowell. Besides the critical-autobiographical pieces of *The Man on the Horse* and *Aspects of Poetry in New Zealand*, those years in Dunedin witnessed the flowering of Baxter's career as a playwright. During 1967 and 1968, Patric Carey at the Globe Theatre produced seven Baxter plays, including all the most important. Although secondary to the poetry, those plays make it a reasonable claim that, besides being the country's foremost poet, Baxter is the most productive and interesting New Zealand playwright up to the present.

The Dunedin years also led him more deeply into religious and social concerns. After a period of catechetical work in the city, he went into solitude for some months at Jerusalem (Hiruharama), a tiny religious settlement on the Wanganui River. Later he founded a commune there for troubled youths and social drop-outs, and he was also the moving spirit in setting up doss-houses in both Auckland and Wellington. These ventures, pursued in a Franciscan spirit, including a vow of poverty, took much of his energy, but the commitment also carried over into his vocation as poet and this period witnessed a further remarkable shift in the development of his writing, especially in the Jerusalem writings, *Jerusalem Sonnets*, *Jerusalem Daybook*, and *Autumn Testament*. He developed a very personal "sonnet" form, in fluid pentameter couplets, and, particularly in *Jerusalem Daybook*, made effective use of an amalgam of prose and verse.

Baxter was also important in his community as a man. His best poems have a natural incandescence which partly derives from his being permeated from boyhood with the finest poetry of the British tradition, but which also comes from a human commitment based on religion. New Zealand is a relatively successful social welfare state, secular in spirit. Baxter, notably, brought to it a strong religious consciousness. A literary talent with a touch of genius was deepened and strengthened by the religious element in his character. That this did not escape the notice of his fellow-countrymen is evident from the crowds which thronged to his funeral and memorial services. Baxter's legacy to his country is a double one, a substantial amount of first-rate writing, especially poems, and the example of a man able to carry the spiritual life as far as it can go.

—Charles Doyle

BECKETT, Samuel (Barclay).   Irish.   Born in Foxrock, County Dublin, 13 April 1906. Educated at Portora Royal School, Enniskillen, County Fermanagh; Trinity College, Dublin, B.A. in French and Italian 1927, M.A. 1931. Worked at the Irish Red Cross Hospital, St. Lô, France, 1945. Married Suzanne Dechevaux-Dumesnil in 1948. Lecturer in English, Ecole Normale Supérieure, Paris, 1928–30; Lecturer in French, Trinity College, Dublin, 1930–32. Closely associated with James Joyce in Paris in the late 1920's and 1930's. Settled in Paris in 1937, and has written chiefly in French since 1945; translates his own work into English. Recipient: *Evening Standard* award, 1955; Obie Award, 1958, 1960, 1962, 1964; Italia Prize, 1959; Prix Formentor, 1959; International Publishers Prize, 1961; Prix Filmcritice, 1965; Tours Film Prize, 1966; Nobel Prize for Literature, 1969. D.Litt.: University of Dublin, 1959. Member, American Academy of Arts and Letters, 1968. Lives in Paris.

PUBLICATIONS

Plays

    Le Kid, with Georges Pelorson (produced 1931).
    En Attendant Godot (produced 1953).   1952; as *Waiting for Godot: Tragicomedy* (produced 1955), 1954.
    Fin de Partie, Suivi de Acte sans Paroles (produced 1957).   1957; as *Endgame, Followed by Act Without Words* (*Endgame* produced 1958, *Act Without Words* produced 1960), 1958.
    All That Fall (broadcast 1957).   1957.
    Krapp's Last Tape (produced 1958).   With *Embers,* 1959.
    Embers (broadcast 1959).   With *Krapp's Last Tape,* 1959.
    Act Without Words II (produced 1959).   In *Krapp's Last Tape and Other Dramatic Pieces,* 1960.
    Happy Days (produced 1961).   1961; bilingual edition edited by James Knowlson, 1978.
    Words and Music (broadcast 1962).   In *Play,* 1964.
    Cascando (in French, broadcast 1963).   1963; in English (broadcast 1964; produced on stage 1970), in *Play,* 1964.
    Play (produced 1963).   1964.
    Eh Joe (televised 1966).   In *Eh Joe and Other Writings,* 1967.
    Come and Go: Dramaticule (produced 1966).   1967.
    Film.   1969.
    Breath (produced 1970).   In *Breath and Other Shorts,* 1971.
    Not I (produced 1972).   1973.
    That Time (produced 1976).   1976.
    Footfalls (produced 1976).   1976.
    Tryst (televised 1976).   In *Ends and Odd,* 1976.
    Ends and Odd: Dramatic Pieces.   1976.

    Screenplay: *Film,* 1965.

    Radio Plays: *All That Fall,* 1957; *Embers,* 1959; *The Old Tune,* 1960; *Words and Music,* 1962; *Cascando,* 1963.

    Television Plays: *Eh Joe,* 1966; *Tryst,* 1976; *Shades (Ghost Trio, Not I, … But the Clouds …),* 1977.

Fiction and Texts

    More Pricks Than Kicks (stories).   1934.

Murphy.   1938.
Molloy (in French).   1951; translated by the author and Patrick Bowles, 1955.
Malone Meurt.   1951; as *Malone Dies,* 1956.
L'Innommable.   1953; as *The Unnamable,* 1958.
Watt (in English).   1953.
Nouvelles et Textes pour Rien.   1955; as *Stories and Texts for Nothing,* 1967.
From an Abandoned Work.   1958.
Comment C'Est.   1961; as *How It Is,* 1961.
Imagination Morte Imaginez.   1965; as *Imagination Dead Imagine,* 1965.
Assez.   1966; as *Enough,* in *No's Knife,* 1967.
Bing.   1966; as *Ping,* in *No's Knife,* 1967.
No's Knife: Selected Shorter Prose 1945–1966.   1967.
L'Issue.   1968.
Sans.   1969; as *Lessness,* 1971.
Mercier et Camier.   1970; as *Mercier and Camier,* 1974.
Séjour.   1970.
Premier Amour.   1970; as *First Love,* 1973.
Le Depeupleur.   1971; as *The Lost Ones,* 1972.
The North.   1973.
First Love and Other Shorts.   1974.
Fizzles.   1976.
For to End Yet Again and Other Fizzles.   1977.
Four Novellas.   1977.
Residua.   1978.

Verse

Whoroscope.   1930.
Echo's Bones and Other Precipitates.   1935.
Gedichte (collected poems in English and French, with German translations) 1959.
Poems in English.   1961.
Collected Poems in English and French.   1977.

Other

Proust.   1931; with *Three Dialogues with Georges Duthuit,* 1965.
Bram van Welde, with Georges Duthuit and J. Putman.   1958.
A Beckett Reader.   1967.
I Can't Go On: A Selection from the Work of Beckett, edited by Richard W.
    Seaver.   1976.

Translator, *Anthology of Mexican Poetry,* edited by Octavio Paz.   1958.
Translator, *La Manivelle/The Old Tune,* by Robert Pinget.   1960.
Translator, *Zone,* by Guillaume Apollinaire.   1960.
Translator, *Drunken Boat,* by Arthur Rimbaud, edited by James Knowlson and Felix
    Leakey.   1977.

Bibliography: *Beckett: His Work and His Critics: An Essay in Bibliography* by Raymond
Felderman and John Fletcher, 1970.

Reading List: "Beckett Issue" of *Perspective 11,* 1959, and of *Modern Drama 9,* 1966, both
edited by Ruby Cohn, and *Beckett: The Comic Gamut,* 1962, and *Back to Beckett,* 1973, both
by Cohn; *Beckett: A Critical Study,* 1961, revised edition, 1968, and *A Reader's Guide to
Beckett,* 1973, both by Hugh Kenner; *Beckett* by William York Tindall, 1964; *The Novels of*

Beckett by John Fletcher, 1964; *Beckett: A Collection of Critical Essays* edited by Martin Esslin, 1965; *Beckett at Sixty: A Festschrift,* 1967; *Beckett* by Ronald Hayman, 1968; *Beckett/Beckett: The Truth of Contradictories* by Vivian Mercier, 1977; *Beckett: A Biography* by Deirdre Bair, 1978.

*   *   *

No living author in English or French has molded words so skillfully in fiction and drama, while paradoxically protesting his own failure. Better appreciated as a playwright, Beckett himself has taken deepest pains with his fiction – most of it originally written in French but self-translated into his native English. Most of his drama, in contrast, was translated into French from English. "English is a good theatre language," he has said, "because of its concreteness, its close relationship between thing and vocable." Two languages and two genres have been indelibly marked by Beckett's vision – a reaching toward human essence or elemental being.

Beckett broke into print in 1929 with a piece on *Finnegans Wake,* written at Joyce's request, with a pastiche dialogue on contraception in Ireland, with a cryptic short story "Assumption." Supercilious mannerism mars the three pieces, and yet they predict Beckett's generic variety. From 1929 to 1977 no year has passed without his contribution to some literary or theatre genre. Nearly half a century of creative activity, however his characters may yearn for indolence.

In the early 1930's, in English, Beckett wavered between obscure verse and satiric short fiction, publishing a volume of each. At about the time he settled in Paris, he published his first English novel, *Murphy* – traditional in its coherence and comic omniscience. It was perceptively reviewed by Dylan Thomas: "[*Murphy*] is serious because it is, mainly, the study of a complex and oddly tragic character who cannot reconcile the unreality of the seen world with the reality of the unseen, and who, through scorn and neglect of 'normal' society, drifts into the society of the certified abnormal in his search for 'a little world.' " The sentence also describes Beckett's next very untraditional novel, *Watt,* and it is relevant too to Beckett's French fiction, where "the seen world" recedes toward a vanishing point.

Watt is a less finished but more important novel than *Murphy* because it predicts the anarchic immediacy of most of the French fiction. Watt carries the Beckettian burden of solitude, attracted and rejected as he is by the inscrutable Mr. Knott. A would-be Cartesian, Watt thinks in order to try to be, but his French successors, adopting the language of Descartes, will try *not* to think in order to be. Beckett revised *Watt* several times during a four-year period in which he fled from his Paris home to a Free French farm. Back in Paris, forty years old when World War II ended, Beckett wrote with prolific zest, producing four long stories, four novels, and two plays. He has never again attained such fluidity.

The French fiction, considered by many to be his most important work, is a shifting soulscape painted by a narrating "I." But "I" 's identity changes in the stories, in the novels, and in the works that grow out of them – *Texts for Nothing* and *How It Is.* The story narrators are nameless social outcasts, old and ill, inventing their ways of survival. Conflict and climax do not structure these alogical cumulations of passionate language. But common to all of them is the overriding sense that they are stories.

The reach toward formal fiction is inherited by the novel heroes Molloy, Moran, Malone, and the Unnamable – four narrators of three books that Beckett himself calls a trilogy. Molloy seeks his mother, and Moran seeks Molloy; both write an account of a fruitless search. Malone writes so as to fill the time of his dying. The Unnamable disowns the written for the spoken discourse, whosoever the voice that speaks it. Even more aural is *How It Is,* whose narrator/narrated tries to order chaos through a few images, many numbers, and skeletal story remnants rising from ubiquitous mud. Probably the most difficult sustained work in the Beckett canon, *How It Is* invents a language rhythmically if not lexically, a language that conveys the body's movements through its mud and the mind's movements through its mud. After *How It Is* Beckett discards first-person fiction and assumes resolute objectivity for the short rending fictions of the late 1960's.

It is a critical convenience to discuss Beckett's fiction and drama as though each had an independent development, but this is inaccurate. Not only did Beckett zigzag from drama to fiction and back (from 1948 to 1971, at any rate), but he frequently translated in the one genre while producing original work in the other. He himself has stated that drama is a relaxation for him: "You have a definite space and people in this space. That's relaxing." In relaxation he has created a spate of works in dramatic form; the list of those published and/or produced includes fourteen plays for the stage, six for radio, three for television, two mime plays, and one film script.

The stage images are at once visually arresting and metaphysically meaningful: two frayed comedians by a tree, a throned and shabby ruler with two ashbins, a prattling blonde buried in the ground, an unkempt old man bent over a tape recorder, three grey faces atop three grey urns, three stately faceless women, a mouth adrift in the dark, a whitehaired head turned up to the light, "a faint tangle of pale grey tatters." The radio plays introduce a rare verbal music to the medium. The television plays are at once paintings through the camera eye and soul searches beyond the camera's power.

Though Beckett does not speak of a stage trilogy, one might so view his three full-evening plays, *Waiting for Godot*, *Endgame*, *Happy Days*. All three are plays in which the main action is waiting; all three are plays in which the stage day is ending without quite coming to an end. Rather than follow the plays chronologically, however, a Beckett baptism might well begin with simpler pieces. In *Breath* a faint cry signals an increase of light and breath to a maximum in about ten seconds, holds for five seconds, and fades to the cry "*as before*." Vagitus and death-rattle are barely distinguishable in the black depths of eternity. This Beckett obsession is dramatized far more memorably in the plays of the 1970's. *Not I* embraces an asyntactical incantation of a life from premature birth to compulsive speech at age seventy, that biblical terminus. *That Time* looks back on three ages of man, finally giving to dust the pronouncement of human brevity. *Footfalls* paces through human pain, unable to escape it even beyond the grave, but always and forever revolving it all in the mind.

Brief as human life may be, Beckett theatricalizes it. The mime plays do this in almost allegorical fashion, the first teaching its arotagonist what Beckett in *Proust* calls the "oblation of desire," and the second demonstrating the repetitive futility of contrasting life-processes. *Come and Go*, less absolute than *Breath*, links childhood and age in a beautifully regular pattern; it is the first of several Beckett stage plays to dramatize the mystery at the heart of being. With the exception of *Not I*, Beckett's stage plays end in a stasis that confirms mystery.

Though Beckett's recent plays hover at death's threshold, he is more widely known for the theater trilogy that is absorbed in life. *Happy Days* implies courage even as Winnie sinks ever deeper into that old extinguisher, the earth. *Endgame*'s four characters reflect on each expiring moment. Liveliest of all Beckett's plays, and living on many stages in many languages is that contemporary classic, *Waiting for Godot*.

The impact of *Godot* is immediate; the impact of *Godot* is inexhaustible. Vaudeville turns are threaded on philosophic nihilism and a classico-Christian tradition. The seed of *Godot* is Luke's account of the crucifixion, as summarized by St. Augustine: "Do not despair: one of the thieves was saved. Do not presume: one of the thieves was damned." The two thieves are Vladimir and Estragon; the two thieves are Pozzo and Lucky; the two thieves are Godot's boy and his brother. On the stage, characters divide into two inseparable couples; action divides into two repetitive acts. The two friends are conscientious about trying to live through each disappointing evening, for Godot may always come tomorrow. In the meantime they volley routines with Wimbledon finesse. In their dogged invention lies the delight of *Godot*. Each act ends: "Well, shall we go?" "Yes, let's go," but the friends "*do not move*." They do not move, but they have moved audiences and readers the world over.

—Ruby Cohn

BEHAN, Brendan (Francis). Irish. Born in Dublin, 9 February 1923. Educated at the French Sisters of Charity School, Dublin. Married Beatrice ffrench-Salkeld in 1955; one daughter. Joined the Irish Republican Army, 1937; sent to a British borstal (correctional school) for attempting to blow up a Liverpool shipyard, 1939; sentenced to 14 years for the attempted murder of two detectives, 1942; released in general amnesty, 1946; in prison, Manchester, 1947, deported, 1952; worked as housepainter and journalist. Recipient: Obie Award, 1958; Paris Festival Award, 1958; French Critics' Award, 1962. *Died 20 March 1964.*

PUBLICATIONS

Collections

    The Wit of Behan, edited by Sean McCann. 1968.
    The Complete Plays. 1978.

Plays

    The Quare Fellow (produced 1954). 1956.
    The Hostage (produced 1958). 1958; revised version, 1962.
    The Big House (broadcast 1957; produced 1963). In *Evergreen Review,* September–October 1961.
    Moving Out, and A Garden Party, edited by Robert Hogan. 1967.
    Richard's Cork Leg, edited and completed by Alan Simpson (produced 1972). 1973.
    Time for a Gargle (produced 1973).

    Radio Play: *The Big House,* 1957.

Fiction

    The Scarperer. 1964.

Verse

    Life Styles: Poems, with Nine Translations from the Irish of Brendan Behan, translated by Ulick O'Connor. 1973.

Other

    Borstal Boy (autobiography). 1958.
    Behan's Ireland: An Irish Sketch-Book. 1962.
    Hold Your Hour and Have Another (articles). 1963.
    Behan's New York. 1964.
    Confessions of an Irish Rebel. 1965.

Reading List: *My Brother Brendan Behan* by Dominic Behan, 1965; *The World of Behan,* edited by Sean McCann, 1965; *Behan, Man and Showman* by Rae Jeffs, 1966; *Behan* by Ted E. Boyle, 1969; *Behan* by Ulick O'Connor, 1970; *The Major Works of Behan* by Peter Gerdes, 1973; *My Life with Brendan* by Beatrice Behan, Des Hickey, and Gus Smith, 1974.

*   *   *

Brendan Behan's fame within his own lifetime, and his abiding reputation, depends on his merits as a dramatist. The two internationally successful plays, *The Quare Fellow* and *The Hostage*, share a theme which is central to all his work – the paradox of man's urge towards love and fellowship on the one hand and his persistent practice of inhumanity on the other. Imprisonment – which the playwright had himself experienced – concentrates these complementary features, providing a graphic account of institutional violence and degradation, and the incidental redeeming evidence of individual human kindness and sympathy. In *The Quare Fellow* the emotional atmosphere of a prison on the eve of an execution is sustained with subtle and humorous control; in *The Hostage*, on the other hand, sentiment intrudes to falsify the real strength of the play. Why should two plays, written within a few years of each other differ so markedly; why should the second fall short so distressingly?

The Quare Fellow impresses with the inhuman logic of inevitable death, whereas *The Hostage* (in which an English soldier is held in Dublin by republican subversives) is based on uncertainty, chance, flux. The "quare fellow" (who is tantalisingly kept off stage) is finally murdered by law, whereas the Tommy in *The Hostage* is accidentally shot in a raid by police trying to rescue him. But beyond this elementary explanation there lies a more significant one. In *The Quare Fellow* Behan's satirical humour is directed very exactly against specific social conditions – the tyranny of officials, the hypocrisy of respectable folk, and the cruelty of faceless law. Each of these is present in the play in concrete and individual characters. *The Hostage*, in contrast, tackles a larger and more abstract problem – the discovery of a basic humanity in people of different nationalities and cultures. And the didacticism of the later play is reflected in the new role adopted by song; in *The Quare Fellow* song had provided mood in a manner which integrated the various levels of society implicated in the drama, in *The Hostage* it adds a neat commentary – nothing more. A third play, *Richard's Cork Leg* (posthumously prepared for the stage) contributes little to Behan's reputation as a serious dramatist.

Of the prose works, *Borstal Boy* is outstanding, with its attention to imprisonment as the epitome of human perversity. It belongs to a sub-genre which has been for many years important in Irish writing – the fictionalised autobiography. And significantly, it proved successful when adapted for the stage. Much of the remainder of Behan's work rises only occasionally above the level of good, original journalism. Behan gives the appearance, consequently, of being an untutored sporadic genius for whom literary tradition meant nothing. In fact, he had a lively (if unconventional) appreciation of literature: the influence of Oscar Wilde, André Gide, and Sean O'Casey can be readily charted. In addition, he wrote occasionally in Gaelic, and was affected by the peculiar power of folk literature both urban and rural. To appreciate his best work one must read it in conjunction with the essays and tape-recorded fragments, the ballads and the wonderfully disrespectful gossip with which he spiced his Spoken Arts record.

—W. J. McCormack

BEHRMAN, S(amuel) N(athaniel).   American.   Born in Worcester, Massachusetts, 9 June 1893. Educated at Clark College, now Clark University, Worcester, 1912–14; Harvard

University, Cambridge, Massachusetts, B.A. 1916 (Phi Beta Kappa); Columbia University, New York, M.A. 1918. Married Elza Heifetz in 1936; one son, two step-children. Book Reviewer for the *New Republic*, New York, and the *New York Times*; Columnist, *The New Yorker*. Founder, with Robert E. Sherwood, Elmer Rice, Maxwell Anderson, Sidney Howard, and John F. Wharton, Playwrights Company, 1938. Trustee, Clark University. Recipient: American Academy of Arts and Letters grant, 1943; New York Drama Critics Circle Award, 1944; Brandeis University Creative Arts Award, 1962. LL.D.: Clark University, 1949. Member, National Institute of Arts and Letters, and American Academy of Arts and Sciences. *Died 9 September 1973.*

PUBLICATIONS

Plays

Bedside Manners: A Comedy of Convalescence with J. Kenyon Nicholson (produced 1923).   1924.
A Night's Work, with J. Kenyon Nicholson (produced 1924).   1926.
The Man Who Forgot, with Owen Davis (produced 1926).
The Second Man (produced 1927).   1927.
Love Is Like That, with J. Kenyon Nicholson (produced 1927).
Serena Blandish, from the novel by Enid Bagnold (produced 1929).   In *Three Plays*, 1934.
Meteor (produced 1929).   1930.
Brief Moment (produced 1931).   1931.
Biography (produced 1932).   1933.
Love Story (produced 1934).
Three Plays: Serena Blandish, Meteor, The Second Man.   1934.
Rain from Heaven (produced 1935).   1935.
End of Summer (produced 1936).   1936.
Amphitryon 38, with Roger Gellert, from a play by Jean Giraudoux (produced 1937).   1938.
Wine of Choice (produced 1938).   1938.
No Time for Comedy (produced 1939).   1939.
The Talley Method (produced 1941).   1941.
The Pirate, from a work by Ludwig Fulda (produced 1942).   1943.
Jacobowsky and the Colonel, with Franz Werfel (produced 1944).   1944.
Dunnigan's Daughter (produced 1945).   1946.
Jane, from a story by W. Somerset Maugham (produced 1946; as *The Foreign Language*, produced 1951).   1952.
I Know My Love, from a play by Marcel Achard (produced 1949).   1952.
Let Me Hear the Melody (produced 1951).
Fanny, with Joshua Logan, music by Harold Rome, from a trilogy by Marcel Pagnol (produced 1954).   1955.
Four Plays: The Second Man, Biography, Rain from Heaven, End of Summer.   1955.
The Cold Wind and the Warm (produced 1958).   1959.
The Beauty Part (produced 1962).
Lord Pengo: A Period Comedy, based on his book *Duveen* (produced 1962).   1963.
But for Whom Charlie (produced 1964).   1964.

Screenplays: *Liliom*, with Sonya Levien, 1930; *Lightnin'*, with Sonya Levien, 1930; *The Sea Wolf*, with Ralph Block, 1930; *The Brat*, with others, 1931; *Surrender*, with Sonya

Levien, 1931; *Daddy Long Legs,* with Sonya Levien, 1931; *Rebecca of Sunnybrook Farm,* with Sonya Levien, 1932; *Tess of the Storm Country,* with others, 1932; *Brief Moment,* 1933; *Queen Christina,* 1933; *Cavalcade,* 1933; *Hallelujah, I'm a Bum,* 1933; *My Lips Betray,* 1933; *Biography of a Bachelor Girl,* 1934; *As Husbands Go,* with Sonya Levien, 1934; *The Scarlet Pimpernel,* with others, 1934; *A Tale of Two Cities,* with W. P. Lipscomb, 1935; *Conquest,* with others, 1937; *Parnell,* with John Van Druten, 1937; *The Cowboy and the Lady,* with Sonya Levien, 1938; *No Time for Comedy,* 1940; *Waterloo Bridge,* with others, 1940; *Two-Faced Woman,* with others, 1941; *Quo Vadis,* with others, 1951; *Me and the Colonel,* with George Froeschel, 1958; *Fanny,* with Joshua Logan, 1961.

Fiction

The Burning-Glass.   1968.

Other

Duveen.   1952.
The Worcester Account (*New Yorker* sketches).   1954.
Portrait of Max: An Intimate Memoir of Sir Max Beerbohm.   1960; as *Conversation with Max,* 1960.
The Suspended Drawing Room.   1965.
People in a Diary: A Memoir.   1972; as *Tribulations and Laughter: A Me...,* 1972.

Bibliography: *Maxwell Anderson and Behrman: A Reference Guide* by William Klink, 1977.

Reading List: "Behrman: The Quandary of the Comic Spirit" by Charles Kaplan, in *College English 9,* 1950.

*   *   *

It is now 50 years since S. N. Behrman's *The Second Man* was produced by the Theatre Guild and made him famous. Even by the 1950's the material was old-hat, and writers of comedies of manners (even better ones, such as Philip Barry) are now quite out of date. Behrman's work after the 1930's was fairly unimportant, largely adaptations. His sophisticated comedy belongs to an earlier generation. A recent revival of *The Second Man* looked very old-fashioned. It, of course, lacked the Lunts, who created roles in it (and Noël Coward and Raymond Massey, who played it in London), and it needed them.

In his time Behrman also had the assistance of stars like Greta Garbo, Ina Claire, Katherine Cornell, and Laurence Olivier. He, like the blasé and aphoristic writer Clark Storey in *The Second Man,* said "*(Seriously)* Life is sad. I know it's sad. But I think it's gallant to pretend that it isn't." In the 1930's this approach made him an American Noël Coward and gave him "perhaps the most considerable reputation" among young playwrights (A. H. Quinn). But soon proletarian and "socially significant drama" was to render inoperable the approach of the heroine of *Biography,* which was to laugh at injustice because nothing could be done about it, and the hero of *No Time for Comedy,* who chose to write light comedy instead of propagandist melodrama. The depression and World War II wiped out Behrman's impassive, indifferent, intellectual sophisticates who gracefully soared above reality. In *Rain from Heaven,* even though it revolves around Fascists and German refugees, the sophisticates are still doing arabesques on the thin ice of political problems.

Behrman wrote a number of screenplays, including such movies as *Queen Christina* and

Anna Karenina, both with Garbo, *Waterloo Bridge*, and *Quo Vadis*. For the *New Yorker* he wrote the sketches that became *Duveen* (about the art dealer who became Lord Millbank) and *The Worcester Account* (about his boyhood in Worcester, Massachusetts). These, I think, surpass his original comedies of manners, his adaptation of Giraudoux (*Amphytrion 38*) or his collaboration with Franz Werfel (*Jacobowsky and the Colonel*), his dramatization of stories by Enid Bagnold (*Serena Blandish*) and W. Somerset Maugham (*Jane*), all his theatre work, and his cinema writing. It is unfortunate that he did not find time in his 80 years to write a work for the stage about the sort of people who enliven *The Worcester Account*. His cosmopolitan intellectuals may be well observed for a "Brief Moment" (as a 1931 play of his was called), but they are seen by a stranger, however clever. The people of Providence Street in Worcester, Behrman knew.

—Leonard R. N. Ashley

BOND, Edward.   English.   Born in London, 18 July 1934. Educated in state schools to age 14. Served in the British Army for two years. Married Elisabeth Pablé in 1971. Member of the Writers Group of the Royal Court Theatre, London. Recipient: George Devine Award, 1968; John Whiting Award, 1969.

PUBLICATIONS

Plays

   The Pope's Wedding (produced 1962).   In *The Pope's Wedding and Other Plays*, 1971.
   Saved (produced 1965).   1966.
   The Three Sisters, from a play by Chekhov (produced 1967).
   Narrow Road to the Deep North (produced 1968).   1968; revised version, as *The Bundle* (produced 1978), 1978.
   Early Morning (produced 1968).   1968.
   Black Mass (produced 1970).   In *The Pope's Wedding and Other Plays*, 1971.
   Passion (produced 1971).   In *Plays: Two*, 1978.
   Lear (produced 1971).   1972.
   The Pope's Wedding and Other Plays (includes *Mr. Dog, The King with Golden Eyes, Sharpville Sequence, Black Mass*).   1971.
   The Sea (produced 1973).   1973.
   Bingo: Scenes of Money and Death (and Passion) (produced 1973).   1974.
   Spring Awakening, from a play by Frank Wedekind (produced 1974).
   The Fool: Scenes of Bread and Love (produced 1975).   In *The Fool, and We Come to the River*, 1976.
   We Come to the River: Actions for Music, music by Hans Werner Henze (produced 1976).   1976.
   A-A-America: Grandma Faust, and The Swing (produced 1976).   In *Stone, and A-A-America*, 1976.
   The White Devil, from the play by Webster (produced 1976).
   Stone (produced 1976).   In *Stone, and A-A-America*, 1976.

The Fool, and We Come to the River.   1976.
Stone, and A-A-America.   1976.
The Woman: Scenes of War and Freedom (produced 1978).

Screenplays: *Blow-Up,* with Michelangelo Antonioni and Tonino Guerra, 1967; *Laughter in the Dark,* 1969; *The Lady of Monza* (English dialogue), 1970; *Walkabout,* 1971.

Radio Play: *Badger by Owl-Light,* 1975.

Verse

Theatre Poems and Songs.   1978.

Reading List: *Bond* by Simon Trussler, 1976; *The Plays of Bond* by Richard Scharine, 1977; *The Plays of Bond* by Tony Coult, 1978.

*   *   *

In a relatively brief dramatic career, and little over half-a-dozen full-length plays, Edward Bond has emerged as a distinctive yet wholly representative voice in the British theatre – representative not of a school of dramatists, but of that growing concern for ecological values which became widespread in the early 1970's, and of which Bond emerged as an early prophet. Not that he engages in the immediacies of the debate: but from the first his plays have had to do with the "quality of life," in a sense far wider than would have been understood by dramatists a generation earlier. He is concerned with the effects an increasingly technological society has had upon the relations between man and man, and between man and his environment, while recognising that there can be no return to the superficially attractive values of a rustic past.

In the earliest plays, *The Pope's Wedding* and *Saved,* these issues were presented through a direct reflection of two contrasting but contemporary social settings – respectively, deprived rural and urban working-class communities, in East Anglia and South London. Primarily, however, both plays held a compelling narrative line: whether in the slow, hermit-like withdrawal of a once braggardly country youth in *The Pope's Wedding,* or the slender hope represented in *Saved* by the survival of one man's inarticulate sense of goodness amidst moral and social lethargy, they sustained the interest on the simple level of event succeeding event. And, of course, both contained an element of violence which for some has given a misleading emphasis to Bond's work: for the dramatist himself, the violence is a consequence of the state of society and (more to the point dramatically) it is also consequential.

These early plays were already assured in their self-developing episodic structures, precise in their very different but distinctive verbal idioms, and, incidentally, often very funny indeed. In all his later work Bond has abandoned contemporary for semi-historical – and sometimes fully mythic – settings. Although *Early Morning,* his third play, is apparently identifiable with a precise historical period, the mid-Victorian age, its surreal combination of anachronism and total moral anarchy quickly (too quickly) lifts it to a symbolic level. Its nightmarish sequence of plots and counter-plots involving many Victorian archetypes (and not a few of Bond's own) has its compulsive quality, but *Early Morning* remains the only one of Bond's plays where the lack of moral co-ordinates blurs the impact of the statements he is making.

It is thus in marked contrast to *Narrow Road to the Deep North* – whose setting in "seventeenth, eighteenth, or nineteenth century" Japan is also anachronistic, but here for the purpose of establishing a clear counterpoint between oriental and western values. The poet

Basho seeks ivory-towered enlightenment as the balance of power shifts between home-grown and imported modes of oppression: yet while Christian imperialism is lampooned, the alternative is in no way romanticised, and the stylised slaughter by the Japanese tyrant Shogo of the children of a mission school is a remarkable theatrical moment, incongruous yet immensely moving. The play is structured throughout with an austere fluidity, and marked a further progression in Bond's sure feeling for formal propriety.

His next work moved from the quasi-historical to the truly mythic. And, fine as some of his more recent plays have been, *Lear* must stand as his highest artistic achievement to date. The play had its beginnings in Bond's dissatisfaction with various elements in Shakespeare's version, but it stands entirely in its own right in its vision of the once authoritarian, dispossessed Lear travelling a lonely road of self-discovery as his daughters do battle for his kingdom, and the revolutionary leader Cordelia perpetuates Lear's mistakes. He dies in a futile attempt to dismantle the wall into whose "defensive" construction he had diverted the energies of his kingdom.

Lear is a very personal achievement, yet persuades one of its dramatic rightness, and impels with its moral force. The ghost who has to die a second time is a recurrent figure in Bond's plays – yet here it is no idiosyncratic ingredient, but an entirely appropriate embodiment of an insidiously attractive way of living in which Lear once found refuge, but which ultimately, like the ghost, must be allowed to die. On paper, the symbolism may intrude: but Bond writes for the stage, and the increasingly skeletal visual image is perhaps the only possible "companion" for Lear on his lonely journey.

In *The Sea*, Bond apparently transposes Chekhov to an English seaside resort, evoking an atmosphere of Edwardian self-assurance overshadowed by tidings of war and social unrest. An accidental drowning brings together a young man and woman, and gives focus to a convergence of local eccentrics, a sort of gauntlet for the couple to run – the aristocratic Mrs. Rafi, the ur-fascist shopkeeper Hatch, the seashore hermit Evens, and many lesser grotesques who merge with everyday elements to form a vision that is, again, fully self-sufficient, yet wholly individual.

This is less true, however, of *Bingo*, in which Shakespeare's historical complicity in the Welcombe enclosures is seen as a betrayal of his art. Perhaps because the incidental events and characters here *seem* incidental to the dramatist's self-determined death, the play lacks the integration of *The Sea* – as it also denies its central character the redemption of *Lear*. *The Fool* is a much more satisfying recreation of a poet's relationship to his society: in this case the poet is John Clare, and he too is caught in the upheavals of an age of enclosures. Here, the environment is fully realized, as is Clare's withdrawal into madness, and a complex balance of sympathies is struck. An opening mumming scene, a boxing match in Hyde Park, the final scene in the madhouse – all bear witness alike to Bond's vividly *theatrical* vision, and to his ability to weave such disparate threads into a unified work of dramatic art. In the blending of satisfaction with an artistic experience and dissatisfaction with the society it has evoked, Bond comes closer to Brecht than any other writer in the modern British theatre.

—Simon Trussler

BOTTOMLEY, Gordon. English. Born in Keighley, Yorkshire, 20 February 1874. Educated at Keighley Grammar School. Married Emily Burton in 1905 (died, 1947). President, Scottish Community Drama Association; Vice-President, British Drama League. Recipient: Femina-Vie Heureuse Prize, 1923; Royal Society of Literature Benson Medal, 1928. LL.D: University of Aberdeen, 1930; D.Litt.: University of Durham, 1940; Litt.D.: University of Leeds, 1944. Fellow, Royal Society of Literature, 1926. *Died 25 August 1948.*

PUBLICATIONS

Collections

Poems and Plays, edited by Claude Colleer Abbott.   1953.

Plays

The Crier by Night (produced 1916).   1902.
Midsummer Eve (produced 1930).   1905.
Laodice and Danaë (produced 1930).   1909.
The Riding to Lithend (produced 1928).   1909.
King Lear's Wife (produced 1915).   1920.
Britain's Daughter (produced 1922).   With *Gruach*, 1921.
Gruach (produced 1923).   1921.
A Parting, and The Return.   1928.
Scenes and Plays (includes *A Parting, The Return, The Sisters, The Widow, Towie Castle, Merlin's Grave, Ardvorlich's Wife, The Singing Sands*).   1929.
Lyric Plays (includes *Marsaili's Weeping, Culbin Sands, The Bower of Wandel, Suilven and the Eagle, Kirkconnel Lea, The Women from the Voe*).   1932.
The Acts of Saint Peter: A Cathedral Festival Play (produced 1933).   1933.
The White Widow (produced 1936).   In *Scottish One-Act Plays*, edited by J. M. Reid, 1935.
The Falconer's Lassie (as *The Falconer's Daughter*, produced 1936).   In *Choric Plays*, 1939.
Ealasaid (produced 1939).   In *50 One-Act Plays*, second series, edited by Constance M. Martin, 1940.
Choric Plays and a Comedy (includes *Fire at Calbart, The Falconer's Lassie, Dunaverty*).   1939.
Fire at Calbart (produced 1944).   In *Choric Plays*, 1939.
Deirdre, from works by Alexander Carmichael.   1944.
Kate Kennedy (produced 1944).   1945.
Maids of Athens.   1945.
Crookback's Crown.   1947.

Verse

The Mickle Drede and Other Verses.   1896.
Poems at White-Nights.   1899.
The Gate of Smaragdus.   1904.
Chambers of Imagery.   2 vols., 1907–12.
A Vision of Giorgione: Three Variations on Venetian Themes.   1910; revised edition, 1922.
Poems of Thirty Years.   1925.
Frescoes from Buried Temples, drawings by James Guthrie.   1927.
Festival Preludes.   1930.

Other

A Note on Poetry and the Stage.   1944(?).

A Stage for Poetry: My Purposes with My Plays. 1948.
Poet and Painter, Being the Correspondence Between Bottomley and Paul Nash 1910–46,
  edited by Claude Colleer Abbott and Anthony Bertram. 1955.

Editor, *Poems,* by Isaac Rosenberg. 1922; revised edition, with D. Harding, as
  Collected Poems, 1949.
Editor, with D. Harding, *The Collected Works of Isaac Rosenberg.* 1937.
Editor, *Essays by Divers Hands.* 1944.
Editor, *The Madness of Merlin,* by Laurence Binyon. 1947.

Reading List: "Bottomley" by A. J. Farmer, in *Etudes Anglaises 9,* 1956; *The Christian Tradition in Modern British Drama* by William V. Spanos, 1967.

*   *   *

The outstanding playwright among Georgian poets, Gordon Bottomley may be ranked as one of the most accomplished verse dramatists of the twentieth century after Yeats and Eliot. Never a popular writer, his reputation has not noticeably revived since his death, although his grave, polished poems recall Edward Thomas's ability to convey a complex sensibility through simple statement, a talent far removed from the *faux naïf* manner and thinness of texture commonly associated with Georgianism. That his work was largely insulated from modern life was perhaps inevitable: forced by illness to dwell remote from cities and find solace in contemplation and meditation, he was also led to reject everyday subjects by influences which included Rossetti and Morris. He maintained a wide circle of correspondents, notably Thomas and the painter Paul Nash, whose published exchanges with the poet contain valuable comments on art, literature, and drama.

It was with his plays that Bottomley discovered a public voice and gained such measure of public attention as was accorded him. The earliest dramas preserve a strong literary element, but the firm control, concentrated psychological interest, narrative tension, and interplay of forceful personalities indicate a true dramatist rather than a mere lyrical decorator. A powerful example is *The Crier by Night,* in which sexual rivalry between a farmer's sadistic wife and a proud Irish bondmaid is resolved by a supernatural water-spirit who draws husband and girl to their deaths in Lake Windermere. Comparable images of physical cruelty are found in *King Lear's Wife,* which, given pride of place in Marsh's second anthology of *Georgian Poetry,* was adversely criticized for its calculated brutality: the play offers a prologue to Shakespeare postulating an adulterous love-affair between the king and an attendant at Lear's wife's death-bed; Goneril, on discovering their clandestine relationship, kills the girl as the queen's body is prepared for burial. In summary the action sounds intolerably crude, but Bottomley invests the dialogue with the required degree of primitive splendour, and the boldly drawn figures are something more than feebly grandiloquent replicas of their Jacobean counterparts. The less sensational *Gruach,* which describes the swift courtship of the Macbeths, is an equally daring and assured performance in a more minor key. By contrast, *Britain's Daughter* is theatrical and over-wrought.

Bottomley's plays were always concerned with far-off periods and regions; in his later plays he turned to esoteric forms, choosing to work with private and amateur groups. Under the influence of Yeats's *Plays for Dancers,* from which he adopted the devices of masks, choric figures, and the concealment of the stage by unfolding a cloth, he composed a number of plays dramatizing incidents from Celtic folklore and history, in which the diction is leaner and less overtly lyrical than formerly. Of these the best are found in *Lyric Plays,* among which are *Marsaili's Weeping,* which recreates a sixteenth-century Highland tragedy, and *The Woman from the Voe,* a beautiful adaptation of a Shetland legend in which a Seal-

Woman marries a mortal. *A Stage for Poetry* sets out Bottomley's views on drama, and forms an admirable record of his achievements.

—William M. Tydeman

BRIDIE, James.   Pseudonym for Osborne Henry Mavor.   Scottish.   Born in Glasgow, 3 January 1888. Educated at Glasgow Academy; Glasgow High School; University of Glasgow (Editor, *University Magazine*); qualified as a physician; Fellow of the Royal Faculty of Physicians and Surgeons, Glasgow. Served with the Royal Army Medical Corps, 1914–19, 1939–42. Married Rona Bremner; two sons. Professor of Medicine, Anderson College, Glasgow; Honorary Consulting Physician, and Governor, Victoria Infirmary, Glasgow. Founder, with Paul Vincent Carroll, Glasgow Citizen's Theatre, 1943; Founder, Glasgow College of Drama, 1950. Member of the Council, League of Dramatists; Scottish Chairman, Arts Council of Great Britain. LL.D.: University of Glasgow, 1939. Fellow, Royal Society of Literature. C.B.E. (Commander, Order of the British Empire), 1946. *Died 29 January 1951.*

PUBLICATIONS

Plays

The Jackals of Lone Pine Gulch (produced 1918).
The Sunlight Sonata; or, To Meet the Seven Deadly Sins (produced 1928).   In *The Switchback* ..., 1930.
The Switchback (produced 1929).   In *The Switchback* ..., 1930; revised version (produced 1931).
What It Is to Be Young (produced 1929).   In *Colonel Wotherspoon and Other Plays*, 1934.
The Anatomist: A Lamentable Comedy of Know, Burke, and Hare, and the West Port Murders (produced 1930).   In *The Anatomist and Other Plays*, 1931.
The Girl Who Did Not Want to Go to Kuala Lumpur (produced 1930).   In *Colonel Wotherspoon and Other Plays*, 1934.
Tobias and the Angel (produced 1930).   In *The Anatomist and Other Plays*, 1931.
The Switchback, The Pardoner's Tale, The Sunlight Sonata.   1930.
The Dancing Bear (produced 1931).   In *Colonel Wotherspoon and Other Plays*, 1934.
The Anatomist and Other Plays (includes *Tobias and the Angel* and *The Amazed Evangelist*).   1931.
The Amazed Evangelist (produced 1932).   In *The Anatomist and Other Plays*, 1931.
Jonah and the Whale: A Morality (produced 1932).   1932; revised version, as *The Sign of the Prophet Jonah* (broadcast, 1942), in *Plays for Plain People*, 1944.
A Sleeping Clergyman (produced 1933).   1933.
Marriage Is No Joke (produced 1934).   1934.
Colonel Wotherspoon; or, The Fourth Way of Greatness (produced 1934).   In *Colonel Wotherspoon and Other Plays*, 1934.
Mary Read, with Claud Gurney (produced 1934).   1935.
Colonel Wotherspoon and Other Plays (includes *What It Is to Be Young, The Dancing Bear, The Girl Who Did Not Want to Go to Kuala Lumpur*).   1934.

The Black Eye (produced 1935).   1935.

Mrs. Waterbury's Millennium.   1935.

The Tragic Muse, in *Scottish One-Act Plays*, edited by J. M. Reid.   1935.

Storm in a Teacup, from a play by Bruno Frank (produced 1936; as *Storm over Patsy*, produced 1937).   1936.

Susannah and the Elders (produced 1937).   In *Susannah and the Elders and Other Plays*, 1940.

Roger – Not So Jolly, with Ronald Mavor.   1937.

The King of Nowhere (produced 1938).   In *The King of Nowhere and Other Plays*, 1938.

Babes in the Wood (produced 1938).   1938.

The Last Trump (produced 1938).   In *The King of Nowhere and Other Plays*, 1938.

The Kitchen Comedy (broadcast 1938).   In *Susannah and the Elders and Other Plays*, 1940.

The King of Nowhere and Other Plays (includes *The Last Trump* and *Babes in the Wood*).   1938.

The Letter-Box Rattles.   1938.

The Golden Legend of Shults (produced 1939).   In *Susannah and the Elders and Other Plays*, 1940.

What Say They? (produced 1939).   1939.

Susannah and the Elders and Other Plays (includes *What Say They?*, *The Golden Legend of Shults*, *The Kitchen Comedy*).   1940.

The Niece of the Hermit Abraham (produced 1942; revised version, as *The Dragon and the Dove; or, How the Hermit Abraham Bought the Devil for his Niece*, produced 1943).

Jonah 3 (produced 1942).   In *Plays for Plain People*, 1944.

Holy Isle (produced 1942).   In *Plays for Plain People*, 1944.

A Change for the Worse (produced 1943).   In *Tedious and Brief*, 1944.

Mr. Bolfry (produced 1943).   In *Plays for Plain People*, 1944.

It Depends What You Mean: An Improvisation for the Glockenspiel (produced 1944).   1948.

The Forrigan Reel (produced 1944; revised version, produced 1945).   In *John Knox and Other Plays*, 1949.

Plays for Plain People (includes *Lancelot*, *Holy Isle*, *Mr. Bolfry*, *Jonah 3*, *The Sign of the Prophet Jonah*, *The Dragon and the Dove*).   1944.

Lancelot (produced 1945).   In *Plays for Plain People*, 1944.

The Pyrate's Den (produced 1946).

The Wild Duck, from a play by Ibsen (produced 1946–47?).

Dr. Angelus (produced 1947).   In *John Knox and Other Plays*, 1949.

Gog and Magog (produced 1948).

Daphne Laureola (produced 1949).   1949.

John Knox and Other Plays (includes *Dr. Angelus*, *It Depends What You Mean*, *The Forrigan Reel*).   1949.

The Tintock Cup, with George Munro (produced 1949).

Mr. Gillie (produced 1950).   1950.

Red Riding Hood, with others (produced 1950).

The Baikie Charivari; or, The Seven Prophets (produced 1952).   1953.

Meeting at Night, edited by Archibald Batty (produced 1954).   1956.

Screenplays: *Under Capricorn*, with Hume Cronyn, 1949; *Stage Fright*, with Alma Reville and Whitfield Cook, 1950.

Fiction

The Christmas Card (story).   1949.

Other

Some Talk of Alexander: A Revue with Interludes in the Antique Mode.   1926.
The Perilous Adventures of Sir Bingo Walker of Alpaca Square (juvenile).   1931.
Alphabet for Little Glasgow Highbrows (essays).   1934.
One Way of Living (autobiography).   1939.
Tedious and Brief (miscellany).   1944.
The British Drama.   1945.
A Small Stir: Letters on the English, with M. McLaren.   1949.

Reading List: *Bridie and His Theatre: A Study of Bridie's Personality, His Stage Plays, and His Work for the Foundation of a Scottish National Theatre* by Winifred Bannister, 1955; *Bridie: Clown and Philosopher* by Helen L. Luybem, 1965.

*   *   *

O.H. Mavor (James Bridie) is an elusive man: unlike some of his contemporaries who shunned publicity and deliberately kept their private lives private (one could cite Edwin Muir), he appears to have enjoyed public life, yet to have cultivated an impish sense of humour to disconcert would-be critics and reviewers. This is especially obvious in his scintillating autobiographical sketch *One Way of Living*, which gives the picture of a clever medical student and practising doctor with a preference for literature, but the need for a more profitable source of income. Bridie's output was prodigious, its quality inevitably uneven, but at his best he is a notable figure in modern British drama and some of his work stands up to revival exceptionally well.

The theatre in Scotland for which Bridie worked inherited neither a strong corps of Scottish-born actors of first talent, nor a tradition of Scottish dramatic writing. For many years frowned on by civic and religious authority, the theatre in Scotland was a late developer. Bridie found it difficult to have his plays performed to his satisfaction, despite some very fortunate choices of actors, but eventually he conquered London's West End, and by the time of his death was a widely-accepted household name.

Comparison with Barrie is impossible to avoid. Barrie aimed openly for London and big-time success, and his plays are professional in appealing to a wide audience and, particularly in his fantasy plays, in achieving a state of emotional involvement on the part of the audience which suspends disbelief. Barrie's great contemporary is quite opposite: Bridie is a confirmed satirist (though always a serious playwright), a man in whose work reality intrudes painfully. Impatient and brusque with those whose ideologies or religious orthodoxies are second-hand or uncritical, like Mr. McCrimmon in *Mr. Bolfry*, iconoclastic − to the medical profession in *The Anatomist* and *A Sleeping Clergyman*, to educationists in *Mr. Gillie*, and to the Old Testament in the delightful skit *Tobias and the Angel* − Bridie is out to startle and to challenge rather than to achieve Barrie's successes simply by imitation. The parallel can be carried too far: Bridie uses his Scottish backgrounds when it suits him to establish an identifiable atmosphere and control the emotional response in consequence (he does this in *Mr. Gillie* shamelessly), and Barrie, of course, has moments of tough self-analysis, particularly in his fiction. Yet the main point emerges strongly that Bridie is a masterful manipulator of dialogue and comic effect, clearly indebted to Shaw in the mischievous puncturing of affectation and arrogance, and the neatness with which he does it. He knows his stage well − he handles the crowds of *The Anatomist* or *Tobias* excellently; he masterfully makes the Devil's umbrella walk off-stage at the end of *Mr. Bolfry*, when the characters are convincing themselves they had not seen the Devil, but merely had a nightmare; he very neatly uses the sleeping clergyman (who takes no part in the action) as a frame for several generations of family interaction and at the same time as comment on the slumbering moral guardians of an age. His moral range encompasses the passionate inhuman ambitions of Dr. Knox in *The*

Anatomist, the cool angel who guides Tobias, the devil-may-care Dr. Cameron who scorns his doctor's etiquette yet develops the serum to save the world from plague, the emptiness of the failed teacher in *Mr. Gillie* who sees his creature move away from the dreams he had planned for him. There are odd moments of anticipation, of Muriel Spark's Miss Brodie, of Edward Albee's handling of disembodied characters as spectators of their own deaths. The form of the enclosed stage is stretched as far as it can go, the comment on society as wide as possible.

The variety of his achievement, often touching on sensitive moral issues, is easy to overlook because of the genial humour which never deserts him, and which expresses itself in light and well-handled humorous dialogue. But the satirist is always waiting in the wings, and the simplest speeches have currents of irony. The man who wrote "Some generalisations, even if they are made about women, are true. At least, they are what are called facts" can never be taken at face value.

In his preface to *Colonel Wotherspoon and Other Plays* Bridie confessed himself a professional playwright, and acknowledged his indebtedness to actors and producers, and he disclaimed writing either an overtly moral play, or what he mockingly called "the first Great Scottish Play." "The truth is that Scotland does not yet deserve a great play.... She is due, however, a little amusement; and the only Scottish dramatist who has reached the very first rank (if we except Ben Jonson) doesn't bother himself much with morals or greatness. Indeed, if we dive for a moral in any one of the plays of Sir James Barrie, we are running the risk of a very horrid surprise." Such a man neatly defies simple description, yet such was the character of the dramatist who has so far dominated the Scottish stage in the present century.

—Ian Campbell

BRIGHOUSE, Harold. Pseudonym, with John Walton: Olive Conway. English. Born in Eccles, Lancashire, 26 July 1882. Educated at Manchester Grammar School. Served in the Royal Air Force, attached to the Intelligence Staff, Air Ministry, during World War I. Associated with Gilbert Cannan and Stanley Houghton in the repertory theatre movement in England; director of a Manchester cotton mill; Drama Critic, Manchester *Guardian*. Chairman of the Dramatic Committee, Author's Society, 1930–31. *Died 25 July 1958.*

PUBLICATIONS

Plays

The Doorway (produced 1909).   1913.
Dealing in Futures (produced 1909).   1913.
The Price of Coal (produced 1909).   1911.
Graft (as *The Polygon,* produced 1911).   1913.
Lonesome-Like (produced 1911).   1914.
Spring in Bloomsbury (produced 1911).   1913.
The Oak Settle (produced 1911).   1911.
The Scaring Off of Teddy Dawson (produced 1911).   1911.

The Odd Man Out (produced 1912).   1912.

Little Red Shoes (produced 1912).   1925.

The Game (produced 1913).   In *Three Lancashire Plays*, 1920.

Garside's Career (produced 1914).   1914.

The Northerners (produced 1914).   In *Three Lancashire Plays*, 1920.

Followers: A "Cranford" Sketch (produced 1915).   1922.

The Hillarys, with Stanley Houghton (produced 1915).

Converts (produced 1915).   1920.

Hobson's Choice (produced 1915).   1916; edited by E. R. Wood, 1964.

The Road to Raebury (produced 1915).   1921.

Zack: A Character Comedy (produced 1916).   In *Three Lancashire Plays*, 1920.

The Clock Goes Round (produced 1916).

Maid of France (produced 1917).   1917.

The Bantam V.C. (produced 1919).   1925.

Other Times (produced 1920).

The Starlight Widow, with John Walton.   1920.

Plays for the Meadow and Plays for the Lawn (includes *Maypole Morning, The Paris Doctor, The Prince Who Was a Piper, The Man about the Place*).   1921.

Once a Hero (produced 1922).   1922.

The Happy Hangman: A Grotesque (produced 1925).   1922.

Once a Year (produced 1923).

The Apple Tree; or, Why Misery Never Dies.   1923.

The Happy Man.   1923.

A Marrying Man (produced 1924).   1924.

Mary's John (produced 1924).   1925.

Becky Sharp, with John Walton, from the novel *Vanity Fair* by Thackeray (produced 1924).   1924.

Open Air Plays (includes *The Laughing Mind, The Oracles of Apollo, The Rational Princess, The Ghosts of Windsor Park, How the Weather Is Made*).   1926.

Costume Plays, with John Walton (includes *Becky Sharp, Mimi, Prudence Corner, The King's Waistcoat*).   1927.

What's Bred in the Bone (produced 1927).   1927.

The Little Liberty.   1927.

Fossie for Short, from his own novel.   1927.

The Might of "Mr. H.": A Charles Lamb Pastiche.   1927.

When Did They Meet Again?   1927.

The Witch's Daughter, in *One-Act Plays for Stage and Study 4.*   1928.

It's a Gamble (produced 1928).

Safe Amongst the Pigs (produced 1929).   1930.

Behind the Throne.   1929.

Coincidence.   1929.

The Sort-of-a-Prince.   1929.

The Stoker.   1929.

Four Fantasies for the Open Air (includes *The Exiled Princess, The Ghost in the Garden, The Romany Road, Cupid and Psyche*).   1931; augmented edition, as *Six Fantasies* (includes *The Ghosts of Windsor Park* and *The Oracles of Apollo*), 1931.

A Bit of War.   1933.

Smoke-Screens.   1933.

Exhibit C., in *Best One-Act Plays of 1933*, edited by J. W. Marriott.   1934.

Tip and Run, in Three Sections, with John Walton, in *The One-Act Theatre 1.*   1934.

The Dye-Hard, in *One-Act Plays of Today 6*, edited by J. W. Marriott.   1934.

The Great Dark, from a play by Don Totheroh.   1934.

The Boy: What Will He Become?, in *Best One-Act Plays of 1934*, edited by J. W. Marriott.   1935.

The Friendly King. 1935.
Back to Adam: A Glimpse of Three Periods. 1936.
The Wish Shop. 1936.
Mr. Somebody, from a play by Molnar (produced 1936).
Modern Plays in One Act, with John Walton (includes *One of Those Letters, Dux, When the Bells Rang, The Bureaucrats, The Desperationist, Wireless Can't Lie, Women Do Things Like That*). 1937.
Below Ground, in *Eight One-Act Plays of 1936,* edited by William Armstrong. 1937.
New Leisure, in *The Best One-Act Plays of 1936,* edited by J. W. Marriott. 1937.
Passport to Romance. 1937.
Under the Pylon, in *One-Act Plays for Stage and Study 9.* 1938.
The Funk-Hole: A Farce of the Crisis. 1939.
British Passport. 1939.
The Man Who Ignored the War. 1940.
The Golden Ray: An Idealistic Melodrama. 1941.
London Front. 1941.
Hallowed Ground, in *The Best One-Act Plays of 1941,* edited by J. W. Marriott. 1942.
Sporting Rights. 1943.
Albert Gate. 1945.
The Inner Man. 1945.
Let's Live in England, in *The Best One-Act Plays of 1944–45,* edited by J. W. Marriott. 1946.
Alison's Island, in *The Best One-Act Plays of 1946–47,* edited by J. W. Marriott. 1948.
Above Rubies, in *The Best One-Act Plays of 1952–53,* edited by H. Miller. 1954.

Fiction

Fossie for Short. 1917.
Hobson's, with Charles Forrest. 1917.
The Silver Lining. 1918.
The Marbeck Inn. 1920.
Hepplestall's. 1922.
Captain Shapely. 1923.
The Wrong Shadow: A Romantic Comedy. 1923.
Hindle Wakes. 1927.

Other

What I Have Had: Chapters in Autobiography. 1953.

Editor, *The Works of Stanley Houghton.* 3 vols., 1914.

*   *   *

It is understandable that in the public mind Harold Brighouse should be associated with the "Manchester School" of playwrights nurtured by Miss Annie Elizabeth Horniman, but unfortunate that his reputation should derive almost exclusively from a lone play, *Hobson's Choice.* His achievements were far more varied both in range and content than such a narrow view suggests. Born in Eccles, educated at Manchester Grammar School where Stanley Houghton, Ben Iden Payne, and James Agate were contemporaries, and then entering the cotton business, Brighouse was only discovered as a playwright with the opening of the Gaiety Theatre, Manchester, for repertory drama in 1908, and with Miss Horniman's determined encouragement for new authors who would supply her with plays reflecting life in the local community. His indigenous experience made him the ideal Lancastrian dramatist, but, in fact, many of his plays did not receive their premieres at the Gaiety, but at other repertory theatres in Britain; nonetheless it was to Miss Horniman that Brighouse recorded his gratitude for the opportunity to learn his craft.

It was in the demanding field of the one-act play that he first revealed his ability to handle working-class situations and characters with sensitivity and restraint, combining a tenderness which never degenerates into sentimentality with an eye for humorous quirks of personality and an ear for the turns of regional dialect. While his early full-length plays such as *Dealing in Futures*, *The Polygon*, and even *Garside's Career* tend to blend psychological observation and social criticism somewhat uneasily, *The Doorway*, *The Price of Coal*, and *Lonesome-Like* are masterly in their economy of construction and ease of dialogue, and in their subtle shifts of mood. Yet Brighouse's dramatic range is far from negligible: of his four full-length plays staged between 1912 and 1914, *The Odd Man Out* was a witty farce, *Garside's Career* a Lancashire comedy with education as its theme, *The Game* a spirited but somewhat improbable comedy with a professional footballing background, and *The Northerners* a grim drama based on the Luddite riots of the 1820's, somewhat hampered by its indebtedness to Victorian melodramatic conventions. And there are features in *Zack* and his post-war dramas to command interest and respect. In a number of collections, published from 1921 onwards, Brighouse's talent for charming fantasy was especially evident, although the temptation to substitute whimsy for fantasy was not always resisted. After about 1930 he tended to concentrate almost entirely on the short play and continued to enjoy success with this form.

Yet the fact remains that Brighouse never quite equalled the success of his comedy of Lancastrian manners, *Hobson's Choice*, and its perennial appeal is not hard to explain: it contains almost text-book examples of comic reversal in the "taming" of the bullying Hobson and the regeneration of the downtrodden Will Mossop by the Shavian yet humane heroine, while its essentially gentle view of lower-middle-class marriage contrasts with that presented in the plays of D. H. Lawrence written at roughly the same time. It is a beautifully structured play, full of quietly observant humour, and, while it points a moral, it does so kindly and without malice. Its place in the modern repertory seems assured.

—William M. Tydeman

BULLINS, Ed.   American.   Born in Philadelphia, Pennsylvania, 2 July 1935. Educated in Philadelphia public schools; William Penn Business Institute, Philadelphia; Los Angeles City College; San Francisco State College. Served in the United States Navy. Playwright-in-Residence, 1967–71, and since 1967, Associate Director, The New Lafayette Theatre, Harlem, New York. Editor, *Black Theatre* magazine, Harlem, 1969–74. Recipient: Rockefeller grant, 1968; Vernon Rice Award, 1968; American Place grant, 1968; Obie Award, 1971; Guggenheim grant, 1971; National Endowment for the Arts grant, 1974; New York Drama Critics Circle Award, 1975, 1977. D.L.: Columbia College, Chicago, 1976. Lives in Brooklyn, New York.

PUBLICATIONS

Plays

Clara's Ole Man (produced 1965).   In *Five Plays,* 1969.
How Do You Do: A Nonsense Drama (produced 1969).   1965.
Dialect Determinism (produced 1965).   In *Spontaneous Combustion: Eight New American Plays,* edited by Rochelle Owens, 1972.
In New England Winter (produced 1967).   In *New Plays from the Black Theatre,* edited by Bullins, 1969.
In the Wine Time (produced 1968).   In *Five Plays,* 1969.
A Son, Come Home (produced 1968).   In *Five Plays,* 1969.
The Electronic Nigger (produced 1968).   In *Five Plays,* 1969.
Goin' a Buffalo: A Tragifantasy (produced 1968).   In *Five Plays,* 1969.
The Gentleman Caller (produced 1969).   In *Illuminations 5,* 1968.
Five Plays.   1969; as *The Electronic Nigger and Other Plays,* 1970.
The Game of Adam and Eve, with Shirley Tarbell (produced 1969).
It Has No Choice (produced 1969).
The Corner (produced 1969).   In *Black Drama Anthology,* edited by Woodie King and Ron Milner, 1972.
Street Sounds (produced 1970).
The Fabulous Miss Marie (produced 1970).   In *The New Lafayette Theatre Presents,* edited by Bullins, 1974.
It Bees Dat Way (produced 1970).   In *Four Dynamite Plays,* 1971.
The Pig Pen (produced 1970).   In *Four Dynamite Plays,* 1971.
Death List (produced 1970).   In *Four Dynamite Plays,* 1971.
State Office Building Curse, in *The Drama Review,* September 1970.
The Duplex: A Black Love Fable in Four Movements (produced 1970).   1971.
The Devil Catchers (produced 1971).
Night of the Beast (screenplay), in *Four Dynamite Plays,* 1971.
Four Dynamite Plays (includes *It Bees Dat Way, Death List, The Pig Pen, Night of the Beast*).   1971.
The Psychic Pretenders (produced 1972).
You Gonna Let Me Take You Out Tonight, Baby (produced 1972).
House Party, music by Pat Patrick, lyrics by Bullins (produced 1973).
The Taking of Miss Janie (produced 1975).
The Mystery of Phyllis Wheatley (produced 1976).
Jo Anne!!! (produced 1976).
Home Boy, music by Aaron Bell, lyrics by Bullins (produced 1976).
Michael (produced 1978).

Screenplays: *Night of the Beast,* 1971; *The Ritual Masters,* 1972.

Fiction

The Hungered One: Early Writings (stories).   1971.
The Reluctant Rapist.   1973.

Verse

To Raise the Dead and Foretell the Future.   1971.

Other

Editor, *New Plays from the Black Theatre.*   1969.
Editor, *The New Lafayette Theatre Presents: Plays with Aesthetic Comments by 6 Black Playwrights.*   1974.

Bibliography: in *Black Image on the American Stage* by James V. Hatch, 1970.

Reading List: "The Polished Reality: Aesthetics and the Black Writer" in *Contact Magazine,* 1962; "The Theatre of Reality" in *Black World,* 1966; "Up from Politics" in *Performance,* 1972.

*   *   *

Ed Bullins is the most original and prolific playwright of the American Black Theatre movement. To quote him: "To make an open secret more public: in the area of playwrighting, Ed Bullins, at this moment in time, is almost without peer in America – black, white or imported." Written in 1973, the statement exaggerates little. Included in a volume *The Theme Is Blackness,* Bullins's title polemically reduces his actual thematic range; he dramatizes many relationships of black people – family, friendship, business, the business of crime. From urban black ghettos Bullins draws characters who speak with humor, obscenity, and sophistication. Whereas Langston Hughes had to strain to capture underworld idiom in Harlem, Bullins modulates a language that ignores the black as the white middle-class.

As ambitious as O'Neill, Bullins has embarked on a Twentieth Century Cycle of twenty plays, to depict the lives of certain Afro-Americans between 1900 and 1999. Five of these plays have been completed to date (1977), very loosely tracing the experiences of the Dawson – it would be inaccurate to call them a family, since the men found households, abandon them, disappear, reappear. Even incomplete, the cycle stresses the necessarily fragmentary nature of relationships of black urban males in twentieth-century America. Each of the plays focuses on a complete action, free in dramatic form, often embellished with song and dance, rich in rhythmic speech and terse imagery which Bullins crafts so beautifully. Indefatigable, Bullins has also written agit-prop Dynamite Plays, in which his anti-white rage is indistinguishable from that of LeRoi Jones. Other extra-cycle plays resemble Chekhov in their evocation of a dying class, e.g., *Clara's Ole Man* and *Goin' a Buffalo.* Like Chekhov, Bullins dramatizes the foibles of his people, endearing them to us through a poignant humor.

—Ruby Cohn

CHAYEFSKY, Paddy.   American.   Born Sidney Chayefsky in the Bronx, New York, 29 January 1923. Educated at DeWitt Clinton High School, Bronx, graduated 1939; City College of New York, B.S. 1943. Served as a Private First Class in the United States Army, 1943–45: Purple Heart. Married Susan Sackler in 1949; one son. President, Sudan Productions, New York, 1956, and Carnegie Productions, New York, 1957. Since 1959,

President of S.P.D. Productions; since 1967, President of Sidney Productions; since 1971, President of Simcha Productions – all New York. Since 1962, Member of the Council of the Dramatists Guild. Recipient: Screen Writers Guild Best Screenplay Award, 1954, 1971; Academy Award, 1955, 1972; New York Film Critics Award, 1956, 1971; Cannes Film Festival Award, 1955; Brussels, Venice and Edinburgh film festivals awards, 1958. Lives in New York City.

PUBLICATIONS

Plays

> *Printer's Measure* (televised 1953).   In *Television Plays*, 1955.
> *Middle of the Night* (televised 1954; revised version, produced 1956).   1957.
> *Televison Plays* (includes *The Bachelor Party, The Big Deal, Holiday Song, Marty, The Mother*, and *Printer's Measure*).   1955.
> *The Bachelor Party* (screenplay).   1957.
> *The Goddess* (screenplay; stage version produced 1971).   1958.
> *The Tenth Man* (produced 1959).   1960.
> *Gideon* (produced 1961).   1962.
> *The Passion of Josef D* (produced 1964).   1964.
> *The Latent Heterosexual* (produced 1968).   1967.

> Screenplays: *As Young as You Feel*, with Lamar Trotti, 1951; *Marty*, 1955; *The Bachelor Party*, 1957; *The Goddess*, 1958; *Middle of the Night*, 1959; *The Americanization of Emily*, with Alan Jay Lerner, 1964; *Paint Your Wagon*, 1969; *The Hospital*, 1971; *Network*, 1975.

> Television Plays: *Holiday Song*, 1952; *The Reluctant Citizen*, 1953; *Printer's Measure*, 1953; *Marty*, 1953; *The Big Deal*, 1953; *The Bachelor Party*, 1953; *The Sixth Year*, 1953; *Catch My Boy on Sunday*, 1953; *The Mother*, 1954; *Middle of the Night*, 1954; *The Catered Affair*, 1955.

Fiction

> *Altered States*.   1978.

*   *   *

Paddy Chayefsky was nurtured in television. There, he says, he learned to concentrate on "small moments in people's lives" and no more than "four people at the same time. TV drama cannot expand in breadth, so it must expand in depth." His first TV drama, *Holiday Song*, was set in a synagogue and based on a *Reader's Digest* story. The next year he was even more successful with *Marty*: the *New Yorker* described it as the story of "a shy, portly, and homely butcher of thirty-four, whose chief problem in life is to find a girl" (calling the plot "not only simple but even outlandish"). But Chayefsky, as he said, was "determined to shatter the shallow and destructive illusions ... that love is simply a matter of physical attraction."

Harriet Van Horne, TV critic for the *New York World Telegram and Sun*, thought Chayefsky "as important to television drama in the 1950's as was Ibsen to the stage in the 1890's. He has broken new ground, introduced a new realism, and resolutely turned his back on some of the old, constricting conventions" (27 July 1955). The famous "tape-recorder" ear for dialogue helped a great deal to make Chayefsky's reputation, but it was nothing new. It was Bronx Odets without quite so much pretension, and was familiar from Arthur Laurents's *Home of the Brave* (1946). Walter Kerr commented in his pointed *How Not to Write a Play* (1955): "He is on the side of the angels; so am I. He is going to develop his argument along certain lines; I know them. He is going to complete his charge to the jury in a burst of warm rhetoric; I can recite it in my sleep."

More recently, in films like *Hospital* and *Network*, Chayefsky has adopted still another device which connects him with television, the commercial, and indeed the television commercial. The larger screen has enabled him, in several ways, to turn up the volume.

The still minor art of television drama derived much benefit from this minor playwright. That he works long and hard and deftly with inarticulate characters and semi-hysterical situations is interesting. But what increasingly emerges is that he has really very little to say.

—Leonard R. N. Ashley

COHAN, George M(ichael).   American.   Born in Providence, Rhode Island, 3 July 1878; son of the vaudevillians Jerry and Helen Cohan. Briefly attended two elementary schools in Providence; received no formal education after age 8. Married 1) Ethelia Fowler (the actress Ethel Levey) in 1899, one daughter; 2) Agnes Nolan in 1907, two daughters and one son. Travelled with his parents as a child, and made his stage debut with them in 1887; thereafter regularly appeared with his parents and sister as The Four Cohans; appeared as an actor in *Peck's Bad Boy*, in New York, 1890; toured America, with The Four Cohans, throughout the 1890's, and was appearing with them in leading vaudeville houses in New York and Chicago by the turn of the century; produced first musical for the New York stage, starring The Four Cohans and his wife, in 1901; formed producing partnership with Sam Harris, 1904, and wrote, presented, and starred in number of musical hits on Broadway; presented plays, with Harris, at the New Gaiety Theatre, New York, 1908–10, and at the George M. Cohan Theatre, New York, 1910–20; lived in semi-retirement after 1920, occasionally appearing on the New York stage. Produced 150 plays, and wrote more than 500 songs. Recipient: United States Congress gold medal, 1940. *Died 5 November 1942.*

PUBLICATIONS

Plays

The Governor's Son (produced 1901).   Songs published 1901(?).
Running for Office (produced 1903); revised version, as The Honeymooners (produced 1907).
Little Johnny Jones (produced 1904).
Popularity (produced 1906).
Forty-Five Minutes from Broadway (produced 1906).
George Washington, Jr. (produced 1906).
Fifty Miles from Boston (produced 1907).
The Talk of New York (produced 1907).

The American Idea (produced 1908).   1909.

The Yankee Prince (produced 1908).

The Man Who Owns Broadway (produced 1909).   Songs published 1909(?).

Get-Rich-Quick Wallingford, from a story by George Randolph Chester (produced 1910).

The Little Millionaire (produced 1911).   1911.

Broadway Jones (produced 1912).   1923; revised version, music by the author, as *The Two of Us* (as *Billie,* produced 1928), 1928.

Seven Keys to Baldpate, from the novel by Earl Derr Biggers (produced 1913).   1914.

The Miracle Man, from a story by Frank L. Packard (produced 1914).

Hello, Broadway!, music by the author (produced 1914).

What Advertising Brings, with L. Grant (produced 1915).

Hit-the-Trail Holliday (produced 1915).   1916.

The Cohan Revue 1916 (produced 1916).

Honest John O'Brien (produced 1916).

The Cohan Revue 1918 (produced 1918).

The Voice of McConnell (produced 1918).

The Fireman's Picnic.   1918.

A Prince There Was, from the novel *Enchanted Hearts* by Darragh Aldrich (produced 1918).   1927.

The Royal Vagabond, with Stephen Ivor-Szinny and William Cary Duncan, music by Anselm Goetzl (produced 1919).   1919.

The Farrell Case: A One Act Mystery (produced 1919).

Madeleine and the Movies (produced 1922).

Little Nelly Kelly (produced 1922).

The Song and Dance Man (produced 1923).

The Rise of Rosie O'Reilly (produced 1923).   Songs published 1923(?).

American Born (produced 1925).

The Home-Towners (produced 1926).

The Baby Cyclone (produced 1927).   1929.

The Merry Malones (produced 1927).

Whispering Friends (produced 1928).

Gambling (produced 1929).

Friendship (produced 1931).

Confidential Service.   1932.

Pigeons and People (produced 1933).   1941.

Dear Old Darling (produced 1935).

Fulton of Oak Falls, from a story by Parker Fennelly (produced 1936).

The Return of the Vagabond (produced 1940).   1940.

Verse

Songs of Yesteryear.   1924.

Other

Twenty Years on Broadway, and the Years It Took to Get There.   1925.

*   *   *

Cohan the dramatist? Surely not. Cohan the Yankee Doodle Dandy, the song and dance man, the song writer (not only "Yankee Doodle Dandy" but also "Mary's a Grand Old

Name" and "Give My Regards to Broadway"). But Cohan the playwright is as unknown today as Cohan the vaudevillean and Cohan the movie star. The only play of his that is still remembered is probably *Seven Keys to Baldpate*, a comedy-thriller filmed five times.

In his own time, however, Cohan was significant not only as an actor but as a playwright. As Alan S. Downer puts it (in *Fifty Years of American Drama*, 1951), "Out of the variety houses and into the legitimate theatre came George M. Cohan, the apostle of rampant Americanism. With a sharp ear for the colloquial speech of New York ... , with his single-minded devotion to the color combination in Old Glory, he created a wise-cracking, quick-footed, dashing young hero who could instantaneously declare and prove his superiority to all lesser mortals, 'reubens' or 'limeys' or both." From his success derive plays such as those of Winchell Smith and George Kelly, the tough talk of the 1930's films, the snappy wisecracks of Kaufman and Dorothy Parker.

The best of the plays are probably *Little Johnny Jones*, *Forty-Five Minutes from Broadway*, *Get-Rich-Quick Wallingford*, *Seven Keys to Baldpate*, *The Miracle Man*, and *Gambling*. Cohan learned his craft in the 1880's and 1890's and seldom went beyond what he learned. He used theatrical tricks in many of the plays, shocked the audience by putting Billy Sunday on the stage in *Hit-the-Trail Holliday*, kept the title character offstage in *The Miracle Man*, had no intermission in *Pigeons and People*, revealed the identity of the robber in the first act of *Confidential Service*, always with an eye on theatrical effect. His one rule was to "wow them." When he died, he had long outlasted his time as a personality and writer.

— Leonard R. N. Ashley

CONNELLY, Marc(us Cook). American. Born in McKeesport, Pennsylvania, 13 December 1890. Educated at Trinity Hall, Washington, Pennsylvania, 1902–07. Married Madeline Hurlock in 1930 (divorced, 1935). Reporter and Drama Critic for the Pittsburgh *Press* and *Gazette-Times*, 1908–15; moved to New York, 1915: free-lance writer and actor, 1915–33; Reporter, New York *Morning Telegraph*, 1918–21; associated with *The New Yorker* in the 1920's; wrote screenplays and directed in Hollywood, 1933–44; Professor of Playwriting, Yale University Drama School, New Haven, Connecticut, 1947–52. United States Commissioner to UNESCO, 1951; Adviser, Equity Theatre Library, 1960. Since 1920, Member of the Council of the Dramatists Guild; Member, Executive Committee, United States National Committe for UNESCO. Recipient: Pulitzer Prize, 1930; O. Henry Award, for short story, 1930. Litt.D.: Bowdoin College, Brunswick, Maine, 1952; Baldwin-Wallace College, Berea, Ohio, 1962. Past President, Authors League of America; President, National Institute of Arts and Letters, 1953–56. Lives in New York City.

PUBLICATIONS

Plays

$2.50 (produced 1913).
The Lady of Luzon (lyrics only; produced 1914).
Follow the Girl (lyrics only, uncredited; produced 1915).
The Amber Express, music by Zoel Joseph Parenteau (produced 1916).
Dulcy, with George S. Kaufman (produced 1921). 1921.
Erminie, revised version of the play by Henry Paulton (produced 1921).

To the Ladies!, with George S. Kaufman (produced 1922).   1923.

No, Sirree!, with George S. Kaufman (produced 1922).

The 49ers, with George S. Kaufman (produced 1922).

West of Pittsburgh, with George S. Kaufman (produced 1922; revised version, as *The Deep Tangled Wildwood,* produced 1923).

Merton of the Movies, with George S. Kaufman, from the story by Harry Leon Wilson (produced 1922).   1925.

A Christmas Carol, with George S. Kaufman, from the story by Dickens, in *Bookman,* December 1922.

Helen of Troy, N.Y., with George S. Kaufman, music and lyrics by Harry Ruby and Bert Kalmar (produced 1923).

Beggar on Horseback, with George S. Kaufman, music by Deems Taylor, from a play by Paul Apel (produced 1924).   1925.

Be Yourself, with George S. Kaufman (produced 1924).

The Wisdom Tooth: A Fantastic Comedy (produced 1925).   1927.

The Wild Man of Borneo, with Herman J. Mankiewicz (produced 1927).

How's the King? (produced 1927).

The Green Pastures: A Fable Suggested by Roark Bradford's Southern Sketches "Ol' Man Adam an' His Chillun" (produced 1930).   1929.

The Survey (skit), in *New Yorker,* 1934.

The Farmer Takes A Wife, with Frank B. Elser, adaptation of the novel *Rome Haul* by Walter D. Edmonds (produced 1934).   Abridgement in *Best Plays of 1934–1935,* edited by Burns Mantle, 1935.

Little David: An Unproduced Scene from "The Green Pastures."   1937.

Everywhere I Roam, with Arnold Sundgaard (produced 1938).

The Traveler.   1939.

The Mole on Lincoln's Cheek (broadcast 1941).   In *The Free Company Presents,* edited by James Boyd, 1941.

The Flowers of Virtue (produced 1942).

The Good Earth, with others, in *Twenty Best Film Plays,* edited by John Gassner and Dudley Nichols.   1943.

A Story for Strangers (produced 1948).

Hunter's Moon (produced 1958).

The Portable Yenberry (produced 1962).

Screenplays: *Whispers,* 1920; *Exit Smiling,* with others, 1926; *The Bridegroom, The Burglar, The Suitor,* and *The Uncle* (film shorts), 1929; *The Unemployed Ghost* (film short), 1931; *The Cradle Song,* 1933; *The Little Duchess* (film short), 1934; *The Green Pastures,* 1936; *The Farmer Takes a Wife,* 1937; *Captains Courageous,* 1937; *The Good Earth,* with others, 1937; *I Married a Witch,* 1942; *Reunion (Reunion in France),* 1942; *The Imposter* (additional dialogue), 1944; *Fabiola* (English dialogue), 1951; *Crowded Paradise* (additional scenes), 1956.

Radio Play: *The Mole on Lincoln's Cheek,* 1941.

Fiction

A Souvenir from Qam.   1965.

Other

Voices Off-Stage: A Book of Memoirs.   1968.

Reading List: *Connelly* by Paul T. Nolan, 1969.

*   *   *

Born to parents who had both had stage careers, Marc Connelly early became dedicated to the theatre. As a young child, he says in his memoirs, he got the "feeling that going to the theater is like going to an unusual church, where the spirit is nourished in mystical ways, and pure magic may occur at any moment." Connelly has spent his life as a man of the theatre seeking to produce that pure magic – as actor, director, and playwright.

Convinced that there was much to be enjoyed in life, Connelly as a young man fell in naturally with the famed "Round Table" of the 1920's at New York's Algonquin Hotel. His first New York stage venture had been the lyrics for the musical *The Amber Express* (1916), but success did not come until the collaborations with George S. Kaufman. In 1921 their *Dulcy*, a mixture of gentle satire and fun, helped to set the standard for the Broadway comedy of the 1920's. They collaborated on six other plays. Their *Merton of the Movies*, based on the story by Harry Leon Wilson, inaugurated an era of Broadway satires on Hollywood. The play's success was marked by Hollywood's turning it into a movie.

The most important play of the Kaufman-Connelly collaboration was *Beggar on Horseback*, a masterpiece of American expressionism and a fitting symbol of the *joie de vivre* the collaborators consistently sought to bring to the stage. The play is based on Paul Apel's *Hans Sonnestössers Höllenfahrt*, but it is no slavish copy of the German play – the expressionism has been completely Americanized in technique and in its satiric ends. Framed by scenes of comic realism, the visual and audial effects of the expressionism, helped by cinematic techniques, are more varied than those of Elmer Rice's *The Adding Machine* (1923).

After the success of *Beggar on Horseback*, the collaborators decided to pursue their careers apart. Connelly wrote musicals and plays (most successfully *The Wisdom Tooth*) and wrote short stories for *The New Yorker* (he was on the editorial board of the struggling new magazine), but it was not until he read Roark Bradford's *Ol' Man Adam an' His Chillun* that he wrote the play that insured his unique position in twentieth-century drama. In Bradford's rendering of Old Testament stories from the viewpoint of uneducated Louisiana Negroes, Connelly immediately perceived the basis of a drama where pure magic might nourish the human spirit. The result was *The Green Pastures*, a work which, while it contained much of the fun of Bradford, gave it a greater dignity and a greater vision. Connelly's Lawd is a growing protagonist; his play's action concerns man's search for God and God's search for man. Connelly enhanced his episodically structured play through the use of Negro spirituals, suggesting other aspects of the folk longings. By framing the play with a children's Sunday School, Connelly conveyed the value of his material: unless one becomes as a little child, the play's vision would be beyond him. Broadway had long been without a religious play, and an all-Negro cast was also unusual. Connelly had difficulty getting backing for the play, but the production (directed by himself) proved the sceptics wrong. The play ran for five years, totalling 1642 performances.

Connelly was in Hollywood often in the 1930's, writing screenplays (some of the best of the period) and directing. (He would later act in *Our Town* and in other plays.) While he wrote some scripts and other plays, none has matched his earlier successes. He published *A Souvenir from Qam*, his only novel, in 1965. He reminisced about his many years on the stage and in the movies in *Voices Off-Stage*, which gives brief glimpses of famous contemporaries but is most valuable in its story of *The Green Pastures*.

—Joseph M. Flora

COWARD, Sir Noël (Pierce). English. Born in Teddington, Middlesex, 16 December 1899. Educated at Chapel Road School, Clapham, London, and privately; studied acting at the Italia Conti Academy, Liverpool. Served in the Artists' Rifles, British Army, 1918; in the British Information Service, 1939–40; entertained troops during the Second World War. Actor, producer and director: made London debut in 1911, and thereafter appeared on the London and New York stage, often in productions of his own works; also composer, lyricist, night-club entertainer, and film actor. President, Actors Orphanage, 1934–56. Recipient: New York Drama Critics Circle Award, 1942. D.Litt.: University of Sussex, Brighton, 1972. Fellow, Royal Society of Literature. Knighted, 1970. *Died 26 March 1973.*

PUBLICATIONS

Collections

Cowardy Custard: The World of Coward, edited by John Hadfield.   1973.

Plays

Ida Collaborates, with Esme Wynne (produced 1917).
Woman and Whisky, with Esme Wynne (produced 1917).
Sketches in *Tails Up!* (produced 1918).
I'll Leave It to You (produced 1920).   1920.
Bottles and Bones (produced 1921).
The Better Half (produced 1922).
Sketches in *The Co-Optimists: A Pierrotic Entertainment* (produced 1922; revised version, produced 1924).
The Young Idea: A Comedy of Youth (produced 1922).   1922.
London Calling!, with Ronald Jeans (revue; produced 1923; revised versions produced 1923, 1924).   Some items in *The Collected Sketches and Lyrics,* 1931, and *The Noël Coward Song-Book,* 1953.
The Vortex (produced 1924).   1925.
Sketches in *Charlot's London Revue of 1924* (produced 1924).
The Rat Trap (produced 1926).   1924.
Sketches in *Yoicks!* (produced 1924).
Sketches in *Charlot's Revue of 1926* (produced 1925).
On with the Dance, music by Philip Braham (revue; produced 1925).   Some items in *The Collected Sketches and Lyrics,* 1931, and *The Noël Coward Song-Book,* 1953.
Hay Fever (produced 1925).   1925.
Fallen Angels (produced 1925; revised version, produced 1967).   1925.
Easy Virtue (produced 1925).   1926.
Three Plays: The Rat Trap, The Vortex, Fallen Angels, With the Author's Reply to His Critics.   1925.
The Queen Was in the Parlour (produced 1926).   1926.
This Was a Man (produced 1926).   1926.
The Marquise (produced 1927).   1927.
Home Chat (produced 1927).   1927.
Sirocco (produced 1927).   1927.
Sketches in *White Birds* (produced 1927).
This Year of Grace! (revue; produced 1928).   In *Play Parade II,* 1939.
Bitter-Sweet, music by the author (produced 1929).   1929.

Private Lives: An Intimate Comedy (produced 1930). 1930.

Sketches in *Charles B. Cochran's 1931 Revue* (produced 1931).

Sketches in *The Third Little Show* (produced 1931). 1931.

Post-Mortem. 1931.

The Collected Sketches and Lyrics. 1931.

Cavalcade (produced 1931). 1932.

Weatherwise (produced 1932). In *The Collected Sketches and Lyrics,* 1931.

Words and Music (revue; produced 1932; revised version, as *Set to Music,* produced 1938). In *Play Parade II,* 1939.

Design for Living (produced 1933). 1933.

Play Parade:

   I.   *Cavalcade, Bitter-Sweet, The Vortex, Hay Fever, Design for Living, Private Lives, Post-Mortem.* 1933.

   II. *This Year of Grace!, Words and Music, Operette, Conversation Piece.* 1939; augmented edition, including *Fallen Angels* and *Easy Virtue,* 1950.

   III. *The Queen Was in the Parlour, I'll Leave It to You, The Young Idea, The Rat Trap, Sirocco, This Was a Man, Home Chat, The Marquise.* 1950.

   IV. *Tonight at 8:30, Present Laughter, This Happy Breed.* 1954.

   V.   *Pacific 1860, Peace in Our Time, Relative Values, Quadrille, Blithe Spirit.* 1958.

   VI. *Point Valaine, South Sea Bubble, Ace of Clubs, Nude with Violin, Waiting in the Wings.* 1962.

Conversation Piece (produced 1934). 1934.

Point Valaine (produced 1934). 1935.

Tonight at 8:30 (includes *We Were Dancing, The Astonished Heart, Red Peppers: An Interlude with Music, Hands Across the Sea, Fumed Oak: An Unpleasant Comedy, Shadow Play, Family Album: A Victorian Comedy with Music, Star Chamber, Ways and Means, Still Life*) (produced in three programmes 1935). 3 vols., 1936 (*Star Chamber* unpublished).

Operette, music by the author (produced 1938). 1938.

Sketches in *All Clear* (produced 1939).

Blithe Spirit: An Improbable Farce (produced 1941). 1941.

Present Laughter (produced 1942). 1943.

This Happy Breed (produced 1942). 1943.

Sigh No More (revue; produced 1945). Some items in *The Noël Coward Song-Book,* 1953.

Pacific 1860: A Musical Romance, music by the author (produced 1946). In *Play Parade V,* 1958.

Peace in Our Time (produced 1947). 1947.

Brief Encounter, in *Three British Screen Plays,* edited by Roger Manvell. 1950.

Ace of Clubs, music by the author (produced 1950). In *Play Parade VI,* 1962.

Relative Values (produced 1951). 1954.

Sketches in *The Lyric Revue* (produced 1951).

South Sea Bubble (as *Island Fling,* produced 1951; as *South Sea Bubble,* produced 1956). 1954.

Quadrille (produced 1952). 1952.

Sketches in *The Globe Revue* (produced 1952).

After the Ball, music by the author, from the play *Lady Windermere's Fan* by Wilde (produced 1954). 1954.

Nude with Violin (produced 1956). 1957.

Look after Lulu, from a play by Feydeau (produced 1959). 1959.

Waiting in the Wings (produced 1960). 1960.

Sail Away, music by the author (produced 1961).

The Girl Who Came to Supper (composer and lyricist only; produced 1963).

Suite in Three Keys: A Song at Twilight, Shadows of the Evening, Come into the Garden Maud (produced in two programmes, 1966).   1966.
Semi-Monde (produced 1977).

Screenplays: *In Which We Serve* 1942; *This Happy Breed,* 1944; *Blithe Spirit,* 1945; *Brief Encounter,* with others, 1946; *The Astonished Heart,* with others, 1950; *Meet Me Tonight,* 1952.

Radio Play: *The Kindness of Mrs. Redcliffe,* 1951.

Ballet Scenario: *London Morning* (also composer), 1959.

Fiction

To Step Aside: Seven Short Stories.   1939.
Star Quality: Six Stories.   1951.
Pomp and Circumstance.   1960.
The Collected Short Stories.   1962.
Seven Stories.   1963.
Pretty Polly Barlow and Other Stories.   1964; as *Pretty Polly and Other Stories,* 1965.
Bon Voyage and Other Stories.   1967.

Verse

Poems by Hernia Whittlebot.   1923.
Chelsea Buns (as Hernia Whittlebot).   1925.
Spangled Unicorn: An Anthology.   1932.
The Coward Song-Book.   1953.
The Lyrics of Coward.   1965.
Not Yet the Dodo and Other Verses.   1967.

Other

A Withered Nosegay: Imaginary Biographies.   1922; augmented edition, as *Terribly Intimate Portraits,* 1922.
Present Indicative (autobiography).   1937.
Australian Broadcast.   1941; as *Australia Visited 1940,* 1941.
Middle East Diary, July to October 1943.   1944.
Future Indefinite (autobiography).   1954.
Short Stories, Short Plays, and Songs, edited by Gilbert Millstein.   1955.
The Wit of Coward, edited by D. Richards.   1968.

Editor, *The Last Bassoon: From the Diaries of Fred Bason.*   1960.

Bibliography: *Theatrical Companion to Coward: A Pictorial Record of the First Performances of the Theatrical Works of Coward* by Raymond Mander and Joe Mitchenson, 1957.

Reading List: *The Art of Coward* by Robert Greacen, 1953; *Coward* by Milton Levin, 1968; *A Talent to Amuse: A Biography of Coward* by Sheridan Morley, 1969; *Noël* by Charles Castle, 1972; *The Life of Coward* by Cole Lesley, 1976, as *Remembered Laughter,* 1976.

*   *   *

Noël Coward was an actor, a nightclub performer, a singer who managed to overcome the lack of a good voice, a director, a producer, a screenwriter, a lyricist and composer, a raconteur and bon vivant, a short-story writer and occasional poet, the author of a couple of autobiographies, a man who gave a style to a whole era, and a dramatist. I must have left out a lot.

His work is essentially moralistic, for all its shock in the 1920's. He was, as St. John Ervine noted (in *Essays by Divers Hands*, 1935), "a Savanarola in evening dress." He is often nostalgic and sentimental but a native cynicism keeps the effect from being cloying. He is one of the great masters of drawing-room comedy and the well-made play but equally at home in revue and musical comedy and the cinema. John Bowen (in *Contemporary Dramatists*, 1973) wrote of him: "Coward is like Mozart — graceful, decorative, logical, witty and above all a craftsman." It is probably this craftsmanship, the finish, the polish, evident in everything from *The Lyrics of Noël Coward* to *The Collected Short Stories* to the forgotten novel and verse, not to mention his sparkling comedies and his acting and singing (marked with a peculiarly refreshing precision of enunciation, said to be due to coping with his mother's deafness, but probably deriving from a determination to do everything definitively) — this *professionalism* that is Coward's hallmark. Mander and Mitchenson's *Theatrical Companion to Coward* is a pictorial record of a career, whatever its ups and downs, of a multi-talented and joyful perfectionist.

His "serious" plays show him as hardworking as ever but perhaps not at the top of his form. *The Rat Trap* ("my first really serious attempt at psychological conflict") of 1926 cannot compare to the dazzling comedies of 1925: *Fallen Angels* and *Hay Fever*. *The Vortex* (1924) was a deft problem play which established him on the theatrical scene, but it was with comedies of the 1930's (such as *Private Lives*) and the 1940's (such as *Blithe Spirit*) that he built a lasting fame. I like *Easy Virtue* (1926), and see in it more real sympathy with his characters than in *A Song at Twilight* (1966), though in the latter play the aged homosexual writer is drawn with great skill. The basic patriotism of Coward is better seen in that "big play on a big scale" *Cavalcade* (1931) than in the England-between-the wars of *This Happy Breed* (1942) or England-after-the-war (as if Hitler had won) in *Peace in Our Time* (1947). The sentimental Englishness is best when tempered by wry humor, as in songs like "There Are Bad Times Just Around the Corner," "Mad Dogs and Englishmen," "Let's Not Be Beastly to the Germans," and raucous music-hall airs ("Saturday Night at the Rose and Crown"). "London Pride" and "London at Night" are a whit less witty, therefore a smidgen more schmaltzy. But in the end it is only fair that he loved his country. It loved him. Only a Lady Mayoress in New Zealand thought "The Stately Homes of England," Coward reported, "let down the British Empire." The Empire is now gone. The melody lingers on....

"The whole Edwardian era," wrote Coward, "was saturated with operetta and musical comedy. In addition to the foreign imprintations, our own native music was of a quality never equalled in this country since.... I was born into a generation whose parents still took light musicals seriously." Coward's contribution to it has been immense and may well prove to be his most lasting memorial. Waltzes such as "I'll See You Again," "Ziguener," "Some Day I'll Find You" and "I'll Follow My Secret Heart" sing in everyone's memory. And the comic songs! No wonder Benny Green has nominated him as "the best British composer of the last fifty years ... the best lyricist this country has produced, certainly since Wodehouse, perhaps since Gilbert."

Coward embodied a whole era. His boyhood friend Micheál Mac Liammóir said on a BBC series on "The Master" that "Noël Coward invented the 20's, just as Oscar Wilde invented the 90's."

The lifestyle presented in *Hay Fever*, *Design for Living*, *Private Lives* and *Blithe Spirit* is somewhat more acceptable now than it was in Coward's day, but the plays can never be either controversial or dated. Coward emphasized entertainment, not message, and the principal appeal of these scintillating comedies arises from their bantering dialogue (with just a touch of malice and cynicism) and their amusing situations (with just a touch of sexual spice). The artificiality of both is part of their charm. The carefully wrought machine runs on jewels of wit, and charming little figures parade before us at the appropriate times with striking effect. That it also indicates The Times is almost incidental, but useful.

In *Hay Fever* Judith Bliss, a retired actress, runs through a few of her favorite roles (glamorous star, neglected wife, self-sacrificing mother, flirt) during one hectic weekend. In *Design for Living* we have a *ménage à trois* and *la vie de Bohème* among the artists: "Otto who loved Gilda, Leo who loved Gilda, Otto who loved Leo, Leo who loved Otto, and Gilda who loved them both." *Private Lives* does something to illustrate Coward's personal credo that "the fewer illusions that I have about me or the world around me, the better company I am for myself."

Coward himself said of *Bitter-Sweet*: "disdaining archness and false modesty, I knew it was witty, I knew it was well constructed, and I also knew it would be a success." That description can suffice for a great many Coward plays (and other achievements) and makes the main points. That comedy, and not tragedy, should have been his *métier* may convince the injudicious that he is brittle and trivial – but neither the chic nor the wise can trouble themselves about people like that.

—Leonard R. N. Ashley

CROTHERS, Rachel. American. Born in Bloomington, Illinois, 12 December 1878. Educated at Illinois State Normal School, Bloomington, graduated 1892; Wheatcroft School of Acting, New York, 1893. Acted with an amateur dramatic society in Bloomington; with Felix Morris's Company; directed and staged all her own plays. Founder and First President, American Theatre Wing. Recipient: Megrue Prize, 1933; Chi Omega National Achievement Award, 1939. *Died in 1958.*

PUBLICATIONS

Plays

    Nora (produced 1903).
    The Point of View (produced 1904).
    Criss Cross. 1904.
    The Rector. 1905.
    The Three of Us (produced 1906). 1916.
    The Coming of Mrs. Patrick (produced 1907).
    Myself, Bettina (produced 1908).
    Kiddie. 1909.
    A Man's World (produced 1910). 1915.
    He and She (as *The Herfords,* produced 1912; as *He and She,* produced 1920). 1932.
    Young Wisdom (produced 1914). 1913.
    Ourselves (produced 1913).
    The Heart of Paddy Whack (produced 1914). 1925.

Old Lady 31, from the novel by Louise Forsslund (produced 1916).   In *Mary the Third*
    ..., 1923.
Mother Carey's Chickens, with Kate Douglas Wiggin, from the novel by Wiggin
    (produced 1917).   1925.
Once upon a Time (produced 1918).   1925.
39 East (produced 1919).   In *Expressing Willie* ..., 1924.
Everyday (produced 1921).   1930.
Nice People (produced 1921).   In *Expressing Willie* ..., 1924.
Mary the Third (produced 1923).   In *Mary the Third* ..., 1923.
Mary the Third, Old Lady 31, A Little Journey: Three Plays.   1923.
Expressing Willie (produced 1924).   In *Expressing Willie* ..., 1924.
Expressing Willie, Nice People, 39 East: Three Plays.   1924.
Six One-Act Plays (includes *The Importance of Being Clothed, The Importance of Being
    Nice, The Importance of Being Married, The Importance of Being a Woman, What
    They Think, Peggy*).   1925.
A Lady's Virtue (produced 1925).   1925.
Venus (produced 1927).   1927.
Let Us Be Gay (produced 1929).   1929.
As Husbands Go (produced 1931).   1931.
Caught Wet (produced 1931).   1932.
When Ladies Meet (produced 1932).   1932.
The Valiant One.   1937.
Susan and God (produced 1937).   1938.

*   *   *

Rachel Crothers was that rarity, a total woman of the theatre. Not since the Duke of Saxe-Meiningen and André Antoine in the last quarter of the 19th century had such a complexity of personal supervision over an entire theatrical production been seen. She was even more commanding than these two estimable and influential gentlemen since this complete control was exercised over her *own* plays which were generally directed, and occasionally even acted in, by her. Most extraordinary was the fact that it was a woman who had such a multi-leveled theatrical success and over so long a period of time. Altogether, the career of Rachel Crothers was unparalleled.

As a writer, she was a playwright and a playwright only, and the singlemindedness of her literary style also became the singlemindedness of her essential theme, that of woman emerging from the oppressions of society. Her "problem comedies" – which were notable for their witty and natural dialogue – dealt with such themes as career versus marriage (*He and She*), the "liberated" girl of the 1920's (*Nice People*), the generation gap (*Mary the Third*), divorce (*Let Us Be Gay*), adultery (*When Ladies Meet*), and emotional-cum-spiritual restlessness (*Susan and God*).

Miss Crothers was critically and popularly acclaimed as America's foremost woman playwright for over thirty years. Always concerned with human dignity, Miss Crothers organized war relief committees in both world wars. This patriotism carried into her work, for, in addition to her depiction of her theme of the feminine view of life in many variations, she was a very endemically American playwright. Speaking of her play on love firmly rooted in Yankee soil (*Old Lady 31*), a *New York Times* article of 9 February 1919 compared her to Booth Tarkington, saying "Rachel Crothers must be admitted to the small and select group of those who tend to reveal America to the Americans."

In her time she was enormously successful, and perhaps the wholesomeness of her approach and the sound common sense and decency of spirit underlying all her plays (which stand up theatrically because of their timely situations and excellent dialogue) are the essential reasons behind this resounding success. Her interest in the "balanced or everyday life" was epitomized in her work: it is her plea for "sanity in all art," as she herself termed it, which her plays so ably exemplify.

—Zoë Coralnik Kaplan

DANE, Clemence. Pseudonym for Winifred Ashton. English. Born in Blackheath, London, in 1887. Educated at various private schools, and at the Slade School of Art, London, 1904–06; also studied art in Dresden, 1906–07. Taught French in Geneva, 1903, and in Ireland, from 1907; left teaching for the stage, 1913: actress, as Diana Portis, 1913–18; playwright from 1921. President, Society of Women Journalists, 1941. C.B.E. (Commander, Order of the British Empire), 1953. *Died 28 March 1965.*

PUBLICATIONS

Plays

A Bill of Divorcement (produced 1921). 1921.
The Terror (produced 1921).
Will Shakespeare: An Invention (produced 1921). 1921.
The Way Things Happen: A Story, from her own novel Legend (produced 1923). 1924.
Shivering Shocks; or, The Hiding Place: A Play for Boys. 1923.
Naboth's Vineyard. 1925.
Granite (produced 1926). 1927.
Mariners (produced 1927). 1927.
Mr. Fox: A Play for Boys. 1927.
A Traveller Returns. 1927.
Adam's Opera, music by Richard Addinsell (produced 1928). 1928.
Gooseberry Fool (produced 1929).
Wild Decembers (produced 1933). 1932.
Come of Age, music by Richard Addinsell (produced 1934). 1933.
L'Aiglon, music by Richard Addinsell, from the play by Rostand (produced 1934). 1934.
Moonlight Is Silver (produced 1934). 1934.
The Happy Hypocrite, from the story by Max Beerbohm (produced 1936).
Herod and Mariamne, from the play by Hebbel (produced 1938). 1938.
England's Darling. 1940.
Cousin Muriel (produced 1940). 1940.
The Saviours: Seven Plays on One Theme (broadcast 1940–41). 1942.
The Golden Reign of Queen Elizabeth (produced 1941). 1941.
Alice's Adventures in Wonderland and Through the Looking-Glass, music by Richard Addinsell, from the novels by Lewis Carroll (produced 1943). 1948.
The Lion and the Unicorn. 1943.
Call Home the Heart (produced 1947). 1947.
Scandal at Coventry (broadcast 1958). In Collected Plays, 1961.
Eighty in the Shade (produced 1958). 1959.

Till Time Shall End (televised 1958).   In *Collected Plays*, 1961.
Collected Plays 1 (all published).   1961.
The Godson: A Fantasy.   1964.

Screenplays: *The Tunnel* (*Transatlantic Tunnel*), with Kurt Siodmak, and L. DuGarde Peach, 1935; *Anna Karenina*, 1935; *The Amateur Gentleman*, with Edward Knoblock, 1936; *Farewell Again* (*Troopship*), with Patrick Kirwan, 1937; *Fire over England*, with Sergei Nolbandov, 1937; *St. Martin's Lane* (*Sidewalks of London*), 1938; *Salute John Citizen*, with Elizabeth Baron, 1942; *Perfect Strangers* (*Vacation from Marriage*), with Anthony Pelissier, 1945; *Bonnie Prince Charlie*, 1948; *Bride of Vengeance*, with Cyril Hume and Michael Hogan, 1949; *The Angel with the Trumpet*, with Karl Hartl and Franz Tassie, 1950.

Radio Plays: *The Scoop* (serial), with others, 1931; *The Saviours* (7 plays), 1940–41; *Henry VIII*, from the play by Shakespeare, 1954; *Don Carlos*, from the play by Schiller, 1955; *Scandal at Coventry*, 1958.

Television Play: *Till Time Shall End*, 1958.

Fiction

Regiment of Women.   1917.
First the Blade: A Comedy of Growth.   1918.
Legend.   1919.
Wandering Stars, with The Lover.   1924.
The Dearly Beloved of Benjamin Cobb.   1927.
The Babyons: A Family Chronicle.   1928.
Enter Sir John, with Helen Simpson.   1928.
The King Waits.   1929.
Printer's Devil, with Helen Simpson.   1930; as *Author Unknown*, 1930.
Broome Stages.   1931.
Re-Enter Sir John, with Helen Simpson.   1932.
Fate Cries Out: Nine Tales.   1935.
The Moon Is Feminine.   1938.
The Arrogant History of White Ben.   1939.
He Brings Great News.   1944.
The Flower Girls.   1954.

Verse

Trafalgar Day 1940.   1940.

Other

The Woman's Side.   1926.
Tradition and Hugh Walpole.   1929.
Recapture (miscellany).   1932.
London Has a Garden.   1964.

Editor, *A Hundred Enchanted Tales.*   1937.
Editor, *The Shelter Book.*   1940.

Editor, *The Nelson Touch: An Anthology of Nelson Letters.* 1942.

Reading List: *Some Modern Authors* by S. P. B. Mais, 1923; *Some Contemporary Dramatists* by G. Sutton, 1924.

*   *   *

Clemence Dane was one of the lesser luminaries among a group of talented women writers of middle-class origin who, emerging during or shortly after the First World War, formed an important feature of the English literary scene until the 1950's. Lacking the ironic wit of a Rose Macaulay or the intuitive sensibility of a Rosamond Lehmann or an Elizabeth Bowen, she had the most vigorous talent of them all, being the author of some dozen popular novels, several collections of essays and short stories, and a large number of successful West-End dramas. Educated in England and abroad, trained at the Slade School of Art, Clemence Dane was herself on the stage for some time, acting under the name Diana Portis, before gaining celebrity as a writer. A large, generous, and energetic personality, and a distinguished sculptor and painter, her real name was Winifred Ashton, her pseudonym being adapted from St. Clement Danes church in London.

Her first novel, *Regiment of Women*, is a story of life (and especially emotional life) in a girls' boarding school, where a close relationship between two teachers is impaired by the death of a pupil and by the younger teacher's love affair, while *Legend* satirizes effectively if mildly the London literary jungle, where the bickering intimates of a young woman novelist unfeelingly dissect her life and work on the night of her death. With *The Babyons* Clemence Dane turned to the familiar romantic family chronicle, and her strong sense of historical continuity was further exploited in two lengthy, highly-acclaimed novels with theatrical backgrounds, *Broome Stages*, which charts the fortunes of a stage dynasty through seven generations, and *The Flower Girls*. While the sense of period is not very highly developed in these works, they possess a good deal of authenticity alongside their somewhat contrived "charm."

But it is primarily as a playwright that Clemence Dane is remembered. Her first play, *A Bill of Divorcement*, presenting sympathetically the case for the annulment of marriage on the grounds of insanity, is simply an updating of the topical late-Victorian "problem play" of Jones and Pinero, with a similarly unlikely, sentimental resolution of the moral dilemma. But *Will Shakespeare*, a highly-fictionalized "Invention" principally concerning the dramatist's relations with Anne Hathaway, Mary Fitton, Marlowe, and his queen, is a courageous venture into the dangers of sham-Tudor blank-verse and prose, and its style, in adorning simple sentiments in colourful language, couples a genuine beauty and bravura with un-Elizabethan decorousness. *The Way Things Happen* and *Mariners* were plays in the contemporary drawing-room convention, but *Granite*, a powerful tragedy of marital cruelty, adulterous desires, and primitive jealousies culminating in murder, set on Lundy Island in the 1810's, is perhaps Clemence Dane's finest single achievement, its skilfully constructed plot rich in ironies unfortunately unmatched by the dialogue. She returned to literary subjects with the Brontës in *Wild Decembers* and Thomas Chatterton in *Come of Age*, while historical figures are central to *England's Darling* (Alfred), *Scandal at Coventry* (Godiva) and *Till Time Shall End* (Elizabeth I). Her last stage play, *Eighty in the Shade*, took place in an Old People's Home, and starred Sybil Thorndike and Lewis Casson, who had both appeared in *Granite* in 1926.

—William M. Tydeman

DRINKWATER, John. English. Born in Leytonstone, Essex, 1 June 1882. Educated at the City of Oxford High School. Married 1) Kathleen Walpole in 1906 (divorced, 1924); 2) Daisy Kennedy in 1924, one daughter. Worked for the Northern Assurance Company in Nottingham, 1897–1901, and in Birmingham, 1901–09. Co-Founder with Sir Barry Jackson, Pilgrim Players, later Birmingham Repertory Theatre, 1907, and Manager of the theatre from 1910; also, Editor, Pilgrim Players *Scallop Shell* magazine, 1911. Ph.D.: University of Athens; M.A.: University of Birmingham. *Died 25 March 1937.*

PUBLICATIONS

Plays

Ser Taldo's Bride, with B. V. Jackson (produced 1911).
Cophetua (produced 1911).   1911.
An English Medley, music by Rutland Boughton (produced 1911).   1911.
Puss in Boots (produced 1911; revised version, produced 1916, 1926).   1911.
The Pied Piper: A Tale of Hamelin City, music by F. W. Sylvester (produced 1912).   1912.
The Only Legend: A Masque of the Scarlet Pierrot (produced 1913).   1913.
Rebellion (produced 1914).   1914.
Robin Hood and the Pedlar, music by James Brier (produced 1914).   1914.
The Storm (produced 1915).   1915.
The God of Quiet (produced 1916).   1916.
The Wounded, with R. De Smet (produced 1917).
X = O: A Night of the Trojan War (produced 1917).   1917.
Pawns: Three Poetic Plays.   1917.
Abraham Lincoln (produced 1918).   1918.
Mary Stuart (produced 1921).   1921.
Oliver Cromwell (produced 1923).   1921.
Robert E. Lee (produced 1923).   1923.
Collected Plays.   2 vols., 1925.
Robert Burns.   1925.
The Mayor of Casterbridge, from the novel by Hardy (produced 1926).
Bird in Hand (produced 1927).   1927.
John Bull Calling: A Political Parable (produced 1928).   1928.
Holiness (produced 1928).
Napoleon: The Hundred Days, from a play by Benito Mussolini and Giovacchino Forzano (produced 1932).   1932.
Midsummer Eve (broadcast 1932).   1932.
Laying the Devil (produced 1933).   1933.
A Man's House (produced 1934).   1934.
Garibaldi.   1936.

Screenplays: *The King of Paris*, with W. P. Lipscomb and Paul Gangelin, 1934; *Blossom Time (April Romance),* with others, 1934; *Pagliacci (A Clown Must Laugh),* with others, 1936; *The King's People,* 1937; *The Mill on the Floss,* with others, 1937.

Radio Play: *Midsummer Eve,* 1932.

Fiction

Robinson of England.   1937.

Verse

Poems. 1903.
The Death of Leander and Other Poems. 1906.
Lyrical and Other Poems. 1908.
Poems of Men and Hours. 1911.
Poems of Love and Earth. 1912.
Cromwell and Other Poems. 1913.
Swords and Ploughshares. 1915.
Olton Pools. 1916.
Poems 1908–1914. 1917.
Tides. 1917; revised edition, 1917.
Loyalties. 1918.
Poems 1908–1919. 1919.
Seeds of Time. 1921.
Cotswold Characters. 1921.
Preludes 1921–1922. 1922.
Selected Poems. 1922.
Collected Poems. 3 vols., 1923–27.
From an Unknown Isle. 1924.
From the German: Verses Written from the German Poets. 1924.
New Poems. 1925.
All about Me: Poems for a Child. 1928.
Poems (selection). 1928.
More about Me: Poems for a Child. 1929.
American Vignettes 1860–65. 1931.
Christmas Poems. 1931.
Summer Harvest: Poems 1924–1933. 1933.

Other

William Morris: A Critical Study. 1912.
Swinburne: An Estimate. 1913.
The Lyric. 1915.
Rupert Brooke: An Essay. 1916.
Prose Papers. 1917.
Lincoln, The World Emancipator. 1920.
Claud Lovat Fraser: A Memoir, with Albert Rutherston. 1923.
Victorian Poetry. 1923.
Patriotism in Literature. 1924.
The Muse in Council. 1925.
The Pilgrim of Eternity: Byron: A Conflict. 1925.
A Book for Bookmen. 1926.
Mr. Charles, King of England. 1926.
Cromwell: A Character Study. 1927.
The Gentle Art of Theatre-Going. 1927; as *The Art of Theatre-Going,* 1927.
Charles James Fox. 1928.
The World's Lincoln. 1928.
Story-Folk (juvenile), with E. Terriss. 4 vols., 1929.
Pepys: His Life and Character. 1930.
Inheritance, Discovery (autobiography). 2 vols., 1931–32.
The Life and Adventures of Carl Laemmle. 1931.
John Hampden's England. 1933.

Shakespeare. 1933.
This Troubled World. 1933.
The King's Reign: A Commentary in Prose and Pictures. 1935.
English Poetry: An Unfinished History. 1938.

Editor, *Poems, Letters, and Prose Fragments,* by Henry Kirke White. 1907.
Editor, *The Poems of Sidney.* 1910.
Editor, *The Way of Poetry* (juvenile). 1920.
Editor, *The Outline of Literature.* 26 vols., 1923–24.
Editor, *Select Poems of Lord De Tabley.* 1924.
Editor, *An Anthology of English Verse.* 1924.
Editor, *The Way of Prose* (juvenile). 4 vols., 1924.
Editor, *Little Nineteenth Century Classics.* 3 vols., 1925.
Editor, with William Rose Benét and Henry Seidel Canby, *Twentieth-Century Poetry.* 1929.
Editor, *The Eighteen-Sixties.* 1932.
Editor, *A Pageant of English Life.* 1934.

Bibliography: *Drinkwater: Catalogue of an Exhibition,* 1962; "Drinkwater: An Annotated Bibliography of Writings about Him" by Peter Berven, in *English Literature in Transition 21,* 1978.

Reading List: *The Poetry of Drinkwater* by Godfrey W. Matthews, 1925; *Drinkwater and His Historical Plays* by C. Ghidelli, 1937.

*   *   *

John Drinkwater first gained attention as a poet in the first decade of the present century and between 1910 and 1930 added to this a considerable reputation as author of plays in verse and prose, many of them composed for performance at the Birmingham Repertory Theatre, in which Drinkwater served as (in his own words) "actor, producer, manager, and odd-job man." His father, Alfred, had made a career on the stage after an Oxford education and some years of school-teaching, and Drinkwater was brought up by his grandfather in Oxford, attending the High School and spending summers with farming relations in the local countryside. After leaving school, he spent twelve years in the Northern and other assurance companies in Nottingham and Birmingham, writing verse after office hours and helping to found the Pilgrim Players, an amateur dramatic society, with Barry Jackson in 1907, becoming their full-time manager in 1910. He was a contributor to all five volumes of Sir Edward Marsh's *Georgian Poetry* between 1912 and 1922, and a prolific writer of literary and historical biographies, studies, and sketches. Two volumes of rather tame autobiography appeared in 1931 and 1932.

As a poet Drinkwater displays the typical virtues and deficiencies of the Georgian school as a whole: his lyrics and poems in blank verse are often successful in celebrating predictable aspects of the rural scene or human relationships, but in a calculatedly unsophisticated, self-consciously timeless, and frequently ponderous vein, contriving to be simultaneously simple in diction and imprecise in meaning. He is inspired to poetry by the carefully observed beauty of natural objects, by a delighted consciousness of historical continuity, by rustic encounters and strong but restrained sexual emotion, and by national crisis, but his tendency to choose the readiest and most conventional image in preference to the most telling one results in mere confirmation of the reader's own perceptions and responses rather than their extension or controversion. Drinkwater's highly-developed sense of poetic decorum, his air of "talking down" to his audience, his taste for extracting profound sentiments from commonplace experiences, have all served to obscure his human sensitivity, his poetic sincerity, and his complete devotion to his craft.

His plays are a curiously mixed collection, the earliest compositions being mainly short experimental verse-dramas such as *Cophetua, The Storm, The God of Quiet*, and *X = O*, all of which may be more accurately described as dramatic poems rather than true dramas. However, with *Abraham Lincoln* (1918) Drinkwater embarked on a more satisfactory sequence of historical plays, unromanticized, semi-documentary, episodic presentations of the problems of leadership encountered by Lincoln, Cromwell, and Robert E. Lee. Despite the author's declared intention of retaining "something of the enthusiasm and poignancy of verse" in these plays, they are actually in slightly stiff but workmanlike modern prose; if they are a little dry and circumspect, they remain absorbing theatre, hampered slightly by their earnest didactic tone. With them may be linked the more sentimentalized portrayal of Mary Stuart, itself in total contrast to Drinkwater's last significant play, *Bird in Hand*, a cheerful but conventional love-comedy unlike anything he had attempted before.

—William M. Tydeman

DUNCAN, Ronald (Frederick Henry). English. Born in Salisbury, Rhodesia, 6 August 1914. Educated in Switzerland and at Downing College, Cambridge, M.A. 1936. Married Rose Marie Theresa Hansom in 1941; one son and one daughter. Farmer in Devon since 1939. Poetry Editor, *The Townsman*, London, 1938–46; Columnist ("Jan's Journal"), *Evening Standard*, London, 1946–56. Founder, Devon Festival of the Arts, Bideford, 1953; Co-Founder, English Stage Company at the Royal Court Theatre, London, 1955.

PUBLICATIONS

Plays

Birth (produced 1937).
The Dull Ass's Hoof (includes *The Unburied Dead: Pimp, Skunk and Profiteer; Ora Pro Nobis*). 1940.
This Way to the Tomb: A Masque and Anti-Masque, music by Benjamin Britten (produced 1945). 1946.
The Eagle Has Two Heads, from a play by Jean Cocteau (produced 1946). 1948.
The Rape of Lucretia, music by Benjamin Britten, from a play by André Obey (produced 1946). 1946; augmented edition, 1948.
Amo Ergo Sum (cantata), music by Benjamin Britten (produced 1948).
The Typewriter, from a play by Jean Cocteau (produced 1950). 1948.
Stratton, music by Benjamin Britten (produced 1949). 1950.
St. Spiv (as *Nothing up My Sleeve*, produced 1950; revised version, as *St. 'Orace*, music by Jerry Wayne, produced 1964). In *Collected Plays*, 1971.
Our Lady's Tumbler, music by Arthur Oldham (produced 1950). 1951.
Don Juan (produced 1953). 1954.
The Death of Satan (produced 1954). 1955.

A Man Named Judas, from a play by C. A. Puget and Pierre Bost (produced 1956).
The Cardinal, with Hans Keuls, from a play by Harald Bratt (produced 1957).
The Apollo de Bellac, from a play by Jean Giraudoux (produced 1957).   1958.
The Catalyst (produced 1958; revised version, as *Ménage à Trois*, produced 1963).   1964.
Christopher Sly, music by Thomas Eastwood (produced 1960).
Abélard and Héloise: A Correspondence for the Stage (produced 1960).   1961.
The Rabbit Race, from a play by Martin Walser (produced 1963).   In *Plays, vol. I* by Walser, 1963.
O-B-A-F-G: A Play in One Act in Stereophonic Sound (produced 1964).   1964.
The Trojan Women, from a play by Jean-Paul Sartre based on the play by Euripides (produced 1967).   1967.
The Seven Deadly Virtues: A Contemporary Immorality Play (produced 1968).   In *Collected Plays*, 1971.
The Gift (produced 1968).   In *Collected Plays*, 1971.
The Rehearsal (as *Still Life*, televised 1970).   In *Collected Plays*. 1971.
Collected Plays (includes *This Way to the Tomb, St. Spiv, Our Lady's Tumbler, The Rehearsal, The Seven Deadly Virtues, O-B-A-F-G, The Gift*).   1971.

Screenplay: *Girl on a Motorcycle*, 1968.

Television Plays: *The Portrait*, 1954; *The Janitor*, 1955; *Preface to America*, 1959; *Not All the Dead Are Buried*, 1960; *The Rebel*, music by Thomas Eastwood, 1969; *Still Life*, 1970; *Mandala*, 1972.

Fiction

The Last Adam.   1952.
Saint Spiv.   1961.
The Perfect Mistress and Other Stories.   1969.
A Kettle of Fish (stories).   1971.
The Tale of Tails: Ten Fables.   1977.

Verse

Postcards to Pulcinella.   1941.
The Mongrel and Other Poems.   1950.
The Solitudes.   1960.
Judas.   1960.
Unpopular Poems.   1969.
Man, parts 1–5.   4 vols., 1970–74.
For the Few.   1977.

Other

The Complete Pacifist.   1937.
The Rexist Party Manifesto.   1937.
Strategy in War.   1937.
Journal of a Husbandman.   1944.
Home-Made Home (on architecture).   1947.
Jan's Journal 1–2.   2 vols., 1949–54.

Tobacco Cultivation in England.   1951.
The Blue Fox (newspaper articles).   1951.
Jan at the Blue Fox (newspaper articles).   1952.
Where I Live.   1953.
All Men Are Islands: An Autobiography.   1964.
Devon and Cornwall.   1966.
How to Make Enemies (autobiography).   1968.
Obsessed: A Third Volume of Autobiography.   1977.

Editor, *Songs and Satires of John Wilmot, 2nd Earl of Rochester.*   1948.
Editor, *Selected Poems,* by Ben Jonson.   1949.
Editor, *Selected Writings of Mahatma Gandhi.*   1951.
Editor, with the Countess of Harewood, *Classical Songs for Children.*   1965.
Editor, with Marion Harewood, *The Penguin Book of Accompanied Songs.*   1973.
Editor, with Miranda Weston-Smith, *The Encyclopedia of Ignorance.*   2 vols., 1977.

Translator, *Diary of a Film: La Belle et le Bête,* by Jean Cocteau.   1950.

Reading List: *Duncan* by Max Walter Haueter, 1969 (includes bibliography); *A Lone Wolf Howling: The Thematic Content of Duncan's Plays,* 1973, and *Duncan Interviewed,* 1973, both by William B. Wahl; *Tribute to Duncan* by Lord Harewood and others, 1974.

*   *   *

Despite its variety, Ronald Duncan's work has shown a marked consistency and steadfastness of purpose. His first love was poetry, and significantly the fruit of his late middle-age was the epic *Man,* one of the longest poems in the English language. Uniting the wisdom of the humanities with the knowledge and insight gained by science, this five-part work is paralleled, at least in content, only by Lucretius's *De Rerum Natura,* Victor Hugo's *La Légende des Siècles,* and, among modern productions, Alfred Noyes's *The Torch-Bearers.* As it remains virtually "undiscovered," its literary merits have still to be debated. Better known to the public, and of admitted dramatic merit, are the plays, especially *This Way to the Tomb,* which brought Duncan fame, *The Death of Satan,* and *The Catalyst,* which have been performed throughout the world. The fact that most of his best dramatic works are in verse (and this includes *The Catalyst*) bears out his steadfastness, since the vogue for verse-drama has waned. Duncan has also written several volumes of short stories, some sketches of rural life of great charm, and three volumes of controversial and unfinished autobiography.

Ezra Pound, a lifelong friend and a powerful influence, called Duncan "the lone wolf of English letters." The description is apt: for Duncan continued to write in studied poetic forms when his contemporaries were experimenting in obscurity and incoherence; to pursue traditional dramatic form when others were cultivating "the absurd"; and to broaden his scope by composing 63 cantos when his fellows were convinced that the epic was long dead. Moreover, Duncan specialized in both adaptation and translation – once a respectable literary art – in *The Eagle Has Two Heads,* when he brought Cocteau to the English stage; in *Our Lady's Tumbler,* and in the highly effective dialogue, *Abélard and Héloise.* He also wrote opera librettos, the best known being that for Britten's opera *The Rape of Lucretia.*

It must not be forgotten that Duncan was a farmer as well as a writer, and that his knowledge of the land and his empathic understanding of animals (he once worked with pit ponies) was fed into his writing. The following is from *This Way to the Tomb:*

And look, there by the brook
A hot-blooded mare
Has lost her leggy foal,

Watch how her head's thrust back,
On her neck's great muscles;
And the white panic of her eyes.
Her nostrils dilate, she calls, and the furious engine stamps the earth.

Indeed, his non-literary experiences often afforded him insight into the nature of writing techniques. In his revulsion against free verse, he sought a more exact form of expression which should nevertheless avoid being "poetic." "It was an incident in my garden which solved this technical problem for me. I was watering the vegetable garden. I observed that the intensity of the jet of water was governed by restricting the outlet. Though obvious to me, this was a revelation; I realized that intensity in language can only be achieved by running it against a defined form, otherwise you get a dribble and not a jet" (Introduction to *Collected Plays*). At their best, Duncan's verse and prose show, besides wit, a capacity for the direct and illuminating *aperçu*.

—E. W. F. Tomlin

DUNSANY, Lord; Edward John Moreton Drax Plunkett, 18th Baron Dunsany. Irish. Born in London, 24 July 1878; succeeded to the barony, 1899. Educated at Cheam School, Surrey; Eton College; Sandhurst. Served as 2nd Lieutenant in the Coldstream Guards in the Boer War, 1899–1902; Captain in the Royal Inniskilling Fusiliers in World War I; wounded, 1916. Associated with Yeats in the Irish theatre movement, Dublin; Byron Professor of English Literature, University of Athens, 1940–41. President, Kent County Chess Association. Recipient: Harmsworth Literary Award. Follow, Royal Society of Literature, and Royal Geographical Society; Member, Irish Academy of Letters; Honorary Member, Institut Historique et Heraldique de France. *Died 25 October 1957.*

PUBLICATIONS

Plays

The Glittering Gate (produced 1909). In Five Plays, 1914.
The Gods of the Mountain (produced 1911). In Five Plays, 1914.
King Argimines and the Unknown Warrior (produced 1911). In Five Plays, 1914.
The Sphinx at Gizeh, in Tripod, May 1912.
The Golden Doom (produced 1912). In Five Plays, 1914.
The Lost Silk Hat (produced 1913). In Five Plays, 1914.
Five Plays. 1914.
The Tents of the Arabs (produced 1914). In Plays of Gods and Men, 1917.
A Night at an Inn (produced 1916). 1916.
The Queen's Enemies (produced 1916). In Plays of Gods and Men, 1917.
Plays of Gods and Men. 1917.
The Laughter of the Gods (produced 1919). In Plays of Gods and Men, 1917.
The Murderers (produced 1919).
The Prince of Stamboul (produced 1919?).

If (produced 1921).   1921.
Cheezo (produced 1921).   In *Plays of Near and Far*, 1922.
Plays of Near and Far (includes *The Compromise of the King of the Golden Isles, The Flight of the Queen, Cheezo, A Good Bargain, If Shakespeare Lived Today, Fame and the Poet*).   1922.
Fame and the Poet (produced 1924).   In *Plays of Near and Far*, 1922.
Lord Adrian (produced 1923).   1933.
Alexander and Three Small Plays (includes *The Old King's Tale, The Evil Kettle, The Amusement of Khan Kharuda*).   1925.
Alexander (produced 1938).   1925.
His Sainted Grandmother (produced 1926).   In *Seven Modern Comedies*, 1928.
Mr. Faithful (produced 1927).   1939.
Seven Modern Comedies (includes *Atalanta in Wimbledon, The Raffle, The Journey of the Soul, In Holy Russia, His Sainted Grandmother, The Hopeless Passion of Mr. Bunyon, The Jest of Hahalaba*).   1928.
The Old Folks of the Centuries.   1930.
Plays for Earth and Air (includes *Fame Comes Late, A Matter of Honour, Mr. Sliggen's Hour, The Pumpkin, The Use of Man, The Bureau de Change, The Seventh Symphony, Golden Dragon City, Time's Joke, Atmospherics*).   1937.
The Strange Lover.   1939.

Fiction

The Gods of Pegāna.   1905.
Time and the Gods.   1906.
The Sword of Welleran and Other Stories.   1908.
A Dreamer's Tales.   1910.
The Book of Wonder: A Chronicle of Little Adventures at the Edge of the World.   1912.
Fifty-One Tales.   1915.
Tales of Wonder.   1916; as *The Last Book of Wonder*, 1916.
Tales of War.   1918.
Tales of Three Hemispheres.   1919.
The Chronicles of Rodriguez.   1922; as *Don Rodriguez: Chronicles of Shadow Valley*, 1922.
The King of Elfland's Daughter.   1924.
The Old Woman's Tale.   1925.
The Charwoman's Shadow.   1926.
The Blessing of Pan.   1927.
The Travel Tales of Mr. Joseph Jorkens.   1931.
The Curse of the Wise Woman.   1933.
Mr. Jorkens Remembers Africa.   1934.
Mr. Faithful.   1935.
Up in the Hills.   1935.
Rory and Bran.   1936.
The Story of Mona Sheehy.   1939.
Jorkens Has a Large Whisky (stories).   1940.
Guerilla.   1944.
The Fourth Book of Jorkens.   1948.
The Man Who Ate the Phoenix.   1949.
The Strange Journeys of Colonel Polders.   1950.
His Fellow Men.   1952.
The Little Tales of Smethers.   1952.
Jorkens Borrows Another Whisky.   1954.

Verse

Fifty Poems. 1929.
Mirage Water. 1938.
War Poems. 1941.
A Journey. 1943.
Wandering Songs. 1943.
The Year. 1946.
To Awaken Pegasus and Other Poems. 1949.

Other

Selections. 1912.
Nowadays. 1918.
Unhappy Far-Off Things. 1919.
If I Were Dictator. 1934.
My Talks with Dean Spanley. 1936.
My Ireland. 1937.
Patches of Sunlight (autobiography). 1938.
The Donellan Lectures 1943. 1945.
While the Sirens Slept (autobiography). 1944.
A Glimpse from a Watchtower: A Series of Essays. 1945.
The Sirens Wake (autobiography). 1945.
The Last Revolution. 1951.

Translator, *The Odes of Horace.* 1947.

Bibliography: *Bibliographies of Modern Authors 1,* by H. Danielson, 1925.

Reading List: *Dunsany the Dramatist* by Edward H. Bierstadt, 1917; *Lord Dunsany, King of Dreams: A Personal Portrait* by Hazel Smith, 1959.

*   *   *

Lord Dunsany, poet, novelist, essayist, and dramatist, began his theatrical career at The Abbey Theatre with *The Glittering Gate*, featuring two dead burglars who break into heaven, only to find a glittering void and much laughter. Dunsany, whose first literary heroes were the brothers Grimm, Andersen, and the Greek Olympians, achieves his crushingly ironic, frequently terrifying effects by quiet, witty, concise understatement and "free-swinging fantasy," especially in his best plays. *King Argimines and the Unknown Warrior* features a deposed monarch who, through discovery of a mystical sword in the slave fields, regains his kingdom because Darniak's profligate court ignores the prophet's Old-Testament hellfire-and-brimstone warnings. Darniak's god is broken into seven pieces, as the tear song of the downtrodden overwhelms the wine song of royalty at orgy, in a play asking what is majesty, what is nobility. A better play is *The Gods of the Mountain*, which displays the fatalism and hubris of Greek tragedy. It presents a group of beggars impersonating the gods of the mountain (to obtain the good life), being challenged by the worshipping public, then to their terror being turned to stone by the enraged gods, moving the populace to tears for having killed them through their doubts, and begging their forgiveness for having doubted them. *A Night at an Inn* is an eerie study of horrible vengeance by an angry oriental god and its priests who methodically destroy the helpless jewel thieves, in an increasingly crushing, terrifying display of perfect dramatic form, dialogue, and suspense. All three are plays which act as well now as they ever have.

Dunsany's mythological world seen in the plays and tales is wild, grotesque, primitive, suggestive of William Blake's universe; his prose style is admittedly influenced by Herodotus, the King James Bible, and William Morris. One must expend intellectual energy (well worth the effort) to grasp the symbolic meaning underlying Dunsany's frequently stormy gods and hopeless-looking mortals. Edwin Bjorkman (in his introduction to *Five Plays*, 1914) finds the weird beauty, the exuberant imagination based on solid observation, and the exquisite fantasy, characteristic of the poetic rebirth of Ireland. The characters in this beautiful, dreamlike world of cosmic, universal gods, where mortals may indeed be measured against monsters, fairies, and gods (and where Dunsany may be highly interested in ideas), though living at the edge of the world, are as familiar as if they were on an Irish or English street.

Dunsany's fiction continues to enthrall us (we read, dream, then enter into the worlds created) whether it be the story of the beginnings of the world in which creator Mana-Yood-Sushai sleeps (don't pray to him), Fate and Chance play their mist-shrouded game, Mung "signs" mortals to oblivion, Limpang-tung takes his music to the grass and winds and ocean, or Yoharnath-Lahai gives the cities peaceful sleep at night, while Skarl drums incessantly to keep Mana-Yood-Sushai asleep lest the world and the gods be forced to enter their golden galleons and glide down to the sea (*The Gods of Pegāna*); or whether the great spirits of Merimna's warriors inspire Rold to activate the spirit and sword of Welleran to save the city, or whether we weep with the little wild thing giving back her soul because self-centered, materialistic Christians made it impossible to worship God in perfect joy (*The Sword of Welleran*); or whether we "sail" with the bad ship *Desperate Lark* across the Sahara Desert (on wheels) to escape jail for piracy on the high seas and a massacre by the desert Arabs ("A Story of Land and Sea," *The Book of Wonder*).

—Louis Charles Stagg

ELIOT, T(homas) S(tearns).   English.   Born in St. Louis, Missouri, U.S.A., 26 September 1888; naturalized, 1927. Educated at Smith Academy, St. Louis, 1898–1905; Milton Academy, Massachusetts, 1905–06; Harvard University, Cambridge, Massachusetts (Editor, *Harvard Advocate*, 1909–10; Sheldon Fellowship, for study in Munich, 1914), 1906–10, 1911–14, B.A. 1909, M.A. 1910; the Sorbonne, Paris, 1910–11; Merton College, Oxford, 1914–15. Married 1) Vivienne Haigh-Wood in 1915 (died, 1947); 2) Esmé Valerie Fletcher, 1957. Teacher, High Wycombe Grammar School, Buckinghamshire, and Highgate School, London, 1915–17; Clerk, Lloyds Bank, London, 1917–25; Editor, later Director, Faber and Gwyer, later Faber and Faber, publishers, London, 1926–65. Assistant Editor, *The Egoist*, London, 1917–19; Founding Editor, *The Criterion*, London, 1922–39. Clark Lecturer, Trinity College, Cambridge, 1926; Charles Eliot Norton Professor of Poetry, Harvard University, 1932–33; Page-Barbour Lecturer, University of Virginia, Charlottesville, 1933; Theodore Spencer Memorial Lecturer, Harvard University, 1950. President, Classical Association, 1941, Virgil Society, 1943, and Books Across the Sea, 1943–46. Resident, Institute for Advanced Study, Princeton University, New Jersey, 1950; Honorary Fellow, Merton College, Oxford, and Magdalene College, Cambridge. Recipient: Nobel Prize for Literature, 1948; New York Drama Critics Circle Award, 1950; Hanseatic Goethe Prize,

1954; Dante Gold Medal, Florence, 1959; Order of Merit, Bonn, 1959; American Academy of Arts and Sciences Emerson-Thoreau Medal, 1960. Litt.D.: Columbia University, New York, 1933; Cambridge University, 1938; University of Bristol, 1938; University of Leeds, 1939; Harvard University, 1947; Princeton University, 1947; Yale University, New Haven, Connecticut, 1947; Washington University, St. Louis, 1953; University of Rome, 1958; University of Sheffield, 1959; LL.D.: University of Edinburgh, 1937; University of St. Andrews, 1953; D.Litt.: Oxford University, 1948; D.Lit.: University of London, 1950; Docteur-ès-Lettres, University of Aix-Marseille, 1959; University of Rennes, 1959; D.Phil.: University of Munich, 1959. Officer, Legion of Honor; Honorary Member, American Academy of Arts and Letters; Foreign Member, Accademia dei Lincei, Rome, and Akademie der Schönen Künste. Order of Merit, 1948. *Died 4 January 1965.*

PUBLICATIONS

Collections

Selected Prose, edited by Frank Kermode.   1975.

Plays

The Rock: A Pageant Play (produced 1934).   1934.
Murder in the Cathedral (produced 1935).   1935; revised version, as *The Film of Murder in the Cathedral,* 1952.
The Family Reunion (produced 1939).   1939.
The Cocktail Party (produced 1949).   1950; revised version, 1950.
The Confidential Clerk (produced 1953).   1954.
The Elder Statesman (produced 1958).   1959.
Collected Plays: Murder in the Cathedral, The Family Reunion, The Cocktail Party, The Confidential Clerk, The Elder Statesman.   1962; as *The Complete Plays,* 1969.

Verse

Prufrock and Other Observations.   1917.
Poems.   1919.
Ara Vos Prec.   1920; as *Poems,* 1920.
The Waste Land.   1922; *A Facsimile and Transcripts of the Original Drafts Including the Annotations of Ezra Pound,* edited by Valerie Eliot, 1971.
Poems 1909–1925.   1925.
Ash-Wednesday.   1930.
Sweeney Agonistes: Fragments of an Aristophanic Melodrama.   1932.
Collected Poems 1909–1935.   1936.
Old Possum's Book of Practical Cats.   1939.
The Waste Land and Other Poems.   1940.
East Coker.   1940.
Later Poems 1925–1935.   1941.
The Dry Salvages.   1941.
Little Gidding.   1942.
Four Quartets.   1943.
A Practical Possum.   1947.

Selected Poems. 1948.
The Undergraduate Poems of T. S. Eliot. 1949.
Poems Written in Early Youth, edited by John Hayward. 1950.
Collected Poems 1909–1962. 1963.

Other

Ezra Pound: His Metric and Poetry. 1917.
The Sacred Wood: Essays on Poetry and Criticism. 1920.
Homage to John Dryden: Three Essays on Poetry in the Seventeenth Century. 1924.
For Lancelot Andrewes: Essays on Style and Order. 1928.
Dante. 1929.
Thoughts after Lambeth. 1931.
Selected Essays 1917–1932. 1932; revised edition, 1950.
John Dryden: The Poet, The Dramatist, The Critic. 1932.
The Use of Poetry and the Use of Criticism: Studies in the Relation of Criticism to Poetry in England. 1933.
After Strange Gods: A Primer of Modern Heresy. 1934.
Elizabethan Essays. 1934; as *Elizabethan Dramatists,* 1963.
Essays Ancient and Modern. 1936.
The Idea of a Christian Society. 1939.
Points of View, edited by John Hayward. 1941.
Reunion by Destruction: Reflections on a Scheme for Church Unity in South India Addressed to the Laity. 1943.
Notes Towards the Definition of Culture. 1948.
The Complete Poems and Plays. 1952.
Selected Prose, edited by John Hayward. 1953.
On Poetry and Poets. 1957.
George Herbert. 1962.
Knowledge and Experience in the Philosophy of F. H. Bradley (doctoral dissertation). 1964.
To Criticize the Critic and Other Writings. 1965.
The Literary Criticism of Eliot: New Essays, edited by David Newton de-Molina. 1977.

Editor, *Selected Poems,* by Ezra Pound. 1928; revised edition, 1949.
Editor, *A Choice of Kipling's Verse.* 1941.
Editor, *Introducing James Joyce.* 1942.
Editor, *Literary Essays of Ezra Pound.* 1954.
Editor, *The Criterion 1922–1939.* 18 vols., 1967.

Translator, *Anabasis: A Poem,* by St.-John Perse. 1930; revised edition, 1938, 1949, 1959.

Bibliography: *Eliot: A Bibliography* by Donald Gallup, 1952, revised edition, 1969; *The Merrill Checklist of Eliot* by B. Gunter, 1970.

Reading List: *The Achievement of Eliot: An Essay on the Nature of Poetry* by F. O. Matthiessen, 1935, revised edition, 1947, with additional material by C. L. Barber, 1958; *Four Quartets Rehearsed* by R. Preston, 1946; *Eliot: The Design of His Poetry* by Elizabeth Drew, 1949; *The Art of Eliot* by Helen Gardner, 1949; *The Poetry of Eliot* by D. E. S. Maxwell, 1952; *Eliot's Poetry and Plays: A Study in Sources and Meaning* by Grover Smith, 1956, revised edition, 1975; *The Invisible Poet: Eliot* by Hugh Kenner 1959; *Eliot: A*

Collection of Critical Essays edited by Hugh Kenner, 1962; *Eliot's Dramatic Theory and Practice* by Carol H. Smith, 1963; *Eliot* by Northrop Frye, 1963; *Eliot: Movements and Patterns* by Leonard Unger, 1966; *Eliot* by Bernard Bergonzi, 1972; *Eliot in His Time: Essays on the Occasion of the Fiftieth Anniversary of the Waste Land* edited by A. Walton Litz, 1973; *Eliot: The Longer Poems* by Derek A. Traversi, 1976.

*   *   *

T. S. Eliot's influence was predominant in English poetry in the period between the two World Wars. His first small volume of poems, *Prufrock and Other Observations*, appeared in 1917. The title is significant. Eliot's earliest verse is composed of *observations*, detached, ironic, and alternately disillusioned and nostalgic in tone. The prevailing influence is that of French poetry, and in particular of Jules Laforgue; the mood is one of reaction against the comfortable certainties of "Georgian" poetry, the projection of a world which presented itself to the poet and his generation as disconcerting, uncertain, and very possibly heading for destruction.

The longest poem in the volume, "The Love Song of J. Alfred Prufrock," shows these qualities, but goes beyond them. The speaker is a kind of modern Hamlet, a man who after a life passed in devotion to the trivial has awakened to a sense of his own futility and to that of the world around him. He feels that some decisive act of commitment is needed to break the meaningless flow of events which his life offers. The question, however, is whether he really dares to reverse the entire course of his existence by a decision the nature of which eludes him:

> And indeed there will be time
> To wonder, "Do I dare?" and, "Do I dare?"
> Time to turn back and descend the stair,
> With a bald spot in the middle of my hair ...
> Do I dare
> Disturb the universe?

The answer, for Prufrock, is negative. Dominated by his fear of life, misunderstood when he tries to express his sense of a possible revelation, Prufrock concludes "No! I am not Prince Hamlet, nor was meant to be," refuses to accept the role which life for a moment seemed to have thrust upon him, and returns to the stagnation which his vision of reality imposes.

After a second small volume, published in 1919, which shows, more especially in its most impressive poem, "Gerontion," a notable deepening into tragedy, the publication in 1922 of *The Waste Land* burst upon its readers with the effect of a literary revolution. Many of its first readers found the poem arid and incomprehensible, though it was in fact neither. The poet tells us that he is working through "a heap of broken images." He does this because it is a world of dissociated fragments that he is describing; but his aim, like that of any artist, is not merely an evocation of chaos. The poem is built on the interweaving of two great themes: the broken pieces of the present, as it presents itself to a disillusioned contemporary understanding, and the significant continuity of tradition. These two strains begin apart, like two separate themes in a musical composition, but the poem is animated by the hope, the *method*, that at the end they will converge into some kind of unity. Some critics, reading it in the light of Eliot's later development, have tried to find in the poem a specifically "religious" content, which however is not there. At best, there is a suggestion at the close that such a content, were it available, might provide a way out of the "waste land" situation, that the life-giving rain *may* be on the point of relieving the intolerable drought; but the poet cannot honestly propose such a resolution and the step which might have affirmed it is never rendered actual.

For some years after 1922, Eliot wrote little poetry and the greater part of his effort went into critical prose, much of it published in *The Criterion*, the literary quarterly which he edited until 1939. Eliot's criticism, which profoundly affected the literary taste of his generation, contributed to the revaluation of certain writers – the lesser Elizabethan dramatists, Donne, Marvell, Dryden – and, more controversially, to the depreciation of others, such as Milton (concerning whom, however, Eliot later modified his views) and some of the Romantic poets. It was the work of a poet whose interest in other writers was largely conditioned by the search for solutions to the problems raised by his own art; and, as such, it was marked by the idiosyncracies which constitute at once its strength and its limitation.

In 1928, in his preface to the collection of essays *For Lancelot Andrewes*, Eliot declared himself Anglo-Catholic in religion, royalist in politics, classicist in literature: a typically enigmatic statement which indicated the direction he was to give to the work of his later years. 1930 saw the publication of *Ash-Wednesday*, his first considerable poem of explicitly Christian inspiration: a work at once religious in content and modern in inspiration, personal yet without concession to sentiment. The main theme is an acceptance of conversion as a necessary and irretrievable act. The answer to the question posed by Prufrock – "Do I dare/ Disturb the universe?" – is seen, in the translation of the first line of the Italian poet Guido Cavalcanti's ballad, "Because I do not hope to turn again," as an embarkation, dangerous but decisive, upon the adventure of faith.

The consequences of this development were explored in the last and in some respects the most ambitious of Eliot's poetic efforts: the sequence of poems initiated in 1935 and finally published, in 1943, under the title of *Four Quartets*. The series opens, in *Burnt Norton*, with an exploration of the *possible* significance of certain moments which seem to penetrate, briefly and elusively, a reality beyond that of normal temporal experience. "To be conscious," the poem suggests, "is not to be in time": only to balance that possibility with the counter-assertion that "Only through time time is conquered." The first step towards an understanding of the problems raised in the *Quartets* is a recognition that time, though inseparable from our human experience, is not the whole of it. If we consider time as an ultimate reality, our spiritual intuitions are turned into an illusion: whereas if we seek to deny the reality of time, our experience becomes impossible. The two elements – the temporal and the timeless – need to be woven together in an embracing pattern of experience which is, in fact, the end to which the entire sequence points.

The later "quartets" build upon this provisional foundation in the light of the poet's experience as artist and human being. The impulse to create in words reflects another, still more fundamental, impulse which prompts men to seek *form*, coherence, and meaning in the broken intuitions which their experience offers them. The nature of the search is such that it can never be complete in time. The true value of our actions only begins to emerge when we abstract ourselves from the temporal sequence – "time before and time after" – in which they were realized; and the final sense of our experience only reveals itself when the pattern is completed, at the moment of death. This moment, indeed, is not properly speaking a single final point, but a reality which covers the whole course of our existence.

These reflections lead the poet, in the last two poems of the series, *The Dry Salvages* and *Little Gidding*, to acceptance and even to a certain optimism. The end of the journey becomes the key to its beginning, and this in turn an invitation to confidence: "Not fare well,/But fare forward, voyagers." The doctrine of detachment explored in the second poem, *East Coker*, becomes an "expanding" one of "love beyond desire." The conclusion stresses the continuity between the "birth" and "death" which are simultaneously present in each moment, in each individual life, and in the history of the human race. It is true, as the closing section of *Little Gidding* puts it, that "we die with the dying"; but it is equally true, as it also goes on to say, that "we are born with the dead." We die, in other words, as part of the tragedy which the fact of our humanity implies, but we are born again when, having understood the temporal process in its true light, we are ready to accept our present position within a still-living and continually unfolding tradition.

Eliot's poetic output was relatively small and intensely concentrated: a fact which at once confirms its value and constitutes, in some sense, a limiting factor. It should be mentioned that in his later years he devoted himself to the writing of verse plays, in an attempt to create a contemporary mode of poetic drama. The earlier plays, *Murder in the Cathedral* and *The Family Reunion*, which are also the best, take up the themes which were being explored at the same time in his poetry and develop them in ways that are often interesting. *The Cocktail Party*, though still a skilful work, shows some decline in conception and execution, and the later plays – *The Confidential Clerk* and *The Elder Statesman* – can safely be said to add little to Eliot's achievement.

—Derek A. Traversi

ERVINE, St. John (Greer).   Irish.   Born in Belfast, Northern Ireland, 28 December 1883. Served as a Lieutenant in the Royal Dublin Fusiliers in France during World War I; wounded, 1918. Married Leonora Mary Davis in 1911. Drama Critic for *The Labour Leader*, 1910, *The Daily Citizen*, 1911, and *The Weekly Despatch*, 1912, all in Dublin; associated with the Abbey Theatre, Dublin: Manager, 1915–16; settled in London after World War I: Drama Critic for *The Observer*, 1919–23, *The Morning Post*, 1925, and *The Daily Express*, 1929; also, Guest Critic, *New York World*, 1928–29; critic/commentator with the BBC from 1932; Professor of Dramatic Literature for the Royal Society of Literature, 1933–36. President, Critics' Circle, 1929. LL.D.: University of St. Andrews. Fellow of the Royal Society of Literature; Member of the Irish Academy. *Died 24 January 1971.*

PUBLICATIONS

Plays

   Mixed Marriage (produced 1911).   1911.
   Compensation (produced 1911).
   The Magnanimous Lover (produced 1912).   1912.
   The Orangeman (produced 1913).   In *Four Irish Plays*.   1914.
   Jane Clegg (produced 1913).   1914.
   The Critics; or, A New Play at the Abbey Theatre (produced 1913).   In *Four Irish Plays*, 1914.
   Four Irish Plays (includes *The Magnanimous Lover, Mixed Marriage, The Critics, The Orangeman*). 1914.
   John Ferguson (produced 1915).   1915.
   The Island of Saints, and How to Get Out of It (produced 1920).
   The Wonderful Visit, with H. G. Wells, from the novel by Wells (produced 1921).
   The Ship (produced 1922).   1922.
   Progress (produced 1922).   In *Four One-Act Plays*, 1928.
   Mary, Mary, Quite Contrary (produced 1923).   1923.
   The Lady of Belmont (produced 1924).   1923.
   Anthony and Anna (produced 1926).   1925; revised version, 1930.
   Ole George Comes to Tea (produced 1927).   In *Four One-Act Plays*, 1928.
   She Was No Lady (produced 1927).   In *Four One-Act Plays*, 1928.
   Four One-Act Plays (includes *Ole George Comes to Tea, Progress, She Was No Lady, The Magnanimous Lover*).   1928.

The First Mrs. Fraser (produced 1929).   1929.
People of Our Class (produced 1937).   1936.
Boyd's Shop (produced 1936).   1936.
Robert's Wife (produced 1937).   1938.
William John Mawhinney (produced 1940).
Friends and Relations (produced 1941).   1947.
Private Enterprise (produced 1947).   1948.
The Christies (produced 1947; revised version, produced 1948).   1949.
My Brother Tom (produced 1952).   1952.

Fiction

Mrs. Martin's Man.   1914.
Alice and the Family: A Story of South London.   1915.
Changing Winds.   1917.
The Foolish Lovers.   1920.
The Wayward Man.   1927.
The Mountain and Other Stories.   1928.
The First Mrs. Fraser.   1931.
Sophia.   1941.

Other

Francis Place, The Tailor of Charing Cross.   1912.
Eight O'Clock and Other Studies.   1913.
Sir Edward Carson and the Ulster Movement.   1915.
Some Impressions of My Elders.   1922.
The Organized Theatre: A Plea in Civics.   1924.
Parnell.   1925.
How to Write a Play.   1928.
The Theatre in My Time.   1933.
The Future of the Press.   1933.
God's Soldier: General William Booth.   2 vols., 1934.
If I Were Dictator.   1934.
A Journey to Jerusalem.   1936.
Is Liberty Lost?   1941.
Craigavon, Ulsterman.   1949.
Oscar Wilde: A Present Time Appraisal.   1951.
Bernard Shaw: His Life, Work, and Friends.   1956.

*   *   *

St. John Ervine's early work is nearly all in the socio-realistic mode in vogue in Britain until the First World War, employing settings from the writer's native Ulster as well as his adopted London where he arrived to work as an insurance clerk in 1900. Of his novels, *Mrs. Martin's Man* was praised by H. G. Wells, and *Alice and a Family: A Story of South London* was considered by *The Daily News* to be the work of "one of our wisest and most brilliant young novelists." But it was as a dramatist that Ervine made his principal impact. His first play, staged at the Abbey Theatre in 1911, was *Mixed Marriage*, in which the precarious alliance between a Belfast Protestant and a Catholic is shattered when the Orangeman's son proposes to marry a Catholic girl, the father's subsequent inflammatory speeches causing riots and the fiancée's death. Ervine's next major success came with *Jane Clegg*, excellently presented at the Gaiety, Manchester, with Sybil Thorndike as the wife who, after loyally condoning her worthless commercial traveller husband's infidelities and financial irresponsibility, finally breaks with him. With *John Ferguson*, another fine Abbey Theatre play, Ervine returned to an Irish Protestant setting, his powerful presentation of unquenchable religious faith and stoicism in adversity somewhat weakened by the melodramatic elements in the plot.

After World War I, Ervine discovered a forte for light comedy, although *The Ship* is a strong, Ibsenesque portrayal of conflict between a materialistic shipbuilder and his rebellious son. Audiences of the inter-war years, however, preferred such well-groomed Knightsbridge ephemera as *The First Mrs. Fraser*, in which a charming, ruthless divorcée detaches her former husband from his youthful second wife with the help of a little blackmail, or humorous depictions of Ulster country life, as in *Boyd's Shop*, which centres on an old-fashioned village shop, and rivalries for the hand of the shopkeeper's daughter. A better play than these is *Robert's Wife*, a somewhat wordy piece that is slow to develop, but which contains much character interest and presents an engrossing theme: in it the birth-control clinic run by the doctor-wife of the popular local parson becomes the subject of much controversy, especially when the Vicar is offered a Deanery and his pacifist stepson is imprisoned for sedition. Ervine's most intriguing post-war play was perhaps *The Christies*, which turns on an embezzler's release from gaol and its impact on his family, particularly his wife now grown independent of him, and his pious mother who is shocked to find him unrepentant.

Novelist, critic, playwright, theatre manager, biographer, and polemicist, Ervine combined a long life with a remarkably varied literary output which incorporated a volume on writing a successful play, a topical study entitled *If I Were Dictator*, a sequel to *The Merchant of Venice*, and a life of the founder of the Salvation Army. To this medley may be added short stories, essays, reminiscences, as well as pungent reviews contributed to *The Observer* and *The Morning Post*, and innumerable prefaces and introductions, Irish political studies of Carson, Parnell, and Lord Craigavon, a trenchant critical biography of Oscar Wilde, and an immensely long and laudatory one of Shaw.

—William M. Tydeman

FITZMAURICE, George. Irish. Born in Listowel, County Kerry, 28 January 1877. Served in the British Army during World War I. Clerk in the Irish Civil Service, Dublin. Contributed sketches of Kerry peasant life to the popular press, 1900–07; wrote for the stage from 1907. *Died 12 May 1963*.

PUBLICATIONS

Collections

Plays. 3 vols., 1967–70.

Plays

> *The Country Dressmaker* (produced 1907).   In *Five Plays*, 1914.
> *The Pie-Dish* (produced 1908).   In *Five Plays*, 1914.
> *The Magic Glasses* (produced 1913).   In *Five Plays*, 1914.
> *Five Plays* (includes *The Country Dressmaker, The Moonlighter, The Pie-Dish, The Magic Glasses, The Dandy Dolls*).   1914.
> *The Moonlighter* (produced 1948).   In *Five Plays*, 1914.
> *The Dandy Dolls* (produced 1969).   In *Five Plays*, 1914.
> *'Twixt the Giltinans and the Carmodys* (produced 1923).   In *Plays 3*, 1970.
> *One Evening Gleam* (produced 1952).   In *Plays 3*, 1970.
> *There Are Tragedies and Tragedies* (produced 1952).   In *Plays 2*, 1970.
> *The Ointment Blue; or, The King of the Barna Men* (as *The King of the Barna Men*, produced 1967).   In *Plays 2*, 1970.
> *The Linnaun Shee, The Green Stone, The Enchanted Land, The Waves of the Sea, The Terrible Baisht, The Toothache, The Simple Hanrahans*, and *The Coming of Ewn Andzale*, in *Plays*.   1967–70.

Fiction

> *The Crows of Mephistopheles and Other Stories*.   1970.

Reading List: *Fitzmaurice and His Enchanted Land* by Howard K. Slaughter, 1972 (includes bibliography); *Fitzmaurice* by Arthur E. McGuinness, 1974.

*   *   *

George Fitzmaurice was born in County Kerry, Ireland, the son of a Protestant clergyman and a Catholic mother. This, for that time, quite unusual union may partly explain his eccentric habits and rather reclusive life. Fitzmaurice's comedies, whether nominally realistic or grotesquely fanciful, are almost all about Kerry peasants, but his birth prevented him from knowing them intimately, as his personal diffidence prevented him from participating in the literary life of Dublin. His early writings were broad comic sketches of the Kerry peasant and appeared in the popular press from about 1900 to 1907. Ten of these stories have so far come to light, and none is of great literary value, but they do prefigure the content of some of his early plays.

Fitzmaurice's first produced play, the comedy *The Country Dressmaker*, was done at the Abbey Theatre in 1907, where it was quite successful and remained for years a staple of the theatre's repertory. This quite broad comedy, like some of Synge's and many of Lady Gregory's, did not so much celebrate as exaggerate the Irish peasant. That exaggeration became even more queerly pronounced in Fitzmaurice's finest work – *The Dandy Dolls, The Enchanted Land*, and *The Ointment Blue; or, The King of the Barna Men*. In such plays, Fitzmaurice did not proceed ever further into broad quaintness as did many popular Abbey dramatists. Rather, he transformed Kerry in these plays into an inimitably personal landscape that owed more to his own fantastic imagination than it did to sociology or geography. Also, these plays have a rather mature dourness of theme that is startlingly counter-pointed against a gaily playful, if sometimes over-embroidered dialogue. One other fault of some of the plays is an awkwardly handled plot structure which emphasises exposition at the expense of dramatisation. However, Fitzmaurice's work is of a consistently high level, and scarcely poorer than the above-mentioned plays are the sombre four-act tragedy, *The Moonlighter*; several grotesque farces, such as *The Simple Hanrahans, The Terrible Baisht*, and *The Green*

Stone; and the two extraordinary one-act tragi-comedies *The Pie-Dish* and *The Magic Glasses*.

In the early 1920's, Fitzmaurice withdrew his plays from the Abbey Theatre, and in the last forty years of his life received only a handful of productions. Indeed, he actually resisted production of his work. His friend, Seumas O'Sullivan, the poet and editor, did persuade him to allow several plays to be published in *The Dublin Magazine*; nevertheless, when Fitzmaurice died in Dublin in 1963, he was virtually forgotten. The posthumous publication of his seventeen plays in a collected edition revived interest in his work, and since the late 1960's there have been several productions of his plays at the Abbey Theatre. Fitzmaurice is probably now regarded not so much as a follower of Synge, as, indeed, almost an equal. His view of Ireland is as individual as was that of Synge, or of James Stephens, or of Flann O'Brien. Like them, he did not so much report Ireland in his work, as transform it.

—Robert Hogan

FRY, Christopher. English. Born in Bristol, 18 December 1907. Educated at the Bedford Modern School, 1918–26. Served in the Non-Combatant Corps, 1940–44. Married Phyllis Marjorie Hart in 1936; one son. Teacher, Bedford Froebel Kindergarten, 1926–27; Actor and Office Worker, Citizen House, Bath, 1927; Schoolmaster, Hazelwood School, Limpsfield, Surrey, 1928–31; Secretary to H. Rodney Bennett, 1931–32; Founding Director, Tunbridge Wells Repertory Players, Kent, 1932–35; Lecturer and editor of schools magazine, Dr. Barnardo's Homes, 1934–39; Director, 1939–40, and Visiting Director, 1945–46, Oxford Playhouse; Visiting Director, 1946, and Staff Dramatist, 1947, Arts Theatre Club, London. Recipient: Shaw Prize Fund Award, 1948; Foyle Poetry Prize, 1951; New York Drama Critics Circle Award, 1951, 1952, 1956; Queen's Gold Medal for Poetry, 1962; Heinemann Award, 1962. Fellow, Royal Society of Literature, 1962. Lives in Sussex.

PUBLICATIONS

Plays

> *Youth and the Peregrines* (produced 1934).
> *To Sea in a Sieve* (produced 1935).
> *She Shall Have Music*, with F. Eyton and M. Crick (produced 1935).
> *Open Door* (produced 1936). N.d.
> *The Boy with a Cart: Cuthman, Saint of Sussex* (produed 1938). 1939.
> *The Tower* (pageant; produced 1939).
> *Thursday's Child: A Pageant*, music by Martin Shaw (produced 1939). 1939.
> *A Phoenix Too Frequent* (produced 1946). 1946.
> *The Firstborn* (broadcast 1947; produced 1948). 1946; revised version (produced 1952). 1952, 1958.
> *The Lady's Not for Burning* (produced 1948). 1949; revised version, 1950, 1958.
> *Thor, With Angels* (produced 1948). 1948.
> *Venus Observed* (produced 1950). 1950.
> *Ring round the Moon: A Charade with Music*, from a play by Jean Anouilh (produced 1950). 1950.

A Sleep of Prisoners (produced 1951).   1951.
The Dark Is Light Enough: A Winter Comedy (produced 1954).   1954.
The Lark, from a play by Jean Anouilh (produced 1955).   1955.
Tiger at the Gates, from a play by Jean Giraudoux (produced 1955).   1955.
Duel of Angels, from a play by Jean Giraudoux (produced 1958).   1958.
Curtmantle (produced 1961).   1961.
Judith, from a play by Jean Giraudoux (produced 1962).   1962.
The Bible: Original Screenplay, assisted by Jonathan Griffin.   1966.
Peer Gynt, from the play by Ibsen (produced 1970).   1970.
A Yard of Sun: A Summer Comedy (produced 1970).   1970.
The Brontës of Haworth (televised 1973).   2 vols., 1975.
Cyrano de Bergerac, from the play by Edmond Rostand (produced 1975).   1975.

Screenplays: The Beggar's Opera, with Denis Cannan, 1953; *The Queen Is Crowned* (documentary), 1953; *Ben Hur,* 1959; *Barabbas,* 1962; *The Bible: In the Beginning,* 1966.

Radio Plays: *The Tall Hill,* 1939; for *Children's Hour* series, 1939–40; *The Firstborn,* 1947; *Rhineland Journey,* 1948.

Television Plays: *The Canary,* 1950; *The Tenant of Wildfell Hall,* 1968; *The Brontës of Haworth* (four plays), 1973; *The Best of Enemies,* 1976; *Sister Dora,* from work by Jo Manton, 1977.

Verse

Root and Sky: Poetry from the Plays of Fry.   1975.

Other

An Experience of Critics, with *The Approach to Dramatic Criticism* by W. A. Darlington
   and others.   1952.
The Boat That Mooed (juvenile).   1966.
Can You Find Me: A Family History.   1978.

Translator, *The Boy and the Magic,* by Colette.   1964.

Bibliography: "A Bibliography of Fry" by B. L. Schear and E. G. Prater, in *Tulane Drama Review 4,* March 1960.

Reading List: *Fry* by Derek Stanford, 1954, revised edition, 1962; *The Drama of Comedy: Victim and Victor* by Nelson Vos, 1965; *Creed and Drama* by W. M. Merchant, 1965; *The Christian Tradition in Modern Verse Drama* by William V. Spanos, 1967; *Fry* by Emil Roy, 1968; *Fry: A Critical Essay* by Stanley M. Wiersma, 1970.

*   *   *

Familiar with every aspect of stage technique, and with poetry in his plays sounding like poetry, not prose, Christopher Fry burst upon the Bristol theatrical scene in 1946 as a major poetic dramatist with *A Phoenix Too Frequent,* one of the best comedies of manners since the Restoration, a creation with marvelous merits in language as well as drama. Haunting beauty of verse, epigram, and symbolism marks his dialogue as distinctly poetic and his own. At no time did he try to compete with Shakespeare in style, romance, or characterization, as did others at this period, but he preferred developing what has been called "mature contemporary poetry," which took him into the experimental realm, yet which did not hinder his dramatic effects. Fry was concerned about the beauty of life and spiritual validity apart from materialistic reality (his "principle of mystery" according to Derek Stanford), no matter how much Dynamene protested she wanted to die (a rebirth cycle lasting 30 minutes rather than the traditional 500 years), where the rescuer was named Chromis for the color he brought into Dynamene's drab life within the depths of her deceased husband's tomb. Reality, easily identifiable here as Chromis helps life triumph, is not always so easily detected, however.

Fry's first major success, *The Lady's Not for Burning*, won the Shaw Prize and boosted his career throughout the English-speaking theatre world. Fry was intensely concerned about the beauty of life, no matter how often Mendip demanded to be hanged. The poetic drama carries well, as a whole, but the longer, more earnest dialogues and speeches can seem heavy. Fry has abandoned rigid forms and probabilities for the symbolic, and seems at times far from reality, but produced exciting, gripping incidents to create suspense, not only in *The Lady's Not for Burning* but also in *A Phoenix Too Frequent*, *Venus Observed*, and *A Sleep of Prisoners*. Jennet Jourdemayne would confess to nothing concerning being a witch, and Thomas Mendip wouldn't stop confessing to reasons as to why he should die. Jennet, who vowed that facts and facts alone should rule her life, suddenly had to face the prospect that Thomas, trying to protect her by claiming he had murdered the man she was supposed to have turned into a dog, had fallen in love with her. Finally faced with the prospect of having to live, when the "murder victim" turned up alive – of having to face life with the beautiful Jennet, who now would accept him – he stole away into the night with her.

Venus Observed is much more than a mere gathering of the Duke's mistresses to see the eclipse and to review his past life; it is an analysis of the autumn of life, Fry tells us, as *A Phoenix Too Frequent* was of summer, *The Lady's Not for Burning* spring, and *The Dark Is Light Enough* winter. *Venus Observed*, considering the Duke's declining years, is like a musical composition keyed to the slow fading out of life, a definite autumnal mood, dialogue describing the autumn wind in the leaves, and entire scenes (like the first one in the Temple of the Ancient Verities) proclaiming it, in addition to the Duke's description of the planet called Venus as it rises, but Lucifer as it sets, going from goddess to demon. The Duke's telescope hangs ominously over the heads of his guests, cutting him off from a meaningful relationship with his mistresses. The essence of reality is as hard to pinpoint here as it is in the strange event when Pebbleman and the Duke safely escape down the stairs previously consumed by flames.

Fry's major appeal is to the ear, so the action is at times suspended in favor of vigorous clashes of ideas, which are as fierce as anyone's swords, yet there are intensely dramatic moments when the incendiary Rosabel determines to destroy the Duke's astronomy laboratory and when, in *Thor, With Angels*, the Christian waits to be sacrificed if the missionaries fail to persuade his Norse captors to save his life. Intensity concerning the plagues and what they will do to or for the Hebrews, and for the relationship between Moses and Rameses, develops in *The Firstborn*. Fry said that this play featured the movement of Moses to maturity, "towards a balancing of life within the mystery, where the conflicts and dilemmas are the trembling of the balance." The death of Rameses, the firstborn, he suggested, gave the Hebrews freedom and created Moses a great leader. Rameses's qualities of innocence, humanity, vigour, and worth (on the enemy's side) failed to alter the justice of or the need for Moses's cause but asked deep questions about the relationship between the ways of God and the ways of men, as the very dramatic ending shattered the audience.

Significant among his later works is *A Sleep of Prisoners*, a psychological reincarnation of the medieval mystery cycle episodes, set in the dreams of four prisoners in a German-occupied cathedral in France during World War II: with Cain and Abel in the first murder; King David, Joab, and Absalom, in Absalom's rebellion; the Abraham-Isaac story; and the adventure of the three Hebrews – Shadrac, Meshac, and Abednego – in Nebuchadnezzar's fiery furnace. One prisoner "stars" in each of the first three dreams, but all four participate in the last. Also notable are the additional songs and lyrics Fry wrote for the filming of *The Beggar's Opera* and his adaptation of Giraudoux's *La Guerre de Troie n'aura pas lieu* (*Tiger at the Gates*), a view of Helen and the Trojan War debunking the "kidnapped" theory, among other things.

—Louis Charles Stagg

FUGARD, Athol. South African. Born in Middleburg, Cape Province, 11 June 1932. Educated at Port Elizabeth Technical College; Cape Town University, 1950–53. Married Sheila Meiring in 1955; one daughter. Worked as a seaman, journalist, and stage manager; since 1959, actor, director, playwright; Director, Serpent Players, Port Elizabeth, since 1965; Co-Founder, The Space experimental theatre, Cape Town, 1972. Recipient: Obie Award, 1971. Lives in Port Elizabeth.

PUBLICATIONS

Plays

Nongogo (produced 1957). In *Dimetos and Two Early Plays*, 1977.
No-Good Friday (produced 1958). In *Dimetos and Two Early Plays*, 1977.
The Blood Knot (produced 1961). 1963.
Hello and Goodbye (produced 1965). 1966.
People Are Living There (produced 1968). 1969.
The Occupation, in *Ten One Act Plays*, edited by Cosmo Pieterse. 1968.
Boesman and Lena (produced 1969). 1969.
Statements after an Arrest under the Immorality Act (produced 1972). In *Statements*, 1974.
Sizwe Bansi Is Dead, with John Kani and Winston Ntshona (produced 1972). In *Statements*, 1974.
The Coat, with *The Third Degree* by Don MacLennan. 1973.
The Island, with John Kani and Winston Ntshona (produced 1974). In *Statements*, 1974.
Statements: Two Workshop Productions Devised by Fugard, John Kani and Winston Ntshona, Sizwe Bansi Is Dead and The Island, and a New Play, Statments after an Arrest under the Immorality Act. 1974.
Dimetos (produced 1975). In *Dimetos and Two Early Plays*, 1977.
Botticelli (produced 1976).
Dimetos and Two Early Plays. 1977.
The Guest (screenplay). 1977.

Screenplays: *Boesman and Lena*, 1972; *The Guest at Steenkampskraal*, 1977.

Television Play: *Mille Miglia*, 1968.

*   *   *

Athol Fugard has emerged as the major South African dramatist. His particular strength lies in a unique combination of a specific social protest and a universal concern with the human condition. Each of his plays deals with one or several aspects of apartheid, and they all carry a strong condemnation of its inhumanity – *Statements after an Arrest under the Immorality Act* is concerned with the immorality act and *The Island* with prison conditions on Robben Island. To that extent his plays fall under the heading of protest literature, but the protest is in each case widened out to include comments and reflections on aspects of human nature, in particular on the problem of identity.

In this as well as in his use of the Open Space theatre technique (theatre of the mind) Fugard owes much to Samuel Beckett. This is most obvious in *Boesman and Lena*, which has strong overtones of *Waiting for Godot*. The set of apartheid laws dealt with in this play are the ones designed to prevent squatting on South African-owned land by homeless migratory workers. Thus the coloured couple Boesman and Lena wake up one morning to find that bulldozers have arrived to destroy their shack, and they wander off in search of somewhere to sleep for the night. Boesman takes his frustrations out on Lena and beats her. In his excessive emotional cruelty he is a convincing psychological portrait of a victim of a cruel society. Lena on the other hand is beset by the problem of her identity. Stranded on featureless mudflats where they spend the night she is disorientated in time and space and she sees the clue to her identity in recognition by others, "Another pair of eyes," to acknowledge her existence. She establishes a relationship with a dog and a dying old African, but even this meagre contact is destroyed by Boesman who chases the dog away and kills the old man, thus forcing them to flee from the law, the system, and themselves.

In *Sizwe Bansi Is Dead* the problem of identity is further exacerbated by the pass laws. A black migratory worker Robert Swelinzima is "endorsed out" of Johannesburg, i.e., sent back to his homeland because his passbook is out of order. He is naive and honest, and therefore helpless in the maze of South African pass laws, but his smart city friend persuades him to steal the identity-card from the body of a dead man they find lying in the street. Robert thus changes his identity and becomes Sizwe Bansi. This creates great confusion in his mind, and he makes a bid to maintain his name because to him it carries his dignity and human worth mainly in his role as a husband and father. He is, however, persuaded to change his mind by his cynical friend who has become totally disillusioned: he has realized that as black men in South Africa they have no dignity to preserve, and the struggle to simply maintain life must take priority over concerns with dignity and identity.

These problems are, however, not confined to the blacks in South Africa; in *Hello and Goodbye* Fugard explores the effect of Calvinism and the resulting Boer morality on the poor section of the white community. Hester and her brother Johnnie search through their late father's belongings looking for a sum of money they think he has received as compensation for the loss of his leg while working on the railway. They are both prisoners of their society; Hester is a prostitute, and her brother is drawing near to madness as a result of the loneliness he feels as a result of the father's death. The search for the compensation becomes a search for a memory of just one act of love or kindness to compensate for the coldness and sterility of their Boer upbringing. Needless to say they do not find it: Hester returns to her life as a prostitute devoid of all illusions of love, and Johnnie takes the final step into madness and assumes the father's identity because it provides him with a past and thereby an identity. "I'm a man with a story," he says. Thus their attempts to establish an identity through memory are thwarted.

The Blood Knot explores what in the world of today can only be termed a myth – that all men are brothers, we are all descendants of Adam and share a universal mother. Morrie and Zachariah share the same mother but not father: Zachariah is black, and Morrie light enough to pass for a white. The entire action of the play takes place in a one-room shack in the Non-White location of Korsten, near Port Elizabeth. On the realistic level it is Zach's home which is now being shared by Morrie, while on the symbolic level it is a microcosm of South Africa.

Zach, who is illiterate, has acquired a penpal whom Morrie writes to; from her letters it becomes obvious that she is white, and this polarizes them into black and white attitudes. Prompted by this event they explore their roles in a series of games. They leave behind their identities and in suspended time act out the archetypal roles of black and white, forcing each other into extreme caricature. The play acting is stopped by the ringing of an alarm clock, bringing them back to time, history, and reality. The games they play perform a psychological function. Insofar as they force each other into their stereotyped roles and compel each other to see themselves as black or white society sees them, they are in effect acting as Freudian analysts on each other, exposing their neuroses and hopefully, through exposure, curing them. Fugard does not, however, offer this as a solution to the South African problem. He is merely reflecting on the situation, and his preoccupation with role playing and identity problems is a logical result of a situation where – in his own words – "people have lost their faces and have become just literally the colour of their skins."

—Kirsten Holst Petersen

GALSWORTHY, John.   English.   Born in Combe, Surrey, 14 August 1867. Educated at the Sangeen School, Bournemouth, 1876; Harrow School, Middlesex, 1881–86; New College, Oxford, 1886–89; entered Lincoln's Inn, London, 1889: called to the Bar, 1890. Married Ada Cooper in 1905. Travelled in the United States, Canada, Australia, New Zealand, and the South Seas, then briefly practised law until 1895; thereafter a full-time writer. President, P.E.N. Club, 1921. Recipient: Nobel Prize for Literature, 1932. D.Litt.: Oxford University, 1931. Honorary Fellow, New College, Oxford. Honorary Member, American Academy of Arts and Sciences, 1931. Order of Merit, 1929. *Died 31 January 1933.*

PUBLICATIONS

Collections

   The Galsworthy Reader, edited by Anthony West.   1967.

Plays

   The Silver Box (produced 1906).   1909; edited by John Hampden, 1964.
   Joy: A Play on the Letter I (produced 1907).   1909.
   Strife (produced 1909).   1909.
   Justice (produced 1910).   1910; edited by John Hampden, 1964.
   The Little Dream: An Allegory (produced 1911).   1911; revised edition, 1912.
   The Pigeon: A Fantasy (produced 1912).   1912.
   The Eldest Son: A Domestic Drama (produced 1912).   1912.
   The Fugitive (produced 1913).   1913.

The Mob (produced 1914).   1914.
The Little Man (produced 1915).   In *Six Short Plays*, 1921.
A Bit o' Love (produced 1915).   1915.
The Foundations: An Extravagant Play (produced 1917).   1920.
The Skin Game (produced 1920).   1920.
The Defeat (produced 1920).   In *Six Short Plays*, 1921.
A Family Man (produced 1921).   1922.
The First and the Last (produced 1921).   In *Six Short Plays*, 1921.
Six Short Plays (includes *The First and the Last, The Little Man, Hallmarked, Defeat,
    The Sun, Punch and Go*).   1921.
The Sun (produced 1922).   In *Six Short Plays*, 1921.
Punch and Go (produced 1924).   In *Six Short Plays*, 1921.
Loyalties (produced 1922).   1922.
Windows: A Comedy for Idealists and Others (produced 1922).   1922.
The Forest, from his own story "A Stoic" (produced 1924).   1924.
Old English (produced 1924).   1924.
The Show (produced 1925).   1925.
Escape: An Episodic Play (produced 1926).   1926; edited by John Hampden, 1964.
Plays.   1928.
Exiled: An Evolutionary Comedy (produced 1929).   1929.
The Roof (produced 1929).   1929.
Carmen, with Ada Galsworthy, from the opera by Henri Meilhac and Ludovic Halévy,
    music by Bizet.   1932.
The Winter Garden: Four Dramatic Pieces (includes *Escape – Episode VII, The Golden
    Eggs, Similes, The Winter Garden*).   1935.

Fiction

From the Four Winds (stories).   1897.
Jocelyn.   1898.
Villa Rubein.   1900; revised edition, 1909.
A Man of Devon.   1901; revised edition, with *Villa Rubein*, 1909.
The Island Pharisees.   1904; revised edition, 1908.
The Man of Property.   1906; *In Chancery*, 1920; *Awakening*, 1920; *To Let*, 1921;
    complete version as *The Forsyte Saga*, 1922.
The Country House.   1907.
Fraternity.   1909.
The Patrician.   1911.
The Dark Flower.   1913.
The Freelands.   1915.
Beyond.   1917.
Five Tales.   1918; as *The First and the Last*, and *The Stoic*, 2 vols., 1920; as *The Apple
    Tree and Other Tales*, 1965.
The Burning Spear, Being the Adventures of Mr. John Lavender in Time of War.   1919.
Saint's Progress.   1919.
Tatterdemalion (stories).   1920.
Captures (stories).   1923.
The White Monkey.   1924; *The Silver Spoon*, 1926; *Swan Song*, 1928; complete
    version as *A Modern Comedy*, 1929.
Caravan: The Assembled Tales.   1925.
Two Forsyte Interludes.   1927.
On Forsyte 'change.   1930.
Soames and Flag.   1930.

Maid in Waiting. 1931; *Flowering Wilderness,* 1932; *Over the River,* 1933 (as *One More River,* 1933); complete version as *End of the Chapter,* 1934.
Corduroys. 1937.
The Rocks. 1937.
'Nyasha. 1939.

Verse

Moods, Songs and Doggerels. 1912.
Five Poems. 1919.
Verses New and Old. 1926.
Collected Poems, edited by Ada Galsworthy. 1934.

Other

A Commentary. 1908.
A Justification of the Censorship of Plays. 1909.
A Motley. 1910.
The Inn of Tranquillity: Studies and Essays. 1912.
The Little Man and Other Satires. 1915; as *Abracadabra and Other Satires,* 1924.
A Sheaf. 1916.
The Land: A Plea. 1917.
Addresses in America. 1919.
Another Sheaf. 1919.
Memorable Days. 1924.
Castles in Spain and Other Screeds. 1927.
Works. 26 vols., 1927–34.
Two Essays on Conrad. 1930.
Author and Critic. 1935.
Glimpses and Reflections. 1937.
Forsytes, Pendyces, and Others, edited by Ada Galsworthy. 1935.
Autobiographical Letters: A Correspondence with Frank Harris. 1933.
Letters 1900–1932, edited by Edward Garnett. 1934.
My Galsworthy Story (letters), by Margaret Morris. 1967.

Editor, with Ada Galsworthy, *Ex Libris John Galsworthy.* 1933.

Bibliography: *A Bibliography of the Works of Galsworthy* by H. V. Marrot, 1928; *Galsworthy: His First Editions* by G. H. Fabes, 1932; "Galsworthy: An Annotated Bibliography of Writings about Him" by H. E. Gerber, with continuation by E. E. Stevens, in *English Literature in Transition 1* and *7,* 1958, 1967; *Galsworthy the Dramatist: A Bibliography of Criticism* by E. H. Mikhail, 1971.

Reading List: *The Life and Letters of Galsworthy* by H. V. Marrot, 1935; *Galsworthy* by Ralph H. Mottram, 1953; *The Man of Principle: A View of Galsworthy,* by Dudley Barker, 1963; *Galsworthy* by David Holloway, 1968; *Galsworthy: A Biography* by Catherine Dupré, 1976.

*   *   *

As is the fate of many writers', Galsworthy's reputation fell steeply in the twenty years after his death, partly for the purely snobbish reason that he was not born working-class. Today it has greatly recovered, and he is recognized as standing no less high than such of his near-contemporaries as Wells, Ford, and Bennett, and in the theatrical field not so far below the mighty Shaw. Galsworthy's recovery of reputation is in part due to the immensely successful television dramatization of *The Forsyte Saga* which went – and is probably still going – round the world. In addition, there has recently been a more sober reassessment of writers of Galsworthy's heyday. The former glib dismissals of him as genteel, a moralising humanitarian, a man too aware of the "claims of niceness" will not do for those who have been reawakened to *The Forsyte Saga*, or who have seen some of the splendid revivals of his plays.

The Forsyte Saga itself and its pendants (two trilogies and additional single works) gradually written and assembled over more than twenty years, is far from consistent in tone and style. Its early volumes picture a largely departed way of life – of the upper business and professional classes in late Victorian and early Edwardian times – and its later books are a unique evocation of the lives of those same classes in the 1920's. But today's fashionable interest in Victoriana, and nostalgia generally – including perhaps a bit of envy among middle-class readers in the picture of a spacious and expansive world – are not enough to explain the interest in Galsworthy's novels. The books are full of interesting characters in a changing and developing time, resulting in an almost documentary view of the period. There are strong dramatic situations, with a highly rich series of plots. And though Galsworthy is short on humour, he is strong on irony. Even outside the strongly focused story of *The Forsyte Saga* itself (*The Man of Property, In Chancery, Awakening,* and *To Let*), the story of the family and its acquaintances and relations continue in later volumes far from negligible as fiction.

His plays have made an even greater come-back in the 1960's and 1970's, largely based on successes on the stage. Young critics acclaim his dramatic talent, his rich and subtle realism and, as Gareth Lloyd Evans in *The Language of Modern Drama* says, "a quality of associativeness in the language." Evans notes that he is a great master of the pause in dialogue, in creating *tableaux vivants*, and in stage directions which are both evocative and of great practical help to the actor.

Often his plays take a theme of the day, almost from a newspaper account, and present it as a problem, but with a wide imaginative and intellectual breadth. The treatment sometimes attains something approaching poetry, and one may detect the cadences of Synge. In this, in fact, he has been compared to Pinter. Galsworthy himself points out in an essay in the collection *Candelabra* (in *Works,* 1932) that though he sets problems in many of his best plays – *Strife, Justice, The Silver Box,* and *The Skin Game* – he does not try to solve them or to effect direct reform; he seeks only "to present truth and, gripping with it his readers or his audience, to produce in them a sort of mental and moral fermenting, whereby vision may be enlarged, imagination livened, and understanding promoted." Like Shaw, Galsworthy shows society to itself. "He was perhaps," writes Gareth Lloyd Evans, "the last prose dramatist of undoubted importance who realized that prose itself need not be the servant alone of the world of public man but can minister to matters more deeply interfused and less palpable."

—Kenneth Young

GLASPELL, Susan (Keating).   American. Born in Davenport, Iowa, 1 July 1882. Educated at Drake University, Des Moines, Iowa, 1897–99, Ph.B. 1899; did graduate work at the University of Chicago, 1903. Married 1) the writer George Cram Cook in 1913 (died, 1923);

2) the writer Norman Matson in 1925 (divorced 1931). State House and Legislative Reporter, *Daily News* and *The Capital*, Des Moines, 1899–1901; returned to Davenport, 1901, to concentrate on writing: supported himself by writing stories for *Harper's*, the *American*, and other magazines; moved to Provincetown, Massachusetts, 1911; with her husband helped found the Provincetown Players, 1915, and wrote for the company, in Provincetown and New York, 1916–22; lived in Greece, 1922–24. Recipient: Pulitzer Prize, 1931. *Died 27 July 1948.*

PUBLICATIONS

Plays

    Suppressed Desires, with George Cram Cook (produced 1915).   1916.
    Trifles (produced 1916).   1916.
    The People (produced 1917).   1918.
    Close the Book (produced 1917).   With *The People*, 1918.
    The Outside (produced 1917).   In *Plays*, 1920.
    Woman's Honor (produced 1918).   In *Plays*, 1920.
    Tickless Time, with George Cram Cook (produced 1918).   In *Plays*, 1920.
    Bernice (produced 1919).   In *Plays*, 1920.
    Plays.   1920; as *Trifles and Other Short Plays*, 1926.
    Inheritors (produced 1921).   1921.
    The Verge (produced 1921).   1922.
    Chains of Dew (produced 1922).
    The Comic Artist, with Norman Matson (produced 1928).   1927.
    Alison's House (produced 1930).   1930.

Fiction

    The Glory of the Conquered.   1909.
    The Visioning.   1911.
    Lifted Masks: Stories.   1912.
    Fidelity.   1915.
    A Jury of Her Peers (stories).   1927.
    Brook Evans.   1928; as *The Right to Love*, 1930.
    The Fugitive's Return.   1929.
    Ambrose Holt and Family.   1931.
    The Morning Is near Us.   1939.
    Cherished and Shared of Old.   1940.
    Norma Ashe.   1942.
    Judd Rankin's Daughter.   1945; as *Prodigal Giver*, 1946.

Other

    The Road to the Temple (on George Cram Cook).   1927.

    Editor, *Greek Coins* (verse), by George Cram Cook.   1925.

Reading List: *Glaspell* by Arthur E. Waterman, 1966.

*   *   *

When the Provincetown Players opened a subscription theatre in Greenwich Village in 1916, their two major playwrights were Eugene O'Neill and Susan Glaspell. With her husband, George Cram "Jig" Cook, Glaspell was a founder of the Provincetown Players and, before his dissatisfaction with the direction the theatre was taking and their departure for Greece in 1922, she was a substantial contributor to the success of the group. Although she lacked O'Neill's theatricality, at this time, she was much closer to O'Neill in his concern for intense, meaningful drama than any of their contemporaries.

An intelligent and perceptive person, confident in her art and the values she found meaningful, she was most impressive in her thoughtful and theatrically effective one-act plays. *Suppressed Desires* (written with Cook) is a clever satire on the idea of complete freedom in self-expression. *Trifles* combines mystery with a penetrating understanding of a woman's character in a single tense scene. Other one-act plays performed by the Provincetown Players were *The People*, *The Outside*, and *Woman's Honor*.

Her full-length plays, all of which reveal a liberal woman's approach with force and dignity, never quite reached the quality she seemed destined to produce. *Bernice*, although too conversational and contrived, shows the power and thoughtful ingenuity of a loving wife to effect a dramatic and sustaining change upon her husband after her death. One of her most popular plays from this period is *Inheritors*, which dramatizes the problems of a mid-western college in carrying on the liberal ideas of its founder over the conservatism of its present Board of Trustees. It is mainly in *The Verge* that Glaspell approached the emotional struggles that determined O'Neill's playwriting. Searching for an understanding of herself, the heroine is on the "verge" both of insanity and that answer which eludes her. In language and idea the play suggests a power which was never completely dramatized.

After her husband's death in Greece, Glaspell wrote a moving and interesting biography-autobiography of their work together in theatre and his last years – *The Road to the Temple*. She also produced a number of short stories and novels which did little for her reputation as a writer. Her single outstanding work of this later period was the Pulitzer Prize-winning *Alison's House*, a thought-provoking and beautifully expressed play based on Emily Dickinson's life. Her major contribution to American drama and theatre, however, rests almost entirely on those years of the Provincetown Players, an extremely important time in the growth of American drama.

—Walter J. Meserve

GRANVILLE-BARKER, Harley.   See **BARKER, Harley Granville-.**

GRAY, Simon.   English.   Born on Hayling Island, Hampshire, 21 October 1936. Educated at Westminster School, London; Dalhousie University, Halifax, Nova Scotia, Canada, 1954–57, B.A. (honours) in English 1957; Trinity College, Cambridge, 1958–61, B.A. (honours) in English 1961. Married Beryl Mary Kevern in 1965; one son and one daughter.

Harper-Wood Student, St. John's College, Cambridge, 1961–62; Research Student, Trinity College, Cambridge, 1962–63; Lecturer in English, University of British Columbia, Vancouver, 1963–64; Supervisor in English, Trinity College, Cambridge, 1964–66. Since 1966, Lecturer in English, Queen Mary College, London. Since 1964, Editor of *Delta* magazine, Cambridge. Recipient: *Evening Standard* award, 1972, 1976; New York Drama Critics Circle Award, 1977. Lives in London.

PUBLICATIONS

Plays

Molly (as *Death of a Teddy Bear*, televised 1967; revised version, as *Molly*, produced 1977).   In *The Rear Column and Other Plays*, 1978.
Wise Child (produced 1967).   1968.
Sleeping Dog (televised 1967).   1968.
Spoiled (televised 1968; produced 1970).   1971.
Dutch Uncle (produced 1969).   1969.
The Idiot, from a novel by Dostoevsky (produced 1970).   1971.
Butley (produced 1971).   1971.
Man in a Side-Car (televised 1971).   In *The Rear Column and Others Plays*, 1978.
Dog Days (produced 1975).   1976.
Otherwise Engaged (produced 1975).   1975.
Plaintiffs and Defendants (televised 1975).   In *Otherwise Engaged and Other Plays*, 1976.
Two Sundays (televised 1975).   In *Otherwise Engaged and Other Plays*, 1976.
Otherwise Engaged and Other Plays.   1976.
The Rear Column (produced 1978).   In *The Rear Column and Other Plays*, 1978.
The Rear Column and Other Plays.   1978.

Screenplay: *Butley*, 1975.

Television Plays: *The Caramel Crisis*, 1966; *Death of a Teddy Bear*, 1967; *A Way with the Ladies*, 1967; *Sleeping Dog*, 1967; *Spoiled*, 1968; *Pig in a Poke*, 1969; *The Dirt on Lucy Lane*, 1969; *Style of the Countess*, 1970; *The Princess*, 1970; *Man in a Side-Car*, 1971; *Plaintiffs and Defendants*, 1975; *Two Sundays*, 1975.

Fiction

Colmain.   1963.
Simple People.   1965.
Little Portia.   1967.
A Comeback for Stark.   1969.

Other

Editor, with Keith Walker, *Selected English Prose*.   1967.

*   *   *

> Beth: In other words, you do know.
> Simon: In other words, can't we confine ourselves to the other words.

Simon Gray's characters wear literal disguises or play witty verbal games to hide their unexpressed frustrations; they convey their unhappiness with the current state of England by a nostalgia for the past; and, though often married, they lead unconventional sex lives. *Wise Child*, Gray's first play, depicted a heterosexual criminal wearing female garb to elude the police, while his young associate's wigs and games revealed a desire to revert to childhood and make the criminal his "Mum." Murder and a sexual tangle like a grim parody of *As You Like It* reinforce the ciminal's indictment of the English ("the beggars of Europe as we are now"), however skewed his perspective. In this play and his next, *Dutch Uncle*, Gray's wit seems forced from unsophisticated characters, and he uneasily mixes cartoon-like farce with grotesque comedy. *Dutch Uncle* focuses on the impotent Mr. Godboy, who has miscast himself as a literal lady-killer. Again, Godboy seems an ironical spokesman for the strength of the English past: "Five years ago there wasn't a man in this country wouldn't have laid his life down for Winnie, and glad to do it."

Gray turned to more literate characters in his dramatization of Dostoevsky's *The Idiot*, but eliminated much of their loquacious philosophizing that gave the plot meaning. Characteristically he translates Dostoevsky's young radicals into the students who suggest a bleak present and bleaker future in many of Gray's works: "Louts, Madame! That is to say, students." His next play, *Spoiled*, confronts what the stage directions call "the comfortable, middle-class, intellectual" world of his best plays. The married protagonist, a French teacher, tutors a working-class youth while courting him obliquely with verses from Mallarmé in Gray's funniest, most complex writing thus far. The teacher's Pygmalion-like role foreshadows Ben Butley's shaping the taste of his former male student Joey, while the soured vulnerability of middle-class marriage prefigures the heterosexual Simon Hench's adventures with young girls in *Otherwise Engaged*.

The dazzling wit of Butley, a university literature teacher, gives the illusion of order to the messy reality of his life and hides his confused sexuality. He forgets names, continually and insultingly fusing Joey's new lover Reg with his predecessor Ted, presumably to deny Reg any meaning in Joey's life. Though both Joey and the audience get caught up in Ben's power to transform reality, ultimately reality triumphs: Reg makes Joey move from both Ben's office and flat. And despite Ben's Wildean "After all, a man's bound to be judged by his wife's husband," Ben's wife will marry "the most boring man in London," whose novel will be published by Reg, while Ben's own book on T. S. Eliot remains unfinished. Thus, the other characters occasionally best Ben, who hides behind his "marriage," probably non-sexual: "Reg: ... our Joey will be moving out of figures of speech into matters of fact. Ours will be too much like a marriage to be a metaphor." Helped immeasurably by the warmth of Alan Bates's acting, both Ben and Simon Hench (in *Otherwise Engaged*) tricked the audience into equating wit with strength, until the action forces a re-evaluation of the characters. Ben finally refuses to repeat the Joey pattern with a new student: "You're not what I mean at all, not what I mean at all. I'm too old for the likes of you." But this echo of Eliot reinforces Ben's domination by the English tradition.

Simon Hench prefers to ignore his wife's infidelity, though even his epigrammatic wit cannot disguise her pregnancy. Like Ben, he pounces on verbal ambiguities to trivialize or over-complicate real problems like the loss of his wife. He acknowledges romantic passion only through a new recording of *Parsifal*; he spends the entire play trying to hear the music, and when, just before the final curtain, the opening bars "fill the theatre," they mock his reduction of disorderly passion to the artistic statement of someone else. The audience shares Simon's ridicule of the unhygienic, uneducated student Dave, but it becomes clear that Simon's concern with elegant surfaces allows too little attention to the moral content of anything (Simon, like other Gray adulterers, washes off the "stench" of his affairs with quick showers at his club). Since a character is writing a book on British sadism in colonial Africa (the subject of Gray's play *The Rear Column*), Simon may no longer be able to retreat behind a belief in the English past or European art.

Dog Days shares themes and characters with *Otherwise Engaged* and the television plays *Plaintiffs and Defendants* and *Two Sundays*. The wit of an adulterous publisher hides familiar middle-aged terrors; he impresses his monogamous brother with tales of seducing the daughters of Gide and Cocteau, but fails in his one attempt at infidelity. Though Gray's wit cuts as deep as ever, the play is a bit thin; there are too few characters to provide the social and psychological interplay of *Butley* and *Otherwise Engaged*, and the protagonist is exposed beyond future exploration.

The homosexuality in Gray's plays provides a realistic index to the sophisticated London-Oxbridge world they chronicle, but homosexuality pervades the obviously non-U *Wise Child* as well. The theme is crucially linked to Gray's disguise motif: Joey and his lover apparently fool Reg's family and friends in the hearty masculine world of Reg's hometown. That sexual identity can assume convincing disguises here and in *Wise Child* raises questions about its real nature, and about other forms of behavior or belief, like the obsession with England's past. Deeper even than his characters' habit of mockery, belief in this past, perhaps the final illusion Ben and Simon adopt, helps blot out their chaotic present. Gray, the chronicler of the clever and bitter publishers and teachers who shape England's current intellectual life and precariously support its values, has peopled his world with the most savagely witty characters on the contemporary stage.

—Burton Kendle

GREEN, Paul (Eliot). American. Born in Lillington, North Carolina, 17 March 1894. Educated at Buies Creek Academy, North Carolina, graduated 1914; University of North Carolina, Chapel Hill, A.B. 1921, graduate study 1921–22; Cornell University, Ithaca, New York, 1922–23. Served in the United States Army Engineers, 1917–19: Lieutenant. Married Elizabeth Atkinson Lay in 1922; four children. Lecturer, then Associate Professor of Philosophy, 1923–39, Professor of Dramatic Arts, 1939–44, and Professor of Radio, Television, and Motion Pictures, 1962–63, University of North Carolina. Editor, *The Reviewer* magazine, Chapel Hill, 1925. President, National Folk Festival, 1934–35; President, National Theatre Conference, 1940–42; President, North Carolina State Literary and Historical Association, 1942–43; Member of the United States Executive Committee, and Member of the National Commission, UNESCO, 1950–53, and United States Delegate to the UNESCO Conference, Paris, 1951; Director, American National Theatre Company, 1959–61; Delegate to the International Conference on the Performing Arts, Athens, 1962. Recipient: Pulitzer Prize, 1927; Guggenheim Fellowship, 1928, 1929; Clare M. Senie Drama Study Award, 1939; Freedoms Foundation George Washington Medal, 1951, 1956, 1966; Susanne M. Davis Award, 1966. Litt.D.: Western Reserve University, Cleveland, 1941; Davidson College, North Carolina, 1948; University of North Carolina, 1956; Berea College, Kentucky, 1957; University of Louisville, Kentucky, 1957; Campbell College, Buies Creek, North Carolina, 1969; Moravian College, Bethlehem, Pennsylvania, 1976; D.F.A.: North Carolina School of the Arts, Winston-Salem, 1976. Member, National Institute of Arts and Letters, 1941. Lives in Chapel Hill, North Carolina.

PUBLICATIONS

Plays

Surrender to the Enemy (produced 1917).
The Last of the Lowries (produced 1920).   In *The Lord's Will and Other Carolina Plays*, 1925.
The Long Night, in *Carolina Magazine*, 1920.
Granny Boling, in *Drama*, August–September 1921.
Old Wash Lucas (The Miser) (produced 1921).   In *The Lord's Will and Other Carolina Plays*, 1925.
The Old Man of Edenton (produced 1921).   In *The Lord's Will and Other Carolina Plays*, 1925.
The Lord's Will (produced 1922).   In *The Lord's Will and Other Carolina Plays*, 1925.
Blackbeard, with Elizabeth Lay Green (produced 1922).   In *The Lord's Will and Other Carolina Plays*, 1925.
White Dresses (produced 1923).   In *Lonesome Road*, 1926.
Wrack P'int (produced 1923).
Sam Tucker, in *Poet Lore*, Summer 1923; revised version, as *Your Fiery Furnace*, in *Lonesome Road*, 1926.
Fixin's, with Erma Green (produced 1924).   1934.
The No 'Count Boy (produced 1925).   In *The Lord's Will and Other Carolina Plays*, 1925; revised (white) version, 1953.
In Aunt Mahaly's Cabin: A Negro Melodrama (produced 1925).   1925.
The Lord's Will and Other Carolina Plays.   1925.
Quare Medicine (produced 1925).   In *In the Valley and Other Carolina Plays*, 1928.
The Man Who Died at Twelve O'Clock (produced 1925).   1927.
In Abraham's Bosom (produced 1926).   In *The Field God, and In Abraham's Bosom*, 1927.
Lonesome Road: Six Plays for the Negro Theatre (includes *In Abraham's Bosom*, one-act version; *White Dresses; The Hot Iron; The Prayer Meeting; The End of the Row; Your Fiery Furnace*).   1926.
The Hot Iron, in *Lonesome Road*.   1926; revised version, as *Lay This Body Down* (produced 1972), in *Wings for to Fly*, 1959.
The Field God (produced 1927).   In *The Field God, and In Abraham's Bosom*, 1927.
The Field God, and In Abraham's Bosom.   1927.
Bread and Butter Come to Supper.   1928; as *Chair Endowed* (produced 1954).
In the Valley and Other Carolina Plays (includes *Quare Medicine, Supper for the Dead, Saturday Night, The Man Who Died at Twelve O'Clock, In Aunt Mahaly's Cabin, The No 'Count Boy, The Man on the House, The Picnic, Unto Such Glory, The Goodbye*).   1928.
Supper for the Dead (produced 1954).   In *In the Valley and Other Carolina Plays*, 1928.
Unto Such Glory (produced 1936).   In *In the Valley and Other Carolina Plays*, 1928.
The Goodbye (produced 1954).   In *In the Valley and Other Carolina Plays*, 1928.
Blue Thunder; or, The Man Who Married a Snake, in *One Act Plays for Stage and Study*.   1928.
Old Christmas.   1928.
The House of Connelly (produced 1931).   In *The House of Connelly and Other Plays*, 1931; revised version (produced 1959), in *Five Plays of the South*, 1963.
The House of Connelly and Other Plays.   1931.
Potter's Field (produced 1934).   In *The House of Connelly and Other Plays*, 1931; revised version, as *Roll Sweet Chariot: A Symphonic Play of the Negro People*, music by Dolphe Martin (produced 1934), 1935.

Tread the Green Grass, music by Lamar Stringfield (produced 1932).   In *The House of Connelly and Other Plays*, 1931.

Shroud My Body Down (produced 1934).   1935; revised version, as *The Honeycomb*, 1972.

The Enchanted Maze: The Story of a Modern Student in Dramatic Form (produced 1935).   1939.

Hymn to the Rising Sun (produced 1936).   1936.

Johnny Johnson: The Biography of a Common Man, music by Kurt Weill (produced 1936).   1937; revised version, 1972.

The Southern Cross (produced 1936).   1938.

The Lost Colony (produced 1937).   1937; revised version, 1939, 1946, 1954, 1962.

Alma Mater, in *The Best One-Act Plays of 1938*, edited by Margaret Mayorga.   1938.

Out of the South: The Life of a People in Dramatic Form (includes *The House of Connelly, The Field God, In Abraham's Bosom, Potter's Field, Johnny Johnson, The Lost Colony, The No 'Count Boy, Saturday Night, Quare Medicine, The Hot Iron, Unto Such Glory, Supper for the Dead, The Man Who Died at Twelve O'Clock, White Dresses, Hymn to the Rising Sun*).   1939.

The Critical Year: A One-Act Sketch of American History and the Beginning of the Constitution.   1939.

Franklin and the King.   1939.

The Highland Call: A Symphonic Play of American History (produced 1939).   1941.

Native Son (The Biography of a Young American), with Richard Wright, from the novel by Wright (produced 1941).   1941.

A Start in Life (broadcast 1941).   In *The Free Company Presents*, edited by James Boyd, 1941; as *Fine Wagon*, in *Wings for to Fly*, 1959.

The Common Glory: A Symphonic Drama of American History (produced 1947).   1948; revised version, 1975.

Faith of Our Fathers (produced 1950).

Peer Gynt, from the play by Ibsen (produced 1951).   1951.

The Seventeenth Star (produced 1953).

Serenata, with Josefina Niggli (produced 1953).

Carmen, from the libretto by H. Meilhac and L. Halévy, music by Bizet (produced 1954).

Salvation on a String (includes *The Goodbye, Chair Endowed, Supper for the Dead, The No 'Count Boy*) (produced 1954).

Wilderness Road: A Symphonic Outdoor Drama (produced 1955; revised version, produced 1972).   1956.

The Founders: A Symphonic Outdoor Drama (produced 1957).   1957.

The Confederacy: A Symphonic Outdoor Drama Based on the Life of General Robert E. Lee (produced 1958).   1959.

The Stephen Foster Story: A Symphonic Drama Based on the Life and Music of the Composer (produced 1959).   1960.

Wings for to Fly: Three Plays of Negro Life, Mostly for the Ear But Also for the Eye (includes *The Thirsting Heart, Lay This Body Down, Fine Wagon*).   1959.

The Thirsting Heart (produced 1971).   In *Wings for to Fly*, 1959.

Five Plays of the South (includes *The House of Connelly, In Abraham's Bosom, Johnny Johnson, Hymn to the Rising Sun, White Dresses*).   1963.

Cross and Sword: A Symphonic Drama of the Spanish Settlement of Florida (produced 1965).   1966.

The Sheltering Plaid.   1965.

Texas: A Symphonic Outdoor Drama of American Life (produced 1966).   1967.

Sing All a Green Willow (produced 1969).

Trumpet in the Land (produced 1970).   1972.

Drumbeats in Georgia: A Symphonic Drama of the Founding of Georgia by James Edward Oglethorpe (produced 1973).

Louisiana Cavalier: A Symphonic Drama of the 18th Century French and Spanish Struggle for the Settling of Louisiana (produced 1976).
We the People: A Symphonic Drama of George Washington and the Establishment of the United States Government (produced 1976).

Screenplays: *Cabin in the Cotton*, 1932; *State Fair*, 1933; *Dr. Bull*, 1933; *Voltaire*, 1933; *The Rosary*, 1933; *Carolina*, 1934; *David Harum*, 1934; *Time Out of Mind*, 1947; *Roseanna McCoy*, 1949; *Broken Soil*, 1949; *Red Shoes Run Faster*, 1949.

Radio Play: *A Start in Life*, 1941.

Fiction

Wide Fields (stories).   1928.
The Laughing Pioneer: A Sketch of Country Life.   1932.
This Body the Earth.   1935.
Salvation on a String and Other Tales of the South.   1946.
Dog on the Sun: A Volume of Stories.   1949.
Words and Ways: Stories and Incidents from My Cape Fear Valley Folklore Collection.   1968.
Home to My Valley (stories).   1970.
Land of Nod and Other Stories: A Volume of Black Stories.   1976.

Verse

The Lost Colony Song-Book.   1938.
The Highland Call Song-Book.   1941.
Song in the Wilderness.   1947.
The Common Glory Song-Book.   1951.
Texas Song-Book.   1967.
Texas Forever.   1967.

Other

Contemporary American Literature: A Study of Fourteen Outstanding American Writers, with Elizabeth Lay Green.   1925; revised edition, 1927.
The Hawthorn Tree: Some Papers and Letters on Life and the Theatre.   1943.
Forever Growing: Some Notes on a Credo for Teachers.   1945.
Dramatic Heritage (essays).   1953.
Drama and the Weather: Some Notes and Papers on Life and the Theatre.   1958.
Plough and Furrow: Some Essays and Papers on Life and the Theatre.   1963.

Reading List: *Green* by Barrett H. Clark, 1928; *Green of Chapel Hill* by Agatha Boyd Adams, 1951; *Green* by Walter S. Lazenby, 1970; *Green* by Vincent S. Kenny, 1971.

*   *   *

Paul Green's career as a playwright can be divided conveniently into four overlapping periods. Utilizing the history, dialect, superstitions, customs, and beliefs of both white and black inhabitants of his native region in eastern North Carolina, he began by writing short realistic folkplays, comedies as well as tragedies. Noticeable from the outset was a compassion for society's expendibles, those cast-offs who, though victims of social injustice, held within them the dreams and hopes common to all mankind. The full-length *In Abraham's Bosom*, its protagonist a luckless black schoolteacher, was an extended treatment of a one-act play. It was followed on Broadway by *The Field God*, dealing with the oppressive religious orthodoxy among back-country whites.

Tread the Green Grass, a deliberate experiment, turned from realism toward a mythic non-realistic folk drama, but retained the kind of rustic characters who were now his special province. Green's stylized blend of pantomime, dance, ritual, dream sequences, puppetlike movements, fantasy and legend, with music an integral part of the play as with the Greeks, expanded, he believed, the accepted concepts of time and space on the stage. For those plays by him synthesizing the theatrical arts – plays like *Roll Sweet Chariot* (earlier title, *Potter's Field*), *Shroud My Body Down*, and *Sing All a Green Willow* – Green coined the term "symphonic drama," intending apparently to devise an American *Gesamtkunstwerk*.

Meanwhile he did not abandon the commercial theater. *The House of Connelly*, a dramatization of the fluctuating conditions among aristocrats and "poor whites" in the post-Civil War South, conformed to Broadway standards of what a well-made play should be. The anti-war musical *Johnny Johnson* was a collaborative effort with Kurt Weill, and *Native Son* an adaptation of Richard Wright's tragic story of a black misfit in Chicago. For the New York stage he provided an English version of *Peer Gynt*, and for an opera theater in Colorado a translation of Carmen.

The fourth phase began in 1937 with *The Lost Colony*, an "outdoor symphonic drama" produced on the very spot where Sir Walter Ralegh's colonists landed in 1587. Applying the elements of his experimental plays, and superimposing upon an event in history a tightly drawn plot, Green was finally permitted, on the huge open-air stage, the freedom of sweeping folk dances, large choruses, and broad movements of men, women, and children. The throngs of unsophisticated ticket-buyers who attended *The Lost Colony* inspired him to establish away from Broadway a "theater of the people." In 1947 came *The Common Glory* for Virginia, then *Faith of Our Fathers* (Washington, D.C.), and other plays like *Wilderness Road* (Kentucky), *Cross and Sword* (Florida), *Texas*, and *Trumpets in the Land* (Ohio). Four decades after *The Lost Colony*, Green and his followers had used his "formula" for more than sixty similar works, spread out from the Atlantic coastline to California and Alaska. Never satisfied with his last versions, Green constantly revised the annual summertime repetitions of his outdoor plays.

—Richard Walser

GREGORY, Lady; Isabella Augusta Persse Gregory.   Irish.   Born in Roxborough, County Galway, 5 March 1852. Educated privately. Married Sir William Gregory in 1881 (died, 1892); one son. Co-Founder, with Edward Martyn and William Butler Yeats, Irish Literary Theatre, 1899, which became the Abbey Theatre, Dublin, 1904: Director, with Yeats, and with Synge (to 1909), until her death; toured the United States with the Abbey Players, 1911–13. Lived at Coole Park, County Galway. *Died 22 May 1932*.

PUBLICATIONS

Collections

Selected Plays, edited by Elizabeth Coxhead.   1962.

Works (Coole Edition), edited by T. R. Henn and Colin Smythe.   1970–
(Collected Plays) edited by Ann Saddlemyer, in *Works.*   4 vols., 1971.

Plays

The Twisting of the Rope (produced 1901).   In *Samhain*, October 1901.
A Losing Game.   1902; revised version, as *Twenty-Five* (produced 1903), in *Lost Plays of the Irish Renaissance*, edited by Robert Hogan and J. F. Kilroy, 1970; revised version, as *On the Racecourse*, 1926.
The Lost Saint, in *Samhain*, October 1902.
Spreading the News (produced 1904).   In *Spreading the News ...*, 1906.
The Poorhouse, with Douglas Hyde (produced 1904).   In *Spreading the News ...*, 1906.
Kincora (produced 1905).   1905; revised version, in *Irish Folk-History Plays*, 1912.
The White Cockade (produced 1905).   1905.
Hyacinth Halvey (produced 1906).   1906.
The Rising of the Moon (produced 1906).   In *Spreading the News ...*, 1906.
Spreading the News, The Rising of the Moon, and The Poorhouse, with Douglas Hyde.   1906.
The Doctor in Spite of Himself, from a play by Molière (produced 1906).   In *The Kiltartan Molière*, 1910.
The Canavans (produced 1906).   In *Irish Folk-History Plays*, 1912.
The Gaol Gate (produced 1906).   In *Seven Short Plays*, 1909.
The Unicorn from the Stars, with W. B. Yeats, from the play *Where There Is Nothing* by Yeats (produced 1907).   In *The Unicorn from the Stars*, 1908.
The Jackdaw (produced 1907).   In *Seven Short Plays*, 1909.
Dervorgilla (produced 1907).   In *Irish Folk-History Plays*, 1912.
The Workhouse Ward (produced 1908).   In *Seven Short Plays*, 1909.
Teja, from a play by Sudermann (produced 1908).
The Rogueries of Scapin, from a play by Molière (produced 1908).   In *The Kiltartan Molière*, 1910.
The Miser, from a play by Molière (produced 1909).   In *The Kiltartan Molière*, 1910.
Seven Short Plays (includes *Spreading the News, Hyacinth Halvey, The Rising of the Moon, The Jackdaw, The Workhouse Ward, The Travelling Man, The Gaol Gate*).   1909.
The Travelling Man, with W. B. Yeats (produced 1910).   In *Seven Short Plays*, 1909.
The Image (produced 1909).   1910.
Mirandolina, from a play by Goldoni (produced 1910).   1924.
Coats (produced 1910).   In *New Comedies*, 1913.
The Full Moon (produced 1911).   1911.
The Nativity Play, from a play by Douglas Hyde (produced 1911).
The Deliverer (produced 1911).   In *Irish Folk-History Plays*, 1912.
Irish Folk-History Plays (includes *Grania, Kincora, Dervorgilla, The Canavans, The White Cockade, The Deliverer*).   2 vols., 1912.
The Bogie Man (produced 1912).   In *New Comedies*, 1913.
Damer's Gold (produced 1912).   In *New Comedies*, 1913.
McDonagh's Wife (produced 1912).   In *New Comedies*, 1913.
New Comedies (includes *The Bogie Man, The Full Moon, Coats, Damer's Gold, McDonagh's Wife*).   1913.
The Marriage, from a play by Douglas Hyde (produced 1913).
The Wrens (produced 1914).   In *The Image and Other Plays*, 1922.
Shanwalla (produced 1915).   In *The Image and Other Plays*, 1922.
The Golden Apple: A Play for Kiltartan Children (produced 1920).   1916.
Hanrahan's Oath (produced 1918).   1918.

The Dragon: A Wonder Play (produced 1919). 1920.
Aristotle's Bellows (produced 1921). In *Three Wonder Plays*, 1922.
The Image and Other Plays (includes *The Wrens, Hanrahan's Oath, Shanwalla*). 1922.
Three Wonder Plays (includes *The Dragon, Aristotle's Bellows, The Jester*). 1922.
The Old Woman Remembers (produced 1923).
The Story Brought by Brigit: A Passion Play (produced 1924). 1924.
The Would-Be Gentleman, from a play by Molière (produced 1926). In *Three Last Plays*, 1928.
Sancho's Master (produced 1927). In *Three Last Plays*, 1928.
Dave (produced 1927). In *Three Last Plays*, 1928.
Three Last Plays (includes *Sancho's Master, Dave, The Would-Be Gentleman*). 1928.
My First Play (Colman and Guaire). 1930.

Other

Arabi and His Household. 1882.
Poets and Dreamers: Studies and Translations from the Irish. 1903.
A Book of Saints and Wonders. 1906.
The Kiltartan History Book. 1909.
The Kiltartan Wonder Book. 1910.
Our Irish Theatre: A Chapter of Autobiography. 1913; revised edition, in *Works*, 1972.
Hugh Lane's Life and Achievement. 1921; as *Sir Hugh Lane: His Life and Legacy*, in *Works*, 1973.
Case for the Return of Sir Hugh Lane's Pictures to Dublin. 1926.
Coole. 1931; in *Works*, 1971.
Journals 1916–30, edited by Lennox Robinson. 1946; revised edition, in *Works*, 2 vols., 1978.
Seventy Years (1852–1922), edited by Colin Smythe. 1974.

Editor, *The Autobiography of Sir William Gregory.* 1894.
Editor, *Mr. Gregory's Letter Box 1813–30.* 1898.
Editor, *Ideals in Ireland.* 1901.
Editor, *Visions and Beliefs in the West of Ireland.* 2 vols., 1930; in *Works*, 1970.

Translator, *Cuchulain of Muirthemne: The Story of the Men of the Red Branch of Ulster.* 1902; in *Works*, 1970.
Translator, *Gods and Fighting Men: The Story of the Tuatha De Danaan and of the Fianna of Ireland.* 1904; in *Works*, 1970.
Translator, *The Kiltartan Poetry Book: Prose Translations from the Irish.* 1918.

Reading List: *Lady Gregory: A Literary Portrait*, 1961, and *Synge and Lady Gregory*, 1962, both by Elizabeth Coxhead; *In Defence of Lady Gregory, Playwright* by Ann Saddlemyer, 1966; *Me and Nu: Childhood at Coole* by Anne Gregory, 1970; *Lady Gregory* by Hazard Adams, 1973; *Interviews and Recollections* edited by E. H. Mikhail, 1977.

*   *   *

It is not easy to disentangle the role of doyenne of Coole from the prolific writer whose own publications include memoirs, biographies, political and economic pamphlets, editions of diaries and letters, poetry, essays, translations, and forty plays. Nor would Lady Gregory herself feel it was necessary, for to her the collaborations with Yeats and Douglas Hyde, the advice and sympathy offered to Synge, Joyce and O'Casey, the long struggle to bring back

Hugh Lane's pictures to Ireland, the fund-raising, administration, stage management, translations and plays for the Abbey Theatre, the collecting of folklore and mythology – all were necessary aids to the restoration and reawakening of Ireland's ancient dignity and a preparation for political independence. The translation of epics and mythology, the creation of her folk-history plays, even her later children's wonder plays were conceived as educating her countrymen through simple entertainment. Even the delightful one-act comedies, written to accompany the more poetic dramas of her colleagues, reflect their creator's clear-eyed view of the universe and the judicious blending of apprenticeships both at home and abroad. In the spinning of fresh wonders by the daft, delightfully self-appraising but uncritical Cloonfolk of her early plays, she laid the foundation of all her work: simplicity of fable and action, balance and counterpoint of dialogue, easy transition from spare prose to music and poetry, delicacy of feeling interwoven with farcical horseplay, and, above all, a constant stripping away of easy sentiment. The result in all her writing is a blend of folk tradition with historical fact, inviting the listener to suspend disbelief while acknowledging the greater truth to human nature implicit in the fable. It is this unselfish sincerity of purpose which gives strength to all Lady Gregory's writing, and, on those few occasions when she wrote tragedy, even indeed in those painful evocations of Ireland's image-makers which she aptly labelled "tragic comedies," unflinching truth leads to some of her most moving work. Of the one-act tragedy *The Gaol Gate*, Frank O'Connor wrote in *The Saturday Review*, 10 December 1966, "It makes everything else written in Ireland in our time seem like the work of a foreigner."

Because of her close familiarity with the company and theatre for which she wrote, Lady Gregory's plays, if uneven in literary quality, are nearly always eminently playable; frequently, as in her Kiltartan adaptations from Molière, her experiments are more flexible and demanding than those of Yeats and Synge. Bernard Shaw once wrote of her natural gift for writing dialogue, and the fluency with which she wrote her plays and translations also provided an easy, readable style for her essays and journals. The biography of her nephew, Hugh Lane, is both dignified and simple; *Our Irish Theatre*, her account of the early years of the Abbey Theatre, including the battles she waged against censor (for Shaw's *Shewing-up of Blanco Posnet*) and militant patriot (for Synge's *Playboy of the Western World*), does author and movement credit; occasional articles, such as the description for *The Nation* of the outrages of the Black and Tans, are courageous in their outspoken honesty and accurate reporting.

She applied the same demanding code of standards to those about her, providing fine common-sense criticism and practical physical assistance not only for playwrights but for politicians, philosophers, artists, and players. But with typical generosity of spirit, she herself was proudest of the unbroken friendship and support of her life-long collaborator, W. B. Yeats, who in turn confided to his journal: "She has been to me mother, friend, sister and brother. I cannot realize the world without her – she brought to my wavering thoughts steadfast nobility." The life and the work are one.

—Ann Saddlemyer

HANKIN, St. John (Emile Clavering).   English.   Born in Southampton, Hampshire, 25 September 1869. Educated at Malvern College, Worcestershire (house and foundation scholar), 1883–86; Merton College, Oxford, 1886–90 (Ackroyd scholar), B.A. 1890. Married

Florence Routledge in 1901. Journalist: began career as contributor to the *Saturday Review*, London, 1890–94; member of staff of the *Indian Daily News*, Calcutta, 1894–95; afterwards worked for *The Times*, London, and contributed drama criticism and miscellaneous articles to various London newspapers, and wrote two satiric essay-series for *Punch*, London; wrote for the stage from the 1890's; retired from journalism in 1905, settled in Campden, Gloucestershire, and thereafter devoted himself to writing for the stage. *Died* (by suicide) *15 June 1909.*

PUBLICATIONS

Collections

Dramatic Works.   3 vols., 1912; revised edition, as *Plays,* 2 vols., 1923.

Plays

Andrew Patterson, with N. Vynne (produced 1893).
Mr. Punch's Dramatic Sequels (13 skits).   1901; as *Dramatic Sequels,* 1925.
The Two Mr. Wetherbys (produced 1903).   1907(?).
The Three Daughters of M. Dupont, from a play by Eugène Brieux (produced 1905).   In *Three Plays,* by Brieux, 1911.
The Return of the Prodigal (produced 1905).   1908.
The Charity That Began at Home (produced 1906).   1908.
The Cassilis Engagement (produced 1907).   1908.
The Burglar Who Failed (produced 1908).   In *Dramatic Works,* 1912.
The Last of the De Mullins (produced 1908).   1909.
The Constant Lover (produced 1912).   1912.
Thompson, completed by George Calderon (produced 1913).   1913.

Verse

Lost Masterpieces and Other Verses.   1904.

Reading List: Introduction by John Drinkwater to *Plays,* 1923; *Hankin als Dramatiker* by G. Engel, 1931 (includes bibliography); Introduction by St. John Ervine to *The Return of the Prodigal,* 1949.

*   *   *

St. John Hankin came to the theatre by way of dramatic criticism and some slight pastiche sequels to well-known plays, published in *Punch,* but little of this background is reflected in his major dramas. *The Two Mr. Wetherbys,* contrasting the marital attitudes and fortunes of two brothers, is the most tentative and least satisfying of these, but *The Return of the Prodigal* is a stylishly ironic treatment of the return to his ambitious *nouveau riche* family's bosom of Eustace, its feckless but astute black sheep, who proceeds to achieve a very comfortable accommodation with his pompous if respectable relations by means of social blackmail. In *The Charity That Began at Home* and *The Cassilis Engagement* the satire grows sharper but never grotesque, and it is accompanied by a keen compassion which extends even to the least prepossessing of the *dramatis personae*. The action in both plays involves a potentially disastrous marriage, averted in one case by the hero's recognition that the lives of pure altruism embraced by Lady Denison and her daughter Margery are full of pitfalls and only suit the chosen few, and in the other by the shrewd tactics of Mrs. Cassilis who subjects her son's unsuitable fiancée and her vulgar mother to ordeal by house-party in order to expose their inability to merge happily with their social superiors. Hankin is able to score equally off philanthropists and beneficiaries, and (more bitterly) off *parvenus* and snobs, without entirely alienating our sympathies from them, and the result is two confidently good-humoured comedies whose ethical bases still stimulate debate. Humour is virtually absent from *The Last of the De Mullins*, which explores the impact caused when Janet De Mullins, the liberated mother of an illegitimate son, returns briefly to her family home. Despite the topical indictment of patriarchal tyranny and ancestral tradition, the need for excessive recapitulation unbalances the slight plot development, and in many of Janet's ardent utterances the verbal slackness shows that even Hankin could be betrayed into substituting liberal and feminist clichés for originality of expression.

Three of Hankin's pieces were first presented by the Stage Society and two by the Vedrenne-Barker management at the Court Theatre, but it is doubtful if their author maintained an earnest belief in the social and moral function of the New Drama. However, like Shaw, he did replace the accepted romantically theatrical conventions of the previous age with the truthful presentation of the realities of actual human conduct and character. His work can perhaps be most helpfully viewed as a thorough-going extension of H. A. Jones's and Pinero's commentaries on upper- and middle-class hypocrisies and ruthlessness, unweakened in its unremittingly pragmatic conclusions by Pinero's evasive sentimentality or the complacent conservatism of Jones. Hankin was doubtless encouraged in his approach to drama by the naturalistic movement: his crises are seemingly casually motivated and credibly resolved, his characterisations are generally individualised and wrought with considerable subtlety, and his dialogue is rarely marred by the urge to engineer strongly emphasized dramatic climaxes. He rarely passed judgement: he was normally careful to preserve strict authorial control even while siding with the rebel, and his moral comments are conveyed only by implication. While not the work of a theatrical revolutionary, Hankin's plays deserve recognition as something other than mere muted renderings of Wilde's detached comedy of social observation.

—William M. Tydeman

HANSBERRY, Lorraine (Vivian). American. Born in Chicago, Illinois, 19 May 1930. Educated at the Art Institute, Chicago; University of Wisconsin, Madison, 1948. Married Robert Barron Nemiroff in 1953 (divorced, 1964). Worked as a journalist and editor. Recipient: New York Drama Critics Circle Award, 1959. *Died 12 January 1965.*

Collections

Les Blancs: The Collected Last Plays (includes *Les Blancs, The Drinking Gourd, What Use are Flowers?*), edited by Robert Nemiroff. 1972.

Plays

> *A Raisin in the Sun* (produced 1959).   1959.
> *The Sign in Sidney Brustein's Window* (produced 1964).   1965.
> *To Be Young, Gifted, and Black: A Portrait of Hansberry in Her Own Words*, adapted by Robert Nemiroff (produced 1969).   1971.
> *Les Blancs*, edited by Robert Nemiroff (produced 1970).   In *Les Blancs* (collection), 1972.

Screenplay: *A Raisin in the Sun*, 1961.

Other

> *The Movement: Documentary of a Struggle for Equality.*   1964; as *A Matter of Colour: Documentary of the Struggles for Racial Equality in the USA*, 1965.
> *To Be Young, Gifted, and Black: Hansberry in Her Own Words*, adapted by Robert Nemiroff.   1969.

*   *   *

The importance of Lorraine Hansberry as an American dramatist rests with two plays, *A Raisin in the Sun* and *The Sign in Sidney Brustein's Window*, both produced during her tragically short life of thirty-four years. The first, by all measurements, was a major success. The second was a commercial failure, meeting only limited critical support. There were two posthumous productions, the effective but somewhat pasted-up collection presented as *To Be Young, Gifted, and Black* and *Les Blancs*, more or less complete but obviously still unfinished.

Lorraine Hansberry is an important, though minor, figure in American drama if for no more than the fact that she wrote an outstanding play of substantial popular and critical success as a Black writer contributing to an essentially white-oriented commercial theatre during a period when the Black identity in American letters was at a very delicate stage. It was a period when a strong pull existed between those Blacks who would prefer to stand on their achievements as artists, irrespective of race, and those who would prefer to take a stand, artistic as well as social or political, because of the very fact of their blackness. It is clear, as one encounters the opinions of critics who evaluate Lorraine Hansberry as a Black writer, that a dichotomy exists. While she herself was completely uncontroversial – she was indeed no LeRoi Jones nor Dick Gregory – and avoided the pointedly racial-political involvements associated with Black writers of her era, there is some controversy as to whether or not her two major plays were merely outstanding, relatively conventional, dramatic works of a fine young American playwright of promising talent who happened to be black, or were the works of a dedicated Black playwright treating subjects directly involved in the causes espoused by the writers overtly conscious of their race.

A Raisin in the Sun at first glance would suggest that Hansberry is squarely in the camp of those Black writers choosing to place onstage the social issue of the ghetto-trapped family. The specifications are there from the exasperated young Black male, fumbling and frustrated in The Man's world, to the matriarch holding the fatherless family together. But Lorraine Hansberry has actually composed a solid, almost conventional "well-made" play, centering upon a theme which could have at one time as easily been Irish, Jewish, or Oriental, but which happens, given the time it was written and the knowledge of its creator, to be Black. True, the plight of the Youngers, a serious and prevalent American theme, exists almost entirely *because* they are black, but the confrontations, save for that with the rather pitiful Linder, who brings the outside forces briefly into the Youngers' living room, remain offstage or are postponed until after the curtain falls. Audience interest in the Youngers is in their human, not their racial, qualities.

The Sign in Sidney Brustein's Window is a sensitive comedy far removed in subject and intent from *Raisin*. The world of a white Jewish flat in Greenwich Village, visited by attractive, if not always "normal" characters and centered upon a strictly local political campaign, is not the usual subject associated with a Black writer intent on attacks against the social injustices of a racist society. Hansberry attacks petty individual prejudices, those against Black or sexual deviant, as well as personal selfishness which can be fatal to those one ought to love.

It is impossible to know where Lorraine Hansberry might have gone. Perhaps she would have become "radicalized," or perhaps she was already more radicalized than we recognize. It hardly matters. Judgment of her two important plays shows that she was a writer of singular promise, a very important voice in an uncertain historical and social period.

—Jordan Y. Miller

HART, Moss. American.   Born in New York City, 24 October 1904. Educated in New York public schools. Married the actress Kitty Carlisle in 1946; one son and one daughter. Worked with the Thalian Players, New York, then as a floor walker in a clothing store, and directed little theatre groups in Brooklyn and Newark, New Jersey; full-time playwright from 1930, often in collaboration with George S. Kaufman; later also produced and directed for the Broadway stage. Recipient: Megrue Prize, 1930; Pulitzer Prize, with George S. Kaufman, 1937; New York Drama Critics Circle Award, for direction, 1955; Antoinette Perry Award, for direction, 1957. *Died 20 December 1961.*

PUBLICATIONS

Plays

The Hold-Up Man (produced 1923).
Jonica, with Dorothy Heyward, music by Joseph Meyer, lyrics by William Moll (produced 1930).
No Retreat (produced 1930).
Once in a Lifetime, with George S. Kaufman (produced 1930).   1930.
Face the Music, music by Irving Berlin (produced 1932).
As Thousands Cheer, with Irving Berlin, music and lyrics by Edward Heyman and Richard Myers (produced 1933).
The Great Waltz, from a play by Ernst Marischka and others, music by Johann Strauss (produced 1934).
Merrily We Roll Along, with George S. Kaufman (produced 1934).   1934.
The Paperhanger, with George S. Kaufman.   1935(?).
Jubilee, music by Cole Porter (produced 1935).
The Show Is On (revue), with others (produced 1936).
You Can't Take It with You, with George S. Kaufman (produced 1936).   1937.
I'd Rather Be Right, with George S. Kaufman, music by Richard Rodgers, lyrics by Lorenz Hart (produced 1937).   1937.

The Fabulous Invalid, with George S. Kaufman (produced 1938).   1938.

The American Way, with George S. Kaufman, music by Oscar Levant (produced 1939).   1939.

The Man Who Came to Dinner, with George S. Kaufman (produced 1939).   1940.

George Washington Slept Here, with George S. Kaufman (produced 1940).   1940.

Lady in the Dark, music by Kurt Weill, lyrics by Ira Gershwin (produced 1941).   1941.

Winged Victory (produced 1943).   1943.

Christopher Blake (produced 1946).   1947.

Light Up the Sky (produced 1948).   1949.

The Climate of Eden, from the novel *Shadows Move among Them* by Edgar Mittelholzer (produced 1952).   1953.

Screenplays: *Winged Victory,* 1944; *Gentleman's Agreement,* 1947; *Hans Christian Andersen,* with Myles Connolly, 1952; *A Star Is Born,* 1954; *Prince of Players,* 1954.

Other

Act One (autobiography).   1959.

*   *   *

Moss Hart's first play, *The Hold-Up Man,* written at 19, folded in Chicago, but his *Once in a Lifetime* caught Sam Harris's eye, he was given George S. Kaufman as a collaborator (a story wittily told in Hart's autobiography, *Act One*), and the rest is history. Their play *Once in a Lifetime* was a success and the team continued with *Merrily We Roll Along,* the classic *You Can't Take It With You, The Man Who Came to Dinner,* and *George Washington Slept Here.*

Then Hart, never secure alone, sought other collaborators and produced important work. Having written *Face the Music* and *As Thousands Cheer* with Irving Berlin, *Jubilee* with Cole Porter, and *I'd Rather Be Right* with Kaufman and Rodgers and Lorenz Hart, he carried on his musical success in 1941 with Kurt Weill and Ira Gershwin: *Lady in the Dark.* This was probably the highlight of his own musical work though he directed such hits by others as Irving Berlin's *Miss Liberty* (1949) and the Lerner and Loewe blockbusters *My Fair Lady* (1956) and *Camelot* (1960). In 1943 he created a "spectacle in two acts and seventeen scenes" for the USAF called *Winged Victory,* starring 300 servicemen, including Red Buttons and Lee J. Cobb. "The Army Emergency Relief Fund needs the money," was Lewis Nichols' review in *The Times,* but he patriotically if not critically added that it was "a wonderful show." After World War II Hart gave us *Christopher Blake* (1946) – which can be forgotten. *Light Up the Sky,* however, is one of my favorite plays about theatre folk – slick, sentimental, simplistic, and very funny. It is a delightful expansion of real life. In *The Climate of Eden,* "Eden" turns out to be the British Guiana mission of Gregory Hawke's uncle, and there our hero, feeling guilty for his wife's death, is obsessed with various problems. More interesting are Hart's films such as *Gentleman's Agreement* and *A Star Is Born.*

Moss Hart was always the innovative sort of theatre man who could call for four revolving stages where no one had ever used more than two before – and the dependent sort of theatre man that leaned on collaborators but also got four times as much out of them, and himself, as had ever been obtained before. He was also the sort who could submit *Once in a Lifetime* to six managers (all of whom accepted it) and then sell it to Sam Harris with the understanding that Kaufman would collaborate.

That collaboration produced one of the best comedies of the American theatre, *The Man Who Came to Dinner.* Of course, "real life" made them a gift of the inimitable Alexander Woollcott, but *they* knew what to do with him. It also takes a crack at Noël Coward, one of the Marx Brothers, the Lizzie Borden story (which is rather ineptly worked in), and the Middle West, would-be writers, fussy nurses, "the most chic actress on the New York or

London stage," etc. The plot (largely Hart's?) is carpentry, but the wisecracks (mostly Kaufman's) are pure gold. Add Monty Woolley (who, said Richard Severo in *The New York Herald Tribune* of 7 May 1963, "wore his beard with the aplomb of a Madison Ave. Santa Claus," brought from Yale some "class" Kaufman and Hart always lacked, and "reduced the nurse ... to the potency of a pound of wet Kleenex") and the audience was limp with laughter. Without him the play is inevitably much less, but is still runs beautifully.

—Leonard R. N. Ashley

HECHT, Ben. American. Born in New York City, 28 February 1894; moved with his family to Chicago, then to Racine, Wisconsin. Educated at Racine High School. Married 1) Marie Armstrong in 1915 (divorced, 1925), one daughter; 2) Rose Caylor in 1925. Journalist, *Chicago Journal*, 1910–14; Reporter, 1914–18, Correspondent in Berlin, 1918–19, and Columnist, 1919–23, *Chicago News*; Founding Editor and Publisher, *Chicago Literary Times*, 1923–25; thereafter a full-time writer for the stage, and for motion pictures from 1933; formed a production company with Charles MacArthur, 1934; Columnist ("1001 Afternoons in Manhattan") *PM* newspaper, Long Island, New York, 1940–41. Active Zionist from 1946: Co-Chairman, American League for a Free Palestine. Recipient: Academy Award, 1928, 1936. *Died 18 April 1964.*

PUBLICATIONS

Plays

The Wonder Hat: A Harlequinade, with Kenneth Sawyer Goodman (produced 1916). 1920.
The Hero of Santa Maria, with Kenneth Sawyer Goodman (produced 1916–17?). 1920.
The Master Poisoner, with Maxwell Bodenheim, in *Minna and Myself,* by Bodenheim. 1918.
The Hand of Siva, with Kenneth Sawyer Goodman. 1920.
The Egoist (produced 1922).
The Wonder Hat and Other One-Act Plays (includes *The Two Lamps, An Idyll of the Shops, The Hand of Siva, The Hero of Santa Maria*), with Kenneth Sawyer Goodman. 1925.
The Stork, from a play by Laszlo Fodor (produced 1925).
Christmas Eve: A Morality Play. 1928.
The Front Page, with Charles MacArthur (produced 1928). 1928.
Twentieth Century, with Charles MacArthur (produced 1932). 1932.
The Great Magoo, with Gene Fowler (produced 1932). 1933.
Jumbo, with Charles MacArthur, music by Richard Rodgers, lyrics by Lorenz Hart (produced 1935). 1935.
To Quito and Back (produced 1937). 1937.
Ladies and Gentlemen, with Charles MacArthur, from a play by Ladislas Bush-Fekete (produced 1939). 1941.

Fun to Be Free: A Patriotic Pageant, with Charles MacArthur (produced 1941). 1941.
Lily of the Valley (produced 1942).
We Will Never Die (produced 1943). 1943.
Wuthering Heights (screenplay), with Charles MacArthur, in *Twenty Best Film Plays,* edited by John Gassner and Dudley Nichols. 1943.
A Tribute to Gallantry, in *The Best One-Act Plays of 1943,* edited by Margaret Mayorga. 1943.
Miracle of the Pullman (broadcast 1944). In *The Best One-Act Plays of 1944,* edited by Margaret Mayorga, 1945.
Swan Song, with Charles MacArthur, from a story by Ramon Romero and Harriett Hinsdale (produced 1946). In *Stage Works of MacArthur,* 1974.
A Flag Is Born, music by Kurt Weill (produced 1946).
Spellbound (screenplay), with Angus MacPhail, in *Best Film Plays 1945,* edited by John Gassner and Dudley Nichols. 1946.
Hazel Flagg, music by Jule Styne, lyrics by Bob Hilliard, from a story by James Street and the screenplay *Nothing Sacred* (produced 1953). 1953.
Winkelberg (produced 1958). 1958.

Screenplays: *Underworld,* with others, 1927; *The Big Noise,* with George Marion, Jr., and Tom J. Geraghty, 1928; *The Unholy Night,* with others, 1929; *Roadhouse Nights,* with Garrett Fort, 1930; *The Great Gabbo,* with Hugh Herbert, 1930; *The Front Page,* with Charles MacArthur, 1931; *Scarface, Shame of the Nation,* 1932; *Design for Living,* 1933; *Hallelujah, I'm a Bum,* 1933; *Topaze,* 1933; *Viva Villa!,* 1934; *Twentieth Century,* with Charles MacArthur, 1934; *Crime Without Passion,* with Charles MacArthur, 1934; *The Scoundrel,* with Charles MacArthur, 1935; *Barbary Coast,* with Charles MacArthur, 1935; *The Florentine Dagger,* 1935; *Once in a Blue Moon,* with Charles MacArthur, 1935; *Soak the Rich,* with Charles MacArthur, 1936; *Nothing Sacred,* 1937; *Goldwyn Follies,* with others, 1938; *Gunga Din,* with others, 1939; *Lady of the Tropics,* 1939; *Wuthering Heights,* with Charles MacArthur, 1939; *It's a Wonderful World,* with Herman J. Mankiewicz, 1939; *Let Freedom Ring,* 1939; *Until I Die,* with Charles MacArthur, 1940; *Angels over Broadway,* 1940; *Comrade X,* with Charles Lederer and Walter Reisch, 1940; *Lydia,* with others, 1941; *Tales of Manhattan,* with others, 1942; *The Black Swan,* with Seton I. Miller, 1942; *China Girl,* with Melville Crossman, 1942; *Spellbound,* with Angus MacPhail, 1945; *Specter of the Rose,* 1946; *Notorious,* 1946; *Her Husband's Affairs,* with Charles Lederer, 1947; *Kiss of Death,* with Charles Lederer and Eleazar Lipsky, 1947; *Ride the Pink Horse,* with Charles Lederer, 1947; *The Miracle of the Bells,* with Quentin Reynolds, 1948; *Whirlpool,* with Andrew Solt, 1950; *Where the Sidewalk Ends,* with others, 1950; *Actors and Sin,* 1952; *The Indian Fighter,* with Frank Davis and Ben Kadish, 1955; *Ulysses,* with others, 1955; *Miracle in the Rain,* 1956; *The Iron Petticoat,* 1956; *Legend of the Lost,* with Robert Presnell, Jr., 1957; *A Farewell to Arms,* 1957; *Queen of Outer Space,* with Charles Beaumont, 1958; *Mutiny on the Bounty* (uncredited), with others, 1962; *Circus World,* with others, 1964; *Casino Royale* (uncredited), with others, 1967.

Radio Play: *Miracle of the Pullman,* 1944.

Fiction

Erik Dorn. 1921.
Fantazius Mallare: A Mysterious Oath. 1922.
A Thousand and One Afternoons in Chicago (stories). 1922.
Gargoyles. 1922.
The Florentine Dagger. 1923.

Humpty Dumpty. 1924.
The Kingdom of Evil: A Continuation of the Journal of Fantazius Mallare. 1924.
Cutie, A Warm Mamma, with Maxwell Bodenheim. 1924.
Broken Necks, Containing More 1001 Afternoons (stories). 1926.
Count Bruga. 1926.
A Jew in Love. 1931.
The Champion from Far Away (stories). 1931.
Actor's Blood (stories). 1936.
A Book of Miracles (stories). 1939.
1001 Afternoons in New York. 1941.
Miracle in the Rain. 1943.
I Hate Actors! 1944; as *Hollywood Mystery!,* 1946.
The Collected Stories. 1945.
Concerning a Woman of Sin and Other Stories. 1947.
The Cat That Jumped Out of the Story (juvenile). 1947.
The Sensualists. 1959.
In the Midst of Death. 1964.

Other

A Guide for the Bedevilled. 1944.
A Child of the Century (autobiography). 1954.
Charlie: The Improbable Life and Times of Charles MacArthur. 1957.
A Treasury of Ben Hecht. 1959.
Perfidy. 1961.
Gaily, Gaily (autobiography). 1963.
Letters from Bohemia. 1964.

*   *   *

Ben Hecht began his writing career before the "audience renaissance," a term he used in a 1963 *Theatre Arts* article for the evolution of "play lovers" into "play decipherers," a process which undermined the status of the theatre as "our most ancient bridgehead of lucidity." Hecht's earliest literary values, influenced by his career in journalism, taught him that "whatever confusions possessed the other arts, the art of the theatre remained basically that of a Western Union telegram – terse and informative." These principles were to govern most of his dramatic output, and partially explain why such a disciplined, intelligent, and prolific writer has only intermittently attracted critical attention.

The journalist's attention to incident and detail, the "katatonic armor" that shields him in daily contact with the extremes and eccentricities of life, and the pragmatism of shaping these into a "story" are all prominent factors in his plays. Hecht's most famous collaboration with Charles MacArthur, *The Front Page,* has often been dismissed as a romantic melodrama about journalism; however, it also generates a poignant dilemma between individual values and public significance, articulated with a vigorous realism that was all but unique on Broadway in 1928. *To Quito and Back,* considered by many to be the best play that Hecht wrote alone, also introduces a journalist as a secondary character to sift out a situation in Ecuador similar to that of the Spanish Civil War. However, the diversity of content and style in Hecht's drama is almost as great as in his screenplays. His early one-act plays (written 1914–18) show experimentation with various types of stylisation then fashionable in "art theatres," a tendency which declines after the death of his first collaborator, the more experienced playwright Kenneth Sawyer Goodman, in 1918. Working with MacArthur, Hecht produced the Hollywood satire *Twentieth Century,* the musical extravaganza *Jumbo,* and the murder melodrama *Swan Song*; with Gene Fowler, he wrote the "dramatic cartoon"

The Great Magoo; with Kurt Weill, he collaborated in the pageant of Jewish history *A Flag Is Born*, which gave a starring part to the young Marlon Brando and netted nearly one million dollars for the Zionist cause in 1946. Several of Hecht's later plays are also graveyard dramas: *Lily of the Valley* is a purgatorial allegory, and his last play, *Winkelberg*, is a work of expressionistic nostalgia. This stylistic eclecticism of Hecht's drama is reflected in the range of collaborators with whom he proved compatible, but his claim to a place in American dramatic history must rest on his tough, anecdotal realism.

Antedating Hecht's "audience renaissance" was the "Chicago literary renaissance" to which he was a central contributor, and which provided the context of *Winkelberg*. Criticism of the "clever saccharinity" of the Chicago school is substantiated by a reading of his earliest prose fiction, from *Erik Dorn* to *Gargoyles*. Hecht's foundation editorship of the *Chicago Literary Times* (which he also printed, published, managed, proofed, and helped distribute) was a watershed in his career, and it was a much less pretentious Hecht who emerged to write *The Front Page*; his original purpose in that play was to reflect his "intellectual disdain of and superiority to the Newspaper," but a much more honest, frontal attitude to his writing developed, resulting in his finest novel, *A Jew in Love*, as well as the best of his short stories.

Ironically, it was only late in his career that Hecht found a commitment that would have given cohesive solidity to his central output. Jews and journalists abound in his early novels and plays, but it is only in his later autobiographical writings that he deliberately anatomises his own identity as an American Jew. However, the growth of this commitment during World War II resulted in one of his finest books: *A Guide for the Bedevilled* confronts anti-Semitism with a sense of stylistic strategy and a passionate urbanity that recall the best prose writing of Bernard Shaw.

—Howard McNaughton

HELLMAN, Lillian (Florence).   American.   Born in New Orleans, Louisiana, 20 June 1907. Educated at New York University, 1923–25; Columbia University, New York, 1926. Married the writer Arthur Kober in 1925 (divorced, 1932). Reader, Horace Liveright, publishers, New York, 1924–25; Reviewer, New York *Herald Tribune*, 1925–28; Theatrical Play Reader, 1927–30; Reader, MGM, 1930–32. Taught at Yale University, New Haven, Connecticut, 1966; and at Harvard University, Cambridge, Massachusetts; Massachusetts Institute of Technology, Cambridge; and the University of California, Berkeley. Recipient: New York Drama Critics Circle Award, 1941, 1960; Brandeis University Creative Arts Award, 1960; National Institute of Arts and Letters Gold Medal, 1964; Paul Robeson Award, 1976. M.A.: Tufts College, Medford, Massachusetts, 1940; LL.D.: Wheaton College, Norton, Massachusetts, 1961; Rutgers University, New Brunswick, New Jersey, 1963; Brandeis University, Waltham, Massachusetts, 1965; Yale University, 1974; Smith College, Northampton, Massachusetts, 1974; New York University, 1974; Franklin and Marshall College, Lancaster, Pennsylvania, 1975; Columbia University, 1976. Member, National Institute of Arts and Letters; American Academy of Arts and Sciences. Lives in New York City.

PUBLICATIONS

Plays

The Children's Hour (produced 1934).   1934.

Days to Come (produced 1936).   1936.
The Little Foxes (produced 1939).   1939.
Watch on the Rhine (produced 1941).   1941.
The North Star: A Motion Picture about Some Russian People.   1943.
The Searching Wind (produced 1944).   1944.
Watch on the Rhine (screenplay), with Dashiell Hammett, in *Best Film Plays of 1943–44*, edited by John Gassner and Dudley Nichols.   1945.
Another Part of the Forest (produced 1946).   1947.
Montserrat, from a play by Emmanuel Roblès (produced 1949)   1950.
Regina, music by Marc Blitzstein (produced 1949).
The Autumn Garden (produced 1951).   1951.
The Lark, from a play by Jean Anouilh (produced 1955).   1955.
Candide, music by Leonard Bernstein, lyrics by Richard Wilbur, John LaTouche and Dorothy Parker, from the novel by Voltaire (produced 1956).   1957.
Toys in the Attic (produced 1960).   1960.
My Mother, My Father and Me, from the novel *How Much?* by Burt Blechman (produced 1963).   1963.
The Collected Plays.   1972.

Screenplays: *The Dark Angel*, with Mordaunt Shairp, 1935; *These Three*, 1936; *Dead End*, 1937; *The Little Foxes*, with others, 1941; *Watch on the Rhine*, with Dashiell Hammett, 1943; *The North Star*, 1943; *The Searching Wind*, 1946; *The Children's Hour*, with John Michael Hayes, 1961; *The Chase*, 1966.

Other

An Unfinished Woman: A Memoir.   1969.
"Pentimento": A Book of Portraits.   1973.
Scoundrel Time.   1976.

Editor, *Selected Letters*, by Chekhov, translated by Sidonie Lederer.   1955.
Editor, *The Big Knockover: Selected Stories and Short Novels*, by Dashiell Hammett.   1966; as *The Dashiell Hammett Story Omnibus*, 1966.

Reading List: *Hellman, Playwright* by Richard Moody, 1971; *The Dramatic Works of Hellman* by Lorena R. Holmin, 1973; *Hellman* by Doris V. Falk, 1978.

*   *   *

Lillian Hellman is one of America's major dramatists. She entered a male-dominated field when she was nearly thirty and wrote some dozen plays in three decades. Her early model was Ibsen, and she shared his love of tightly knit plots and emphasis on sociological and psychological forces. Her best plays, like Ibsen's, are those in which a powerful character cuts loose and transcends the limitations of the play's rigid symmetry and plot contrivance. Along with Clifford Odets, the other significant writing talent of the 1930's, Hellman showed a keen interest in Marxist theory and explored the relationship between the nuclear family and capitalism. Hellman, more than Odets, held ambiguous views of man and society. Her antagonists are not wholly the products of environment but seem at times innately malicious. The quest for power fascinated the author and her characters became famous for their ruthlessness and cunning. Most of her plays verge on melodrama but are admired for their energetic protagonists and swift-moving plots.

In her first play, *The Children's Hour*, Hellman showed how the capricious wielding of power could ruin innocent people. Two young women at a girl's school are falsely accused of having a lesbian relationship by a disturbed child. They are brought to trial by outraged parents and eventually lose their case – and their school. One of the teachers commits suicide and, too late, the child's treachery is discovered. The homosexual motif, though discreetly handled, accounted for the play's notoriety in 1934; but the abuse of power by an arrogant elite is its enduring theme.

Usurping power is also the motivating force in Hellman's best-known play, *The Little Foxes*, at once a political statement and a complex study of family dynamics. The rapacious Hubbard family represents a new brand of Southern capitalist who subordinates all traditions and human values to the goal of acquiring wealth and property. The strength of the play lies in Hellman's implicit comparison of the Hubbard siblings' rivalries with the competitiveness of Americans in the free enterprise system. The role of Regina Hubbard, who withholds her dying husband's heart medicine and who outwits her equally greedy brothers in a major business coup, has become a favorite vehicle for American actresses.

At the beginning of World War II Hellman wrote *Watch on the Rhine* and *The Searching Wind* which both dealt with the fascist menace. The former play contains some witty repartee and suspenseful moments; but its solutions to the international crisis are simplistic, and it is better described as an adventure story than a thesis play.

When the war ended, Hellman returned to the easy-to-hate Hubbard family in *Another Part of the Forest*. Unfortunately the exaggerated spitefulness and hysteria of the characters and the unrelieved high-tension atmosphere of this play become nearly ludicrous. The concept of personal manipulation had become an obsession with the author, and a correlation seemed to have developed between her studies of social and societal exploitation and her own excessive control over plot characterization and stage effects. Perhaps the playwright realized this, because in her last plays she turned from Ibsen to Chekhov for inspiration. Both *The Autumn Garden* and *Toys in the Attic* recall the mood and ambiguous moral judgments of the great Russian dramatist. Neither of these plays has a truly pernicious villain, and most of the characters seem to be suffering from a Chekhovian paralysis of will. The atmosphere is deterministic and the plots are truer to life. What has changed is that all bids for personal power prove self-defeating – the predatory are caught in traps of their own making and hardly struggle before acknowledging defeat. Nevertheless these plays also include sharp, amusing verbal exchanges and the famous blackmail scenes associated with Hellman. Blackmail, present in all of her plays, is Hellman's favorite metaphor for personal manipulation; but in the later works she uses blackmail and other devices with greater subtlety, and presents a somewhat blurred but more convincing vision of stumbling modern man and his society.

Hellman's dramatic mode, based on her adherence to continental models, is bound to an earlier era. Most of her experiments with film-writing proved frustrating. Her best recent works have been autobiographical sketches. In *An Unfinished Woman*, *Pentimento*, and *Scoundrel Time* she reveals her penetrating intelligence but tacitly acknowledges that her insights and talents are presently better suited to the historical memoir.

—Kimball King

HOME, William Douglas. Scottish. Born in Edinburgh, 3 June 1912. Educated at Eton College; New College, Oxford, B.A. in history 1935; Royal Academy of Dramatic Art, London, 1935–37. Served in the Royal Armoured Corps, 1940–44: Captain. Married Rachel Brand in 1951; one son and three daughters. Progressive Independent candidate for

Parliament, for the Cathcart division of Glasgow, April 1942, Windsor division of Berkshire, June 1942, and Clay Cross division of Derbyshire, April 1944; Liberal candidate for South Edinburgh, 1957. Lives in Hampshire.

PUBLICATIONS

Plays

Great Possessions (produced 1937).
Passing By (produced 1940).
Now Barabbas ... (produced 1947). 1947.
The Chiltern Hundreds (produced 1947). 1949; as *Yes, M'Lord* (produced 1949), 1949.
Ambassador Extraordinary (produced 1948).
Master of Arts (produced 1949). 1950.
The Thistle and the Rose (produced 1949). In *The Plays,* 1958.
Caro William (produced 1952).
The Bad Samaritan (produced 1952). 1954.
The Manor of Northstead (produced 1954). 1956.
The Reluctant Debutante (produced 1955). 1956.
The Iron Duchess (produced 1957). 1958.
The Plays (includes *Now Barabbas* ..., *The Chiltern Hundreds, The Thistle and the Rose, The Bad Samaritan, The Reluctant Debutante).* 1958.
Aunt Edwina (produced 1959). 1960.
Up a Gum Tree (produced 1960).
The Bad Soldier Smith (produced 1961). 1962.
The Cigarette Girl (produced 1962).
The Drawing Room Tragedy (produced 1963).
The Reluctant Peer (produced 1964). 1964.
Two Accounts Rendered: The Home Secretary and Lady J.P.2 (produced 1964).
A Friend Indeed (produced 1965). 1966.
Betzi (produced 1965).
The Queen's Highland Servant (produced 1967).
The Secretary Bird (produced 1968). 1968.
The Grouse Moor Image (produced 1968).
The Bishop and the Actress (televised 1968). 1969.
Uncle Dick's Surprise (produced 1970).
The Jockey Club Stakes (produced 1970). 1973.
The Editor Regrets (televised 1970; produced 1978).
The Douglas Cause (produced 1971).
Lloyd George Knew My Father (as *Lady Boothroyd of the By-Pass,* produced 1972; as *Lloyd George Knew My Father,* produced 1972). 1973.
The Bank Manager (produced 1972).
At the End of the Day (produced 1973).
The Dame of Sark (produced 1974).
The Lord's Lieutenant (produced 1974).
In the Red (produced 1977).
The Kingfisher (produced 1977).
Rolls Hyphen Royce (produced 1977).
The Perch (produced 1977).

Screenplays: *Sleeping Car to Trieste,* with Allan Mackinnon, 1948; *For Them That*

Trespass, with J. Lee-Thompson, 1949; *The Chiltern Hundreds (The Amazing Mr. Beecham),* with Patrick Kirwan, 1949; *Your Witness (Eye Witness),* with Hugo Butler and Ian Hunter, 1950; *Made in Heaven,* 1952; *The Colditz Story,* with others, 1955; *The Reluctant Debutante,* 1959; *Follow That Horse!,* with Howard Mason and Alfred Shaughnessy, 1960.

Television Plays: *The Bishop and the Actress,* 1968; *The Editor Regrets,* 1970; *On Such a Night,* 1974.

Verse

Home Truths. 1939.

Other

Half-Term Report: An Autobiography. 1954.

*   *   *

William Douglas Home is a dramatist of considerable range and variety. Whether he is writing a play that has an historical setting (e.g., *The Thistle and the Rose*) or one that is modern in setting and theme, Home displays a keen sense of what is telling on the stage. In fact, his comedies have often been the vehicles for actors of great distinction. It is this latter sort of play, rather than the rather episodic historical spectacles, which constitute Home's claim to attention. In general, Home's imagination moves with facility in the medium of upper-class British life; the plays suggest that he is a sympathetic and yet mildly critical observer of that life. The plays also suggest that Home has also looked with attention at the plays of Maugham and Lonsdale.

Sometimes Home indicates that the world he depicts best is changing, as in *The Chiltern Hundreds* and *The Jockey Club Stakes.* In the former play an election reminds upper-class persons that it is the middle of the twentieth century and change is imminent; butlers as well as masters aspire to political power. *The Jockey Club Stakes* shows the entrenched directors of a sporting club threatened by a parvenu; with a characteristic *coup de théâtre*, the upstart who challenges the closed circle discovers that his wife is as dishonest as the men he is confronting. The result, here and elsewhere in his plays, is a draw, if not a full return to the status quo. The same can be said of other plays. *Lloyd George Knew My Father* begins with a piquant situation: a noble lady threatens suicide if a freeway crosses her acres. Of course, she does not do away with herself. But her protests provide entertainment and a mild consideration of the costs of social change.

Sometimes only the former benefit – entertainment – marks a particular play. *The Reluctant Debutante* shows prosperous parents in London attempting to find a suitable mate for their daughter. And *The Secretary Bird* is a neat and diverting linkage of adultery and conventional morality. A clever husband brings his wife, his wife's lover, his own secretary, and himself together for a typical English stage weekend. By the time Monday morning comes, it is certain that the husband will keep his wife. After a great deal of brittle talk and suspect behavior, the characters – and the audience – exit by familiar doors.

In short, Home is a careful craftsman of the not quite obvious – a not quite obvious that resolves itself, by the end of the play, into shapes that have been long familiar.

—Harold H. Watts

HOUGHTON, (William) Stanley. English. Born in Ashton-upon-Mersey, Cheshire, 22 February 1881. Educated at Bowdon School; Stockport Grammar School; West Imslow Grammar School; Manchester Grammar School, 1896–97. Worked in his father's cotton business in Manchester, 1897–1912; Dramatic Critic, *Manchester City News*, 1905–06; Feature Writer and Literary/Dramatic Critic, *Manchester Guardian*, 1905–13; settled in Paris, 1913, then, because of illness, returned to Manchester. *Died 11 December 1913.*

PUBLICATIONS

Collections

    Works, edited by Harold Brighouse. 3 vols., 1914.

Plays

    The Intriguers, with Frank G. Naismith (produced 1906).
    The Reckoning, with Frank G. Naismith (produced 1907; as *The Day of Reckoning*, produced 1912).
    The Dear Departed (produced 1908).   1910.
    Independent Means (produced 1909).   1911.
    The Master of the House (produced 1910).   1913.
    The Younger Generation (produced 1910).   1910.
    Fancy Free (produced 1911).   1912; revised version, as *Partners* (produced 1915), in *Works 2*, 1914.
    Hindle Wakes (produced 1912).   1912.
    Phipps (produced 1912).   1913.
    Pearls (produced 1912).
    Trust the People (produced 1913).
    The Fifth Commandment (produced 1913).   1913; revised version, as *The Perfect Cure* (produced 1913), in *Works 2*, 1914.
    Ginger (produced 1913).
    The Old Testament and the New (produced 1914).   In *Works 3*, 1914.
    Marriages in the Making, in *Works 1*.   1914.
    The Hillarys, with Harold Brighouse (produced 1915).

Reading List: *Houghton: Eine Untersuchung Seiner Dramen* by Marcel Gaberthuel, 1973.

*   *   *

    Stanley Houghton came to prominence with a series of neatly constructed, shrewd comedies of provincial life, written for Miss Horniman's pioneering repertory company at the Gaiety Theatre, Manchester, and, although his plays were indebted to the new "intellectual" iconoclastic drama of Shaw and Hankin, Houghton's affinities and insights were exclusively confined to the Lancastrian milieu, and he was ill-at-ease when portraying conditions elsewhere. His strength as a dramatist lay in his keen eye for human pretensions, hypocrisies, and evasions, his skilful depiction of psychological reactions to crises resulting from changing standards of morality and behaviour, and an ability to extract ironic resonances from domestic situations and dry humour from everyday dialogue. Admittedly he never exploited the richness of regional dialect, his dramatic expositions could lack subtlety, and his subject-matter was sometimes ephemeral, but his best plays transcended these blemishes, and Houghton is now regarded as one of the most interesting playwrights of his decade.
    His first solo play to be staged, *The Dear Departed*, now has the status of a classic one-act comedy: the presumed death of an aged man permits the merciless exposure of the

"departed" one's mercenary daughters, to whose predations their spineless husbands are compliant accessories. The "corpse's" subsequent discomfiture of the rival sisters provides a satisfying conclusion to a small masterpiece of economy and observation. *Independent Means*, Houghton's first full-length play, is unsatisfactory, being less securely rooted in accurate scrutiny of character and environment: its subject is bankruptcy in a well-to-do Manchester suburb, and part of its theme is women's rights, but there is an air of contrivance about the piece and the dialogue is flat to the point of banality. However, the independent-minded, resourceful girl, the shiftless son, and the dominating father recur to greater effect in *The Younger Generation* and *Hindle Wakes*, where their actions are less unconvincing and their creator's touch more assured. *The Younger Generation* presents youth rebelling in support of freedom from repressive parental restrictions, and its encouragement by the liberal-minded, expatriate brother of the chapel-going teetotaller Mr. Kennion: here the characterization is rounder, the humour riper, and the plot development less predictable, even if the theme is not uncommon.

But his major triumph is indubitably *Hindle Wakes*. This play attracted some notoriety for its daringly explicit sexual matter when first produced (Oxford students were banned from attending performances). It is an impeccably told story of a boldly self-reliant mill-girl who spends a hotel week-end with the spoiled son of her employer, and then successfully resists both families' efforts to force the couple into a face-saving marriage. It challenged traditional propriety by arguing that women too might have a voice in their own sexual activities and marital destinies, and that the "New Woman" was not found exclusively among the leisured and educated classes. Yet the play's message never dominates the dramatic narration, and the unforced quality of writing which rarely sinks to the melodramatic, coupled with Houghton's restraint, sincerity, and wry comic intelligence, makes *Hindle Wakes* an absorbing play of considerable power.

—William M. Tydeman

HOUSMAN, Laurence. English. Born in Bromsgrove, Worcestershire, 18 July 1865; brother of the poet A. E. Housman. Educated at Bromsgrove School; moved to London, 1883, and studied painting at Lambeth School of Art and the National Art Training College. Contributor, as author and illustrator, to the *Universal Review*, London; Art Critic for the *Manchester Guardian*, 1895–1911; began writing for the theatre c. 1900; lived in Somerset from 1924. Noted for espousal of liberal causes: member of the men's section of the Women's Social and Political Union; pacifist; supporter of the League of Nations, on which he lectured in the United States. *Died 20 February 1959.*

PUBLICATIONS

Plays

> *Bethlehem: A Nativity Play*, music by Joseph Moorat (produced 1902). 1902; revised version, music by Rutland Boughton (produced 1923), 1927.
> *Prunella; or, Love in a Dutch Garden*, with Harley Granville-Barker (produced 1904). 1906; revised version, 1930.
> *The Vicar of Wakefield*, music by Liza Lehmann, from the novel by Goldsmith (produced 1906). 1906.

The Chinese Lantern: A Fairy Play, music by Joseph Moorat (produced 1908). 1908.

A Likely Story (produced 1910). 1916.

The Lord of the Harvest (produced 1910). 1916.

Lysistrata, from the play by Aristophanes (produced 1910). 1911.

Alice in Ganderland: A Political Skit (produced 1911). 1911.

Pains and Penalties: The Defence of Queen Caroline (produced 1911). 1911.

The Return of Alcestis. 1916.

Nazareth. 1916.

As Good as Gold. 1916.

The Snow Man. 1916.

Bird in Hand: A Fairy Play (produced 1918). 1916.

The Wheel (includes *Apollo in Hades, The Death of Alcestis, The Doom of Admetus*). 1919.

Angels and Ministers: Three Plays of Victorian Shade and Character (includes *The Queen, God Bless Her!; His Favourite Flower; The Comforter*). 1921; augmented version (includes *Possession, The King-Maker, The Man of Business, The Instrument*), 1922.

The Queen, God Bless Her! (produced 1929). In *Angels and Ministers*, 1921.

The Comforter (as *Mr. Gladstone's Comforter*, produced 1929). In *Angels and Ministers*, 1921.

The House Fairy (as *The Fairy*, produced 1921). In *False Premises*, 1922.

The Death of Orpheus. 1921; revised version, 1925.

Possession: A Peep-Show in Paradise (produced 1923). In *Angels and Ministers*, 1922.

Dethronements: Imaginary Portraits of Political Characters. 1922.

False Premises: Five One-Act Plays (includes *The Christmas Tree, The Torch of Time, Moonshine, A Fool and His Money, The House Fairy*). 1922.

Little Plays of St. Francis. 1922; second series, 1931; augmented edition, 3 vols., 1935.

Echo de Paris: A Study from Life. 1923.

Followers of St. Francis. 1923.

The Death of Socrates. 1925.

The Comments of Juniper. 1926.

Ways and Means: Five One Act Plays of Village Characters. 1928.

Cornered Poets: A Book of Dramatic Dialogues. 1929.

The New Hangman. 1930.

Palace Plays. 1930; *The Queen's Progress*, 2nd series, 1932; *Victoria and Albert*, 3rd series, 1933; complete series, as *Victoria Regina* (produced 1937), 1934.

Ye Fearful Saints! Plays of Creed, Custom, and Credulity. 1932.

Nunc Dimittis: An Epilogue to Little Plays of St. Francis. 1933.

Four Plays of St. Clare. 1934.

Palace Scenes. 1937.

The Golden Sovereign. 1937.

Glorious Majesty. 1941.

Palestine Plays. 1942.

Samuel the Kingmaker. 1944.

Happy and Glorious (selected from *Victoria Regina, The Golden Sovereign*, and *Glorious Majesty*). 1945.

The Family Honour (produced 1948). 1950.

Old Testament Plays. 1950.

Fiction

All-Fellows: Seven Legends of Lower Redemption. 1896.

Gods and Their Makers. 1897.

An Englishwoman's Love-Letters.   1900.
Blind Love (story).   1901.
The Tale of a Nun, with L. Simons.   1901.
A Modern Antaeus.   1901.
Sabrina Warham: The Story of Her Youth.   1904.
The Blue Moon and Other Tales.   1904.
The Cloak of Friendship (story).   1905.
John of Jingalo: The Story of a Monarch in Difficulties.   1912; as *King John of Jingalo,*
   1937.
The Royal Runaway and Jingalo in Revolution.   1914.
*The Sheepfold: The Story of a Shepherdess and Her Sheep, and How She Lost
   Them.*   1918.
The Wheel.   1919.
Trimblerigg: A Book of Revelation.   1924.
Odd Pairs: A Book of Tales.   1925.
Ironical Tales.   1926.
Uncle Tom Pudd: A Biographical Romance.   1927.
The Life of H.R.H. the Duke of Flamborough.   1928.
Hop-o'-Me-Heart: A Grown Up Fairy Tale.   1938.
What Next: Provocative Tales of Faith and Morals.   1938.
Strange Ends and Discoveries: Tales of This World and the Next.   1948.
The Kind and the Foolish: Short Tales of Myth, Magic, and Miracle.   1952.

Verse

Green Arras.   1896.
Spikenard: A Book of Devotional Love-Poems.   1898.
Rue.   1899.
The Little Land, with Songs from Its Four Rivers.   1899.
Mendicant Rhymes.   1906.
Selected Poems.   1908.
The Heart of Peace and Other Poems.   1918.
The Love Concealed.   1928.
Collected Poems.   1937.
Cynthia.   1947.

Other

A Farm in Fairyland (juvenile).   1894.
The House of Joy (juvenile).   1895.
The Field of Clover (juvenile).   1898.
The Story of the Seven Young Goslings (juvenile).   1899.
The Missing Answers to An Englishwoman's Love-Letters.   1901.
Stories from the Arabian Nights, Retold.   1907.
Articles of Faith in the Freedom of Women.   1910.
*The New Child's Guide to Knowledge: A Book of Poems and Moral Lessons for Old and
   Young.*   1911.
The Immoral Effects of Ignorance in Sex Relations.   1911.
The Bawling Brotherhood.   1913.
The "Physical Force" Fallacy.   1913.
The Law-Abiding.   1914.
Great Possessions.   1915.

The Winners. 1915.
Christianity a Danger to the State. 1916.
The Relation of Fellow-Feeling to Sex. 1917.
St. Francis Poverello. 1918.
Ploughshare and Pruning-Hook (lectures). 1919.
Moonshine and Clover (selections). 1922.
A Doorway in Fairyland (selections). 1922.
The New Humanism. 1923.
The Open Door (juvenile), with *Toffee Boy* by Mabel Marlowe. 1925.
Puss-in-Boots (juvenile). 1926.
A Thing to Be Explained (juvenile). 1926.
Wish to Goodness! (juvenile), with *The Dragon at Hide and Seek* by G. K. Chesterton. 1927.
The "Little Plays" Handbook. 1927.
Etheldrinda's Fairy (juvenile), with *The Tame Dragon* by A. V. Leaper. 1928.
The Religious Advance Toward Rationalism. 1929.
The Boiled Owl (juvenile). 1930.
Busybody's Land (juvenile). 1930.
Cotton-Woolleena (juvenile). 1930.
A Gander and His Geese (juvenile). 1930.
Little and Good (juvenile). 1930.
Turn Again Tales (juvenile). 1930.
A Clean Sweep: A Tale of a Cat and a Broomstick (juvenile). 1931.
Histories, Introductory to Marten and Carter's Histories, with C. H. K. Marten. 4 vols., 1931–32.
What O'Clock Tales (juvenile). 1932.
The Long Journey: The Tale of Our Past, with C. H. K. Marten. 1933.
The Unexpected Years (autobiography). 1937.
What Can We Believe? (correspondence with Dick Sheppard). 1939.
The Preparation of Peace. 1940.
Military Necessity in the Middle Ages. 1941.
Back Words and Fore Words: An Author's Year-Book 1893–1945 (miscellany). 1945.
What Price Salvation Now? 1949.
Moonlight and Fairyland (juvenile). 1978.

Editor, with W. Somerset Maugham, *Venture: An Annual of Art and Literature.* 2 vols., 1903–05.
Editor, *War Letters of Fallen Englishmen.* 1930.
Editor, *A. E. Housman: Some Poems, Some Letters, and a Personal Memoir.* 1937.

Translator, *Of Aucassin and Nicolette, with Annabel and Amoris.* 1902.

Bibliography: *Housman: A Brief Catalogue of the Collection Presented to the Street [Somerset] Library* by Ivor Kemp, 1965.

Reading List: *Die Dichtung von Housman* by A. Rudolf, 1930.

*　　*　　*

Laurence Housman was an extremely prolific writer whose work spread itself over many categories. The abundance and versatility were paid for in the lack of real tension and conflict in most of his work. Known among his contemporaries as the most censored of dramatists, he brought this fate on himself not in his character as a sexual reformer, but through his presentation of sacred and royal personages on the stage. Apart from this violation of protocol in the days of the Lord Chamberlain's power over the theatre, *Bethlehem*, the medieval-style Christian play best remembered because Gordon Craig produced it, and *Pains and Penalties*, concerned with the public humiliation of Queen Caroline, were surely always innocuous enough.

If there is a consistency to be found throughout Housman's work, it is probably a matter of temperament, a bias towards the feminine and towards the domestic, combined with a rationalism that accommodates a desire for spiritual values. His early poetry has a ninetyish contrived simplicity about it and recalls aspects of Rossetti's poetry; other influences are Matthew Arnold (evident in such verse plays as *The Death of Orpheus*) and, persistently, George Herbert. Although he wrote of it in his autobiography, *The Unexpected Years*, as work he was rather ashamed of, his anonymously published best-seller, *An Englishwoman's Love Letters*, remains of some interest for the skill with which the epistolary form is used to create a novel of temperament and emotion which almost entirely dispenses with plot and subsidiary characters. There is more to its febrile lyricism, also, than a response to Meredith's *Ordeal of Richard Feverel*. Its theme of love doomed to premature ending without fulfilment associates it with the largely autobiographical novel of childhood and youth ending in premature death, *A Modern Antaeus*. Housman's series of plays about the Royal Family, including the selection of episodes from the life of Queen Victoria which had considerable theatrical success under the title *Happy and Glorious*, when the ban on performance was lifted at the time of the silver jubilee of George V, is marked by indifference to historical accuracy, but concern to break through reverential mists to the truth of human personalities. In this series and his *Little Plays of St. Francis*, which became a favourite for amateur production, he followed a design since made very familiar through television: the series of short plays linked together by centring on the same character, or group of characters, which can be multiplied indefinitely. The artist and spiritual man combined to create the plays of Saint Francis, which are mildly pleasing and show the author's virtuosity in a tradition that has little to do with modern life or modern art forms. The Housman who embroiled himself in feminist and pacificist causes is more easily identified in the author of the political playlets published as *Dethronements* and the satirical novels *John of Jingalo* and *Trimblerigg*, a stinging satire on Lloyd George. *Echo de Paris* stands on its own, an effective and moving one-act play based on an actual meeting between Laurence Housman and a friend with Robert Ross and Oscar Wilde. *The Unexpected Years* refers to a number of plays that Housman worked on with Granville-Barker, but the delicate and bittersweet *commedia dell'arte* pastiche, *Prunella*, was the only one produced and published under both their names.

—Margery Morgan

HOWARD, Sidney (Coe). American. Born in Oakland, California, 26 June 1891. Educated at the University of California, Berkeley, B.A. 1915; studied with George Pierce Baker at Harvard University, Cambridge, Massachusetts, 1915–16. Served in the American Ambulance Corps, and later in the United States Army Air Corps, in World War I: Captain. Married 1) the actress Clare Jenness Eames in 1922 (divorced, 1930), one daughter; 2) Leopoldine Blaine Damrosch in 1931, one daughter and one son. Member of the Editorial Staff, 1919–22, and Literary Editor, 1922, *Life* magazine, New York; Special Investigator and Feature Writer, *New Republic* and *Hearst's International Magazine*, New York, 1923; full-time playwright from 1923; Founder, with Robert E. Sherwood, Elmer Rice, Maxwell Anderson, S. N. Behrman, and John F. Wharton, Playwrights Company, 1938. Member, Board of Directors, American Civil Liberties Union; President, American Dramatists Guild. Recipient: Pulitzer Prize, 1925. Litt.D.: Washington and Jefferson College, Washington, Pennsylvania, 1935. Member, American Academy of Arts and Letters. *Died 23 August 1939.*

PUBLICATIONS

Plays

    Swords (produced 1921).   1921.
    Casanova, from a play by Lorenzo de Azertis (produced 1923).   1924.
    Lexington (produced 1925).   1924.
    They Knew What They Wanted (produced 1924).   1925.
    Bewitched, with Edward Sheldon (produced 1924).
    Lucky Sam McCarver (produced 1925).   1926.
    Ned McCobb's Daughter (produced 1926).   1926.
    The Silver Cord (produced 1926).   1927.
    Salvation, with Charles MacArthur (produced 1928).   In *Stage Works of MacArthur,* 1974.
    Olympia, from a play by Molnar (produced 1928).   1928.
    Half Gods (produced 1929).   1930.
    Lute Song, with Will Irwin (as *Pi-Pa-Ki,* produced 1930); revised version, as *Lute Song,* music by Raymond Scott, lyrics by Bernard Hanighen (produced 1946).   1955.
    The Late Christopher Bean, from a play by René Fauchois (produced 1932).   1933.
    Alien Corn (produced 1933).   1933.
    Ode to Liberty, from a play by Michel Duran (produced 1934).
    Dodsworth, from the novel by Sinclair Lewis (produced 1934).   1934.
    Yellow Jack, with Paul de Kruif, from a work by de Kruif (produced 1934).   1934.
    Paths of Glory, from the novel by Humphrey Cobb (produced 1935).   1935.
    The Ghost of Yankee Doodle (produced 1937).   1938.
    Madam, Will You Walk? (produced 1953).   1955.

    Screenplays: *Bulldog Drummond,* with Wallace Smith, 1929; *Condemned,* 1929; *A Lady to Love,* 1930; *Free Love,* 1930; *Raffles,* 1930; *Arrowsmith,* 1931; *One Heavenly Night,* 1931; *The Greeks Had a Word for It,* 1932; *Dodsworth,* 1936; *Gone with the Wind,* 1939; *Raffles,* with John Van Druten, 1939.

Fiction

    Three Flights Up (stories).   1924.

Other

    The Labor Spy: A Survey of Industrial Espionage.   1921; revised edition, 1924.
    Professional Patriots, with John Hearley, edited by Norman Hapgood.   1927.

*   *   *

The first major writer of social drama after American drama approached the age of maturity following World War I, Howard mixed melodrama and comedy with the established mode of realism in literature to reflect a dominant social idea of the 1920's – *They Knew What They Wanted*. As the title of one of his best plays, it presented the positive individualism of his generation which other playwrights (Philip Barry, S. N. Behrman, Maxwell Anderson, Paul Green) soon emphasized. In contrast to some of his outstanding contemporaries, Howard was not an innovator in dramatic form nor a particularly profound writer. He readily admitted such shortcomings, if indeed, they were that. Instead, he was a substantial playwright of considerable theatrical skill and imagination who stepped into the ongoing stream of social drama in America and produced at least two major plays in that genre.

They Knew What They Wanted is a modern version of the Paolo-Francesca love story but with a modern twist that none of those who told the story from Dante to Wagner would have accepted. But Howard's intelligently expedient people, battling the exigencies of the modern world, know what they want, and his hero, Tony, can become, as Frank Loesser's musical adaptation made him, "The Most Happy Fella." In *The Silver Cord* Howard took advantage of ideas propounded by Strindberg and Freud. With a diabolic cunning worthy of Strindberg's Laura, Howard's protagonist fights for the control of her sons in an emotion-packed drama that remains one of America's best thesis plays. Emotion and spectacle are always major aspects of a Howard play. He wrote about people, frequently with a strong sense of irony, and all of his plays held at least one spectacular scene which he handled with a craftsmanship critics have admired. The best include *Lucky Sam McCarver*, *Ned McCobb's Daughter*, and *The Late Christopher Bean*; he also adapted Sinclair Lewis's *Dodsworth* to the stage.

During a life cut short by a farm accident in 1939 Howard wrote some twenty plays, most of them either adaptations or collaborations. But his reputation in American drama rests solidly upon the plays he wrote by himself, the best of which appeared during the 1920's. He seemed unable to relate successfully to the social atmosphere of the Depression years which followed.

—Walter J. Meserve

HUNTER, N(orman) C(harles). English. Born in Derbyshire, 18 September 1908. Educated at Repton School; Royal Military College, Sandhurst. Commissioned in the Dragoon Guards, 1930; relinquished commission, 1933; served in the Royal Artillery during World War II. Married Germaine Marie Dachsbeck in 1933. Staff Member of the BBC, 1934–39. Lived in Montgomeryshire. *Died 19 April 1971.*

PUBLICATIONS

Plays

The Merciless Lady, with John Ferguson (produced 1934).
All Rights Reserved (produced 1935).   1935.
Ladies and Gentlemen (produced 1937).

Little Stranger, from a play by Katherine Hilliker and H. H. Caldwell (produced 1938).
A Party for Christmas (produced 1938).   1938.
Grouse in June (as *Galleon Gold,* produced 1939; as *Grouse in June,* produced
    1939).   1939.
Smith in Arcady (produced 1947).
The Affair at Assino (produced 1950).
A Picture of Autumn (produced 1951).   1957.
Waters of the Moon (produced 1951).   1951.
Adam's Apple: A Victorian Fairy Tale (produced 1951; as *Now the Serpent,* produced
    1951).   1953.
A Day by the Sea (produced 1953).   1954.
A Touch of the Sun (produced 1958).   1958.
A Piece of Silver (produced 1960).   1961.
The Tulip Tree (produced 1962).   1963.
The Excursion (produced 1964).   1964.
Adventures of Tom Random (produced 1967).
One Fair Daughter (produced 1970).

Screenplay: *Poison Pen,* with others, 1939.

Radio Plays: *The Coneen Ghost,* 1939; *The Phantom Island,* 1941; *The Clerk's Story,*
1958; *Henry of Navarre,* from book by Hesketh Pearson, 1966.

Fiction

Let's Fight till Six.   1933.
The Servitors.   1934; as *Marriage with Nina,* 1934.
Riot.   1935.
The Ascension of Mr. Judson.   1950.
The Romsea Romeo.   1950.
The Losing Hazard.   1951.

Other

Translator, *The Fight in the Forest,* by Victor Eloy.   1949.

*   *   *

N. C. Hunter came to prominence as a dramatist in the early 1950's after producing a
number of unremarkable light comedies and novels, and achieved his greatest successes at a
time when the dominant British theatrical form was still the well-made naturalistic play of
middle-class life, featuring articulate and generally unextraordinary characters who conveyed
their beliefs and attitudes through the vocabulary of bourgeois reticence and understatement.
Hunter's distinction, however, lay in largely dispensing with incidents resulting from the
conventional pressures exerted by a formal plot, so that his plays appeared more genuinely
"true to life" than those of his contemporaries, especially when complemented by the
seeming inconsequentiality of everyday conversations, and by an atmosphere of stoical
endurance typical of the national mood during and after the Second World War. Hunter's
elegies for the educated middle class in post-war decline are in a very attenuated sense
reminiscent of Chekhov's presentation of the last days of the Russian aristocracy, and it was
almost inevitable that his mature works with their note of autumnal sadness and their gallery
of gentle eccentrics should have been accorded the epithet Chekhovian.

The first of this group, aptly entitled *A Picture of Autumn*, is set in a decaying Wiltshire manor, where, against a background of Edwardian recollections and reminders of the modern social revolution, the older and younger generations confront the abandonment of the ancestral residence with its mixture of memories and inconveniences. Next followed Hunter's major success, *Waters of the Moon*, performed by a distinguished cast in 1951, in which a wealthy but insensitive woman contrives to unsettle the shabby and disillusioned inmates of a snowbound hotel on Dartmoor by offering them a glimpse of a comfortable world to which they cannot return or aspire. The same air of resignation is evident in *A Day by the Sea*, which brings together an intense but arid diplomat and his childhood sweetheart defeated after two unsatisfactory marriages, only to frustrate a lasting reunion, but arguing that consolation lies in acceptance of one's own limitations and of life's continuity. *A Touch of the Sun* contrasts respectable and impecunious righteousness with affluent vulgarity, by charting the effect on a priggish, idealistic preparatory schoolmaster and his family of a Riviera holiday with his materialistic brother and rich American wife: again the playwright opts for moral courage and personal integrity as the best available lifelines in despair. In *The Tulip Tree* an estranged couple are shown gradually reconciling themselves to the death of a beloved son, to the inevitable onset of advancing age, and to each other, a further instance of Hunter's emphasis on honesty in human relationships, and the central importance of not evading unpalatable truths about oneself or one's dependents.

Any vogue for Hunter's plays has now declined, but such excellent examples of an outmoded dramatic form should not be judged by inappropriate criteria of more recent origin. A valid critical assessment must weigh Hunter's unquestioning preference for traditional liberal values and conventional models, and his plays' too-accurate reflection of the concerns of one social class at one period in history, against his careful characterisations and finely orchestrated dialogue, his immaculate control of exposition and *dénouement*, his overall craftsmanship. Hunter's work may yet receive that fuller appraisal its quality still merits.

—William M. Tydeman

INGE, William (Motter). American. Born in Independence, Kansas, 3 May 1913. Educated at the University of Kansas, Lawrence, A.B. 1935; Peabody Teachers College, Nashville, Tennessee, M.A. 1936; Yale University, New Haven, Connecticut, Summer 1940. Taught at Columbus High School, Kansas, 1937–38, and Stephens College, Columbia, Missouri, 1938–43; Art Critic, St. Louis *Star-Times*, 1943–46; taught at Washington University, St. Louis, 1946–49, University of North Carolina, Chapel Hill, 1969, and the University of California at Irvine, 1970. Recipient: George Jean Nathan Award, 1951; Pulitzer Prize, 1953; New York Drama Critics Circle Award, 1953; Donaldson Award, 1953; Academy Award, 1962. *Died 10 June 1973.*

PUBLICATIONS

Plays

The Dark at the Top of the Stairs (as *Farther Off from Heaven*, produced 1947; revised version, as *The Dark at the Top of the Stairs*, produced 1957). 1958.

Come Back, Little Sheba (produced 1950).   1950.

Picnic: A Summer Romance (produced 1953).   1953; revised version, as *Summer Brave* (produced 1962), in *Summer Brave and Eleven Short Plays,* 1962.

Bus Stop (produced 1955).   1955.

Glory in the Flower (produced 1959).   In *24 Favorite One-Act Plays,* edited by Bennett Cerf and Van H. Cartmell, 1958.

The Tiny Closet (produced 1959).   In *Summer Brave and Eleven Short Plays,* 1962.

A Loss of Roses (produced 1959).   1960.

Splendor in the Grass: A Screenplay.   1961.

Natural Affection (produced 1962).   1963.

Summer Brave and Eleven Short Plays (includes *To Bobolink, For Her Spirit; A Social Event; The Boy in the Basement; The Tiny Closet; Memory of Summer; The Rainy Afternoon; The Mall; An Incident at the Standish Arms; People in the Wind; Bus Riley's Back in Town; The Strains of Triumph*).   1962.

Where's Daddy? (as *Family Things Etc.,* produced 1965; as *Where's Daddy?*, produced 1966).   1966.

The Disposal (as *Don't Go Gentle,* produced 1967–68?; as *The Last Pad,* produced 1972). In *Best Short Plays of the World Theatre 1958–1967,* edited by Stanley Richards, 1968; revised version, as *The Disposal,* music by Anthony Caldarella, lyrics by Judith Gero (produced 1973).

Two Short Plays: The Call, and A Murder.   1968.

Midwestern Manic, in *Best Short Plays 1969,* edited by Stanley Richards.   1969.

Caesarian Operation (produced 1972).

Overnight (produced 1974).

Love Death Plays: Dialogue for Two Men, Midwestern Music, The Love Death, Venus and Adonis, The Wake, The Star (produced 1975).

Screenplays: *Splendor in the Grass,* 1961; *All Fall Down,* 1962.

Television Play: *On the Outskirts of Town,* 1964–65?

Fiction

Good Luck, Miss Wyckoff.   1971.
My Son Is a Splendid Driver.   1972.

Reading List: *Inge* by Robert B. Shuman, 1965.

*   *   *

William Inge remains an interesting phenomenon in American drama. His impact upon critic and public alike demands that he be included in any serious consideration of the post-war theatre, but in subject matter and in style he was so counter to the patterns of his contemporaries as to seem from quite another generation. Leaving behind a minimal impression upon the development of recent American drama, his name rapidly fading, he was nonetheless a major figure for almost a decade and wrote some of the most appealing dramatic pieces of the fifteen post-war years.

William Inge's place in American drama is limited to four plays: *Come Back, Little Sheba, Picnic, Bus Stop,* and *The Dark at the Top of the Stairs.* His first, *Farther Off from Heaven,* produced by Margo Jones in Dallas, got to New York only in a much-revised version. *A Loss of Roses* failed completely, as did *Natural Affection* and *Family Things, Etc.* His screenplays brought no added fame, and his prose fiction is limited in appeal.

While Tennessee Williams, Arthur Miller, and Eugene O'Neill dwelt upon the tragic nature of their often inauspicious characters, Inge chose to emphasize his characters' fundamentally pathetic and frequently comic nature. The tragic fates are nowhere in evidence. Inge's appeal lies in a compassionate understanding of and a great sensitivity toward his petty little people, as he conveys successfully to his audiences the universally amusing and simultaneously agonizing quality of ordinary human nature under very ordinary circumstances. Furthermore, at a time when his major contemporaries favored impressionistic stagings, stylized settings, politico-historical themes, and regional emphases, Inge remained consistently a writer of straightforward, single-set plays of Ibsenesque realism. His characters, straight from the unprepossessing streets and towns of the vast mid-section of contemporary America, moved within settings, both geographical and theatrical, remarkable for their unobtrusive, innocuous nature. Inge is one of the most regional of dramatists, but he is emphatically not a "regionalist"; that is, his chosen locale is so lacking in specific regional association and importance, and hence influence upon his characters, as to be virtually neutral. The importance of the surroundings into which Inge places his characters lies precisely in their lack of any importance at all.

Nor does Inge permit the many individual problems of his characters to become the central "problem" of the plays as a whole. His first success, *Come Back, Little Sheba*, is a fine case in point. For instance, we learn a great deal about A.A. and alcoholism, but it is not a play *about* alcoholism. Sexual restraints, taboos, and frustrations, past and present, cause serious personal problems for Doc and Lola, but the play is in no way *about* sex. The air of pessimistic hopelessness surrounding the Delaneys may be the strongest theme, but the play refuses to dwell upon the subject and, in fact, displays a considerable·awareness of the positive aspect of human resilience *and* ultimate hope. *Come Back, Little Sheba* is, then, a play which sends out strong shock waves from all of these problems, permitting none of them to dominate the action. The audience finds itself attracted to these wholly undistinguished people in this undistinguished small town by bonds of mutual sympathy and understanding, together with an appreciation of Inge's outstanding ability to demonstrate what human love, patience, and endurance really mean to virtually all of us. Much has been lost by Doc and Lola in the course of the action, but much has been gained in return. Everybody, at the final curtain, is back at the beginning, more or less, and that, in the end, is far more the way of the world than otherwise. Inge's characters, here and elsewhere, will move no mountains in their lifetimes, but they are, as one critic has said, the salt of the earth, their importance lying almost entirely in the fact of their being human.

Picnic, as one opening night critic observed, is still "basic Inge." The sensation of the season, the play won a Pulitzer Prize and remains probably Inge's most famous play. Adding a few characters and moving them from kitchen to back yard, Inge proved that his formula for the dramatic impact of *Sheba* had been no fluke. "Affectionate, understanding, interesting, engagingly funny, emotionally touching, with fascinating characters" were the critical terms that greeted the play's portrayal of what happens on a Labor Day weekend in a Kansas back yard among a group of almost embarrassingly stock stage figures from clucking-hen mother to sexually frustrated old-maid schoolteacher. Highly emotional things happen in *Picnic*, as they do in *Sheba*, caused mainly by the intrusion of the handsome semi-clad drifter who causes a general loosening of assorted libidos, culminating in fornication, drunkenness, and elopement. But none of these things in themselves, any more than in *Sheba*, is the point. What matters is Inge's highly skilled and absolutely convincing portrayal of the driving human forces of underlying desires, frustrations, fears, and joys of these routinely bland people in an equally bland environment.

In *Bus Stop* Inge falls back on a device that worked for Shakespeare on Prospero's island, for Melville aboard the *Pequod*, and for James Jones in his pre-Pearl Harbor army. Into Grace's microcosmic lunchroom, driven by the unalterable force of a prairie blizzard, the playwright sends a group of individuals as stereotyped and undistinguished as anything he or many another artist has attempted. What emerges, for all that, is a wholly delightful human comedy with an underlying drama of deep human pathos. The pursuit and capture of the pitifully floozy "chantoosie" by the frantically infatuated, rambunctious but innocent cowboy is superbly comic, beautifully controlled. Simultaneously, the parallel affair of the decadent professor and the naive waitress, while ever on the edge of the pit of gratuitous sensation, carries the more serious theme with touching effectiveness. Before he is through with us, Inge has made us care a great deal about Bo, Cherie, Lyman, Elma, and Virgil. Normally we, as well as the rest of the world, would take little note of them, but Inge has shown us that they are highly important people to themselves and in many ways to each other. Cherie, hopelessly tarnished, artistically a fiasco, has stood her ground with dignity while vigorously defending her womanly honor against the onrushing Bo. He, in turn, literally forced to bow before her, has learned, to his wondering astonishment, that women are not calves to be bulldogged, hogtied, and subdued. Elma has come dangerously close to the total destruction of her innocence, but that very innocence has given the aging sensualist pause enough to permit both of them, for the time, to escape. By the time Inge returns all on stage to equilibrium and sends his bus on its journey, we have encountered a touching human experience of lasting impressiveness.

In his final and least noteworthy "success," *The Dark at the Top of the Stairs*, Inge unfortunately surrenders to artificialities of plot, less than subtle symbolism, gratuitous violence, and remarkably unconvincing characters. There is much of the "basic Inge" to be seen and, upon occasion, praised, but the strong human appeal of the first three plays is lost amid generally unsatisfactory handling of marital problems, racial prejudices, and parent–child relationships. We may still understand some of the reasons for Rubin Flood's infidelity and Sonny's mamma's boy behavior, as well as little Sammy's suicide, but, on the whole, there is too much of the trite and unimaginative to be as convincing as we would like.

The ultimate appeal of William Inge seems to lie in his ability to transform the lives and behavior of drab people in drab surroundings into a significant drama of human experience. Taking us inside and outside the houses most of us pass every day down the block and around the corner, he reveals some rather profound human truths, and he grips us in fascination as he does so.

—Jordan Y. Miller

JOHNSTON, (William) Denis. Irish. Born in Dublin, 18 June 1901. Educated at St. Andrew's College, Dublin; Merchiston Castle School, Edinburgh; Christ's College, Cambridge (President of the Union), 1921–23, M.A., LL.M. 1926; Harvard Law School, Cambridge, Massachusetts (Pugsley Scholar), 1923–24; Barrister, Inner Temple, London, and King's Inns, Dublin, 1925, and Northern Ireland, 1926. Married 1) Shelah Richards in 1928 (divorced), one son and one daughter, the novelist Jennifer Johnston; 2) Betty Chancellor in 1945, two sons. Producer, Dublin Drama League, and Abbey Theatre, Dublin, and the Dublin Gate Theatre, 1927–36, also a Member of the Board of Directors of the Dublin Gate Theatre, 1931–36; Features Producer, BBC, Belfast, 1936–38; Television Producer, BBC, London, 1938–39; BBC Correspondent, in the Middle East, Italy, France, and Germany, 1942–45: mentioned in despatches; O.B.E. (Officer, Order of the British Empire), 1946; Director of Television Programmes, BBC, London, 1945–47; Visiting Director, Kirby Memorial Theatre, Amherst, Massachusetts, 1950; Professor of English, Mount Holyoke College, South Hadley, Massachusetts, 1950–60; Chairman of the Department of Theatre and Speech, Smith College, Northampton, Massachusetts, 1960–66; Visiting Professor, Amherst College, Massachusetts, 1966–67, University of Iowa, Iowa City, 1967–68, and the University of California at Davis, 1970–71; Berg Professor, New York University, 1971–72; Arnold Professor, Whitman College, Walla Walla, Washington, 1972–73. Literary Editor, Abbey Theatre, Dublin, 1975. Recipient: Guggenheim Fellowship, 1954. Lives in County Dublin.

PUBLICATIONS

Plays

The Old Lady Says "No!" (produced 1929).   In *The Moon in the Yellow River and The Old Lady Says "No!,"* 1932.
The Moon in the Yellow River (produced 1931).   1931.
The Moon in the Yellow River and The Old Lady Says "No!": Two Plays.   1932.
A Bride for the Unicorn (produced 1933).   In *Storm Song and A Bride for the Unicorn*, 1935.
Storm Song (produced 1934).   In *Storm Song and A Bride for the Unicorn*.   1935.
Storm Song and A Bride for the Unicorn: Two Plays.   1935.
Blind Man's Buff, with Ernst Toller, from a play by Toller (produced 1936).   1938.
The Golden Cuckoo (produced 1938).   In *The Golden Cuckoo and Other Plays*, 1954; revised version, 1971.
The Dreaming Dust (as *Weep for Polyphemus*, broadcast 1938; revised version, as *The Dreaming Dust*, produced 1940).   In *The Golden Cuckoo and Other Plays*, 1954.
A Fourth for Bridge (as *The Unthinking Lobster*, televised 1948).   In *The Golden Cuckoo and Other Plays*, 1954.
Six Characters in Search of an Author, from a play by Pirandello (produced 1950); revised version, music by Hugo Weisgall (produced 1956).   1957.
The Golden Cuckoo and Other Plays.   1954.
Strange Occurrence on Ireland's Eye (produced 1956).   In *Collected Plays II*, 1960.
Tain Bo Cuailgne (pageant; produced 1956).
The Scythe and the Sunset (produced 1958).   In *Collected Plays I*, 1960.
Ulysses in Nighttown, adaption of parts of *Ulysses* by James Joyce (produced 1958).
Finnegans Wake, from the novel by James Joyce (produced 1959).
Collected Plays I–II.   2 vols., 1960.
Nine Rivers from Jordan, music by Hugo Weisgall (produced 1969).   1969.
Dramatic Works 1.   1977.

Screenplays: *Guests of the Nation*, 1933; *River of Unrest*, 1937; *Ourselves Alone*, 1937.

Radio Plays: *Death at Newtownstewart*, 1937; *Lillibulero*, 1937; *Weep for Polyphemus*, 1938; *Multiple Studio Blues*, 1938; *Nansen of the "Fram,"* 1940; *The Gorgeous Lady Blessington*, 1941; *The Autobiography of Mark Twain*, 1941; *Abraham Lincoln*, 1941; *In the Train*, 1946; *Not One Returns to Tell*, 1946; *Verdict of the Court* series, 1960.

Television Plays: *The Last Voyage of Captain Grant*, 1938; *The Parnell Commission*, 1939; *Weep for the Cyclops*, 1946; *The Unthinking Lobster*, 1948; *The Call to Arms*, 1949; *Siege at Killyfaddy*, 1960.

Ballet: *The Indiscreet Goat*, Dublin, 1931.

Other

Dionysia.   1949.
Nine Rivers from Jordan: The Chronicle of a Journey and a Search (wartime autobiography).   1953.
In Search of Swift.   1959.
John Millington Synge.   1965.
The Brazen Horn (autobiographical).   1968; revised edition, 1976.

Reading List: *Johnston's Irish Theatre* by Harold Ferrar, 1975.

*   *   *

Denis Johnston was trained for the law at Cambridge and Harvard, but he found the drama a more absorbing pursuit, and became involved as actor and director with the Dublin Drama League and the new Dublin Gate Theatre of Hilton Edwards and Micheál Mac Liammóir. His subsequent career has been extraordinarily varied, and has embraced acting, directing, and writing for radio, films, and television. As a playwright, Johnston was much less influenced by the peasant drama of the Abbey Theatre than he was by the experimental drama of the continent. However, his restless search for form has militated against a recognisable "Johnston" play – as, for instance, there is the recognisable early O'Casey and late O'Casey. His plays were produced by both the Gate and the Abbey theatres, the Gate doing the more unconventional ones and the Abbey the seemingly more traditional.

His first play, *The Old Lady Says "No!,"* produced by the Gate, was a satiric expressionistic play about contemporary Ireland which stunningly used the technique of allusion that T. S. Eliot had popularised in poetry and James Joyce in fiction. For years the play seemed both too baffling and too Irish to travel well outside of Ireland, but in Ireland its sophisticated technique was wedded to such a broad theatricality that it remained an important item of the Gate's repertory for almost thirty years. The play's day may now have passed, for in a 1977 revival by the Abbey it seemed not only somewhat dated but, surprisingly, a bit superficial.

Johnston's keen satiric mind and enormous technical expertise have made even such nominally realistic plays as *The Moon in the Yellow River* and *The Scythe and the Sunset* as complex yet smooth as Chekhov, but as rarely produced as Turgenev or Granville-Barker. Although *The Moon in the Yellow River* is tied to the aftermath of the Irish Civil War and *The Scythe and the Sunset* to the 1916 Rising, both plays have a density of theme, a complexity of plot, a comic theatricality, and even intermittently a humanity that make them transcend their time and place.

The best of Johnston's minor work is almost as good as his very best, and would certainly include the symbolic fantasy *A Bride for the Unicorn*, the sardonic farce *The Golden Cuckoo*, and perhaps the best dramatic treatment yet of Jonathan Swift, *The Dreaming Dust*. His chief non-dramatic work includes a work on Swift, a war memoir, and a dubious philosophic treatise. Despite his bold experiments, he will probably be most remembered for the two social-political comedies which broadened the possibilities of realism, and which have not yet been assimilated by the modern theatre.

—Robert Hogan

JONES, (Everett) LeRoi. Pseudonym: Amiri Baraka. American. Born in Newark, New Jersey, 7 October 1934. Educated at the Central Avenue School, and Barringer High School, Newark; Howard University, Washington, D.C. Served in the United States Air Force, 1954–56. Married 1) Hettie Cohen in 1958 (divorced, 1965), two daughters; 2) Sylvia Robinson (Bibi Amina Baraka) in 1966, five children. Taught at the New School for Social Research, 1961–64; State University of New York at Buffalo, Summer 1964; Columbia University, 1964; Visiting Professor, San Francisco State College, 1966–67. Founder, *Yugen* magazine and Totem Press, New York, 1958; Editor, with Diane di Prima, *Floating Bear* magazine, New York, 1961–63. Founding Director, Black Arts Repertory Theatre, Harlem, New York, 1964–66. Since 1966, Founding Director, Spirit House, Newark. Involved in Newark politics: Member of the United Brothers, 1967, and Committee for Unified Newark, 1968. Member of the International Coordinating Committee, Congress of African Peoples; Chairman, Congress of Afrikan People; Secretary-General, National Black Political

Assembly. Recipient: Whitney Fellowship, 1961; Obie Award, 1964; Guggenheim Fellowship, 1965; Dakar Festival Prize, 1966; National Endowment for the Arts grant, 1966. Member, Black Academy of Arts and Letters. Lives in Newark, New Jersey.

PUBLICATIONS

Plays

A Good Girl is Hard to Find (produced 1958).
Dante (produced 1961; as *The 8th Ditch*, produced 1964).   In *The System of Dante's Hell*, 1965.
The Toilet (produced 1962).   In *The Baptism and The Toilet*, 1967.
Dutchman (produced 1964).   In *Dutchman and The Slave*, 1964.
The Slave (produced 1964).   In *Dutchman and The Slave*, 1964.
Dutchman, and The Slave.   1964.
The Baptism (produced 1964).   In *The Baptism and The Toilet*, 1967.
Jello (produced 1965).   1970.
Experimental Death Unit No. 1 (produced 1965).   In *Four Black Revolutionary Plays*, 1969.
A Black Mass (produced 1966).   In *Four Black Revolutionary Plays*, 1969.
The Baptism and The Toilet.   1967.
Arm Yrself or Harm Yrself (produced 1967).   1967.
Slave Ship: A Historical Pageant (produced 1967).   1967.
Madheart (produced 1967).   In *Four Black Revolutionary Plays*, 1969.
Home on the Range (produced 1968).   In *Drama Review*, Summer 1968.
Police, in *Drama Review*, Summer 1968.
The Death of Malcolm X, in *New Plays from the Black Theatre*, edited by Ed Bullins.   1969.
Great Goodness of Life (A Coon Show) (produced 1969).   In *Four Black Revolutionary Plays*, 1969.
Four Black Revolutionary Plays.   1969.
Junkies Are Full of (SHHH ...), and Bloodrites (produced 1970).   In *Black Drama Anthology*, edited by Woodie King and Ron Milner, 1971.
BA-RA-KA, in *Spontaneous Combustion: Eight New American Plays*, edited by Rochelle Owens.   1972.
A Recent Killing (produced 1973).
Sidnee Poet Heroical (produced 1975).
S-1 (produced 1976).   In *The Motion of History and Other Plays*, 1978.
The Motion of History (produced 1977).   In *The Motion of History and Other Plays*, 1978.
The Motion of History and Other Plays (includes *S-1* and *Slave Ship*).   1978.

Other plays: *Columbia the Gem of the Ocean; Resurrection of Life.*

Screenplays: *Dutchman*, 1967; *A Fable*, 1971.

Fiction

The System of Dante's Hell.   1965.
Tales.   1967.

Verse

Preface to a Twenty Volume Suicide Note.   1961.
The Dead Lecturer.   1964.
Black Art.   1966.
Black Magic: Poetry 1961–1967.   1969.
It's Nation Time.   1970.
In Our Terribleness: Some Elements of Meaning in Black Style, with Billy
   Abernathy.   1970.
Spirit Reach.   1972.
Afrikan Revolution.   1973.
Hard Facts.   1976.

Other

Cuba Libre.   1961.
Blues People: Negro Music in White America.   1963.
Home: Social Essays.   1966.
Black Music.   1968.
A Black Value System.   1970.
Raise Race Rays Raze: Essays since 1965.   1971.
Strategy and Tactics of a Pan-African Nationalist Party.   1971.
The Creation of the New Ark.   1975.

Editor, *Four Young Lady Poets.*   1962.
Editor, *The Moderns: New Fiction in America.*   1964.
Editor, with Larry Neal, *Black Fire: An Anthology of Afro-American Writing.*   1968.
Editor, *African Congress: A Documentary of the First Modern Pan-African
   Congress.*   1972.
Editor, with Diane di Prima, *The Floating Bear: A Newsletter, Numbers 1–37.*   1974.

Bibliography: *Jones (Imamu Amiri Baraka): A Checklist of Works by and about Him* by Letitia Dace, 1971.

Reading List: *From LeRoi Jones to Amiri Baraka: The Literary Works* by Theodore R. Hudson, 1973; *Baraka: The Renegade and the Mask* by Kimberly W. Benston, 1976; *Baraka/Jones: The Quest for a "Populist Modernism"* by Werner Sollors, 1978.

*   *   *

LeRoi Jones – now known as Amiri Baraka – says he has "always tried to be a revolutionary." That is the consistent quality in a twenty-year career which has included writing in every literary genre and representing contradictory points of view.

The rebel in Jones led him in his youth to prefer running with the ghetto gangs to remaining in his respectable middle-class home. At Howard University, which he found distastefully bourgeois, it led him to quit college after his junior year to join the Air Force. In New York in the late 1950's, it prompted him to become a Greenwich Village bohemian and a disciple of Allen Ginsberg and Jack Kerouac, to turn out lyric poetry and surreal fiction expressing the romantic *angst* and waggish frivolity which permitted publication under titles such as *The System of Dante's Hell* and *Preface to a Twenty Volume Suicide Note*: "My wife is left-handed./which implies a fierce de-/termination. ITS WEIRD BABY./The way some folks are always trying to be/different. A sin & a shame."

Jones in the late 1950's and early 1960's possessed a boundless energy and an extraordinarily diverse talent. He was still speaking to white people and writing for a racially mixed audience. He founded periodicals with two white women, the magazine *Yugen* with his wife Hettie Cohen and the newsletter *The Floating Bear* – its title derived from an A. A. Milne Winnie the Pooh story – with the poet Diane di Prima. His saturation in the western literary tradition (William Carlos Williams, Whitman, Eliot, Yeats, Pound, and the Black Mountain poets) was clearly discernible in his poetry and novel. At that time Jones did not write specifically ethnic literature. Indeed, he alleged in 1959 that "Negro writing" can at best be folklore, for what is written out of racial consciousness cannot achieve literary status. In 1961 his poetry muses "Africa/is a foreign place. You are/as any other sad man here/american."

Yet even in the early work techniques analogous to black music – jazz and the blues – are evident, and Jones was also writing music criticism and essays expressing an increasingly inflammatory political consciousness. He was becoming politicized as early as 1960, when he visited Cuba and wrote the essay *Cuba Libre* in praise of Castro and that island's revolution. His verse became edgy, uneasy with his white life, and his essays and plays began to express an urgency which was turning, by 1964, to racial militancy.

Although a portion of his novel and the play *The Toilet* had been produced earlier, 1964 was the year that Baraka really won attention as a playwright. In March *The Eighth Ditch* (his *Dante* play) opened and was quickly closed by police on grounds of obscenity. Within a week *The Baptism*, an equally startling play, this one a religious satire which drew charges of both obscenity and blasphemy, jarred and amused its spectators. The very next day *Dutchman* opened, and later that year a double bill of *The Toilet* and *The Slave* further solidified Baraka's reputation. (A full-length play, *A Recent Killing*, which was written in this year but not produced until a decade later, dramatizes an inter-racial cooperation in which Jones was already losing faith.)

These plays are blistering in their dramatization of raw racial tensions on a realistic level, but they also function on an allegorical plane. *Dutchman*, in particular, is generally acknowledged to be his finest achievement. The Flying Dutchman constitutes one of the more obvious symbolic references in this play about a woman picking up a man on a New York City subway, but critical opinion has been divided over whether white Lula or black Clay embodies the legendary captain who is doomed to roam until his final peace can be purchased by a lover willing to die with him. Perhaps it is white racism, as exemplified by the murderous Lula, that won't die, or possibly the swallowing of pride and suppression of rage which the superficially assimilated Clay practices represents what Jones had in mind. Whatever the parallel, a double death does not occur, so the spectre of racism is not exorcised.

Dutchman can also be interpreted as a modernization of the Adam and Eve story in which Lula – who keeps eating and offering apples – is a corrupter of the innocent, natural man of Africa and the cause of his expulsion from the paradise of the American dream. Other religious parables which have been discerned include that of Clay as Christ and Lula as Satan (with the young man at the end representing the resurrection) and the idea that Clay is being baptized in hell-fire. *Dutchman* can therefore be viewed as a reference to disguise and the voluntary assumption of roles. Lula is an author creating a series of characters for herself. When Clay stops concealing his blackness behind white clothes, intellectual interests, and a courteous demeanor, Lula rewards his self-assertion with murder.

Equally playable and nearly equally subject to glosses (sometimes more arcane than illuminating), *The Toilet* and *The Slave* take somewhat different approaches to racial conflict. The earlier play, *The Toilet*, depicts interracial relations in a fashion which Jones later came to regard as more sentimental than realistic, for the black gang leader really loves the white boy who is beaten up in the lavatory, and he returns to comfort Karolis when the bullies have left. A major factor in the play's appeal is Jones's embodiment in his protagonist of a universal conflict between the gentle, nurturing, reflective aspect of the character (the "Ray" side of us) and the belligerent, aloof, authoritative aspect (the "Foots" side). The split in this particular temperament, of course, sets up a conflict between the assimilationist with aspirations to white goals (Ray, the good student who is attracted to Karolis) and the true black man (Foots, the natural leader).

Although *The Toilet* is milder than *Dutchman*, *The Slave* finds its protagonist has progressed beyond the birth of militance, which Clay barely reaches, to full leadership in a race war. Walker has left the insurgents just long enough to visit a white couple, his ex-wife and her new husband, the latter a college professor who represents the western culture to which Walker has bidden farewell. That he would pay such a call at all suggests that Walker is still something of a slave to the white liberal heritage, and the old slave whom Walker becomes in a long monologue reinforces that notion. Still, Walker is wiping out, literally, the old associations, and he, like Jones himself at this time of his life, sets a new, independent course.

Jones's drama had been by and large realistic and by and large addressed to a white or racially mixed audience. But the radical changes in his life – his departure in 1965 for Harlem and soon thereafter for the Newark ghetto, his divorce (subsequent to the prophetic *The Slave*) from the white wife (who now felt she was the enemy) and his remarriage to a black woman, his conversion to the Kawaida sect of Muslim and his adoption of an African name, Amiri (prince) Baraka (blessedness), preceded for a time by the religious title Imamu (spiritual leader) – all reflect an ideological transformation which had a profound effect upon all his writing. The essays grew violent, the poetry took on the dialect of black speech, and the plays increasingly spoke only to blacks and were presented in segregated theatres. Realism was generally rejected in favor of a technique sometimes expressionistic and sometimes a montage of brief episodes, cinematic juxtapositions.

The first plays of this black militant period, including *Experimental Death Unit No. 1*, *Jello*, *A Black Mass*, and *Madheart*, explicitly proclaim the superiority of black to white, of black revolutionist to assimilationist, and of male to female. *Jello* is also a quite funny parody of Jack Benny's radio show in which Rochester stops serving Benny and starts asserting his new-found black manhood, and *A Black Mass* is a lyrical evocation of a misguided black man's creation of the white race. While some later black nationalist plays by Baraka – *Arm Yrself or Harm Yrself*, for instance – are simple didactic dramas with lines which preach the point, others make considerable use of nonverbal techniques and are theatrical in ways Antonin Artaud would have appreciated. *Slave Ship*, for instance, forces its spectators to feel they themselves are manacled in the hold of that ship, and it employs Swahili and moans and groans quite as much as English dialogue. The play's spectacle of human suffering is marvelously powerful drama. Some other plays of the late 1960's are cinematic or surreal, and some experiment with language in ways outside the tradition of mainstream American drama.

A recent resurgence of the polemical in Baraka's dramaturgy has followed another political change. The creator of and foremost writer in the black arts movement by 1973 had become a Communist leader and had rejected his nationalist rage and rancor toward whites as racist. Therefore, *S-1* and *The Motion of History* employ agit-prop techniques, in the former to attack the proposed Senate Bill 1, the Federal Criminal Code reform bill which opponents feel would abridge freedom of speech and assembly, and in the latter to urge the solidarity of blacks and whites in a revolution to overthrow their oppressors. *The Motion of History* dramatizes instances from the past four centuries in which the ruling class has pitted poor blacks and whites against each other so as to obscure their common interests in ending exploitation. This play even ridicules the black militant, who is represented as a mindless robot chanting "the white man is the devil."

In 1961, LeRoi Jones was president of the Fair Play for Cuba Committee. He strayed far afield from such politics, but has returned now to a Marxist-Leninist-Maoist stance. Whatever his particular affiliation, he continues to be one of the foremost of contemporary committed writers.

—Tish Dace

KAUFMAN, George S(imon). American. Born in Pittsburgh, Pennsylvania, 16 November 1889. Educated at Liberty School, New Castle School, and Central High School, Pittsburgh, graduated 1907; Western University of Pennsylvania Law School, 1907. Married 1) Beatrice Bakrow in 1917 (died, 1945), one adopted daughter; 2) the writer Leueen MacGrath in 1949 (divorced, 1957). Worked as a surveyor, clerk in the Allegheny County Tax Office, and stenographer in the Pittsburgh Coal Company; travelling salesman for the Columbia Ribbon Company, Paterson, New Jersey; Jornalist: Columnist, *Washington Times*, 1912–13; Drama Critic, New York *Tribune*, 1914–15; Columnist, New York *Evening Mail*, 1915; Drama Critic, *New York Times*, 1917–30. Writer for the stage from 1918, often in collaboration; stage director from 1928. Chairman of the Board, Dramatists' Guild 1927. Recipient: Megrue Prize, 1931; Pulitzer Prize, 1932, 1937. *Died 2 June 1961.*

PUBLICATIONS

Plays

  Among Those Present, with Larry Evans and Walter C. Percival (produced 1918; as *Someone in the House,* produced 1918).
  Jacques Duval, with Hans Mueller (produced 1919).
  Dulcy, with Marc Connelly (produced 1921). 1921.
  To the Ladies!, with Marc Connelly (produced 1922). 1923.
  No, Sirree!, with Marc Connelly (produced 1922).
  A Christmas Carol, with Marc Connelly, from the story by Dickens, in *Bookman,* December 1922.
  The 49ers, with Marc Connelly (produced 1922).
  West of Pittsburgh, with Marc Connelly (produced 1922); revised version, as *The Deep Tangled Wildwood* (produced 1923).
  Merton of the Movies, with Marc Connelly, from the story by Harry Leon Wilson (produced 1922). 1925.
  Helen of Troy, N.Y., with Marc Connelly, music and lyrics by Harry Ruby and Bert Kalmar (produced 1923).
  Beggar on Horseback, with Marc Connelly, music by Deems Taylor, from a play by Paul Apel (produced 1924). 1925.
  Sketches, in *'Round the Town* (produced 1924).
  Be Yourself, with Marc Connelly (produced 1924).
  Minick, with Edna Ferber, from the story "Old Man Minick" by Ferber (produced 1924). 1925.
  The Butter and Egg Man (produced 1925). 1925.
  The Cocoanuts, music by Irving Berlin (produced 1925). 1925.
  If Men Played Cards Like Women Do. 1926.
  The Good Fellow, with Herman J. Mankiewicz (produced 1926). 1931.
  The Royal Family, with Edna Ferber (produced 1927). 1928; as *Theatre Royal* (produced 1935), 1936.
  Animal Crackers, with Morrie Ryskind, music and lyrics by Harry Ruby and Bert Kalmar (produced 1928).
  The Still Alarm (sketch), in *The Little Show* (produced 1929). 1930.
  June Moon, with Ring Lardner, from the story "Some Like Them Cold" by Lardner (produced 1929). 1931.
  The Channel Road, with Alexander Woollcott (produced 1929).
  Strike Up the Band, book by Morrie Ryskind from a libretto by Kaufman, music by George Gershwin, lyrics by Ira Gershwin (produced 1930).

Once in a Lifetime, with Moss Hart (produced 1930).   1930.

The Band Wagon, with Howard Dietz, music by Arthur Schwartz (produced 1931).

Eldorado, with Laurence Stallings (produced 1931).

Of Thee I Sing, with Morrie Ryskind, music by George Gershwin, lyrics by Ira Gershwin (produced 1931).   1932.

Dinner at Eight, with Edna Ferber (produced 1932).   1932.

Let 'em Eat Cake, with Morrie Ryskind, music by George Gershwin, lyrics by Ira Gershwin (produced 1933).   1933.

The Dark Tower, with Alexander Woollcott (produced 1933).   1934.

Merrily We Roll Along, with Moss Hart (produced 1934).   1934.

Bring on the Girls, with Morrie Ryskind (produced 1934).

Prom Night.   1934.

Cheating the Kidnappers.   1935.

The Paperhanger, with Moss Hart.   1935(?).

First Lady, with Katharine Dayton (produced 1935).   1935.

Stage Door, with Edna Ferber (produced 1936).   1939.

You Can't Take It with You, with Moss Hart (produced 1936).   1937.

I'd Rather Be Right, with Moss Hart, music by Richard Rodgers, lyrics by Lorenz Hart (produced 1937).   1937.

The Fabulous Invalid, with Moss Hart (produced 1938).   1938.

The American Way, with Moss Hart, music by Oscar Levant (produced 1939).   1939.

The Man Who Came to Dinner, with Moss Hart (produced 1939).   1939.

George Washington Slept Here, with Moss Hart (produced 1940).   1940.

The Land Is Bright, with Edna Ferber (produced 1941).   1946.

Six Plays, with Moss Hart.   1942.

The Late George Apley, with John P. Marquand, from the novel by Marquand (produced 1944).   1946.

Hollywood Pinafore (produced 1945).

Park Avenue, with Nunnally Johnson, music by Arthur Schwartz, lyrics by Ira Gershwin (produced 1946).

Bravo!, with Edna Ferber (produced 1948).   1949.

The Small Hours, with Leueen MacGrath (produced 1951).   1951.

Fancy Meeting You Again, with Leueen MacGrath (produced 1952).   1952.

The Solid Gold Cadillac, with Howard Teichmann (produced 1953).   1954.

Silk Stockings, with Leueen MacGrath and Abe Burrows, music by Cole Porter, suggested by Melchior Lengyel (produced 1955).   1955.

Amicable Parting, with Leueen MacGrath (produced 1957).   1957.

Screenplays: *Business Is Business,* with Dorothy Parker, 1925; *If Men Played Cards As Women Do,* 1929; *Roman Scandals,* with others, 1933; *A Night at the Opera,* with Morrie Ryskind, 1935; *Star Spangled Rhythm,* with others, 1943.

Reading List: *Kaufman: An Intimate Portrait,* by Howard Teichmann, 1972; *Kaufman and His Friends* by Scott Meredith, 1974, abridged version, as *Kaufman and the Algonquin Round Table,* 1977.

*   *   *

George S. Kaufman was a devastating wit and a serious satirist who worked, almost always in collaboration, on successful plays, musicals, and films. He was especially effective with Moss Hart, a productive blend of talents much studied and much admired: "Their most distinguished works, *You Can't Take It with You* and *The Man Who Came to Dinner,* reveal Kaufman and Hart," says Milton Levin (in *The Reader's Encyclopedia of World Drama*), "as the best satirists in American drama."

Kaufman's first play was with the team of Larry Evans and Walter Percival. Then he and Marc Connelly (another newspaperman from Pennsylvania active in New York) entered on a series of collaborations: *Dulcy*, *To the Ladies*, *Merton of the Movies*, *The Deep Tangled Wildwood*, and *Beggar on Horseback*. Of these only *The Deep Tangled Wildwood* (a satire "upon the Winchell-Smith type of play") was a failure. *Merton of the Movies*, the story of a movie-struck clerk who achieves success because he, unconsciously, burlesques serious roles, was a delight. The dream sequence of *Beggar on Horseback* (a penniless composer, Neil McRae, is given a sedative and has nightmares about having to work in a "widget" factory and then a Consolidated Art Factory, where he has to write music for songs like: "You've broken my heart like you broke my heart/So why should you break it again?") was considered "a fine expression of the resentment of the artist" for those who are "contemptuous of those who show originality" (A. H. Quinn). *Beggar on Horseback* is considered a milestone in American expressionism. The team broke up and Kaufman wrote his one unaided work, *The Butter and Egg Man* (1925), and Connelly tried an original also, *The Wisdom Tooth* (1926). Neither was much good, for Kaufman's farce and Connelly's fantasy did not seem to work separately.

"I have always been smart enough to attach myself to the most promising lad that came along in the theater," said Kaufman, and he joined forces with a number of burgeoning, bright talents. With Edna Ferber he wrote *Minick*, *The Royal Family*, *Dinner at Eight*, *Stage Door*, and *The Land is Bright*. With Herman J. Mankiewicz, another journalist and wit, he wrote *The Good Fellow*, which flopped (Mankiewicz went on to success as a screenwriter, probably writing most of *Citizen Kane*, though that is still argued), but the same year Kaufman had a hit with Ring Lardner, that "wonderful man" with such a great ear for American speech, in an hilarious take-off of Tin-Pan Alley, *June Moon*. About the same time Kaufman began to work with one of the madcap writers behind the Marx Brothers, the too-little-acknowledged zany genius, Morrie Ryskind. With Ryskind Kaufman entered the world of Broadway musicals, starting with *Animal Crackers*. Their collaboration was later to produce *Of Thee I Sing* (with the Gershwins; Pulitzer Prize 1932) and *Let 'em Eat Cake* (with the Gershwins), satires of politics and revolutionaries. With Alexander Woollcott, Kaufman wrote *The Channel Road* and, not much better, *The Dark Tower*. With Katharine Dayton he did a comedy of Washington politics and social life, *First Lady*. In the 1930's he was at his best with Moss Hart. *Once in a Lifetime* was a facile but funny satire on Hollywood. *Merrily We Roll Along* cleverly told its story backwards, taking the middle-aged failure back to the promise of his youth. *I'd Rather Be Right* took its title from a Henry Clay speech of 1850 ("I would rather be right than be President"), but attacked the administration of Franklin Delano Roosevelt. *You Can't Take It with You* well deserved its Pulitzer Prize for 1936, for the crazy Sycamore family creates one of the fastest, most furious, funniest farces ever and manages to effect a sweet, sentimental ending as well. The musicals *Strike Up the Band* and *The Band Wagon* (with Howard Dietz) were fun – but *The Man Who Came to Dinner*, with Hart, was fabulous. At the center of the chaos stands (or sits, in a wheelchair) Sheridan Whiteside, described by Monty Woolley in the film biography of Cole Porter as "an intolerable ass." As Woolley played him on stage and screen, this caricature of Alexander Woollcott was irresistible and, though the play is cluttered with other matters (such as cartoons of Noël Coward, one of the Marx Brothers, and a Lizzie Borden character), he delightfully dominates the action as he dominates the poor family who were unlucky enough to have him break a hip on their premises. The play contains some of the best single lines in American comedy.

The Man Who Came to Dinner may be the highspot of Kaufman's career. *George Washington Slept Here* was accurately reviewed as "George Kaufman slipped here" and later work such as *The Late George Apley* (with novelist J. P. Marquand) and *The Solid Gold Cadillac* (with Howard Teichmann) were a part of Kaufman's long career as a play doctor, though much of their success was no doubt due to his expertise. He also worked with other play doctors (such as Abe Burrows) and with Nunnally Johnson, Leueen MacGrath, and others.

Kaufman gained various strengths from various collaborators – farce, fantasy, satire, structure – but, to put it briefly, he can best be understood if one thinks of him as a Jewish comedian. He was a leader among the "Broadway intellectuals" (with Hart, Dorothy Parker, S. N. Behrman, George Jean Nathan) and a master of the wisecrack. His is the *echt* Jewish humor that plays with language (as in Goodman Ace); often sees the world as *ash und porukh* (ashes and dust) but will hang on to see what happens ("You might as well live" – Dorothy Parker); deals in insult; sometimes takes off into nonsense, intoxicated by words (S. J. Perelman), and sometimes into sentimentality (Sam Levine), attracted to nostalgia for better times; is repelled by pretension and more than a little attracted to cynism (though not at Kaufman's time going as far as the Shock Schlock of Lenny Bruce) and always loves to tinker with logic until it explodes (you had best read Leo Rosten's *The Joys of Yiddish* rather than Freud on humor). In *World of Our Fathers* (1977), Irving Howe dissects this Jewish humor which chooses laughter as the alternative to tears and often uses satire as both a defensive and an offensive weapon. Professor Howe quotes Gilbert Seldes, who claimed that the Jewish entertainers' "daemonic" approach was traceable to "their fine carelessness about our superstitions of politeness and gentility ... contempt for artificial notions of propriety."

Kaufman was businessman enough to know that an all-out assault on The Establishment would not pay off. His pose was that of the hero of *The Butter and Egg Man*, the naïf in the big city. His targets were the obvious, safe ones that are best suited to musical comedy and farce. When he tried something "positive," like *The American Way* (a patriotic panorama), he was at his weakest. A wisecrack has to be a *zinger*, not a compliment. He never let himself get bitter: *that* was the kind of satire, as he said, which "closes on Saturday night." He wasn't a *kvetch* or a nag or a moralist, just a very funny wisecracking wit, one of the best.

—Leonard R. N. Ashley

KELLY, George (Edward). American. Born in Philadelphia, Pennsylvania, 16 January 1887. Educated privately. Actor as a young man: debut, 1908; subsequently played in touring companies and vaudeville; playwright from 1916. Recipient: Pulitzer Prize, 1926; Brandeis University Creative Arts Award, 1959. D.F.A.: LaSalle College, Philadelphia, 1962. *Died 18 June 1974.*

PUBLICATIONS

Plays

> *Mrs. Ritter Appears* (produced 1917); revised version, as *The Torchbearers: A Satirical Comedy* (produced 1922). 1923; revised version of Act III, as *Mrs. Ritter Appears*, 1964.
> *Poor Aubrey* (produced 1922). In *The Flattering Word and Other One-Act Plays*, 1925; revised version, as *The Show-Off: A Transcript of Life* (produced 1924), 1924.
> *Mrs. Wellington's Surprise* (produced 1922).
> *Finders-Keepers*. 1923.
> *The Flattering Word and Other One-Act Plays* (includes *Smarty's Party, The Weak Spot, Poor Aubrey*). 1925.
> *Craig's Wife* (produced 1925). 1926.

Daisy Mayme (produced 1926).   1927.
One of Those Things, in *One-Act Plays for Stage and Study, Third Series.*   1927.
Behold the Bridegroom (produced 1927).   1928.
A La Carte (sketches and lyrics only; produced 1927).
Maggie the Magnificent (produced 1929).
Philip Goes Forth (produced 1931).   1931.
Reflected Glory (produced 1936).   1937.
The Deep Mrs. Sykes (produced 1945).   1946.
The Fatal Weakness (produced 1946).   1947.

Screenplay: *Old Hutch,* 1936.

Bibliography: "Kelly: An Eclectic Bibliography" by Paul A. Doyle, in *Bulletin of Bibliography,* September-December 1965.

Reading List: *Kelly* by Foster Hirsch, 1975.

*   *   *

George Kelly had a lot of brothers and sisters and he followed his older brother Walter ("The Virginia Judge" of vaudeville) into the theatre. In those days it was not quite so unusual a place to find a moralist, even an anti-romantic, deeply-puritanical one.

Kelly played juveniles in the Keith and Orpheum circuits and began to write playlets, sketches really, such as *One of Those Things, Finders-Keepers, The Flattering Word,* and *Poor Aubrey.* They were light little satires on character flaws such as vanity and bragging. People who overstepped the accepted moral code were given their comeuppance, like the adventuress who outsmarts herself in *Smarty's Party.* They were popular enough: really trenchant satire (as George S. Kaufman remarked) "closes on Saturday night," but audiences like to see obvious targets hit skilfully and wittily.

But then Kelly expanded *Poor Aubrey* into the full-length play of *The Show-Off,* in which Aubrey Piper's bragging and bluffing are exposed and his lies and pretensions exploded. It was Kelly's first success, for *The Torchbearers,* a rather gentle send-up of the pretensions of Little Theatres with even littler talents in them, did not catch on at first, though it later was to achieve some recognition.

Kelly achieved the height of his career (and the Pulitzer Prize) with *Craig's Wife.* The vanity of *Flattering Word* and the manipulator defeated of *Smarty's Party* combine in the well-constructed but rather grimly determined story of a woman whose concern with appearances and control of her sterile environment give "Good Housekeeping" a bad name. But character study is confused with the problem play and Kelly is no Ibsen. Mrs. Craig (mordantly played by Chrystal Herne) was unforgettable but essentially just revealed, not developed. A revival of the play in the 1970's made the theatrical success of a half century before look too theatrical and the character of Mrs. Craig too static and that of her long-suffering husband too trivial.

After *Craig's Wife,* Kelly was on the slide. He had four failures in a row: *Daisy Mayme* was talky; *Behold the Bridegroom* was worse, preachy; *Maggie the Magnificent* and *Philip Goes Forth* convinced the dramatist to give up Broadway, though he returned with *Reflected Glory,* and *The Deep Mrs. Sykes.*

After the poor reception of *The Fatal Weakness* in 1946, he seemed to recognize his own fatal weaknesses as a playwright – getting in the way of the characters, imposing himself and his views on the situation and using the stage as a soapbox without the brilliance of Shaw or the cleverness of Brecht – and retired. Today he is known as the author of *Craig's Wife* and *The Torchbearers.*

—Leonard R. N. Ashley

KINGSLEY, Sidney. American. Born Sidney Kieschner in New York City, 22 October 1906. Educated at Townsend Harris Hall, New York, 1920–24; Cornell University, Ithaca, New York (state scholarship), 1924–28, B.A. 1928. Served in the United States Army, 1941–43: Lieutenant. Married the actress Madge Evans in 1939. Worked as an actor in the Tremont Stock Company, Bronx, New York, 1928; thereafter worked as a play-reader and scenario-writer for Columbia Pictures; full-time writer and stage director from 1934. Past President, Dramatists Guild. Recipient: Pulitzer Prize, 1934; New York Theatre Club Medal, 1934, 1936, 1943; New York Drama Critics Circle Award, 1943, 1951; New York Newspaper Guild Front Page Award, 1943, and Page One Citation, 1949; Edgar Allan Poe Award, 1949; Donaldson Award, 1951; American Academy of Arts and Letters Award of Merit Medal, 1951. Lives in New Jersey.

PUBLICATIONS

Plays

    Men in White (produced 1933).   1933.
    Dead End (produced 1935).   1936.
    Ten Million Ghosts (produced 1936).
    The World We Make, from the novel *The Outward Room* by Millen Brand (produced
       1939).   1939.
    The Patriots (produced 1943).   1943.
    Detective Story (produced 1949).   1949.
    Darkness at Noon, from the novel by Arthur Koestler (produced 1951).   1951.
    Lunatics and Lovers (produced 1954).   Condensed version in *Theater 1955*, 1955.
    Night Life (produced 1962).   1966.

Screenplay: *Homecoming*, with Paul Osborn and Jan Lustig, 1948.

*   *   *

Sidney Kingsley was one of "the young radicals our colleges are said to be full of nowadays" (as S. N. Berhman put it in *End of Summer*). His agit-prop approach to theatre was a bit less strident than that of some other proletarian dramatists, but sufficient to endear him to the famous Group Theater, whose financial life he saved early in its career with the success of his first play, *Men in White*.

The story of the Group Theater is brilliantly told by Harold Clurman in *The Fervent Years*. The story of *Men in White* is accurately told by John Mason Brown (*Two on the Aisle*, 1938): it "is a piffling script, mildewed in its hokum, childishly sketchy in its characterization, and so commonplace in its every written word that it in no way justifies its own unpleasantness." Moreover, "the finished result, as Arthur Hopkins once observed when Mr. [David] Belasco converted his stage into a Child's Restaurant, is *only remarkable because it is not real.*" Very just; but just also to add that Kingsley's approach has since been copied, in its dab-hand dramaturgy and somewhat fuzzy concern with ethical standards, in Paddy Chayefsky's *Hospital* and *Network* and in many television soap operas and feature films.

Also seminal was *Dead End*, establishing for the cinema many of the clichés of slum-life sociology, "a raucous tone-poem of the modern city" (Brooks Atkinson), a shaky melodrama set down in a handsome set (by Norman Bel Geddes) with a pier-head jutting right into the orchestra pit. The contrived plot brings the Dead End kids and other poor folk into contact with some rich East Siders in New York: the façade of the wealthy apartment house is under repair, which brings the rich people round to the back and right on stage. Unfortunately for

Kingsley, he does not seem to remember poverty without sentimentality and, at least before the considerable success of *Dead End*, seems never to have met anyone rich. His sociology is superficial and his dramaturgy profoundly pedestrian.

Ten Million Ghosts is a confused discussion of munitions magnates. Kingsley was well out of his intellectual depth. *The World We Make* was not much better, although for once in the 1930's the emphasis is upon character rather than upon "The System" and environment. *The Patriots* is about a decade in the life of Thomas Jefferson. In none of these plays did Kingsley have the advantages he had in *Dead End*. He desperately needed stars and set designers and a whole team to "make something" of his scripts. He once half perceived this when he said: "When two people have a baby, the baby is a bit of a surprise. In the theater we have a marriage of many people. I can't really tell how the baby will come out."

Kingsley was once a leading Broadway playwright. He became known to a wider audience through such films as *Men in White*, *Dead End*, and *Detective Story*. He was at his best whenever he had help: the committed cast of *Men in White*, the street arabs and street scene of *Dead End*, Millen Brand's novel *The Outward Room* as a basis for *The World We Make*, Madge Evans to help with *The Patriots*, Arthur Koestler's novel behind *Darkness at Noon*. *Crowell's Handbook of Contemporary Drama* (1971) give as fair an estimate as any: "In most of his work Kingsley relies on a sense of atmosphere generated by realistic re-creation of a particular world – hospitals, slums, police stations, prisons – a vivid milieu that supplies much of the vivid impact of the play and also constitutes its limitation. The plays are frequently melodramatic in plot and sketchy in characterization; timely issues have made them at first appear more substantial than they later are seen to be."

—Leonard R. N. Ashley

KOPIT, Arthur (Lee).   American.   Born in New York City, 10 May 1937. Educated at Lawrence High School, New York, graduated 1955; Harvard University, Cambridge, Massachusetts, B.A. (cum laude) 1959 (Phi Beta Kappa). Married Leslie Ann Garis. Recipient: Vernon Rice Award, 1962; Outer Circle Award, 1962; Guggenheim Fellowship, 1967; Rockefeller grant, 1968; National Institute of Arts and Letters award, 1971; National Endowment for the Arts grant, 1974; Wesleyan University Center for the Humanities Fellowship, 1974. Lives in Connecticut.

PUBLICATIONS

Plays

> *The Questioning of Nick* (produced 1957).   In *The Day the Whores Came Out to Play Tennis and Other Plays*, 1965.
> *Gemini* (produced 1957).
> *Don Juan in Texas*, with Wally Lawrence (produced 1957).
> *On the Runway of Life, You Never Know What's Coming Off Next* (produced 1957).
> *Across the River and into the Jungle* (produced 1958).
> *To Dwell in a Place of Strangers*, Act I published in *Harvard Advocate*, May 1958.
> *Aubade* (produced 1959).

Sing to Me Through Open Windows (produced 1959; revised version, produced
    1965).   In *The Day the Whores Came Out to Play Tennis and Other Plays*, 1965.
*Oh Dad, Poor Dad, Mama's Hung You in the Closet and I'm Feelin' So Sad: A
    Pseudoclassical Tragifarce in a Bastard French Tradition* (produced 1960).   1960.
Mhil'daim (produced 1963).
Asylum; or, What the Gentlemen Are Up To, and And As for the Ladies (produced 1963;
    And As for the Ladies produced, as *Chamber Music*, 1971).   *Chamber Music* in *The
    Day the Whores Came Out to Play Tennis and Other Plays*, 1965.
The Conquest of Everest (produced 1964).   In *The Day the Whores Came Out to Play
    Tennis and Other Plays*, 1965.
The Hero (produced 1964).   In *The Day the Whores Came Out to Play Tennis and Other
    Plays*, 1965.
The Day the Whores Came Out to Play Tennis (produced 1965).   In *The Day the Whores
    Came Out to Play Tennis and Other Plays*, 1965.
The Day the Whores Came Out to Play Tennis and Other Plays.   1965; as *Chamber
    Music and Other Plays*, 1969.
Indians (produced 1968).   1969.
An Incident in the Park, in *Pardon Me, Sir, But Is My Eye Hurting Your Elbow?*, edited
    by Bob Booker and George Foster.   1968.
What's Happened to the Thorne's House (produced 1972).
Louisiana Territory; or, Lewis and Clark – Lost and Found (produced 1975).
Secrets of the Rich (produced 1976).   1978.
Wings (produced 1978).   1978.

*   *   *

A brilliant satirist with a highly developed sense of the theatrical, Arthur Kopit has been concerned from the time of his earliest plays with America's continuing need to create myth and mythic heroes in order to justify its barbaric cruelty and unlimited greediness. He is deeply disturbed by the power of these myths to shape its actions, to destroy its people's ability to make moral judgements, and to transform its real heroes into garish, bewildered caricatures of human beings.

In his first play, *The Questioning of Nick*, Kopit develops the crude prototype of his later mythic heroes. Nick Carmonatti, a high school basketball player "named in *Sport* as one of the five hun'red leading basketball prospects in the whole country," is so overpowered by the illusion of his importance that he not only admits that he accepted a bribe to throw a game but also brags that he was the only player good enough to be offered one.

In such early farces as *Don Juan in Texas* and *Across the River and into the Jungle*, as well as in *The Conquest of Everest* and *The Day the Whores Came Out to Play Tennis*, Kopit creates outrageously funny characters – "eighteen bare assed" whores who invade the staid atmosphere of the Cherry Valley Country Club; a soap salesman who is mistaken for Billy the Kid; two American barefooted tourists in Florida garb who climb Everest without realizing what they've accomplished, who eat sandwiches and drink cokes, and who then rejoin their tour for dinner. Through these characters he ridicules such minor American flaws as stuffiness, cowardice, provincialism, and prudishness.

In his more serious works, the ridicule is underscored with a strong sense of menace. *Chamber Music*, for example, features eight hilarious madwomen, each of whom believes she is a well-known historical figure. These women convince themselves that they are in danger of being attacked by the inmates of the men's ward. Then, using logic appropriate to the asylum, they decide to protect themselves by a show of strength, by a sign of their ferocity. So they kill Amelia Earhart, one of their own, and are satisfied that they have thus protected themselves from danger. *Oh Dad, Poor Dad*, Kopit's most vicious satire, again combines the ludicrous and the terrifying. Focusing on the myth of Supermom, Kopit creates Madame Rosepettle, a woman who hangs the stuffed corpse of her husband in her closet, locks her adult son Jonathan in her apartment, keeps a piranha in her living room, and grows Venus's-flytraps on her balcony. When Jonathan rebels – kills the piranha, the Venus's-flytraps, and his seductive babysitter, who is herself a potential supermom – Madame Rosepettle is shocked into a state of bewilderment. She cannot understand the meaning of his action.

Kopit carries the bewildered mythic hero a step further in his best work, *Indians*, where the genocide practiced against the American Indians is used as the metaphor for the American violence in Vietnam. William Cody's frantic struggle to live up to the myth of Buffalo Bill and his futile attempt to regain his own identity, once the barbaric cruelty of the conquest of the West and the bizarre sham of the Wild West Show threaten to destroy all sense of his humanity, epitomize for Kopit the continuing struggle of contemporary America. Thus, he demonstrates most powerfully here what he has already said in his earlier plays and what he reiterates in his most recent works: America has created the wrong kinds of heroes in order to justify the wrong kinds of actions, and it is trapped by its need to perpetuate the myth of its glorious past.

—Helen Houser Popovich

LAURENTS, Arthur. American. Born in Brooklyn, New York, 14 July 1918. Educated at Cornell University, Ithaca, New York, B.A. 1937. Served in the United States Army, rising to the rank of Sergeant, 1940–45: Radio Playwright, 1943–45 (Citation, Secretary of War, 1945). Director, Dramatists Play Service, New York, 1961–66. Since 1955, Member of the Council of the Dramatists Guild. Recipient: National Institute of Arts and Letters grant, 1946; Sidney Howard Memorial Award, 1946; Antoinette Perry Award, 1967. Lives on Long Island, New York.

PUBLICATIONS

Plays

    Now Playing Tomorrow (broadcast 1939).   In *Short Plays for Stage and Radio,* edited by Carless Jones, 1939.
    Western Electric Communicade (broadcast 1944).   In *The Best One-Act Plays of 1944,* edited by Margaret Mayorga, 1944.
    The Last Day of the War (broadcast 1945).   In *Radio Drama in Action,* edited by Erik Barnouw, 1945.
    The Face (broadcast 1945).   In *The Best One-Act Plays of 1945,* edited by Margaret Mayorga, 1945.
    Home of the Brave (produced 1945; as *The Way Back,* produced 1946).   1946.
    Heartsong (produced 1947).
    The Bird Cage (produced 1950).   1950.
    The Time of the Cuckoo (produced 1952).   1953.
    A Clearing in the Woods (produced 1957).   1957.
    West Side Story, music by Leonard Bernstein (produced 1957).   1958.
    Gypsy, music by Jule Styne, lyrics by Stephen Sondheim, from a book by Gypsy Rose Lee (produced 1959).   1960.

Invitation to a March (produced 1960).   1961.
Anyone Can Whistle, music by Stephen Sondheim (produced 1964).   1965.
Do I Hear a Waltz?, music by Richard Rodgers, lyrics by Stephen Sondheim (produced 1965).   1966.
Hallelujah, Baby!, music and lyrics by Jule Styne, Betty Comden and Adolph Green (produced 1967).   1967.
The Enclave (produced 1973).   1974.

Screenplays: *The Snake Pit*, with Frank Partos and Millen Brand, 1948; *Rope*, with Hume Cronyn, 1948; *Anna Lucasta*, with Philip Yordan, 1949; *Caught*, 1949; *Anastasia*, 1956; *Bonjour Tristesse*, 1958; *The Way We Were*, 1973; *The Turning Point*, 1977.

Radio Plays: *Now Playing Tomorrow*, 1939; *Hollywood Playhouse, Dr. Christian, The Thin Man, Manhattan at Midnight*, and other series, 1939–40; *The Last Day of the War, The Face, Western Electric Communicade*, 1944, and other plays for *The Man Behind the Gun, Army Service Force Presents* and *Assignment Home* series, 1943–45; *This Is Your FBI* series, 1945.

Fiction

The Way We Were.   1972.

*   *   *

Brooklyn-born, Hollywood-bred, Arthur Laurents is best known for his work in the two most successful American art forms, the Broadway musical and the Hollywood film.

His films include *Caught* and *The Snake Pit* and versions of two of his stage plays, *Home of the Brave* and *Time of the Cuckoo* (filmed as *Summertime*). All tend to prove Samuel Beckett's thesis: "We are all born mad. Some remain so." Psychology, especially self-realization, is Laurents's major interest and it runs through all of his serious work, even getting into musicals.

His musicals are *West Side Story* (*Romeo and Juliet* updated), *Gypsy* (based on the life of stripper Gypsy Rose Lee), *Do I Hear a Waltz?* and *Hallelujah, Baby!* These musicals show all the inventiveness and commercial savvy one would expect from a writer whose work ranges from adapting Marcel Maurette's TV play *Anastasia* for Ingrid Bergman's return to the screen to a modern version of the Sleeping Beauty legend in which the heroine refuses to tread boring conventional paths and takes off with a plumber (*Invitation to a March*). Laurents attempted to make Broadway musicals in some way more serious. He didn't always succeed. As Walter Kerr put it in *Thirty Plays Hath November*, "if a musical is going to be as serious as *Do I Hear a Waltz?* it has got to be more serious than *Do I Hear a Waltz?* ... Half measures taken toward sobriety tend to leave us all halfhearted, torn between an elusive passion on the one hand and a lost playfulness on the other." Shall we settle for the *ersatz*, typically Broadway idea of the serious (especially in diversions such as *A Chorus Line*) and not strive for reality?

Laurents's plays do make a serious effort at seriousness: in a sense they are religious, if psychology is the New Religion. In *The Bird Cage* downtrodden employees of a dictatorial employer fly their nightclub cage. We sense Symbolism and are tempted to ask, like the psychoanalyst greeted with a "hello" in the street: What Does That *Mean*? In *A Clearing in the Woods* a woman yearns "to rise in the air just a little, to climb, to reach a branch, even the lowest" and this bird learns to accept herself as "an imperfect human being," thus escaping the cage of her past. If Tom Driver is right (in *Romantic Quest and Modern Theory*, 1970) that in *West Side Story* "adult authority does not exist ... [and] there is more 'order' in the improvised life of the young than in public institutions," can it be that Laurents, for all his interest in psychology, is telling us in *A Clearing in the Woods* that we should avoid all the psychiatrists who want to adjust us, and achieve "mental health" just by learning to be happy with our craziness, accepting ourselves as "imperfect human beings"? In *Home of the Brave* (which Kenneth Tynan found pat but promising), an Army shrink copes with Coney, a soldier who learns that though he is Jewish he is just another "imperfect human being" like Mingo and everyone else who is secretly glad that it was The Other Guy who got killed, regardless of race, color, or creed. In *Time of the Cuckoo* the uptight New England spinster Leona Samish has to work out for herself the appropriate reactions to a brief encounter in Venice with a dashing (but married) Italian. Predictably, "those louses/Go back to their spouses" (as *Diamonds Are a Girl's Best Friend* teaches) and Ms. Samish realizes, reviewing her Puritan Code, that he wasn't such a nice man, after all. This psychologizing may not be as broad as a barn door, nor so deep as a well, but it will serve in the theatre, where Thornton Wilder once got away with summing up all of Freud in a single sentence: "We're all just as wicked as we can be." Well, not wicked, imperfect.

In 1960, Henry Hewes introducing *Famous American Plays of the 1940's* wrote about Laurents:

> In form it is the sort of play that has become an increasingly popular stereotype for American drama. Someone in trouble reviews the reasons for his trouble to find something he has not been facing up to. Because Mr. Laurents introduced the psychiatrist himself and had the answer up his sleeve all the time, some critics found the play too clinical. However, *Home of the Brave* contains the driving theme which seems to motivate most of this young writer's work. It is the acceptance of our imperfections in a society where everyone expects the ideal.

That is a nice, comforting thought! And we can go to movies and musicals and enjoy ourselves and rest very content with our human, albeit imperfect, selves.

—Leonard R. N. Ashley

LAWLER, Ray(mond Evenor).   Australian.   Born in Footscray, Melbourne, Victoria, in 1921. Left school at age 13. Married Jacklyn Kelleher; three children. Worked in a factory; then as an actor in variety, Brisbane; as actor and producer, National Theatre Company, Melbourne; and as Director, Melbourne University Repertory Company. Recipient: *Evening Standard* award, 1957.

PUBLICATIONS

Plays

    Cradle of Thunder (produced 1949).
    Summer of the Seventeenth Doll (produced 1955).   1957.
    The Piccadilly Bushman (produced 1959).   1961.
    The Unshaven Cheek (produced 1963).

A Breach in the Wall (televised 1967; produced 1970).
The Man Who Shot the Albatross (produced 1972).
Kid Stakes (produced 1975).
Other Times (produced 1976).

Television Plays: *A Breach in the Wall*, 1967; *Cousin Bette* (serialization), from the novel by Balzac, 1971; *The Visitors* (serialization), from the novel by Mary McMinnies, 1972; *Two Women* (serialization), from the novel by Alberto Moravia, 1972; *Mrs. Palfrey at the Claremont*, from the novel by Elizabeth Taylor, 1973; *Seeking the Bubbles*, in *The Love School* series, 1975; *True Patriots All*, 1975; *Husband to Mrs. Fitzherbert*, 1975.

*   *   *

With his first professionally produced play, *Summer of the Seventeenth Doll*, Ray Lawler established a landmark in Australian drama. The play awakened his country's theatre from a prolonged sleep of adolescence through an incisive attack on national myths, stereotypes, and the clichéd language of earlier plays. Although Lawler's later work has not had the same power or effect, Australian drama unquestionably owes him an enormous debt.

The Doll, as it is known, explores the "mateship" of two sugarcane cutters who work half the year, and their carefree life with their women during the "layoff." This idyllic society, symbolized by the kewpie doll brought home each summer, is torn apart on its seventeenth anniversary, when the characters are forced to see the insubstantiality of their relationships. Blinded by the Australian national myths of male friendship, the submissiveness of women, and the superiority of the country over the city, they are helpless before the inexorable advance of their own lives. Lawler's precise use of the understatement inherent in Australian colloquial speech and his relentless exposure of the myths and illusions surrounding the characters, as well as his strong dramatic construction, give the play the ring of authenticity and an intense power.

After *The Doll*, Lawler left Australia, settling ultimately in Ireland, and his next play, *The Piccadilly Bushman*, examined the ambivalent attachment of Australians to their mother country. Although it reflects Lawler's continuing investigation of national myths, it is weakened first by the already-diminished force of the very myth he was attacking, and second by a failure to weld his theme to his characters, who remain at such a distance from one another that the play's resolution seems contrived and unsatisfying.

Although most of Lawler's work has been realistic, he has worked in other styles. *The Unshaven Cheek*, for example, progresses largely through flashbacks, but his most serious experiment with non-realistic drama has been *The Man Who Shot the Albatross*. This study of Captain Bligh (of the *Bounty*), who served as governor of New South Wales from 1806 to 1808, mixes present experience, memory, and fantasy on a stage divided into several performance areas, and provides a fascinating look at this curious man's mind.

Lawler's most recent work, however, *Kid Stakes* and *Other Times* (known with *The Doll* as *The Doll Trilogy*) marks a return, both theatrically and dramatically to his first success. The new plays mirror the realism and the structure of *The Doll*, and deal with the same characters in years previous to that play's action, but neither has the intensity and life of before. Despite his lack of development, Ray Lawler is nonetheless a talented and able dramatist, whose place in Australian drama is secure.

—Walter Bode

LAWSON, John Howard. American. Born in New York City, 25 September 1894. Educated at Yonkers High School, New York; Cutler School, New York, graduated 1910;

Williams College, Williamstown, Massachusetts, 1910–14, B.A. 1914. Served in the American Ambulance Service in France and Italy during World War I. Married 1) Kathryn Drain in 1919 (divorced, 1923), one son; 2) Susan Edmond in 1925, one son and one daughter. Cable Editor, Reuters Press, New York, 1914–15; lived in Paris for two years after the war; a Director, New Playwrights Theatre, New York, 1927–28; film writer in Hollywood, 1928–47. Member of the Council of the Authors League of America, 1930–40; Founding President, 1933–34, and Member of the Executive Board, 1933–40, Screen Writers Guild. One of the "Hollywood Ten": served a one-year sentence for contempt of the House Un-American Activities Committee, 1950–51. *Died 11 August 1977.*

PUBLICATIONS

Plays

Servant-Master-Lover (produced 1916).
Standards (produced 1916).
Roger Bloomer (produced 1923).   1923.
Processional: A Jazz Symphony of American Life (produced 1925).   1925.
Nirvana (produced 1926).
Loudspeaker (produced 1927).   1927.
The International (produced 1928).   1928.
Success Story (produced 1932).   1932.
The Pure in Heart (produced 1934).   In *With a Reckless Preface,* 1934.
Gentlewoman (produced 1934).   In *With a Reckless Preface,* 1934.
With a Reckless Preface: Two Plays.   1934.
Marching Song (produced 1937).   1937.
Algiers (screenplay), with James M. Cain, in *Foremost Films of 1938,* edited by Frank
    Vreeland.   1939.
Parlor Magic (produced 1963).

Screenplays: *Dream of Love,* with others, 1928; *The Pagan,* with Dorothy Farnum, 1929; *Dynamite,* with Jeanie Macpherson and Gladys Unger, 1929; *The Sea Bat,* with others, 1930; *Our Blushing Brides,* with Bess Meredyth and Helen Mainard, 1930; *The Ship from Shanghai,* 1930; *Bachelor Apartment,* 1931; *Success at Any Price,* with others, 1934; *Blockade,* 1938; *Algiers,* with James M. Cain, 1938; *They Shall Have Music,* with Irmgard Von Cube, 1939; *Four Sons,* with Milton Sperling, 1940; *Earthbound,* with Samuel C. Engel, 1940; *Sahara,* with others, 1943; *Action in the North Atlantic,* with others, 1943; *Counter-Attack,* 1945; *Smashup – The Story of a Woman,* with others, 1947.

Other

Theory and Technique of Playwriting.   1936; revised edition, as *Theory and Technique
    of Playwriting and Screenwriting,* 1949.
*The Hidden Heritage: A Rediscovery of the Ideas and Forces That Link the Thought of
    Our Time with the Culture of the Past.*   1950.
Film in the Battle of Ideas.   1953.
*Film: The Creative Process: The Search for an Audio-Visual Language and
    Structure.*   1964; revised edition, 1967.

* * *

John Howard Lawson was one of the "Hollywood Ten" who went to jail rather than tell the House Un-American Activities Committee about their Marxist views. HUAC need not have asked. They could have read his plays or seen his movies. Whether he belonged to the Communist Party or not is basically none of our business. That his work is imbued with Marxism and that he is characteristic of a period in which (as the Garment Workers' musical *Pins and Needles* put it) many sang "Sing Me a Song of Social Significance," is abundantly clear. In his time, it gave him strength. Now it makes all but a few of his film works look impossibly dated.

Servant-Master-Lover, *Standards*, and *Roger Bloomer* gave him his start, and with *Processional* his left-wing sympathies were expressed in the story of "the West Virginia coal fields during a strike" told in "this new technique ... essentially vaudevillesque in character." The theory is adumbrated in a Preface (more of his interesting ideas appear in prefatory material to *The Pure in Heart* and *Gentlewoman* and in the excellent textbook *Theory and Technique of Playwriting*) and illustrated in a series of scenes which recall the Living Newspaper of the depression, the propaganda techniques of agitprop, and other attempts at "an immediate emotional response across the footlights." All the force and all the faults of the left-wing theatre tracts of the 1920's and 1930's, "the fervent years" (as Harold Clurman calls them), are here: the party-line dogmatism and narrow vision; the confusion of tragedy and pathos; the axe-to-grind earnestness, where comedy (and everything else that relates to a sense of proportion) perishes; and so on, down to the stereotyped characters: Cohen the Jewish comedian, Rastus the minstrel clown, the hard-boiled Sheriff, the city-slicker newspaperman Phillpots, the woman called Mrs. Euphemia Stewart Flimmins, even a Man in a Silk Hat.

George Abbott played Dynamite Jim in *Processional*, but only in the last act did he soar for a moment above what Stark Young called "antagonisms, bad taste and crass thinking." The critics thought it basically an amateur play "conceived with varying degrees of taste, intelligence, insight and imagination." When it is good it is very, very good – Stark Young risked "streaked with genius" – and when it is bad it's as foolish as Odets without his primitive charm. It is not that the characters are unrealistic – "Mr. Lawson," reported Watson and Pressey in *Contemporary Drama*, "says that he can find vaudeville characters on every street corner, whereas the so-called realistic characters he sees on the stage he never meets in life" – but that the politics distort the truth.

Processional was produced by the Theatre Guild and ran 96 performances in 1925 and 81 more when The Federal Theatre revived it in 1937. Today it would not run any more than would *Nirvana*, *Loudspeaker*, *The International* (a musical), *Success Story*, *Marching Song*, or other Lawson efforts. "All great art and literature," boomed Shaw, "is propaganda," but that does not mean that all propaganda is great art.

Some of Lawson's films have survived better. Very typical are, say, *Blockade* and *Smashup*. The cinema was more congenial to Lawson's talents, though *Theory and Technique of Playwriting* amply demonstrates that, as Théophile Gautier said of drama critics and eunuchs in harems, those who see it done every night may know all about it but be quite unable to do it themselves.

—Leonard R. N. Ashley

LONSDALE, Frederick. English. Born Lionel Frederick Leonard in St. Helier, Jersey, Channel Islands, 5 February 1881; adopted the name Lonsdale, 1908. Educated in schools in

St. Helier. Served as a private in the South Lancashire Regiment. Married Leslie Brook Hoggan in 1904; three daughters. Worked as a railway clerk in St. Helier; worked passage to Canada as a steward on a liner, then worked at odd jobs on the Southampton docks; wrote for the theatre from 1906; lived in the United States, 1938–45, and in France, 1950 until his death. *Died 4 April 1954.*

PUBLICATIONS

Plays

Who's Hamilton? (produced 1906).
The Early Worm (produced 1908).
The King of Cadonia, music by Sidney Jones (produced 1908).
Aren't We All? (as *The Best People,* produced 1909; revised version, as *Aren't We All?,* produced 1923). 1924.
The Balkan Princess, with Frank Curzon, music by P. A. Rubens (produced 1910).
The Woman of It (produced 1913).
Betty, with Gladys Unger, music by P. A. Unger (produced 1914).
The Patriot (produced 1915).
High Jinks, from a play by P. Bilhaud and M. Hennequin (produced 1916).
Waiting at the Church (produced 1916).
The Maid of the Mountains, music by H. Fraser-Simson, lyrics by Harry Graham (produced 1916). 1949.
Monsieur Beaucaire, music by André Messager, from the novel by Booth Tarkington (produced 1919).
The Lady of the Rose, music by J. Gilbert, from a work by R. Schanzer and E. Welisch (produced 1921).
Spring Cleaning (produced 1923). 1925.
Madame Pompadour, with Harry Graham, music by Leo Fall (produced 1923).
The Street Singer, music by H. Fraser-Simson, lyrics by P. Greenbank (produced 1924). 1929.
The Fake (produced 1924). 1926.
Katja the Dancer, with Harry Graham, music by J. Gilbert, from a play by L. Jacobsohn and R. Osterreicher (produced 1924).
The Last of Mrs. Cheyney (produced 1925). 1925.
On Approval (produced 1926). 1927.
The High Road (produced 1927). 1927.
Lady Mary, with J. Hastings Turner, music by A. Sirmay (produced 1928).
Canaries Sometimes Sing (produced 1929). 1929.
Never Come Back (produced 1932).
The Foreigners (produced 1939). 1932.
Once Is Enough (produced 1938). 1939; revised version, as *Let Them Eat Cake* (produced 1959), in *Plays of the Year 1958–59,* 1961.
Another Love Story (produced 1934). 1948.
But for the Grace of God (produced 1946).
The Way Things Go (produced 1950). 1951.

Screenplays: *The Devil to Pay,* 1930; *Lovers Courageous,* 1932; *The Private Life of Don Juan,* with Lajos Biro, 1934; *Forever and a Day,* with others, 1944.

Reading List: *Freddy Lonsdale* (biography) by Frances Donaldson, 1957.

*   *   *

Some might think that Frederick Lonsdale is as dated as the Manchester School of Alan Monkhouse, Harold Brighouse, Stanley Houghton, but the comedies of the 1920's have survived better than most of the other plays of the period. He has not weathered as well as Noël Coward, whose *Private Lives* of 1930 is an interesting comparison with Lonsdale's *On Approval* of several years earlier, but non-dramatic considerations must be taken into account there; it is really with W. Somerset Maugham's plays that his work invites consideration. The "Bright Young Thingery" of Lonsdale's clever *Spring Cleaning* relies not so much on what we have come to think of as Coward characters as on a Maugham situation, and Lonsdale lacked not so much Coward's insouciance and wit as the stronger satire and "seriousness" of, say, Maugham's *For Services Rendered*. In his time he was one of the mainstays of West End theatre, easily as important as William Douglas Home and similar box-office draws of our own period.

His greatest success was probably with musicals such as the comic opera *The Maid of the Mountains* (1352 performances) and the Ruritanian divertissement of *The Balkan Princess*, but the best-remembered of his hits was the romantic comedy *The Last of Mrs. Cheyney*. That displays an unquestioned technical brilliance and produces an electrifying scene in the reading of Lord Elton's foolish letter, even though the ending is marred by sentimentality. Otherwise, it might well have ranked with *The Circle* and *The Constant Wife*, whose salt of cynicism have preserved them better. *The Last of Mrs. Cheyney*, along with *Aren't We All?*, established Lonsdale in the middle of the 1920's as a popular playwright. From then on it was more or less downhill, for times changed and Lonsdale did not.

It is a combination of talented actors and actresses, familiar themes, and craftsmanship (all too unfamiliar in some plays since the war) that endeared Lonsdale to audiences. More recent writers have tried to copy some of his farce techniques, and some turn up in "serious" comedies such as Tennessee Williams's *A Period of Adjustment*, not to mention inferior works. We recall the story of Walter Scott as a boy lying out on the hillside in a thunderstorm and greeting each flash of lightning with delighted cries of "Bonny, bonny!" So too with unabashed and brilliant *coups de théâtre*.

If the plays of Lonsdale's prime seem less impressive in content than in technique, we must recall that playwrights as talented as Maugham and St. John Ervine were content with the titillations of bright boulevard comedy. Maugham wrote: "Plays will only succeed if they amuse. The drama is just as ephemeral as the newspaper, and must reflect the passions and foibles of the day." In the 1920's the passions were trivial: "We just want to have a good time," said Galsworthy's Fleur, "because we don't believe anything can last." *The Last of Mrs. Cheyney* – the story of a shop girl turned crook turned honorable – was perfect for Terence Rattigan's "Aunt Edna" starting out her theatre-going career as a young embodiment of the middle class. The play was full of glittering make-believe people in the tinsel world of theatre, a world of matinée idols and leading actresses in egret feathers and the very latest fashions, of handsome profiles and good lines.

Frederick Lonsdale flourished. When cataclysm swept it all away, he went with it. Whenever it suits us to recall those carefree if confused years between the wars, we could do worse than to revive one of his light but not necessarily flimsy comedies. They are the brief chronicles of the time. I suggest a sounder play then *The Last of Mrs. Cheyney*, the more astringent *On Approval*. Two couples go away to the wilds of Scotland "on approval," considering marriage. The "two even-tempered experimenters withdraw in dismay," as critic Henry Popkin has put it, "leaving the quarrelsome and utterly impossible man and woman to each other." This might be where a Coward of Maugham play would begin, but it is where Lonsdale's audience was pleased to have the curtain drop.

—Leonard R. N. Ashley

MacARTHUR, Charles.   American.   Born in Scranton, Pennsylvania, 5 November 1895. Educated at the Wilson Memorial Academy, Nyack, New York. Served as a trooper in the 1st Illinois Cavalry, Mexican Border, 1916; Private in the 149th Field Artillery of the United States Army, 1917–19; Assistant to the Chief of the Chemical Warfare Service, Washington, D.C., with rank of Lieutenant Colonel, 1942–45. Married 1) Carol Frink (divorced); 2) the actress Helen Hayes in 1928, one daughter and one son, the actor James MacArthur. Reporter, City News Bureau, Chicago, 1914, *Herald and Examiner*, Chicago, 1915–16, and the *Chicago Tribune*, 1916–17; worked on the New York *American*, 1921–23; Special Writer, *Hearst's International Magazine*, New York, 1924; full-time writer and producer from 1929; screen writer and director from 1930; formed a production company with Ben Hecht, 1934. *Died 21 April 1956.*

PUBLICATIONS

Collections

    The Stage Works (includes *Lulu Belle; Salvation; The Front Page; Twentieth Century; Ladies and Gentlemen; Swan Song; Johnny on a Spot; Stag at Bay,* with Nunnally Johnson), edited by Arthur Dorlag and John Irvine.   1974.

Plays

    My Lulu Belle, with Edward Sheldon (as *Lulu Belle,* produced 1926).   1925; in *Stage Works,* 1974.
    Salvation, with Sidney Howard (produced 1928).   In *Stage works,* 1974.
    The Front Page, with Ben Hecht (produced 1928).   1928; in *Stage Works,* 1974.
    Twentieth Century, with Ben Hecht (produced 1932).   1932; in *Stage Works,* 1974.
    Jumbo, with Ben Hecht, music by Richard Rodgers, lyrics by Lorenz Hart (produced 1935).   1935.
    Ladies and Gentlemen, with Ben Hecht, from a play by Ladislas Bush-Fekete (produced 1939).   1941; in *Stage Works,* 1974.
    Fun to Be Free: A Patriotic Pageant, with Ben Hecht (produced 1941).   1941.
    Johnny on a Spot, from a story by Parke Levy and Alan Lipscott (produced 1942).   In *Stage Works,* 1974.
    Wuthering Heights (screenplay), with Ben Hecht, in *Twenty Best Film Plays,* edited by John Gassner and Dudley Nichols.   1943.
    Swan Song, with Ben Hecht, from a story by Ramon Romero and Harriett Hinsdale (produced 1946).   In *Stage Works,* 1974.
    Stag at Bay, with Nunnally Johnson (produced 1976).   In *Stage Works,* 1974.

Screenplays: *Billy the Kid,* with Wanda Tuckock and Laurence Stallings, 1930; *The King of Jazz,* with others, 1930; *Paid,* with Lucien Hubbard, 1930; *Way for a Sailor,* with others, 1930; *The Girl Said No,* with Sarah Y. Mason and A. P. Younger, 1930; *New Adventures of Get-Rich-Quick Wallingford,* 1931; *The Sin of Madelon Claudet,* 1931; *The Front Page,* with Ben Hecht, 1931; *Rasputin and the Empress,* 1933; *Twentieth Century,* with Ben Hecht, 1934; *Crime Without Passion,* with Ben Hecht, 1934; *The Scoundrel,* with Ben Hecht, 1935; *Barbary Coast,* with Ben Hecht, 1935; *Once in a Blue Moon,* with Ben Hecht, 1936; *Soak the Rich,* with Ben Hecht, 1936; *Wuthering Heights,* with Ben Hecht, 1939; *Gunga Din,* with others, 1939; *I Take This Woman,* with James Kevin McGuinness, 1940; *Until I Die,* with Ben Hecht, 1940; *The Senator Was Indiscreet,* with Edwin Lanham, 1947.

Other

A Bug's-Eye View of the War.   1919.
War Bugs.   1928.

Reading List: *Charlie: The Improbable Life and Times of MacArthur* by Ben Hecht, 1957.

*   *   *

The young Charles MacArthur was a reporter for the City News Bureau, the *Herald and Examiner*, and the *Tribune* in Chicago, worked on the *New York American*, and contributed to Hearst's *International Magazine* and other journals. From their Chicago journalism experience, but chiefly from Jed Harris traditions of Broadway melodrama, MacArthur and Ben Hecht created the famous play, *The Front Page*. The *New York Times* (15 August 1928) liked this sensational and sentimental, if somewhat raucous and callous hymn to the antics of the working press. It said the play opened the season "noisily": "By superimposing a breathless melodrama upon a good newspaper play the authors and directors [actually George S. Kaufman] of 'The Front Page' ... have packed an evening with loud, rapid, coarse and unfailing entertainment ... have told a racy story with all the tang of front-page journalism ... [and] convey the rowdy comedy of the pressroom, the whirr of excitement, of nerves on edge ... in the hurly-burly of a big newspaper yarn."

MacArthur's unaided work (such as the forced farce of *Johnny on a Spot*) was undistinguished, but in collaboration he did well. In collaboration he also wrote *Lulu Belle* (with Edward Sheldon), *Salvation* (with Sidney Howard), and *Twentieth Century* (with Ben Hecht, 1932). All were solid Broadway vehicles. With Hecht he also wrote the spectacular *Jumbo, Ladies and Gentlemen, Swan Song*, and several film scripts.

MacArthur married as his second wife Helen Hayes, later to be queen of the legitimate stage, but professionally after 1928 he was more or less married to the movies. He began with several scripts in 1930, but hit the jackpot with a vehicle for Helen Hayes, *The Sin of Madelon Claudet*. Later films include *Rasputin and the Empress* (with the Barrymores), *Crime Without Passion* (writer, producer, director), *The Scoundrel, Gunga Din*, and *Wuthering Heights*. When he died he was working with Anita Loos on a vehicle for Miss Hayes. He was by then one of Hollywood's most respected writers.

His service with the Rainbow Division in France in World War I led to *A Bug's-Eye View of the War* and *War Bugs*. It is too bad he did not do more humorous prose. He brought together a nice combination of sentiment and wit and a touch of irony with a raucous sense of fun and irreverence. All these elements are at their best in *The Front Page*. Brooks Atkinson (in his introduction to *Sixteen Famous American Plays*, 1946) wrote that "*The Front Page* is to journalism what *What Price Glory?* is to the marines – rudely realistic style but romantic in its loyalties, and also audaciously profane." Actually, the "baldest profanity and most slatternly jesting as has ever been heard on the public stage" (as the *New York Times* had it in 1928) today sounds rather tame – and the play is not as realist as it seemed then. But some reporters still at least attempt to sound like MacArthur-Hecht characters (for nature imitates art), and *The Front Page* still has life in it, while *Five Star Final, Press Time, The Squeaker, Freedom of the Press*, and *Kiss the Boys Goodbye* and a host of other newspaper plays are long dead.

—Leonard R. N. Ashley

MacKAYE, Percy (Wallace).   American.   Born in New York City, 16 March 1875; son of the dramatist Steele MacKaye. Educated at Harvard University, Cambridge, Massachusetts,

A.B. 1897; studied at the University of Leipzig, 1898–1900. Married Marion Homer Morse in 1898 (died, 1939), two daughters and one son. Teacher, Craigie School for Boys, New York, 1900–04; full-time writer from 1904; Fellow in Poetry, Miami University, Ohio, 1920–24; Advisory Editor, *Folk-Say* journal, from 1929; Teacher of poetry and folk backgrounds, Rollins College, Winter Park, Florida, 1929–31; Visiting Professor of the creative aspects of drama, Sweet Briar College, Virginia, 1932–33; Director, White Top Mountain Folk Festival, Virginia, 1933; engaged in research into folklore in the Appalachian Mountains, 1933–35, and in Switzerland and the British Isles, 1936–37. Founder Member, Phi Beta Kappa Associates, 1941; President, Pan American Poets League of North America, 1943; Founder, Marion Morse-Percy MacKaye Collection at Harvard University Library, 1943. Recipient: Shelley Memorial Award, 1943; Academy of American Poets Fellowship, 1948. M.A.: Dartmouth College, Hanover, New Hampshire, 1914; Litt.D.: Miami University, 1924. Member, National Institute of Arts and Letters. *Died 31 August 1956.*

PUBLICATIONS

Plays

Kinfolk of Robin Hood (as *Inhabitants of Carlysle*, produced 1901).   1924.
The Canterbury Pilgrims (produced 1903).   1903; revised version, music by Reginald DeKoven, 1916.
Fenris the Wolf. 1905.
St. Gaudens Masque-Prologue (produced 1905).   1910.
Jeanne d'Arc (produced 1906).   1906.
Sappho and Phaon (produced 1907).   1907.
Mater: An American Study in Comedy (produced 1908).   1908.
The Scarecrow, from the story "Feathertop" by Hawthorne (produced 1908).   1908.
A Garland to Sylvia: A Dramatic Reverie. 1910.
Anti-Matrimony (produced 1910).   1910.
Hannele, with Mary Safford, from a play by Gerhart Hauptmann (produced 1910).
A Masque of Labor. 1912.
Tomorrow (produced 1913).   1912.
Yankee Fantasies (includes *Chuck, Gettysburg, The Antick, The Cat-Boat, Sam Average*). 1912.
Chuck (produced 1912).   In *Yankee Fantasies,* 1912.
Sam Average (produced 1912).   In *Yankee Fantasies,* 1912.
Gettysburg (produced 1912).   In *Yankee Fantasies,* 1912.
The Antick (produced 1915).   In *Yankee Fantasies,* 1912.
Sanctuary: A Bird Masque (produced 1913).   1914.
A Thousand Years Ago: A Romance of the Orient (produced 1913).   1914.
St. Louis: A Civic Pageant, with Thomas Wood Stevens (produced 1914).   1914.
The Immigrants, music by Frederick Converse.   1915.
The New Citizenship: A Civic Ritual (produced 1916).   1915.
Caliban, By the Yellow Sands (produced 1916).   1916.
The Evergreen Tree (produced 1917).   1917.
Sinbad the Sailor. 1917.
The Roll Call: A Masque of the Red Cross (produced 1918).   1918.
The Will of Song: A Dramatic Service of Community Singing, music by Harry Barnhart (produced 1919).   1919.
Washington, The Man Who Made Us (produced 1920).   1919; shortened versions published, as *George Washington,* 1920, *Washington and Betsy Ross,* 1927, and *Young Washington at Mt. Vernon,* 1927.

Rip Van Winkle, music by Reginald DeKoven (produced 1920).   1919.
The Pilgrim and the Book.   1920.
This Fine-Pretty World (produced 1923).   1924.
Kentucky Mountain Fantasies (includes *Napoleon Crossing the Rockies, The Funeralizing of Crickneck, Timber*).   1928; revised edition, 1932.
The Sphinx.   1929.
Wakefield: A Folk-Masque of America, music by John Tasker Howard (produced 1932).   1932.
The Mystery of Hamlet, Prince of Denmark; or, What We Will: A Tetralogy (produced 1949).   1950.

Fiction

Tall Tales of the Kentucky Mountains.   1926.
Weathergoose Woo!   1929.

Verse

Johnny Crimson: A Legend of Hollis Hall.   1895.
Ode on the Centenary of Abraham Lincoln.   1909.
Poems.   1909; as *The Sistine Eve and Other Poems*, 1915.
Uriel and Other Poems.   1912.
The Present Hour.   1914.
Dogtown Common.   1921.
The Skippers of Nancy Gloucester.   1924.
April Fire.   1925.
Winged Victory.   1927.
The Gobbler of God: A Poem of the Southern Appalachians.   1928.
Songs of a Day.   1929.
William Vaughn Moody, Twenty Years After.   1930.
Moments en Voyage: Nine Poems for the Harvard Class of 1897.   1932.
In Another Land, with Albert Steffen.   1937.
The Far Familiar.   1938.
Poem-Leaflets in Remembrance of Marion Morse MacKaye.   1939.
My Lady Dear, Arise! Songs and Sonnets in Remembrance of Marion Morse MacKaye.   1940.
What Is She? A Sonnet of Sonnets to Marion Morse.   1943.
Rememberings 1895–1945: Four Poems.   1945.
The Sequestered Shrine.   1950.
Discoveries and Inventions: Victories of the American Spirit.   1950.

Other

The Playhouse and the Play, and Other Addresses Concerning the Theatre and Democracy in America.   1909.
The Civic Theatre in Relation to the Redemption of Leisure.   1912.
The New Citizenship.   1915.
A Substitute for War.   1915.
Poems and Plays.   2 vols., 1916.
Epoch: The Life of Steele MacKaye.   2 vols., 1927.
American Theatre-Poets.   1935.

Poesia Religio.   1940.
Poog's Pasture: The Mythology of a Child: A Vista of Autobiography.   1951.
Poog and the Caboose Man: The Mythology of a Child: A Vista of Autobiography.   1952.

Editor, *Letters to Harriet,* by William Vaughn Moody.   1935.
Editor, *An Arrant Knave and Other Plays,* by Steele MacKaye.   1941.

Translator, *The Canterbury Tales of Chaucer: A Modern Rendering into Prose of the Prologue and Ten Tales.*   1904.
Translator, with John S. P. Tatlock, *The Modern Reader's Chaucer: Complete Poetical Works Now First Put into Modern English.*   1912; selection as *Canterbury Tales,* edited by Carl W. Ziegler, 1923.

Reading List: *MacKaye: A Sketch of His Life with Bibliography of His Works,* 1922; *Dipped in Sky* by Frank A. Doggett, 1930; *Annals of an Era: Percy MacKaye and the MacKaye Family* edited by E. O. Grover, 1932.

*   *   *

As the son of Steele MacKaye, Percy MacKaye might have been expected to show an interest in experimental drama. And he did, beginning with his graduation speech from Harvard in 1897 entitled "The Need of Imagination in the Drama of Today." Early in his career he added his efforts to the work of a small group of poetic dramatists – William Vaughn Moody, Josephine Peabody Marks, George Cabot Lodge – who were attempting to offset the excess of Realism on the American stage with something of the artistry which Yeats and Maeterlinck were creating abroad. MacKaye's poetic dramas, however – *The Canterbury Pilgrims, Jeanne d'Arc, Sappho and Phaon* – were minor contributions to the genre.

It was with pageant drama and community theatre that MacKaye trod most successfully in the steps of his father, generally celebrating America's heritage on the grand scale his father envisioned. As a crusader for community theatre he wrote several books and numerous articles – *The Playhouse and the Play, The Civic Theatre.* One of his most successful pageants – allegorical masques is a more accurate descriptive term: he called his work "poetry for the masses; the drama of democracy" – was *St. Louis: A Civic Pageant* which had a cast of 7,500 and attracted over half a million people to its five performances. *Caliban, By the Yellow Sands,* produced on the 300th anniversary of Shakespeare's death, was an elaborate pageant using various scenes from Shakespeare's plays to humanize Caliban, to suggest, as MacKaye explained, "the slow education of mankind through the influences of cooperative art." His other pageants included *The Roll Call,* requested by the American Red Cross, and *Wakefield,* in which he attempted to dramatize the effect of "the Folk-Spirit of America" on American freedom.

For the historian of American drama one of MacKaye's particular contributions is his definitive two-volume biography of his father, *Epoch,* a man Percy worshipped and with whom he shared the dream of creating drama for the people. As a poet and a dramatist, MacKaye's best and most enduring work was his dramatization of Nathaniel Hawthorne's "Feathertop" which he called *The Scarecrow.* Created before the audience's eyes with a display of imagination and theatrical skill, the scarecrow comes to life as Lord Ravensbane and achieves a considerable sense of humanity before it succumbs to the wiles of mankind and its own artificial construction. It is a fine example of MacKaye's commentary on the "need of imagination" and still retains its theatrical magic for modern audiences.

—Walter J. Meserve

MacLEISH, Archibald. American. Born in Glencoe, Illinois, 7 May 1892. Educated at the Hotchkiss School, Lakeville, Connecticut; Yale University, New Haven, Connecticut, A.B. 1915; Harvard University, Cambridge, Massachusetts, LL.B. 1919. Served in the United States Army, 1917–19: Captain. Married Ada Hitchcock in 1916; three children. Lecturer in Government, Harvard University, 1919–21; Attorney, Choate, Hall, and Stewart, Boston, 1920–23; Editor, *Fortune* magazine, New York, 1929–38; Curator of the Niemann Foundation, Harvard University, 1938; Librarian of Congress, Washington, D.C., 1939–44; Director, United States Office of Facts and Figures, 1941–42, Assistant Director of the Office of War Information, 1942–43, and Assistant Secretary of State, 1944–45, Washington, D.C. Chairman of the United States Delegation to the Unesco drafting conference, London, 1945, and Member of the Executive Board, Unesco, 1946. Rede Lecturer, Cambridge University, 1942; Boylston Professor of Rhetoric and Oratory, Harvard University, 1949–62; Simpson Lecturer, Amherst College, Massachusetts, 1964–67. Recipient: Shelley Memorial Award, 1932; Pulitzer Prize, 1933, 1953, for drama, 1959; New England Poetry Club Golden Rose, 1934; Bollingen Prize, 1952; National Book Award, 1953; Sarah Josepha Hale Award, 1958; Antoinette Perry Award, 1959; National Association of Independent Schools Award, 1959; Academy of American Poets Fellowship, 1965; Academy Award, 1966; National Medal for Literature, 1978. M.A.: Tufts University, Medford, Massachusetts, 1932: Litt.D.: Wesleyan University, Middletown, Connecticut, 1938; Colby College, Waterville, Maine, 1938; Yale University, 1939; University of Pennsylvania, Philadelphia, 1941; University of Illinois, Urbana, 1947; Rockford College, Illinois, 1952; Columbia University, New York, 1954; Harvard University, 1955; Carleton College, Northfield, Minnesota, 1956; Princeton University, New Jersey, 1965; University of Massachusetts, Amherst, 1969; York University, Toronto, 1971; LL.D.: Dartmouth College, Hanover, New Hampshire, 1940; Johns Hopkins University, Baltimore, 1941; University of California, Berkeley, 1943; Queen's University, Kingston, Ontario, 1948; University of Puerto Rico, Rio Piedras, 1953; Amherst College, Massachusetts, 1963; D.C.L.: Union College, Schenectady, New York, 1941; L.H.D.: Williams College, Williamstown, Massachusetts, 1942; University of Washington, Seattle, 1948. Commander, Legion of Honor; Commander, El Sol del Peru. President, American Academy of Arts and Letters, 1953–56. Lives in Massachusetts.

Plays

Nobodaddy. 1926.
Union Pacific (ballet scenario; produced 1934). In *The Book of Ballets,* 1939.
Panic: A Play in Verse (produced 1935). 1935.
The Fall of the City: A Verse Play for Radio (broadcast 1937). 1937.
Air Raid: A Verse Play for Radio (broadcast 1938). 1938.
The States Talking (broadcast 1941). In *The Free Company Presents,* edited by James Boyd. 1941.
The American Story: Ten Radio Scripts (includes *The Admiral; The American Gods; The American Name; Not Bacon's Bones; Between the Silence and the Surf; Discovered; The Many Dead; The Names for the Rivers; Ripe Strawberries and Gooseberries and Sweet Single Roses; Socorro, When Your Sons Forget*) (broadcast 1944). 1944.
The Trojan Horse (broadcast 1952). 1952.
This Music Crept by Me upon the Waters (broadcast 1953). 1953.
J.B.: A Play in Verse (produced 1958). 1958.
The Secret of Freedom (televised 1959). In *Three Short Plays,* 1961.
Three Short Plays: The Secret of Freedom, Air Raid, The Fall of the City. 1961.

Our Lives, Our Fortunes, and Our Sacred Honor (as *The American Bell,* music by David Amram, produced 1962). In *Think,* July-August 1961.
Herakles: A Play in Verse (produced 1965).   1967.
An Evening's Journey to Conway, Massachusetts: An Outdoor Play (produced 1967).   1967.
Scratch, suggested by *The Devil and Daniel Webster* by Stephen Vincent Benét (produced 1971).   1971.
The Great American Fourth of July Parade (produced 1975).   1975.

Screenplays: *Grandma Moses,* 1950; *The Eleanor Roosevelt Story,* 1965.

Radio Plays: *The Fall of the City,* 1937; *King Lear,* from the play by Shakespeare, 1937; *Air Raid,* 1938; *The States Talking,* 1941; *The American Story* series, 1944; *The Son of Man,* 1947; *The Trojan Horse,* 1952; *This Music Crept by Me upon the Waters,* 1953.

Television Play: *The Secret of Freedom,* 1959.

Verse

Songs for a Summer's Day (A Sonnet-Cycle).   1915.
Tower of Ivory.   1917.
The Happy-Marriage and Other Poems.   1924.
The Pot of Earth.   1925.
Streets in the Moon.   1926.
The Hamlet of A. MacLeish.   1928.
Einstein.   1929.
New Found Land: Fourteen Poems.   1930.
Before March.   1932.
Conquistador.   1932.
Frescoes for Mr. Rockefeller's City.   1933.
Poems 1924–1933.   1933; as *Poems,* 1935.
Public Speech: Poems.   1936.
Land of the Free – U.S.A.   1938.
America Was Promises.   1939.
Actfive and Other Poems.   1948.
Collected Poems 1917–1952.   1952.
Songs for Eve.   1954.
Collected Poems.   1963.
"The Wild Old Wicked Man" and Other Poems.   1968.
The Human Season: Selected Poems 1926–1972.   1972.
New and Collected Poems 1917–1976.   1976.

Other

Housing America, by the Editors of *Fortune.*   1932.
Jews in America, by the Editors of *Fortune.*   1936.
Background of War, by the Editors of *Fortune.*   1937.
The Irresponsibles: A Declaration.   1940.
The Next Harvard, As Seen by MacLeish.   1941.
A Time to Speak: The Selected Prose.   1941.
The American Cause.   1941.
A Time to Act: Selected Addresses.   1943.

*Poetry and Opinion: The Pisan Cantos of Ezra Pound: A Dialogue on the Role of
   Poetry.* 1950.
*Freedom Is the Right to Choose: An Inquiry into the Battle for the American
   Future.* 1951.
Poetry and Journalism. 1958.
Emily Dickinson: Papers Delivered at Amherst College, with others.   1960.
Poetry and Experience. 1961.
The Dialogues of MacLeish and Mark Van Doren, edited by Warren V. Busch.   1964.
The Eleanor Rossevelt Story. 1965.
A Continuing Journey. 1968.
The Great American Frustration. 1968.
Riders of the Earth: Essays and Reminiscences. 1978.

Editor, *Law and Politics,* by Felix Frankfurter.   1962.

Bibliography: *A Catalogue of the First Editions of MacLeish* by Arthur Mizener, 1938;
MacLeish: A Checklist by Edward J. Mullahy, 1973.

Reading List: *MacLeish* by Signi Lenea Falk, 1965; *MacLeish* by Grover G. Smith, 1971.

*   *   *

By 1940, Archibald MacLeish had written numerous books of poems, and was a well-known writer. He was also the target of adverse criticism. MacLeish's early work is too derivative. It abounds with the distracting influence of Eliot and Pound, among others. MacLeish writes on the same subjects as Eliot and Pound and from exactly their point of view. MacLeish's early long poems proved very weak. His most famous one is *Conquistador*, which won him the first of three Pulitzer Prizes. It is a verbose, unqualified glorification of Spain's slaughter and enslavement of Mexican natives, and is, at best, unthinkingly adolescent. Other works in this period are marred by the confusing about-face MacLeish executes concerning the role of the poet. In his "Invocation to the Social Muse," MacLeish criticizes those who would urge the poet to concentrate on social issues. These issues, however, soon become central to his own work. MacLeish proceeds to sermonize, harangue – and produced much poor poetry, especially in *Public Speech* and his plays for radio.

Yet, despite the inferior work written in these decades, MacLeish was beginning to compile an outstanding body of lyric poetry. Some of the short poems in *Streets in the Moon* and *New Found Land* hold up very well. "L'an trentiesme de mon eage" is a superior presentation on the subject of the lost generation. Other fine poems include "Eleven," "Immortal Autumn," and "Memorial Rain." "Ars poetica" develops the stimulating idea that "A poem should not mean/But be." Perhaps the best of all is "The End of the World," a dramatization of the belief that the universe is basically meaningless. *Poems 1924–1933* brought together such superior lyrics as "Pony Rock," "Unfinished History," and "Lines for an Interment."

What became increasingly apparent in the 1940's and thereafter is that MacLeish's primary strength as a writer resides in the lyric form. In fact, MacLeish has done most of his best work after the age of fifty.

Even some of MacLeish's later plays and long poems, two genres he never really excels at, rise above the mediocre. The full-length play *J.B.*, despite its bland poetry and tepid main character, effectively dramatizes the tragedies that engulf J.B. and offers a frequently rousing debate between Mr. Zuss (representing orthodox religion) and Nickles (representing a pragmatic outlook). MacLeish's one-act play *This Music Crept by Me upon the Waters* is also successful. The main characters, Peter and Elizabeth, are interesting; the plot builds in suspense; and the poetry and the theme (a preference for the present over the past) are powerful. *Actfive* is MacLeish's best long poem. The first section, which delineates modern man's basic predicament, is quite absorbing.

Still, it is MacLeish's lyric poetry that will be remembered the longest. Starting with the poems collected in 1948, the number of excellent lyrics mounts steadily. For this reason, the critical neglect MacLeish has suffered in recent years is unjust. These later lyrics center on three sometimes overlapping subjects. One presents MacLeish's increasing awareness of the mystery that permeates human experience. Earlier in his life, he wrote several poems that spoke confidently, if not cockily about setting out on explorations; now he writes "Voyage West," a sensitive expression of the uncertainty involved in a journey. Significantly, "Poet's Laughter" and "Crossing" are full of questions, while "The Old Man to the Lizard" and "Hotel Breakfast" end with questions, not answers. MacLeish sums up his sense of the mysterious in "Autobiography" when he says, "What do I know of the mystery of the universe?/Only the mystery."

MacLeish has also written several tender eulogies and epitaphs. Two such poems about his mother are "The Burial" and "For the Anniversary of My Mother's Death." A pair of even finer poems, "Poet" and "Hemingway," have Ernest Hemingway for their subject. Other outstanding poems in this vein include "Edwin Muir," "Cummings," and "The Danger in the Air."

Finally, MacLeish has written a host of fine poems about old age. The difficulty of creativity when one is no longer young is described in "They Come No More, Those Words, Those Finches." Tiredness is poignantly depicted in "Waking" and "Dozing on the Lawn." "Ship's Log" records the narrowing awareness of the old. Here, MacLeish states: "Mostly I have relinquished and forgotten/Or grown accustomed, which is a way of forgetting." Yet " 'The Wild Old Wicked Man' " presents an old person's wisdom and passion. In the two poems concerning "The Old Gray Couple," he offers the reader a moving portrait of the final, deepest stage of human love. Lastly, using Odysseus as narrator, MacLeish chooses human love (symbolized by his aging wife) and mortal life over love for the abstract (symbolized by the goddess Calypso) and the metaphysical in his lovely poem "Calypso's Island." This poem declares, "I long for the cold, salt,/Restless, contending sea and for the island/Where the grass dies and seasons alter."

—Robert K. Johnson

MARTYN, Edward (Joseph). Irish. Born in Galway, 31 January 1859. Educated at Christ Church, Oxford, left without taking a degree. Settled in Dublin, and began to write for the theatre, 1899; Co-Founder, with William Butler Yeats and Lady Gregory, Irish Literary Theatre, 1899, which became the Abbey Theatre, Dublin, 1904; Founder, Palestrina Society, Dublin, 1901; left the Irish Literary Theatre after a quarrel with Yeats, 1902, and abandoned the theatre for the next decade; returned to the theatre when he began writing plays for the Independent Theatre Company, from 1912; founded the Irish Theatre, to present plays in Gaelic, 1914. *Died 5 December 1923.*

PUBLICATIONS

Plays

The Heather Field (produced 1899). In *The Heather Field, and Maeve*, 1899.

Maeve (produced 1900).   1899.
The Tale of a Town, and An Enchanted Sea.   1902.
The Place-Hunters, in *Leader,* 26 July 1902.
Romulus and Remus.   1907.
Grangecolman (produced 1912).   1912.
The Dream Physician (produced 1914).   1918.
Privilege of Place (produced 1915).
Regina Eyre (produced 1919).

Fiction

Morgante the Lesser, His Notorious Life and Wonderful Deeds.   1890.

Reading List: *Martyn and the Irish Revival* by Denis R. Gwynn, 1930; *Martyn and the Irish Theatre* by Marie-T. Courtney, 1956.

*   *   *

Edward Martyn was one of the founders of the Irish Literary Theatre, which performed his *The Heather Field* as its second production in 1899. The declared aim of the Literary Theatre was to break with the crude sensationalism of commercial theatre. By appealing to the intellect and spirit it would furnish a vehicle for the literary expression of the national thought and ideals of Ireland. This was the movement which, under the inspiration of W. B. Yeats and Lady Gregory, was to lead to the foundation of the Abbey Theatre, and to the work of Synge and O'Casey.

Although the theme of *The Heather Field* is Irish (it describes the infatuated attempt of Carden Tyrrel to reclaim waste land for agriculture), the main influence upon Martyn was Ibsen. He follows closely Ibsen's attempts to introduce poetic and symbolic elements within a naturalistic setting. In *Maeve* the heroine proves a reincarnation of an ancient Irish queen, and in *An Enchanted Sea* the sinister deities of the ocean bring tragedy to an old family. Partly because of his concern with the life of the middle and upper classes, Martyn broke from the Abbey Theatre which had become preoccupied with peasant plays and heroic fantasies, and he satirised Yeats and his circle in *Romulus and Remus* and *The Dream Physician.*

Although Martyn associated with figures in the Irish political movement such as Constance Markievicz and Thomas MacDonagh, his national idealism is haunted by the shades of Pater (whose early influence he had felt at Oxford – especially the essay on Winckelmann), and it was the hard gemlike flame of intellectual abstraction his plays seek to kindle. Lord Mask's praise of Ireland in *An Enchanted Sea* may serve an example: "Here in the Insula Sacra – the Ogygia of Homer and our Hellenic ancestors – the genius is here and will soon awaken, and he will revive arts, and trades, and letters in our ancient tongue which all will speak again. Let us be ready to minister." Besides generously patronising theatre in Ireland, Martyn was active also in his support of music, the Catholic Church, and the Gaelic League.

—Malcolm Kelsall

MASON, Bruce (Edward George).   New Zealander.   Born in Wellington, 28 September 1921.   Educated at Takapuna Grammar School, Auckland; Wellington Boys' College;

Victoria University College, now Victoria University of Wellington, B.A. 1945. Served in the New Zealand Army, 1941–45; Royal New Zealand Naval Volunteer Reserve, 1943–45: Sub-Lieutenant. Married Dr. Diana Manby Shaw in 1945; one son and two daughters. Research Assistant, War History Branch, Wellington, 1946–48; Assistant Curator of Manuscripts, Alexander Turnbull Library, Wellington, 1948–49; travelled in Europe, 1949–51; Public Relations Officer, New Zealand Forest Service, Wellington, 1951–57; Radio Critic, 1955–61, Record Critic, 1961–62, and Music Critic, 1964–69, *New Zealand Listener*, Wellington; Senior Journalist, *Tourist and Publicity*, Wellington, 1957–58; Drama Critic, *Dominion*, Wellington, 1958–60; Editor, *Te Ao Hou* (Maori Affairs), Wellington, 1960–61; Editor, *Act*, Wellington, 1967–70; Senior Copywriter, Wood and Mitchell Advertising, Wellington, 1969–71. President, Secretary, and Committee Member, Unity Theatre, Wellington, 1948–60. New Zealand Delegate, International Drama Conference, Edinburgh, 1963. Full-time actor, producer and director: has directed first productions of most of his own plays, operas for the New Zealand Opera Company, and revues for the Unity Theatre and Downstage, Wellington; has appeared in his own plays for solo actor, in New Zealand, England, and the United States. Recipient: British Drama League Playwriting Competition Prize, five times; Auckland Festival Society National Playwriting Competition Prize, 1958; State Literary Fund Scholarship in Letters, 1973. Lives in Wellington.

PUBLICATIONS

Plays

> *The Bonds of Love* (produced 1953).
> *The Evening Paper* (produced 1953).
> *The Verdict* (produced 1955).
> *The Licensed Victualler,* music by Mason (produced 1955).
> *A Case in Point* (produced 1956).
> *Wit's End* (revue; produced 1956).
> *The Light Enlarging* (produced 1957).
> *Birds in the Wilderness* (produced 1957).
> *The Pohutukawa Tree* (produced 1957).   1960.
> *The End of the Golden Weather* (produced 1960).   1962.
> *We Don't Want Your Sort Here,* music by Mason (cabaret; produced 1961).
> *Awatea* (broadcast 1964; produced 1968).   1969.
> *Swan Song* (broadcast 1964; produced 1965).
> *The Hand on the Rail* (broadcast 1964; produced 1965).
> *The Counsels of the Wood* (produced 1965).
> *The Waters of Silence,* from a work by Vercors (produced 1965).
> *Hongi* (broadcast 1967; produced 1968).   In *Contemporary New Zealand Plays,* edited
>   by Howard McNaughton, 1974.
> *Zero Inn* (produced 1970).   1970.
> *Not Christmas, But Guy Fawkes* (produced 1976).
> *Courting Blackbird* (produced 1976).

> Radio Plays: *The Cherry Orchard,* from a play by Chekhov, 1960; *Awatea,* 1964; *Swan Song,* 1964; *The Hand on the Rail,* 1965; *Hongi,* 1967.

Verse

> *We Don't Want Your Sort Here: A Collection of Light Verse.*   1963.

Other

Theatre in Danger, with John Pocock.   1957.
New Zealand Drama: A Parade of Forms and a History.   1972.

Reading List: *Mason* by Howard McNaughton, 1975.

*   *   *

The artistic career of Bruce Mason reflects, in its breadth, the resourcefulness which until recently has been essential to the professional artist in New Zealand. While his earliest short stories were establishing his literary reputation in the late 1940's, he was already gaining the intimate knowledge of all aspects of stage production that was to enable him to write, direct, and act in most of his early plays, in the 1950's. *The Bonds of Love, The Evening Paper,* and *The Verdict* brought a new intensity and severity to New Zealand realistic drama, while *The Light Enlarging* and the full-length *Birds in the Wilderness* educated audiences to subtleties of stylised comedy. The constrictions of domestic drama, however, proved increasingly frustrating to a writer with more epic propensities, and an expansion of professional production resources on both radio and stage stimulated Mason into his most ambitious series of plays, the five dramas on Maori themes.

The Pohutukawa Tree quickly became famous through stage, radio, and television productions, and remains the seminal dramatic portrayal of the corrosion between Maori and European culture. Other plays offer a more optimistic resolution to such an issue, all of them written for radio in 1964–5: the controversial *Awatea,* conceived on a scale as grand as that of *The Pohutukawa Tree, Swan Song,* a more stylised treatment of the cultural impasse, and *The Hand on the Rail,* an intimate study of the tensions within a bicultural family. Reverting to a more pessimistic tone, *Hongi* is a historical drama with a highly resonant core of ethnic pageantry. All of these later Maori plays have also been radically reshaped and rescripted for the stage, but their production has been limited because they were originally written with lead parts for the great Maori bass singer, the late Inia Te Wiata; only *Awatea* is familiar to theatre audiences, and more subtle plays like *The Hand on the Rail* and *Hongi* have been undeservedly neglected.

Mason's most dramatically innovative work, however, lies in his plays for solo actor. Initially inspired by Emlyn Williams's Dickens performances, he wrote and performed *The End of the Golden Weather,* a study of New Zealand boyhood; between 1959 and 1962 he was engaged in extensive internal tours, and after appearances in London, at the Edinburgh Festival, and in the U.S.A., the popularity of the work is unabated. In 1965, he extended his solo repertoire with *The Counsels of the Wood* and *The Waters of Silence* (adapted from Vercors); though the more exotic content of these works has limited their stage popularity, he has combined them under the title of *Men of Soul* and continues to present the programme during his larger seasons. For his two most recent solo works, both premiered in 1976, Mason has returned to New Zealand material; *Not Christmas, But Guy Fawkes* is based on some of his own short stories and autobiographical pieces, while *Courting Blackbird* is a swift-moving, well-integrated, highly comic anecdotal piece about an expatriate eccentric.

Since the Maori works, Mason's output of plays has been limited, with only *Zero Inn* (1970) making an impact on the stage. His solo theatre, however, has flourished, and his tours continue to be among the most remarkable feats of sustained creativity that the New Zealand stage has seen.

—Howard McNaughton

MAUGHAM, W(illiam) Somerset. English. Born in Paris, 25 January 1874, of English parents. Educated at King's School, Canterbury, Kent, 1887–91; University of Heidelberg, 1891–92; studied medicine at St. Thomas's Hospital, London, 1892–97; interned in Lambeth London; qualified as a surgeon, L.R.C.P., M.R.C.S., 1897, but never practised. Served with the Red Cross Ambulance Unit, later with the British Intelligence Corps, in World War I. Married Syrie Barnardo Wellcome in 1915 (divorced, 1927); one daughter. Writer from 1896; lived abroad, mainly in Paris, 1897–1907; successful dramatist for the London stage, 1907–33; travelled widely during the 1920's, in the South Seas, Malaya, and China; lived at Cap Ferrat in the south of France from 1928; lived in the United States during World War II; instituted annual prize for promising young British writer, 1947. D.Litt.: Oxford University; University of Toulouse. Fellow, and Companion of Literature, 1961, Royal Society of Literature. Commander, Legion of Honour; Honorary Senator, University of Heidelberg; Honorary Fellow, Library of Congress, Washington, D.C.; Honorary Member, National Institute of Arts and Letters. Companion of Honour, 1954. *Died 16 December 1965.*

PUBLICATIONS

Plays

> *Marriages Are Made in Heaven* (as *Schiffbrüchig,* produced 1902). Published in *Venture,* 1903.
> *A Man of Honour* (produced 1903). 1903.
> *Mademoiselle Zampa* (produced 1904).
> *Lady Frederick* (produced 1907). 1912.
> *Jack Straw* (produced 1908). 1911.
> *Mrs. Dot* (produced 1908). 1912.
> *The Explorer: A Melodrama* (produced 1908). 1912.
> *Penelope* (produced 1909). 1912.
> *The Noble Spaniard,* from a work by Ernest Grenet-Dancourt (produced 1909). 1953.
> *Smith* (produced 1909). 1913.
> *The Tenth Man* (produced 1910). 1913.
> *Landed Gentry* (as *Grace,* produced 1910). 1913.
> *Loaves and Fishes* (produced 1911). 1924.
> *A Trip to Brighton,* from a play by Abel Tarride (produced 1911).
> *The Perfect Gentleman,* from a play by Molière (produced 1913). Published in *Theatre Arts,* November 1955.
> *The Land of Promise* (produced 1913). 1913.
> *The Unattainable* (as *Caroline,* produced 1916). 1923.
> *Our Betters* (produced 1917). 1923.
> *Love in a Cottage* (produced 1918).
> *Caesar's Wife* (produced 1919). 1922.
> *Home and Beauty* (produced 1919; as *Too Many Husbands,* produced 1919). 1923.
> *The Unknown* (produced 1920). 1920.
> *The Circle* (produced 1921). 1921.
> *East of Suez* (produced 1922). 1922.
> *The Camel's Back* (produced 1923).
> *The Constant Wife* (produced 1926). 1927.
> *The Letter,* from his own story (produced 1927). 1927.
> *The Sacred Flame* (produced 1928). 1928.
> *The Bread-Winner* (produced 1930). 1930.
> *Dramatic Works.* 6 vols., 1931–34; as *Collected Plays,* 3 vols., 1952.

For Services Rendered (produced 1932).   1932.
The Mask and the Face: A Satire, from a play by Luigi Chiarelli (produced 1933).
Sheppey (produced 1933).   1933.
Trio: Stories and Screen Adaptations, with R. C. Sherriff and Noel Langley.   1950.

Screenplay: *The Verger,* in *Trio,* 1950.

Fiction

Liza of Lambeth.   1897; revised edition, 1904.
The Making of a Saint.   1898.
Orientations (stories).   1899.
The Hero.   1901.
Mrs. Craddock.   1902.
The Merry-Go-Round.   1904.
The Bishop's Apron: A Study in the Origins of a Great Family.   1906.
The Explorer.   1907.
The Magician.   1908.
Of Human Bondage.   1915.
The Moon and Sixpence.   1919.
The Trembling of the Leaf: Little Stories of the South Sea Islands.   1921; as *Sadie Thompson and Other Stories,* 1928; as *Rain and Other Stories,* 1933.
The Painted Veil.   1925.
The Casuarina Tree: Six Stories.   1926; as *The Letter: Stories of Crime,* 1930.
Ashenden; or, The British Agent.   1928.
Cakes and Ale; or, The Skeleton in the Cupboard.   1930.
Six Stories Written in the First Person Singular.   1931.
The Book-Bag.   1932.
The Narrow Corner.   1932.
Ah King: Six Stories.   1933.
The Judgement Seat (story).   1934.
East and West: The Collected Short Stories.   1934; as *Altogether,* 1934.
Cosmopolitans (stories).   1936.
Favorite Short Stories.   1937.
Theatre.   1937.
Princess September and the Nightingale (juvenile).   1939.
The Round Dozen (stories).   1939.
Christmas Holiday.   1939.
The Mixture as Before: Short Stories.   1940; as *Great Stories of Love and Intrigue,* 1947.
Up at the Villa.   1941.
The Hour Before the Dawn.   1942.
The Unconquered (story).   1944.
The Razor's Edge.   1944.
Then and Now.   1946.
Creatures of Circumstance: Short Stories.   1947.
Catalina: A Romance.   1948.
East of Suez: Great Stories of the Tropics.   1948.
Here and There (stories).   1948.
Complete Short Stories.   3 vols., 1951.
The World Over: Stories of Manifold Places and People.   1952.
Selected Novels.   3 vols., 1953.
Best Short Stories, edited by John Beecroft.   1957.

Malaysian Stories, edited by Anthony Burgess.   1969.
Seventeen Lost Stories, edited by Craig V. Showalter.   1969.

Other

The Land of the Blessed Virgin: Sketches and Impressions of Andalusia.   1905.
On a Chinese Screen.   1922.
The Gentleman in the Parlour: A Record of a Journey from Rangoon to Haiphong.   1930.
Non-Dramatic Works.   28 vols., 1934–69.
Don Fernando; or, Variations on Some Spanish Themes.   1935.
My South Sea Island.   1936.
The Summing Up.   1938.
Books and You.   1940.
France at War.   1940.
Strictly Personal.   1941.
The Somerset Maugham Sampler, edited by Jerome Weidman.   1943; as *The Somerset Maughan Pocket Book,* 1944.
Great Novelists and Their Novels: Essays on the Ten Greatest Novels of the World and the Men and Women Who Wrote Them.   1948; revised edition, as *Ten Novels and Their Authors,* 1954; as *The Art of Fiction,* 1955.
A Writer's Notebook.   1949.
The Maugham Reader, edited by Glenway Wescott.   1950.
The Vagrant Mood: Six Essays.   1952.
Mr. Maugham Himself, edited by John Beecroft.   1954.
The Partial View (includes *The Summing Up* and *A Writer's Notebook*).   1954.
The Travel Books.   1955.
Points of View.   1958.
Purely for Pleasure.   1962.
Selected Prefaces and Introductions.   1963.
Essays on Literature.   1967.

Editor, with Laurence Housman, *Venture: An Annual of Art and Literature.*   2 vols., 1903–05.
Editor, *The Truth at Last,* by Charles Hawtrey.   1924.
Editor, *The Travellers' Library.*   1933; as *Fifty Modern English Writers,* 1933.
Editor, *Tellers of Tales: 100 Short Stories.*   1939; as *The Greatest Stories of All Time,* 1943.
Editor, *A Choice of Kipling's Prose.*   1952; as *Maugham's Choice of Kipling's Best: Sixteen Stories,* 1953.

Bibliography: *A Bibliography of the Works of Maugham* by Raymond Toole Stott, 1956; revised edition, 1973.

Reading List: *The Maugham Enigma,* 1954, and *The World of Maugham,* 1959, both edited by K. W. Jonas; *Maugham* by J. Brophy, revised edition, 1958; *Maugham: A Candid Portrait* by K. G. Pfeiffer, 1959; *Maugham: A Guide* by Laurence Brander, 1963; *The Two Worlds of Maugham* by W. Menard, 1965; *Maugham* by M. K. Naik, 1966; *The Dramatic Comedy of Maugham* by R. E. Barnes, 1968; *Maugham: A Biographical and Critical Study* by R. A. Cordell, revised edition, 1969; *Maugham and the Quest for Freedom* by Robert L. Calder, 1972; *The Pattern of Maugham: A Critical Portrait,* 1974, and *Maugham,* 1977, both by Anthony Curtis; *Maugham and His World* by Frederic Raphael, 1976.

*   *   *

"Every writer who has any sense," said Somerset Maugham in a press interview, "writes about the circumstances in which he himself has lived. What else can he write about with authority?" That statement is well illustrated by the closeness with which a long and varied life is reflected in Maugham's equally versatile achievement as short-story writer, novelist, dramatist, critic, essayist, and autobiographer. Upbringing in Paris and an early familiarity with the work of the French naturalists profoundly influenced his style and method, giving him a classical sense of form, lucidity, and Gallic detachment of attitude to human frailty and the ironies of existence. Later experiences as a medical student in London provided material for a realistic portrayal of slum life in his first novel, *Liza of Lambeth*, and, as a British intelligence agent during the First World War, for the Ashenden stories. Above all Maugham's extensive foreign travels, in search of new backgrounds and ways of life, proved inexhaustibly fruitful. He paints exotic Eastern scenes with economy and exactitude; and observes a wealth of bizarre incident and human idiosyncrasy – on liners, in clubs, in the bungalows of the white man in the tropics, where passions are stripped of the masks of conformity and convention demanded by more civilized communities – with amused tolerance and an unerring eye for the significant detail. Unlike his contemporaries Bennett, Galsworthy, and Wells, Maugham was not interested in fiction as the vehicle of social criticism. Savouring instead the singularity, paradox, and sheer unexpectedness of individual lives, he proclaimed his subject, in his short stories, novels, and plays alike, "the personal drama of human relationships."

Maugham's career as a dramatist spanned three decades, beginning with *A Man of Honour* in 1903 and ending in 1933 with *Sheppey*. His comedies of manners in the tradition of Oscar Wilde were less immediately successful than his fiction. Within a year of the production of *Lady Frederick* in 1907, however, he was rivalling the popularity of Shaw with four plays running in London. Such caustic, wittily satirical portrayals of elegant society as *Home and Beauty*, *The Circle*, *Our Betters*, and *The Bread-Winner*, with their dexterous craftsmanship and sparkling epigrammatic dialogue, continued to enjoy a steady stage success.

Maugham's achievement as a novelist is distinctly uneven. The authenticity of deep feeling in perhaps his most popular work, the long autobiographical *Of Human Bondage*, is vitiated by prolixity and that sentimentality which in many of his short stories masquerades as cynicism. In *The Razor's Edge*, written when he was over seventy, and *Catalina*, he is perceptibly out of his native element in ambitious explorations of uncharacteristic themes. The moral confusions and simplifications, lapses in taste, and overall implausibility in these novels show Maugham less at ease as an anatomist of spiritual struggles and values than in his accustomed role of shrewd and worldy observer of his fellow men. Essentially a master of shorter forms of fiction, he makes far greater impact in *The Moon and Sixpence*, based on the career of Gauguin, and *Cakes and Ale*, his own favourite. This astringent picture of London literary life introduces thinly disguised, maliciously acute portraits of two eminent contemporaries; and the engaging personality of Rosie, the maternal, warm-hearted barmaid, is in a clear line of descent from an earlier Maugham heroine, Liza. In its narrative expertise, perception, and credibility of characterization, *Cakes and Ale* is indisputably Maugham's most completely realized novel.

But it is in the short story form that his individual gifts are most satisfyingly exemplified. Temperamentally and technically out of tune with Chekhov and his methods, Maugham from the first made Maupassant his model. His avowed aim was the "compact, dramatic story," tightly knit, sharply characterized, ending "with a fullstop rather than a straggle of dots," which could hold the attention of listeners over a dinner-table or in a ship's smoking room. To this end he developed with consummate skill the device of the narrator: his own urbane, ubiquitous presence, as ringside spectator rather than active participant, lending his tales the heightened verisimilitude of the conversational eye-witness account. Maugham's factual first-person narratives not only invest with veracity what might otherwise seem incredible (as he cunningly allows at the opening of "The Kite"); the deliberate tone of dry understatement intensifies by contrast the violent, often tragic events related by this suave, unobtrusive commentator. Sometimes, indeed, his "shock" climax seems calculated enough to be over-simplified and superficial. Compared with the psychological penetration and compassion in a story like Maupassant's "Boule de Suif," Maugham's situations and characterization lack subtlety and depth. His ironical revelations can be more effective in such lighter vein as the delectable disclosure of "The Colonel's Lady."

One of Maugham's favourite and most typical themes, in his sardonic clinical diagnoses of human folly in "Before the Party," "The Door of Opportunity," "The Lion's Skin," and many other stories, is the disillusioning disparity between the outward appearances of a relationship and its underlying reality. Not only amorous frailty is relentlessly exposed, but also the humbug of moral conventions and literary pretentiousness. Yet Maugham never explicitly moralizes. He presents life, as he sees it, dispassionately: almost – for his very lack of comment can carry its own acid implication. His cool, fastidious detachment is that of the outsider remote from the complexities and disasters of ordinary living. Disarmingly aware of his own limitations, both personal and literary, he acknowledges in his autobiographies his lack of that emotional warmth and sympathetic involvement which would, as he says, have given his work "intimacy, the broad human touch."

Maugham saw himself primarily as an entertainer; and he was indeed a supremely successful one, with his work broadcast, televised, filmed, and translated into many languages. In the light of his serious lifelong dedication to the writer's craft, he felt he had been consistently undervalued by the "intellectual" critics. Certainly his reputation has always stood higher abroad than in England; but an appreciative world-wide readership has made him possibly the most popular storyteller who has ever lived.

—Margaret Willy

MERCER, David. English. Born in Wakefield, Yorkshire, 27 June 1928. Educated at King's College, Newcastle upon Tyne, University of Durham, B.A. (honours) in fine art 1953. Served as a laboratory technician in the Royal Navy, 1945–48. Two daughters. Worked as a laboratory technician, 1942–45; Supply Teacher, 1955–59; Teacher, Barrett Street Technical College, 1959–61. Full-time writer since 1962. Recipient: Writer's Guild Award, for television play, 1962, 1967, 1968; *Evening Standard* award, 1965; British Film Academy Award, 1966. Lives in London.

PUBLICATIONS

Plays

The Governor's Lady (broadcast 1960; produced 1965). 1968.
The Buried Man (produced 1962).
The Generations: Three Television Plays (includes *Where the Difference Begins, A Climate of Fear, The Birth of a Private Man*). 1964.
Ride a Cock Horse (produced 1965). 1966.
Belcher's Luck (produced 1966). 1967.
Three TV Comedies (includes *A Suitable Case for Treatment, For Tea on Sunday, And Did Those Feet*). 1966.

In Two Minds (televised 1967; produced 1973).   In *The Parachute with Two More TV Plays*, 1967.

The Parachute with Two More TV Plays: Let's Murder Vivaldi, In Two Minds.   1967.

Let's Murder Vivaldi (televised 1968; produced 1972).   In *The Parachute with Two More TV Plays*, 1967.

On the Eve of Publication and Other Plays (television plays: includes *The Cellar and the Almond Tree* and *Emma's Time*).   1970.

White Poem (produced 1970).

Flint (produced 1970).   1970.

After Haggerty (produced 1970).   1970.

Blood on the Table (produced 1971).

Duck Song (produced 1974).   1974.

The Bankrupt and Other Plays (includes *You and Me and Him, An Afternoon at the Festival, Find Me*).   1974.

Huggy Bear and Other Plays (television plays: includes *The Arcata Promise* and *A Superstition*).   1977.

Shooting the Chandelier (televised, 1977).   With *Cousin Vladimir*, 1978.

Cousin Vladimir (produced 1978).   1978.

Screenplays: *Ninety Degrees in the Shade* (English dialogue), 1965; *Morgan! A Suitable Case for Treatment*, 1966; *Family Life*, 1972; *A Doll's House*, 1973; *Providence*, 1977.

Radio Plays: *The Governor's Lady*, 1960; *Folie à Deux*, 1974.

Television Plays: *Where the Difference Begins*, 1961; *A Climate of Fear*, 1962; *A Suitable Case for Treatment*, 1962; *The Birth of a Private Man*, 1963; *For Tea on Sunday*, 1963; *The Buried Man*, 1963; *A Way of Living*, 1963; *And Did Those Feet*, 1965; *In Two Minds*, 1967; *Let's Murder Vivaldi*, 1968; *The Parachute*, 1968; *On the Eve of Publication*, 1968; *The Cellar and the Almond Tree*, 1970; *Emma's Time*, 1970; *The Bankrupt*, 1972; *You and Me and Him*, 1973; *An Afternoon at the Festival*, 1973; *Barbara of the House of Grebe*, from a story by Hardy, 1973; *Find Me*, 1974; *The Arcata Promise*, 1974; *Huggy Bear*, 1976; *A Superstition*, 1977; *Shooting the Chandelier*, 1977; *The Ragazza*, 1978.

Fiction

The Long Crawl Through Time (story) in *New Writers 3*.   1965.

Bibliography: *The Quality of Mercer: Bibliography of Writings by and about the Playwright Mercer*, edited by Francis Jarman, 1974.

Reading List: *The Second Wave* by John Russell Taylor.   1971.

*   *   *

David Mercer's hallmark for many years was his opposition to repression, whether political or psychological. In plays sometimes Marxist in ideology, sometimes in keeping with R. D. Laing's precepts on psychology, he championed the individual in opposition to the political and/or psychiatric establishment's authoritarian pressures to conform. Repeatedly he favored the anarchic or aberrant over the pedestrian and normal. Mercer's plays in the 1960's frequently reflected his socialist allegiance, but they were not simplistic in content or truly social realist in style, and as the years passed, his anti-Stalinism and individualism have more and more alienated those he once called comrades. His interest in psychopathology, which has caused him to examine and re-examine the origin, development, and manifestations of mental illness from a distinctly maverick perspective that virtually denies the existence of abnormality, has always set him apart from the purely politically partisan playwright. His allegiance to personal freedom precluded his becoming a party member or taking a party line.

Mercer began writing plays when he discovered in psychoanalysis that he was fascinated with stateless wanderers because he had strayed from his working class origins and simple upbringing to a sophisticated, intellectual life. So he wrote his television play *Where the Difference Begins*. This play and the subsequent *A Climate of Fear* and *The Birth of a Private Man* examine the conflicts of working-class children educated into the middle class. Like so many of Mercer's subsequent plays, they are domestic dramas, the first probing the dilemma's roots, the second considering family crisis during the campaign for nuclear disarmament, and the third examining a man disillusioned with his communist affiliations.

In the last play of this trilogy, Colin goes mad from his loss of political faith, and what most people would term insanity or neurosis – often involving violence between the sexes or violence turned inward – figured in most of Mercer's plays for more than a decade to come. *The Buried Man* suggested the preoccupation by taking as its protagonist a boilerman judged mad when found crying over his machinery, but *A Suitable Case for Treatment*, established the quintessential Mercer hero. Illustrating his premise that aberrance "may be a necessary, meaningful and creative means by which the personality reveals its relationship to the world, and the 'breakdown' may be on the world's side," Mercer in Morgan fashions a character who has an understanding with the gorilla at the zoo and with animals in general. Though Morgan is in some way's Rousseau's noble savage, his relations with his wife Leonie have deteriorated to the point that he's living in her car. When Leonie divorces Morgan and tries to remarry, he kidnaps her. After his abduction is circumvented, he dresses in a gorilla suit to disrupt the wedding reception and then, costume ablaze, careens on a stolen motorcycle into the Thames. Morgan lies delirious on riverbank garbage till carted off to an institution, where he cheerfully ascertains that he fathered the baby his ex-wife carries. The film's final image – more symbol of rebellion than political statement – is the asylum's flower bed, which Morgan has planted in the shape of hammer and sickle.

Mercer's fascination with animals and their contrast to less genuine, more duplicitous and barbaric people are likewise featured in *The Governor's Lady* and in *And Did Those Feet*. In the latter the twin zoo-keepers even release their animals and then emigrate to the African jungle. In *Belcher's Luck*, the natural and fecund Belcher and his horses are foils to the impotent and rapacious patricians, and in *For Tea on Sunday* the psychotic hero who identifies with animals explains that his body contains a harmless leopard.

Other Mercer plays depict, not animals or the animal-obsessed, but abnormal characters whom he seems to regard as superior to or more sympathetic than the beastly normal folk around them. Even those who suffer total mental collapse – Peter, the regressive paranoid in *Ride a Cock Horse*, for instance, or the schizophrenic Kate of *In Two Minds* – are clearly favored by Mercer over more ordinary mortals. Peter's setting his wife's clothes and paintings and books afire and his eventual donning of an SS uniform bring spectators nearer to tears than to derision. And as for Kate, she is unquestionably more sinned against than sinning, having been driven into psychosis by repressive parents and the insensitive psychiatric establishment. Unable to please both herself and her parents, she succumbs to guilt feelings, and, deprived of the supportive treatment of one renegade therapist, she is drugged into submission and eventual catatonia. In Morgan Mercer admires abnormality, but here he laments the loss of mental health. One of Mercer's major tenets is that psychiatric care must treat, not symptoms, but causes. Kate suffers from unenlightened sedation and a dullard doctor who leaves her a zombie because he thinks her illness bears no relation to her family environment.

Although the outlook for aberrance there is bleak, the obverse to that prognosis comes in *Flint*, where the rapscallion hero, whose name suggests striking sparks to create fire, is a promethean, seventy-year-old Anglican priest who is all libido. As devoid of repression or inhibitions as he is free of religious convictions, Flint is sleeping with a pregnant girl who tried to kill herself in his church. After he has dissuaded Dixie from self-destruction, the adventures of this formidable proponent of the joy of life comprise affirmative but iconoclastic farce far removed from the harrowing documentary treatment of schizophrenia.

For the first decade, Mercer's plays of political and psychological disorientation were life-affirming. When a character suffers, the blame is usually to be laid upon some interference with his or her personal freedom by malicious or misguided social units or institutions or because inhibitions – as with Bernard Link in *After Haggerty* – reduce a character to phlegmatic ineffectuality. During this period, Mercer was a playwright of compassionate optimism, one who believed in the individual if not in the social order. Harold Hobson could write, with some justification, "Mr. Mercer is a dramatist whose generosity of spirit strengthens and breathes life into those who come into contact with it. He writes of the universe as an experiment that is justified, because he instinctively finds in it so much of good."

Recent developments, however, would prevent such an assessment. The disorientation of which he writes is now more frequently metaphysical, as his fear of totalitarianism and repression has receded in the wake of troubling anxieties on the basic human condition. A profoundly Beckettian pessimism about birth, death, the quest for meaning and purpose, and the fear of futility pervade the recent plays and films. Often employing daring dramatic techniques, Mercer does combat with ontological despair in *An Afternoon at the Festival, The Bankrupt, Find Me, Ducksong, The Arcata Promise, Providence* and *A Superstition.*

Among the recent works, the teleplay *The Arcata Promise*, the film *Providence* (written for Alain Resnais), and the stage work *Ducksong* are especially durable drama. The destructive and self-destructive dissociated actor – actually named John, but called "Gunge" by the Voice with which he pursues interior dialogue – about whom Mercer writes in *The Arcata Promise*, haunted by imagined failures in his distinguished acting career and the real failure of his relations with a woman, suffers a collapse – as much moral as mental – which leads to murder and suicide. Mercer is no longer enjoying eccentricity and condoning aberrance here; Morgan was a charming zany, but Gunge's self indulgence, past and present, prompts sympathy mixed with revulsion.

Resnais has not altogether realised the more whimsical aspects of the surreal comedy *Providence*, in which ageing novelist Clive Langham as creator – a sort of god or providence over his imagination's issue – asserts control in unexpected ways. He thinks up a nubile young thing to be his son's mistress, decides she'd be wasted on priggish Claud, and substitutes a middle-aged, intellectual journalist. The creative process may get out of hand: while imagining a scene between Claud and the fictive mistress, Clive bemusedly watches a rugger jog through towards the shower; to wrench the intruder out of the frame, he instantly resets the scene in another hotel room. Although the film's visual and verbal surprises, as well as the self-importance and bombast of its dream characters, are flippant, serious revulsion at mortality is as fundamental to the screenplay as to *Ducksong*. The sundrenched verdant festivities at the end hardly erase the terminally ill Langham's nightmarish night.

Ducksong dramatizes one family's efforts to come to terms with death, or perhaps with their failures in life, since the title refers to their rather ordinary attempts at swansongs. A cuckoo clock, a sort of *memento mori*, goads a man who dreads dying into hurling walnuts at its bobbing bird. Soon, forced to confront an entropic universe, all the characters' real needs and obsessions emerge. Some are topical issues – class conflicts, women's liberation, red power – but others are the more universal matters of transience, futility, and violence which Mercer summarizes as "the terrible poetry of doom."

In *Where the Difference Begins* Richard worried over the Communist ideal of feeding the body without regard for the soul. Mercer is still, in his latest plays, worried that the consumer society fails to provide spiritual nourishment. And he still sees the fanatical individualist as our last, best hope in a grim cosmos.

—Tish Dace

MILLER, Arthur. American. Born in New York City, 17 October 1915. Educated at the University of Michigan, Ann Arbor (Hopwood Award, 1936, 1937), 1934–38, A.B. 1938. Married 1) Mary Slattery in 1940 (divorced, 1956), one son and one daughter; 2) the actress Marilyn Monroe in 1956 (divorced, 1961) ; 3) Ingeborg Morath in 1962, one daughter. Member of the Federal Theatre Project, 1938. Wrote for the CBS and NBC Radio Workshops. International President, P.E.N., London and New York, 1965–69. Recipient: Theatre Guild Award, 1938; New York Drama Critics Circle Award, 1947, 1949; Antoinette Perry Award, 1947, 1949, 1953; Pulitzer Prize, 1949; National Association of Independent Schools Award, 1954; American Academy of Arts and Letters Gold Medal, 1959; Brandeis University Creative Arts Award, 1969. D.H.L.: University of Michigan, 1956. Member, American Academy of Arts and Letters, 1971.

PUBLICATIONS

Plays

> *Honors at Dawn* (produced 1936).
> *No Villains (They Too Arise)* (produced 1937).
> *The Pussycat and the Expert Plumber Who Was a Man* and *William Ireland's Confession*, in *100 Non-Royalty Radio Plays*, edited by William Kozlenko. 1941.
> *The Man Who Had All the Luck* (produced 1944). In *Cross-Section 1944*, edited by Edwin Seaver, 1944.
> *That They May Win* (produced 1944). In *Best One-Act Plays of 1944*, edited by Margaret Mayorga, 1945.
> *Grandpa and the Statue*, in *Radio Drama in Action*, edited by Erik Barnouw. 1945.
> *The Story of Gus*, in *Radio's Best Plays*, edited by Joseph Liss. 1947.
> *The Guardsman*, radio adaptation of a play by Ferenc Molnar, in *Theatre Guild on the Air*, edited by H. William Fitelson. 1947.
> *Three Men on a Horse*, radio adaptation of the play by George Abbott and John Cecil Holm, in *Theatre Guild on the Air*, edited by H. William Fitelson. 1947.
> *All My Sons* (produced 1947). 1947.
> *Death of a Salesman: Certain Private Conversations in Two Acts and a Requiem* (produced 1949). 1949.
> *An Enemy of the People*, from a play by Ibsen (produced 1950). 1951.
> *The Crucible* (produced 1953). 1953.
> *A View from the Bridge, and A Memory of Two Mondays: Two One-Act Plays* (produced 1955). 1955; revised version of *A View from the Bridge* (produced 1956), 1956.
> *Collected Plays* (includes *All My Sons, Death of a Salesman, The Crucible, A Memory of Two Mondays, A View from the Bridge*). 1957.
> *After the Fall* (produced 1964). 1964.
> *Incident at Vichy* (produced 1964). 1965.
> *The Price* (produced 1968). 1968.
> *Fame, and The Reason Why* (produced 1970). *Fame* in *Yale Literary Magazine*, March 1971.
> *The Creation of the World and Other Business* (produced 1972). 1973.
> *Up from Paradise* (produced 1974).
> *The Archbishop's Ceiling* (produced 1976).

Screenplay: *The Misfits*, 1961.

Radio Plays: *The Pussycat and the Expert Plumber Who Was a Man, William Ireland's Confession, Grandpa and the Statue*, and *The Story of Gus*, in early 1940's.

Fiction

Focus. 1945.
The Misfits (screenplay in novel form).   1961.
I Don't Need You Any More: Stories.   1967.

Other

Situation Normal.   1944.
Jane's Blanket (juvenile).   1963.
In Russia, photographs by Inge Morath.   1969.
The Portable Miller, edited by Harold Clurman.   1971.
In the Country, photographs by Inge Morath.   1977.
The Theatre Essays of Miller, edited by Robert A. Martin.   1978.

Bibliography: "Miller: The Dimension of His Art: A Checklist of His Published Works," in *The Serif,* June 1967, and *Miller Criticism (1930–1967),* 1969, both by Tetsumaro Hayashi.

Reading List: *Miller,* 1961, and *Miller: A Study of His Plays,* 1979, both by Dennis Welland; *Miller* by Robert G. Hogan, 1964; *Miller: The Burning Glass* by Sheila Huftel, 1965; *Miller* by Leonard Moss, 1967 (includes bibliography); *Miller, Dramatist* by Edward Murray, 1967; *Miller: A Collection of Critical Essays* edited by Robert W. Corrigan, 1969; *Miller: Portrait of a Playwright* by Benjamin Nelson, 1970; *Miller* by Ronald Hayman, 1970.

*   *   *

In "On Social Plays," the introduction to the 1955 edition of *A View from the Bridge,* Arthur Miller expressed his dissatisfaction with the subjective play so popular on Broadway in the 1950's. At the same time, he rejected the customary definition of the social play ("an arraignment of society's evils") and identified his own work as "the drama of the whole man," an inextricable mixture of the social and the psychological. The emphasis on one side or the other varied over the years and his conception of the nature of man underwent a change in the 1960's, but his 1955 sense of his work is a useful description of the whole career of Arthur Miller as a social playwright.

In his student plays, his wartime one-acters, his early radio plays, even his first Broadway offering, *The Man Who Had All the Luck,* Miller can be seen working his way toward the theme that was to dominate his early plays. From *All My Sons* through *A View from the Bridge,* Miller places his protagonist in a setting in which society functions as a creator of images, and the hero-victim is destroyed because, as he says in the essay quoted above, "the individual is doomed to frustration when once he gains a consciousness of his own identity." Ironically, the destruction comes whether a man accepts or rejects the role that society asks or demands that he play. Joe Keller, in *All My Sons,* is a good man, a loving husband and father, a successful business man who believes that his responsibility ends "at the building line"; when his son teaches him that neither the welfare of his family nor the self-protective impulse of conventional business ethics can excuse a shipment of faulty airplane parts, he commits suicide. Willy Loman, in *Death of a Salesman,* embraces the American dream, assumes that success is not only possible, but inevitable, and, faced with his failure, kills himself; the irony of the final suicide and the strength of the play is that Willy goes to his death, his dream still intact, convinced that the elusive success will be visited on his son, Biff, a man already crippled by society's neatly packaged ideas. In *The Crucible,* the victim becomes a romantic hero. John Proctor, guilty of adultery, confuses his accusing wife with an accusing society and admits to practicing witchcraft, but, finally unwilling to sign his name, he rejects society's demand for ritual confession, regains his identity, and dies, purely, in an act of defiance. Eddie Carbone, in *A View from the Bridge*, dies crying out for his name, too, but he wants a lie, the pretense that he has not violated the neighborhood ethic; like Joe Keller and Willy Loman, he accepts his society, but he breaks its rules when his desire for his niece and his attraction to her sweetheart threaten him with labels more frightening than informer. The explicit assumption of all these plays is that, win or lose, in contemporary society you can't win; the implicit assumption is that the individual is at his strongest, philosophically and dramatically, when the tensions between self and society are made manifest by a revealing crisis. The artistic result of the twin assumptions is a group of remarkably effective plays, reflecting Miller's theatrical skill as clearly as they do his moral concerns. In the best of them, *Death of a Salesman*, Miller's social-psychological mix has given birth, in Willy Loman, to one of the richest characters in American drama.

Between 1956, when the revised version of *A View from the Bridge* appeared, and 1964, Miller was inactive in the theater. During those years he published a number of short stories, later collected in *I Don't Need You Any More*, including "The Misfits," which was the basis for the short novel and screenplay, written for his wife Marilyn Monroe. The most startling thing about the work is that in it Miller seems to be accepting the concept of the curative power of love in a way that recalls the prevailing cliché of Broadway in the 1950's; he had already given the idea explicit statement in two essays published a few years before the story-novel-film – the introduction to *Collected Plays* and "Bridge to a Savage World" (*Esquire*, October 1958).

When Miller returned to the theater with *After the Fall* and *Incident at Vichy*, he had put aside the momentary softness of *The Misfits*, but he had also discarded the concept of man as an admirable loser which marked his earlier plays. "The first problem," he wrote in "Our Guilt for the World's Evil" (*New York Times Magazine*, 3 January 1965), "is ... to discover our own relationship to evil, its reflection of ourselves." Quentin in *Fall* learns to live and Von Berg in *Vichy* to die by the process of self-discovery already familiar in Miller's work, but identity is no longer individual. Miller, like the Salem of *The Crucible*, is now forcing an image of guilt on his characters. Finally in 1972, with *The Creation of the World and Other Business*, Miller makes obvious what has already been stated in the title *After the Fall*, that his post-1964 subject is original sin translated into the psychological commonplace that makes everyone responsible for "the World's Evil." Miller does not try to dramatize the corollary, that when everyone is guilty no one is, but it is possible – or so the autobiographical elements in *After the Fall* suggest – that the idea is working on the author if not within the play. One result of Miller's new concept of man is that the later plays have a schematic look to them; the characters lack the vitality of Miller's early protagonists and often appear to be simply figures in an exemplum. *The Price* is the only one of the later plays that escapes the look of drama as demonstration. Ideologically one with the other post-1964 plays, it returns to the domestic setting familiar with Miller as far back as the time of his student work *They Too Arise*. Whether it is the inherent drama of two brothers at odds or the presence of the old furniture dealer, Miller's only successful comic figure, *The Price* escapes Significance with a capital S and finds theatrical validity. In his most recent work, *The Archbishop's Ceiling*, Miller seems to have moved away from the ideological concerns that marked his drama from *After the Fall* to *Creation of the World*, but the play is more intellectual than dramatic and the characters are more complex in conception than in presentation.

Since Miller is a playwright of ideas, it is perhaps fitting that I have largely stuck to his themes in discussing his work, stopping occasionally to suggest that the ideational content of a play can interfere with the dramatic action or dehumanize character. These strictures are valid only to the extent that Miller is a realistic playwright in the American tradition, a dramatist who wants to create psychologically valid characters with whom audiences can identify directly. That is Miller's tradition, although he is one of a number of postwar American playwrights who recognize that that kind of character can exist outside a conventional realistic play. *Death of a Salesman* and *After the Fall* are examples of domesticated American Expressionism in which realistic scenes are played in an anti-realistic context. *The Crucible* is a romantic history play with a consciously artificial language, and Alfieri's stilted speeches in *A View from the Bridge*, which turn into free verse in the original version, are an attempt to impose the label *tragedy* on the play. *The Creation of the World* is an unhappy mixture of philosophical drama and Jewish low comedy. *Incident at Vichy* is a roundtable discussion and *The Price* is a debate of sorts with exits and entrances so artificially conceived that Miller surely means them to be seen as devices. The playwright's nearest approaches to traditional realism are *All My Sons* and the affectionate short play *A Memory of Two Mondays*.

Aside from his plays, Miller's work includes not only the short stories and screenplay mentioned above, but a novel, *Focus*; a report on Americans in training during World War II, *Situation Normal*; a children's book, *Jane's Blanket*; two volumes in which his text shares space with photographs by his wife Inge Morath, *In Russia* and *In the Country*; and a great many articles and essays, most of them about the theater. The chief value of these works lies less in their specific generic virtues than in those analogies – in theme, in method – that heighten our appreciation of the plays. After all, Arthur Miller is pre-eminently a playwright, one of the best the American theater has produced.

—Gerald Weales

MOODY, William Vaughn. American. Born in Spencer, Indiana, 8 July 1869; grew up in New Albany, Indiana. Educated at New Albany High School; Harvard University, Cambridge, Massachusetts (an editor of the *Harvard Monthly*), 1889–94, B.A. 1893, M.A. 1894. Married Harriet Tilden Brainard in 1909. Taught in a high school in Spencer, 1885–89; Instructor in English, Harvard University and Radcliffe College, Cambridge, Massachusetts, 1894–95; Instructor in English and Rhetoric, 1895–99, and Assistant Professor of English, 1901–07, University of Chicago; full-time writer, 1907 until his death. Litt.D.: Yale University, New Haven, Connecticut, 1908. Member, American Academy of Arts and Letters, 1908. *Died 17 October 1910.*

PUBLICATIONS

Collections

Selected Poems, edited by Robert Morss Lovett. 1931.

Plays

The Masque of Judgment: A Masque-Drama. 1900.
The Fire-Bringer. 1904.
The Great Divide (as *A Sabine Woman*, produced 1906; as *The Great Divide*, produced 1906). 1909.
The Faith Healer. 1909.

Verse

Poems. 1901; as *Gloucester Moors and Other Poems,* 1909.

Other

A History of English Literature, with Robert Morss Lovett. 1902; revised edition, 1918; simplified edition, as *A First View of English Literature,* 1905; as *A First View of English and American Literature,* 1909.
Poems and Plays, edited by John M. Manly. 2 vols., 1912.
Some Letters, edited by Daniel Gregory Mason. 1913.
Letters to Harriet, edited by Percy MacKaye. 1935.

Editor, *The Pilgrim's Progress,* by Bunyan. 1897.
Editor, *The Rime of the Ancient Mariner by Coleridge and The Vision of Sir Launfal by Lowell.* 1898.
Editor, *The Lady of the Lake,* by Scott. 1899.
Editor, with Wilfred Wesley Cressy, *The Iliad of Homer,* books 1, 6, 22, 24. 1899.
Editor, *The Complete Poetical Works of Milton.* 1899.
Editor, with George Cabot Lodge and John Ellerton Lodge, *The Poems of Trumbull Stickney.* 1905.
Editor, *Selections from De Quincey.* 1909.

Reading List: *Moody: A Study* by David D. Henry, 1934; *Moody* by Martin Halpern, 1964; *Estranging Dawn: The Life and Works of Moody* by Maurice F. Brown, 1973.

*   *   *

After William Vaughn Moody's early death, Edwin Arlington Robinson, his close friend and literary ally, wrote Harriet Moody, "Thank God he lived to do his work – or enough of it to place him among the immortals." While that assessment now seems exaggerated, Moody's work, as a scholar, poet, and dramatist, is sufficient to give him a firm place in literary history. As the author of *The Great Divide,* he is considered the first playwright to provide the American stage with a serious, realistic, modern drama, thus ushering in the new age in American theatre. Critics have speculated that had he lived to realize his full potential, his only rival would have been Eugene O'Neill.

Martin Halpern, in his critical biography of Moody, has suggested that his literary career falls into two periods: from 1890 until the publication of *The Masque of Judgment* and *Poems,* in 1900 and 1901 respectively, his primary interest was poetry; from then until his final illness debilitated him in 1909 he worked consciously as a practicing dramatist. Although *The Masque of Judgment* is the first part of a projected dramatic trilogy, it is a closet drama in verse. And while two of the four plays he wrote during the last decade of his life are also verse dramas, they were intended for the stage.

Moody's poems have few admirers today, largely because they seem imitative of the English romantics in inflated diction and archaic subject matter. Some of his poems are innovative, however, notably his poems that involve social commentary or those that are conscious attempts to use the vernacular. "On a Soldier Fallen in the Philippines," for instance, is an ironic attack on American foreign policy. Perhaps his most celebrated poem today is "The Menagerie," a comic soliloquy in which the inebriated speaker speculates on how the animals in the zoo regard the putative fulfillment of the evolutionary process, man. The psychologically honest "The Daguerreotype," a tribute to his mother, and the ambiguous "I Am the Woman" are two disparate treatments of the symbolic and psychic implications of the feminine principle, an interest that informs "The Death of Eve." Generally his poems, like his poetic trilogy, are full of high seriousness, frequently devolving upon theological, especially eschatological, matters.

Moody's two prose plays successfully combine realistic and symbolic dramatic techniques. Originally produced as *A Sabine Woman* in Chicago, *The Great Divide* was a commercial as well as a critical success, playing for two years in New York. The play deals with the conflicting cultures of the eastern and western United States, symbolized by the abduction and eventual marriage of a woman from Massachusetts to a rough but honest man from Arizona. The less well-received *Faith Healer* deals with the conflict between human and spiritual passions; the conflict is resolved when the protagonist discovers that his religious work is effective only when he has accepted human love.

Although *The Fire-Bringer*, Moody's verse play based on the Prometheus legend, and the fragment, *The Death of Eve*, were not produced commercially, critics have found them to be more artistically interesting than the prose plays. Moody was able to complete only one act of *The Death of Eve*, but the poem by the same title and his recorded plans for the play suggest that with it he might have achieved his dream of making verse drama a viable theatrical experience. Even so, his contribution to American drama and poetry is considerable.

—Nancy C. Joyner

MORTIMER, John (Clifford). English. Born in Hampstead, London, 21 April 1923. Educated at Harrow School, 1937–40; Brasenose College, Oxford, 1940–42, B.A. 1947; called to the Bar, 1948. Served with the Crown Film Unit as a scriptwriter during World War II. Married the writer Penelope Dimont, i.e., Penelope Mortimer, in 1949 (divorced, 1971); Penny Gollop in 1972; three children. Has practised law in London since 1948: noted for his defense in free speech and civil liberties cases; Queen's Counsel, 1966; Master of the Bench, Inner Temple, London, 1975. Drama Critic, *New Statesman, Evening Standard*, and *Observer*, 1972, all in London. Chairman, League of Dramatists. Recipient: Italia Prize, for radio play, 1958; Screenwriters Guild Award, for television play, 1970. Lives in Henley on Thames, Oxfordshire.

PUBLICATIONS

Plays

    The Dock Brief (broadcast 1957; produced 1958). In *Three Plays*, 1958.
    I Spy (broadcast 1957; produced 1959). In *Three Plays*, 1958.
    What Shall We Tell Caroline? (produced 1958). In *Three Plays*, 1958.
    Three Plays. 1958.
    Call Me a Liar (televised 1958; produced 1968). In *Lunch Hour and Other Plays*, 1960.
    Sketches in *One to Another* (produced 1959). 1960.
    The Wrong Side of the Park (produced 1960). 1960.

Lunch Hour (broadcast 1960; produced 1960).   1960.

David and Broccoli (televised 1960).   In *Lunch Hour and Other Plays*, 1960.

Lunch Hour and Other Plays.   1960.

Collect Your Hand Baggage (produced 1963).   In *Lunch Hour and Other Plays*, 1960.

Sketches in *One over the Eight* (produced 1961).

Two Stars for Comfort (produced 1962).   1962.

A Voyage round My Father (broadcast 1963; produced 1970).   1971.

Sketches in *Changing Gear* (produced 1965).

A Flea in Her Ear, from a play by Feydeau (produced 1966).   1967.

A Choice of Kings (televised 1966).   In *Playbill Three*, edited by Alan Durband, 1969.

The Judge (produced 1967).   1967.

Desmond (televised 1968).   In *The Best Short Plays 1971*, edited by Stanley Richards, 1971.

Cat among the Pigeons, from a play by Feydeau (produced 1969).   1970.

Come As You Are: Four Short Plays (includes *Mill Hill, Bermondsey, Gloucester Road, Marble Arch*) (produced 1970).   1971.

The Captain of Köpenick, from a play by Carl Zuckmayer (produced 1971).   1971.

Conflicts, with others (produced 1971).

I, Claudius, from the novels *I, Claudius* and *Claudius the God* by Robert Graves (produced 1972).

Knightsbridge (televised 1972).   1973.

Collaborators (produced 1973).   1973.

Heaven and Hell (includes *The Fear of Heaven* and *The Prince of Darkness*) (produced 1976); revised version of *The Prince of Darkness*, as *The Bells of Hell* (produced 1977).

The Lady from Maxim's, from a play by Feydeau (produced 1977).   1978.

Screenplays: *Ferry to Hong Kong*, with Lewis Gilbert and Vernon Harris, 1959; *The Innocents*, with Truman Capote and William Archibald, 1961; *Guns of Darkness*, 1962; *I Thank a Fool*, with others, 1962; *Lunch Hour*, 1962; *The Running Man*, 1963; *Bunny Lake Is Missing*, with Penelope Mortimer, 1964; *A Flea in Her Ear*, 1967; *John and Mary*, 1969.

Radio Plays: *Like Men Betrayed*, 1955; *No Hero*, 1955; *The Dock Brief*, 1957; *I Spy*, 1957; *Three Winters*, 1958; *Call Me a Liar*, 1958; *Lunch Hour*, 1960; *The Encyclopedist*, 1961; *A Voyage round My Father*, 1963; *Personality Split*, 1964; *Education of an Englishman*, 1964; *A Rare Device*, 1965; *Mr. Luby's Fear of Heaven*, 1976.

Television Plays: *Call Me a Liar*, 1958; *David and Broccoli*, 1960; *A Choice of Kings*, 1966; *The Exploding Azalea*, 1966; *The Head Waiter*, 1966; *Hughie*, 1967; *The Other Side*, 1967; *Desmond*, 1968; *Infidelity Took Place*, 1968; *Married Alive*, 1970; *Swiss Cottage*, 1972; *Knightsbridge*, 1972; *Rumpole of the Bailey*, 1975, and series, 1978; *A Little Place off Edgware Road, The Blue Film, The Destructors, The Case for the Defence, Chagrin in Three Parts, The Invisible Japanese Gentlemen, Special Duties*, and *Mortmain*, all from stories by Graham Greene, 1975–76; *Will Shakespeare* series, 1978.

Ballet Scenario: *Home*, 1968.

Son et Lumière script: *Hampton Court*, 1964.

Fiction

Charade.   1947.

Rumming Park.   1948.
Answer Yes or No.   1950; as *The Silver Hook,* 1950.
Like Men Betrayed.   1953.
The Narrowing Stream.   1954.
Three Winters.   1956.
Will Shakespeare: The Untold Story.   1977.

Other

No Moaning at the Bar.   1957.
With Love and Lizards (travel), with Penelope Mortimer.   1957.

Reading List: *Anger and After* by John Russell Taylor, 1962.

*   *   *

Although his first writing was for film, a medium more visual than verbal, John Mortimer then devoted a decade to the novel. This proficiency at prose fiction, taken with a degree of education which for a contemporary British playwright is unusual, may be responsible for the dramatist's felicitous style. If the drama in a Mortimer play is sometimes thin, the language in which it is orchestrated, at its most urbane, boasts cunning cadenzas and playful arabesques; even at its more mundane the Mortimer speech is literate and sensitive to both cerebral quirk and linguistic nuance.

This verbal urbanity is accompanied by a sophistication of viewpoint. Q.C. Mortimer's distinguished career in jurisprudence has found him repeatedly as defense attorney in film and literary prosecutions on grounds of obscenity or blasphemy. As a stalwart champion of freedom of press and speech, he has denied any danger inherent in the magazine *Oz,* the books *Last Exit to Brooklyn* and *Inside Linda Lovelace,* and a poem about Christ published in *Gay News.* As a vocal opponent of stage censorship, his testimony against the Lord Chamberlain's bowdlerizing function was instrumental in bringing an end to that practice. Yet for all his theoretical permissiveness, Mortimer has never written what the censorious could label lewd or profane. He defends hedonism in plays of the utmost civility.

Mortimer's allegiance to the pleasure principle is part of a larger worldview which prefers the joy of life to propriety and requires him to side habitually with the underdog. In the courtroom, he is a defense attorney; in the theatre, he is an advocate for those he describes as "the lonely, the neglected, the unsuccessful," for people engaged "in the war against established rules." He cannot take middle-class conventionality seriously. He delights in pricking the pretensions of the pompous and exposing repression or hypocrisy cloaked though it is in the mantle of respectability, but more often still he's engaged in opening viewers' hearts to sympathy for the simple or the forlorn.

Thus in *The Dock Brief* the life's losers for whom Mortimer wins our sympathy are a woebegone wife murderer and his court-appointed attorney who has long awaited a case. In the first scene the barrister brags of how he'll secure his client's acquittal; in the second we learn the accused has been saved all right – by his counsel's incompetence. In the equally whimsical *What Shall We Tell Caroline?,* an irascible husband seemingly unbearable to his wife reveals his true sympathy for her when he bullies their friend into continuing a pretended flirtation with her so she shan't be hurt. Mortimer's optimism for those willing to leave the shelter of tradition for the risk of independence imbues this study of the eighteen-year-old Caroline's escape from over-protective parents, and his philosophy is nowhere articulated more clearly than in the family friend's admonition "Every day she should collect some small pleasure to keep her warm ... because when she reaches our age, it won't be the things she's done she'll regret, it will be the things she hasn't done."

The zest for life lived fully and the compassion for crippled souls are apparent in other plays. The proprietor of the hotel in *Two Stars for Comfort* – a rating earned for lodging and for the comforts of reassurance and sexual pleasure as well – is a free spirit not treated with the same tolerance and affection which he offers the world. The title character's dour view in *The Judge*, who is as repressed as the law he administers is repressive, contrasts with the acceptance of life practised by his former mistress. In *Mr. Luby's Fear of Heaven*, the pompous old Byron scholar who wakes in a hospital with a ceiling painting of heaven so beautiful he thinks he has died comes to realize he is "sexually underprivileged" when he contrasts his merely literary sensuality with the unrepressed enjoyments of the practicing sensualist in the adjacent bed. *The Bells of Hell* finds the devil is "a gentleman," one who can perform the miracles of putting sin back in sex and otherwise feeding the emotionally malnourished. And the old defense lawyer in *Rumpole of the Bailey* triumphantly secures acquittal for a black teenager accused in a stabbing by proving the lad couldn't have read his signed confession since he is illiterate.

Mortimer usually writes comedy, but within this genre he has permitted himself considerable stylistic latitude. Not surprisingly for a translator of Feydeau, he has mastered the sex farce in a play like *Marble Arch*. Actress Laura is being kept by a married Labor peer who appears to die in her loo. It's not the lines which convulse us but the exits and entrances mere seconds apart of characters who must not meet. Similarly, in *Mill Hill* a husband interrupts an illicit rendezvous but the wife's subterfuge preserves the appearance of decorum.

It's usually the situation, rather than plot or character, which especially takes our fancy in a Mortimer play, and many of them might most fairly be termed situation comedies. In *Bermondsey*, a wife and a homosexual, for their mutual benefit, connive to keep the man in their life out of the arms of a young barmaid. The detective of *I Spy* falls in love with the woman he's observing and conspires with her falsely to impugn her virtue so as to win her for himself following the divorce proceedings. *The Wrong Side of the Park* gives us a decaying family in a crumbling house where a hysterical woman, of the type its originator Margaret Leighton did so well, seeks to bring some glamor into her humdrum life only to discover the real excitement in her own husband. Similar genial fun is had with gentility in *A Voyage round My Father*, a charming ramble down memory lane without pretension to plot. This play includes recollections of Mortimer's boyhood, his early experiences of women, and his film-making during the war, but mostly it is a loving tribute to his father, the barrister whose blindness prompted the program's solicitation for "The Prevention of Blindness Fund." *Collaborators* is a domestic comedy about a barrister and his wife who are collaborating on a film. Both the play by Mortimer and the film his characters are concocting examine another kind of collaboration, modern marriage.

Indeed marriage, love and sex, and failure are Mortimer's repeated subjects, whether the style is relatively representational – as in the early plays – or more presentational, as in *I, Claudius*, *A Voyage round My Father*, *The Judge*, and *Rumpole of the Bailey*. The characteristic Mortimer atmosphere is mildly Chekhovian, and he is more often than not ironic. We expect from Mortimer eloquence in middle-class speech, idiosyncratic character parts, freedom of thought, and humor aimed at evoking grins more often than guffaws. He shares his wry amusement at people lovingly created and brought to life with understated but inventive theatricality.

—Tish Dace

O'CASEY, Sean.   Irish.   Born in Dublin, 30 March 1880. Attended a school in Dublin for three years; lived in extreme poverty as a child: largely self-educated. Married Eileen Reynolds in 1927; two sons and one daughter. Began working at age 13 in a Dublin chandlery; thereafter worked as a docker, hod carrier, stone breaker on road-building crews; and for a news agency; involved in the Dublin transport strike in 1913, and served in the Irish Citizen Army; associated with the Abbey Theatre, Dublin, from 1923; settled in England, 1926. Recipient: Hawthornden Prize, 1926. *Died 18 September 1964.*

PUBLICATIONS

Collections

The O'Casey Reader, edited by Brooks Atkinson.   1968.
The Letters 1910–41, edited by David Krause.   Vol. 1 (of 3), 1975.

Plays

The Shadow of a Gunman (produced 1923).   In *Two Plays,* 1925.
Cathleen Listens In: A Phantasy (produced 1923).   In *Feathers from the Green Crow,* 1962.
Juno and the Paycock (produced 1924).   In *Two Plays,* 1925.
Nannie's Night Out (produced 1924).   In *Feathers from the Green Crow,* 1962.
Two Plays: Juno and the Paycock, The Shadow of a Gunman.   1925.
The Plough and the Stars (produced 1926).   1926.
The Silver Tassie (produced 1929).   1928.
Within the Gates (produced 1934).   1933.
The End of the Beginning (produced 1937).   In *Windfalls,* 1934.
A Pound on Demand (produced 1939).   In *Windfalls,* 1934.
The Star Turns Red (produced 1940).   1940.
Purple Dust: A Wayward Comedy (produced 1943).   1940.
Red Roses for Me (produced 1943).   1942.
Oak Leaves and Lavender; or, A World on Wallpaper (produced 1947).   1946.
Cock-a-Doodle Dandy (produced 1949).   1949.
Collected Plays.   4 vols., 1949–51.
Bedtime Story: An Anatole Burlesque (produced 1952).   In *Collected Plays 4,* 1951.
Hall of Healing: A Sincerious Farce (produced 1952).   In *Collected Plays 3,* 1951.
Time to Go: A Morality Comedy (produced 1952).   In *Collected Plays 4,* 1951.
The Bishop's Bonfire (produced 1955).   1955.
The Drums of Father Ned: A Mickrocosm of Ireland (produced 1959).   1960.
The Moon Shines on Kylenamoe (produced 1961).   In *Behind the Green Curtains ...,* 1961.
Behind the Green Curtains, Figaro in the Night, The Moon Shines on Kylenamoe: Three Plays.   1961.
Behind the Green Curtains (produced 1962).   In *Behind the Green Curtains ...,* 1961.
Figaro in the Night (produced 1962).   In *Behind the Green Curtains ...,* 1961.

Screenplay: *Juno and the Paycock (The Shame of Mary Boyle),* with Alma Reville and Alfred Hitchcock, 1929.

Verse

Songs of the Wren.   2 vols., 1918.
More Wren Songs.   1918.

Other

> *The Sacrifice of Thomas Ashe.* 1918.
> *The Story of Thomas Ashe.* 1918.
> *The Story of the Irish Citizen Army.* 1919.
> *Windfalls: Stories, Poems, and Plays.* 1934.
> *The Flying Wasp* (on theatre). 1937.
> Autobiography:
> 1. *I Knock at the Door: Swift Glances Back at Things That Made Me.* 1939.
> 2. *Pictures in the Hallway.* 1942.
> 3. *Drums under the Window.* 1945.
> 4. *Inishfallen, Fare Thee Well.* 1949.
> 5. *Rose and Crown.* 1952.
> 6. *Sunset and Evening Star.* 1956.
> *The Green Crow* (essays and stories). 1956.
> *Feathers from the Green Crow 1905–15* (miscellany), edited by Robert Hogan. 1962.
> *Under a Colored Cap: Articles Merry and Mournful with Comments and a Song.* 1963.
> *Blasts and Benedictions: Articles and Stories,* edited by Ronald Ayling. 1967.
> *The Sting and the Twinkle: Conversations with O'Casey,* edited by E. H. Mikhail and John O'Riordan. 1974.

Bibliography: *O'Casey: A Bibliography* by Ronald Ayling and Michael J. Durkan, 1977.

Reading List: *The Green and the Red: O'Casey, The Man and His Plays* by Jules Koslow, 1950, revised edition, 1966; *The Experiments of O'Casey* by Robert Hogan, 1960; *O'Casey, The Man and His Work,* 1960, revised edition, 1976, and *O'Casey and His World,* 1976, both by David Krause; *O'Casey, The Man Behind the Plays,* 1963, revised edition, 1965, and *O'Casey,* 1966, both by Saros Cowasjee; *The World of O'Casey* edited by S. McCann, 1966; *O'Casey* by W. A. Armstrong, 1967; *A Self-Portrait of the Artist as a Man: O'Casey's Letters* edited by David Krause, 1968; *The Plays of O'Casey* by Maureen Malone, 1969; *The Early Life of O'Casey* by Martin B. Margulies, 1970; *Sean* by Eileen O'Casey, edited by J. C. Trewin, 1971; *O'Casey: A Collection of Critical Essays* edited by Thomas Kilroy, 1974; *O'Casey* by Doris Darin, 1975; *O'Casey* by C. Desmond Greaves, 1978.

*   *   *

Fame came to Sean O'Casey at the age of forty-three when the Abbey Theatre, after rejecting four of his "apprentice" plays, accepted *The Shadow of a Gunman* in 1923. Set during the Anglo-Irish wars, the play deals with a pseudo-poet Donal Davoren who pretends, with tragic consequences, to be a gunman to win the affections of Minnie Powell – one of the tenement residents. The immediate success of the play paved the way for *Juno and the Paycock* and *The Plough and the Stars.* The former, with the Irish Civil War as its backdrop, is the story of the Boyle family trapped between events they themselves have precipitated and others over which they have no control. While Captain Jack Boyle, the dry-land sailor, struts about the snugs saturating himself on stout with his "butty" Joxer Daly, Juno, his hardworking wife, keeps the home together. But misfortunes move in fast: their son Johnny is shot as a traitor, their daughter Mary is left pregnant by her suitor, and the promise of the expected legacy is not fulfilled. The latter play, to my mind O'Casey's finest work, is about the tenement dwellers caught in the 1916 Easter Rising. While a few idealistic Irishmen strike a blow for freedom, the vast majority of the Dubliners loot, swear, gamble, and applaud the fighters from a safe distance. The result is as one would expect: the Rising fails; the hero,

Jack Clitheroe, and his wife, Nora, die, while the braggarts and the good-for-nothings live on. Among them is Fluther Good, a veritable Falstaff, some of whose wildness O'Casey saw in himself and whose name he sprawls all over his autobiographies.

The above three plays have many features in common. They have a war period for background, and O'Casey views the war strictly from the angle of the slum dweller. He condemns all wars, and shows their horrible impact on people who have the least to do with fighting. The evils of tenement life are depicted with frightening realism and accuracy. Characters generally take precedence over plot: in the main his women are brave and earthy, his men are dreamers and braggarts. Through the interaction of his male and female characters (many of them modelled on people from real life), O'Casey offers a juxtaposition of tragedy and comedy rarely rivalled in English dramatic literature. But his main concern is to give an honest and unflinching portrayal of his countrymen and times. It is no exaggeration to say that these plays are a suitable appendix to any political and social history of Ireland between the years 1916 and 1923.

Realism had never strongly appealed to O'Casey in spite of the success it had brought him. His lost play, *The Robe of Rosheen*, was according to him "in the 'first principle' of a fantasy," and his one-actor *Cathleen Listens In* was also a fantasy with symbolic characters. But his first conscious experiment in symbolism and expressionism was *The Silver Tassie*. It is the story of the footballer Harry Heegan who goes unthinkingly to the trenches. He returns an invalid to discover that the man who saved his life has been awarded the Victoria Cross and has won the affection of the girl he loves. Through the agony of the crippled hero, O'Casey voices his hatred of warfare. To show the colossal nightmare war is, O'Casey makes the second act totally expressionistic and juxtaposes it with other acts written in the naturalistic manner. The setting of the act (a ruined monastery), the intoning of the prophecies of doom (parodies from the Book of Ezekiel), the fantastic chanted poetry, the stylisation of characters and dialogue, all go to make the play, in the words of John Gassner, "one of the most trenchant pacifist protests of the generation."

Having seen the possibilities of symbolic drama in *The Silver Tassie*, O'Casey went on to write a completely expressionistic play, *Within the Gates*. The setting is no longer Dublin but Hyde Park, London, and the three principal characters are the Bishop, the Dreamer, and the Young Woman. The Young Woman is torn between conflicting emotions: on the one hand she wishes to live a life of joy, sex, and unrestrained youth; on the other hand she seeks the salvation which her mode of life denies her. The Bishop and the Dreamer, holding views that are diametrically opposite, struggle to win her to their respective beliefs. In a way they both succeed, for O'Casey gets the Bishop to bless her as she dies dancing in the arms of the Dreamer. The message of the play seems to be that God should be approached through joy, not fear.

What is unique about this play is its design. Its four scenes, Morning, Noon, Evening, and Night, correspond to the four seasons, Spring, Summer, Autumn, and Winter. These blend with the changing colours of flowers and trees. Close significance is implicit in chosen moments of bird-song and sunshine; human action in all instances is related to seasonal references. The dialogue is stylised, and the entry and exit of the numerous characters and their positions on the stage are expertly controlled. Music and dance are closely woven into the symbolic pattern of the drama — they do not merely further the theme but contain it as well. The whole play is a triumph of technique and stagecraft.

With a couple of exceptions, O'Casey's remaining plays are less successful. They may conveniently be divided into two groups, plays concerned primarily with Communism and plays expressing his views of life in Ireland. Technique, characterisation, humour, and a strong urge to promote happiness for all are common to these two groups.

In the first group falls *The Star Turns Red*, *Red Roses for Me*, and *Oak Leaves and Lavender*. Of these only *Red Roses for Me* has distinctive merit. The background of the play is the Irish Transport Workers' strike of 1913; the hero is a doomed idealist called Ayamonn Breydon, a Protestant, in love with a Catholic girl, Shiela Moorneen. A strike is organised by the workers for a shilling-a-week increase in wages, and Shiela begs him to take no part in it.

But Ayamonn ignores her entreaties, and is killed in a clash with the police. Dying, he sends words to his friend, the parish Rector: "this day's but a day's work done, an' it'll be begun again tomorrow."

In *Red Roses for Me*, O'Casey returns to Dublin for his *milieu*. Slum life is depicted with its accompanying poverty and hunger; there is the same lack of privacy to be found in his Abbey plays. But the most moving thing here is the expressionistic third act. The dull and dismal quays of Dublin are transformed into a vision of beauty as Ayamonn unfolds to the people his dream of the city's hidden splendour. Under the stress of genuine poetry the Party Line disappears, and we have a political play which is no facile propaganda.

The second group comprises *Purple Dust*, *Cock-a-Doodle Dandy*, *The Bishop's Bonfire*, *The Drums of Father Ned*, and *Behind the Green Curtains*. They are all set in "imaginary" Irish villages, and among the things they have in common are O'Casey's attack on the Irish clergy and a vibrant plea for joy, sex, and sanity. Of these, *Purple Dust* is the gayest. It deals with the efforts of two Englishmen to transplant themselves to a Tudor mansion in the west of Ireland to enjoy the pleasures of country life. Their manners, temperaments, and outlook clash with those of the Irish, till the whole house becomes a bedlam. *Cock-a-Doodle Dandy*, the author's favourite, is an uproarious fantasy that most sharply defines O'Casey's view of Ireland in particular and life in general. The all-out battle waged by the priest and his puritanical crew against the indefatigable Cock (symbolic of joy, courage, and sexual ecstasy) is the play's highlight and shows O'Casey at his funniest. *The Bishop's Bonfire* centres on the preparations being made to receive Bishop Bill Mullarkey in his home town of Ballyoonagh. A lesser play that the preceding two, it tackles the problems of Ireland more pointedly by its vigorous condemnation of men and institutions that stand between the individual and his right to happiness.

Among O'Casey's prose works, his six volumes of autobiography are a notable achievement. Each volume covers a 12-year span of his life, beginning with *I Knock at the Door*, and continuing with *Picture in the Hallway*, *Drums under the Window*, *Inishfallen, Fare Thee Well*, *Rose and Crown*, and *Sunset and Evening Star*. Written in the third person, and in a variety of styles, the work is, as one reviewer puts it, "one of the most astonishing and appalling documents of poverty, failure, success, and then the poverty and failure of success itself, written in the last half century." They also throw enormous light on the Dublin of O'Casey's youth and are an indispensable source-book for the study of his plays.

Of the six books, the first four dealing with his hard struggle to survive and become a great dramatist are the best. And of these four, *Inishfallen, Fare Thee Well* is the most impressive. He recalls with great clarity the year immediately following the Easter Rising, his grief at his mother's death and the pauper's funeral that accompanied it, the fight against the Black and Tans, and the heart-rending Civil War. He tells us of his meeting with Yeats and Lady Gregory, and the circumstances that forced him into exile. Any account following those memorable years and events was sure to be an anti-climax, and it is not surprising that the last two volumes are the least successful. But they still make fascinating reading because of the old O'Casey traits: narrative detail, sharp observation, comic invective, incisive humour, and glorious puns and malapropisms.

—Saros Cowasjee

ODETS, Clifford.   American.   Born in Philadelphia, Pennsylvania, 18 July 1906; grew up in the Bronx, New York. Educated at Morris High School, New York, 1921–23. Married 1) the actress Luise Rainer in 1937 (divorced, 1941); 2) Betty Grayson in 1943 (died, 1954), one son and one daughter. Actor on radio and on Broadway, 1923–28, and with Theatre Guild Productions, New York, 1928–30; Co-Founder, Group Theatre, New York, 1930; wrote for the stage from 1933; film writer and director. Recipient: New Theatre League prize, 1935; Yale drama prize, 1935; American Academy of Arts and Letters Award of Merit Medal, 1961. *Died 15 August 1963.*

PUBLICATIONS

Plays

Waiting for Lefty (produced 1935).   In *Three Plays*, 1935.
Awake and Sing! (produced 1935).   In *Three Plays*, 1935.
Till the Day I Die (produced 1935).   In *Three Plays*, 1935.
I Can't Sleep: A Monologue (produced 1935).   1936.
Paradise Lost (produced 1935).   1936.
Golden Boy (produced 1937).   1937.
Rocket to the Moon (produced 1938).   1939.
Night Music (produced 1940).   1940.
Clash by Night (produced 1941).   1942.
The Russian People, from a play by Konstantin Simonov (produced 1942).
None But the Lonely Heart (screenplay), in *Best Film Plays 1945*, edited by John Gassner
   and Dudley Nichols.   1946.
The Big Knife (produced 1949).   1949.
The Country Girl (produced 1950).   1951; as *Winter Journey* (produced 1952), 1953.
The Flowering Peach (produced 1954).   1954.
The Silent Partner (produced 1972).

Screenplays: *The General Died at Dawn*, 1936; *Black Sea Fighters*, 1943; *None But the Lonely Heart*, 1944; *Deadline at Dawn*, 1946; *Humoresque* with Zachery Gold, 1946; *Sweet Smell of Success*, with Ernest Lehman, 1957; *The Story on Page One*, 1960; *Wild in the Country*, 1961.

Television Plays: *Big Mitch*, 1963; *The Mafia Man*, 1964.

Other

Rifle Rule in Cuba, with Carleton Beals.   1935.

Reading List: *Odets* by R. Baird Shuman, 1963; *Odets: The Thirties and After* by Edward Murray, 1968; *Odets, Humane Dramatist* by Michael J. Mendelsohn, 1969; *Odets* by Gerald Weales, 1971; *Odets, Playwright-Poet* by Harold Cantor, 1978.

*   *   *

Clifford Odets's first produced play was *Waiting for Lefty*, a one-act agitprop drama based on the New York City taxi strike of 1934. It is uncharacteristic Odets in both form and intention. A group of naturalistic dramatic sketches set within a union meeting, still visible while the more intimate scenes are being played, *Waiting for Lefty* is non-realistic theater that breaks the conventional frame to invite the audience to join in the final call for a strike. Aside from this play, Odets remained within the American realistic tradition even when he attempted to open the form with cinematic techniques (*Golden Boy*), visual and musical devices (*Night Music*) and Yiddish-Biblical fantasy (*The Flowering Peach*). Although most of his plays, particularly the early ones like *Awake and Sing!* and *Paradise Lost*, have the mandatory optimistic ending decreed by the American Left in the 1930's, *Waiting for Lefty* is the only overt propaganda play Odets wrote, except for *Till the Day I Die*, an ineffective anti-fascist piece hastily written to fill out the bill when *Lefty* moved to Broadway. He did do a few sketches, like "I Can't Sleep," for benefit performances and he worked at two political plays, *The Cuban Play* and *The Silent Partner*, which he never got into final form. If *Waiting for Lefty* is uncharacteristic in some ways, it is also unmistakable Odets. Scenes like "Joe and Edna" and "The Young Hack and His Girl" show that Odets's political and social concerns look their best transformed into domestic conflict, and the language of those scenes set the tone for the Odets work to come. When Edna says "Get out of here!" meaning "I love you" and Sid, in affectionate exasperation, calls his brother, "that dumb basketball player," we get a first taste of the Odets obliquity – the wisecrack as lament, slang as lyricism – that, trailing its Yiddish and urban roots, enriches *Awake and Sing!* and *Paradise Lost* before it peters out in the self-parody of some of the lines in the screenplay *Sweet Smell of Success*.

Although *Waiting for Lefty* introduced Odets to audiences and critics, it was not his first play. *Awake and Sing!* was already written and about to open when *Lefty* was produced. *Awake and Sing!*, Odets's most enduring work, is *the* American depression play, a still vital example of the 1930's conviction that, however terrible the situation, it could be rectified by an infusion of idealistic rhetoric administered at the final curtain. Although Odets was a Communist when he wrote it (and the play carries a few verbal indications of that fact), its optimism is more generalized, tied into the historical American penchant for possibility which, battered by the first years of the depression, had begun to revive with the election of Franklin D. Roosevelt in 1932. Not only is Odets hooked into the American ideational mainstream in *Awake and Sing!* but he recalls earlier American drama in his choice of a family setting for his play and in his willing employment of melodramatic commonplaces – the suicide of Jacob, the pregnancy of Hennie. He transcends the structural weaknesses in the play with the creation of a milieu so real that an audience feels it can be touched; this texture – partly verbal, partly emotional – is probably a product not simply of Odets's talent but of the context in which the play was written. Odets was a member of the Group Theatre, an acting company that was a family of sorts, and his Bergers are an echo of the loving, quarreling Group company which was a home for Odets, one that – reacting like Ralph and Hennie to Bessie Berger's Bronx – he sometimes saw as a trap. All of his plays through *Night Music* were written for the Group actors, but *Paradise Lost*, which Odets once correctly described as "a beautiful play, velvety ... gloomy and rich," and *Rocket to the Moon* come closest in texture to *Awake and Sing!*

When the success of *Awake and Sing!* was followed by the failure of *Paradise Lost*, Odets went to Hollywood to work on *The General Died at Dawn*. After that, he vacillated between Hollywood and New York, commerce and art, guilt and regeneration. These terms suit his view of the matter as reflected in *The Big Knife*, in which the Odets surrogate, the actor Charlie Castle, is destroyed as man and artist by the movie business. Despite this gloomy view of Hollywood Odets constantly returned to a suspicion that the movies too were an art, all the more attractive for the size of the audience. Ironically, the movies he worked on were conventional Hollywood products; even the two he directed as well as wrote, *None But the Lonely Heart* and *The Story on Page One*, are interesting primarily for their attempt at poetic verisimilitude, the visual equivalent of the sense of milieu created by other means in *Awake and Sing!* and *Paradise Lost*.

Odets's greatest commercial successes were *Golden Boy*, a parable in boxing gloves about the destructiveness of the American success ethic, and *The Country Girl*, an effective sentimental melodrama about an alcoholic actor's attempt to recover his career and his life. Both plays show Odets's theatrical skill, but his most attractive failures, *Paradise Lost* and *Night Music*, display a bumbling sweetness that is as important a part of Odets's talent as his technical proficiency. Both the staccato dialogue of *Golden Boy* and the rambling non sequiturs of *Paradise Lost* are aspects of the authentic Odets voice which can still be heard at its purest in *Awake and Sing!*

—Gerald Weales

O'NEILL, Eugene (Gladstone).   American.   Born in New York City, 16 October 1888; son of the actor James O'Neill. Toured with his father as a child, and educated at Catholic boarding schools, and at Betts Academy, Stamford, Connecticut; attended Princeton University, New Jersey, 1906–07, and George Pierce Baker's "47 Workshop" at Harvard University, Cambridge, Massachusetts, 1914–15. Married 1) Kathleen Jenkins in 1909 (divorced, 1912), one son; 2) Agnes Boulton in 1918 (divorced, 1929), one son and one daughter; 3) the actress Carlotta Monterey in 1929. Worked in a mail order firm in New York, 1908; gold prospector in Honduras, 1909; advance agent and box-office man for his father's company, and seaman on a Norwegian freighter to Buenos Aires, 1910–11; Reporter for the *New London Telegraph*, Connecticut, 1912; patient in a tuberculosis sanitarium, where he began to write, 1912–13; full-time writer from 1914; associated with the Provincetown Players, New York, and Provincetown, Massachusetts, as actor and writer, 1914–20; wrote for the Theatre Guild; Manager, with Kenneth Macgowan and Robert Edmond Jones, Greenwich Village Theatre, New York, 1923–27; a Founding Editor, *American Spectator*, 1934; in ill-health from 1934: in later years suffered from Parkinson's Disease. Recipient: Pulitzer Prize, 1920, 1922, 1928, 1957; American Academy of Arts and Letters Gold Medal, 1922; Nobel Prize for Literature, 1936; New York Drama Critics Circle Award, 1957. Litt.D.: Yale University, New Haven, Connecticut, 1926. Member, National Institute of Arts and Letters, and Irish Academy of Letters. *Died 27 November 1953.*

PUBLICATIONS

Plays

>   *Thirst and Other One Act Plays* (includes *The Web, Warnings, Fog, Recklessness*).   1914.
>   *Thirst* (produced 1916).   In *Thirst and Other Plays*, 1914.
>   *Fog* (produced 1917).   In *Thirst and Other Plays*, 1914.
>   *Bound East for Cardiff* (produced 1916).   In *The Moon of the Caribbees* ..., 1919.
>   *Before Breakfast* (produced 1916).   1916.
>   *The Sniper* (produced 1917).   In *Lost Plays*, 1950.
>   *In the Zone* (produced 1917).   In *The Moon of the Caribbees* ..., 1919.
>   *The Long Voyage Home* (produced 1917).   In *The Moon of the Caribbees* ..., 1919.
>   *Ile* (produced 1917).   In *The Moon of the Caribbees* ..., 1919.
>   *The Rope* (produced 1918).   In *The Moon of the Caribbees* ..., 1919.
>   *Where The Cross Is Made* (produced 1918).   In *The Moon of the Caribbees* ..., 1919.
>   *The Moon of the Caribbees* (produced 1918).   In *The Moon of the Caribbees...*, 1919.
>   *The Moon of the Caribbees and Six Other Plays of the Sea.*   1919.
>   *The Dreamy Kid* (produced 1919).   In *Complete Works 2*, 1924.

Beyond the Horizon (produced 1920).   1920.

Anna Christie (as *Chris*, produced 1920; revised version, as *Anna Christie*, produced 1921).   With *The Hairy Ape, The First Man*, 1922.

Exorcism (produced 1920).

The Emperor Jones (produced 1920).   With *Diff'rent, The Straw*, 1921.

Diff'rent (produced 1920).   With *The Emperor Jones, The Straw*, 1921.

The Straw (produced 1921).   With *The Emperor Jones, Diff'rent*, 1921.

Gold (produced 1921).   1921.

The First Man (produced 1922).   With *The Hairy Ape, Anna Christie*, 1922.

The Hairy Ape (produced 1922).   With *The First Man, Anna Christie*, 1922.

Welded (produced 1924).   With *All God's Chillun Got Wings*, 1924.

All God's Chillun Got Wings (produced 1924).   With *Welded*, 1924.

Desire under the Elms (produced 1924).   In *Complete Works 2*, 1924.

Complete Works.   2 vols., 1924.

The Fountain (produced 1925).   With *The Great God Brown, The Moon of the Caribbees*, 1926.

The Great God Brown (produced 1926).   With *The Fountain, The Moon of the Caribbees*, 1926.

Marco Millions (produced 1928).   1927.

Lazarus Laughed (produced 1928).   1927.

Strange Interlude (produced 1928).   1928.

Dynamo (produced 1929).   1929.

Mourning Becomes Electra: A Trilogy (produced 1931).   1931.

Ah, Wilderness! (produced 1933).   1933.

Days Without End (produced 1934).   1934.

The Iceman Cometh (produced 1946).   1946.

Lost Plays (includes *Abortion, The Movie Man, The Sniper, Servitude, Wife for a Life*), edited by Lawrence Gellert.   1950.

A Moon for the Misbegotten (produced 1957).   1952.

Long Day's Journey into Night (produced 1956).   1956.

A Touch of the Poet (produced 1957).   1957.

Hughie (produced 1958).   1959.

More Stately Mansions (produced 1962).   1964.

Ten "Lost" Plays.   1964.

Children of the Sea and Three Other Unpublished Plays (includes *Bread and Butter, Now I Ask You, Shell Shock*), edited by Jennifer McCabe Atkinson.   1972.

Other

Inscriptions: O'Neill to Carlotta Monterey O'Neill, edited by Donald Gallup.   1960.

Bibliography: *O'Neill and the American Critic: A Summary and Bibliographical Checklist* by Jordan Y. Miller, 1973; *O'Neill: A Descriptive Bibliography* by Jennifer McCabe Atkinson, 1974.

Reading List: *The Haunted Heroes of O'Neill* by Edwin A. Engel, 1955; *O'Neill and His Plays: Four Decades of Criticism* edited by Oscar Cargill and other, 1961; *O'Neill* (biography) by Arthur and Barbara Gelb, 1962, revised edition, 1973; *The Tempering of O'Neill* by Doris Alexander, 1962; *O'Neill* by Frederic I. Carpenter, 1964; *O'Neill: A Collection of Critical Essays* edited by John Gassner, 1964; *The Plays of O'Neill* by John Henry Raleigh, 1965; *Playwright's Progress: O'Neill and the Critics* by Jordan Y. Miller, 1965; *O'Neill* by John Gassner, 1965; *O'Neill's Scenic Images* by Timo Tiusanen, 1968; *O'Neill: Son and*

Playwright, 1968, and *O'Neill: Son and Artist*, 1973, both by Louis Sheaffer; *A Drama of Souls: Studies in O'Neill's Super-Naturalistic Techniques* by Egil Törnqvist, 1969; *O'Neill* by H. Frenz, 1971; *Contour in Time* by T. M. Bogard, 1972; *O'Neill: A Collection of Criticism* edited by Ernest Griffin, 1976.

*   *   *

Eugene O'Neill, writing dramas comparable to the best available overseas models, brought the American Theater of his actor-father's *Monte Cristo* into the twentieth century. He acknowledged (1936) drawing from the Greeks, Strindberg, and Nietzsche. Nietzsche gave this romantic pessimist a usable theory of classical tragedy: the Apollonian mask with the Dionysian force behind it.

The stage sea caught the real and the poets' seas in 1916 in O'Neill's first production. *Bound East for Cardiff* compresses the international crew of the *S.S. Glencairn* into the wedge of a forecastle. Around Yank's dying, a rusting freighter continues toward Wales, the sea-sounds adding density to the squalid realism. Yet somehow, for the attentive Driscoll and audience, something spacious has been shown through or behind the seaman-life image that contains it. The play opened the Provincetown Players' new Playwrights' Theater in New York that fall, and within the next year three new scripts completed the *S.S. Glencairn* series. In *The Long Voyage Home* deliberate and casual inhumanity (Fate?) allows a shipmate to be shanghaied. Theatricality builds mood in all four *Glencairn* plays, but their author found the tropical night and carousing seamen of *Moon of the Caribbees* more poetic than the war-hysteria of *In the Zone* for conveying "the compelling inscrutable forces behind life."

O'Neill aspired to be a poet – to catch unexpected "rhythms" and to show man's "glorious self-destructive struggle to make the Force express him." A too "acutely conscious," too articulate protagonist or heavy schematization undermines many of the heroic searches in O'Neill's plays during the 1920's. Though thematically prophetic, *Diff'rent* and *Gold* blare out the undeniability of Life and the power of "the hopeless hope." They share with many O'Neill one-acters of 1916–20 a hammering illustrativeness. Still, O'Neill's purposefulness salvages moments in faulty plays like *Lazarus Laughed* and justifies even his overblown experiments. Spectacle and comedy in *Marco Millions* cannot make delightful the overwritten dialectic, as in *Fog* earlier, between Eastern poetry and Western business; yet Marco's epilogue journey from puzzlement to complacency comments expressively on a new function of O'Neill's theater. He insisted on testing forms and tampering with his audience.

The Pulitzer Prizes for *Beyond the Horizon* and *Anna Christie* designated O'Neill the outstanding American dramatist. The former, alternating indoor–outdoor scenes for affecting "rhythm," wrings two brothers and a wife through ironic choices of farm or sea. Still challenging for top actresses, *Anna Christie* sets an ex-prostitute, her barge-skipper father, and a hesitant seaman awash together in the rhythms of that "ole davil sea." *Strange Interlude*, awarded his third Pulitzer Prize of the decade, alternates outer, realistic dialogue with inner monologues to portray the figure of (O'Neill's) Woman. A nostalgic comedy, *Ah, Wilderness!* celebrates the happier side of the autobiographical setting of *Long Day's Journey into Night*, the tragedy which would win O'Neill his fourth Pulitzer Prize, posthumously. With Aeschylus's *Oresteia* lending substance and stature, *Mourning Becomes Electra* is a modern psychological myth placed in New England after the Civil War. His drafts show masks and asides abandoned once they have helped raise the three-play drama to the desired level of formal realism. Though finally unsatisfying to O'Neill in its language and melodrama, it was the basis for his Nobel Prize.

O'Neill's socially angry 1919 portrayals of Black Americans in *The Dreamy Kid* suffer from the lurid extremities of their situation, at the terrifying juncture of religion and criminality in a New York flat. A shared "Lawd Jesus!" signals the approach of the dark God; the all-black cast was another breakthrough. *All God's Chillun Got Wings* welds black Jim and white Ella into a Strindberg marriage; their love-hate festers ever more privately upon the racial violence of their destructive self-images. That the protagonists have O'Neill's parents' names adds another dimension of identification and concern. Watching *The Emperor Jones*, an audience awaiting the irregular firing of the hero's six bullets shares his panic in the increasing pulse-rate of the incessant drums and his dread of his next night vision. The final scene returns the audience to its daily (theatrical) reality, but with emotional overtones making them more aware than those who have not undergone the stripping away of the hero.

The Hairy Ape further dislocates hero and audience in each of eight scenes. Below decks, Yank epitomizes power among the half-naked crew members and identifies himself with steel, coal, and speed. The stokers move with demonic rhythm. When a young lady descends to call Yank a hairy ape, the titanic figure falls out of the rhythm of his own life. Yank's displacements accelerate until his love-death embrace of the gorilla at the zoo satisfies the play's imagery and demand for tragic inevitability, but also looses upon the city another sinister, unthinking force.

When after tiresome grandiloquence the artist Dion(-ysus) dies three-fourths of the way through *The Great God Brown*, the play actually shifts the character beneath the protagonist's mask. Brown, a businessman, puts on Dion's mask, and accepts his wife Margaret and mother-mistress Cybel. Shot as Brown's murderer and unmasked, he speaks his last ecstatic vision in a pietà with Cybel. She croons the eternal recurrence of spring, while upstage Margaret hymns her love to Dion's mask. Reenter the cop with *"grimy notebook"* to ask, "Well, what's his name?" "Man!" answers Cybel. "How d'yuh spell it?" The accumulated rhythms press this joking question into brute fact and poetic theater. Its hard mask distances those who cannot see the tragedy behind, but also drops an audience abruptly back into everyday rhythms. *Desire under the Elms* sets the same pattern more grimly and solidly in the dialect and rock farms of the New England in the gold-fevered 1850's. Ephraim Cabot, 75, returns with "God's message t'me in the spring" – a new wife, Abbie. Finally prisoners for murdering their love-child, she and mother-haunted Eben pause, *"strangely aloof and devout,"* to repeat the play's first line: "Purty, hain't it?" Then, as in *The Great God Brown* and later *The Iceman Cometh* the cop comes in at the normal level of greedy imperception: "Wished I owned it." With an ironic chuckle of recognition, an audience rejects the tragic imperception.

"A Tale of Possessors Self-Dispossessed," O'Neill's name for his 11-play cycle, would have traced an American family from pre-Revolution to 1932. In the fifth (the only one finished), *A Touch of the Poet*, Major Cornelius Melody, an immigrant Irish tavern-keeper near Boston, 1828, remembers heroics, recites Byron, and resents the Irish. His cruel pretensions victimize his wife and embarrass his daughter Sara, who sees a "poet" only in the wealthy Harfords' son. Americanization destroys Con's special dignity and vitality. Historical details and Irish humour enrich the tragic shift of power to a less noble generation. A double-length manuscript intended for destruction, *More Stately Mansions* dandles Simon Harford between his mother's symbolic garden and the realistic world of his mistress-wife Sara, 1832–41. In the edited and produced versions, artistic styles clash more than characters do. Another projected series has left only *Hughie* and the pattern of a dead title character, a talkative central character (Erie Smith), and a listener (the new nightclerk). Night sounds press New York upon the 1928 dialogue with multimedia effect.

The autobiographical plays that interrupted his cycle work have climactic monologues. *The Iceman Cometh* gathered the political, social, and psychological dreams-deferred into a period piece of 1912. All the characters and pipedreams of Harry Hope's flophouse bar had been New York familiars of O'Neill's. Everyone awaits the salesman Theodore Hickman who cometh, like Dionysus, every spring with drinks for Hope's birthday binge. This spring Hickey pushes the inhabitants into testing and destroying their pipedreams. Hickey's own mask of delusion is that he has murdered his wife out of love. The cops lead Hickey away; life returns to the booze and a kind of peace to everyone but Larry Slade, the sensitive O'Neill type. He recognizes death in disillusion but cannot die. *A Moon for the Misbegotten* is an often comic, sometimes lyric tragedy of entropy. On a Connecticut pigfarm soaked in September moonlight and an alcoholic haze, James plays out his 1923 epilogue to the story told in *Long*

Day's Journey into Night and receives from huge Josie Hogan an absolution and benediction. O'Neill wrote *Long Day's Journey into Night* with "deep pity and understanding and forgiveness for *all* the four haunted Tyrones." The characters' self-indulgences are objectified as though "the Force behind" had become the playwright's own perspective. An opium-addicted mother, miserly father, alcoholic and tubercular sons use humor and hurting wit to sustain their tragedy. Conventional artistry and deeply felt characters keep the relentless exposition moving for almost five hours. Dope-dreaming Mary Tyrone – behind her, her family – finishes it: "... so happy for a time." Her line is a delicate mask of glass, cracking.

O'Neill thought drama began "in the worship of Dionysus," and critics have generally granted his plays this big, dark, tragic vision along with stage-worthy melodrama. A wild Celtic humor couches the inevitable destruction in his last tragedies. A period-richness informs them with a sense of history, and a more quietly compassionate understanding cleanses the combatants. Excellent posthumous productions and revivals showed unexpected delicacy in feeling and expression. This secured for the plays, more excruciatingly and less ironically, that massive "Force behind" which a younger playwright had often sought too directly. Outside his grandest schemes, he worked his Apollonian images with a finer, richer sensitivity.

—John G. Kuhn

ORTON, Joe (John Kingsley Orton). English. Born in Leicester, 1 January 1933. Educated at the Royal Academy of Dramatic Art, London (Leicester Council grant), for 2 years. Actor at the Ipswich Repertory Theatre. Recipient: *Evening Standard* award, 1966. *Died 9 August 1967.*

PUBLICATIONS

Collections

   The Complete Plays.   1976.

Plays

   Entertaining Mr. Sloane (produced 1964).   1964.
   The Ruffian on the Stair (broadcast 1964; produced 1966).   In *Crimes of Passion,* 1967.
   Loot (produced 1965).   1967.
   Crimes of Passion: The Ruffian on the Stair, and The Erpingham Camp (produced 1967).   1967.
   The Good and Faithful Servant (televised 1967; produced 1971).   In *Funeral Games, and The Good and Faithful Servant,* 1970.
   Funeral Games (televised 1968; produced 1970).   In *Funeral Games, and The Good and Faithful Servant,* 1970.
   What the Butler Saw (produced 1969).   1969.
   Funeral Games, and The Good and Faithful Servant.   1970.

Radio Play: *The Ruffian on the Stair*, 1964.

Television Plays: *The Good and Faithful Servant*, 1967; *Funeral Games*, 1968.

Other

Head to Toe. 1971.

Reading List: *Prick Up Your Ears: The Biography of Orton* by John Lahr, 1978.

*   *   *

When Joe Orton rewrote his first play, *The Ruffian on the Stair*, he removed the element of mystification. It was a conscious attempt to restrict the influence of Pinter. Even so, both this play and his first theatrical success, *Entertaining Mr. Sloane*, are centred on the familiar room with its alien visitor. The manifest sexuality and the preparedness to vilify are Orton's emendation of his model. The resolution of *Entertaining Mr. Sloane* is achieved when brother and sister come to an agreement to take turns in sleeping with the smooth-skinned young man who has just murdered their father.

The "combination of elegance and crudity," which Orton observed in Genet, and noted in his diary as "irresistibly funny," became increasingly a characteristic of his own style. The language is polished and the sentence-structure artful, however vulgar the subject. In *Loot*, Hal tips his mother's body out of its coffin in order to conceal in its place the swag from a bank-raid. The corpse becomes a comic property, gleefully exploited in defiance of "good taste." In the decade of the "sick" joke, Orton was the "sick" dramatist. His malice – towards the church, the police force, intellectuals, supporters of routine – gives edge to the carefully planted and highly polished jokes with which his plays are littered. The wild and whirling climax of *The Erpingham Camp* seems almost to endorse anarchic violence as a response to the respectable rituals of the establishment. This short play turns on an incident in a holiday camp in which religion and clean chalets are complementary offshoots of patriotism. The sudden death of the Entertainments Organiser at the beginning of the play, and the emergency substitution of Chief Redcoat Riley, lead through some physically punishing farce-scenes to the climactic death of Erpingham himself. It is a much wittier farce than *Funeral Games*, in which death and religion again provide a framework.

But Orton's talent was not on the decline. *What the Butler Saw*, his last play, is also his finest farce. Set in a private clinic, it describes a lunatic day in which the sexual desires of the proprietary psychiatrist fall foul of his nymphomaniac wife's to the confusion of everything, including sex. Transvestite disguise is the running joke, and the tangle is finally resolved when it is discovered that the twins who resulted from a thoughtless indiscretion in the Station Hotel during a black-out have been reunited before our very eyes. The psychiatrist, then, has been narrowly denied the chance of seducing his daughter, while his wife has succeeded in seducing her son – who took pictures in order to blackmail her. The play's final image is a mischievous parody of a Greek apotheosis, Orton cocking a snook at cultural snobs.

—Peter Thomson

OSBORNE, John (James).   English.   Born in London, 12 December 1929. Educated at Belmont College, Devon. Married 1) Pamela Lane in 1951 (divorced, 1957); 2) the actress

Mary Ure in 1957 (divorced, 1963); 3) the writer Penelope Gilliatt in 1963 (divorced, 1968), one daughter; 4) the actress Jill Bennett in 1968 (divorced, 1977). Journalist, 1947–48; toured as an actor, 1948–49; actor-manager, Ilfracombe Repertory, 1951; also in repertory, as actor and stage manager, in Leicester, Derby, Bridgewater and London. Since 1958, Co-Director, Woodfall Films; since 1960, Director, Oscar Lewenstein Plays Ltd., London. Member of the Council, English Stage Company, London, since 1960. Recipient: *Evening Standard* award, 1956, 1965, 1968; New York Drama Critics Circle Award, 1958, 1965; Antoinette Perry Award, 1963; Academy Award, 1964. Honorary doctor: Royal College of Art, London, 1970. Lives in Sussex.

PUBLICATIONS

Plays

The Devil Inside Him, with Stella Linden (produced 1950).
Personal Enemy, with Anthony Creighton (produced 1955).
Look Back in Anger (produced 1956).   1957.
The Entertainer (produced 1957).   1957.
Epitaph for George Dillon, with Anthony Creighton (produced 1957).   1958.
The World of Paul Slickey, music by Christopher Whelan (produced 1959).   1959.
A Subject of Scandal and Concern (as *A Matter of Scandal and Concern*, televised 1960; as *A Subject of Scandal and Concern*, produced 1962).   1961.
Luther (produced 1961).   1961.
Plays for England: The Blood of the Bambergs, Under Plain Cover (produced 1963).   1963.
Tom Jones: A Film Script.   1964.
Inadmissible Evidence (produced 1964).   1965.
A Bond Honoured, from a play by Lope de Vega (produced 1966).   1966.
A Patriot for Me (produced 1966).   1966.
The Hotel in Amsterdam (produced 1968).   In *Time Present, The Hotel in Amsterdam*, 1968.
Time Present (produced 1968).   In *Time Present, The Hotel in Amsterdam*, 1968.
The Right Prospectus: A Play for Television (televised 1969).   1970.
Very Like a Whale (televised 1970).   1971.
West of Suez (produced 1971).   1971.
Hedda Gabler, from the play by Ibsen (produced 1972).   1972.
The Gift of Friendship (televised 1972).   1972.
A Sense of Detachment (produced 1972).   1973.
A Place Calling Itself Rome, from the play *Coriolanus* by Shakespeare.   1973.
The Picture of Dorian Gray: A Moral Entertainment, from the novel by Oscar Wilde (produced 1975).   1973.
Jill and Jack (as *Ms.; or, Jill and Jack*, televised 1974).   In *The End of Me Old Cigar, and Jill and Jack*, 1975.
The End of Me Old Cigar (produced 1975).   In *The End of Me Old Cigar, and Jill and Jack*, 1975.
The End of Me Old Cigar, and Jill and Jack: A Play for Television.   1975.
Watch It Come Down (produced 1976).   1975.
You're Not Watching Me, Mummy, and Try a Little Tenderness (television plays).   1978.

Screenplays: *Look Back in Anger*, with Nigel Kneale, 1959; *The Entertainer*, with Nigel

Kneale, 1960; *Tom Jones,* 1963; *Inadmissible Evidence,* 1968; *The Charge of the Light Brigade,* with Charles Wood, 1968.

Television Plays: *For the Children* series: *Billy Bunter,* 1952, and *Robin Hood,* 1953; *A Matter of Scandal and Concern,* 1960; *The Right Prospectus,* 1969; *Very Like a Whale,* 1970; *The Gift of Friendship,* 1972; *Ms.; or, Jill and Jack,* 1974.

Reading List: *Anger and After* by John Russell Taylor, 1962; *Osborne* by Ronald Hayman, 1968; *Osborne* by Martin Banham, 1969; *Osborne* by Alan Carter, 1969; *The Plays of Osborne* by Simon Trussler, 1969; *Theatre Language: A Study of Arden, Osborne, Pinter, and Wesker* by John Russell Brown, 1972; *Osborne* by Harold Ferrar, 1973; *Anger and Detachment: A Study of Arden, Osborne, and Pinter* by Michael Anderson, 1976.

*   *   *

It is easy to be glib, in retrospect, about John Osborne's decline from spokesmanship for his intellectual generation to his present role as a sniper from the sidelines of disgruntled middle age. Arguably, this is only a sideways shift – from the sympathetic treatment of nostalgic values which informed even his earliest work to an overt declaration of hatred for contemporary values in the later plays. After all, the work by which he is still best known had us *look back* in anger.

Such an interpretation depends, however, on a response that is limited to the social standpoint of his work – and Osborne has always been least assured in that area. Although for many young people of the 1950's *Look Back in Anger* induced a shock of recognition such as most had despaired of ever receiving from a theatrical experience, the effect of that shock, assisted by the other political realignments of that post-war watershed, 1956, was an upsurge of political and social activity. Jimmy Porter, the central character of *Look Back in Anger*, had long since abandoned any such activity, to retreat into his own necessary sexual fantasies – and it is difficult to image Alison and Jimmy Porter trudging the road from Aldermaston with a scruffy toddler in their wake.

Thus, *Look Back in Anger* was only accidentally a clarion call to action: primarily, it was a perceptive (but structurally conventional) psychological drama, in which a couple who found it necessary to tear each other's hearts out for their mutual satisfaction happened also to live in a provincial garret, share their bed-sit with an ironing board, and strew the posh Sunday papers over the floor. Their political disillusion was inward-turning: it was the physical trappings of that disillusion with which the activists could identify.

Osborne's dramatic career has, it is true, witnessed an apparent change of political mind: more important, it has witnessed a failure to achieve maturity of craftsmanship, and this has inevitably made the plays less interesting as the purely imaginative impulse behind them has become ... not necessarily reactionary, but merely commonplace.

Even in the early years of his career, for every work of major theatrical significance there was an equally resounding disappointment. After *The Entertainer* – in which the decline of empire was microcosmically reflected through the prism of the dying music-hall tradition – came the broken-backed *The World of Paul Slickey*, one-third musical, one-third diffuse satire on gossip columnists, one-third rambling comedy about an attempt to evade death duties. Such a wavering of narrative line has often flawed Osborne's writing – just as, in *Luther* and *A Patriot for Me*, his attempts to take his characters through extended time spans were weakened by his showing each stage of their development fully accomplished, rather than dramatically evolved.

Luther is also weakened by a would-be epic structure which is ostensibly appropriate for so public a figure, yet which Osborne's actual concentration on the intensely private person renders unnecessary, and positively distracting. Of the two *Plays for England* which followed, *The Blood of the Bambergs* was an essentially occasional piece (the occasion being the flummery of a royal wedding), while *Under Plain Cover* began as a compassionate cameo study of a shared sexual fantasy, but changed direction half-way with the heavy-footed intrusion of a hack journalist, and thereafter focused on the easier, pock-marked target.

Osborne is not readily able to find the appropriate form for his plays – yet when he does so, by accident or intention, as in *Inadmissible Evidence*, the result is striking. This is a brilliant study of one man's loss of touch with reality, its style increasingly impressionistic as its peripheral characters become more and more enmeshed in the personal endgame being played out by the central character, the solicitor Bill Maitland. This is a bourgeois tragedy of the stature of Miller's *Death of a Salesman* – and the more compelling in that Maitland remains, always, aware of the wasted potential, and of exactly what is happening to him.

In spite of the defeat already noted, *A Patriot for Me*, which followed, is much more successful than *Luther* in its realization of a broad social context – that of the decaying Austro-Hungarian Empire, in the twilight period before the First World War. The play now seems somewhat dated in its (then daring) treatment of homosexuality, and, yet again, changes direction half way, to become virtually a period spy-thriller, complete with an honourable suicide as its climax. *A Bond Honoured* began, interestingly, as a study of incest, but splurged itself over a broad canvas of depravity, reducing its original – Lope de Vega's *La Fianza Satisfecha* – from a masterly portrayal of Christian redemption to an orgy of adolescent existentialism, strong on action, short on philosophic justification.

In many ways Osborne's most mature work, *The Hotel in Amsterdam* is a surely-paced evocation of the satisfaction and insidious dangers of close friendship, spread over a single weekend jaunt to Amsterdam. Its three couples eat, drink, see sights – and, mainly, just talk. Patterns of mutual dependence and affection are traced, and the play is remarkable for allowing unremarkable characters to relate on equal terms to extraordinary ones, rather than to exist (as in many of the earlier plays) in a different dimension.

West of Suez set old imperial against new anarchic values in the location its title suggests, but was fatally flawed by simplistic dialectical short-cuts. The ironically titled *A Sense of Detachment* set about all and sundry in a style half way between Pirandello and the Living Theatre, but carrying the conviction of neither. And an assortment of pieces for television, adaptations, and lightweight stage plays has completed the canon to date. Since Osborne's work has never been technically remarkable, the lack of a redeeming imaginative spark has reduced it recently to little more than run-of-the-mill, though the occasional rhetorical flares remind one of a potential for mature greatness that might yet be realized.

—Simon Trussler

PINTER, Harold. English. Born in Hackney, London, 10 October 1930. Educated at Hackney Downs Grammar School, 1943–47; Royal Academy of Dramatic Art, London, 1948. Married the actress Vivien Merchant in 1956 (divorced, 1976); one son. Professional actor since 1949; writer for the stage since 1957. Since 1973, Associate Director of the National Theatre, London. Member, Drama Panel, Arts Council of Great Britain. Recipient: *Evening Standard* award, 1960; Newspaper Guild of New York Award, 1962; Italia Prize, for television play, 1962; Screenwriters Guild Award, for television play, 1963, for screenplay, 1963; Guild of Televison Producers and Directors Award, 1963; New York Film Critics Award, 1964; British Film Academy Award, 1965, 1971; Antoinette Perry Award, 1967; Whitbread Award, 1967; New York Drama Critics Circle Award, 1967; Shakespeare Prize, Hamburg, 1970; Writers Guild Award, 1971. C.B.E. (Commander, Order of the British Empire), 1966. Lives In London.

PUBLICATIONS

Plays

The Room (produced 1957).   In *The Birthday Party and Other Plays*, 1960.
The Birthday Party (produced 1958).   1959; revised version, 1965.
Sketches in *One to Another* (produced 1959).   1960.
Sketches in *Pieces of Eight* (produced 1959).   In *A Slight Ache and Other Plays*, 1961.
A Slight Ache (broadcast 1959; produced 1961).   In *A Slight Ache and Other Plays*, 1961.
The Dwarfs (broadcast 1960; produced 1963; revised version, produced 1966).   In *A Slight Ache and Other Plays*, 1961.
The Dumb Waiter (produced 1960).   In *The Birthday Party and Other Plays*, 1960.
The Birthday Party and Other Plays.   1960; as *The Birthday Party and The Room* (includes *The Dumb Waiter*), 1961.
The Caretaker (produced 1960).   1960.
Night School (televised 1960).   In *Tea Party and Other Plays*, 1967.
A Night Out (broadcast 1960; produced 1961).   1961.
The Collection (televised 1961; produced 1962).   1962.
The Lover (televised 1963; produced 1963).   1965.
Tea Party (televised 1965; produced 1968).   1965; revised version, 1968.
The Homecoming (produced 1965).   1965; revised version, 1968.
The Dwarfs and Eight Revue Sketches.   1965.
The Collection and The Lover (includes the prose piece *The Examination*).   1966.
The Basement (televised 1967; produced 1968).   In *Tea Party and Other Plays*, 1967.
Tea Party and Other Plays.   1967.
Early Plays: A Night Out, Night School, Revue Sketches.   1968.
Sketches by Pinter (produced 1969).   In *Early Plays*, 1968.
Landscape (broadcast 1968; produced 1969).   1968.
Silence (produced 1969).   In *Landscape and Silence*, 1969.
Landscape and Silence.   1969.
Night, in *Mixed Doubles* (produced 1969).   In *Landscape and Silence*, 1969.
Five Screenplays (includes *The Caretaker, The Servant, The Pumpkin Eater, Accident, The Quiller Memorandum*).   1971; modified version, omitting *The Caretaker* and including *The Go-Between*, 1973.
Old Times (produced 1971).   1971.
Monologue (televised 1973; produced 1973).   1973.
No Man's Land (produced 1975).   1975.
Pinter Plays 1-3.   3 vols., 1975–78.
Complete Works 1 and *2*.   2 vols., 1977.
The Proust Screenplay: A la Recherche du Temps Perdu.   1977.
Betrayal (produced 1978).   1978.

Screenplays: *The Servant*, 1963; *The Guest (The Caretaker)*, 1964; *The Pumpkin Eater*, 1964; *The Quiller Memorandum*, 1966; *Accident*, 1967; *The Birthday Party*, 1968; *The Go-Between*, 1971; *The Homecoming*, 1971.

Radio Plays: *A Slight Ache*, 1959; *The Dwarfs*, 1960; *A Night Out*, 1960; *Landscape*, 1968.

Television Plays: *Night School*, 1960; The Collection, 1961, revised version, 1978; *The Lover*, 1963; *Tea Party*, 1965; *The Basement*, 1967; *Monologue*, 1973; *Langrishe, Go Down*, from the novel by Aidan Higgins, 1978.

Verse

Poems, edited by Alan Clodd.   1968; revised edition, 1970.

Other

Mac (on Anew McMaster).   1968.
Poems and Prose 1949–1977.   1978.

Editor, with others, *New Poems 1967.*   1968.

Bibliography: *Pinter: A Bibliography: His Works and Occasional Writings with a Comprehensive Checklist of Criticism and Reviews of the London Productions* by Rudiger Imhof, 1975.

Reading List: *Pinter* by Ronald Hayman, 1968; *Pinter* by John Russell Taylor, 1969; *The Peopled Wound: The Work of Pinter* by Martin Esslin, 1970, as *Pinter: A Study of His Plays,* 1973; *Strategems to Uncover Nakedness: The Dramas of Pinter* by Lois Gordon, 1970; *Pinter* by Alrene Sykes, 1970; *Pinter: A Study of His Reputation, 1956–1969* by Herman T. Schroll, 1971; *Pinter: A Collection of Critical Essays* edited by Arthur Ganz, 1972; *The Plays of Pinter: An Assessment* by Simon Trussler, 1973; *Pinter* by William Baker and Stephen E. Tabachnick, 1973; *The Pinter Problem* by Austin E. Quigley, 1975.

*   *   *

Harold Pinter's plays at first acquaintance bear a deceptive resemblance to conventional realistic fare: almost all are set in a room, the dialogue appnily close to actual desultory chit-chat, and the characters seem simple slice-of-life folks drawn from Pinter's observation of his own associates of the working classes and, eventually, the upper-middle class.

Yet so rich are his plays with inscrutable motivations and latent or ambiguous import that a whole industry has arisen in the explication of his art, and his name has entered the critical lexicon in order to deal with those derivative dramas now termed "Pinteresque."

Most writers of realistic drama feel obliged to explain their characters' behavior. Even the first few minutes of a Pinter play, however, suggest that further exposure to the situation will merely compound the conundrum, heighten the obscurity, elaborate the elusive hints at the sources of his characters' anxiety or bereavement. Early in his career, Pinter defended the seemingly impenetrable nature of his work by asserting "The assumption that to verify what has happened and what is happening presents few problems I take to be inaccurate. A character on the stage who can present no convincing argument or information as to his past experience, his present behaviour or his aspirations, nor give a comprehensive analysis of his motives is as legitimate and as worthy of attention as one who, alarmingly, can do all these things. The more acute the experience the less articulate its expression."

Where most other playwrights set out to bring clarity, shape, and order to what they dramatize, Pinter may seem to delight in slyly selecting exactly what will appear most cryptic, vague or even contradictory. His substitution of hints for exposition and intangible menace for explicit confrontation has set directors to worrying over how to convey the "subtext" and critics to contriving exegeses which more often than not reveal more about themselves than about their subjects.

Symbol hunters enter a nirvana where they can deduce ever more ingenious significance. Pinter's eponymous dwarfs have been identified in the quest for allegory as tycoons, dictators, poetic genius, the tensions of friendship, or projection of the protagonists' anxieties or sense of inadequacy. All the titles have been subjected to such scrutiny. *The Dumb Waiter,* literally the restaurant lift to transport food between floors, is seen figuratively as mute service expected by a hired killer, or a description of the psyche's operation, or even a frightened child who wakes in the night needing to go to the toilet. Critics have labored over the nature of the slight ache, debated whose homecoming is intended, examined the landscape of the mind, the no man's land of the soul, and the old times recalled or imagined or fabricated.

Religion, philosophy, and psychology have been scavanged for evidence that Teddy is the prodigal son, Riley a messenger from the dead, Edward and Flora gods of the dying year and of fertility, and the lift in *Tea Party* a rising into consciousness of repressed desires. One critic has devoted an entire book to identifying Freudian symbolic content just as though the plays were dreams. Anal and oedipal imagery are deemed ubiquitous: the most innocuous exchanges perform sexual service here, the "sit down-stand up" dialogue in *The Room* for example, demonstrating penis envy. Even playwright Terence Rattigan propounded an allegorical interpretation, opining *The Caretaker* was about the God of the Old Testament, the God of the New Testament, and Humanity.

Pinter, who insisted to Rattigan that his subject was simply a caretaker and two brothers, has resisted the imposition of the unduly arcane abstraction on what can be accounted for on an immediate human level. On the other hand, frugality in supplying us with details in the text, his acknowledgment of such obscure references as the naming of everyone in *No Man's Land* after Edwardian cricketers, and his flippancy with critics, to one of whom he suggested he was writing about "the weasel under the cocktail cabinet," have encouraged a probing for clues to withheld information or keys to unspecified puzzles.

Instead of supplying us with the neat solutions usually contrived for plays, Pinter artfully deploys menace (in the early plays) and mystery (in the later work) to tantalize our attention. He creates myths of the modern psyche which seem to touch universal responses in men and women reared to repress violence, rage, fear, and sexuality and to substitute guilt for joy. A sort of poet laureate to the age of anxiety, Pinter substitutes indefinable dread for more routine dramatic action.

Dialogue in such drama takes on the character of combat, with words the weapons. No ordinary debate this, but power struggles in which even seeming non-sequiturs, delivered with sufficient conviction, can best an adversary. Stanley in *The Birthday Party* succumbs to an assault of this sort by McCann and Goldberg. Conversations which defy the analysis appropriate to ordinary discursive prose but which have the suggestive value and the rhythmic force of poetry orchestrate each Pinter play. Moving quickly from giggles to gasps, veering off into digression, repetition, and the most halting or elliptical approach to what must really most concern the speaker, Pinter's dialogue suggests that we often chatter without any intention of conveying an idea.

The degree to which Pinter sees people as inarticulate, either unable to communicate or unwilling to chance it, is exemplified by the amount of silence his plays require. Moments in which speech stalls he indicates by three of four dots, and these ellipses run into the thousands in a single play. Longer periods when no sound is uttered number, in *The Caretaker* alone, 17 long silences and 170 or so extended pauses. And Pinter insists that speech itself, as a "strategem to cover nakedness," is a kind of silence. He has even named one play about three loquacious though isolated characters (on the pattern of Beckett's *Play*) simply *Silence*. Whether his characters are using language to evade others or to manipulate them, what they speak of is often only indirectly indicative of the real subject of the scene. Thus Ruth and Lennie ostensibly discuss a glass of water and Ben and Gus quibble over the terminology of the tea kettle when control of the relationship is the real issue of both scenes.

In the early plays this struggle is rather more overt than in the later work. The proportion of physical violence and other threats to security likewise diminishes. In *The Room*, Rose fears the loss of her womb-like retreat even though her curiosity about outsiders leaves her ambivalent towards those who visit her. Ironically, it is the blind Riley, not Rose, who is victimized and Rose's husband Bert, rather than a stranger, who proves the real danger. In *The Birthday Party*, Stanley's haven is violated by mysterious intruders who reduce the poor fellow (often regarded as a symbol of individual creative talent) to catatonia. *The Dumb Waiter* works still another variation on the inhabitants-of-a-room-threatened-by-menace formula by turning the tables on a hired killer who suddenly finds that he is a menacer himself menaced, the target he and his partner were engaged to kill.

The work grows more subtle. Although most of Pinter's stage plays are set in a room which is visited by an alien spirit, mere menace is rejected in favor of less simple sources of dramatic tension. Thus in *The Caretaker* and *The Homecoming* visitors Davies and Teddy, having lost much of their dignity and status, are pathetic by play's end, and in *Landscape*, *Silence*, *Old Times*, and *No Man's Land*, the characters' past anxieties have long since given way to loneliness, sterility, even despair.

By the late 1960's Pinter was using a form almost as spare as that of Beckett. The womb room is now more of a tomb for the living dead, and characters are more likely to fear, not what is outside the room, but what's inside it or inside themselves. The considerable activity of the earlier plays has been reduced to a mere hint of change or conflict glossing a substance so static, indeed so private, that the terrain is nearly inaccessible. The danger of writing about people who are numb is that of leaving the audience also in that state, and late Pinter may touch the heart less than do his masterpieces *The Caretaker* and *The Homecoming*.

Although on the printed page this is not always evident, in the theatre even the serious plays prompt some laughter, and lighter work such as *The Collection* and *The Lover* amuse for long stretches. The humor of *No Man's Land* is one of the factors which renders its stasis an artistic success. And one of the theatre's finest comic scenes is the opening of *The Basement*, in which Law, the bewildered host, makes polite small talk while his guests strip and have sexual relations.

Critics fascinated by the puzzles in Pinter often advance hypotheses which neglect the broader human issues. Pinter is above all a playwright fascinated by man's metaphysical isolation, evanescence, futility, hostility, and narcissism. Frequently the characters suffer from a sort of ontological hysteria. Unsure of who or what they are, they seek to learn this by examining their reflections in others' eyes or by confirming their roles as these relate to their companions' functions. Rose plays "wife" to Bert's reluctant "husband" and Duff babbles to Beth in much the same spirit. Because Edward operates on the premise "You hear me, therefore I am," his failure to elicit a response from the Matchseller costs him his whole personality and his position in the house.

The derelict Davies uses an assumed name, reminds Mick of three other men, has no papers proving his identity. This ineffectual nonentity has no firm grasp on his place in the universe. He mistrusts those who are trustworthy and attempts to manipulate those who can best him at that game. The insight into aggression's source in insecurity, into the ways in which we might be our brother's keeper, and into the compulsion to undermine relationships, is much more important than some rigidly allegorical reading. Ungrateful, self-seeking Davies, by betraying Aston's friendship, does precisely what is contrary to his best interests. The universality of this experience is expressed in the old saw about the dog that bites the hand that feeds it and also that of doing unto others what you would have them do unto you. Eugene O'Neill's title for his abandoned cycle, *Dispossessors Self-Dispossessed*, would express one of the play's archetypical aspects.

Likewise, in *The Homecoming* just who comes home – Teddy to a house, Ruth to a past profession in another kind of house, or Max and his other sons to their need of dominance by a madonna-whore – is less significant than the universal elements of impotence, frustration, and the territorial disputes which are also waged in *The Basement* and *Night School*, among others. Repressed Disson in *Tea Party*, superfluous Deeley in *Old Times*, and sodden Hirst in *No Man's Land* are particularly poignant variations on the financially successful men who are nevertheless among life's losers.

Pinter's vision is archetypically male. He epitomizes the view of woman as the Other, a figure to be desired and feared, venerated, reviled and, often, lost. The maternal figures – Rose, Meg, Flora, Mrs. Stokes, Wally's aunts, even Ruth as a substitute for Jessie – are emasculating or suffocating or both. The younger women often are disguised mother-figures, and they disconcert their men by withholding information (Stella or Sally) or sexual favors (Ruth) or affection (Beth, Ellen, Kate). Women are objects invested with unfathomable allure, danger, and mystery who evade all male attempts to comprehend or control them, whether, like Kate or Diana, they prompt the repression of eroticism, or, as in *No Man's Land*, the effort to confront them and the whole matter of sensuality has been dropped, as forever unprofitable, in favor of acquiescence to alcohol. Pinter's recent women tend to be unresponsive to their men or arouse a compulsion to debase them as well as a feeling of guilt over the sensuality they inspire.

For Pinter, the world may be unstable, uncertain, unpredictable, and inhospitable. At best, memory surpasses present experience and mutability is our inescapable lot. Verification, communication, cooperation, satisfaction are equally unlikely. The pleasantries and amenities of civilisation provide only temporary buffers against a terror of both death and life itself.

—Tish Dace

PRIESTLEY, J(ohn) B(oynton). English. Born in Bradford, Yorkshire, 13 September 1894. Educated in Bradford schools, and at Trinity Hall, Cambridge, M.A. Served with the Duke of Wellington's and the Devon Regiments, 1914–19. Married 1) Patricia Tempest (died, 1925), two daughters; 2) Mary Wyndham Lewis (divorced, 1952), two daughters and one son; 3) the writer Jacquetta Hawkes in 1953. Writer from 1925; Director of the Mask Theatre, London, 1938–39; radio lecturer on the BBC programme "Postscripts" during World War II; regular contributor to the *New Statesman*, London. President, P.E.N., London, 1936–37; United Kingdom Delegate, and Chairman, UNESCO International Theatre Conference, Paris, 1947, and Prague, 1948; Chairman, British Theatre Conference, 1948; President, International Theatre Institute, 1949; Member, National Theatre Board, London, 1966–67. Recipient: Black Memorial Prize, 1930; Ellen Terry Award, 1948. LL.D.: University of St. Andrews; D.Litt.: University of Birmingham; University of Bradford. Honorary Freeman of the City of Bradford, 1973. Order of Merit, 1977. Lives in Alveston, Warwickshire.

PUBLICATIONS

Plays

   The Good Companions, with Edward Knoblock, from the novel by Priestley (produced 1931).   1935.
   Dangerous Corner (produced 1932).   1932.
   The Roundabout (produced 1932).   1933.
   Laburnum Grove: An Immoral Comedy (produced 1933).   1934.
   Eden End (produced 1934).   1934.
   Cornelius: A Business Affair in Three Transactions (produced 1935).   1935.
   Duet in Floodlight (produced 1935).   1935.
   Bees on the Boat Deck: A Farcical Tragedy (produced 1936).   1936.
   Spring Tide, with George Billam (produced 1936).   1936.
   The Bad Samaritan (produced 1937).
   Time and the Conways (produced 1937).   1937.

I Have Been Here Before (produced 1937).   1937.
I'm a Stranger Here (produced 1937).
People at Sea (produced 1937).   1937.
Mystery at Greenfingers: A Comedy of Detection (produced 1938).   1937.
When We Are Married: A Yorkshire Farcical Comedy (produced 1938).   1938.
Music at Night (produced 1938).   In *Three Plays*, 1943.
Johnson over Jordan (produced 1939).   Published as *Johnson over Jordan: The Play,
    And All about It (An Essay)*, 1939.
The Long Mirror (produced 1940).   In *Three Plays*, 1943.
Good Night Children: A Comedy of Broadcasting (produced 1942).   In *Three Comedies*,
    1945.
Desert Highway (produced 1943).   1944.
They Came to a City (produced 1943).   In *Three Plays*, 1943.
Three Plays.   1943.
How Are They at Home? A Topical Comedy (produced 1944).   In *Three Comedies*,
    1945.
The Golden Fleece (as *The Bull Market*, produced 1944).   In *Three Comedies*, 1945.
Three Comedies.   1945.
An Inspector Calls (produced 1945).   1945.
Jenny Villiers (produced 1946).
The Rose and Crown (televised 1946).   1947.
Ever Since Paradise: An Entertainment, Chiefly Referring to Love and Marriage
    (produced 1946).   1949.
The Linden Tree (produced 1947).   1948.
The Plays of J. B. Priestley.   3 vols., 1948–50; vol. 1 as *Seven Plays*, 1950.
Home Is Tomorrow (produced 1948).   1949.
The High Toby: A Play for the Toy Theatre (produced 1954).   1948.
Summer Day's Dream (produced 1949).   In *Plays III*, 1950.
The Olympians, music by Arthur Bliss (produced 1949).   1949.
Bright Shadow: A Play of Detection (produced 1950).   1950.
Treasure on Pelican (as *Treasure on Pelican Island*, televised 1951; as *Treasure on
    Pelican*, produced 1952).   1953.
Dragon's Mouth: A Dramatic Quartet, with Jacquetta Hawkes (produced 1952).   1952.
Private Rooms: A One-Act Comedy in the Viennese Style.   1953.
Mother's Day.   1953.
Try It Again (produced 1965).   1953.
A Glass of Bitter.   1954.
The White Countess, with Jacquetta Hawkes (produced 1954).
The Scandalous Affair of Mr. Kettle and Mrs. Moon (produced 1955).   1956.
These Our Actors (produced 1956).
Take the Fool Away (produced 1956).
The Glass Cage (produced 1957).   1958.
The Thirty-First of June (produced 1957).
The Pavilion of Masks (produced 1963).   1958.
A Severed Head, with Iris Murdoch, from the novel by Murdoch (produced
    1963).   1964.

Screenplays: *Sing As We Go*, 1934; *We Live in Two Worlds*, 1937; *Jamaica Inn*, with
Sidney Gilliat and Joan Harrison, 1939; *Britain at Bay*, 1940; *Our Russian Allies*, 1941;
The Foreman Went to France (Somewhere in France), with others, 1942; *Last Holiday*,
1950.

Radio Plays: *The Return of Jess Oakroyd*, 1941; *The Golden Entry*, 1955; *End Game at
the Dolphin*, 1956; *An Arabian Night in Park Lane*, 1965.

Television Plays: *The Rose and Crown*, 1946; *Treasure on Pelican Island*, 1951; *The Stone Face*, 1957; *The Rack*, 1958; *Doomsday for Dyson*, 1958; *The Fortrose Incident*, 1959; *Level Seven*, 1966; *The Lost Peace* series, 1966; *Anyone for Tennis*, 1968; *Linda at Pulteneys*, 1969.

Fiction

Adam in Moonlight. 1927.

Benighted. 1927; as *The Old Dark House*, 1928.

Farthing Hall, with Hugh Walpole. 1929.

The Good Companions. 1929.

The Town Major of Miraucourt (story). 1930.

Angel Pavement. 1930.

Faraway. 1932.

Albert Goes Through (story). 1933.

I'll Tell You Everthing: A Frolic, with Gerald Bullett. 1933.

Wonder Hero. 1933.

They Walk in the City: The Lovers in the Stone Forest. 1936.

The Domesday Men: An Adventure. 1938.

Let the People Sing. 1939.

Black-Out in Gretley: A Story of – and for – Wartime. 1942.

Daylight on Saturday: A Novel about an Aircraft Factory. 1943.

Three Men in New Suits. 1945.

Bright Day. 1946.

Jenny Villiers: A Story of the Theatre. 1947.

Going Up: Stories and Sketches. 1950.

Festival at Farbridge. 1951; as *Festival*, 1951.

The Other Place and Other Stories of the Same Sort. 1953.

The Magicians. 1954.

Low Notes on a High Level: A Frolic. 1954.

Saturn over the Water: An Account of His Adventures in London, South America and Australia by Tim Bedford, Painter; Edited, with Some Preliminary and Concluding Remarks, By Henry Sulgrave and Here Presented to the Reading Public. 1961.

The Thirty-First of June: A Tale of True Love, Enterprise and Progress in the Arthurian and ad-Atomic Ages. 1961.

The Shapes of Sleep: A Topical Tale. 1962.

Sir Michael and Sir George: A Tale of COMSA and DISCUS and the New Elizabethans. 1964; as *Sir Michael and Sir George: A Comedy of the New Elizabethans*, 1965(?).

Lost Empires, Being Richard Herncastle's Account of His Life on the Variety Stage from November 1913 to August 1914, Together with a Prologue and Epilogue. 1965.

Salt Is Leaving. 1966.

It's an Old Country. 1967.

The Image Men: Out of Town, and London End. 2 vols., 1968.

The Carfitt Crisis and Two Other Stories. 1975.

Found, Lost, Found; or, The English Way of Life. 1976.

Verse

The Chapman of Rhymes (juvenilia). 1918.

Other

Brief Diversions, Being Tales, Travesties, and Epigrams. 1922.
Papers from Lilliput. 1922.
I for One. 1923.
Figures in Modern Literature. 1924.
Fools and Philosophers: A Gallery of Comic Figures from English Literature. 1925; as *The English Comic Characters,* 1925.
George Meredith. 1926.
Talking: An Essay. 1926.
(Essays). 1926.
Open House: A Book of Essays. 1927.
Thomas Love Peacock. 1927.
The English Novel. 1927; revised edition, 1935.
Too Many People and Other Reflections. 1928.
Apes and Angels: A Book of Essays. 1928.
The Balconinny and Other Essays. 1929; as *The Balconinny,* 1930.
English Humour. 1929.
Self-Selected Essays. 1932.
Four-in-Hand (miscellany). 1934.
English Journey, Being a Rambling But Truthful Account of What One Man Saw and Heard and Felt and Thought During a Journey Through England During the Autumn of the Year 1933. 1934.
Midnight on the Desert: A Chapter of Autobiography. 1937; as *Midnight on the Desert, Being an Excursion into Autobiography During a Winter in America, 1935–36.* 1937.
Rain upon Godshill: A Further Chapter of Autobiography. 1939.
Britain Speaks (radio talks). 1940.
Postscripts (radio talks). 1940.
Out of the People. 1941.
Britain at War. 1942.
British Women Go to War. 1943.
Here Are Your Answers. 1944.
Letter to a Returning Serviceman. 1945.
The Secret Dream: An Essay on Britain, America and Russia. 1946.
Russian Journey. 1946.
Theatre Outlook. 1947.
Delight. 1949.
A Priestley Companion: A Selection from the Writings. 1951.
Journey down a Rainbow, with Jacquetta Hawkes (travel). 1955.
All about Ourselves and Other Essays, edited by Eric Gillett. 1956.
Thoughts in the Wilderness (essays). 1957.
Topside; or, The Future of England: A Dialogue. 1958.
The Story of Theatre (juvenile). 1959; as *The Wonderful World of the Theatre,* 1959; revised edition, 1969.
Literature and Western Man. 1960.
William Hazlitt. 1960.
Charles Dickens: A Pictorial Biography. 1961; as *Dickens and His World,* 1969.
Margin Released: A Writer's Reminiscences and Reflections. 1962.
Man and Time. 1964.
The Moments and Other Pieces. 1966.
The World of Priestley, edited by D. G. MacRae. 1967.
All England Listened: Priestley's Wartime Broadcasts. 1968.
Essays of Five Decades, edited by Susan Cooper. 1968.

Trumpets over the Sea, Being a Rambling and Egotistical Account of the London Symphony Orchestra's Engagement at Daytona Beach, Florida, in July–August 1967.   1968.

The Prince of Pleasure and His Regency, 1811–1820.   1969.

The Edwardians.   1970.

Snoggle (juvenile).   1971.

Victoria's Heyday.   1972.

Over the Long High Wall: Some Reflections and Speculations on Life, Death and Time.   1972.

The English.   1973.

Outcries and Asides.   1974.

A Visit to New Zealand.   1974.

Particular Pleasures, Being a Personal Record of Some Varied Arts and Many Different Artists.   1975.

The Happy Dream (biography).   1976.

English Humour.   1976.

Instead of the Trees (autobiography).   1977.

Editor, *Essayists Past and Present: A Selection of English Essays.*   1925.

Editor, *Tom Moore's Diary: A Selection.*   1925.

Editor, *The Book of Bodley Head Verse.*   1926.

Editor, *The Female Spectator: Selections from Mrs. Eliza Haywood's Periodical, 1744–1746.*   1929.

Editor, *Our Nation's Heritage.*   1939.

Editor, *Scenes of London Life, From Sketches by Boz by Charles Dickens.*   1947.

Editor, *The Best of Leacock.*   1957; as *The Bodley Head Leacock,* 1957.

Editor, with O. B. Davis, *Four English Novels.*   1960.

Editor, with O. B. Davis, *Four English Biographies.*   1961.

Editor, *Adventures in English Literature.*   1963.

Editor, *An Everyman Anthology.*   1966.

Reading List: *Priestley* by Ivor Brown, 1957, revised edition, 1964; *Priestley: An Informal Study of His Work* by David Hughes, 1958; *Mensch und Gesellschaft bei Priestley* by L. Löb, 1962 (includes bibliography); *Priestley the Dramatist* by G. L. Evans, 1964; *Priestley: Portrait of an Author* by Susan Cooper, 1970.

*   *   *

J. B. Priestley, born as long ago as 1894, is not only jack of most literary trades but master of quite a few: novels, plays, essays both historical and literary. He fully deserved his Order of Merit in 1977. During the second world war he became a skilled broadcaster with a large following.

After the first world war he was a widely appreciated essayist and reviewer. More recently he completed a remarkably readable autobiography. He was a superb journalist as he showed in the now classic *English Journey*.

But it is probably as a novelist, translated into almost every known language and in the best-seller class, that he is best known. *The Good Companions*, a picaresque novel without a real picaro (rogue), describes on a broad Victorian-style canvas the adventures of a travelling concert party and those who attach themselves to it. It has a not quite happy ending. No less successful a year or two later was *Angel Pavement* which had no happy ending at all and concerned the disasters brought upon a group of lower middle-class clerical workers in a City of London veneer firm by a predatory "sharp Alec" from the Baltic. There are a dozen or more pieces of fiction he wrote in the ensuing years, notably the superbly, though gently satirical, study of the new universities and the advertising business in *The Image Men* and *Bright Day*, which some regard as his best post-war novel. It harks back, as so often in his work, to the experiences of a family and others the narrator has known before the overwhelming and shattering experience of the First World War (in which Priestley fought) and which changed so many lives in many countries. Almost all his novels continue to be readable and are often stimulating, for example, *Let the People Sing*, *Daylight on Saturday*, and *Festival at Farbridge*. He discovered a fluent and often witty narrative style. He was obscure neither in subject matter nor character portrayal; yet he did not lack psychological penetration.

It is, however, for certain of his plays that he would claim real originality. Some, excellent though they are – and continually performed all over the world – are conventional in format: *Eden End*, *Laburnum Grove*, and the moving *The Linden Tree*. But he carried out such stage experiments as *Ever Since Paradise*, a comedy about love and marriage where each set of three couples are both actors and soliloquising commentators. The most powerful of the experimental plays is *Johnson over Jordan*, a sort of dramatic obituary of a recently-deceased business man which has moments of great insight and moving intensity. It is full of Johnson's hopes and fears and, now, vain regrets. Difficult, indeed, to stage but as moving as any mid-20th century drama.

Priestley's plays and other works were often centred on the theories popularized by J. W. M. Dunne, Carl Jung, and others about the nature of time, on which Priestley wrote with intelligence and imagination. Priestley has also always been sensitive to, as he would regard it, the untoward interference of politics in men's lives. He is not a party man, though until latter years he would have regarded himself as anti-Conservative. From 1950 or so, his essays became more and more polemical and anti-authoritarian Socialism. He may be summed up as a centre radical if that is not a contradiction in terms. Radical, however, he certainly is in the sense that he believes changes may quickly be made to improve matters rather than having to wait for the slow processes of evolution. He has invented words which became part and parcel of the common talk of his time; one such word was "admass" which conveyed the idea of the mindless majorities of "civilised" mankind helplessly persuaded by subtle advertising schemes to buy more and more goods they did not require.

By some of his contemporaries he was reputed to be of a contumacious nature. Certainly he was not, either as a man or writer, one to be over-ruled or to allow his views to go unheard – and he had views and preferences on pictures (he himself painted) and on music as well as, of course, on the arts he himself practised. But despite his bluntness of speech he was not – as he himself repeatedly declared – quarrelsome. Most who knew him enjoyed his company; and to his millions of devoted followers he was a source of delight on the page and stage, a superb entertainer full of talent, and here and there something of genius.

—Kenneth Young

RATTIGAN, Sir Terence (Mervyn).   English.   Born in London, 10 June 1911. Educated at Harrow School (scholar), 1925–30; Trinity College, Oxford (history scholar), B.A. 1933. Served as a Flight Lieutenant in the Coastal Command of the Royal Air Force, 1940–45. Full-time playwright, 1934 until his death. Recipient: Ellen Terry Award, 1947; New York Drama Critics Circle Award, 1948. C.B.E. (Commander, Order of the British Empire), 1958. Knighted, 1971. *Died 30 November 1977.*

PUBLICATIONS

Plays

First Episode, with Philip Heimann (produced 1933).
French Without Tears (produced 1936). 1937; revised version, music by Robert Stolz, lyrics by Paul Dehn, as Joie de Vivre (produced 1960).
After the Dance (produced 1939). 1939.
Follow My Leader, with Anthony Maurice (produced 1940).
Grey Farm, with Hector Bolitho (produced 1940).
Flare Path (produced 1942). 1942.
While the Sun Shines (produced 1943). 1945.
Love in Idleness (produced 1944). 1945; as O Mistress Mine (produced 1946), 1949.
The Winslow Boy (produced 1946). 1946.
Playbill: The Browning Version and Harlequinade (produced 1948). 1949.
Adventure Story (produced 1949). 1950.
Who Is Sylvia? (produced 1950). 1951.
The Deep Blue Sea (produced 1952). 1952.
The Sleeping Prince (produced 1953). 1954.
Collected Plays 1–4. 4 vols., 1953–78.
Separate Tables: Two Plays (produced 1954). 1955.
The Prince and the Showgirl: The Script for the Film. 1957.
Variation on a Theme (produced 1958). 1958.
Ross: A Dramatic Portrait (produced 1960). 1960.
Heart to Heart (televised 1962). In Collected Plays 3, 1964.
Man and Boy (produced 1963). 1963.
A Bequest to the Nation (as Nelson, televised 1966; revised version, as A Bequest to the Nation, produced 1970). 1970.
All on Her Own (televised 1968; produced 1974; as Duologue, produced 1976). In The Best Short Plays 1970, edited by Stanley Richards, 1970.
High Summer (televised 1972). In The Best Short Plays 1973, edited by Stanley Richards, 1973.
In Praise of Love: Before Dawn, and After Lydia (produced 1973). 1973; (After Lydia produced, as In Praise of Love, 1974), 1975.
Cause Célèbre (broadcast 1975; produced 1977). 1978.

Screenplays: The Belles of St. Clement's, 1936; Gypsy, with Brock Williams, 1937; French Without Tears, with Anatole de Grunwald and Ian Dalrymple, 1939; Quiet Wedding, with Anatole de Grunwald, 1941; The Day Will Dawn (The Avengers), with Anatole de Grunwald and Patrick Kirwan, 1942; Uncensored, with Rodney Ackland and Wolfgang Wilhelm, 1942; English Without Tears (Her Man Gilbey), with Anatole de Grunwald, 1944; The Way to the Stars (Johnny in the Clouds), with Anatole de Grunwald, 1945; Journey Together, with John Boulting, 1946; Brighton Rock (Young Scarface), with Graham Greene, 1947; While the Sun Shines, with Anatole de Grunwald, 1947; The Winslow Boy, with Anatole de Grunwald and Anthony Asquith, 1948; Bond Street, with Rodney Ackland and Anatole de Grunwald, 1948; The Browning Version, 1951; The Sound Barrier (Breaking the Sound Barrier), 1952; The Final Test, 1953; The Deep Blue Sea, 1955; The Man Who Loved Redheads, 1955; The Prince and the Showgirl, 1957; Separate Tables, 1958; The VIPs, 1963; The Yellow Rolls-Royce, 1964; Goodbye Mr. Chips, 1969; A Bequest to the Nation (The Nelson Affair), 1973.

Radio Plays: A Tale of Two Cities, from the novel by Dickens, 1950; Cause Célèbre, 1975.

Television Plays: *The Final Test*, 1951; *Heart to Heart*, 1962; *Ninety Years On*, 1964; *Nelson*, 1966; *All on Her Own*, 1968; *High Summer*, 1972.

Reading List: *Rattigan: The Man and His Work* by Michael Darlow and Gillian Hodson, 1978.

*   *   *

Few playwrights (or critics) would agree with American dramatist Eugene Walter's statement that "in essence, play writing is a trade," but if it is, one would be hard pressed to name a more craftsmanlike and artistic artisan than Terence Rattigan.

His career began inauspiciously with a collaboration with Philip Heimann (*First Episode*) and five unproduced plays in which Rattigan learned his craft slowly but thoroughly. Then with *French Without Tears* he began an unusually long and successful career of "sheer theatre" which Kenneth Tynan in *Curtains* (1961) translates as "How well these old craftsmen knew their jobs!" Rattigan is the professional playwright supreme. His brilliant introduction to his collected plays stresses the ideal of "good theatre," and it is true that he has appealed to many more than merely the middle-class theatre-goer, and that without sensationalism or "the 'gilded phrase.' "

Along the way Rattigan has given us several first-rate plays, standards of the modern theatre, among them *The Deep Blue Sea*, with a full-length portrait of a woman even better than that of the Grand Duchess in his *The Sleeping Prince*, and *Separate Tables*, which contrives to educate the audience in emotion without attempting, as Rattigan says, "to 'instruct' it in taste"). His *Ross* was better than his play about Alexander (*Adventure Story*) and typically Rattigan in its treatment of humiliation, an episodic and rather Freudian dramatic portrait of the enigmatic Lawrence of Arabia that almost explained that entertaining enigma (and, perhaps, fascinating fraud). *Man and Boy* was a perceptive study of an absconding financier and his son. *Variation on a Theme* a clever discussion of a boy living off an older woman, and these and other plays (even including *Cause Célèbre*) amply demonstrate Rattigan's rare ability to please the public without ever falling into a rut or repeating himself. Nor does he ever stoop to shocking the audience with fake "revolution" aimed at the Establishment or trying to bore or baffle them. In an age when art involves John Cage's music, minimalist art and Pinter (characterized by Bernard Levin as "seeking answers to questions that were never asked, and the questions to answers that were found"), not to mention the shrill or shoddy or senseless works of artists far less talented than Pinter, Rattigan went sincerely and solidly on with good, solid plays, plays with dialogue that may not be eminently quotable but is invariably effective, plays with themes and characters and beginnings, middles, and ends.

This put Rattigan somewhat out of favor in the 1950's but the public has loved him (on and off) from the start. His "power of implication," as he would say, makes his message clear without frills, and the audience always loves a good story or a decent laugh. James Agate thundered against *French Without Tears*: "Nothing. It has no wit, no plot, no characterization, nothing."

But Agate was off the mark on almost every count. Rattigan is not without wit, though his is not a show-off kind of verbal skill: he makes his points with great economy. He is one of the great masters of exposition. His plots are deftly crafted, even those of *The Deep Blue Sea* and *The Browning Version* which he admits are "unsatisfactory to an audience because of their inconclusiveness." He is a genius at weaving together stray characters (as in *Separate Tables*) or disconnected episodes (as in *Ross*). His forte is character and plot rather than ideas, which in the long run will probably keep his plays from dating as fast as the pieces of his colleagues of the 1950's and 1960's. He can handle a sentimental story without getting soppy and he can dish up "a soufflé" of a farce like *Harlequinade* (designed as a dessert after *The Browning Version*) with dazzling ease. He can be as effective on television or in the cinema.

His best works will long be studied as models of playwriting and also as mirrors of the times. Rattigan can capture the social outlook of a whole period in a *Cause Célèbre* (or the *cause célèbre* of *The Winslow Boy*). He can plumb the depths of obsessions rampant in a sedate residential hotel near Bournemouth, a crummy North London flat, a Public School, the active lives of Alexander the Great or T. E. Lawrence or Lord Nelson, the twisted lives of a financier with a charming but weak son or a rapacious woman out to snare her fifth and richest man who falls prey (willingly, self-destructively) to an ambiguous little ballet dancer. *Variation on a Theme* (whose plot is the last of those situations mentioned) is closely based on Dumas *fils' La Dame aux Camélias* – but it is based on a steady and shrewd observation of English life in Rattigan's own time.

Undoubtedly, Rattigan can capture the surface of life; many critics would add that he is all surface, that his works lack profundity. I do not think this charge of superficiality can be made to stick. What is true is that Rattigan's scope is narrow, but where he touches he goes very deep. What he does delve into he will not abandon until he has explored the very depths, and what he finds there he brings to the audience with some reticence but unalloyed honesty. He can make folly funny and pathos poignant and what some would dismiss as "a purely theatrical experience" deeply moving and quite unforgettable.

—Leonard R. N. Ashley

REANEY, James (Crerar).   Canadian.   Born near Stratford, Ontario, 1 September 1926. Educated at Elmhurst Public School, Easthope Township, Perth County; Stratford High School; University College, University of Toronto (Epstein Award, 1948), B.A. in English 1948, M.A. 1949, Ph.D. 1956. Married Colleen Thibaudeau in 1951; one son and one daughter. Member of the English faculty, 1949–57, and Assistant Professor of English, 1957–60, University of Manitoba, Winnipeg. Associate Professor, 1960–63, and since 1964 Professor of English, Middlesex College, University of Western Ontario, London. Founding Editor, *Alphabet* magazine, London, Ontario, 1960–71. Active in little theatre groups in Winnipeg and London. Recipient: Governor-General's Award, 1950, 1959, 1963; President's Medal, University of Western Ontario, 1955, 1958; Chalmers Award, 1975, 1976. Lives in Ontario.

PUBLICATIONS

Plays

Night-Blooming Cereus (broadcast 1959; produced 1960).   In *The Killdeer and Other Plays*, 1962.
The Killdeer (produced 1960).   In *The Killdeer and Other Plays*, 1962; revised version (produced 1970), in *Masks of Childhood*, 1972.
One-Man Masque (produced 1960).   In *The Killdeer and Other Plays*, 1962.
The Easter Egg (produced 1962).   In *Masks of Childhood*, 1972.
The Killdeer and Other Plays.   1962.
Sun and Moon (produced 1972).   In *The Killdeer and Other Plays*, 1962.
Names and Nicknames (produced 1963).   In *Apple Butter and Other Plays*, 1973.

Apple Butter (puppet play; produced 1965).   In *Apple Butter and Other Plays*, 1973.
Let's Make a Carol: A Play with Music for Children, music by John Beckwith.   1965.
Listen to the Wind (produced 1965).   1972.
Colours in the Dark (produced 1967).   1970.
Three Desks (produced 1967).   In *Masks of Childhood*, 1972.
Masks of Childhood (includes *The Killdeer, Three Desks, The Easter Egg*), edited by
    Brian Parker.   1972.
Apple Butter and Other Plays for Children (includes *Names and Nicknames, Ignoramus,
    Geography Match*).   1973.
The Donnellys: A Trilogy:
    1. Sticks and Stones (produced 1973).   1975.
    2. The Saint Nicholas Hotel (produced 1974).   1976.
    3. Handcuffs (produced 1975).   1977.
All the Bees and All the Keys (for children), music by John Beckwith.   1976.
The Dismissal.   1978.

Radio Play: *Night-Blooming Cereus*, 1959.

Verse

The Red Heart.   1949.
A Suit of Nettles.   1958.
Twelve Letters to a Small Town.   1962.
The Dance of Death at London, Ontario.   1963.
Poems, edited by Germaine Warkentin.   1972.
Selected Longer Poems, edited by Germaine Warkentin.   1976.
Selected Shorter Poems, edited by Germaine Warkentin.   1976.

Other

The Boy with an "R" in His Hand (juvenile).   1965.
Twenty Barrels.   1976.

Reading List: *Reaney* by Alvin A. Lee, 1968; *Reaney* by Ross G. Woodman, 1971; *Reaney*
by James Stewart Reaney, 1976.

*   *   *

James Reaney is probably the best Canadian playwright writing today, yet, paradoxically, his plays are less performed than those of many other dramatists. This is so largely because the conception that Reaney has of the theatre does not accord well with the taste for either naturalism – the theatre of social comment – or surrealism – the theatre of the absurd. Not only do his plays have many and rapidly shifting scenes, but his characters inhabit a world of fragile Proustian nostalgic fantasy that is almost operatic.

It is easy to see Reaney as outside the mainstream not only of Canadian playwriting and literature, but of modern English literature generally. (This may in part account for his former neglect among the fashionable theatrical circles of Toronto – a city he long ago came to think of as Blake's City of Destruction.) But his debt is to a tradition of fantasy that is preeminently late nineteenth century. This influence comes strongly from the early Yeats, but it is also indebted to the Brontës (Reaney takes the name Branwell in his long poem *A Suit of Nettles*), and, one can't help feeling, to the Henry James of *The Turn of the Screw* and *Owen*

Wingrave. Indeed, in *Listen to the Wind*, the protagonist is called Owen and proceeds to stage within the play another play called *The Saga of Caresfoot Court*. Reaney based this on his own childhood experience of reading Rider Haggard's *Dawn*, but it owes a good deal also to the tradition of the Gothic tale out of *Wuthering Heights*.

Indeed, it is in Reaney's taste for melodrama – the sudden reversals in the last acts, for instance – that he is weakest. His attempt to justify melodrama by claiming for it another and truer world – "the patterns in it are not only sensational but deadly accurate" – is only partly succesful. The "strong pattern" of melodrama can easily obscure the significant moral exploration of the play, as the exterior story of *Listen to the Wind* very nearly does.

But if the theatre of fantasy works against naturalism, it also, allied with strong lexical whimsy, works against the excesses of melodrama. The playbox of *Colours in the Dark* is not only a way of explaining the longing to get back home to childhood's Eden; it is also an outward and visible sign of those wordlists that Reaney loves – the inventory of the world. The naming of things is as important to him as it is for Eliot in *Old Possum's Book of Practical Cats*, and shares something of that whimsical attitude to the serious matter of language. "What did the Indians call you?/For you do not flow/With English accents," asks Reaney addressing the Avon River in his set of poems *Twelve Letters to a Small Town*. And this concern with names is uppermost in *Names and Nicknames* especially. But it is a characteristic concern of all his plays and poetry. We never forget Reaney the classicist by training. "Most of those words you've no idea of their meaning, but we're sowing them in your mind anyhow," says Polly in *Easter Egg*; and elsewhere, in *Masks of Childhood*, we have a fantasia on the street names of Winnipeg, ending in a whoop – "I Winnipeg ... She Winnipeggied ... They Winnipugged."

Reaney's language spars with his imagery and by its whimsy prevents the apocalyptic metaphors from becoming bombastic. The verse many be Blakean but it is spoken in the dialect of John Clare. Reaney's debt to Blake, via Frye's *Fearful Symmetry*, is a stated one, but Walt Disney and Mother Goose are there as well. This is most obvious in his poem sequence, *A Suit of Nettles* in which barnyard animals become part of a complex allegory that owes something to Spenser and mediaeval flyting. Reaney has a sense of the landscape that reminds us more of Palmer than of Blake, though it is the voice of the *Prophetic Books* that speaks in *Colours in the Dark*:

> We sit by the fire and hear the rushing sound
> Of the wind that comes from Temiskaming
> Algoma, Patricia
> Down from the north over the wilderness.

But for Reaney there is none of Blake's sense of contraries or great loss and fall. Innocence is accessible if we can but find the way, or rather listen to the children who, like the children in *Burnt Norton*, know it. Their music has the apocalyptic quality of the poetry of Leonard Cohen: "I saw the sundogs barking/On either side of the sun." This surrealist strain in him combines with his other theme, death, in a sequence of poems, *The Dance of Death at London, Ontario*, illustrated by the well-known Canadian painter Jack Chambers. In the same year that *Nettles* was published, a critic said of Chambers that he too had captured in his paintings "The Life of Death in London Ontario." Chambers insisted that he was not a surrealist or even a hyper-realist but a "perceptual realist," and doubtless this is a more accurate term for Reaney's work as well.

In that world objects have a life that is almost Dickensian (again the connection to Victorian fantasy). "I'll be the orange devil waiting in the stove/I'll be the chimney trumpeting the night," says Madam Fay in *The Killdeer*. And it is the cry of the killdeer – plaintive (like Reaney's search for the ancestors and the past that will make sense of the present) and deceiving (as Eli in that play recognizes, "It's another clock in another time") – that is a paradigm of Reaney's work. In that sense he speaks for the English Canada that he knows and loves – one of great farmhouses surrounded by large trees on summer afternoons among musty books where "long, long ago" is as real as here and now, the world of Blake and Spenser, Yeats and Rider Haggard, as immediate as the killdeer and the barnyard geese.

Reaney's major achievement has been his recently completed Donnellys trilogy. In those plays he has managed to capture a myth that is both poetic and destructive, universal and local – and for the first time in English Canadian culture. For Reaney James Donnelly is still there in Biddulph Township, not a ghost but a myth. The shifts through time and game and song achieve this in the plays.

The drift from real to fantasy in most of his plays (*The Dismissal* is an exception) is encouraged by the elements – the wind to which the children listen or the detailed catalogues of flowers and animals. It shares something with O'Neill and Miller, but its closest analogy is the late Shakespearean romances where Illyria is a pattern of England as Caresfoot Court becomes a way of understanding Ontario, and Pericles goes searching for the lost child, Marina, that is himself.

—D.D.C. Chambers

RICE, Elmer. American. Born Elmer Leopold Reizenstein in New York City, 28 September 1892. Educated at a high school in New York; studied law in night school, LL.B. (cum laude), New York Law School, 1912; admitted to the New York Bar, 1913, but never practiced. Married 1) Hazel Levy in 1915 (divorced, 1942), one son and one daughter; 2) the actress Betty Field in 1942 (divorced, 1956), two sons and one daughter; 3) Barbara A. Marshall in 1966. Claims Clerk, Samstag and Hilder Brothers, New York 1907; Law Clerk, 1908–12; began writing and producing for the theatre, 1914, as Dramatic Director, University Settlement, and Chairman, Inter-Settlement Dramatic Society, New York; Scenarist, Samuel Goldwyn Pictures Corporation, Hollywood, 1918–20; freelance writer for Famous Players, the Lasky Corporation, and Real Art Films, Hollywood, 1920; returned to New York and organized the Morningside Players, with Hatcher Hughes; purchased and operated the Belasco Theatre, New York, 1934–37; Regional Director, Works Progress Administration Federal Theatre Project, New York, 1935–36; Founder, with Robert E. Sherwood, Maxwell Anderson, S. N. Behrman, Sidney Howard, and John F. Wharton, Playwrights Company, 1938; Lecturer in English, University of Michigan, Ann Arbor, 1954; Adjunct Professor of English, New York University, 1957–58. President, Dramatists Guild, 1939–43; President, Author's League of America, 1945–46; International Vice-President, and Vice-President of the New York Center, P.E.N., 1945–46. Recipient: Pulitzer Prize, 1929. Litt.D.: University of Michigan, 1961. Member, National Institute of Arts and Letters. *Died 8 May 1967.*

PUBLICATIONS

Plays

On Trial (produced 1914).   1919.
The Iron Cross (produced 1917).   1965.
The Home of the Free (produced 1917).   1934.
For the Defense (produced 1919).

Wake Up, Jonathan, with Hatcher Hughes (produced 1921).   1928.

It Is the Law, from a novel by Hayden Talbot (produced 1922).

The Adding Machine (produced 1923).   1923.

The Mongrel, from a play by Hermann Bahr (produced 1924).

Close Harmony; or, The Lady Next Door, with Dorothy Parker (produced 1924).   1929.

The Blue Hawaii, from a play by Rudolph Lothar (produced 1927).

Cock Robin, with Philip Barry (produced 1928).   1929.

Street Scene (produced 1929).   1929; revised version, music by Kurt Weill, lyrics by Langston Hughes (produced 1947).   1948.

The Subway (produced 1929).   1929.

A Diadem of Snow, in *One-Act Plays for Stage and Study 5*.   1929.

See Naples and Die (produced 1929).   1930.

The Left Bank (produced 1931).   1931.

Counsellor-at-Law (produced 1931).   1931.

The House in Blind Alley.   1932.

Blacksheep (produced 1932).   1938.

We, The People (produced 1933).   1933.

The Gay White Way, in *One-Act Plays for Stage and Study 8*.   1934.

Judgment Day (produced 1934).   1934.

The Passing of Chow-Chow (produced 1934).   1934.

Three Plays Without Words (includes *Landscape with Figures, Rus in Urbe, Exterior*).   1934.

Between Two Worlds (produced 1934).   In *Two Plays*, 1935.

Two Plays: Not for Children, and Between Two Worlds.   1935.

Not for Children (as *Life Is Real*, produced 1937; revised version, as *Not for Children*, produced 1951).   In *Two Plays*, 1935.

American Language (produced 1938).   1939.

Two on an Island (produced 1940).   1940.

Flight to the West (produced 1940).   1941.

A New Life (produced 1943).   1944.

Dream Girl (produced 1945).   1946.

The Grand Tour (produced 1951).   1952.

The Winner (produced 1954).   1954.

Cue for Passion (produced 1958).   1959.

Love among the Ruins (produced 1963).   1963.

Screenplays: *Help Yourself*, with others, 1920; *Rent Free*, with Izola Forrester and Mann Page, 1922; *Doubling for Romeo*, with Bernard McConville, 1922; *Street Scene*, 1931; *Counsellor-at-Law*, 1933; *Holiday Inn*, with Claude Binyon and Irving Berlin, 1942.

Fiction

A Voyage to Purilia.   1930.

Imperial City.   1937.

The Show Must Go On.   1949.

Other

The Supreme Freedom.   1949.

The Living Theatre.   1959.

Minority Report: An Autobiography.   1963.

Bibliography: "Rice: A Bibliography" by Robert Hogan, in *Modern Drama*, February 1966.

Reading List: *The Independence of Rice* by Robert Hogan, 1965; *Rice* by Frank Durham, 1970.

*   *   *

Elmer Rice was one of the most prolific and technically proficient of modern American dramatists, as well as, in many of his plays, an eclectic experimenter and an outspoken social spokesman. Although he graduated from law school *cum laude* and was admitted to the New York Bar, he gave up law to write plays; and one of his early pieces, a deftly constructed thriller entitled *On Trial*, achieved a rather spectacular success in 1914. For the next nine years, Rice wrote two kinds of plays – commercial potboilers, some of which were produced, and experimental plays with social themes, which were generally not produced. In 1923, however, he had a critical success when the Theatre Guild staged his Expressionistic satire about the automated modern world, *The Adding Machine*. This play is one of Rice's few to retain its popularity and effectiveness over the years, and is considered one of the significant modern American plays. A companion piece, *The Subway*, did not receive a production until 1929; although somewhat dated, it has some remarkable strengths and has been unfairly neglected. Rice's other plays until 1929 were either adaptations or collaborations (one with Dorothy Parker and one with Philip Barry) of little importance.

In 1929, after much difficulty in finding a producer, Rice's *Street Scene* opened in New York, ran for 602 performances, and won the Pulitzer Prize. The play is a realistic depiction of life on a segment of a New York street, with something of a melodramatic plot to tie its many diverse strands together. Its powerful impact was that of a "shock of recognition"; and only a huge cast requirement (more than eighty characters) has prevented its more frequent revival. Rice also directed this play, and was thereafter to direct all of his New York productions, as well as some by Behrman and Sherwood. Also in 1929 Rice produced a trivial light comedy, *See Naples and Die*, and, in 1931, a somewhat more substantial study of American expatriates in Paris, *The Left Bank*. The same year saw one of Rice's most durable pieces, *Counsellor-at-Law*. Somewhat akin in tone and pace to *The Front Page*, the play is full of hectic activity and a vehicle for a strong actor.

Three other plays of the 1930's show Rice's pre-occupation with social issues. *We, The People* is a sprawling "panoramic presentation" of American life, specifically critical but generally affirmative. Its large cast and many issues make it thin in characterisation and rather more akin to a movie scenario than to a play. In novel form, such as his novels *Imperial City* and *The Show Must Go On*, Rice was able to be fuller and more effective. In 1934 Rice acquired the Belasco Theatre in New York, intending to produce a season of his own work. The first play, *Judgment Day*, a serious melodrama based somewhat on the Reichstag fire trial, was an indictment of Fascism; it was a failure in New York, but a distinct success in London. Rice's second play at the Belasco, *Between Two Worlds*, was even less successful with the New York critics, though a better play. It is a thickly drawn Chekhovian drama of ideas, containing some of the playwright's best work. Set on an ocean liner and with the usual large cast, the play contrasts the values of capitalistic and communistic societies, and suggests that the best of two worlds must somehow be welded together. Rice was to have produced a third play, *Not for Children*, at the Belasco, but, disheartened by the critical response to the first two plays, he announced his disenchantment with the commercial stage and turned to travel and to writing a novel. The unproduced play (done some years later in an inferior revised version) is a richly droll, technically dazzling attack on the inadequacies and superficialities of the drama as an artistic form. Successful really only in its Dublin production at the Gate Theatre, the play remains a seriously neglected tour de force.

In 1938 Rice returned to the theatre as a partner in the Playwrights Company. Most of the plays he wrote for the company were patriotic social commentaries, such as *American*

Landscape and *Flight to the West*, and thin work compared to the Belasco plays. One comedy, *Dream Girl*, which starred his second wife, Betty Field, was successful theatre; and his panoramic paean to New York City, *Two on an Island*, contains some excellent satiric writing in a rather trite plot.

Rice's last commercially produced plays were less ambitious in scope, but more thoughtful in content. *The Grand Tour* and *The Winner* were about the relation of morality to money, and, although not his most memorable work and set on a much smaller scale, both were quite craftsmanlike. *Cue for Passion* was a psychoanalytic version of the Hamlet story, set in California, and is really too weak in characterization to be successful. *Love among the Ruins* is a thoughtful contemplation of the contemporary world, in which a group of American tourists in Lebanon look back on America. Rather more ambitious than *The Winner*, the play is also somewhat dull.

When Rice died in 1967, he had written over fifty plays (of which about forty were published or produced), two long novels, a satire on the early movies, a knowledgeable book about the professional theatre, and a long autobiography. He will, however, be remembered primarily as a playwright, as one of the men who transformed the American theatre from the gentility of Clyde Fitch and the entertainment of David Belasco into a form for the serious depiction of life, the critical social statement, and the broadening of technique. Not as powerful as Eugene O'Neill, sometimes deficient in character drawing, and often simplistic in statement, Rice nevertheless left a handful of plays which must be considered part of the permanent American repertory.

—Robert Hogan

SAROYAN, William. American. Born in Fresno, California, 31 August 1908. Educated in Fresno public schools. Served in the United States Army, 1942–45. Married Carol Marcus in 1943 (divorced, 1949; remarried, 1951; divorced, 1952); one daughter and one son, the poet Aram Saroyan. Past occupations include grocery clerk, vineyard worker, post office employee; Clerk, Telegraph Operator, then Office Manager of the Postal Telegraph Company, San Francisco, 1926–28; Co-Founder, Conference Press, Los Angeles, 1936; Founder and Director, Saroyan Theatre, New York, 1942; Writer-in-Residence, Purdue University, Lafayette, Indiana, 1961. Recipient: New York Drama Critics Circle Award, 1940; Pulitzer Prize, 1940 (refused). Member, National Institute of Arts and Letters. Lives in Fresno, California.

PUBLICATIONS

Plays

> *The Man with the Heart in the Highlands,* in *Contemporary One-Act Plays,* edited by William Kozlenko. 1938; revised version, as *My Heart's in the Highlands* (produced 1939), 1939.
> *The Time of Your Life* (produced 1939). 1939.
> *The Hungerers* (produced 1945). 1939.

A Special Announcement (broadcast 1940).   1940.

Love's Old Sweet Song (produced 1940).   In *Three Plays*, 1940.

Three Plays: My Heart's in the Highlands, The Time of Your Life, Love's Old Sweet Song.   1940.

Subway Circus.   1940.

Something about a Soldier (produced 1940).

Hero of the World (produced 1940).

The Great American Goof (ballet scenario; produced 1940).   In *Razzle Dazzle*, 1942.

Radio Play (broadcast 1940).   In *Razzle Dazzle*, 1942.

The Ping Pong Game (produced 1945).   1940.

Sweeney in the Trees (produced 1940).   In *Three Plays*, 1941.

The Beautiful People (produced 1941).   In *Three Plays*, 1941.

Three Plays: The Beautiful People, Sweeney in the Trees, Across the Board on Tomorrow Morning.   1941.

Across the Board on Tomorrow Morning (produced 1941).   In *Three Plays*, 1941.

The People with Light Coming Out of Them (broadcast 1941).   In *The Free Company Presents*, edited by James Boyd, 1941.

There's Something I Got To Tell You (broadcast 1941).   In *Razzle Dazzle*, 1942.

Hello, Out There (produced 1941).   In *Razzle Dazzle*, 1942.

Jim Dandy (produced 1941).   1941; as *Jim Dandy: Fat Man in a Famine*, 1947.

Talking to You (produced 1942).   In *Razzle Dazzle*, 1942.

Razzle Dazzle; or, The Human Opera, Ballet, and Circus; or, There's Something I Got to Tell You: Being Many Kinds of Short Plays As Well As the Story of the Writing of Them (includes *Hello, Out There, Coming Through the Rye, Talking to You, The Great American Goof, The Poetic Situation in America, Opera, Opera, Bad Men in the West, The Agony of Little Nations, A Special Announcement, Radio Play, The People with Light Coming Out of Them, There's Something I Got to Tell You, The Hungerers, Elmer and Lily, Subway Circus, The Ping Pong Players*).   1942.

Opera, Opera (produced 1955).   In *Razzle Dazzle*, 1942.

Get Away Old Man (produced 1943).   1944.

Sam Ego's House (produced 1947–48?).   In *Don't Go Away Mad and Two Other Plays*, 1949.

Don't Go Away Mad (produced 1949).   In *Don't Go Away Mad and Two Other Plays*, 1949.

Don't Go Away Mad and Two Other Plays: Sam Ego's House; A Decent Birth, A Happy Funeral.   1949.

The Son (produced 1950).

The Slaughter of the Innocents (produced 1957).   1952.

The Oyster and the Pearl: A Play for Television (televised 1953).   In *Perspectives USA*, Summer 1953.

Once Around the Block (produced 1956).   1959.

The Cave Dwellers (produced 1957).   1958.

Ever Been in Love with a Midget (produced 1957).

Cat, Mouse, Man, Woman; and The Accident, in *Contact I*, 1958.

Settled Out of Court, with Henry Cecil, from the novel by Henry Cecil (produced 1960).   1962.

The Dogs; or, The Paris Comedy (as *Lily Dafon*, produced 1960).   In *The Dogs; or, The Paris Comedy and Two Other Plays*, 1969.

Sam, The Highest Jumper of Them All; or, The London Comedy (produced 1960).   1961.

High Time along the Wabash (produced 1961).

Ah Man, music by Peter Fricker (produced 1962).

Four Plays: The Playwright and the Public, The Handshakers, The Doctor and the Patient, This I Believe, in *Atlantic*, April 1963.

Dentist and Patient, and Husband and Wife, in *The Best Short Plays 1968,* edited by
   Stanley Richards. 1968.
*The Dogs; or, The Paris Comedy and Two Other Plays: Chris Sick; or, Happy New Year
   Anyway, Making Money, and Ninteen Other Very Short Plays.* 1969.
The New Play, in *The Best Short Plays 1970,* edited by Stanley Richards. 1970.
Armenians (produced 1974).
The Rebirth Celebration of the Human Race at Artie Zabala's Off-Broadway Theatre
   (produced 1975).

Screenplay: *The Good Job,* 1942.

Radio Plays: *Radio Play,* 1940; *A Special Announcement,* 1940; *There's Something I Got
to Tell You,* 1941; *The People with Light Coming Out of Them,* 1941.

Television Plays: *The Oyster and the Pearl,* 1953; *Ah Sweet Mystery of Mrs. Murphy,*
1959; *The Unstoppable Gray Fox,* 1962.

Ballet Scenario: *The Great American Goof,* 1940.

Fiction

The Daring Young Man on the Flying Trapeze and Other Stories. 1934.
Inhale and Exhale (stories). 1936.
Three Times Three (stories). 1936.
Little Children (stories). 1937.
A Gay and Melancholy Flux: Short Stories. 1937.
Love, Here Is My Hat (stories). 1938.
A Native American (stories). 1938.
The Trouble with Tigers (stories). 1938.
Peace, It's Wonderful (stories). 1939.
3 Fragments and a Story. 1939.
My Name Is Aram (stories). 1940.
Saroyan's Fables. 1941.
The Insurance Salesman and Other Stories. 1941.
48 Saroyan Stories. 1942.
31 Selected Stories. 1943.
Some Day I'll Be a Millionaire: 34 More Great Stories. 1943.
The Human Comedy. 1943.
Dear Baby (stories). 1944.
The Adventures of Wesley Jackson. 1946.
The Saroyan Special: Selected Short Stories. 1948.
The Fiscal Hoboes (stories). 1949.
*The Twin Adventures: The Adventures of Saroyan: A Diary; The Adventures of Wesley
   Jackson: A Novel.* 1950.
The Assyrian and Other Stories. 1950.
Rock Wagram. 1951.
Tracy's Tiger. 1951.
The Laughing Matter. 1953; as *The Secret Story,* 1954.
The Whole Voyald and Other Stories. 1956.
Mama, I Love You. 1956.
Papa, You're Crazy. 1957.
Love (stories). 1959.
Boys and Girls Together. 1963.

One Day in the Afternoon of the World. 1964.
After Thirty Years: The Daring Young Man on the Flying Trapeze (includes essays). 1964.
Best Stories of Saroyan. 1964.
My Kind of Crazy Wonderful People: 17 Stories and a Play. 1966.

Other

The Time of Your Life (miscellany). 1939.
Harlem as Seen by Hirschfeld. 1941.
Hilltop Russians in San Francisco. 1941.
Why Abstract?, with Henry Miller and Hilaire Hiler. 1945.
The Bicycle Rider in Beverly Hills (autobiography). 1952.
Saroyan Reader. 1958.
Here Comes, There Goes, You Know Who (autobiography). 1961.
A Note on Hilaire Hiler. 1962.
Me (juvenile). 1963.
Not Dying (autobiography). 1963.
Short Drive, Sweet Chariot (autobiography). 1966.
Look at Us: Let's See: Here We Are: Look Hard: Speak Soft: I See, You See, We All See; Stop, Look, Listen; Beholder's Eye; Don't Look Now But Isn't That You? (us? U.S.?). 1967.
Horsey Gorsey and the Frog (juvenile). 1968.
I Used to Believe I Had Forever; Now I'm Not So Sure. 1968.
Letters from 74 rue Taitbout; or, Don't Go But if You Must Say Hello to Everybody. 1969; as *Don't Go But If You Must Say Hello to Everybody,* 1970.
Days of Life and Death and Escape to the Moon. 1970.
Places Where I've Done Time. 1972.
The Tooth and My Father (juvenile). 1974.
Famous Faces and Other Friends: A Personal Memoir. 1976.
Morris Hirshfield. 1976.
Sons Come and Go, Mothers Hang In Forever (memoirs). 1976.
Chance Meetings. 1978.

Editor, *Hairenik 1934–1939: An Anthology of Short Stories and Poems.* 1939.

Bibliography: *A Bibliography of Saroyan 1934–1963* by David Kherdian, 1965.

Reading List: *Saroyan* by Howard R. Floan, 1966.

*   *   *

Hailed by some as the greatest writer to come out of San Francisco since Frank Norris, William Saroyan is one of the striking paradoxes in 20th-century literary writing in America. If he has been dismissed for being non-literary, a critic of the eminence of Edmund Wilson has lauded him for his uncanny gift for creating atmosphere in his books: "Saroyan takes you to the bar, and he creates for you there a world which is the way the world would be if it conformed to the feeling instilled by drinks. In a word, he achieves the feat of making and keeping us boozy without the use of alcohol and purely by the action of art."

Saroyan never went beyond high school and thus exemplifies the successful homespun writer. *The Daring Young Man on the Flying Trapeze, and Other Stories* was his first collection of short fiction, and many still consider it to be among his finest writing. A breathtakingly prolific writer (he produced about five hundred stories between 1934 and 1940), Saroyan is a short story writer, playwright, and novelist, but his claim to greatness rests essentially on plays like *My Heart's in the Highlands* and *The Time of Your Life* and on his short stories. He has been criticized for his pervasive sentimentality, but his retort to the charge is that it is a very sentimental thing to be a human being. And to the charge that his style is careless and sloppy, he responded: "I do not know a great deal about what the words come to, but the presence says, Now don't get funny; just sit down and say something: it'll be all right. Say it wrong; It'll be all right anyway. Half the time I *do* say it wrong, but somehow or other, just as the presence says, it's right anyway. I am always pleased about this."

One of his best stories, "A Daring Young Man on the Flying Trapeze," is an interior monologue revealing the recollections of a poor writer who lives in the troubled present while achieving distance from it by reaching back into the past centuries. Unperturbed on the conscious level by his problems, occasionally the young writer is embittered by such experiences as the need to sell his books to buy food. Finally, on returning to his room in the afternoon from his wanderings he dies a sudden and painless death. Saroyan's identification with his young protagonist is evident, despite the author's disclaimers. The story is suffused with pathos, though there is clearly an attempt to hold the sentimentality in check. The story would also appear to be a plea for sympathy and support for deprived writers. Among his plays, *The Time of Your Life* is the one that probably most fully reflects Saroyan the artist. It received both the Drama Critics Circle Award and the Pulitzer Prize, but Saroyan refused the latter as an expression of his contempt for commercial patronage of art. Despite its melodramatic plot the play, as Howard R. Floan admirably sums up, is "about a state of mind, illusive but real, whose readily recognizable components are, first, an awareness of America's youth – its undisciplined swaggering, unregulated early life – and, secondly, a pervasive sense of America in crisis: an America of big business, of labor strife, of depersonalized government, and, above all, of imminent war."

At seventy, Saroyan's interest in the comedy-tragedy of life remains undiminished: "Living is the only thing. It is an awful pain most of the time, but this compels comedy and dignity." What makes Saroyan stand out in American literary writing is his optimism about life despite the evidence to the contrary in the world around, especially as perceived by most American writers; and his buoyancy seems to work with his considerable reading public. But the major appeal of his writing comes from his characters, who are common people like gas station attendants, and from his heavily romantic emphasis on the individuality of man. With charming candour Saroyan not too long ago declared that his main purpose was to earn as much money as possible – a confession that has been used by adverse criticism to exaggerate the casualness of his writing and to withhold due recognition from him.

—J. N. Sharma

SHAFFER, Peter (Levin).   English.   Born in Liverpool, Lancashire, 15 May 1926; twin brother of the playwright Anthony Shaffer. Educated at St. Paul's School, London; Trinity College, Cambridge, 1947–50, B.A. 1950. Served as a conscript in coal mines in England, 1944–47. Worked in the acquisitions department of the New York Public Library, 1951–54; worked for Boosey and Hawkes, music publishers, London, 1954–55; Literary Critic, *Truth*, London, 1956–57; Music Critic, *Time and Tide*, London, 1961–62. Recipient: *Evening Standard* award, 1958; New York Drama Critics Circle Award, 1960, 1975; Antoinette Perry Award, 1975. Lives in London.

PUBLICATIONS

Plays

Five Finger Exercise (produced 1958).   1958.
The Private Ear and The Public Eye (produced 1962).   1962.
The Merry Roosters Panto, with the Theatre Workshop (produced 1963).
Sketch in *The Establishment* (produced 1963).
The Royal Hunt of the Sun: A Play Concerning the Conquest of Peru (produced 1964).   1965.
Black Comedy (produced 1965).   In *Black Comedy, Including White Lies,* 1967.
A Warning Game (produced 1967).
White Lies (produced 1967).   In *Black Comedy, Including White Lies,* 1967; as *The White Liars* (produced 1968), 1967; (revised version, produced 1976).
Black Comedy, Including White Lies: Two Plays.   1967; as *The White Liars, Black Comedy: Two Plays,* 1968.
It's about Cinderella (produced 1969).
Shrivings (as *The Battle of Shrivings,* produced 1970).   1974.
Equus (produced 1973).   1973.

Screenplays: *Lord of the Flies,* with Peter Brook, 1963; *The Public Eye (Follow Me!),* 1972.

Radio Play: *The Prodigal Father,* 1957.

Television Plays: *The Salt Land,* 1955; *Balance of Terror,* 1957.

Fiction

How Doth the Little Crocodile?, with Anthony Shaffer.   1951.
Woman in the Wardrobe, with Anthony Shaffer.   1952.
Withered Murder, with Anthony Shaffer.   1955.

Reading List: *Shaffer* by John Russell Taylor, 1974.

*   *   *

Four of Peter Shaffer's plays have had considerable success in the theatre and have given him a misleading reputation for versatility without personal commitment. Furthermore, comparisons with Brecht and Rattigan have obscured deeper affinities with the "total theatre" of Paul Claudel and the intimate savagery of O'Neill's or Albee's drama. Certainly his work ranges from farce to tragedy, but it is criss-crossed with recurrent images, and the same basic structures emerge in secular and religious transformations. A line from *Shrivings,* "The most anyone can say in the end to God or Man is 'Let us see!' " is crucially pertinent to all the plays, both one-act and full-length. An allusion to self-blinded Oedipus, planted early in *Five Finger Exercise,* anticipates the blackened sun of *The Royal Hunt of the Sun* and the blinded horses of *Equus*; there seems to be a connection with the owl image of dim-sighted innocence in *Five Finger Exercise* and *Shrivings* with the unilluminating crystal ball in *White Liars* and, in reversal, the casting of stage light on what the characters of *Black Comedy* get up to in the dark. The Oedipal family situation which is exposed in *Five Finger Exercise* and *Equus,* and resides as a phantasm in the background of *Shrivings,* has its maturer variant in the situation of the sceptic who is faced by an impossible choice between a Christianity he loathes and a humaner faith he cannot trust: Pizarro, in *Royal Hunt of the Sun*, caught between the greed and cruelty of the Church and a sixteenth-century equivalent of the Marxist dream; Mark Askelon, in *Shrivings* (the re-written, published text of the theatrical failure, *The Battle of Shrivings*), who plays the Devil to Gideon Petrie's humanist saint in longing for a defeat that will save him from taking hopeless refuge in traditional religion; the psychiatrist, Dysart, in *Equus*, who sees the issues but evades battle and makes do with a nostalgia for the Greek world at the price of self-contempt. The visionary dream of faith takes alternative form as music in some of the plays (*Five Finger Exercise*, *The Private Ear*), and the apparent conflict between culture and philistinism seems to be an obscurer enactment of the alternatives of belief or destructive nihilism.

Shaffer has declared his aesthetic predilection for "the cold which burns," and the emotions that give power and intensity to the verbal battles and the pursuit of ultimates in his plays are the cold ones of guilt, envy, disgust, despondency, hatred. (The author's loathing is most consistently projected on the adult female characters in the plays, who range from tiresome and stupid to nauseating, though Shaffer can also be arraigned for some degree of contempt for the lower middle class.) Pizarro's cry, "Where can a man live, between two hates?" defines the quest of a playwright whose recognition of man's spiritual nature springs from an agonised consciousness of original sin. This has been an unfashionable viewpoint in the 1960's and 1970's, and in technique also Peter Shaffer stands apart from any school or group of contemporary dramatists.

The plays are firmly and ingeniously structured and ask to be met by creative collaboration from designers and choreographers, as well as directors and actors. The result has been a degree of physical stage action unusual in modern drama. Shaffer has a liking for multiple sets, or at least two acting areas, which allow for the counterpointing of different lines of dialogue, or of dialogue and action, and set up a convention in which long rhetorical speeches, and even soliloquies, are acceptable. The action is deftly farcical in *Black Comedy* and grandly spectacular in *Royal Hunt of the Sun* – but not epic in the Brechtian sense, as Shaffer maintains theatrical illusion and does not use his period setting to give a provocatively estranged view of modern issues. Indeed it may be a weakness of both *Royal Hunt of the Sun* and *Equus* that there is some muffling of the contemporary and personal anguish by elements that have led to the work's success with the general public. In *Equus*, the elucidation of the mystery which gives the play its plot is a more unfortunate reminder than the comic fantasy of a detective in *The Public Eye* that Peter and Anthony Shaffer had collaborated on several detective novels; for this interferes with the proper relation of the play's lyrical core to its true protagonist, Dysart. Perhaps significantly, it is in passages of the least-liked major play, *Shrivings*, that the emotional urgency is strongest.

Shaffer is never a meticulous naturalist; he is not concerned to make it credible that the parents in *Five Finger Exercise* should have such a wise and happy child as Pamela, or that the ex-teacher and the left-wing printer of *Equus* have an illiterate son; more obviously deliberate is the morality-play element in *Shrivings*, and this, apart from the embarrassing way in which the characters take theatrically ineffective symbols out of parcels, may account for the hostile reception given to the original staged version of this work. He has an unreliable ear for colloquial speech. But this weakness is venial in a writer whose concern with society is indirect and secondary. Even the undistinguished prose of his more formal dialogue does not cancel out the genuine dramatic gift, the courage and ability to tackle large subjects, and the force of conviction.

—Margery Morgan

SHAW, George Bernard. Irish. Born in Dublin, 26 July 1856. Educated privately and at the Wesleyan Connexional School and elsewhere in Dublin. Married Charlotte Payne-

Townshend in 1898 (died, 1943). Office boy and cashier for Charles Townshend, estate agent, Dublin, 1871–76; settled in London, 1876; worked briefly for the Edison Telephone Company, 1879; wrote novels and literary and art criticism for various newspapers, 1879–83; became a socialist in 1882: speaker for the Social Democratic Federation: joined the Fabian Society in 1884: Member of the Executive Committee for many years; Music Critic (as "Corno di Bassetto"), *The Star*, 1888–1890, and *The World*, 1890–94; began writing for the stage in the 1890's; Drama Critic, *The Saturday Review*, 1895–98; Member of the Borough Council of St. Pancras, London, 1900–03; Founder, with Sidney and Beatrice Webb, *The New Statesman*, 1913, and helped establish the London School of Economics; drafted his last manifesto for the Fabian Society in 1929; lifelong advocate of spelling reform. Recipient: Nobel Prize for Literature, 1925; Irish Academy of Letters medal, 1934. Declined a peerage and the Order of Merit. *Died 2 November 1950.*

Publications

Collections

> *Collected Letters*, edited by Dan H. Laurence.   2 vols. only, 1965–72.
> *The Bodley Head Shaw* (plays and prefaces).   7 vols., 1970–74.
> *The Portable Shaw*, edited by Stanley Weintraub.   1977.

Plays

> *Widowers' Houses: A Didactic Realistic Play* (produced 1892).   1893; revised version, in *Plays Unpleasant*, 1898.
> *Arms and the Man* (produced 1894).   In *Plays Pleasant*, 1898.
> *Candida* (produced 1897).   In *Plays Pleasant*, 1898.
> *The Devil's Disciple* (produced 1897).   In *Three Plays for Puritans*, 1901.
> *The Man of Destiny* (produced 1897).   In *Plays Pleasant*, 1898.
> *The Gadfly; or, The Son of the Cardinal*, from the novel by Ethel Voynich (produced 1898).   In *Bodley Head Shaw 7*, 1974.
> *You Never Can Tell* (produced 1899).   In *Plays Pleasant*, 1898.
> *Mrs. Warren's Profession* (produced 1902).   In *Plays Unpleasant*, 1898.
> *The Philanderer* (produced 1905).   In *Plays Unpleasant*, 1898.
> *Captain Brassbound's Conversion* (produced 1900).   In *Three Plays for Puritans*, 1901.
> *Caesar and Cleopatra* (produced 1907).   In *Three Plays for Puritans*, 1901.
> *The Admirable Bashville; or, Constancy Rewarded*, from his novel *Cashel Byron's Profession* (produced 1902).   In *Cashel Byron's Profession*, 1901.
> *Man and Superman: A Comedy and a Philosophy* (produced 1905).   1903; excerpt, as *Don Juan in Hell: A Dream* (produced 1907).
> *How He Lied to Her Husband* (produced 1904).   With *John Bull's Other Island, Major Barbara*, 1907.
> *John Bull's Other Island* (produced 1904).   With *How He Lied to Her Husband, Major Barbara*, 1907.
> *Passion, Poison, and Petrification; or, The Fatal Gazogene* (produced 1905).   1905.
> *Major Barbara* (produced 1905).   With *How He Lied to Her Husband, John Bull's Other Island*, 1907; revised version (screenplay), 1945.
> *The Doctor's Dilemma* (produced 1906).   With *Getting Married, The Shewing Up of Blanco Posnet*, 1911.
> *The Interlude at the Playhouse* (produced 1907).   In *Behind the Scenes with Cyril Maude*, 1927.

Getting Married (produced 1908).   With *The Doctor's Dilemma, The Shewing Up of Blanco Posnet*, 1911.

The Shewing Up of Blanco Posnet (produced 1909).   With *The Doctor's Dilemma, Getting Married*, 1911.

Press Cuttings (produced 1909).   1909.

Misalliance (produced 1910).   With *The Dark Lady of the Sonnets, Fanny's First Play*, 1914.

The Dark Lady of the Sonnets (produced 1910).   With *Misalliance, Fanny's First Play*, 1914.

Fanny's First Play (produced 1911).   With *Misalliance, The Dark Lady of the Sonnets*, 1914.

Overruled (produced 1912).   With *Androcles and the Lion, Pygmalion*, 1916.

Androcles and the Lion (produced 1913).   With *Overruled, Pgymalion*, 1916.

Pygmalion (produced 1913).   With *Overruled, Androcles and the Lion*, 1916; revised version (screenplay), 1941.

Great Catherine (produced 1913).   With *Heartbreak House, Playlets of the War*, 1919.

The Music Cure (produced 1914).   In *Translations and Tomfooleries*, 1926.

The Inca of Perusalem (produced 1916).   With *Great Catherine, Heartbreak House, Playlets of the War*, 1919.

Augustus Does His Bit (produced 1917).   With *Great Catherine, Heartbreak House, Playlets of the War*, 1919.

O'Flaherty, V.C. (produced 1917).   With *Great Catherine, Heartbreak House, Playlets of the War*, 1919.

Annajanska, The Bolshevik Empress (produced 1918).   With *Great Catherine, Heartbreak House, Playlets of the War*, 1919.

Heartbreak House (produced 1920).   With *Great Catherine, Playlets of the War*, 1919.

Back to Methuselah (produced 1922).   1921.

Jitta's Atonement, from a work by Siegfried Trebitsch (produced 1923).   In *Translations and Tomfooleries*, 1926.

Saint Joan (produced 1923).   1924; revised version (screenplay), 1968.

The Glimpse of Reality (produced 1927).   In *Translations and Tomfooleries*, 1926.

Translations and Tomfooleries.   1926.

The Fascinating Foundling (produced 1928).   In *Translations and Tomfooleries*, 1926.

The Apple Cart (produced 1929).   1930.

Complete Plays.   1931; revised edition, 1934, 1938, 1950, 1952, 1965.

Too True to Be Good (produced 1932).   With *Village Wooing, On the Rocks*, 1934.

On the Rocks (produced 1933).   With *Village Wooing, Too True to Be Good*, 1934.

Village Wooing (produced 1934).   With *Too True to Be Good, On the Rocks*, 1934.

The Six of Calais (produced 1934).   With *The Simpleton of the Unexpected Isles, The Millionairess*, 1936.

The Simpleton of the Unexpected Isles (produced 1935).   With *The Six of Calais, The Millionairess*, 1936.

The Millionairess (produced 1936).   With *The Six of Calais, The Simpleton of the Unexpected Isles*, 1936.

Cymbeline Refinished (produced 1937).   With *Geneva, In Good King Charles's Golden Days*, 1946.

Geneva (produced 1938).   1939.

In Good King Charles's Golden Days (produced 1939).   1939.

Buoyant Billions (produced 1948).   1949.

Shakes Versus Shav: A Puppet Play (produced 1949).   With *Buoyant Billions, Far-Fetched Fables*, 1950.

Far-Fetched Fables (produced 1950).   With *Buoyant Billions, Shakes Versus Shav*, 1950.

Why She Would Not (produced 1957).   In *Ten Short Plays*, 1960.

Ten Short Plays.   1960.
Passion Play: A Dramatic Fragment, 1878, edited by Jerald E. Bringle.   1971.

Screenplays: *Pygmalion,* with others, 1938; *Major Barbara,* with Anatole de Grunwald, 1941; *Caesar and Cleopatra,* with Marjorie Deans and W. P. Lipscomb, 1946.

Fiction

Cashel Byron's Profession.   1886; revised edition, 1889, 1901.
An Unsocial Socialist.   1887.
Love among the Artists.   1900.
The Irrational Knot.   1905.
Immaturity, in *Works.*   1930.
The Adventures of the Black Girl in Her Search for God.   1932.
My Dear Dorothea: A Practical Guide of Moral Education for Females, edited by Stephen Winsten.   1956.
An Unfinished Novel, edited by Stanley Weintraub.   1958.

Other

The Quintessence of Ibsenism.   1891; revised edition, 1913.
The Perfect Wagnerite: A Commentary on the Ring of the Niblungs.   1898; revised edition, 1907.
Dramatic Opinions and Essays.   2 vols., 1906.
The Sanity of Art.   1908.
Common Sense about the War.   1914.
How to Settle the Irish Question.   1917.
Ruskin's Politics.   1921.
Letters to Miss Alma Murray.   1927; *More Letters,* 1932.
The Intelligent Woman's Guide to Socialism and Capitalism.   1928; revised edition, 1937.
Works.   33 vols., 1930–38.
Ellen Terry and Shaw: A Correspondence.   1931.
Works (Standard Edition).   34 vols., 1931–51.
What I Really Wrote about the War.   1931.
Doctors' Delusions, Crude Criminology, Sham Education, in *Works* (Standard Edition).   1931.
Pen Portraits and Reviews, in *Works* (Standard Edition).   1931.
Our Theatre in the Nineties, in *Works* (Standard Edition).   3 vols., 1932.
Essays in Fabian Socialism, in *Works* (Standard Edition).   1932.
The Political Madhouse in America and Nearer Home, in *Works* (Standard Edition).   1933.
Prefaces.   1934; revised edition, 1938, 1965.
Short Stories, Scraps, and Shavings, in *Works* (Standard Edition).   1934.
London Music in 1888–89 as Heard by Corno di Bassetto, in *Works* (Standard Edition).   1937.
Shaw Gives Himself Away: An Autobiographical Miscellany.   1939.
Florence Farr, Shaw, and W. B. Yeats Letters, edited by Clifford Bax.   1941.
Everybody's Political What's What.   1944.
Sixteen Self Sketches, in *Works* (Standard Edition).   1949.
Shaw on Vivisection, edited by G. H. Bowker.   1949.
Rhyming Picture Guide to Ayot Saint Lawrence.   1950.

Correspondence Between Shaw and Mrs. Patrick Campbell, edited by A. Dent.   1952.
Advice to a Young Critic and Other Letters, edited by E. J. West.   1955.
Letters to Granville Barker, edited by C. B. Purdom.   1957.
To a Young Actress: Letters to Molly Tompkins, edited by P. Tompkins.   1960.
The Matter with Ireland, edited by Dan H. Laurence and D. H. Greene.   1962.
The Rationalization of Russia, edited by H. M. Geduld.   1964.
Non-Dramatic Literary Criticism, edited by Stanley Weintraub.   1972.
Shaw 1914–1918: Journey to Heartbreak (from Shaw's journals), edited by Stanley Weintraub.   1973.

Editor, *Fabian Essays on Socialism.*   1889; revised edition, 1908, 1931, 1948.
Editor, *Fabianism and the Empire: A Manifesto.*   1900.

Bibliography: *A Bibliography of the Books and Pamphlets of Shaw* by G. H. Wells, 1925, supplements in *Bookman's Journal,* 1925, 1928; *The Rehearsal Copies of Shaw's Plays* by F. E. Loewenstein, 1950; *Shaw: An Exhibit, A Catalogue* by Dan H. Laurence, 1977.

Reading List: *Shaw, Playboy and Prophet,* 1932, and *Shaw, Man of the Century,* 1956, both by Archibald Henderson; *Shaw: A Reconsideration* by Eric Bentley, 1947, revised edition, 1957; *A Good Man Fallen among Fabians* by Alick West, 1950; *Shaw: A Critical Survey* edited by Louis Kronenberger, 1955; *Shaw: The Style and the Man* by Richard M. Ohmann, 1962; *Shaw and the Nineteenth Century* by Martin Meisel, 1963; *Shaw of Dublin: The Formative Years* by B. C. Rosset, 1964; *Twentieth Century Views of Shaw* edited by R. J. Kaufmann, 1965; *Shaw and the Charlatan Genius* by John O'Donovan, 1965; *Shaw and the Art of Destroying Ideals* by Charles A. Carpenter, 1969; *The Shavian Background* by Margery Morgan, 1972; *Shaw, Playwright* by Bernard F. Dukore, 1973; *Shaw and the Art of Drama* by Charles A. Berst, 1973; *The Cart and the Trumpet* by Maurice Valency, 1973; *Shaw's Moral Vision: The Self and Salvation* by Alfred Turco, Jr., 1976; *Shaw: The Critical Heritage* edited by T. F. Evans, 1976.

*   *   *

George Bernard Shaw achieved the status of a classic dramatist in his life-time, yet the question of how good he is still perplexes criticism. One reason for this is undoubtedly the suspicion that attaches to commercial success in the arts. Another is the idiosyncratic nature of his comic genius: on his own admission, childhood experience of a drunken father and a coolly indifferent mother blocked his capacity for feeling as other men do, and a long virginity followed by deliberate entry on a sexless yet happy marriage mark him out as further removed from the apotheosis of the normal which is the least disturbing form of greatness. His unflagging sense of the ridiculous, his gift of the gab, even the rationality that brought opprobrium on him amid the mass hysteria of the First World War (see *Common Sense about the War*), can be seen as grotesque over-developments of particular faculties in an unbalanced personality. His love of horseplay may strike grown men and women as juvenile. It seems easier to acknowledge a supreme clown if he is inarticulate and his art seems largely instinctive, and if he stays in the "primitive" ambience of circus or music hall. The clown as political theorist, intellectual leader, and religious visionary, invading the realms of literature and the serious, "legitimate" stage, throws all civilised activities anarchically into doubt. It is not even as though Shaw's satire had the savagery of Swift's; at his most vituperative he has an air of only playing and enjoying his own jokes. When turned by others, against his intentions, into a librettist of musical comedy (*The Chocolate Soldier* and *My Fair Lady*), he has provided smash hits easier to categorise and assimilate.

He first made his reputation as a journalist, writing music criticism under the name of "Corno di Bassetto," and he went on to become theatre critic to *The Saturday Review,* writing plays at the same time. His reviews combine technical knowledge with acute judgment and an extremely lively, exaggerative style, and his example did much to raise the standard of criticism in both fields. He had already written five novels, which have been most fully and sympathetically discussed by Alick West in *A Good Man Fallen among Fabians*. In these he attempts a panoramic view of society and tackles some of the large themes that are to occupy him in his plays, among them marriage (*The Irrational Knot*), genius and class distinctions (*Immaturity* and *Cashel Byron's Profession*), the politician as Don Juan (*An Unsocial Socialist*). In all, he presents the independent professional woman in contrast to the conventionally domesticated type, and studies (especially in *Love among the Artists*) examples of men and women on whom the impersonal claims of work, art, or science are stronger than those of personal relationships. These novels are brimming with current ideas and abound in entertaining passages, but the sense of direction is usually uncertain and the impulse to break into self-parody is strongly marked, appearing most oddly in the antics of Trefusis *alias* Smilash, the self-ironical clown of a hero in *An Unsocial Socialist*. *Cashel Byron's Profession* stands apart as the briefest and most evenly sustained, and here Shaw first tries out the satiric formula to be used as a basis for *Mrs. Warren's Profession* and *Major Barbara*. Here his hero is an innocent who speaks out the literal truth of his experience as a prize-fighter and is heard as a philosopher spinning metaphors of the competitive society and its economic system. Shaw later drew on this novel for his burlesque in heroic couplets, *The Admirable Bashville*.

Interest in the less intellectual forms of nineteenth-century theatre surfaces in *Immaturity* and in *The Irrational Knot*, where one of the principal characters is a star of burletta, admired by an upper-class, amateur comedian who plays the banjo. This strain in his work is kept relatively subdued in Shaw's earliest published plays: the blue-book themes of slum landlordism (*Widowers' Houses*) and prostitution (*Mrs. Warren's Profession*) advertised the Fabian socialist's reforming purpose and were associated with his lecture to the Fabian Society, later expanded into *The Quintessence of Ibsenism*, introducing the Norwegian dramatist as a social iconoclast. Structural features of the Ibsen social play are imitated in several early Shavian dramas: the retrospective action, involving interpretation and re-interpretation of the past, is clear in *Mrs. Warren's Profession*; the extended *raisonnement* with which Ibsen ended *A Doll's House* also marks the end of *Candida* (which Shaw described as an English version of the same situation, but with the man as the doll); the Dickensian caricature-figure that intrudes into Act I and reappears, perhaps transformed, towards the end of the play (Lickcheese in *Widowers' Houses* and later Doolittle in *Pygmalion*, recalling Ibsen's Engstrand and Brendel). But it is for a strictly philosophical, not stylistic, naturalism that Shaw declares himself in the Preface to *Plays Pleasant*: "To me the tragedy and comedy of life lie in the consequences ... of our persistent attempts to found our institutions on the ideals suggested to our imaginations by our half-satisfied passions, instead of on a genuinely scientific natural history." Indeed Ibsen as author of *Peer Gynt* offered a major precedent for the blending of fantasy with moral allegory which is characteristic of so much of Shaw's later work.

Failure to secure more than a few private performances of his "Unpleasant" plays led Shaw to change his tactics and strengthen the comic element in his work. He turned to the mock-heroic variety of burlesque in *Arms and the Man*, and the piece calls for an evidently artificial, exaggerated style of acting in most of its roles. *You Never Can Tell* has taken a hint from the phase in the development of pantomime when the characters of the opening story doubled with those of the attached harlequinade, and both action and dialogue are devised to suggest the stock situations and sprightly stock types of the *commedia dell'arte* tradition. Not until *The Apple Cart* and *Geneva* did Shaw describe his work as "political extravaganza," but already in the 1890's he was establishing a continuity with the theatrical entertainments most skilfully devised in the middle of the nineteenth century by J. R. Planché. *Androcles and the Lion* includes the simplest Shavian variation on the extravaganza mode; *Caesar and Cleopatra* manages to combine historical and Shakespearian burlesque; the early scenes, the epilogue, and some of the characters in *Saint Joan*, including the Dauphin and intermittently Joan herself, belong to the same theatrical category. The capacity of parody to retain some distillation of mood from the original it travesties is already realised in the anti-romanticism of *Arms and the Man*; it is outstandingly illustrated, in a more limited instance, in Bloomfield-Bonnington's muddled and misapplied quotations from Shakespeare, in *The Doctor's Dilemma*. This seems to give Shaw the medium in which he is best able to convey the often poignant human emotions at the heart of his plays, and stage presentations of his drama succeed to the measure that they realise the pure grain of truthful feeling among the absurdities.

A substratum of burlesque may be concealed under the superficial naturalism of contemporary situations and characters. The secret is revealed in the detachable hell scene of *Man and Superman*, in which Tanner dreams of himself as Don Juan. *Candida* guards its secret in an almost obscurantist way, linked with Shaw's personal ambivalence towards mother figures which emerges in play after play. The subcategory of burlesque which embodies classical myth in familiar domestic form serves him as a means of portraying the hold of the domestic ideal, with its virtual worship of virgin-mother goddesses, on late Victorian society. In *Pygmalion* he uses classical myth as a form of metaphor, in combination with a fairy extravaganza of Cinderella. When he came to write *Heartbreak House*, mythological burlesque emerged in a more grandiose form under the influence of Wagnerian music-drama. Then in *Back to Methuselah*, the "metabiological pentateuch," parody almost returns to its matrix, becoming the thing it travesties.

It was through the movement to establish a National Theatre that Shaw eventually, in 1904, gained command of a theatre public. With the first of his "national" plays put on by the Court Theatre management of Vedrenne and Granville-Barker, *John Bull's Other Island*, he set about using the stage more blatantly as a forum for public debate, debate, in this instance on the Irish Question. The fluid form, in which comic episodes, character turns, and set discussions were loosely strung together, ensured a mood of relaxation in which ideas could be exploded most forcefully on the governing classes. *Major Barbara*, with a much tighter dialectical structure reinforcing the mythic element, is Shaw's most impressive examination of the theme of political power, and its complex system of ironies makes doubtful the critical reading, not confined to Marxists, which represents it as the author's abandonment of socialism. Playing devil's advocate is a recurrent Shavian intellectual trick which led to unsubtle charges of Fascism against *On the Rocks*. This raises the question of how politically influential Shaw's drama has been, and whether doctrine has been sacrificed to entertainment, or confused in overloaded, overcomplex imaginative structures. The problem has to be considered play by play; but it can be said, as of his nearest European analogue, Brecht, that Shaw's comedic brilliance and his geniality tend to enliven the mind and break down prejudice.

The First World War and Granville-Barker's withdrawal from the theatre left Shaw for a time without access to the stage. One effect of this was the turning of *Back to Methuselah*, in the course of writing, into non-theatrical literature, though even this has managed to hold the stage in a few productions. Barry Jackson, founder of the Malvern Shaw Festival, came to the rescue, but a number of Shaw's later plays have still had little theatrical testing and exploration.

—Margery Morgan

SHEPARD, Sam. American. Born in Fort Sheridan, Illinois, 5 November 1943. Educated at Duarte High School, California; Mount San Antonio Junior College, Walnut, California, 1961–62. Married O-Lan Johnson Dark in 1969; one son. Worked as a "hot walker" at Santa Anita Race Track, a stable hand, sheep shearer, herdsman and orange picker, all in California; car wrecker, Charlemont, Massachusetts; busboy at the Village Gate, a waiter at Marie's Crisis Cafe, and musician with the Holy Modal Rounders, all in New York. Recipient: Obie Award, 1967, 1977; Guggenheim Fellowship, 1968, 1971; National Institute of Arts and Letters award, 1974; Brandeis University Creative Arts Award, 1975.

PUBLICATIONS

Plays

Cowboys (produced 1964).
Rock Garden (produced 1964; excerpt produced in *Oh! Calcutta!*, 1969).   In *The Unseen Hand and Other Plays*, 1971.
Up to Thursday (produced 1964).
Dog (produced 1964).
Rocking Chair (produced 1964).
Chicago (produced 1965).   In *Five Plays*, 1967.
Icarus's Mother (produced 1965).   In *Five Plays*, 1967.
4-H Club (produced 1965).   In *Mad Dog Blues and Other Plays*, 1967.
Fourteen Hundred Thousand (produced).   In *Five Plays*, 1967.
Red Cross (produced 1966).   In *Five Plays*, 1967.
La Turista (produced 1966).   1968.
Forensic and the Navigators (produced 1967).   In *The Unseen Hand and Other Plays*, 1971.
Melodrama Play (produced 1967).   In *Five Plays*, 1967.
Five Plays.   1967.
Cowboys No. 2 (produced 1967).   In *Mad Dog Blues and Other Plays*, 1971.
Shaved Splits (produced 1969).   In *The Unseen Hand and Other Plays*, 1971.
The Unseen Hand (produced 1970).   In *The Unseen Hand and Other Plays*, 1971.
Operation Sidewinder (produced 1970).   1970.
Holy Ghostly (produced 1970).   In *The Unseen Hand and Other Plays*, 1971.
Back Bog Beast Bait (produced 1971).   In *The Unseen Hand and Other Plays*, 1971.
Mad Dog Blues (produced 1971).   In *Mad Dog Blues and and Other Plays*, 1971.
Cowboy Mouth (produced 1971).   In *Mad Dog Blues and Other Plays*, 1971.
The Unseen Hand and Other Plays.   1971.
Mad Dog Blues and Other Plays.   1971.
The Tooth of Crime (produced 1972).   In *The Tooth of Crime, and Geography of a Horse Dreamer*, 1974.
Nightwalk, with Megan Terry and Jean-Claude van Itallie (produced 1973).
Blue Bitch (produced 1973).
Little Ocean (produced 1974).
Geography of a Horse Dreamer (produced 1974).   In *The Tooth of Crime, and Geography of a Horse Dreamer*, 1974.
The Tooth of Crime, and Geography of a Horse Dreamer.   1974.
Action (produced 1974).   In *Action, and The Unseen Hand*, 1975.
Action, and The Unseen Hand.   1975.
Killer's Head (produced 1975).   In *Angel City ...*, 1976.
Angel City (produced 1976).   In *Angel City ...*, 1976.
Angel City, Curse of the Starving Class, and Other Plays (includes *Killer's Head, Action, Mad Dog Blues, Cowboy Mouth, Rock Garden, Cowboys No. 2*).   1976.

Curse of the Starving Class (produced 1977).   In Angel City ..., 1976.
Suicide in B-flat (produced 1976).

Screenplays: Me and My Brother, with Robert Frank, 1967; Zabriskie Point, with
others, 1970; Ringaleevio, with Murray Mednick, 1971.

Fiction

Hawk Moon (stories).   1972.

Other

Rolling Thunder Logbook.   1977.

*   *   *

Sam Shepard shapes the intellectual, physical, and temporal spaces where improvisational
chance must happen for actors and audience. Action's two couples seek through standard
improvisations to re-create lost group or individual identities that would enable them to
combat fear and cold and perhaps to act. The dramatic event characteristically witholds any
genuine resolution and focuses on the procession of images within an occasioning action-
celebration.

Most of Shepard's over thirty tragi-comedies, like Action, are set on a down-slope, "highs"
during the decline of a revolution (Shaved Splits), a literacy-based civilization (Fourteen
Hundred Thousand), or even Fourth-of-July celebrations (Icarus's Mother). Haunting power
plays arise from striking theatrical exercises. Three characters demand attention as
relationships deteriorate in Red Cross. Jim uses role-playing to dominate, until each woman
glides off through her compelling sexual/death aria, down a ski-slope or undersea, to a
private place. Returning to everyday hysteria and complacency, they leave their parasitic
victim-tormentor bleeding and empty. Despite established orders of fundamentalism,
Mariology, and gunslingers in Back Bog Beast Bait, a new beast slouches toward the stage to
be born – with the aid of poisonous mushrooms, totem animals, and a bewitching Cajun
fiddler.

Language is a probe, a veil, an incantation, a mystery of voices. Diction and syntax catch
and flow directly from the styles of different contemporary subcultures. The verbal vitality of
a young man in an electric chair (Killer's Head) ignores and postpones the inevitable with talk
of trucks, rodeos, distances, racing, breeding. Disorganizing-discovering voices often surprise
the speaker. The seventh son of "Holy Ghostly" leads his father through ancient-modern
myths and shamanisms to embrace his own dying. Their languages slip one to another, and
roles slide and erode identities.

In the brilliant, extended battle of words and musical movement of The Tooth of Crime,
Hoss's original, characterizing virtuosity falls to the power-stealing dazzle of Crow's
mimicry. The art-and-power theme – begun in Cowboy Mouth and Melodrama Play, toyed
with in Mad Dog Blues – finally bleeds through its images. Angel City explores the same
theme with movies, instead of pop-rock. Indian magic reinforces its artists' mystery
(intuition-inspiration) until the ultimate disaster film engulfs the audience too: "Even chaos
has a form!" Geography of a Horse Dreamer charts the broken flow of inspiration through
race-track and criminal images, until brothers' shotguns save the dreamer's magic neckbone
from falling into a medicine bundle. Primitive magic that decorates the matched panels of
punning La Turista is the overwhelming ground of power in Operation Sidewinder, Holy
Ghostly, and Back Bog Beast, but it becomes a dangerous net-below in these later, and better,
plays. Rituals cannot prevent the sale and destruction of a California family and farm in

Curse of the Starving Class. Man is caught but falls through the magic charts or totems. Keeping Shepard's special coherence, *Action* and *Curse* somehow make his notoriously bizarre images, arias, and rituals feel inevitable as Russian realism.

This prolific young playwright knowingly freshens the conventions, terror, and pleasure essential to theatre.

—John G. Kuhn

SHERRIFF, R(obert) C(harles).   English.   Born in Kingston upon Thames, Surrey, 6 June 1896. Educated at Kingston Grammar School; New College, Oxford, 1931–34. Served as a Captain in the East Surrey Regiment, 1917. Entered the Sun Insurance Company, 1914. Fellow, Society of Antiquaries; Fellow, Royal Society of Literature. *Died 13 November 1975.*

PUBLICATIONS

Plays

> *Profit and Loss* (produced 1923).
> *Cornlow-in-the-Downs* (produced 1923).
> *Badger's Green* (as *Mr. Birdie's Finger,* produced 1926; revised version, as *Badger's Green*, produced 1930).   1930.
> *Journey's End* (produced 1928).   1929.
> *Windfall* (produced 1934).
> *St. Helena,* with Jeanne de Casalis (produced 1936).   1934.
> *Two Hearts Doubled: A Playlet.*   1934.
> *Goodbye Mr. Chips* (screenplay), with Claudine West and Eric Maschwitz, in *The Best Pictures 1939–1940,* edited by Jerry Wald and Richard Macaulay.   1940.
> *Mrs. Miniver* (screenplay), with others, in *Twenty Best Film Plays,* edited by John Gassner and Dudley Nichols.   1943.
> *Miss Mabel* (produced 1948).   1949.
> *Quartet: Stories by W. Somerset Maugham, Screenplays by Sherriff.*   1948.
> *Trio: Stories and Screen Adaptations,* with W. Somerset Maugham and Noel Langley.   1950.
> *Odd Man Out* (screenplay) with F. L. Green, in *Three British Screen Plays,* edited by Roger Manvell.   1950.
> *Home at Seven* (produced 1950).   1950.
> *The Kite,* in *Action: Beacon Lights of Literature,* edited by Georgia G. Winn and others.   1952.
> *The White Carnation* (produced 1953).   1953.
> *The Long Sunset* (broadcast 1955; produced 1955).   In *Plays of the Year 12,* 1956.
> *The Telescope* (broadcast 1956; produced 1957).   1957.
> *A Shred of Evidence* (produced 1960).   1961.

Screenplays: *The Invisible Man,* 1933; *The Road Back,* with Charles Kenyon, 1937; *Goodbye Mr. Chips,* with Claudine West and Eric Maschwitz, 1939; *The Four Feathers,*

with Arthur Wimperis and Lajos Biro, 1939; *That Hamilton Woman* (*Lady Hamilton*),
with Walter Reisch, 1941; *Unholy Partners,* with others, 1941; *This Above All,* 1942;
Mrs. Miniver, with others, 1942; *Stand By for Action,* with others, 1943; *Forever and a
Day,* with others, 1944; *Odd Man Out,* with F. L. Green, 1947; *Quartet,* 1948; *Mr.
Know-All* (in *Trio*), 1950; *No Highway* (*No Highway in the Sky*), with Alec Coppel and
Oscar Millard, 1951; *The Dam Busters,* 1955; *The Night My Number Came Up,* 1955;
Storm over the Nile, with Lajos Biro and Arthur Wimperis, 1955.

Radio Plays: *The Long Sunset,* 1955; *The Night My Number Came Up,* 1956; *The
Telescope,* 1956; *Cards with Uncle Tom,* 1958.

Television Play: *The Ogburn Story,* 1963.

Fiction

Journey's End, with Vernon Bartlett.   1930.
The Fortnight in September.   1931.
Greengates.   1936.
The Hopkins Manuscript.   1939; revised edition, as *The Cataclysm,* 1958.
Chedworth.   1944.
Another Year.   1948.
The Wells of St. Mary's.   1962.

Other

King John's Treasure: An Adventure Story (juvenile).   1954.
No Leading Lady: An Autobiography.   1968.
The Siege of Swayne Castle (juvenile).   1973.

*   *   *

R. C. Sherriff has been an excellent and prolific screenwriter. Among his first-rate or even
classic films have been *The Invisible Man, Goodbye Mr. Chips, Lady Hamilton* (*That Hamilton
Woman*), *Odd Man Out, Quartet,* and *The Dam Busters.* These and many other cinema
achievements and his fiction are all discussed in his readable autobiography, *No Leading
Lady.* But Sherriff is chiefly known as a playwright, and that for only one of his plays, the
first that took him from amateur theatricals (*Profit and Loss, Mr. Birdie's Finger*) to London.
That is the war drama set in a dugout under fire at St. Quentin in World War I, *Journey's
End.*

Journey's End is a very sentimental play, more sentimental than *What Price Glory?,
Sergeant York,* or *All Quiet on the Western Front,* so (since men tend to be more sentimental
than women, at least when it comes to war) let us quote a couple of women on the subject of
the play's rather unthinking acceptance of sentiment and slaughter. First, Anita Block in *The
Changing World in Plays and Theatre* (1939): "I freely admit all its fine qualities, but it is
important for us to understand that *Journey's End* is an old-fashioned play exhibiting the
time-honored ambivalent emotions of loathing war's cruelty while glorifying its victims as
heroes.... The audience leaves the theatre weeping for dead heroes, but without a single
clarifying or provocative idea on the subject of war." Albert Hunt (*Encore,* December 1959) is
only one of the many who have noted in *Journey's End* "an acceptance of the values that
make war possible."

Dame Rebecca West (in *Ending in Earnest,* 1931) finds *Journey's End* "enormously
impressive and stirring" but also "neurotic" in its inspiration:

To begin with, it is one more expression of the desperate infantilism characteristic of the modern young Englishman. I do not mean by that to quarrel with his emphasis on the tragedy of murdered youth which was the war's foulest offence, for that is legitimate and most beautifully contrived ... but one is disquieted by Mr. Sherriff's assumption that immaturity is the most important phase of existence. The older men in the play are represented as being not only protective to the boys, but deferential to them, as to people of obviously greater importance....

The significance of this can be seen when one considers that there have been three first-rate plays written by young Englishmen since the war – *Prisoners of War*, by J. R. Ackerley; *Young Woodley*, by John Van Druten; and this *Journey's End*; and they all have this obsession with immaturity....

Chambers' Biographical Dictionary puts it succinctly when it notes that Sherriff "achieved an international reputation" with his first play, *Journey's End* but "later plays did not match up to his first." Still, one play as famous as *Journey's End* is no mean achievement and perhaps someday Sherriff's considerable gifts as a screenwriter will be studied.

—Leonard R. N. Ashley

SHERWOOD, Robert E(mmet).   American.   Born in New Rochelle, New York, 4 April 1896. Educated at Milton Academy, Massachusetts, 1909–14; Harvard University, Cambridge, Massachusetts, 1914–17, B.A. 1918. Served in the Canadian Black Watch, 1917–19: wounded in action, 1918; served as Special Assistant to the Secretary of War, Washington, D.C., 1939–42; Director, Overseas Branch, Office of War Information, 1942–44; Special Assistant to the Secretary of the Navy, Washington, D.C., 1945. Married 1) Mary Brandon in 1922 (divorced, 1934), one daughter; 2) Madeline Hurlock Connelly in 1935. Dramatic Editor, *Vanity Fair*, New York, 1919–20; Film Reviewer and Associate Editor, 1920–24, and Editor, 1924–28, *Life* magazine, New York; Literary Editor of *Scribner's Magazine*, New York, 1928–30; full-time playwright from 1930; Founder, with Elmer Rice, Sidney Howard, Maxwell Anderson, S. N. Behrman, and John F. Wharton, Playwrights Company, 1938. Secretary, 1935, and President, 1937–40, Dramatists Guild; President, American National Theatre and Academy, 1940. Recipient: Megrue Prize, 1932; Pulitzer Prize, 1936, 1939, 1941, and, for biography, 1949; American Academy of Arts and Letters Gold Medal, 1941; Academy Award, 1946; Bancroft Prize, for history, 1949; Gutenberg Award, 1949. D.Litt.: Dartmouth College, Hanover, New Hampshire, 1940; Yale University, New Haven, Connecticut, 1941; Harvard University, 1949; D.C.L.: Bishop's University, Lennoxville, Quebec, 1950. *Died 14 November 1955.*

PUBLICATIONS

Plays

The Road to Rome (produced 1926).   1927.
The Love Nest (produced 1927).
The Queen's Husband (produced 1928).   1928.

Waterloo Bridge (produced 1929). 1930.
This Is New York (produced 1930). 1931.
Reunion in Vienna (produced 1931). 1932.
Acropolis (produced 1933).
The Petrified Forest (produced 1935). 1935.
Idiot's Delight (produced 1936). 1936.
The Ghost Goes West (screenplay), with Geoffrey Kerr, in *Successful Film Writing* by Seton Margrave. 1936.
Tovarich, from a play by Jacques Deval (produced 1936). 1937.
The Adventures of Marco Polo (screenplay), in *How to Write and Sell Film Stories* by Frances Marion. 1937.
Abe Lincoln in Illinois (produced 1938). 1939.
There Shall Be No Night (produced 1940). 1940.
An American Crusader (broadcast 1941). In *The Free Company Presents*, edited by James Boyd, 1941.
Rebecca (screenplay), with others, in *Twenty Best Film Plays*, edited by John Gassner and Dudley Nichols. 1943.
The Rugged Path (produced 1945). Shortened version in *The Best Plays of 1945–46*, edited by Burns Mantle, 1946.
Miss Liberty, music by Irving Berlin (produced 1949). 1949.
Second Threshold, from a play by Philip Barry (produced 1951).
Small War on Murray Hill (produced 1957). 1957.

Screenplays: *The Lucky Lady,* with James T. O'Donohoe and Bertram Bloch, 1926; *Oh, What a Nurse!,* with Bertram Bloch and Daryl F. Zanuck, 1926; *Age for Love,* 1931; *Around the World in Eighty Minutes with Douglas Fairbanks,* 1931; *Cock of the Air,* with Charles Lederer, 1932; *Roman Scandal,* with George S. Kaufman, 1933; *The Scarlet Pimpernel,* with others, 1935; *The Ghost Goes West,* with Geoffrey Kerr, 1936; *Over the Moon,* with others, 1937; *Thunder in the City,* with others, 1937; *The Adventures of Marco Polo,* 1938; *The Divorce of Lady X,* with Lajos Biro, 1938; *Idiot's Delight,* 1939; *Abe Lincoln in Illinois,* 1940; *Rebecca,* with others, 1940; *The Best Years of Our Lives,* 1946; *The Bishop's Wife,* with Leonardo Bercovici, 1947; *Man on a Tightrope,* 1953; *Main Street to Broadway,* with Samson Raphaelson, 1953.

Radio Play: *An American Crusader,* 1941.

Television Writing: *The Backbone of America,* 1954.

Fiction

The Virtuous Knight. 1931; as *Unending Crusade,* 1932.

Other

Roosevelt and Hopkins: An Intimate History. 1948; revised edition, 1950; as *The White House Papers of Harry L. Hopkins,* 2 vols., 1948–49.

Editor, *The Best Moving Pictures of 1922–23.* 1923.

Reading List: *Sherwood* by R. Baird Shuman, 1964; *The Worlds of Sherwood: Mirror to His Times 1896–1939,* 1965, and *The Ordeal of a Playwright: Sherwood and the Challenge of*

War, edited by Norman Cousins, 1970, both by John Mason Brown; *Sherwood: Reluctant Moralist* by Walter J. Meserve, 1970.

*   *   *

Though of a generation very often described as "rootless" and "lost," Robert Sherwood was a romantic idealist with a liberal outlook whose plays closely corroborated the assumptions underlying the political philosophy of the Roosevelt administration and gave them powerful artistic expression. Alive to the need of creating an art imbued with a social and moral fervour, he believed that the one determining consideration for the future of the theatre was "its ability to give its audiences something they can't obtain, more cheaply and conveniently, in the neighbouring cinema palaces." The artist's lack of social purpose, he pointed out in his address to the P.E.N. International Congress in 1950, gave him a guilty sense of inadequacy – the uneasy knowledge that reform, though needed, was not taking place. The supreme task of "all writers, young and old" was, therefore, to achieve a reconciliation of the "problems of the human heart with a world state of mind that appears to become increasingly inhuman."

Sherwood's anxious apprehension of the insidious threats posed by a world situation indifferent to finer human sentiments constitutes a dominant resonance of his dramatic art. His realistic problem plays – whether set in Finland under Russian attack (*There Shall Be No Night*), or in a hotel in the Alps (*Idiot's Delight*) or in a gasoline station and lunch room in the Arizona desert (*The Petrified Forest*) – often relied on an extreme situation, a background of war or violence, to highlight his protagonists' search for viable ethical values and their eventual affirmation of freedom and peace. Sherwood's pacifism, though closely attuned to the feeling of liberals during the Roosevelt era, was never parochial or chauvinistic and displayed dynamic, even militant, modulations of growth over the years. If his first play, *The Road to Rome*, dealing comically with Hannibal's decision to defer his march on Rome, represents a plea for absolute peace, his last important play, *There Shall Be No Night*, is characterised by the realisation that freedom has to be defended even at the cost of endangering peace temporarily. In fighting the Russians in Finland, the scientist-protagonist of *There Shall Be No Night*, therefore, fights for the emancipation of all men from oppression and unfreedom. Likewise, *The Rugged Path* can be read, at one level, as an idealist's resolve to join the war in defence of peace and human dignity.

Several of Sherwood's plays exemplify his belief that the ability to make personal sacrifice is an index of moral refinement. Sacrifice appears, in *The Petrified Forest*, as a necessary means of preventing Nature from "taking the world away from the intellectuals and giving it back to the apes." On the other hand, *Abe Lincoln in Illinois*, chronicling Lincoln's struggling years before his election to the presidency, sensitively focuses on the relationship between an individual's sacrifice and national interest. Returning to the same moral issue, *There Shall Be No Night* implies through the fate of its protagonist that "There is no coming to consciousness without pain."

Sherwood's moral bias often made him vulnerable to the charge of overt didacticism – and not without some justification. As one who always had his fingertips on the pulse of his age and depended securely on its grammar of assent, Sherwood, in a literary career spanning nearly three decades, rarely suggested new and daring departures from the opinions current in his milieu. As a result, the moralistic intentions of his plays tended to be so static that their appeal rarely extended beyond their topical issues. But it must also be recognized that his didacticism very often went beyond direct statements to become an integral aspect of dramatic form. In *Abe Lincoln in Illinois*, for example, the curtain is meant to drop just as the farewell crowd, which has been singing "John Brown's Body," reaches the line "His soul goes marching on." Also, his frequent use of comedy, as in *The Road to Rome* and *The Queen's Husband*, helped substantially in relieving the solemnity of potentially moralistic themes. Moreover, one sign of "health" that critics always detected in Sherwood was that his ironic consciousness did not overlook the flaws in his own plays and made him record them with rare candour and precision. To cite one instance, he found *The Road to Rome* defective, because it employed "the cheapest sort of device – making historical characters use modern slang."

Sherwood also experimented with several other kinds of writing, achieving mixed results. *The Virtuous Knight*, his early historic novel about the Third Crusade, was generally regarded as a failure, though its perusal in retrospect does provide useful insights into his treatment of the themes and techniques of character-delineation that were to be employed later in his plays. His scenario *The Best Years of Our Lives* won an Academy Award in 1946, but his TV show, *The Backbone of America* , produced a year before his death, turned out to be a dismal flop. The crowning success of his non-dramatic writing was his biography *Roosevelt and Hopkins*, based on his experience as special assistant to the Secretary of War, director of the Overseas Branch of the Office of War Information, and, more important, as Roosevelt's favourite speechwriter and unofficial adviser. The book, ranked among the finest histories of World War II written in the United States, received several awards.

In spite of his immense popular appeal in his own lifetime, Sherwood does not belong to the same class of playwrights as Eugene O'Neill, Arthur Miller, and Tennessee Williams. For this reason, as time passes, his plays are unlikely to be received witthe same immediacy they once elicited. Still, there can be no denying that his realistic problem plays, inspirited as they were by his passion for freedom and peace, faithfully reflected the urges and anxieties of the American people and, in the attempt, made a significant contribution to American drama in the 1920's and 1930's.

—Chirantan Kulshrestha

SIMPSON, N(orman) F(rederick). English. Born in London, 29 January 1919. Educated at Emanuel School, London, 1930–37; Birkbeck College, University of London, 1950–54, B.A. (honours) 1954. Served in the Royal Artillery, 1941–43, and the Intelligence Corps, 1943–46. Married Joyce Bartlett in 1944; one child. Teacher, City of Westminster College, London, and extra-mural lecturer, 1946–62. Full-time playwright since 1963. Since 1976, Literary Manager of the Royal Court Theatre, London. Lives in London.

PUBLICATIONS

Plays

    A Resounding Tinkle (produced 1957).   In *The Observer Plays*, 1958; shortened version
       included in *The Hole and Other Plays and Sketches*, 1964.
    The Hole (produced 1958).   1958.
    One Way Pendulum (produced 1959).   1960.
    Sketches in *One to Another* (produced 1959).   1960.
    Sketches in *You, Me and the Gatepost* (produced 1960).
    Sketches in *On the Avenue* (produced 1961).
    Sketches in *One over the Eight* (produced 1961).
    The Form (produced 1961).   1961.
    Oh (produced 1961).   In *The Hole and Other Plays and Sketches*, 1964.

The Hole and Other Plays and Sketches (includes shortened version of *A Resounding Tinkle, The Form, Gladly Otherwise, Oh, One Blast and Have Done*). 1964.

The Cresta Run (produced 1965). 1966.

We're Due in Eastbourne in Ten Minutes (televised, 1967; produced 1971). In *Some Tall Tinkles*, 1968.

Some Tall Tinkles: Television Plays (includes *We're Due in Eastbourne in Ten Minutes, The Best I Can Do by Way of a Gate-Leg Table Is a Hundredweight of Coal, At Least It's a Precaution Against Fire*). 1968.

Playback 625, with Leopoldo Maler (produced 1970).

How Are Your Handles? (includes *Gladly Otherwise, Oh, The Other Side of London*) (produced 1971).

Was He Anyone? (produced 1972). 1973.

In Reasonable Shape (produced 1977). In *Play Ten: Ten Short Plays*, edited by Robin Rook, 1977.

Anyone's Gums Can Listen to Reason, in *Play Ten: Ten Short Plays*, edited by Robin Rook. 1977.

Screenplays: *One Way Pendulum*, 1964; *Diamonds for Breakfast*, with Pierre Rouve and Ronald Harwood, 1968.

Radio Plays: *Something Rather Effective*, 1972; *Sketches for Radio*, 1974.

Television Plays: *Make a Man*, 1966; *Three Rousing Tinkles* series: *The Father by Adoption of One of the Former Marquis of Rangoon's Natural Granddaughters, If Those Are Mr. Heckmondwick's Own Personal Pipes They've Been Lagged Once Already*, and *The Best I Can Do by Way of a Gate-Leg Table Is a Hundredweight of Coal*, 1966; *Four Tall Tinkles* series: *We're Due in Eastbourne in Ten Minutes, In a Punt with Friends Under a Haystack on the River Mersey, A Row of Potted Plants*, and *At Least It's a Precaution Against Fire*, 1967; *World in Ferment* series, 1969; *Charley's Grants* series, 1970; *Thank You Very Much*, 1971; *Elementary, My Dear Watson*, 1973; *Silver Wedding*, 1974; *An Upward Fall* (*Crown Court* series), 1977.

Fiction

Harry Bleachbaker. 1976; as *Man Overboard: A Testimonial to the High Art of Incompetence*, 1976.

Reading List: *Curtains* by Kenneth Tynan, 1961; *The Theatre of the Absurd* by Martin Esslin, 1961; *Dramatic Essays* by Nigel Dennis, 1962.

*   *   *

Although a coincidence of chronology tempted critics to pigeonhole N. F. Simpson alongside the dramatists of the absurd, his is a very English style of humour. His sense of man's sublime dependence on the inanimate owes more to Jerome K. Jerome and the early Paul Jennings than to Ionesco, and his plays keep company with Lewis Carroll in their plunges along the Möbius slopes of language, when language gets slightly out of phase with conventional logic.

Simpson's is a world in which effects tend to anticipate their causes. In *One Way Pendulum*, Kirby Groomkirby is thus a multiple murderer because he has a passion for wearing black, and so craves the instant kick of attending funerals. Indeed, he only finds himself on trial because his father has built a courtroom from a do-it-yourself kit in his front parlour, and its presence calls irresistibly for a trial. But this is no Kafkaesque affair: in spite of the damning evidence that not one of Kirby's victims is willing to speak in his defence, he is discharged, and his choir of speak-your-weight machines celebrates the event with a renewed attempt at the Hallelujah Chorus.

One Way Pendulum is the most successful of Simpson's stage plays because it never stretches its ideas too thin. *The Cresta Run* has moments of sublime lunacy, but the tenuous consistency of its "plot" actually weakens its impact – as if a throwaway comic were to attempt an extended monologue. For Simpson has been at his happiest at his most episodic – notably, in the succession of parodic sketches (including a climactic gathering of "The Critics") which added up to *A Resounding Tinkle*. In recent years he has thus tended to concentrate on work for television, and has succeeded in finding visual equivalents to those deftly deflected verbal transitions for which he was surely indebted to that vintage radio comedy, *The Goon Show*.

Thus, critics who have noted a certain pedantry in his humour may only be discerning the inherently more mechanical nature of anarchic comedy in live performance, the resources of the tape and video recorder perhaps offering fuller scope for Simpson's genius. So little comic innovation is there in the broadcasting media that it has to be stressed that this judgement is an attempt to define his art, not to diminish it: the relative infrequency of new work from him in recent years would certainly suggest a writer not quite certain that he has yet found his true medium.

—Simon Trussler

SOYINKA, Wole (Akinwande Oluwole Soyinka). Nigerian. Born in Abeokuta, Western Nigeria, 13 July 1934. Educated at the Government College, Ibadan; University of Leeds, Yorkshire, 1954–57, B.A. (honours) in English. Married; one son and three daughters. Play Reader, Royal Court Theatre, London, 1958–59; Research Fellow in Drama, University of Ibadan, 1960–61; Lecturer in English, University of Ife, 1962–63; Senior Lecturer in English, University of Lagos, 1964–67; Political Prisoner, for alleged pro-Biafra activities, Kaduna Prison, 1967–69; Director of the School of Drama, University of Ibadan, 1969–72. Research Professor in Drama, 1972–75, and since 1975 Professor of Comparative Literature, University of Ife. Founding Director of the Orisun Theatre and The 1960 Masks Theatre, Lagos and Ibadan. Recipient: Dakar Negro Arts Festival award, 1966; John Whiting Award, 1966. D.Litt.: University of Leeds, 1973. Lives in Nigeria.

PUBLICATIONS

Plays

    The Swamp Dwellers (produced 1958). In *Three Plays,* 1963.
    The Lion and the Jewel (produced 1959). 1963.
    The Invention (produced 1959).
    A Dance of the Forests (produced 1960). 1963.
    The Trial of Brother Jero (produced 1960). In *Three Plays,* 1963.
    Camwood on the Leaves (broadcast 1960). 1973.

Three Plays.   1963.
The Strong Breed (produced 1964).   In *Three Plays,* 1963.
Kongi's Harvest (produced 1964).   1967.
Before the Blackout (produced 1964).   N.d. (1965?).
The Road (produced 1965).   1965.
Madmen and Specialists (produced 1970; revised version, produced 1971).   1971.
The Jero Plays: The Trials of Brother Jero and Jero's Metamorphosis.   1973.
The Bacchae: A Communion Rite, from the play by Euripides (produced 1973).   1973.
Collected Plays:
   I. *A Dance of the Forests, The Swamp Dwellers, The Strong Breed, The Road, The Bacchae.*   1973.
   II. *The Lion and the Jewel, Kongi's Harvest, The Trials of Brother Jero, Jero's Metamorphosis, Madmen and Specialists.*   1974.
Death and the King's Horseman.   1975.

Screenplay: *Kongi's Harvest,* 1970.

Radio Play: *Camwood on the Leaves,* 1960.

Television Documentaries: *Joshua: A Nigerian Portrait,* 1962; *Culture in Transition,* 1963.

Fiction

The Interpreters.   1965.
Season of Anomy.   1973.

Verse

Idanre and Other Poems.   1967.
Poems from Prison.   1969.
A Shuttle in the Crypt.   1972.
Ogun Abibiman.   1977.

Other

The Man Died: Prison Notes.   1972.
In Person: Achebe, Awooner, and Soyinka at the University of Washington.   1975.
Myth, Literature, and the African World.   1976.

Editor, *Poems of Black Africa.*   1975.

Translator, *The Forest of a Thousand Daemons: A Hunter's Saga,* by D. A. Fagunwa.   1968.

Reading List: *Mother Is Gold: A Study in West African Literature* by A. Roscoe, 1971; *Soyinka* by Gerald H. Moore, 1971, revised edition, 1978; *The Writing of Soyinka* by Eldred D. Jones, 1973; *The Movement of Transition: A Study of the Plays of Soyinka* by Oyin Ogunba, 1975.

*   *   *

Wole Soyinka is not only Nigeria's leading playwright but possibly the most versatile writer at work in Africa today, having also excelled as a poet, novelist, essayist, critic, editor, and translator. Born in 1934, Soyinka was educated in Ibadan and Leeds. On his return to Nigeria in 1960, after nearly six years in Europe (one result of which was the much-anthologised poem "Telephone Conversation," in which he wittily sums up on the racial prejudice of English landladies), Soyinka was appointed to a number of university posts. These afforded him, particularly at Ibadan and Ife, the chance to produce his own plays, sometimes acting in them himself. He also worked for Nigerian radio and television, and formed an acting company in Lagos called The 1960 Masks. Soyinka was arrested by the Federal Government in 1967 for alleged pro-Biafran activity. The result of his experiences in solitary confinement at Kaduna Prison are recorded with great bitterness in *The Man Died*, a set of prison notes which make little attempt to enter the fashionable spirit of magnanimity which followed the Federal victory.

Soyinka's early work as a dramatist showed his skill as a comic writer. In both *The Swamp Dwellers* and *The Lion and the Jewel* he deals with traditional village life, but in the second he is already experimenting with mime and dance elements as an integral part of the comedy.

Soyinka's plays have subsequently become more technically daring. In *A Dance of the Forests*, his highly ambiguous celebration of Nigerian independence, the mortal world and the divine are brought into conjunction in a half-satirical, half-fantastic blend of traditional Yoruba imagery, dance motifs, and masque. Soyinka has written ironic comedies like his Jero plays, where the main character is a charlatan preacher all too easily exploiting the gullibility of his fellow countrymen, but his most significant dramatic work in recent years is probably *Madmen and Specialists*. This play arises from the mood of war, and the aftermath of war, but the form it takes shows the influence of experimental drama in America (where an early version was first staged) and Europe. Recent work, such as *Death and the King's Horseman* and his new version of *The Bacchae* of Euripides, commissioned for performance by the National Theatre in London, show a growing concern to relate African experience with European.

Soyinka has always tried to express a broad humanity in his work which will not be narrowly nationalistic. Many of his cultural principals are set out in an illuminating critical book, *Myth, Literature, and the African World*. Here he admits a recognizable distinction between African and European aesthetics but believes that they should not operate in isolation from each other.

As a novelist Soyinka has been the subject of some controversy. *The Interpreters* has probably gained in reputation in recent years as African fiction in English has faced up to more contemporaneous themes and more complex relationships. The book concerns a group of young Nigerian intellectuals, capturing, largely through dialogue, their idealism and anticipation about the development of the new Africa. *Season of Anomy* may seem to possess a Joycean difficulty of presentation, but it corresponds to *Madmen and Specialists* in its attempts to make sense of the recent devastations of war. The publisher's description is apt – "an expression of the affirmative, humane response to chaos and blind social forces." Soyinka has also translated *The Forest of a Thousand Daemons*, a Yoruba novel by D. O. Fagunwa. The folk and fantasy material with which it deals has often been reflected in Soyinka's plays.

Idanre and *A Shuttle in the Crypt* are two collections of verse, written over several years. The tone of the second collection is even bleaker than the first, distilling not just the horror and pity of war but the sterility of modern politics:

> They do not bleed
> On whom the dunghill falls, nor they
> Whose bones are sucked of marrow
> In noon perversions of inhuman tongues.
> They do not bleed whose breaths are stilled
> In sludges or sewers, who slither down
> To death on the burst tumour of hate's

Inventive mind, through chasms of the flight
Of earth from rites of defilement,
Dark of abomination. They do not bleed
Whose wombs are bared to leprous lust

This extract from the long poem "Conversation at Night with a Cockroach" captures the morbid pessimism out of which Soyinka is only just beginning to emerge through the affirmative quality of works like *Season of Anomy*.

—Alastair Niven

STEWART, Douglas (Alexander).   Australian.   Born in Eltham, New Zealand, 6 May 1913. Educated at New Plymouth Boys High School; Victoria University College, Wellington. Married Margaret Coen in 1946; one daughter. Literary Editor, *The Bulletin*, Sydney, 1940–61; Literary Advisor, Angus and Robertson Ltd., publishers, Sydney, 1961–73. Recipient: *Encyclopaedia Britannica* Award, 1968; Wilke Award, for non-fiction, 1975. O.B.E. (Officer, Order of the British Empire). Lives in Sydney.

PUBLICATIONS

Plays

　　Ned Kelly (produced 1944).   1943.
　　The Fire on the Snow and The Golden Lover: Two Plays for Radio.   1944.
　　Shipwreck (produced 1948).   1947.
　　Four Plays (includes *The Fire on the Snow, The Golden Lover, Ned Kelly, Shipwreck*).   1958.
　　Fisher's Ghost: The Historical Comedy (produced 1961).   1960.

　　Radio Plays: *The Fire on the Snow*, 1941; *The Golden Lover*, 1943; *The Earthquake Shakes the Land*, 1944.

Fiction

　　A Girl with Red Hair and Other Stories.   1944.

Verse

　　Green Lions.   1937.
　　The White Cry.   1939.
　　Elegy for an Airman.   1940.
　　Sonnets to the Unknown Soldier.   1941.
　　The Dosser in Springtime.   1946.

Glencoe. 1947.
Sun Orchids. 1952.
The Birdsville Track and Other Poems. 1955.
Rutherford and Other Poems. 1962.
The Garden of Ships: A Poem. 1962.
(Poems). 1963; as *Selected Poems*, 1969, 1973.
Collected Poems, 1936–1967. 1967.

Other

The Flesh and the Spirit: An Outlook on Literature. 1948.
The Seven Rivers (on angling). 1966.
The Broad Stream (criticism). 1975.
Norman Lindsay: A Personal Memoir. 1975.

Editor, *Coast to Coast: Australian Stories.* 1945.
Editor, with Nancy Keesing, *Australian Bush Ballads.* 1955.
Editor, with Nancy Keesing, *Old Bush Songs and Rhymes of Colonial Times, Enlarged and Revised from the Collection by A. B. Paterson.* 1957.
Editor, *Voyager Poems.* 1960.
Editor, *The Book of Bellerive,* by Joseph Tischler. 1961.
Editor, *(Poems),* by A. D. Hope. 1963.
Editor, *Modern Australian Verse: Poetry in Australia II.* 1964.
Editor, *Selected Poems,* by Hugh McCrae. 1966.
Editor, *Short Stories of Australia: The Lawson Tradition.* 1967.
Editor, with Nancy Keesing, *The Pacific Book of Bush Ballads.* 1967.
Editor, with Nancy Keesing, *Bush Songs, Ballads, and Other Verse.* 1968.
Editor, with Beatrice Davis, *Best Australian Short Stories.* 1971.
Editor, *The Wide Brown Land: A New Selection of Australian Verse.* 1971.
Editor, *Australia Fair.* 1976.

Reading List: *Stewart* by Nancy Keesing, 1965; *Stewart* by Clement Semmler, 1975.

*   *   *

Douglas Stewart is one of the most prolific and versatile of Australian writers. Well-known as a poet and radio playwright, he has also written short stories, essays, and biography. His account of the Sydney *Bulletin*, whose Red Page he edited from 1940 to 1960, is lively, informative, and graceful, and an important contribution to local literary history.

Stewart's *Collected Poems* assembled the best of his verse from 1936 onwards, and included some not before published in book-form. Though he is a New Zealander by birth, few native Australians have developed Stewart's feeling for Australian landscape and animal life. His relationship with the natural world has been in turns egocentric, anthropomorphic, even animistic, but in the later poems it has become fraternal and non-attached. Where once he would have wished an insect to look at the world as a man would, he now tries to see the world, not merely as an insect would see it, which would be affectation, but through the eyes of an insect without surrendering the vision of a man. Courtesy is what distinguishes Stewart's atttitude to the non-human world, and the reserve which is part of his own nature is scrupulously respected in other creatures, as the volume *Sun Orchids* makes clear. The mood of his verse is primarily one of good humour and well-being, and, in a darkening world living on the edge of a balance of terror, such a mood strikes many readers as superficial and evasive. The long narrative poem *Rutherford* wrongly attributes to Rutherford misgivings about the outcome of his researches, and in spite of some fine passages, it never really comes to grip with the central moral problem of post-Baconian science, while the weight of the verse suggests that the author shares the fuzzy optimism of his hero. Against this, however, should be set the magnificent ballad-sequence, *Glencoe*, with its fine structural coherence, its dramatic appropriateness and the timeless urgency of its theme: the wanton spirit of senseless faction in mankind which guarantees the suffering of the innocent. The main part of the sequence ends with one of Stewart's finest lyrics, the lament "Sigh, wind in the pine," with its grim warning:

> Oh life is fierce and wild
> And the heart of the earth is stone,
> And the hand of a murdered child
> Will not bear thinking on.
>
> Sigh, wind in the pine,
> Cover it over with snow;
> But terrible things were done
> Long, long ago.

The poem was written not long after another massacre: Hiroshima.

Those who deny Stewart the capacity for reflection must take *Glencoe* into account. They must also consider that his reflective exercises are as a rule conducted far below the surface of his poems, as the early poem "The River" makes plain: what he sees he has no objection to sharing, what he really thinks or feels, he seems to regard as largely his own business. His principal gift as a poet is the ability to transfigure the commonplace, to catch a moment of heightened experience and endow it with a history. The facility with which he seizes the poetic moment has sometimes led him into verbosity through over-exercise, and in some of his occasional verse there is a sense of strain. At times indeed he can degenerate into producing a kind of poetic "chirruping." Stewart's preoccupation with an immediate moment of intense awareness has tended to obscure the metaphysical base from which he works, expressed in paradoxical images of fire and snow, heat and cold, which perhaps hint at a struggle between the rational and the irrational in his own nature. Flame and snow come together in his earliest poem "Day and Night with Snow" and in the latest piece in *Collected Poems*, "Flowering Place," while variants of the same image crop up throughout the work, in "Spider Gums," from *The Birdsville Track*; in "The River," from *The Dosser in Springtime*; and in "Flower of Winter," from *Sun Orchids*. There is nothing static about this symbolism: fire is as much an image of destruction as it is of the continuity of life; snow, cold, as much an image of potentiality, of steadfastness, as of death. His grasp of this archetypal imagery seems to be intuitional rather than intellectual, but for a lyrist, this is hardly a disadvantage. The lack of intellectual rigour however becomes something of an obstacle in his prose work, especially in the literary criticism, in spite of its general good sense. His criticism, in *The Flesh and the Spirit* and *The Broad Stream*, belongs to the same impressionistic genre, without being as captious or exhibitionist, as that of his more famous predecessor on the *Bulletin* A. G. Stephens. It is intuitional, idiosyncratic, intensely subjective, capable of crystallising the essentials of a work under scrutiny, but liable to the temptations of the large, arresting generalisation, which will not stand up to close analysis because it takes little account of what is extra-literary. It is never dull, always stimulating, often prejudiced, on occasions brilliant, and like much of the verse, often humorous.

Stewart's plays, written mainly for radio and all in verse, are strangely static: there is a much more genuinely dramatic element in the *Glencoe* ballads, or the poem "Terra Australis" than in *Fire on the Snow* or *Ned Kelly*. It is odd, for instance, that a dramatist should always choose situations which involve the characters in so much merely waiting around and talking. *Fire on the Snow*, about Scott's last expedition, unlike *Ned Kelly* and *Shipwreck*, is in addition devoid of human conflict; the enemy is nature, and endurance the only possible response. Written for radio, it is not a play for theatre at all; and even *Ned Kelly*, which lends itself more easily to the stage, almost founders from excessive verbalisation. *Shipwreck* is a more shapely drama, in which the tendency to lyric expansion is kept under control. Even so, there is too much reliance at certain points on clumsy reporting of off-stage events. This play, however, is securely founded on a real moral conflict: whether a captain is justified in making a dangerous journey to bring help to his shipwrecked crew and passengers, when he must leave them on the verge of mutiny under precarious control. *Shipwreck* is perhaps the strongest and most interesting of Stewart's plays, though not the most endearing. *The Golden Lover*, on a New Zealand theme, is that. It dramatises the difficulty of choosing between dream and reality, between unearthly, intense love, and domestic security; and in the Maori girl Tawhai, her lumpish husband Ruarangi, and Whana, the "golden lover" from the People of the Mist, Stewart has succeeded in creating three of his most convincing characters. As with *Ned Kelly*, however, the ending is left ambiguous, or rather it seems to be ambiguous, until we reflect that the voices of commonsense have been given all the best tunes. It is difficult to avoid the conclusion, when one considers all the plays together, that the one value Stewart unequivocally endorses is sheer survival.

It is in the prose, finally, especially the biographical writing on Kenneth Slessor and Norman Lindsay, that doubts make themselves felt about Stewart's ultimate seriousness. The weight given to the superficial picturesqueness of some of the figures he admires, the flavour of old boy nostalgia for Bohemia, seem to sort ill with the realities of the life the world has known since Hiroshima. Nevertheless, it is possible that the generally light-hearted and circumspect temper of Stewart's writing may conceal a deep ineradicable pessimism, even disgust, about human nature, and that having a conviction of irremediable original sin, he has turned away to the natural world, content only with the surface pleasures of human society. Two passages in *Shipwreck* may crystallise his view of humanity; when Heynorick, the "observing" butler says suddenly, echoing Hamlet – "The appalling things that happen between sky and earth/Where the beast called man walks upright!" – and when Pelsart tells the condemned sailor: "I cannot pity you, prisoner; but, sometimes, my friends,/I am sorry for the race of men, trapped on this planet."

—Dorothy Green

STOPPARD, Tom. English. Born in Zlin, Czechoslovakia, 3 July 1937; emigrated to Singapore in 1938, and to England in 1946. Educated abroad, and at the Dolphin School, Nottinghamshire, and Pocklington School, Yorkshire. Married 1) Jose Ingle in 1965 (divorced, 1972), two sons; 2) Dr. Miriam Moore-Robinson in 1972, one son. Journalist, *Western Daily Press*, Bristol, 1954–58, and *Bristol Evening World*, 1958–60; free-lance journalist in London, 1960–63. Recipient: John Whiting Award, 1967; *Evening Standard* award, 1967, 1972, 1974; Prix Italia, 1968; Antoinette Perry Award, 1968, 1976; New York Drama Critics Circle Award, 1968, 1976. Lives in Buckinghamshire.

PUBLICATIONS

Plays

 A Walk on the Water (televised 1963; produced 1964); revised version, as *The*

Preservation of George Riley (televised 1964); as *Enter a Free Man* (produced 1968).   1968.
M Is for Moon among Other Things (broadcast 1964; produced 1977).
The Gamblers (produced 1965).
Tango, from a play by Slawomir Mrozek, translated by Nicholas Bethell (produced 1966).   1968.
A Separate Peace (televised 1966).   1978.
Rosencrantz and Guildenstern Are Dead (produced 1966; revised version, produced 1967).   1967.
Albert's Bridge (broadcast 1967; produced 1975).   In *Albert's Bridge and If You're Glad I'll Be Frank,* 1969.
The Real Inspector Hound (produced 1968).   1968.
Albert's Bridge and If You're Glad I'll Be Frank: Two Plays for Radio.   1969.
After Magritte (produced 1970).   1971.
Dogg's Our Pet (produced 1971).   In *Six of the Best,* 1976.
Jumpers (produced 1972).   1972.
The House of Bernarda Alba, from a play by Lorca (produced 1973).
Artist Descending a Staircase, and Where Are They Now? Two Plays for Radio.   1973.
Travesties (produced 1974).   1975.
Dirty Linen, and New-found-land (produced 1976).   1976.
Albert's Bridge and Other Plays.   1977.
Professional Foul (televised 1977). With *Every Good Boy Deserves Favour,* 1978.
Every Good Boy Deserves Favour, music by André Previn (produced 1977).   1978.
Night and Day (produced 1978).   1978.

Screenplays: *The Engagement,* 1969; *The Romantic Englishwoman,* 1975; *Despair,* 1978.

Radio Plays: *The Dissolution of Dominic Boot,* 1964; *M Is for Moon among Other Things,* 1964; *If You're Glad I'll Be Frank,* 1965; *Albert's Bridge,* 1967; *Where Are They Now?,* 1970; *Artist Descending a Staircase,* 1972.

Television Plays: *A Walk on the Water,* 1963 (as *The Preservation of George Riley,* 1964); *A Separate Peace,* 1966; *Teeth,* 1967; *Another Moon Called Earth,* 1967; *Neutral Ground,* 1968; *One Pair of Eyes* (documentary), 1972; *Boundaries,* with Clive Exton, 1975; *Three Men in a Boat,* from the novel by Jerome K. Jerome, 1975; *Professional Foul,* 1977.

Fiction

Lord Malquist and Mr. Moon.   1966.

Reading List: *Stoppard* by C. W. E. Bigsby, 1976; *Stoppard* by Ronald Hayman, 1977.

*   *   *

In Tom Stoppard's early and greatly successful play, *Rosencrantz and Guildenstern Are Dead,* occur examples of the habits of dramatic composition and ways of thinking that appear in all of his plays; habits of thought and dramatic conventions that are taken seriously in many quarters undergo exaggeration, with results that are disconcerting or delightful according to taste. Thus, in *Rosencrantz and Guildenstern Are Dead,* the center of the stage is occupied by Hamlet's two undependable friends, and they watch – but without much comprehension – the Elsinor events. Their paths keep making farcical contact with Hamlet's until he deserts them for their fate in England. Stoppard fashions his drama out of the contrasts between the high-flown language of Hamlet and the groping comment and search for meaning manifest in the speech of Rosencrantz and Guildenstern. For they as well as Hamlet take up the great questions. But they reduce them to triviality, and their failure suggests that Shakespeare's successes with the same questions are more apparent than real.

In other plays, Stoppard mounts dramas that are his non-involved meditations on selected pretensions from the more recent past. Characters better endowed with language than are Stoppard's Rosencrantz and Guildenstern (their language is as restricted as that of Beckett's two who wait for Godot) are harried along very complicated courses. At many points in the chase, Stoppard allows his creatures to define – to themselves and to the audience – the meaning of their flights. But the definition is always one that reaches ridiculous extremes.

The parody of *Hamlet* frees us from *Hamlet*. *The Real Inspector Hound* frees us from a lesser mistress, Agatha Christie. With amusing variations on Rosencrantz and Guildenstern watching a chain of events they can hardly understand, the watchers of the action in *The Real Inspector Hound* observe a play that *they* cannot grasp. The two doltish, pretentious drama critics earnestly discuss a vacuous modern thriller and, by its conclusion, are as much involved in its conventions as were Hamlet's two friends in his tragedy. It is as though Stoppard were saying, "A curse on all your serious dramatic intents."

Elsewhere, Stoppard's entertaining maledictions move outside the theatre itself and reject many of the serious pretensions of this century. In *Jumpers*, a grotesque plot concerning the murder of a modern philosopher unites his survivors not so much in the investigation of the crime as in extreme displays of twentieth-century British philosophical themes: proofs of the existence (or non-existence) of God; the authority (or nullity) of standards of morality and taste; the power of words themselves to represent (or misrepresent) reality. The events that precipitate such discourse are preposterous, and the characters are incredible. But the parodies and the neatly managed distortions of serious modern concerns are not. A retired musical-comedy star, her erudite husband, her sexually active analyst, and the police inspector swing like puppets in the intellectual gusts that Stoppard creates.

Two other examples will indicate how pervasive is Stoppard's habit of mind. In a play written for radio, *Artist Descending a Staircase*, the event is the probable murder of an artist by one of two old friends. But the substance of the play is the wonderfully dextrous reproduction of talk by artists about art during the last half-century. Knowing hearers – and hearers who are not well-informed are given enough buffoonery to make them content – will recognize windy versions of the arguments that have carried painters through several of the currents and counter-currents of modern art: cubism, surrealism, and other tendencies that were first discussed and then only later illustrated by brush.

And in *Travesties* Stoppard mixes up a stew which contains several of the most serious and transforming aspirations of the present era. The years are the war-years of 1914–18, and the scene is Zurich. In that city Joyce was writing *Ulysses*, Tristan Tzara was initiating Dadaism, and Lenin was waiting to bring his kind of revolution to Russia. Responsive to all kinds of pretension (and Stoppard's Zurich is full of pretension's cross-purpose and inconsequence), the mocking dramatist does both justice and injustice to all the artistic and political propaganda. The ridiculous plot is but an ornament to the bravura display of Stoppard's power to hear other voices and to mock them as they pass through the baffle chamber of his own mind.

Some criticism judges that Stoppard is a latter-day G. B. Shaw. This perception occurs because both dramatists are primarily celebrators of ideas. The ideas that Shaw displayed are, roughly speaking, all his own. With Stoppard, the case is altered; the ideas are, without exception, those of others. Shaw delighted the receptive with a display of ideas that were "better"; the cumulative effect of Stoppard's theatre is that there simply are no "better" ideas. One and all, they commit us to imbecility. Perhaps this is a desponding message. But it is one that Stoppard executes with unhalting zest and brilliance.

—Harold H. Watts

STOREY, David (Malcolm). English. Born in Wakefield, Yorkshire, 13 July 1933; brother of the novelist Anthony Storey. Educated at Queen Elizabeth Grammar School, Wakefield, 1943–51; Wakefield College of Art, 1951–53; Slade School of Fine Art, London, 1953–56, diploma in fine arts. Married Barbara Rudd Hamilton in 1956; two sons and two daughters. Played professionally for the Leeds Rugby League Club, 1952–56. Fellow, University College, London, 1974. Recipient: Rhys Memorial Award, for fiction, 1961; Maugham Award, 1963; *Evening Standard* award, 1967, 1970; Variety Club of Great Britain Writer of the Year Award, 1971; New York Drama Critics Circle Award, 1971, 1973, 1974; Faber Memorial Prize, 1973; Obie Award, 1974; Booker Prize, for fiction, 1976. Lives in London.

PUBLICATIONS

Plays

The Restoration of Arnold Middleton (produced 1966).   1967.
In Celebration (produced 1969).   1969.
The Contractor (produced 1969).   1970.
Home (produced 1970).   1970.
The Changing Room (produced 1971).   1972.
The Farm (produced 1973).   1973.
Cromwell (produced 1973).   1973.
Life Class (produced 1974).   1975.
Mother's Day (produced 1976).   1977.

Screenplays: *This Sporting Life*, 1963; *In Celebration*, 1974.

Television Play: *Grace*, from the story by James Joyce, 1974.

Fiction

This Sporting Life.   1960.
Flight into Camden.   1961.
Radcliffe.   1963.
Pasmore.   1972.
A Temporary Life.   1973.
Saville.   1976.

Other

Writers on Themselves, with others.   1964.
Edward, drawings by Donald Parker.   1973.

Reading List: *Revolutions in Modern English Drama* by Katharine J. Worth, 1972; *Storey* by John Russell Taylor, 1974; *Playwrights' Theatre* by Terry Browne, 1975.

*   *   *

It is rare for a writer to claim attention equally as a dramatist and a novelist, but it is impossible to say that David Storey is primarily one or the other. He had already published an accomplished novel of working-class experience, *This Sporting Life*, in 1960, when a group of plays, all presented at the Royal Court Theatre and directed by Lindsay Anderson, established him as one of the two leading figures (Edward Bond, the other) in the "second wave" of contemporary British drama. More recently he has produced a series of further, prize-winning novels. There is considerable variation of tone across his work from the sombreness of *Radcliffe* or *Cromwell* to the sardonic persiflage of *Life Class* or *A Temporary Life*; but reticence and subjectivity complement each other in his writing in both genres.

His undeniable concern with social class has a moral and cultural rather than political focus. *In Celebration* most straightforwardly exposes the strains that social mobility has set up in a family of working-class origins. The influence of D. H. Lawrence shows clearly here, but Storey marks out his individual territory in the expression of bitter and painful feelings and extreme mental turmoil on the edge of breakdown. Though he can recreate social detail precisely, as in *This Sporting Life* and *Saville*, his avoidance of explicit general comment contributes to the impression that the major characters in his novels move somnambulistically through a pattern of events unconsciously chosen. They themselves are manifestations of tradition, or deep-rooted class experience – of manual labour, poverty, and deprivation (Mrs. Hammond, in *This Sporting Life*, an unappeasable figure of suffering and defeat, is an impressive early example). If they find themselves in comfortable middle-class circumstances, they compulsively reject and destroy the conformist role and drift into more fundamentally determined alignments and confrontations. In *Radcliffe*, the strength of the labouring class is seen with fascination from the point-of-view of the opposed and dependent high culture. The titles of the novels, *Radcliffe* and *Saville*, and of the play, *Cromwell*, denote the hold of tradition on individual life: *Saville* presents its main figure living out the experience of a family identified with a particular place in social history; *Radcliffe* is a Gothic novel in which an old house haunts and dominates the minds of a family; *Cromwell* stands for a complex of moral qualities and social ideals.

Though the plots of all Storey's novels and plays are quite distinct from each other, the reader is struck by the reworking of particular episodes (including a beating-up) again and again, in variant order and associated with different characters. The analogy that comes to mind is that of the painter (which Storey also is) who includes a number of motifs idiosyncratically in picture after picture. The play *Life Class* and the novel *A Temporary Life* draw specifically on his familiarity with art schools, and the latter is interestingly structured so that stages of the narrative are linked with current ideas (and practices) of the nature and status of visual art.

If Storey's interest in continuity is reminiscent of Raymond Williams's, his most distinguished plays suggest a structuralist model in the kind of integration they achieve. *The Contractor* and *The Changing Room* dispense with star parts and a conventional narrative plot in favour of theatrical teamwork to create a new version of the ancient notion of the theatre as microcosm. Stage business takes on the status of dramatic action and the dialogue is spare, laconic, half-articulate, close to being a neutral element from which no line can be abstracted and quoted to significant effect. It approximates to "writing degree zero" and serves a drama that has a more than usually tenuous existence as a literary work. In the theatre, the actors create the form of the play and, in *The Contractor*, it is their achievement that stands clear at the climax: the wedding marquee, an image of art and the play itself, not as an individual production, but emerging out of the communal work process. *The Changing Room* excludes the separate achievement, the sacred ritual of the Rugby League game, to trace the emergence – and later dissolution – of the team out of disparate individuals. *Home* moves closer to absurdist drama (though Ewbank is no more the Contractor of the earlier play's title than Pozzo is Godot); but the idea of "home" from which the sense of alienation arises is here replaced by the reality which the characters (the actors in rehearsal and performance) make for themselves: the relationships they build, the communications they effect. The strict observance of the unities works both ways: preserving the effect of extreme naturalism and defining the plays as symbols. The richness of meaning arising from this inexplicit drama recalls Chekhov, as does the degree and quality of theatrical collaboration required.

—Margery Morgan

SUTRO, Alfred. English. Born in London, 7 August 1863. Educated at the City of London School, and in Brussels. Served in the Artists' Rifles, and on the staff of the War Trade Intelligence Department, during World War I: O.B.E. (Officer, Order of the British Empire), 1918. Married Esther Stella Isaacs in 1894. Worked in the City of London for 14 years, first as a clerk, 1880–83, then in partnership with his brother as wholesale merchants, 1883–94; also active in the direction of working men's clubs in London during this period; lived in Paris, 1894, met Maeterlinck and became his translator: devoted himself to the translations, as well as to occasional journalism and to writing plays, 1895–1904; full-time playwright from 1904. *Died 11 September 1933.*

PUBLICATIONS

Plays

The Chili Widow, with Arthur Bourchier, from a play by Alexandre Busson (produced 1895).
Aglavaine and Selysette, from a play by Maeterlinck (produced 1904).   1897.
Alladine and Palomides, Interior, The Death of Tintagiles: Three Little Dramas for Marionettes, from plays by Maeterlinck.   1899.
The Death of Tintagiles, from a play by Maeterlinck (produced 1902).   In *Alladine and Palomides ...*, 1899.
Carrots, from a play by J. Renard (produced 1900).   1904.
The Cave of Illusion.   1900.
A Marriage Has Been Arranged (produced 1902).   1904.
Women in Love: Eight Studies in Sentiment (includes *The Correct Thing, The Gutter of Time, Ella's Apology, A Game of Chess, The Salt of Life, Mr. Steinmann's Corner, Maggie, A Maker of Men*).   1902.
A Maker of Men (produced 1905).   In *Women in Love*, 1902.
The Correct Thing (produced 1905).   In *Women in Love*, 1902.
Ella's Apology (produced 1906).   In *Women in Love*, 1902.
Mr. Steinmann's Corner (produced 1907).   In *Women in Love*, 1902.
The Gutter of Time (produced 1908).   In *Women in Love*, 1902.
A Lonely Life (produced 1907).   1903.
Arethusa (produced 1903).
The Walls of Jericho (produced 1904).   1906.
Monna Vanna, from a play by Maeterlinck (produced 1911).   1904.
Mollentrave on Women (produced 1905).   1905.
The Perfect Lover (produced 1905).   1905.
The Fascinating Mr. Vanderveldt (produced 1906).   1906.
The Open Door.   1906.

The Price of Money (produced 1906).   1906.
The Desperate Duke; or, The Culpable Countess, with R. Marshall (produced 1907).
John Glayde's Honour (produced 1907).   1907.
The Barrier (produced 1907).   1908.
The Romantic Barber (produced 1908).
The Man on the Kerb (produced 1908).   1908.
The Builder of Bridges (produced 1908).   1908.
Making a Gentleman (produced 1909).
The Perplexed Husband (produced 1911).   1913.
The Man in the Stalls (produced 1911).   1911.
The Firescreen (produced 1912).   1912.
The Bracelet (produced 1912).   1912.
Five Little Plays (includes *The Man in the Stalls, A Marriage Has Been Arranged, The Man on the Kerb, The Open Door, The Bracelet*).   1912.
The Two Virtues (produced 1914).   1914.
The Clever Ones (produced 1914).
Rude Min and Christine.   1915; as *Uncle Anyhow* (as *The Two Miss Farndons,* produced 1917, as *Uncle Anyhow,* produced 1918), 1919.
Freedom.   1916.
The Great Redding Street Burglary (produced 1916).
The Marriage Will Not Take Place (produced 1917).   1917.
The Trap (produced 1918).
The Egoist, from the novel by Meredith.   1919.
The Choice (produced 1919).   1920.
The Laughing Lady (produced 1922).   1922.
The Great Well (produced 1922).   1922.
Far above Rubies (produced 1924).   1924.
The Man with a Heart (produced 1925).   1925.
The Desperate Lovers (produced 1927).   1927.
Living Together (produced 1929).   1928.
The Blackmailing Lady.   1929.

Fiction

The Foolish Virgins (stories).   1904.
About Women.   1931.
Which.   1932.

Other

Celebrities and Simple Souls (autobiography).   1933.

Translator, *The Treasure of the Humble,* by Maeterlinck.   1897.
Translator, *Wisdom and Destiny,* by Maeterlinck.   1898.
Translator, *The Life of the Bee,* by Maeterlinck.   1901.
Translator, *Buried Temple,* by Maeterlinck.   1902.
Translator, *Ancient Egypt,* by Maeterlinck.   1925.
Translator, *The Life of the White Ant,* by Maeterlinck.   1927.
Translator, *The Magic of the Stars,* by Maeterlinck.   1930.

Reading List: *Some Modern Authors* by S. P. B. Mais, 1923; "Some Plays by Sutro" by G. Sutton, in *Bookman 63,* 1923.

*   *   *

Alfred Sutro is most well-known for his Maeterlinck translations. But it was his plays that for a time established him as a leading English popular dramatist, though he is now little remembered.

At the time that Henry Arthur Jones was describing *The Renascence of the English Drama* and calling for more serious work, Sutro succeeded with commercial glitter. His earliest plays went unproduced (a collaboration with George Meredith on a dramatization of *The Egoist*) or were tepidly received. A collaboration with actor Arthur Bourchier on *The Chili Widow* (cleaning up Alexandre Busson's *Monsieur le Directeur* as a vehicle) starred Bourchier and Violet Vanbrugh. "Almost sixty years afterwards," wrote Ernest Short in *Sixty Years of Theatre* (1951), "one can remember her play with a parasol and a prospective lover," but that was Miss Vanbrugh's charm, not Sutro's dramaturgy. Sutro did make a splash with *The Walls of Jericho*, though Jones was to employ similar material even better in *The Ogre*. Thereafter Sutro held the boards in the West End year after year with trivial plays. "He has nothing to say that matters," wrote S. P. B. Mais, "but his stagecraft is good. He entertains, but leaves no permanent impression on the mind."

His *coups de théâtre* and starring players kept him going for some time. *John Glayde's Honour* was good enough for the matinée crowd and *The Builder of Bridges* was better, though less popular. Clayton Hamilton found *The Builder of Bridges* "the best of all his plays – better even than that powerful and popular work, *The Walls of Jericho*," but he had to admit (*Forum*, December 1909) that "it was reviewed adversely by nearly all the newspapers of New York, and has also failed to make money with the public."

Commercial failure must have hurt Sutro more than critical gibes. He said in a lecture that "the dramatist should keep one eye raised to heaven and the other on the box-office," and his gaze at the latter was the more steadfast. Throughout his career, charmingly reported in *Celebrities and Simple Souls*, he looked not upward and inward but forward and outward, like a commercial hack. He repackaged some imported tricks (Scribe, Sardou, etc.) and was clever in adapting, solid in construction, deft in dialogue, always innocuous and also inconsequential. By the 1920's he was old-hat: *The Laughing Lady*, *The Man with a Heart*, *The Desperate Lovers* increasingly depend upon an old-fashioned though facile manipulation of "inconsequential and wholly artificial themes" (Mais). His last play, *Living Together* (1929), was "given away with a pound of tea," said Francis Birrell, because it was too contrived, put "too much new wine into old bottles ... tried to sing songs of Cowardice in the tempo of Sardou," too – *theatrical*. "All the brilliant old men have dubbed him out of date."

By the year of Sutro's death the critics were saying frankly that "his plays are uniformly worthless" and that his "method was to produce, merely from the box-office standpoint, more failures than successes." The trick is to be bad but to get *very* old and be revived, like Ben Travers. But *The Walls of Jericho* (with the Australian backwoodsman taking on Lady Alethea and Mayfair society) and *The Laughing Lady* might play now. After all, William Douglas Home is in the West End. *Five Little Plays* and *Carrots* might give those few people who stage one-acters some ideas. *The Perplexed Husband* would be fun: it brings an unwonted (unwanted?) humor to the grimness of Women's Liberation. But do not expect a Sutro revival. Clark and Freedley in their pedestrian *History of the Modern Theatre* (1947) are strolling in the right direction: "Alfred Sutro was a serious writer of the well-made play who moved from drama to light comedy with that expert efficiency which is the hallmark of the second- or third-rate talent. In his more than thirty years of play writing he was one of the most popular dramatists of his day." Since he lacks Jones's craftsmanship, Shaw's genius, Maugham's wit, Pinero's effectiveness with a stagey idea (or even Barrie's with a fuzzy one), perhaps "second- or third-rate" had best be reserved for those admirable Edwardians St. John Hankin and Harley Granville-Barker, and that leaves Alfred Sutro considerably lower in the ranks.

—Leonard R. N. Ashley

SYNGE, (Edmund) J(ohn) M(illington).   Irish.   Born in Newtown Villas, Rathfarnham, near Dublin, 16 April 1871. Educated at private schools until age 14, then with a private tutor for three years, and at Trinity College, Dublin, 1888–92, B.A. 1892; studied piano and violin at the Royal Irish Academy, Dublin, and thereafter studied music and travelled in Germany, Italy, and France; settled in Paris and studied intermittently at the Sorbonne, 1895–97. Met William Butler Yeats, who encouraged him to write, 1896; returned to Ireland, 1897, and summers 1898–1902; with Yeats and Lady Gregory, involved in the initial planning of the Irish Literary Theatre, which became the Abbey Theatre, Dublin; wrote for the stage from 1901; Director, with Yeats and Lady Gregory, of the Abbey Theatre, from 1904. Suffered from Hodgkin's disease: *Died 24 March 1909.*

PUBLICATIONS

Collections

   Poems, edited by Robin Skelton.   1962.
   Prose, edited by Alan Price.   1966.
   Plays, edited by Ann Saddlemyer.   2 vols., 1968.

Plays

   In the Shadow of the Glen (produced 1903).   1904.
   Riders to the Sea (produced 1904).   With *In the Shadow of the Glen,* 1905; edited by
      Robin Skelton, 1969.
   The Well of the Saints (produced 1905).   1905.
   The Playboy of the Western World (produced 1907).   1907; edited by Malcolm Kelsall,
      1974.
   The Tinker's Wedding (produced 1909).   1907.
   Deirdre of the Sorrows (produced 1910).   1910.

Verse

   Poems and Translations.   1909.

Other

   The Aran Islands.   1907.
   In Wicklow, West Kerry, and Connemara.   1911.
   Some Unpublished Letters and Documents.   1959.
   The Autobiography, Constructed from the Manuscripts, edited by Alan Price.   1965.
   Letters to Molly: Synge to Maire O'Neill, edited by Ann Saddlemyer.   1971.
   Some Letters to Lady Gregory and Yeats, edited by Ann Saddlemyer.   1971.

Bibliography: "Bibliographies of Irish Authors: Synge" by M. MacManus, in *Dublin Magazine,* October-December 1930; *Synge: A Bibliography of Criticism* by E. H. Mikhail, 1974.

Reading List: *Synge and Anglo-Irish Literature* by Daniel Corkery, 1931; *Synge* by David H.

Greene and Edward Stephens, 1959; *Synge and Anglo-Irish Drama* by Alan Price, 1961; *Synge and Lady Gregory* by Elizabeth Coxhead, 1962; *Synge* by Denis Johnston, 1965; *Synge* by Donna L. Gerstenberger, 1965; *Synge and Modern Comedy* by Ann Saddlemyer, 1968; *The Writings of Synge* by Robin Skelton, 1971; *Synge Centenary Papers* edited by Maurice Harmon, 1972; *Synge: A Critical Study of the Plays* by Nicholas Greene, 1976; *Interviews and Recollections* edited by E. H. Mikhail, 1977.

*   *   *

Although the bulk of his work was written during the last six years of his life when he was involved in the creation of Dublin's Abbey Theatre, J. M. Synge's preparation as a writer was deliberate, intensive, and lengthy. The poems, plays, travel writings, even his critical essays and translations, were shaped by his early training in music and languages, while his nature mysticism dictated choice and handling of subject matter and formed his aesthetic theory. All his experience was conscientiously woven into his developing philosophy, eventually reappearing in the fabric of his art. Thus, his bitter private struggle as a young adolescent with his mother's evangelical teaching, all the more painful because of his admiration for her strong moral commitment, surfaces in the poignant portrayal of mother and son in *Riders to the Sea*, in the strong simplicity of "Prayer of the Old Woman" after Villon, and in old Mary Byrne's indomitable embrace of life in *The Tinker's Wedding*. Similarly, his fascination for the manufacture of words, which led him to create in any language he studied, is responsible not only for the extraordinary richness and vitality of his dialogue but the conscious conjunction, sometimes harmonic, sometimes contrapuntal, of vivid imagery, exaggerated action, and sweeping rhythmical patterns.

Synge's musical training and correspondingly close study of art and natural history are the foundation also of his attempt to bring into harmony in his writing not only the sound, meaning, colour, and rhythm of language ("every speech should be as fully flavoured as a nut or apple") but a harmony of nature, myth, and passion. Thus the characters of his plays honour the moods of both nature and man and celebrate sounds and senses, while his travel essays evoke the peculiar clarity and intensity of Wicklow's light and atmosphere, Aran's majestic harmony of the supranatural and natural, the exotic grandeur and innate power of Mayo and Kerry. The extraordinary plot of *The Playboy of the Western World*, he insisted to his close friend the translator and journalist Stephen MacKenna, "in its *essence* – is probable given the psychic state of the locality."

Against this background of cosmic orchestration the passions, actions, and dreams of characters in his plays are etched with simple precision. His people experience intensely the incidents of everyday life, while longing equally vividly for the excitement and fulfilment of the unusual or the ideal. In both dream and reality they remain true to themselves; in the resolution of the play we perceive a greater truth to the universe without losing sight of the disparate parts. Thus in *The Tinker's Wedding*, Sarah Casey dreams of acquiring the respectability of marriage, while at the same time refusing to turn her back on the rich joys of the vagrant's unconventional ways; in *The Playboy of the Western World* Pegeen Mike is tempted to "go sailing the seas till I'd marry a Jew-man with ten kegs of gold," but the horror of Christy Mahon's potentially dirty deed is too great for her to face despite her love of the playboy; blind Martin and Mary Doul in *The Well of the Saints* choose certain death and the preservation of their deliberately fostered illusions to the well-meaning Saint's gift of participation in the working world of the sighted; and, in his last play, Deirdre and Naisi embrace both myth and reality by electing a vibrant seven years and an equally resounding death. "On the stage one must have reality, and one must have joy," he wrote in his preface to *The Playboy*, and rejoiced that "in Ireland, for a few years more, we have a popular imagination that is fiery and magnificent, and tender." In Synge's own life, Yeats's famous advice to seek for subject matter in the Aran Islands met with a temperament and personality long prepared for the event.

Synge's travel writings, in particular *The Aran Islands* and his Wicklow essays, reflect these values in a more personal, less artificial style. Where he deliberately objectified feelings and responses in his plays, his essays and poems use his own personal reactions as touchstone. Centering himself in a particular time and place, his descriptions take in the full sweep of horizon and history until the reader shares the flash of illumination achieved at a moment of intense awareness, and is then led, usually through an ironic device, back to the natural and the mundane. In these writings he aligns himself with the wanderer, the vagrant, who views all life and action through the eyes of the self-imposed semi-exile; frequently he signed his love letters to the actress Maire O'Neill (Molly Allgood) "your old Tramp," recognizing not only his affinity with the Stranger in *In the Shadow of the Glen* but with the tinkers, playboys, and beggars celebrated in his other plays.

Constantly striving to distil the essence of experience in his art, he filled thousands of pages with dialogue, critical commentary, made or overheard phrases, lists, analyses, and readings. But his few critical essays and notebook entries are of value primarily to the student of his evolving aesthetic. His experimental scenarios and prose translations, on the other hand, indicate the restlessness with which he approached form and language. Always the student, his method remained one of selectivity and a distant appreciation of other writers. Absorbed in his own vision, sensitive to his private responses, striving towards the perfection of a unique ambition, he preserved to an almost unique extent an individual voice throughout all his work. For Synge, the only arbiter conceivable was the art itself.

—Ann Saddlemyer

TRAVERS, Ben. English. Born in Hendon, London, 12 November 1886. Educated at the Abbey School, Beckenham, Surrey; Charterhouse, Surrey. Served in the Royal Navy Air Service, 1914–17: Squadron Commander; transferred to the Royal Air Force as Major, 1918: Air Force Cross, 1920; rejoined the Royal Air Force in 1939: Squadron Leader, 1940. Married Violet Mouncey in 1916 (died, 1951); two sons and one daughter. Prime Warden of the Fishmongers Company, London, 1946. President, Dramatists Club, 1956–60. Recipient: *Evening Standard* award, 1975. C.B.E. (Commander, Order of the British Empire), 1976. Lives in London.

PUBLICATIONS

Plays

The Dippers, from his own novel (produced 1922).
The Three Graces, from the play by Carl Lombardi and A. M. Willner, music by Franz Lehar (produced 1924).
A Cuckoo in the Nest, from his own novel (produced 1925).   1938.
Rookery Nook, from his own novel (produced 1926).   1930.
Thark (produced 1927).   1932.
Plunder (produced 1928).   1931.
Mischief, from his own novel (produced 1928).
A Cup of Kindness (produced 1929).   1934.
A Night Like This (produced 1930).

Turkey Time (produced 1931).   1934.
Dirty Work (produced 1932).
A Bit of a Test (produced 1933).
Chastity, My Brother (produced 1936).
Nun's Veiling (as *O Mistress Mine*, produced 1936; revised version, as *Nun's Veiling*,
    produced 1953).   1956.
Banana Ridge (produced 1938).   1939.
Spotted Dick (produced 1939).
She Follows Me About (produced 1943).   1945.
Outrageous Fortune (produced 1947).   1948.
Runaway Victory (produced 1949).
Wild Horses (produced 1952).   1953.
Corker's End (produced 1968).
The Bed Before Yesterday (produced 1975).   In *Five Plays*, 1977.
Five Plays (includes *A Cuckoo in the Nest, Rookery Nook, Thark, Plunder, The Bed
    Before Yesterday*).   1977.

Screenplays: *A Little Bit of Fluff (Skirts)*, with Ralph Spence and Wheeler Dryden, 1928;
Rookery Nook (One Embarrassing Night), with W. P. Lipscomb, 1930; *Thark*, 1932; *A
Night Like This*, 1932; *Just My Luck*, 1933; *Turkey Time*, 1933; *A Cuckoo in the Nest*,
with A. R. Rawlinson, 1933; *Up to the Neck*, 1933; *Dirty Work*, 1934; *Lady in Danger*,
1934; *A Cup of Kindness*, 1934; *Fighting Stock*, 1935; *Stormy Weather*, 1935; *Foreign
Affaires*, 1935; *Pot Luck*, 1936; *Dishonour Bright*, 1936; *For Valour*, 1937; *Second Best
Bed*, 1938; *Old Iron*, 1938; *So This Is London*, with others, 1939; *Banana Ridge*, with
Walter C. Mycroft and Lesley Storm, 1941; *Uncle Silas (The Inheritance)*, 1947; *Fast
and Loose*, with A. R. Rawlinson, 1954.

Television Plays: *Potter*, 1948; *Picture Page*, 1949.

Fiction

The Dippers.   1920.
A Cuckoo in the Nest.   1922.
Rookery Nook.   1923.
Mischief.   1925.
The Collection Today (stories).   1929.
The Dippers, Together with Game and Rubber and The Dunkum Jane.   1932.
Hyde Side Up.   1933.

Other

Vale of Laughter (autobiography).   1957.
A-Sitting on a Gate (autobiography).   1978.

Editor, *The Leacock Book*.   1930.
Editor, *Pretty Pictures, Being a Selection of the Best American Pictorial Humour*.   1932.

*   *   *

Educated at Charterhouse, where he showed no particular promise of any sort, Ben
Travers, though he spent his early years in London and the Far East in the family firm, had
an early passion for the theatre. He was not able to indulge this till he had completed his years

with the Royal Naval Air Service during World War I, and big success did not come his way till Tom Walls, who had leased the Aldwych Theatre, took up his early farce *A Cuckoo in the Nest*. From 1922 till 1933, he wrote for the Aldwych company, and his plays were more or less adapted to the cast: the horsy, cunning Tom Walls; the silly ass Ralph Lynn, always dropping his monocle; the bald, clerkish, bespectacled Robertson Hare, always liable at some point in the play to have his trousers removed for perfectly logical reasons; the slim pretty Winifred Shotter, equally liable to dash across the stage in her underclothes; and Mary Brough, the gruff, suspicious landlady. Tom Walls was very much the boss of the show and once made Travers spend fifty-two hours revising, and much improving, a weak third act.

Travers's plays, which were essentially farces of suspense in which the most extravagant pains, lies, deceptions, and assumed identities were used to conceal improprieties that had not taken place, became very popular both with amateur theatrical companies and in their film versions in the 1930's. There was a long silence after 1952, but Travers produced *Corker's End* in 1968 and a serious farce, *The Bed Before Yesterday*, in 1975. In this last play he dealt (setting the scene in 1930) with the predicament of an essentially likable woman who had been put off sex for life by her utter ignorance on her marriage night. Not quite too late, she discovers its delights, but at the end realises that with a new husband of sixty she will have to rely more on affection. The play is more touching than funny (and the younger characters do not really belong to the 1930's), but it shows Travers's good heart. The cult of panic-stricken propriety in the 1920's gives his early work, however, in its very improbability, a more genuinely farcical flavour. There cannot be true farce without taboos.

—G. S. Fraser

USTINOV, Peter (Alexander).   English.   Born in London, 16 April 1921. Educated at Westminster School, London, 1934–37; London Theatre Studio, 1937–39. Served in the Royal Sussex Regiment and the Royal Army Ordnance Corps, 1942–46; Army Kinetograph Service, 1943. Married 1) Isolde Denham in 1940 (divorced, 1950), one daughter; 2) Susanne Cloutier in 1953 (divorced, 1971), two daughters and one son; 3) Helene du Laud-Allemans in 1972. Entered the theatre as an actor, 1939; first appearance in films, 1940. Co-Director of the Nottingham Playhouse, 1963. Rector, University of Dundee, 1968–73; Member, British U.S.A. Bicentennial Liaison Committee, 1973. Goodwill Ambassador for Unicef since 1969. Recipient: Golden Globe Award, 1952; New York Drama Critics Circle Award, 1953; *Evening Standard* award, 1956; Benjamin Franklin Medal, 1957; Emmy Award, for acting, three times; Academy Award, for acting, 1961, 1965. D.L.: University of Dundee, 1969; D.F.A.: LaSalle University, Philadelphia, 1971; D.Litt.: University of Lancaster, 1972. Fellow, Royal Society of Arts. C.B.E. (Commander, Order of the British Empire), 1975. Lives in Switzerland.

PUBLICATIONS

Plays

The Bishop of Limpopoland (sketch; produced 1939).

Sketches in *Diversion* and *Diversion 2* (produced 1940, 1941).
Fishing for Shadows, from a play by Jean Sarment (produced 1940).
House of Regrets (produced 1942).   1943.
Beyond (produced 1943).   1944.
Blow Your Own Trumpet (produced 1943).   In *Plays about People*, 1950.
The Banbury Nose (produced 1944).   1945.
The Tragedy of Good Intentions (produced 1945).   In *Plays about People*, 1950.
The Indifferent Shepherd (produced 1948).   In *Plays about People*, 1950.
Frenzy, from a play by Ingmar Bergman (produced 1948).
The Man in the Raincoat (produced 1949).
Plays about People.   1950.
The Love of Four Colonels (produced 1951).   1951.
The Moment of Truth (produced 1951).   1953.
High Balcony (produced 1952).
No Sign of the Dove (produced 1953).   In *Five Plays*, 1965.
Romanoff and Juliet (produced 1956).   1957; revised version, as *R Loves J*, music by
    Alexander Faris, lyrics by Julian More (produced 1973).
The Empty Chair (produced 1956).
Paris Not So Gay (produced 1958).
Photo Finish: An Adventure in Biography (produced 1962).   1962.
The Life in My Hands (produced 1963).
*Five Plays: Romanoff and Juliet, The Moment of Truth, The Love of Four Colonels,
    Beyond, No Sign of the Dove.*   1965.
*The Unknown Soldier and His Wife: Two Acts of War Separated by a Truce for
    Refreshment* (produced 1967).   1967.
Halfway up the Tree (produced 1967).   1968.
Who's Who in Hell (produced 1974).

Screenplays: *The New Lot* (documentary), 1943; *The Way Ahead,* with Eric Ambler,
1944; *The True Glory,* 1944; *Carnival,* with others, 1946; *School for Secrets,* 1946; *Vice
Versa,* 1948; *Private Angelo,* with Michael Anderson, 1949; *The Secret Flight,* 1952;
School for Scoundrels, with others, 1960; *Romanoff and Juliet,* 1961; *Billy Budd,* with
Robert Rossen and DeWitt Bodeen, 1962; *Lady L.,* 1965; *Hot Millions,* with Ira
Wallach, 1968; *Hammersmith Is Out,* 1972.

Radio Plays: *In All Directions* series.

Television Play: *Ustinov ad lib,* 1969.

Fiction

Add a Dash of Pity: Short Stories.   1959.
The Loser.   1961.
The Frontiers of the Sea (stories).   1966.
Krumnagel.   1971.

Other

Ustinov's Diplomats: A Book of Photographs.   1961.
We Were Only Human (caricatures).   1961.
The Wit of Ustinov, edited by Dick Richards.   1969.
Dear Me (autobiography).   1977.

Reading List: *Ustinov* by Geoffrey Willans, 1957; *Ustinov in Focus* by Tony Thomas, 1971.

*   *   *

The delightful comic vision of Peter Ustinov has been most significantly shaped by his cosmopolitan heritage, his talent for mimicry, his buffeting by the British educational system, his wide reading, and especially by his service in the British army. The son of a Russian journalist-spy-diplomat, who worked for the Germans until he defected to the British, and of a French artist, Ustinov was conceived in Holland and born in London. He claimed in the introduction to *Five Plays* to feel "more emotionally involved in the United Nations than in any individual country." This perspective is reflected throughout his works. The characters in his plays typically represent at least three different countries; their stereotypical provincialism, their jingoistic patriotism, and their pompous posings are major objects of Ustinov's satire. In *Romanoff and Juliet*, for instance, the Russians and the Americans badger each other in the main square of the capital city of the smallest country in the world. And although the families of the two lovers are ideological enemies, their quarrels are reduced to lilliputian insignificance as they crumble in the face of adolescent love.

In *The Love of Four Colonels* an American, an Englishman, a Frenchman, and a Russian are spirited away from their Allied Headquarters in a disputed section of Germany to an enchanted castle where each, in turn, tries to awaken Sleeping Beauty, acting out a fantasy in which he envisions her as his own conception of the ideal woman. The discrepancy between these fantasies and the moralistic proclamations of the four men provide much of the play's best comedy.

In *The Unknown Soldier and His Wife* the central characters repeatedly change their nationalities as Ustinov follows the course of battle from Greece and Rome through England of the Middle Ages to the eighteenth century and finally to the present. In *No Sign of the Dove*, a reworking of the Noah myth, the central characters are Russian and English; the setting is a cosmopolitan mansion whose rooms are designated as the Venetian, the Roman, and the Chinese Regency. Such a mixture of nationalities, such ready combination of the realistic and the supernational, and such disregard for chronology enable Ustinov to satirize the pettiness and prejudice of people everywhere. No one ideology, he seems to say, has a corner on idiocy.

If there is one particular idiocy that people everywhere cling to, it is, in Ustinov's view, the supposition that a country can benefit from the actions of its government and its army. An undistinguished private in the British army during World War II, Ustinov learned that the military was the seat of stupidity, confusion, and waste. His writing consistently reflects this opinion. Military figures appear and play significant roles in virtually every work that he has written. They are usually bumbling incompetents, like the four colonels who seek to maintain the honor of their countries by quibbling over which language will be spoken on which weeks in their shared headquarters; or they are impotent, like Colonel Radley in *Beyond*, who wishes he could have made general, wishes he could have stayed in Africa, wishes he had not been forced to retire, and finally dies because there are no more worlds for him to conquer. When the military figures are perceptive, like General Sir Mallalieu in *Halfway up the Tree*, they perceive that death and bloodshed have done nothing to improve the human condition and that in any war the good and the bad are equally shared by each of the contending forces.

In the military establishment, with its rigid hierarchies, Ustinov found an apt metaphor for all the structured social systems and institutions which stifle creativity and make human beings more uniform and predictable. His belief that such systems should be ridiculed began as early as his grammar school days, when one of his masters reported, "He shows great originality, which must be curbed at all cost." This great originality, which led Ustinov to create brilliant vignettes rather than plays with conventionally unified and carefully developed plots and which caused him to try constantly to dramatize "the comic side of things tragic and the melancholy of things ribald," has accounted for much of the criticism he has received from reviewers who wish his satires were curbed by closer attention to proper form. But the battle against rigidity and preconceptions continues to affect the style as well as the substance of Ustinov's works.

—Helen Houser Popovich

---

van DRUTEN, John (William).   American.   Born in London, England, 1 June 1901; emigrated to the United States, 1926; naturalized, 1944. Educated at University College School, London, 1911–17; subsequently studied law: awarded LL.B., University of London, 1922; Solicitor of the Supreme Court of Judicature, 1923. Special Lecturer in English Law and Legal History, University College of Wales, Aberystwyth, 1923–26; full-time writer from 1928. Recipient: American Academy of Arts and Letters Award of Merit Medal, 1946; New York Drama Critics Circle Award, 1952. *Died 19 December 1957.*

PUBLICATIONS

Plays

> *The Return Half* (produced 1924).
> *Chance Acquaintance* (produced 1927).
> *Diversion* (produced 1928).   1928.
> *Young Woodley* (produced 1928).   1928.
> *The Return of the Soldier,* from the novel by Rebecca West (produced 1928).   1928.
> *After All* (produced 1929).   1929.
> *London Wall* (produced 1931).   1931.
> *Sea Fever,* with Auriol Lee, from a play by Marcel Pagnol (produced 1931).
> *There's Always Juliet* (produced 1931).   1931.
> *Hollywood Holiday,* with Benn Levy (produced 1931).   1931.
> *Somebody Knows* (produced 1932).   1932.
> *Behold We Live* (produced 1932).   1932.
> *The Distaff Side* (produced 1933).   1933.
> *Flowers of the Forest* (produced 1934).   1934.
> *Most of the Game* (produced 1935).   1936.
> *Gertie Maude* (produced 1937).   1937.
> *Leave Her to Heaven* (produced 1940).   1941.
> *Old Acquaintance* (produced 1940).   1941.
> *Solitaire,* from the novel by E. Corle (produced 1942).
> *The Damask Cheek,* with Lloyd R. Morris (produced 1942).   1943.
> *The Voice of the Turtle* (produced 1943).   1944.
> *I Remember Mama,* from the novel *Mama's Bank Account* by Kathryn Forbes (produced 1944).   1945.
> *The Mermaids Singing* (produced 1945).   1946.
> *The Druid Circle* (produced 1947).   1948.
> *Make Way for Lucia,* from novels by E. F. Benson (produced 1948).   1949.
> *Bell, Book, and Candle* (produced 1950).   1951.

I Am a Camera, from *The Berlin Stories* by Christopher Isherwood (produced 1951). 1954.
I've Got Sixpence (produced 1952). 1953.
Dancing in the Chequered Shade (produced 1955).

Screenplays: *Young Woodley*, with Victor Kendall, 1930; *I Loved a Soldier*, 1936; *Parnell*, with S. N. Behrman, 1937; *Night Must Fall*, 1937; *The Citadel*, with others, 1938; *Raffles*, with Sidney Howard, 1939; *Lucky Partner*, with Allen Scott, 1940; *My Life with Caroline*, with Arnold Belgard, 1941; *Johnny Come Lately*, 1943; *Old Acquaintance*, with Lenore Coffee, 1943; *Forever and a Day*, with others, 1944; *Gaslight*, with Walter Reisch and John L. Balderston, 1944; *The Voice of the Turtle*, 1948.

Fiction

Young Woodley. 1929.
A Woman on Her Way. 1930.
And Then You Wish. 1936.
The Vicarious Years. 1955.

Other

The Way to the Present: A Personal Record. 1938.
Playwright at Work. 1953.
Widening Circle (autobiography). 1957.

* * *

A prolific writer – best known for his plays but also recognized as a novelist, screenwriter, and autobiographer – John van Druten delighted audiences for more than thirty years with his polished, urbane comedies. The persistent tone in his works is warm and gentle; his style has been praised for its convincing naturalness and controlled simplicity.

Van Druten's plots are often loosely structured, imitative, and readily forgettable. *I Remember Mama*, one of his most popular works, for example, is structured as a series of vignettes linked together by tone and characters, but scarcely more unified than the collection of Kathryn Forbes's short stories on which it was based.

When there is a developed plot in either his original works or his adaptations, it is usually one of two variations on the same basic action: two people meet, have or contemplate having an affair, discover that they love each other, and then joyfully renounce wantonness and move toward a thoroughly conventional marriage (as in *There's Always Juliet*; *The Distaff Side*; *Bell, Book, and Candle*; *The Damask Cheek*; and *The Voice of the Turtle*); or, sadly, discover that their age, circumstance, or character prevents such a marriage (as in *Young Woodley*, *Old Acquaintance*, *The Mermaids Singing*, and *I Am a Camera*). In developing these plots, van Druten moves perilously close to the brink of sentimentality and heavy-handed moralism; but his wit and determination to master "the difficult art of sincerity" keep him, with rare exceptions, from plunging headlong into the abyss.

Indeed, van Druten's plays were consistently praised for their fresh dialogue, their unforced cleverness, and their sophisticated repartée. His fiction and autobiographies, too, are natural and eminently readable.

His awareness of the importance of style and his concern that his works be well-written are reflected both in his commentary on his own works and in his evaluation of the works of others. For example, he criticizes bad writing, which he describes as that which is filled with bathos, facetiousness, and an endless flow of shop-worn phrases that "produce no effect save that of total weariness." He states that only the immature taste can appreciate great sweetness or a "mustard and vinegar sharpness," which the experienced palate would disdain. And in his own works, from the beginning, he attempted to avoid these excesses.

Van Druten's artistry in writing dialogue brings his characters to life. They are unforgettable. Sally Bowles, the complex, misguided, comical, pathetic American ex-patriate in *I Am a Camera*, who leads the life of the grasshopper as the deadly threat of the Third Reich moves forward; Marta, the warm, clever, protective, stable foundation of her family in *I Remember Mama*; Gillian Holroyd, the thoroughly human witch in *Bell, Book, and Candle* – these are only three who clearly rise above the ordinary to the distinctive.

This ability to create memorable characters, and thus major roles, was early recognized by Hollywood, where van Druten wrote dialogue, adapted his own works and those of others, and collaborated on screen plays for major actors from virtually every important studio. He was largely responsible, for instance, for creating the role of Paula Alquist in *Gaslight*, a role for which Ingrid Bergman won the Academy Award in 1944. It is on such success that his reputation rests.

—Helen Houser Popovich

WALCOTT, Derek (Alton).   Jamaican.   Born in Castries, St. Lucia, West Indies, 23 January 1930. Educated at St. Mary's College, St. Lucia; University of the West Indies, Kingston, Jamaica, B.A. 1953. Married; three children. Taught at St. Mary's College and Jamaica College. Formerly, Feature Writer, *Public Opinion*, Kingston, and *Trinidad Guardian*, Port-of-Spain. Since 1959, Founding Director, Trinidad Theatre Workshop. Recipient: Rockefeller Fellowship, 1957; Guinness Award, 1961; Heinemann Award, 1966; Cholmondeley Award, 1969; Order of the Humming Bird, Trinidad and Tobago, 1969; Obie Award, 1971. Lives in Trinidad.

PUBLICATIONS

Plays

> *Henri Christophe: A Chronicle* (produced 1950).   1950.
> *Henri Dernier: A Play for Radio Production.*   1951.
> *Sea at Dauphin* (produced 1954).   1954.
> *Ione: A Play with Music* (produced 1957).   1954.
> *Drums and Colours* (produced 1958).   In *Caribbean Quarterly 1* and *2*, 1961.
> *Ti-Jean and His Brothers,* music by André Tanker (produced 1958).   In *The Dream on Monkey Mountain and Other Plays,* 1971.
> *Malcochon; or, Six in the Rain* (produced 1959; as *Six in the Rain*, produced 1960; as *Malcochon*, produced 1969).   In *The Dream on Monkey Mountain and Other Plays,* 1971.
> *The Dream on Monkey Mountain* (produced 1967).   In *The Dream on Monkey Mountain and Other Plays,* 1971.
> *In a Fine Castle* (produced 1970).

The Dream on Monkey Mountain and Other Plays (includes *Ti-Jean and His Brothers,*
    Malcochon, Sea at Dauphin, and the essay "What the Twilight Says").   1971.
The Charlatan, music by Galt MacDermot (produced 1974).
The Joker of Seville, and O Babylon! 1978.

Verse

Twenty-Five Poems. 1948.
Epitaph for the Young. 1949.
Poems. 1953.
In a Green Night: Poems 1948–1960. 1962.
Selected Poems. 1964.
The Castaway and Other Poems. 1965.
The Gulf and Other Poems. 1969.
Another Life. 1973.
Sea Grapes. 1976.
Selected Verse. 1976.
Selected Poems, edited by O. R. Dathorne. 1977.

Reading List: *Walcott: "Another Life"* by Edward Baugh, 1978.

*   *   *

The first and simplest pleasure offered by Derek Walcott's poetry is the sense of being alive
and out-of-doors in the West Indies: sand and salt on the skin, sunlight and space and the
open beach, sea-grapes and sea-almonds, liners and islands, where always "The starved eye
devours the seascape for the morsel of a sail,/The horizon threads it infinitely."

Walcott was a painter before he was a poet, and as a youth set off with a friend around his
native island of St. Lucia to put it on canvas and thus create it in the imagination. Later he
found he could do the work of creation better with words and metaphor, and that this too
was needed:

> For no-one had yet written of this landscape
> that it was possible, though there were sounds
> given to its varieties of wood.

Walcott has kept his painter's eye, and is especially aware of effects of light. He often
compares life with art ("Tables in the trees, like entering Renoir"), as indeed he often quotes
or echoes lines from the English Metaphysicals, Tennyson, Eliot, Dylan Thomas, and others.
These things, taken together with the high polish of his verse, have sometimes led to
accusations of virtuoso artificiality and preciosity. But, though there may be some lapses
which deserve such strictures, it is precisely the successful transmuting of life into art which
makes Walcott's achievement so important.

At his best he fuses the outward scene with inward experience and with a form of English
words, resonant within the tradition of literature in English but also appropriate to the
particular occasion, all in one single act of perception. In so doing he enhances and illustrates
(in the Renaissance sense of that word) the landscape and the human lives that are found on
the islands. It is not surprising, perhaps, that he should be such a good love poet, for the
experience of love has this same quality of enhancing places: "But islands can only exist/If
we have loved in them."

Love, the creation of a centre of consciousness and a relationship of security with the place
one lives are particularly important in societies where a history of slavery, cultural

deprivation, colonial dependency, and, latterly, tourism have combined to reinforce the more generalized modern feelings of alienation and contingency. Walcott's work may therefore be quite as socially important as that of more obsessively socially-orientated West Indian writers.

Walcott by no means ignores the well-known dilemmas of the West Indian situation. In "Ruins of a Great House" he works out in a complex fashion his relationship with men like Ralegh, "ancestral murderers and poets," with England and the English language, and with the earlier history of a ruined plantation house. Here and elsewhere he is aware that he has one white grandfather, who like many others "drunkenly seeded their archipelago." When the Mau Mau insurrection in Kenya occurs, he cannot give murderers on either side his blessing though "poisoned with the blood of both," and when he sees television film of the Biafran war he notes "The soldiers' helmeted shadows could have been white." In general his aim seems to be not to make rhetoric out of the past, but to transcend it: "All in compassion ends/So differently from what the heart arranged."

Walcott is also a successful and prolific playwright, the founder-director of the Trinidad Theatre Workshop, a travelling group of players who move around the Caribbean. Whereas the poetry is almost entirely in standard English, the plays are largely in the creole idiom of the West Indies. A further linguistic complication is that the popular language of Walcott's home island is a Creole French (as on Jean Rhys's home island of Dominica) and the French phrases and songs of the islands also find their way in quotation, and, with their special intonations, into his work.

In his best-known play, *Dream on Monkey Mountain*, Makak the charcoal-burner lives in utter degradation, dreams he is king of a united Africa, yet has to go on living in the everyday world. "The problem," Walcott said in an interview (*New Yorker*, 26 June 1971), "is to recognize our African origins but not to romanticize them." Generally, one feels that Walcott has little sympathy for exploitation of the past by modern ideologists, even if they are negro ideologists, and some of his bitterest lines are reserved for post-independence politicians. Against their power and rhetoric he sets out on a subtler and more revolutionary course:

> I sought more power than you, more fame than yours,
> I was more hermetic, I knew the commonweal,
> I pretended subtly to lose myself in crowds
> knowing my passage would alter their reflection

and at the same time to redeem the past

> Its racial quarrels blown like smoke to sea.
> From all that sorrow, beauty is our gain
> Though it may not seem so
> To an old fisherman rowing home in the rain.

—Ned Thomas

WESKER, Arnold.   English.   Born in Stepney, London, 24 May 1932. Educated at Upton House School, Hackney, London, 1943–48; London School of Film Technique, 1956. Served in the Royal Air Force, 1950–52. Married Doreen (Dusty) Bicker in 1958; two sons and one daughter. Worked as a furniture-maker's apprentice and carpenter's mate, 1948, bookseller's assistant, 1949, 1952, plumber's mate, 1952, farm labourer and seed sorter, 1953, kitchen porter, 1953–54, and pastry cook, 1954–58. Founder-Director, Centre 42, London, 1961–70. Former Member, Youth Service Council. Recipient: Arts Council grant, 1958; *Evening Standard* award, 1959; *Encyclopaedia Britannica* Award, 1959; Marzotto Prize, 1964. Lives in London.

PUBLICATIONS

Plays

   The Wesker Trilogy.   1960.
     Chicken Soup with Barley (produced 1958).   In *New English Dramatists, 1959.*
     Roots (produced 1959).   1959.
     I'm Talking about Jerusalem (produced 1960).   1960.
   The Kitchen (produced 1959).   In *New English Dramatists 2,* 1960; expanded version, 1962.
   Chips with Everything (produced 1962).   1962.
   The Nottingham Captain: A Moral for Narrator, Voices and Orchestra, music by Wilfred Josephs and Dave Lee (produced 1962).   In *Six Sundays in January,* 1971.
   Menace (televised 1963).   In *Six Sundays in January,* 1971.
   Their Very Own and Golden City (produced 1965).   1966; revised version (produced 1974).
   The Four Seasons (produced 1965).   1966.
   The Friends (produced 1970).   1970.
   The Old Ones (produced 1972).   1973; revised version, edited by Michael Marland, 1974.
   The Wedding Feast, from a story by Dostoevsky (produced 1974).
   The Journalists.   1975.
   The Plays.   2 vols., 1976–77.
   Love Letters on Blue Paper, from his own story (televised 1976; revised version, produced 1978).
   The Merchant, from the play *The Merchant of Venice* by Shakespeare (produced 1977).

Screenplay: *The Kitchen,* 1961.

Television Plays: *Menace,* 1963; *Love Letters on Blue Paper,* from his own story, 1976.

Fiction

   Love Letters on Blue Paper (stories).   1974.
   Said the Old Man to the Young Man: Three Stories.   1978.

Other

   Labour and the Arts: II; or, What, Then Is to Be Done?   1960.
   The Modern Playwright; or, "O Mother, Is It Worth It?"   1961.
   Fears of Fragmentation (essays).   1970.
   Six Sundays in January (miscellany).   1971.
   Say Goodbye – You May Never See Them Again: Scenes from Two East-End Backgrounds, paintings by John Allin.   1974.

Journey into Journalism.   1977.
Fatlips (juvenile).   1978.

Reading List: *Anger and After* by John Russell Taylor, 1962; *Wesker* by Ronald Hayman, 1970; *The Plays of Wesker* by Glenda Leeming and Simon Trussler, 1971; *Theatre Language: A Study of Arden, Osborne, Pinter, and Wesker* by John Russell Brown, 1972.

*   *   *

Arnold Wesker has suffered from instant critical acclaim for early works which appeared to conform to a fashion for working-class drama – and, conversely, from what he has himself called the "casual condemnation" of later plays which have sought new directions and themes, and so upset critical preconceptions. He is a writer much-hated and much-loved, and it is not difficult to identify the ingredients which his detractors have found superficially irritating: an assumption that answers *may* be there for the seeking, in a theatre where middle-brow nihilism is a dominant force; an unfashionably sincere faith in the power of the written word and, indeed, of literacy itself, at a time when the McLuhanite heresy remains widespread; and a refusal to conceal what is serious beneath a compromising veneer of comedy, where it is modish to argue that existential anguish can only be made bearable by laughter.

Wesker is an autobiographical writer, not (at least, since the early plays) in his choice of plots, but in the sources of the characters from which they spring. He is a skilled but largely instinctive craftsman, with a wide stylistic range, and an expository skill appropriate to all formal requirements. He has a quick, responsive ear for racial or regional idioms. And he is an independent though not entirely an original thinker: thus, while other dramatists were drawing inspiration from Marcuse or R. D. Laing, he was writing *The Merchant* saturated in the works of Ruskin and George Eliot.

He has often been accused of naivety and a simplistic reading of complex social and political issues: yet a closer look at the plays indicts his critics of the very same charges. Alike in *The Kitchen* and the plays which came to comprise *The Wesker Trilogy*, his conclusions show the failure of revolutionary hopes, or, as in *Roots*, reveal a very tiny and particular success which only serves to highlight pervasive apathy and incomprehension. In *The Friends* and *Love Letters on Blue Paper*, a perverse optimism is achieved only through full acceptance of the fact of death. And *The Merchant* rewrites Shakespeare to show Shylock and Antonio intensely individualised, yet trapped by a bond that is a product of the law regulating the relationship between gentile and Jew, and so was intended as a surety for friendship rather than a symptom of hatred.

Why, then, has Wesker found his work since *The Friends* so difficult to get staged in the English-speaking theatre, although in parts of the world as different as Scandinavia, Latin America, and Japan he remains highly regarded and regularly produced? Perhaps it is in part a consequence of his characters' very openness – their lack of decent, British reticence. There is little that remains unspoken in Wesker's plays – and when a character does find an overt expression of feelings difficult, as in *Love Letters on Blue Paper*, an alternative but equally direct mode of expression (as the title here suggests) is found.

This was somehow acceptable in the East End Jewish setting of *Chicken Soup with Barley*, or in the working-class worlds of *The Kitchen*, *Roots*, or *Chips with Everything*, for English middle-class audiences do not expect the lower orders to preserve stiff upper lips (and Wesker's own valiant attempt to broaden the audience for the arts in Britain, through trades-union sponsorship and the Centre 42 movement, was an honourable failure). Although the later plays were written in a period when so many taboos have allegedly been overcome, their themes have nonetheless offended in direct proportion to their unsuitability for a liberal dinner table. Thus, *The Friends* is concerned not only with an awareness of mortality (the ultimate contemporary taboo), but the nature of friendship itself. And *The Journalists* similarly touched raw radical nerves: all very well to question the role of a capitalist-dominated press, but not the ethics of even *being* a journalist, in a society which probably gets the journalism it deserves.

Wesker is an unconscious craftsman, yet has ranged from the almost expressionist dominance of setting over characters in *The Kitchen*, to the "straightforward" naturalism of the Trilogy, to the impressionism of *Their Very Own and Golden City*, to the poetic feeling for *caesurae* in *The Four Seasons*, to the entirely logical yet un-pin-downable narrative flow of *The Wedding Feast*. His other plays are even harder to define stylistically, for he moulds each so closely to its subject that it would take a latter-day Polonius adequately to categorise the barrack-square realism combined with comic-strip caricature in *Chips with Everything*, or the extraordinary blending of minutely researched historical detail with acceptable Shakespearian "givens" in *The Merchant*.

As surely as Wesker has gone out of fashion, yet persevered to produce such master works as *The Friends* and *The Merchant*, almost as surely will he return to critical acclaim, and, one hopes, ignore it, the better to weather the next swing of fashion. He has staying power, stylistic range, and an entirely personal vocabulary and vision. For the discerning, his plays will survive so long as the insidious newspeak of the trendy and the trivial does not entirely overwhelm the English-speaking theatre.

—Simon Trussler

WHITE, Patrick (Victor Martindale). Australian. Born in London, England, 28 May 1912. Educated at schools in Australia, 1919–25; Cheltenham College, 1925–29; King's College, Cambridge, 1932–35, B.A. in modern languages 1935. Served in the Royal Air Force as an Intelligence Officer, in the Middle East, 1940–45. Travelled in Europe and the United States, and lived in London, before World War II; returned to Australia after the war. Recipient: Australian Literary Society Gold Medal, 1956; Miles Franklin Award, 1958, 1962; Smith Literary Award, 1959; National Conference of Christians and Jews' Brotherhood Award, 1962; Nobel Prize for Literature, 1973. A.C. (Companion, Order of Australia), 1975. Lives in Sydney.

PUBLICATIONS

Plays

Return to Abyssinia (produced 1947).
The Ham Funeral (produced 1961). In Four Plays, 1965.
The Season at Sarsaparilla (produced 1962). In Four Plays, 1965.
A Cheery Soul (produced 1963). In Four Plays, 1965.
Night on Bald Mountain (produced 1964). In Four Plays, 1965.
Four Plays. 1965.
Big Toys (produced 1977).

Fiction

Happy Valley.   1939.
The Living and the Dead.   1941.
The Aunt's Story.   1948.
The Tree of Man.   1955.
Voss.   1957.
Riders in the Chariot.   1961.
The Burnt Ones (stories).   1964.
The Solid Mandala.   1966.
The Vivisector.   1970.
The Eye of the Storm.   1973.
The Cockatoos: Shorter Novels and Stories.   1974.
A Fringe of Leaves.   1976.

Verse

The Ploughman and Other Poems.   1935.

Bibliography: *A Bibliography of White* by Janette Finch, 1966.

Reading List: *White* by Geoffrey Dutton, 1961; *White* by Robert F. Brissenden, 1966; *White* by Barry Argyle, 1967; *The Mystery of Unity: Theme and Technique in the Novels of White* by Patricia A. Morley, 1972; *The Eye in the Mandala: White, A Vision of Man and God* by Peter Beatson, 1976.

*   *   *

Patrick White comes from a pioneering Australian family, although he was born in London. He was educated in New South Wales and England, travelled widely in Europe and the U.S.A. before World War II, and also lived in London where he was much involved with the theatre, a life-long passion. Part of the depth and intensity of his view of the world comes from his experience of its newer and older civilizations.

His first novel, *Happy Valley* (which he will not allow to be reprinted), was highly praised by some of the most eminent contemporary English critics and writers. It is an uneven but powerful work, set in the high, cold country of southern New South Wales, where he had worked as a jackeroo (an Australian term for a young man learning the skills of managing sheep or cattle). Its immaturity shows in the strong stylistic influence of Joyce, its maturity in its characteristic searching assessment of the causes of human failure.

The Living and the Dead is set in the England of the second and third decades of the twentieth century, and is a harsh judgement of a society more dead than living, softened by the refusal of some of the characters, especially female, to "behave in the convention of a clever age that encouraged corrosiveness, destruction." It is also the first of White's many onslaughts on "the disgusting, the nauseating aspect of the human ego." White's deepest and most consistent purpose in all his work is the offering of signposts on the road to humility. He is a profoundly religious writer, not bound to any creed.

White's original genius appears unmistakably in his next novel, *The Aunt's Story*. The aunt is a spinster, Theodora Goodman, who although lonely and "leathery" has an extraordinarily rich understanding of life and people. Her story moves from reality to illusion, in Australia, Europe and the U.S.A.; she is broken by her longing, but inability, to reconcile the two.

White's next novel, *The Tree of Man*, is the result of his decision to return to Australia after the War, where he settled on a farm near Castle Hill, on the edge of Sydney, with a Greek friend and partner, Manoly Lascaris. All his subsequent books are, in a sense, his attempts to populate what he once called "The Great Australian Emptiness." His love-hate relationship with his own country (for some years now he has lived in Sydney) has in recent years extended to an active involvement in public issues, especially over the Constitutional crisis of 1975, surprising perhaps in someone who guards his privacy so fiercely. *The Tree of Man* is White's tribute to the ability of ordinary men and women to survive against the elemental and inhuman forces of nature in Australia; ironically, the action takes place on the outskirts of Sydney, and not in the immensities of the outback.

Into these surroundings White plunged his next hero. *Voss* is a novel about a German explorer in New South Wales, Queensland, and the Northern Territory, some of the inspiration for which came from White's reading of the journals of the explorers E. J. Eyre and Ludwig Leichhardt. With *The Tree of Man* and *Voss* White secured his international reputation; both have been translated into many languages. In *The Tree of Man* he attempted to explain the ordinary. In *Voss* he took an extraordinary hero into an extraordinary country, with the Aborigines leading Voss on to further mysteries of magic and death. But the explorer's real journey is in the purification of his soul through torments of both agony and joy, understood only by the partner of his spiritual life, Laura Trevelyan, who remains in Sydney.

However, no discussion of White's work should be involved exclusively with the spiritual. White is also a master of social comedy, with a classical eye and ear for pretension and vulgarity, and an equally classical, if perhaps surprising, love of knockabout farce and bawdry.

White's next novel, *Riders in the Chariot*, brings a European experience of war and racial persecution into the stifling bourgeois normality of White's mythical Sydney suburb, Sarsaparilla. But, as the title indicates, understanding is only achieved by those who see that life is "streaming with implications," those with the vision of the Chariot. The range of the book may be hinted at by the individuality of the "Riders": Himmelfarb, the Jewish migrant; Miss Hare, a slightly dotty old lady; Mrs. Godbold, a working-class woman (and one of White's great gallery of women without whom the world would collapse); and Alf Dubbo, an Aboriginal artist who is also familiar with booze and the brothel.

In the early 1960's White's energies shifted temporarily to the theatre and the short story. An early (1947) play, *The Ham Funeral*, was produced in Adelaide for the first time in 1961, followed in rapid succession by *The Season at Sarsaparilla* (successfully revived in 1977), *A Cheery Soul* (adapted from a short story), and *Night on Bald Mountain*. These plays came from a deep and long-felt passion for the theatre, but White, disillusioned with the intrigues of theatrical life, turned his back on the stage until 1976, when spurred on by contemporary Australian social and political corruption, he wrote *Big Toys*, which had a long run in various Australian capital cities in 1977.

The Solid Mandala, set in Sydney, is perhaps the most tightly knit, difficult, yet rewarding of White's novels. The twin brothers, Waldo and Arthur Brown, are in many ways the two halves of human nature, knowledge and intuition, fancy and imagination.

The Vivisector, a novel about an artist and the nature of art itself, is the most unsparing and uncompromising of White's works. As the title suggests, no compromise is possible for a true artist, doomed to loneliness, uncomforted by love or sex because both are in competition with art. It is a bleak philosophy, but, as so often with White, it must be emphasized that there is always comedy, from wit to bawdry, from irony to hilarity, which is present not for light relief but because White is always conscious of the human comedy beyond the individual tragedy.

White's recent novel *A Fringe of Leaves* is immediately accessible, with an unexpected tenderness considering the violence of the action: 19th-century shipwreck and murder, and the ordeal of a white woman, naked except for a fringe of leaves, among wild Aborigines, who may be "wild" but in fact have plenty to teach her.

White's genius shows no sign of slackening in its attack or invention. He has more novels on the way, and a film (based on a short story), *The Night the Prowler*, was made in 1977. His intense individuality comes in life from his depth and clarity of vision, and in literature from his unmistakable style, which is based on the widest expansion of metaphor; to adapt De Quincey's words, his style "cannot be regarded as a *dress* or alien covering, but it becomes the *incarnation* of his thoughts."

—Geoffrey Dutton

WHITING, John (Robert).   English.   Born in Salisbury, Wiltshire, 15 November 1917. Educated at Taunton School, Somerset; Royal Academy of Dramatic Art, London, 1934–36. Served in the Royal Artillery, 1939–44. Married Asthore Lloyd Mawson in 1940; two sons and two daughters. Actor in repertory and in London, 1936–52; Drama Critic, *London Magazine*, 1961–62. Member, Drama Panel, Arts Council of Great Britain, 1954–63. *Died 16 June 1963.*

PUBLICATIONS

Collections

The Collected Plays, edited by Ronald Hayman.   2 vols., 1969.

Plays

Paul Southman (broadcast 1946; produced 1965).
A Penny for a Song (produced 1951).   In *The Plays,* 1957; revised version (produced 1962), 1964.
Saint's Day (produced 1951).   In *The Plays,* 1957.
Marching Song (produced 1954).   1954.
Sacrifice to the Wind, from a play by André Obey (televised, 1954; produced 1955).   In *Plays for Radio and Television,* edited by Nigel Samuels, 1959.
The Gates of Summer (produced 1956).   In *The Collected Plays,* 1969.
The Plays (includes *Saint's Day, A Penny for a Song, Marching Song).*   1957.
Madame de ... , and *Traveller Without Luggage,* from plays by Jean Anouilh (produced 1959).   1959.
A Walk in the Desert (televised 1960).   In *The Collected Plays,* 1969.
The Devils, from the book *The Devils of Loudun* by Aldous Huxley (produced 1961).   1961.
No Why (produced 1964).   1961.
Conditions of Agreement (produced 1964).   In *The Collected Plays,* 1969.
The Nomads (produced 1965).   In *The Collected Plays,* 1969.
No More A-Roving.   1975.

Screenplays: *The Ship That Died of Shame,* with Michael Relph and Basil Dearden, 1955; *The Good Companions,* with T. J. Morrison and J. L. Hodgson, 1957; *The Captain's Table,* with Bryan Forbes and Nicholas Phipps, 1959; *Young Cassidy,* 1965.

Radio Plays: *Paul Southman,* 1946; *Eye Witness,* 1949; *The Stairway,* 1949; *Love's Old Sweet Song,* 1950.

Television Plays: *A Walk in the Desert,* 1960; *Sacrifice to the Wind,* 1964.

Other

Whiting on Theatre. 1966.
The Art of the Dramatist and Other Pieces, edited by Ronald Hayman.   1969.

Reading List: *Whiting* by Ronald Hayman, 1969; *The Plays of Whiting: An Assessment* by Simon Trussler, 1972; *The Dark Journey: A Critical Survey of Whiting's Plays* by Eric Salmon, 1979.

*   *   *

"I may have been meant for the Drama – God knows! – but I certainly wasn't meant for the theatre." Whiting scribbled this remark in his *Notebook* for 1960. Like Henry James, from whom the remark comes, Whiting saw himself doomed to write plays that would get at best a lukewarm response from an audience – always supposing that they were accepted for production in the first place. And, also like James, he had a deeply ingrained distrust for that popularity which he yet desired. The distrust comes out in a lecture he gave at the Old Vic in 1957, "The Art of the Dramatist." Whiting there prophesies, with stylish gloom, a time shortly to come when the individual voice will have to give way to the voice of the collective, the group, demos: what you will. For Kenneth Tynan, who was present on that very odd occasion, Whiting "seemed to anticipate, even to embrace, defeat. He stood before us like one lately descended from an ivory tower, blinking in the glare and bustle of the day."

It is a perceptive comment. For Whiting was something of an ivory-tower artist. He scorned the naturalism, the kitchen-sink drama, which he saw as the major disease of contemporary British drama; and he took much of his inspiration from the verse dramas of T. S. Eliot. Not that he himself wrote verse drama. But his language, heightened and supercharged as it is, is very clearly not the language of naturalism, his themes are large ones – he had an essentially tragic vision of life – and he never bothered to invent characters with whom an audience could identify or at least sympathise. Now of course all this can be true of writers and plays which find a wide measure of acceptance. How then shall we explain Whiting's unpopularity? In terms of a deficiency in his dramatic art, perhaps?

"I may have been meant for the drama...." But was he really so meant? The question is worth asking, if only because it draws attention to the following facts: that Whiting began his career by writing a novel, *Not a Foot of Land,* which is "a strange and remarkable first work," according to Eric Salmon, but which was never published; that he continued to write and broadcast short stories; that he made most of his money by writing film scripts, for which he seems to have had a real gift; that in November 1956, he began to make notes for a novel called *Noman* which he then tried to turn into a play (he made in all four abortive attempts to finish this play, whose title he changed to *The Nomads*); that in a career spanning the best part of twenty years he completed only nine plays. Does this suggest an uncertainty of direction? Did Whiting know *that* he wanted to write, but not *how,* not what medium would best suit his talents? "I may have been meant for the Drama" includes the possibility that "I may *not* have been meant for the Drama."

At this point it is necessary to quote Ronald Hayman, writing in praise of Whiting: "The turning points in *Saint's Day, Marching Song, The Gates of Summer* and *The Devils* involve personality changes which are so basic it's no exaggeration to call them conversions. The characters fall in and out of love not with each other but with life and death. But these moments of conversion are not directly dramatised." This seems to me more of a flaw than Hayman recognises, or is willing to admit. And indeed he himself appears to be not totally happy with what he has said, for he quickly adds that "we do see how and we do see why these moments of conversion occur. To dramatise them too directly would be to write melodrama." One problem with *The Devils*, for example, is that it *is* often merely melodramatic. Grandier's conversion to a course of self-destruction isn't sufficiently explained to make it at all convincing, though I don't deny that it can be theatrically effective.

Yet having said this much, we must reconsider; after all, Whiting's plays are regarded by a small but constant number as undeniably the work of a major writer. Certainly, the best of them – *Saint's Day* and *Marching Song* – couldn't have been written by anyone else, and have about them a queer, compelling authority. Hayman notes, very shrewdly, that Whiting's work is "characterised by its sensitivity to the violence of unreason and the impossibility of reasoning about violence"; and this is particularly true of *Saint's Day* and *Marching Song*. What is odd about Whiting, of course, and what makes it unlikely that his plays will ever attract a wide audience, is that he seems much more interested in ideas than the people who express them. They are vehicles rather than embodiments. In this, he is perhaps like Ben Jonson: he has something of Jonson's steely integrity, and he shares a measure of Jonson's scornful contempt at the muddle and compromise for which most people settle.

Perhaps a better point of comparison, however, is with Byron. Eric Salmon has remarked that after Whiting's death fifty-four volumes relating to the poet were found on his shelves. "It is easy," Salmon says, "to see why Whiting would feel an instinctive sympathy for Byron and the Byronic hero: many of his own characters have that savage self-disgust, the same contempt for the shoddiness of human society coupled paradoxically with an intuitive belief in what they feel ought to be the nobility of life and man." Given this, and given also Whiting's passion for a system that will somehow permit the nobility to come through – it amounts to a kind of political metaphysic – it is not surprising that his plays shouldn't address themselves to present concerns, shouldn't even *try* to do so, should in a word, lack popular appeal. But this isn't to say that they lack durability.

—John Lucas

WILDER, Thornton (Niven).   American.   Born in Madison, Wisconsin, 17 April 1897. Educated at Oberlin College, Ohio, 1915–17; Yale University, New Haven, Connecticut, A.B. 1920; American Academy in Rome, 1920–21; Princeton University, New Jersey, A.M. 1926. Served in the United States Coast Artillery Corps, 1918–19; in the United States Army Air Intelligence, rising to the rank of Lieutenant-Colonel, 1942–45: honorary M.B.E. (Member, Order of the British Empire), 1945. Teacher, 1921–28, and House Master, 1927–28, Lawrenceville School, New Jersey. Full-time writer from 1928. Lecturer in Comparative Literature, University of Chicago, 1930–36; Visiting Professor, University of Hawaii, Honolulu, 1935; Charles Eliot Norton Professor of Poetry, Harvard University, Cambridge, Massachusetts, 1950–51. United States Delegate: Institut de Cooperation Intellectuelle, Paris, 1937; with John Dos Passos, International P.E.N. Club Congress, England, 1941; UNESCO Conference of the Arts, Venice, 1952. Recipient: Pulitzer Prize, for fiction, 1928, for drama, 1938, 1943; National Institute of Arts and Letters Gold Medal, 1952; Friedenpreis des Deutschen Buchhandels, 1957; Austrian Ehrenmedaille, 1959; Goethe-Plakette, 1959; Brandeis University Creative Arts Award, 1959; Edward MacDowell Medal, 1960; Presidential Medal of Freedom, 1963; National Book Committee's National

Medal for Literature, 1965; Century Association Art Medal; National Book Award, for fiction, 1968. D.Litt.: New York University, 1930; Yale University, 1947; Kenyon College, Gambier, Ohio, 1948; College of Wooster, Ohio, 1950; Northeastern University, Boston, 1951; Oberlin College, 1952; University of New Hampshire, Durham, 1953; Goethe University, Frankfurt, 1957; University of Zurich, 1961; LL.D.: Harvard University, 1951. Chevalier, Legion of Honor, 1951; Member, Order of Merit, Peru; Order of Merit, Bonn, 1957; Honorary Member, Bavarian Academy of Fine Arts; Mainz Academy of Science and Literature. Member, American Academy of Arts and Letters. *Died 7 December 1975.*

PUBLICATIONS

Plays

The Trumpet Shall Sound (produced 1927).
The Angel That Troubled the Waters and Other Plays (includes *Nascuntur Poetae, Proserpina and the Devil, Fanny Otcott, Brother Fire, The Penny That Beauty Spent, The Angel on the Ship, The Message and Jehanne, Childe Roland to the Dark Tower Came, Centaurs, Leviathan, And the Sea Shall Give Up Its Dead, Now the Servant's Name was Malchus, Mozart and the Gray Steward, Hast Thou Considered My Servant Job?, The Flight into Egypt*).   1928.
The Long Christmas Dinner (produced 1931).   In *The Long Christmas Dinner and Other Plays,* 1931; libretto, music by Paul Hindemith (produced 1961), libretto published, 1961.
The Happy Journey to Trenton and Camden (produced 1931).   In *The Long Christmas Dinner and Other Plays,* 1931; revised version, as *The Happy Journey,* 1934.
Such Things Only Happen in Books (produced 1931).   In *The Long Christmas Dinner and Other Plays,* 1931.
Love and How to Cure It (produced 1931).   In *The Long Christmas Dinner and Other Plays.*   1931.
The Long Christmas Dinner and Other Plays in One Act.   1931.
Queens of France (produced 1932).   In *The Long Christmas Dinner and Other Plays,* 1931.
Pullman Car Hiawatha (produced 1962).   In *The Long Christmas Dinner and Other Plays,* 1931.
Lucrece, from a play by André Obey (produced 1932).   1933.
A Doll's House, from a play by Ibsen (produced 1937).
Our Town (produced 1938).   1938.
The Merchant of Yonkers, from a play by Johann Nostroy, based on *A Well-Spent Day* by John Oxenford (produced 1938).   1939; revised version, as *The Matchmaker* (produced 1954), 1955.
The Skin of Our Teeth (produced 1942).   1942.
Our Century.   1947.
The Victors, from a play by Sartre (produced 1949).
A Life in the Sun (produced 1955); as *The Alcestiad,* music by L. Talma (produced 1962).   Published as *Die Alkestiade,,* 1958; as *The Alcestiad; or, A Life in the Sun, and The Drunken Sisters: A Satyr Play,* 1977.
The Drunken Sisters.   1957.
Bernice (produced 1957).
The Wreck of the 5:25 (produced 1957).
Plays for Bleecker Street (includes *Infancy, Childhood,* and *Someone from Assisi*) (produced 1962).   3 vols.,   1960–61.

Screenplays: *Our Town,* 1940; *Shadow of a Doubt,* 1943.

Fiction

The Cabala. 1926.
The Bridge of San Luis Rey. 1927.
The Woman of Andros. 1930.
Heaven's My Destination. 1934.
The Ides of March. 1948.
The Eighth Day. 1967.
Theophilus North. 1973.

Other

The Intent of the Artist, with others. 1941.
Kultur in einer Demokratie. 1957.
Goethe und die Weltliteratur. 1958.

Bibliography: *A Bibliographical Checklist of the Writings of Wilder* by J. M. Edelstein, 1959.

Reading List: *Wilder* by Rex Burbank, 1961; *Wilder* by Helmut Papajewski, 1961, translated by John Conway, 1968; *Wilder* by Bernard Grebanier, 1964; *The Art of Wilder* by Malcolm Goldstein, 1965; *The Plays of Wilder: A Critical Study,* by Donald Haberman, 1967.

*   *   *

Many recent American writers have written both plays and fiction, but no other has achieved such a distinguished reputation for both as Thornton Wilder. He is distinguished also for the uniqueness of his works: each is a fresh formal experiment that contributes to his persistent conception of the artist's re-inventing the world by revivifying our perceptions of the universal elements of human experience.

Wilder's earliest published plays in *The Angel That Troubled the Waters and Other Plays* are short pieces presenting usually fantastic situations in an arch, cryptic style employed by such favored writers of the 1920's as Elinor Wylie. A number of the plays deal with the special burden that falls upon persons who discover that they possess artistic gifts, and most of them demand staging too complex for actual performance.

Before he became a successful playwright, Wilder was a novelist. His first novel *The Cabala*, displays much the same preciosity as the early plays. It describes through loosely linked episodes the effort of an aspiring young American writer to be accepted by the Cabala, "members of a circle so powerful and exclusive that ... Romans refer to them with bated breath." These elegant figures turn out to be contemporary embodiments of the ancient Roman gods, and the veiled point of the work is that the United States is to succeed a decaying Rome as the next abiding place of these gods.

This fantasy did not attract many readers, but Wilder achieved an astonishing success with his next short novel, *The Bridge of San Luis Rey,* which became a surprise best seller. This episodic story about the perishability of material things and the endurance of love is exquisitely structured. It tells the stories of the five persons who die in the collapse of a famous Peruvian bridge with a framework provided by the narrative of a Brother Juniper, who investigates the accident to learn whether "we live by accident and die by accident, or live by plan and die by plan." For his efforts, both he and his book are publicly burned. The last sentence stresses that the only bridge that survives is love.

Wilder's third novel, *The Woman of Andros*, was attacked by social-minded critics of the 1930's for evading present realities and retreating to the classical world; but this subtle fictionalization of Terence's *Andria* actually relates closely to Wilder's own seemingly dying world through its presentation of the death of the Greek world at the time of the coming of Christ because its commercial and artistic communities had become alienated: With his next novel, *Heaven's My Destination*, Wilder returned to contemporary America to create one of his most beguiling characters, George Brush, a high-school textbook salesmen in the midwest, who fails comically and pathetically in his constant efforts to uplift other people and who recovers his faith only when he realizes that he must remain an isolated wanderer, happy only in the world that he makes for himself.

The world that we make for ourselves is the subject again of one of Wilder's most admired works and one of his major contributions to a myth of American community, the play *Our Town*. Wilder explained in *The Intent of the Artist* that he turned from the novel to the stage in the 1930's because "the theater carries the art of narration to a higher power than the novel or the epic poem." He was impatient, however, with the elaborate stage settings of the naturalistic theater, and he had already sought in short plays like *The Long Christmas Dinner* to tell a fundamental human story with only the simplest of props. His culminating experiment with this technique was *Our Town*, a chronicle of the value of "the smallest events in our daily life" in a traditional New England village.

Wilder next experimented with updating a nineteenth-century farce that had been popular in both English and German versions as *The Merchant of Yonkers*. Unsuccessful when first ponderously presented by Max Reinhardt, the play in a revised version entitled *The Matchmaker* was a popular success that subsequently provided the basis for the enormously popular musical comedy, *Hello, Dolly!* Wilder did enjoy enormous immediate success with his third major play, *The Skin of Our Teeth*, an expressionist fantasy about man's struggles for survival through the Ice Age, the Flood, and the Napoleonic Wars as symbolized by the travails of the Antrobus family. Again Wilder's timing was superb. A world reduced to doubt and despair by World War II responded enthusiastically to this affirmative vision of man's possible survival despite his destructive propensities.

Wilder served with American Intelligence units in Italy during World War II, and for his first post-war work returned to the novel and to a classical Roman setting for *The Ides of March*. This pseudo-history, which Malcolm Goldstein compares to "a set of bowls placed one within another," centers on the assassination of Julius Caesar, but traces through four overlapping sections an ever widening circle of events in order to present "the tragic difference between Caesar's idealistic visions and the sordid events for which they are finally responsible" – a subject fraught with implications for the mid-twentieth century.

After the comparatively cool reception of this work, Wilder published little for twenty years. Although his plays remained popular, he was generally too lightly regarded after World War II when existential *angst* dominated in literary criticism. His writings were felt to be too affirmative and optimistic, and his long silence caused him to be regarded as an artist whose time had passed. Literary mandarins were startled, therefore, by the appearance in 1967 of his longest and most complex work, *The Eighth Day*. This novel jumps back and forth in time as it resurrects the events relating to a murder in a southern Illinois coal town early in the twentieth century, the false conviction of a man who escapes, and the eventual solution of the cunning crime. This mystery plot, however, provides only a backdrop for Wilder's observation that all history is one "enormous tapestry" and that "there are no Golden Ages and no Dark Ages. There is the oceanlike monotony of the generations of men under the alternations of fair and foul weather." At the center of the work stands falsely accused John Ashley, who avoids succumbing to despair over this inescapable cycle by "inventing" afresh such fossilized institutions as marriage and fatherhood as he also invents small practical objects to make man's work easier. An old woman whom he meets sums up the sensibility that informs the novel, "The human race gets no better. Mankind is vicious, slothful, quarrelsome, and self-centered....[But] you and I have a certain quality that is rare as teeth in a hen. We work. And we forget ourselves in our work."

The Eighth Day triumphantly capped Wilder's "re-invention" of mankind, but he had one final delight for readers. Perhaps to complement James Joyce's and others' portraits of the artist as a young man *by* a young man, Wilder presented in his last published work, *Theophilus North*, an episodic novel about the artist as a young man *by* an old man. The seemingly loosely connected tales are actually – as in his other works – parts of an intricate mosaic that discloses against a background of the "nine cities" of Newport, Rhode Island, the nine career possibilities that a young man explores before discovering that being a writer will encompass all of them.

—Warren French

WILLIAMS, (George) Emlyn.   Welsh.   Born in Mostyn, Flintshire, 26 November 1905. Educated at Holywell County School, Flintshire; Christ Church, Oxford, M.A. 1927. Married Molly O'Shann in 1935 (died, 1971); two sons. Actor and director: debut as actor, 1927. Recipient: New York Drama Critics Circle Award, 1941. LL.D.: University College of North Wales, Bangor, 1949. C.B.E. (Commander, Order of the British Empire), 1962. Lives in London.

PUBLICATIONS

Plays

Vigil (produced 1925).   In *The Second Book of One-Act Plays,* 1954.
Full Moon (produced 1927).
Glamour (produced 1928).
A Murder Has Been Arranged: A Ghost Story (produced 1930).   1930.
Port Said (produced 1931; revised version, as *Vessels Departing,* produced 1933).
The Late Christopher Bean, from the play by Sidney Howard, based on a play by René Fauchois (produced 1933).   1933.
Josephine, from a work by Hermann Bahr (produced 1934).
Spring 1600 (produced 1934; revised version, produced 1945).   1946.
Night Must Fall (produced 1935).   1935.
He Was Born Gay: A Romance (produced 1937).   1937.
The Corn Is Green (produced 1938).   1938.
The Citadel (screenplay), with others, in *Foremost Films of 1938,* edited by Frank Vreeland.   1939.
The Light of Heart (produced 1940).   1940.
The Morning Star (produced 1941).   1942.
Yesterday's Magic (produced 1942).
Pen Don (produced 1943).
A Month in the Country, from a play by Turgenev (produced 1943).   1943; revised version (produced 1956), 1957.
The Druid's Rest (produced 1944).   1944.
The Wind of Heaven (produced 1945).   1945.
Thinking Aloud: A Dramatic Sketch (produced 1945).   1946.

Trespass: A Ghost Story (produced 1947). 1947.
Pepper and Sand: A Duologue (broadcast 1947). 1948.
Dear Evelyn, from a play by Hagar Wilde and Dale Eunson (produced 1948). N.d.
Accolade (produced 1950). 1951.
Emlyn Williams as Charles Dickens, based on writings by Dickens (produced 1951). Published as *Readings from Dickens*, 1953.
Bleak House, dramatic reading based on the novel by Dickens (produced 1952).
Someone Waiting (produced 1953). 1954.
A Boy Growing Up, dramatic reading based on works by Dylan Thomas (produced 1955; as *Dylan Thomas Growing Up*, produced 1977).
Beth (produced 1958). 1959.
The Master Builder, from a play by Ibsen (produced 1964). 1967.
Saki, dramatic reading based on works by Saki (produced 1977).

Screenplays: *Friday the Thirteenth*, 1933; *Evergreen,* with Marjorie Gaffney, 1934; *The Man Who Knew Too Much*, with A. R. Rawlinson and Edwin Greenwood, 1934; *The Divine Spark*, with Richard Benson, 1935; *Broken Blossoms*, 1936; *Dead Men Tell No Tales,* with others, 1938; *The Citadel*, with others, 1938; *This England*, 1941; *The Last Days of Dolwyn*, 1949.

Radio Play: *Pepper and Sand*, 1947.

Television Plays: *Every Picture Tells a Story*, 1949; *In Town Tonight*, 1954; *A Blue Movie of My Own True Love*, 1968; *The Power of Dawn*, 1975.

Other

George: An Early Autobiography. 1961.
Beyond Belief: A Chronicle of Murder and Its Detection. 1967.
Emlyn: An Early Autobiography 1927–1935. 1973.

Editor, *Short Stories*, by Saki. 1978.

Reading List: *Williams: An Illustrated Study of His Work with a List of His Appearances on Stage and Screen* by Richard Findlater, 1957 (includes bibliography).

*   *   *

Night Must Fall is probably Emlyn Williams's most famous work and has earned him a reputation as a writer of suspense drama, though suspense elements may be traced back to his earliest plays such as *Vigil* and *A Murder Has Been Arranged*. Although he reacted against Strindberg's *Ghost Sonata* as being "too obscurely symbolic," Williams allowed most of his early suspense dramas to pivot on supernatural causation; in *Night Must Fall*, he was able to generate the whole action through plausibly realistic motivation, but later plays such as *The Wind of Heaven* and *Trespass* achieve their resolution only at the convenience of ghosts, mediums, or heavenly intervention. This aspect of Williams's drama has dated fast, and his plays which are dependent on such mechanics generally trivialise his more substantial dramatic talents.

Though a minor, unsuccessful work, *Glamour* anticipated Williams's greatest dramatic achievements. With this play, he decided that his most apposite material was "Wales and the theatre," subjects to which he has returned often. The theatre had already provided the context of *A Murder Has Been Arranged* and was to be dominant in *Spring 1600*, a play about

Burbage's company rehearsing *Twelfth Night* for the opening of the Globe Theatre. In most of Williams's other plays, the theatre has a slighter, though significant, function: *The Light of Heart*, in which the main character is an aging alcoholic actor, typifies his effective exploitation of theatricality as a dramatic energy source.

A related issue, basic to Williams's dramaturgy, was that in *Glamour* he first wrote a lead part specifically for himself, and he has continued to act central roles in most of his major plays. This habit has inevitably resulted in a certain typification: the flamboyant, assertive character is glimpsed on the brink of spectacular success, and, although he tends to have an extraordinary capacity for initiating a central action, an extraneous complicating factor deprives him of the likely consummation. Such is the position of the murderer in *Night Must Fall*, the actor in *The Light of Heart*, the surgeon in *The Morning Star*, the circus owner in *The Wind of Heaven*, the medium in *Trespass*, and the Nobel prize winner in *Accolade*; similar characters appear in the costume drama *He Was Born Gay* and the psychological thriller *Someone Waiting*. Sometimes, this pattern dissolves into sentiment, but it can also work its way out in terms of powerful comedy or irony. A logical extension of Williams's interest in the writer-actor persona may be seen in his Dickens solo performances in the 1950's, virtuoso acting achievements which emphasise a basic propensity in his work.

It is the Welsh content of Williams's plays which may well prove their most lasting element. Almost all of them include a Welsh character, several have Welsh settings, and two are obviously based on Williams's boyhood in Wales: *The Corn Is Green* (about an old schoolmistress), and *The Druid's Rest*. This latter, much-underrated play, with its determinedly English perspective of a doggedly Celtic subject, activates many of the comic ironies to be found in the plays O'Casey wrote in England; if Williams's originative influence on both Welsh and English drama has been slight, he has at least written several plays which deserve to be read as long as O'Casey's *Purple Dust*.

—Howard McNaughton

WILLIAMS, Tennessee (Thomas Lanier Williams).   American.   Born in Columbus, Mississippi, 26 March 1911. Educated at the University of Missouri, Columbia, 1930–32; Washington University, St. Louis, 1936–37; University of Iowa, Iowa City, 1938, A.B. 1938. Clerical Worker and Manual Laborer, International Shoe Company, St. Louis, 1934–36; held various jobs, including waiter and elevator operator, New Orleans, 1939; teletype operator, Jacksonville, Florida, 1940; worked at odd jobs, New York, 1942, and as a screenwriter for MGM, 1943. Full-time writer since 1944. Recipient: Rockefeller Fellowship, 1940; National Institute of Arts and Letters grant, 1944, and Gold Medal, 1969; New York Drama Critics Circle Award, 1945, 1948, 1955, 1962; Pulitzer Prize, 1948, 1955; *Evening Standard* award, 1958; Brandeis University Creative Arts Award, 1964. Member, American Academy of Arts and Letters, 1976. Lives in Key West, Florida, and New York City.

PUBLICATIONS

Plays

Cairo! Shanghai! Bombay! (produced 1936).

The Magic Tower (produced 1936).

Headlines (produced 1936).

Candles in the Sun (produced 1936).

Fugitive Kind (produced 1937).

Spring Song (produced 1938).

The Long Goodbye (produced 1940).   In *27 Wagons Full of Cotton*, 1946.

Battle of Angels (produced 1940).   1945; revised version, as *Orpheus Descending* (produced 1957), published as *Orpheus Descending, with Battle of Angels*, 1958.

At Liberty (produced 1968).   In *American Scenes*, edited by William Kozlenko, 1941.

Stairs to the Roof (produced 1944).

You Touched Me, with Donald Windham, suggested by the story by D. H. Lawrnece (produced 1944).   1947.

The Glass Menagerie (produced 1944).   1945.

27 Wagons Full of Cotton and Other One-Act Plays (includes *The Purification, The Lady of Larkspur Lotion, The Last of My Solid Gold Watches, Portrait of a Madonna, Auto-da-Fé, Lord Byron's Love Letter, The Strangest Kind of Romance, The Long Goodbye, Hello from Bertha*, and *This Property Is Condemned*).   1946; augmented edition (includes *Talk to Me Like the Rain and Let Me Listen* and *Something Unspoken*), 1953.

This Property Is Condemned (produced 1946).   In *27 Wagons Full of Cotton*, 1946.

Portrait of a Madonna (produced 1946).   In *27 Wagons Full of Cotton*, 1946.

The Last of My Solid Gold Watches (produced 1946).   In *27 Wagons Full of Cotton*, 1946.

Lord Byron's Love Letter (produced 1947).   In *27 Wagons Full of Cotton*, 1946; revised version, music by Raffaello de Banfield (produced 1964); libretto published, 1955.

Auto-da-Fé (produced 1947).   In *27 Wagons Full of Cotton*, 1946.

The Lady of Larkspur Lotion (produced 1947).   In *27 Wagons Full of Cotton*, 1946.

The Purification (produced 1954).   In *27 Wagons Full of Cotton*, 1946.

27 Wagons Full of Cotton (produced 1955).   In *27 Wagons Full of Cotton*, 1946.

Hello from Bertha (produced 1961).   In *27 Wagons Full of Cotton*, 1946.

The Strangest Kind of Romance (produced 1969).   In *27 Wagons Full of Cotton*, 1946.

Mooney's Kid Don't Cry (produced 1946).   In *American Blues*, 1948.

A Streetcar Named Desire (produced 1947).   1947.

Summer and Smoke (produced 1947).   1948; revised version, as *The Eccentricities of a Nightingale* (produced 1964), published as *The Eccentricities of a Nightingale, and Summer and Smoke*, 1965; revised version (produced 1976).

American Blues: Five Short Plays.   1948.

Ten Blocks on the Camino Real, in *American Blues*.   1948; revised version, as *Camino Real* (produced 1953), 1953.

The Case of the Crushed Petunias (produced 1957).   In *American Blues*, 1948.

The Dark Room (produced 1966).   In *American Blues*, 1948.

The Long Stay Cut Short; or, The Unsatisfactory Supper (produced 1971).   In *American Blues*, 1948.

The Rose Tattoo (produced 1951).   1951.

I Rise in Flame, Cried the Phoenix: A Play about D. H. Lawrence (produced 1953).   1951.

Talk to Me Like the Rain and Let Me Listen (produced 1958).   In *27 Wagons Full of Cotton*, 1953.

Something Unspoken (produced 1958).   In *27 Wagons Full of Cotton*, 1953.

Cat on a Hot Tin Roof (produced 1955).   1955; revised version (produced 1973), 1975.

Three Players of a Summer Game (produced 1955).

Sweet Bird of Youth (produced 1956).   1959.

Baby Doll: The Script for the Film, Incorporating the Two One-Act Plays Which Suggested It: 27 Wagons Full of Cotton and The Long Stay Cut Short; or, The Unsatisfactory Supper.   1956.

Garden District: Something Unspoken, Suddenly Last Summer (produced 1958).   1958.
The Fugitive Kind: Original Play Title: Orpheus Descending (screenplay).   1958.
A Perfect Analysis Given by a Parrot (produced 1976).   1958.
The Enemy: Time, in *Theatre,* March 1959.
The Night of the Iguana (produced 1959; revised version, produced 1961).   1962.
Period of Adjustment: High Point over a Cavern: A Serious Comedy (produced 1959).   1960.
To Heaven in a Golden Coach (produced 1961).
The Milk Train Doesn't Stop Here Anymore (produced 1962; revised versions, produced 1962, 1963, 1964, 1968).   1964.
Slapstick Tragedy (The Mutilated and *The Gnädiges Fräulein)* (produced 1966).   2 vols., 1967; revised version of *The Gnädiges Fräulein,* as *The Latter Days of a Celebrated Soubrette* (produced 1974).
Kingdom of Earth, in *Esquire,* February 1967; revised version, as *Kingdom of Earth: The Seven Descents of Myrtle* (produced 1968).   1968.
The Two Character Play (produced 1967; revised version, produced 1969).   1969; revised version, as *Out Cry* (produced 1971), 1973; revised version (produced 1974).
In the Bar of a Tokyo Hotel (produced 1969).   1969.
I Can't Imagine Tomorrow (televised 1970; produced 1976).   In *Dragon Country,* 1970.
Dragon Country: A Book of Plays (includes *In the Bar of a Tokyo Hotel, I Rise in Flame, Cried the Phoenix, The Mutilated, I Can't Imagine Tomorrow, Confessional, The Frosted Glass Coffin, The Gnädiges Fräulein, A Perfect Analysis Given by a Parrot).*   1970.
Senso, with Paul Bowles, in *Two Screenplays,* by Luigi Visconti.   1970.
A Streetcar Named Desire (screenplay), in *Film Scripts One,* edited by George P. Garrett, O. B. Harrison, Jr., and Jane Gelfann.   1971.
Small Craft Warnings (produced 1972).   1972.
The Theatre of Williams I–V.   5 vols., 1972–76.
The Red Devil Battery Sign (produced 1974; revised version, produced 1976; revised version, produced 1977).
Demolition Downtown: Count Ten in Arabic – Then Run (produced 1976).
This Is an Entertainment (produced 1976).
Vieux Carré (produced 1977).

Screenplays: *Senso (The Wanton Countess,* English dialogue, with Paul Bowles), 1949; *The Glass Menagerie,* with Peter Berneis, 1950; *A Streetcar Named Desire,* with Oscar Saul, 1951; *The Rose Tattoo,* with Hal Kanter, 1955; *Baby Doll,* 1956; *Suddenly Last Summer,* with Gore Vidal, 1960; *The Fugitive Kind,* with Meade Roberts, 1960; *Boom,* 1968.

Television Play: *I Can't Imagine Tomorrow,* 1970.

Fiction

One Arm and Other Stories.   1948.
The Roman Spring of Mrs. Stone.   1950.
Hard Candy: A Book of Stories.   1954.
Three Players of a Summer Game and Other Stories.   1960.
Grand (stories).   1964.
The Knightly Quest: A Novella and Four Short Stories.   1967; augmented edition, as *The Knightly Quest: A Novella and Twelve Short Stories,* 1968.
Eight Mortal Ladies Possessed: A Book of Stories.   1974.
Moise and the World of Reason.   1975.

Verse

Five Young American Poets, with others.   1944.
In the Winter of Cities: Poems.   1956.
Androgyne, Mon Amour.   1977.

Other

Memoirs.   1975.
Letters to Donald Windham 1940–1965, edited by Windham.   1976.
Where I Live (essays).   1978.

Reading List: *Williams* by Signi Lenea Falk, 1961 (includes bibliography); *Williams: Rebellious Puritan* by Nancy M. Tischler, 1961; *Williams: The Man and His Work* by Benjamin Nelson, 1961; *The Dramatic World of Williams* by Francis Donahue, 1964; *The Broken World of Williams* by Esther M. Jackson, 1965; *Williams* by Gerald Weales, 1965; *Williams: A Tribute* edited by Jac Tharpe, 1977; *Williams: A Collection of Critical Essays* edited by Stephen S. Stanton, 1977; *The World of Williams* by Richard Freeman Leavitt, 1978.

*   *   *

Shortly before *Vieux Carré* opened on Broadway in 1977, Tennessee Williams wrote an article for the New York *Times* which began, "Of course no one is more acutely aware than I that I am widely regarded as the ghost of a writer." So he is. The name Tennessee Williams still conjures up the flamboyant plays of the 1940's and 1950's — *A Streetcar Named Desire*, *Cat on a Hot Tin Roof*, *Suddenly Last Summer*. Except for a period in the mid-sixties when he suffered mental and physical collapse, Williams has been a remarkably busy ghost. Since 1974, he has seen new plays staged in London, San Francisco, and New York, and he has published a novel (*Moise and the World of Reason*), a book of short stories (*Eight Mortal Ladies Possessed*), a book of poems (*Androgyne, Mon Amour*) and *Memoirs.* Artistically and personally, he has become an advertisement for the theme that has obsessed him since Amanda Wingfield tried to hold her disintegrating family together in *The Glass Menagerie* — survival.

When *Vieux Carré* opened, the critics did treat it as a ghost play, a nostalgic look at the New Orleans of Williams's youth, full of echoes of characters, situations, themes relentlessly familiar to Williams admirers. In the *Times* article, in *Memoirs*, in any number of interviews, Williams has attempted to explain how he was transformed from America's most popular serious playwright into an historical figure, inexplicably still active in the real world. His plays through *The Night of the Iguana*, he suggests, shared a similarity of style — "poetic naturalism" he calls it — which became so identified with him that when he made a shift into new styles, his audiences could not or would not follow him. It is true that there are great stylistic similarities among the Williams plays through *Iguana* and it is also true that he has lost the large audiences that once flocked to his work, but the new styles have their roots in his earlier work.

He has never been a realistic playwright, which may be what the phrase *poetic naturalism* is supposed to suggest, but he has always been capable of writing a psychologically valid scene in the American realistic tradition — the breakfast scene in *The Glass Menagerie*, for instance, or the birthday dinner in *A Streetcar Named Desire*. His characters are able to claim the allegiance of audiences who continue to identify with them even after they become larger than life (Big Daddy in *Cat on a Hot Tin Roof*, Alexandra Del Lago in *Sweet Bird of Youth*) or when the use of significant names (Val Xavier in *Orpheus Descending*, Alma in *Summer and*

Smoke) turn them into myth or symbol. However grounded in realistic surface, the events in Williams's plays, particularly the violent events, take on meaning that transcends psychological realism ("Here is your God, Mr. Shannon," says Hannah when the storm breaks in *Night of the Iguana*), and when the violence moves off stage – the cannibalism in *Suddenly Last Summer*, the castration in *Sweet Bird of Youth* – the nonrealistic implications of event are heightened by its transformation into narrative (*Summer and Smoke*) or promise (*Sweet Bird of Youth*). From the glass menagerie through the dressmaker's dummies in *The Rose Tattoo* to the costumes, ritually donned by Shannon and Hannah in *Night of the Iguana*, Williams has always used sets, props, dress as devices whose significance runs deeper than the verisimilitude required by realism. When Williams deserted old forms – or thought he did – he brought two decades of nonrealistic theater with him. *Slapstick Tragedy* may have suggested absurdist drama to some of its viewers, but Polly and Molly, the grotesque comedy team whose voices sustain *The Gnädiges Fräulein*, are variations on Dolly and Beulah, who introduce *Orpheus Descending*, and Flora and Bessie, the "female clowns" of *The Rose Tattoo* and *A Perfect Analysis Given by a Parrot*. When each of the characters in *Small Craft Warnings* takes his place in the spotlight to sound his sorrow – a mechanism which suggests that the title of an earlier version of the play, *Confessional*, is more apt – we have at most an intensification of the device Williams used extensively in his earlier plays, most notably in Maggie's opening speech in *Cat on a Hot Tin Roof* and the soliloquies of Chance and Alexandra in *Sweet Bird of Youth*.

Stylistically, then, the later Williams plays grow out of the early ones. Nor are there surprising shifts in theme. The similarities between the pre- and post-*Night of the Iguana* plays can best be seen in the recurrence of characters. The Blanche of *Streetcar Named Desire*, whose variants people *Summer and Smoke*, *Camino Real*, *Sweet Bird of Youth*, and *Night of the Iguana*, is still visible in Isabel in *Period of Adjustment*, Miriam in *In the Bar of a Tokyo Hotel*, and, bizarrely, in the fish-trapping heroine of *The Gnädiges Fräulein*. Amanda – or at least her comic toughness – is apparent in Flora Goforth in *The Milk Train Doesn't Stop Here Anymore*, Myrtle in *Kingdom of Earth*, and Leona in *Small Craft Warnings*, and Laura, the frightened daughter of *The Glass Menagerie*, is present in characters as different as One in *I Can't Imagine Tomorrow* and Clare in *Out Cry*. Blanche, Amanda, Laura, three aspects of the perennial Williams character, the fugitive kind, who, male and female, has been the playwright's concern from his very early one-act plays to *Vieux Carré*. At first, his characters were simply outsiders, set off from the rest of society by a recognizable difference of one kind or another – Laura's limp, Blanche's defensive sexuality, Alma's pseudo-artistic sensitivity. It became increasingly clear – even as the forces that opposed his protagonists became more violent – that all men are outsiders. The murderous Jabe in *Orpheus Descending* is set apart by the disease that is killing him as obviously as Val is by his priapic aura, his guitar, and his snakeskin jacket, as Lady is by being Italian, as Carol Cutrere is by her unconsoling wealth and self-lacerating sex, as Vee Talbot is by her painting and her religious visions. Chance calls Alexandra "nice monster" in *Sweet Bird of Youth*, and she calls him "pitiful monster," and both are "Lost in the beanstalk country ... the country of the flesh-hungry, blood-thirsty ogre," but the play's ogre, Boss Finley, is supposed to be monster-ridden too and Williams keeps revising the play in the hopes that that point will emerge. The enemy is no longer the ugly other, but a surrogate self, or time (note all those age-obsessed Williams characters, like Mrs. Stone who wanted a Roman spring), or a godless universe. This last is presented most clearly in two plays, *Suddenly Last Summer* and *Night of the Iguana*, which come closest to making specific theological statements. Man, as Tennessee Williams sees him – as Tennessee Williams embodies him – is a temporary resident in a frightening world in an indifferent universe. The best he can hope is the transitory consolation of touching and the best he can do is hang on for dear (and only) life.

In the *Times* article quoted above Williams mentions his "private panic," his dreams "full of alarm and wild suspicion" that he wants to "cry ... out to all who will listen," and his continued revision of *Out Cry* emphasized his urgency. But that cry has always echoed through his work – his novels, his short stories, his poetry, his autobiography and all his plays. In the hope that the cry will come through more clearly, he has always revised and rewritten, turning short stories into plays, short plays into long ones, full-length plays into other full-length plays, as *Battle of Angels* became *Orpheus Descending*, and *Summer and Smoke* became *The Eccentricities of a Nightingale*. Audiences have withdrawn from Williams, I suspect, not because his style has changed or his concerns altered, but because in his desperate need to cry out he has turned away from the sturdy dramatic containers which once gave the cry resonance and has settled for pale imitations of familiar stage images; he has built on the direct address of the early soliloquies and the discursiveness of plays like *Night of the Iguana* and substituted lyric argument for dramatic language. It is a measure of his stature as a playwright and the importance of his central theme that each new play bears the promise of old vigor in new disguise. The promise has not been fulfilled for some years now, but while we wait, we can always turn back to those other Williams plays, elevated now to contemporary classics, which remind us that this ghost just may produce something worth waiting for.

—Gerald Weales

YEATS, William Butler.   Irish.   Born in Sandymount, County Dublin, 13 June 1865; son of the artist John Butler Yeats, and brother of the artist Jack Butler Yeats; lived in London, 1874–83. Educated at Godolphin School, Hammersmith, London; Erasmus Smith School, Dublin; studied art in Dublin, 1883–86; left art school to concentrate on poetry. Married Georgie Hyde-Lees in 1917; one son and one daughter. Lived mainly in London, spending part of each year in Ireland, 1890–1921: a Founder of the Rhymers Club, London, and member of the *Yellow Book* group; met Lady Gregory, 1896, and thereafter spent many of his summer holidays at her home in Sligo; Co-Founder, with Lady Gregory and Edward Martyn, Irish Literary Theatre, 1899, which became the Abbey Theatre, Dublin, 1904: Director, with Lady Gregory (to 1932), until his death; Editor of *Beltaine*, 1899–1900, *Samhain*, 1901–08, and *The Arrow*, 1906–09; settled with his family in Ireland, 1922: Senator of the Irish Free State, 1922–28. Recipient: Nobel Prize, 1923. D.Litt.: Oxford University, 1931; Cambridge University; University of Dublin. *Died 28 January 1939.*

PUBLICATIONS

Collections

> *Letters,* edited by Allan Wade.   1954.
> *Poems, Prose, Plays,* and *Criticism* (selections), edited by A. Norman Jeffares.   4 vols.,
>   1963–64.
> *Variorum Edition of the Plays,* edited by Russell and C. C. Alspach.   1966.
> *Variorum Edition of the Poems,* edited by Peter Allt and Russell Alspach.   1967.

Plays

> *The Countess Kathleen* (produced 1899).   In *The Countess Kathleen and Various
>   Legends and Lyrics,* 1892; revised version, as *The Countess Cathleen,* 1912.

The Land of Heart's Desire (produced 1894).

The Shadowy Waters (produced 1904). 1900; revised version, in *Poems*, 1906.

Diarmuid and Grania, with George Moore (produced 1901). 1951; edited by Anthony Farrow, 1974.

Cathleen ni Hoolihan (produced 1902). 1902.

The Pot of Broth (produced 1902). In *The Hour Glass and Other Plays*, 1904.

Where There Is Nothing (produced 1904). 1902; revised version, with Lady Gregory, as *The Unicorn from the Stars* (produced 1907), 1908.

The Hour Glass: A Morality (produced 1903). 1903; revised version (produced 1913), in *The Mask*, April 1913.

The King's Threshold (produced 1903). 1904; revised version (produced 1913), in *Poems*, 1906.

The Hour Glass and Other Plays, Being Volume 2 of Plays for an Irish Theatre (includes *Cathleen ni Houlihan* and *The Pot of Broth*). 1904.

On Baile's Strand (produced 1904). In *Plays for an Irish Theatre 3*, 1904; revised version, in *Poems*, 1906.

Deirdre (produced 1906). In *Plays for an Irish Theatre 5*, 1907.

The Golden Helmet (produced 1908). 1908; revised version, as *The Green Helmet* (produced 1910), 1910.

At the Hawk's Well; or, Waters of Immortality (produced 1916). In *The Wild Swans at Coole*, 1917.

The Dreaming of the Bones (produced 1931). In *Two Plays for Dancers*, 1919.

Two Plays for Dancers (includes *The Dreaming of the Bones* and *The Only Jealousy of Emer*). 1919.

The Player Queen (produced 1919). 1922.

Four Plays for Dancers (includes *At the Hawk's Well, The Only Jealousy of Emer, The Dreaming of the Bones, Calvary*). 1921.

Plays in Prose and Verse (Collected Works 2). 1922.

Plays and Controversies (Collected Works 3). 1923.

King Oedipus, from the play by Sophocles (produced 1926). 1928.

The Resurrection (produced 1934). 1927.

Oedipus at Colonus, from the play by Sophocles (produced 1927). In *Collected Plays*, 1934.

Fighting the Waves (produced 1929). In *Wheels and Butterflies*, 1934.

The Words upon the Window Pane. 1934.

Collected Plays. 1934; revised edition, 1952.

Nine One-Act Plays. 1937.

The Herne's Egg. 1938.

The Herne's Egg and Other Plays (includes *A Full Moon in March* and *The King of the Great Clock Tower*). 1938.

Purgatory and *The Death of Cuchulain*, in *Last Poems and Two Plays*. 1939.

Verse

Mosada: A Dramatic Poem. 1886.

The Wanderings of Oisin and Other Poems. 1889.

The Countess Kathleen and Various Legends and Lyrics. 1892.

Poems. 1895; revised edition, 1899, 1901, 1904, 1908, 1912, 1913, 1927, 1929.

The Wind among the Reeds. 1899.

In the Seven Woods, Being Poems Chiefly of the Irish Heroic Age. 1903.

Poems 1899–1905. 1906.

Poetical Works: Lyrical Poems, Dramatic Poems. 2 vols., 1906–07.

Poems, Second Series. 1909.

The Green Helmet and Other Poems.   1910; revised edition, 1912.
A Selection from the Poetry.   1913.
A Selection from the Love Poetry.   1913.
Poems Written in Discouragement 1912–13.   1913.
Nine Poems.   1914.
Responsibilities: Poems and a Play.   1914.
Responsibilities and Other Poems.   1916.
The Wild Swans at Coole, Other Verses, and a Play in Verse.   1917; revised edition, 1919.
Nine Poems.   1918.
Michael Robartes and the Dancer.   1921.
Selected Poems.   1921.
Later Poems (Collected Works 1).   1922.
Seven Poems and a Fragment.   1922.
The Cat and the Moon and Certain Poems.   1924.
October Blast.   1927.
The Tower.   1928.
Selected Poems, Lyrical and Narrative.   1929.
The Winding Stair.   1929.
Words for Music Perhaps and Other Poems.   1932.
The Winding Stair and Other Poems.   1933.
Collected Poems.   1933; revised edition, 1950.
Wheels and Butterflies.   1934.
The King of the Great Clock Tower: Commentaries and Poems.   1934.
A Full Moon in March.   1935.
Poems.   1935.
New Poems.   1938.
Last Poems and Two Plays.   1939.
Selected Poems, edited by A. Holst.   1939.
Last Poems and Plays.   1940.
The Poems.   2 vols., 1949.

Fiction

John Sherman and Dhoya.   1891.
The Secret Rose (stories).   1897.
The Tables of the Law; The Adoration of the Magi.   1897.
Stories of Red Hanrahan.   1905.

Other

The Celtic Twilight: Men and Women, Dhouls and Fairies.   1893; revised edition, 1902.
Literary Ideals in Ireland, with AE and John Eglinton.   1899.
Is the Order of R.R. and A.C. to Remain a Magical Order?   1901.
Ideas of Good and Evil.   1903.
Discoveries: A Volume of Essays.   1907.
Collected Works.   8 vols., 1908.
Poetry and Ireland: Essays, with Lionel Johnson.   1908.
Synge and the Ireland of His Time.   1911.
The Cutting of an Agate.   1912; revised edition, 1919.
Reveries over Childhood and Youth.   1915.
Per Amica Silentia Lunae.   1918.

Four Years.   1921.
The Trembling of the Veil.   1922.
Essays (Collected Works 4).   1924.
A Vision.   1925; revised edition, 1937; edited by George Mills Harper and W. K. Hood, 1978.
Early Poems and Stories (Collected Works 5).   1925.
Estrangement, Being Some Fifty Thoughts from a Diary Kept in 1909.   1926.
Autobiographies (Collected Works 6).   1926.
The Death of Synge and Other Passages from an Old Diary.   1928.
A Packet for Ezra Pound.   1929.
Stories of Michael Robartes and His Friends.   1932.
Letters to the New Islands, edited by Horace Reynolds.   1934.
Dramatis Personae.   1935.
Dramatis Personae 1896–1902.   1936.
Essays 1931 to 1936.   1937.
The Autobiography.   1938; revised edition, as *Autobiographies,* 1955.
On the Boiler (essays, includes verse).   1939.
If I Were Four-and-Twenty.   1940.
Pages from a Diary Written in 1930.   1940.
The Senate Speeches, edited by Donald Pearce.   1960.
Reflections, edited by Curtis Bradford.   1970.
Ah, Sweet Dancer: Yeats and Margaret Ruddock: A Correspondence, edited by Roger McHugh.   1970.
Uncollected Prose, edited by John F. Frayne and Colton Johnson.   2 vols., 1970–74.
Interviews and Recollections, edited by E. H. Mikhail.   1977.
The Correspondence of Robert Bridges and Yeats, edited by J. Finneran.   1977.

Editor, *Fairy and Folk Tales of the Irish Peasantry.*   1888; as *Irish Fairy and Folk Tales,* 1893.
Editor, *Stories from Carleton.*   1889.
Editor, *Representative Irish Tales.*   1891.
Editor, *Irish Fairy Tales.*   1892.
Editor, with E. Ellis, *The Works of Blake.*   3 vols., 1893.
Editor, *The Poems of Blake.*   1893.
Editor, *A Book of Irish Verse.*   1895; revised edition, 1900.
Editor, *A Book of Images Drawn by W. Horton.*   1898.
Editor, *Twenty-One Poems,* by Lionel Johnson.   1905.
Editor, *Some Essays and Passages,* by John Eglinton.   1905.
Editor, *Sixteen Poems,* by William Allingham.   1905.
Editor, *Poems of Spenser.*   1906.
Editor, *Twenty-One Poems,* by Katharine Tynan.   1907.
Editor, *Poems and Translations,* by J. M. Synge.   1909.
Editor, *Selections from the Writings of Lord Dunsany.*   1912.
Editor, with F. Higgins, *Broadsides: A Collection of Old and New Songs.*   2 vols., 1935–37.
Editor, *The Oxford Book of Modern Verse 1892–1935.*   1936.
Editor, *The Ten Principal Upanishads,* translated by Shree Purohit Swami and Yeats.   1937.

Bibliography: *A Bibliography of the Writings of Yeats* by Allan Wade, 1951, revised edition, 1958, additions by Russell Alspach, in *Irish Book 2,* 1963; *Yeats: A Classified Bibliography of Criticism* by K. P. S. Jochum, 1978.

Reading List: *The Poetry of Yeats* by Louis MacNeice, 1941; *Yeats: The Man and the Masks,* 1948, and *The Identity of Yeats,* 1954, revised edition, 1964, both by Richard Ellmann; *The Golden Nightingale: Essays on Some Principles of Poetry in the Lyrics of Yeats* by Donald Stauffer, 1949; *Yeats: The Tragic Phase: A Study of the Last Poems* by V. Koch, 1951; *Prolegomena to the Study of Yeats's Poems and Plays* by G. B. Saul, 2 vols., 1957–58; *Yeats the Playwright: A Commentary on Character and Design in the Major Plays* by Peter Ure, 1963; *Between the Lines: Yeats's Poetry in the Making* by Jon Stallworthy, 1963; *Yeats's Vision and the Later Poems* by Helen Vendler, 1963; *Yeats: A Collection of Critical Essays* edited by John Unterecker, 1963; *Yeats's Golden Dawn* by George Mills Harper, 1974; *A Commentary on the Collected Plays of Yeats* by A. Norman Jeffares and A. S. Knowland, 1974; *Yeats's Early Poetry: The Quest for Reconciliation* by Frank Murphy, 1975; *Yeats: The Critical Heritage* edited by A. Norman Jeffares, 1976.

*   *   *

William Butler Yeats wrote his early poetry out of a love of a particular place, Sligo, in the West of Ireland, with its folklore, its belief in the supernatural, and its legends. He found material for his own mythology in translations of the Gaelic tales into English. These tales of the Red Branch cycle and the Fenian cycle became tinged in his handling with *fin de siècle* melancholy, with what was called the Celtic twilight. His first long poem, "The Wanderings of Oisin," was founded upon Gaelic pagan legends and gave an account of Oisin visiting three islands in the other-world. In "The Rose" his poems developed this use of Gaelic material, and his Rose symbolism showed the effect of his editing Blake and his interest in the occult tradition, as well as the effect of his love for Maud Gonne. *The Wind among the Reeds* contains more elaborate poetry, intense, at times obscurely allusive, drawing upon Gaelic mythology and Rosicrucian images ("The Secret Rose"), defeatist in its romantic poems (the devotion of "He wishes for the Cloths of Heaven"), and filled with a delicate melancholic beauty.

He began to change this style; *In the Seven Woods* contains more personal, realistic poems ("The Folly of Being Comforted," "Adam's Curse"). *The Green Helmet* records the emptiness of love, now Maud Gonne had married (there is exalted celebration of her beauty in "No Second Troy" and "Words"). He reflects on how he seemed to have lost spontaneity ("All Things can tempt me from this craft of verse"). His *Collected Works* had appeared in 1908; but he found a new kind of poetic voice in *Responsibilities*; this is the antithesis of his early work; stripped of decoration and mystery it is savagely satiric in its defence of art against the philistines. He draws images of aristocratic patronage from Renaissance Italy, he contrasts contemporary Ireland with the past, filled with brave leaders ("September 1913"), he reflects on Irish ingratitude ("To a Shade"), and in his poems on beggars and hermits transmits enjoyment of coarse vitality. And yet there is still the magnificence of vision in "The Cold Heaven." "A Coat" repudiates the celtic "embroideries out of old mythologies"; now he is walking naked. *The Wild Swans at Coole* continues his praise of Maud Gonne ("The People" and "Broken Dreams"); his elegy on Major Robert Gregory and "An Irish Airman Foresees His Death" mark a new capacity for elevating the personal into heroic stature; and his three poems "Ego Dominus Tuus," "The Phases of the Moon," and "The Double Vision of Michael Robartes" reflect his interest in putting his thoughts into order, into some kind of system. This found its best poetic expression in "The Second Coming" of *Michael Robartes and the Dancer* which also contained his poems (notably "Easter 1916") on the Rising. Other poems record his marriage, and "A Prayer for My Daughter" attacks the intellectual hatred of Maud Gonne.

These two volumes showed Yeats emerging from the wintry rages of *Responsibilities* into a new appreciation of beauty balanced against tragedy. His own life had blossomed: marriage, children, his tower in the west of Ireland, the Nobel Prize for poetry, membership of the Irish Senate – and, above all, the writing of *A Vision* which gave him a "system of symbolism," a structure for his thought, and the confidence to write fully of his interests – he was now a sufficient subject for his poetry. And how superbly he wrote in *The Tower* of his ideas on life, on death. "Sailing to Byzantium," "The Tower," "Meditations in Time of Civil War," "Nineteen Hundred and Nineteen," "Leda and the Swan," "Among School Children," and "All Soul's Night" have a lofty but passionate authority about them. He was discovering his own intellectual ancestry among the eighteenth-century Anglo-Irish, expressed in "Blood and the Man" and "The Seven Sages" of *The Winding Stair*. Here, too, are the extremes of "vacillation," the contemplation of death after life in "Byzantium," and the noble poems on his friends Eva Gore-Booth and Con Markiewicz, and on Lady Gregory at Coole Park in 1929 and again in 1931 – "we were the last romantics," he cried, realising "all is changed." This note is there in *A Full Moon in March*, where "An age is the reversal of an age"; and, as Yeats grows older, the brilliant metaphysical compression of "The Four Ages of Man" strikes a note which runs through *Last Poems*, which records heroic stances in the face of coming death – of civilization and the self. There are, of course, as ever, the poems on love, the celebration of his friends ("The Municipal Galley Revisited" and "Beautiful Lofty Things"), the despairing recognition of the foul rag and bone shop of the heart, the recording of his own views on Ireland, on poetry, and on himself in "Under Ben Bulben" and, most movingly, in "The Man and the Echo."

Yeats began writing plays in his teens – heroic plays with little dramatic content. But he left conventional modes behind with *The Countess Cathleen*, written for Maud Gonne, and with the aim of blending pagan legend with Christian belief. Yeats revised this play extensively, as he did *The Shadowy Waters*, a study of the heroic gesture, carried by somewhat cryptic symbolism. He also wrote some short plays for the Irish National Dramatic Society, notably the revolutionary *Cathleen ni Houlihan*. *The King's Threshold* marks a change in Yeats's heroes from passivity to more active roles – Seanchan the poet hero in this play (founded upon a middle-Irish story) asserts the place of poetry in public life. Yeats was also deeply interested in Cuchulain, the hero of the Red Branch cycle of stories, and in *On Baile's Strand* he used the story of Cuchulain unwittingly killing his own son. In *Deirdre* he conferred a lofty dignity upon Deirdre's suicide after the heroic gesture made by her and Naoise when they realise they are doomed. In *The Golden Helmet*, rewritten in verse as *The Green Helmet*, Yeats used an old Irish tale as basis for an ironical farce, another "moment of intense life." The strangeness of Yeats's imagination and his very real capacity for farce emerged in *The Player Queen*, which is most effective on stage and extends the theories which were first elaborated in the prose work *Per Amica Silentia Lunae*.

Yeats found the Abbey Theatre was not suitable for the plays he wanted to write: his *Four Plays for Dancers* arose in part out of his interest in the Japanese Noh drama to which Ezra Pound had introduced him. He wanted to do without an orthodox theatre, and so the ritual of music and dancing aided the mysterious art he sought. *At the Hawk's Well* and *The Only Jealousy of Emer* develop the Cuchulain mythology, while *The Dreaming of the Bones* blends supernatural with political themes. *Calvary* is more complex, and depends upon *A Vision*'s ideas. A later play, *Resurrection*, is far more effective, being intense and economic in its presentation of abstract ideas against a turbulent background. His versions of *King Oedipus* and *Oedipus at Colonus* capture the essence of the Greek tragedies with success, and his sense of dialogue and neat construction make *The Words upon the Window Pane* a *tour de force*, communicating via a glance the agony in Swift's spirit. After *The King of the Great Clock Tower*, *A Full Moon in March*, and *The Herne's Egg*, another examination of the limitations of the hero's role, came *Purgatory*, a brilliant evocation of the history of a ruined house and its family, bound in a murderous cycle. *The Death of Cuchulain* written just before Yeats's death in 1939 examines the proud disdain of his hero for death.

Yeats wrote a large number of articles and reviews up to the end of the century; these were mainly on Irish writing. His first extended prose work was *John Sherman and Dhoya*, fiction which gave his youthful impressions of Sligo. The essays in *The Celtic Twilight* portrayed the traditional beliefs and scenery of the West of Ireland in limpid prose, but *The Secret Rose* contained more complex stories, a mixture of symbolism and mysticism written in that "artificial elaborate English" which was popular in the 1890's. His mannered prose appeared in *The Tables of the Law* and *The Adoration of the Magi*. By the turn of the century he changed his prose style, revised *The Celtic Twilight* and some of the stories in *The Secret Rose*. *Ideas of Good and Evil* contained essays written earlier in his complex style. The need for propaganda for the Abbey Theatre further simplified his style, and he was influenced by Lady Gregory's use of the idiomatic language of country people in her translations from the Irish.

In his autobiographical writings Yeats created an evocative, richly patterned record of his own unique experience, and of his family and his friends. His diaries, some of which were published in *Estrangement*, show his attempts to achieve unity. And his thought, based on most diverse sources, appeared in *A Vision* which contains many witty as well as profound passages as he got "it all in order." His prose became more flexible, ranging between complexity and simplicity – "The Bounty of Sweden" is a good example. Some of his senate speeches are excellent pieces of rhetoric. His introduction to *The Words upon the Window Pane* (1934) shows his capacity for imaginative meditation and creative criticism. The many introductions he wrote to the work of writers he admired contain a lofty generosity. On the other hand, his airing of opinions – and prejudices – in *On the Boiler* has an engaging touch of the outrageous. His intellectual curiosity, his originality, and his ability to convey his ideas attractively appears in his correspondence, notably in his youthful letters to Katharine Tynan and his later unreserved, lively letters to Mrs. Shakespeare. His criticism is beginning to be appreciated more fully as the complexity and strength of his mind are understood.

—A. Norman Jeffares

NOTES ON CONTRIBUTORS

ASHLEY, Leonard R. N. Professor of English, Brooklyn College, City University of New York. Author of *Colley Cibber*, 1965; *19th-Century British Drama*, 1967; *Authorship and Evidence: A Study of Attribution and the Renaissance Drama*, 1968; *History of the Short Story*, 1968; *George Peele: The Man and His Work*, 1970. Editor of the *Enriched Classics* series, several anthologies of fiction and drama, and a number of facsimile editions. **Essays:** S. N. Behrman; Paddy Chayefsky; George M. Cohan; Noël Coward; Moss Hart; George S. Kaufman; George Kelly; Sidney Kingsley; Arthur Laurents; John Howard Lawson; Frederick Lonsdale; Charles MacArthur; Sir Terence Rattigan; R. C. Sherriff; Alfred Sutro.

BODE, Walter. Editor in the Chemistry Department, University of California, Berkeley; Assistant Editor of *San Francisco Theatre Magazine*, and free-lance theatre and film critic. **Essay:** Ray Lawler.

BRAKE, Laurel. Member of the Department of English, University College of Wales, Aberystwyth. **Essay:** John Arden.

CAMPBELL, Ian. Lecturer in English Literature, University of Edinburgh. Author of *Thomas Carlyle*, 1974, and of articles on Scottish literature since 1750. Associate Editor of the Duke-Edinburgh edition of *Carlyle Letters*, and editor of Carlyle's *Reminiscences* and *Selected Essays*. **Essay:** James Bridie.

CHAMBERS, D. D. C. Associate Professor of English, Trinity College, Toronto. **Essay:** James Reaney.

COHN, Ruby. Professor of Comparative Drama, University of California, Davis; Editor of *Modern Drama*, and Associate Editor of *Educational Theatre Journal*. Author of *Samuel Beckett: The Comic Gamut*, 1962; *Currents in Contemporary Drama*, 1969; *Edward Albee*, 1970; *Dialogue in American Drama*, 1971; *Back to Beckett*, 1973; *Modern Shakespeare Offshoots*, 1976. **Essays:** Edward Albee; Samuel Beckett; Ed Bullins.

COWASJEE, Saros. Professor of English, University of Regina, Saskatchewan. Author of *Sean O'Casey: The Man Behind the Plays*, 1963; *O'Casey*, 1966; *Stories and Sketches*, 1970; *Goodbye to Elsa*, 1974; *Coolie: An Assessment*, 1976; *So Many Freedoms*, 1977; *The Last of the Maharajas*, 1978. Editor of the novels of Mulk Raj Anand. **Essay:** Sean O'Casey.

DACE, Tish. Associate Professor of Speech, Drama and English, John Jay College of Criminal Justice, City University of New York; Theatre Critic, *Soho Weekly News*, and contributor to the *Village Voice*, the *New York Times*, and other newspapers. Author of *LeRoi Jones (Imamu Amiri Baraka): A Checklist of Works by and about Him*, 1971, *The Theatre Student: Modern Theatre and Drama*, 1973, and the article on Baraka in *Black American Writers*, 1978. **Essays:** LeRoi Jones; David Mercer; John Mortimer; Harold Pinter.

DOYLE, Charles. Professor of English, and Director of the Division of American and Commonwealth Literature, University of British Columbia. Author (as Mike Doyle) of several books of poetry, the most recent being *Going On*, 1974, and of critical studies of New Zealand poetry, R. A. K. Mason, and James K. Baxter. Editor of *Recent Poetry in New Zealand*, 1965. **Essay**: James K. Baxter.

DUTTON, Geoffrey. Author of more than 25 books, including verse (most recently *New Poems to 1972*, 1972), novels (most recently *Queen Emma of the South Seas*, 1977), travel books, biographies, art criticism, and critical works, including *Patrick White*, 1961, and *Walt Whitman*, 1961. Editor of anthologies of Australian writing and translator of works by Yevtushenko and Bella Akhmadulina. **Essay**: Patrick White.

FLORA, Joseph M. Professor of English, University of North Carolina, Chapel Hill. Author of *Vardis Fisher*, 1965; *William Ernest Henley*, 1974; *Frederick Manfred*, 1974. Editor of *The Cream of the Jest* by James Branch Cabell, 1975, and *A Biographical Guide to Southern Literature* (with R. A. Bain and Louis D. Rubin, Jr.), 1978. **Essay**: Marc Connelly.

FRASER, G. S. Reader in Modern English Literature, University of Leicester. Author of several books of verse, the most recent being *Conditions*, 1969; travel books; critical studies of Yeats, Dylan Thomas, Pound, Durrell, and Pope; and of *The Modern Writer and His World*, 1953, *Vision and Rhetoric*, 1959, and *Metre, Rhythm, and Free Verse*, 1970. Editor of works by Keith Douglas and Robert Burns, and of verse anthologies. **Essay**: Ben Travers.

FRENCH, Warren. Professor of English and Director of the Center for American Studies, Indiana University-Purdue University, Indianapolis; Member of the Editorial Board, *American Literature* and *Twentieth-Century Literature*; series editor for Twayne publishers. Author of *John Steinbeck*, 1961; *Frank Norris*, 1962; *J. D. Salinger*, 1963; *A Companion to "The Grapes of Wrath,"* 1963; *The Social Novel at the End of an Era*, 1966; and a series on American fiction, poetry, and drama, *The Thirties*, 1967, *The Forties*, 1968, *The Fifties*, 1971, and *The Twenties*, 1975. **Essay**: Thornton Wilder.

GREEN, Dorothy. Member of the Faculty, Humanities Research Centre, Australian National University, Canberra. Author of books of verse, including *The Dolphin*, 1967, and of articles on Australian literature. **Essay**: Douglas Stewart.

GREEN, Roger Lancelyn. Author of more than 50 books including fiction and verse for children and adults, retellings of folk and fairy tales, and critical studies of Andrew Lang, A. E. W. Mason, Lewis Carroll, J. M. Barrie, Mrs. Molesworth, C. S. Lewis, and Rudyard Kipling; also editor of works by these authors and others, and translator of plays by Sophocles. **Essay**: J. M. Barrie.

HOGAN, Robert. Free-lance Writer. Former Professor of English, University of Delaware, Newark. Author of *The Experiments of Sean O'Casey*, 1960; *Arthur Miller*, 1964; *The Independence of Elmer Rice*, 1965; *The Plain Style* (with H. Bogart), 1967; *After the Irish Renaissance*, 1967; *Dion Boucicault*, 1969; *The Fan Club*, 1969; *Lost Plays of the Irish Renaissance* (with James Kilroy), 1970; *Eimar O'Duffy*, 1972; *Mervyn Wall*, 1972; *Conor Cruise O'Brien* (with E. Young-Bruehl), 1974; *The Irish Literary Theatre* (vol. 1 of *A History of the Modern Irish Drama*, with James Kilroy), 1975. Editor of several collections of plays and of anthologies of drama criticism. **Essays**: George Fitzmaurice; Denis Johnston; Elmer Rice.

JEFFARES, A. Norman. Professor of English Studies, University of Stirling, Scotland; Editor of *Ariel: A Review of International English Literature*, and General Editor of the Writers and Critics series and the New Oxford English series. Past Editor of *A Review of English Studies*. Author of *Yeats: Man and Poet*, 1949; *Seven Centuries of Poetry*, 1956; *A Commentary on the Collected Poems* (1958) and *Collected Plays* (1975) *of Yeats*. Editor of

Restoration Comedy, 1974, and *Yeats: The Critical Heritage*, 1977. **Essay:** William Butler Yeats.

JOHNSON, Robert K. Professor of English, Suffolk University, Boston. Author of articles on Richard Wilbur, Wallace Stevens, T. S. Eliot, and William Carlos Williams. **Essay:** Archibald MacLeish.

JOYNER, Nancy C. Member of the Department of English, Western Carolina University, Cullowhee, North Carolina. **Essay:** William Vaughn Moody.

KAPLAN, Zoë Coralnik. Adjunct Assistant Professor of Speech and Theatre, John Jay College of Criminal Justice, City University of New York. **Essay:** Rachel Crothers.

KELSALL, Malcolm. Professor of English, University College, Cardiff; Advisory Editor of *Byron Journal.* Editor of *The Adventures of David Simple* by Sarah Fielding, 1969, *Venice Preserved* by Thomas Otway, 1969, and *Love for Love* by William Congreve, 1970. **Essay:** Edward Martyn.

KENDLE, Burton. Associate Professor of English, Roosevelt University, Chicago. Author of articles on D. H. Lawrence, John Cheever, and Chekhov. **Essay:** Simon Gray.

KING, Kimball. Member of the Department of English, University of North Carolina, Chapel Hill. **Essay:** Lillian Hellman.

KUHN, John G. Professor of English and Director of Theatre, Rosemont College, Pennsylvania. Author of an article in *Walt Whitman Review*, 1962, poems in *Denver Quarterly*, 1973, and a play, *Statu(t)es Like Cartoons*, produced 1976. **Essays:** Eugene O'Neill; Sam Shepard.

KULSHRESTHA, Chirantan. Reader in English, University of Hyderabad, India. Author of *The Saul Bellow Estate*, 1976; *Bellow: The Problem of Affirmation*, 1978; chapters in *Considerations*, edited by Meenakshi Mukherjee, 1977, and *Through the Eyes of the World; International Essays in American Literature*, edited by Bruce A. Lohof, 1978; and articles in *Chicago Review, American Review, Quest, Indian Literature*, and other periodicals. Editor of *Not by Politics Alone!* (with V. V. John), 1978. **Essay:** Robert E. Sherwood.

LUCAS, John. Professor of English and Drama, Loughborough University, Leicestershire; Editor of *Victorian Studies, Literature and History*, and *Journal of European Studies.* Author of *Tradition and Tolerance in 19th-Century Fiction*, 1966; *The Melancholy Man: A Study of Dickens*, 1970; *Arnold Bennett*, 1975; *Egilssaga: The Poems*, 1975; *The Literature of Change*, 1977; *The 1930's: Challenge to Orthodoxy*, 1978. Editor of *Literature and Politics in the 19th Century*, 1971, and of works by George Crabbe and Jane Austen. **Essay:** John Whiting.

McCORMACK, W. J. Member of the Faculty, School of English, University of Leeds. Editor of *A Festschrift for Francis Stuart on His Seventieth Birthday*, 1972. **Essay:** Brendan Behan.

McNAUGHTON, Howard. Senior Lecturer in English, University of Canterbury, Christchurch, New Zealand; Theatre Critic, *The Press* since 1968; Advisory Editor, *Act* since 1976. Author of *New Zealand Drama: A Bibliographical Guide*, 1974, and *Bruce Mason*, 1976. Editor of *Contemporary New Zealand Plays*, 1976. **Essays:** Enid Bagnold; Ben Hecht; Bruce Mason; Emlyn Williams.

MESERVE, Walter J.   Professor of Theatre and Drama, Indiana University, Bloomington. Author of *An Outline of American Drama*, 1965, *Robert Sherwood: Reluctant Moralist*, 1970, and *An Emerging Entertainment: The Drama of the American People to 1828*, 1977. Editor of *The Complete Plays of W. D. Howells*, 1960; *Discussions of Modern American Drama*, 1966; *American Satiric Comedies*, 1969; *Modern Dramas from Communist China*, 1970; *The Rise of Silas Lapham* by W. D. Howells, 1971; *Studies in "Death of a Salesman,"* 1972; *Modern Literature from China*, 1974. **Essays:** Susan Glaspell; Sidney Howard; Percy MacKaye.

MILLER, Jordan Y.   Chairman of the Department of English, University of Rhode Island, Kingston. Exchange Professor, University of East Anglia, Norwich, 1977. Author of *Eugene O'Neill and the American Critic*, 1962; *Maxwell Anderson: Gifted Technician*, 1967; *Eugene O'Neill*, 1968; *The War Play Comes of Age*, 1969; *Expressionism: The Wasteland Enacted*, 1974; *The Other O'Neill*, 1974. Editor of *American Dramatic Literature*, 1961, *Playwright's Progress*, 1965, and *Twentieth-Century Interpretations of "A Streetcar Named Desire,"* 1971. **Essays:** Lorraine Hansberry; William Inge.

MORGAN, Margery.   Reader in English, University of Lancaster. Author of *A Drama of Political Man: A Study of the Plays of Harley Granville-Barker*, 1961, and *The Shavian Playground: An Exploration of the Art of G. B. Shaw*, 1972. Editor of *You Never Can Tell* by Shaw, 1967, and *The Madras House* by Granville-Barker, 1977. **Essays:** Harley Granville-Barker; Laurence Housman; Peter Shaffer; George Bernard Shaw; David Storey.

NIVEN, Alastair.   Member of the Department of English Studies, University of Stirling. Scotland. Author of *D. H. Lawrence: The Novels*, 1978. **Essay:** Wole Soyinka.

PERKINS, Barbara M.   Director of Writing Improvement, Humanities Program, Eastern Michigan University, Ypsilanti. **Essay:** Maxwell Anderson.

PETERSEN, Kirsten Holst.   Member of the Commonwealth Literature Division of the English Department, University of Aarhus, Denmark; reviewer for *Danida*. Editor of *Enigma of Values* (with Anna Rutherford), 1975. **Essay:** Athol Fugard.

POPOVICH, Helen Houser.   Associate Dean of the College of Arts and Sciences and Associate Professor of English, University of South Florida, Tampa. Author of articles on Samuel Beckett in *South Atlantic Bulletin 37*, 1972, and composition in *College Composition and Communication 27*, 1976. **Essays:** Arthur Kopit; Peter Ustinov; John van Druten.

SADDLEMYER, Ann.   Professor of English and Drama, University of Toronto. Author of *The World of W. B. Yeats*, 1965, and *In Defence of Lady Gregory, Playwright*, 1966. Editor of *The Plays of J. M. Synge*, 1968; *The Plays of Lady Gregory*, 1971; *Letters to Molly: Synge to Maire O'Neill*, 1971; *Some Letters of Synge to Lady Gregory and Yeats*, 1971. **Essays:** Lady Gregory; J. M. Synge.

SHARMA, J. N.   Academic Associate, American Studies Research Centre, Hyderabad. **Essay:** William Saroyan.

SMITH, Stan.   Lecturer in English, University of Dundee, Scotland. Author of the forthcoming book *A Superfluous Man* (on Edward Thomas), and of articles on modern literature for *Critical Quarterly, Literature and History, Irish University Review, Scottish International Review*, and other periodicals. **Essay:** W. H. Auden.

STAGG, Louis Charles.   Professor of English, Memphis State University, Tennessee; Member of the Executive Committee, Tennessee Philological Association. Author of *Index to Poe's Critical Vocabulary*, 1966; *Index to the Figurative Language in the Tragedies of*

Webster, Jonson, Heywood, Chapman, Marston, Tourneur, and *Middleton*, 7 vols., 1967–70, revised edition, as *Index to the Figurative Language of the Tragedies of Shakespeare's Chief 17th-Century Contemporaries,* 1977. **Essays:** Lord Dunsany; Christopher Fry.

STEDMAN, Jane W.   Professor of English, Roosevelt University, Chicago. Author of *Gilbert Before Sullivan,* 1967, and of articles on Gilbert, Dickens, and the Brontës. Regular contributor to *Opera News.* **Essay:** David Belasco.

THOMAS, Ned.   Lecturer in English, University College of Wales, Aberystwyth; Founding Editor of *Planet* magazine. Author of *George Orwell,* 1965, and *The Welsh Extremist: Essays on Modern Welsh Literature and Society,* 1971. **Essay:** Derek Walcott.

THOMSON, Peter.   Professor of Drama, University of Exeter, Devon. Author of *Ideas in Action,* 1977. Editor of *Julius Caesar* by Shakespeare, 1970; *Essays on Nineteenth-Century British Theatre* (with Kenneth Richards), 1971; *The Eighteenth-Century English Stage,* 1973; *Lord Byron's Family,* 1975. **Essay:** Joe Orton.

TOMLIN, E. W. F.   Free-lance Writer, Broadcaster, and Lecturer. Author of *The Approach to Metaphysics,* 1947; *The Western Philosophers,* 1950; *The Eastern Philosophers,* 1952; *Simone Weil,* 1954; *Living and Knowing,* 1955; *Wyndham Lewis,* 1955; *R. G. Collingwood,* 1956; *Tokyo Essays,* 1967; and books on Turkey and Japan. Editor of *Wyndham Lewis: An Anthology,* 1969, *Dickens: A Centenary Volume,* 1970, and *Arnold Toynbee: A Selection from His Works,* 1978. **Essay:** Ronald Duncan.

TRAVERSI, Derek A.   Professor of English, Swarthmore College, Pennsylvania. Author of *An Approach to Shakespeare,* 1938 (revised, 1968); *Shakespeare: The Last Phase,* 1954; *Shakespeare: From Richard II to Henry V,* 1957; *Shakespeare: The Roman Plays,* 1963; *T. S. Eliot: The Longer Poems,* 1976. **Essay:** T. S. Eliot.

TRUSSLER, Simon.   Editor of *Theatre Quarterly.* Theatre Critic, *Tribune,* 1969–76. Author of several books on theatre and drama, including studies of John Osborne, Arnold Wesker, John Whiting, Harold Pinter, and Edward Bond, and of articles on theatre bibliography and classification. Editor of two collections of eighteenth-century plays and of *The Oxford Companion to the Theatre,* 1969. **Essays:** Edward Bond; John Osborne; N. F. Simpson; Arnold Wesker.

TYDEMAN, William M.   Senior Lecturer in English, University College of North Wales, Bangor. Author of *The Theatre in the Middle Ages,* 1978, and of the chapter on the earlier 16th century in *Year's Work in English Studies,* 1971–74. Editor of *English Poetry 1400–1800,* 1970, and of casebooks on Wordsworth and Coleridge. **Essays:** Clifford Bax; Gordon Bottomley; Harold Brighouse; Clemence Dane; John Drinkwater; St. John Ervine; St. John Hankin; Stanley Houghton; N. C. Hunter.

WALSER, Richard.   Professor Emeritus of English, North Carolina State University, Raleigh. Author of *North Carolina Drama,* 1956; *Thomas Wolfe: An Introduction and Interpretation,* 1961; *Literary North Carolina,* 1970; *Thomas Wolfe, Undergraduate,* 1977. **Essay:** Paul Green.

WATTS, Harold H.   Professor of English, Purdue University, Lafayette, Indiana. Author of *The Modern Reader's Guide to the Bible,* 1949; *Ezra Pound and the Cantos,* 1951; *Hound and Quarry,* 1953; *The Modern Reader's Guide to Religions,* 1964; *Aldous Huxley,* 1969. **Essays:** William Douglas Home; Tom Stoppard.

WEALES, Gerald.   Professor of English, University of Pennsylvania, Philadelphia; Drama

Critic for *The Reporter* and *Commonweal*. Author of *Religion in Modern English Drama*, 1961; *American Drama since World War II*, 1962; *A Play and Its Parts*, 1964; *The Jumping-Off Place: American Drama in the 1960's*, 1969; *Clifford Odets*, 1971. Editor of *The Complete Plays of William Wycherley*, 1966, and, with Robert J. Nelson, of the collections *Enclosure*, 1975, and *Revolution*, 1975. Recipient of the George Jean Nathan Award for Dramatic Criticism, 1965. **Essays:** Philip Barry; Arthur Miller; Clifford Odets; Tennessee Williams.

WILLY, Margaret.   Free-lance Writer and Lecturer. Author of two book of verse – *The Invisible Sun*, 1946, and *Every Star a Tongue*, 1951 – and of several critical works, including *Life Was Their Cry*, 1950; *Three Metaphysical Poets: Crashaw, Vaughan, Traherne*, 1961; *Three Women Diarists: Celia Fiennes, Dorothy Wordsworth, Katherine Mansfield*, 1964; *A Critical Commentary on "Wuthering Heights,"* 1966; *A Critical Commentary on Browning's "Men and Women,"* 1968. Editor of two anthologies and of works by Goldsmith. **Essay:** W. Somerset Maugham.

YOUNG, Kenneth.   Literary and Political Adviser, Beaverbrook Newspapers. Author of *John Dryden*, 1954; *A. J. Balfour*, 1963; *Churchill and Beaverbrook*, 1966; *The Greek Passion*, 1969; *Stanley Baldwin*, 1976; and other biographies and works on political and social history. Editor of the diaries of Sir R. Bruce Lockhart. **Essays:** John Galsworthy; J. B. Priestley.